LOUIS RIEL.
COMPLIMENTS OF
S & SONS, MONTREAL,
MANUFACTURERS IN

LOUIS RIEL

LOUIS RIEL

George F. G. Stanley

The Ryerson Press
Toronto

To **The Right Reverend Antoine d'Eschambault**

BOOKS BY GEORGE F. G. STANLEY

The Birth of Western Canada
Canada's Soldiers
In Search of the Magnetic North
In the Face of Danger
For Want of a Horse
Louis Riel

Preface

It was during the preparation of my *Birth of Western Canada* in 1935/36 that I first became interested in writing a biography of Louis Riel. It seemed strange to me that, although most of the books about the history of Canada, or the opening of the West, or the relations of the French- and English-speaking peoples had something to say about Riel, there was no book that attempted to deal seriously with the man whose name was so familiar to students. Not even the collection of biographies, the "Makers of Canada" series, included the story of the métis leader. Nevertheless interest in Riel has never flagged—perhaps because he was such a strange and pathetic figure, perhaps because he evoked such strong feelings of sympathy or antagonism. Playwrights, polemicists and even musicians were willing to do something about Riel; historians appeared to hold aloof.

I was unable, however, to devote my full attention to the biography that I hoped to do. Teaching university students, taking part in a war and writing several books on military history intervened to prevent me from bringing my earlier plans to fruition. Then books began to appear about Riel. But not one of these could be regarded as a fully documented or fully credible account of the man who brought Manitoba into Confederation but who ended his career on the scaffold on November 16, 1885. Encouraged by a number of friends, including the late Dr. Lorne Pierce, I resumed my search for new and unfamiliar material relating to Riel. With the assistance of a Canada Council Fellowship and a years' leave of absence from my teaching duties at the Royal Military College, I was finally able to complete the book I had always wanted to see in print.

This work is intended to be an authoritative life of Louis Riel. I hardly imagine that it will be the definitive life, if such a thing is really possible. I know that it will not answer all the questions that Canadians have asked about the métis chief. Nor do I expect that my interpretation will be accepted with complete unanimity on the part of all my readers. When I wrote a pamphlet on Riel several years ago for the Canadian Historical Association, I thought I knew all the answers: now that I know more about Riel, I am less certain what the answers are. This book is a sincere effort however, and it is as complete as time and space will permit. This, then, is the justification for the present study.

II

I am pleased to acknowledge with gratitude the assistance I have received from many sources while preparing this biography. These include both individuals and libraries. In particular, I must mention His Grace, the Most Reverend Maurice Baudoux, Archbishop of St. Boniface; the Rev. A. Champagne and the Rev. P. Picton, St. Boniface; the late Rev. U. Forest, St. Norbert; the late Mgr. Antoine d'Eschambault, Genthon; Mr. H. Bowsfield and Miss C. Combaz, Winnipeg; the Rev. Pierre Breton, O.M.I., Edmonton; the late Rev. D. McAstocker,

PREFACE

S.J., Spokane; Miss Geneva Lent, Victoria; the late Mr. Z. M. Hamilton, Regina; Dr. and Mrs. R. C. Moir, Kenora; Mr. W. A. Stewart, Toronto; Mr. H. P. Gundy, Kingston; Mr. W. G. Ormsby, Ottawa; the Rev. L. Groulx, the Rev. L. Pouliot, S.J., Mr. J. J. Lefebvre, Mr. Emile Falardeau, Major H. Masson and Mr. J. K. Sexton, Montreal; Mgr. P. Décary, Ste. Thérèse; the Rev. A. Pouliot, S.J., and Mr. Antoine Roy, Quebec; Dr. Gabriel Nadeau, Rutland, Massachusetts. I must also thank Miss Kathleen Robb and Mr. George Stansbury of the Royal Military College, Kingston, for typing the manuscript and preparing the maps.

To these names I am happy to add the staffs of the Library of the State Historical Society, Helena, Montana; the Glenbow Foundation, Calgary; the Legislative Library, Edmonton; the Library of the University of Saskatchewan and the Saskatchewan Archives, Saskatoon; the Archiepiscopal Archives, St. Boniface; the Legislative Library and Provincial Archives, Winnipeg; the Library of Queen's University and the Library of the Royal Military College of Canada, Kingston; the Public Archives of Canada, Ottawa; the Episcopal Archives, Montreal; the Library of the Séminaire de Ste. Thérèse, Ste. Thérèse, Quebec; the Archiepiscopal Archives, the Archives of Laval University, and the Provincial Archives, Quebec; the Library of the Union St. Jean-Baptiste, Woonsocket, Rhode Island; the Archives of the State Department, Washington, D.C.; the Public Record Office, and the Governor and Committe of the Hudson's Bay Company, London.

Finally, I acknowledge my indebtedness to the Canada Council for the financial grants that made possible the many journeys I was obliged to take in search of the documentary materials out of which this book has been constructed.

GEORGE F. G. STANLEY

The Royal Military College of Canada
St. Andrew's Day, 1962

Contents

List of Plates

List of Maps

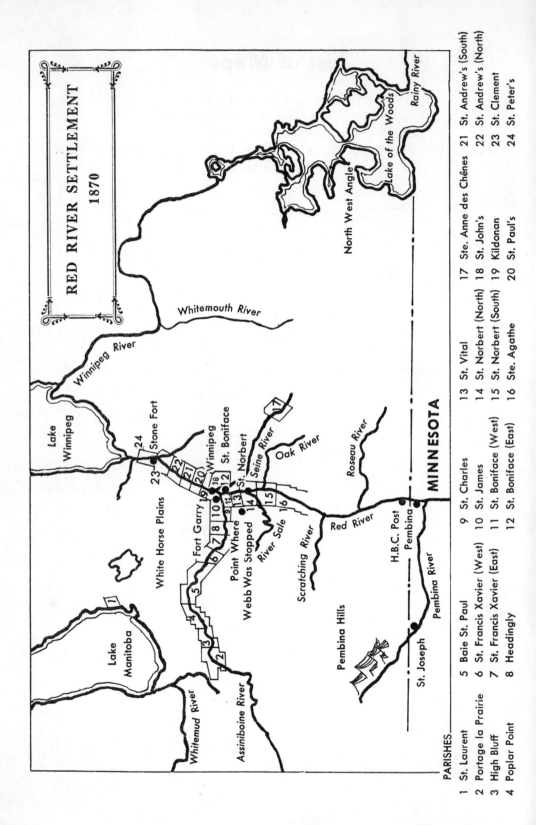

RED RIVER SETTLEMENT
1870

Lake Winnipeg

Lake Manitoba

Whitemouth River

Winnipeg River

Stone Fort

White Horse Plains

Fort Garry

Point Where Webb Was Stopped

River Sale

St. Norbert

St. Boniface

Winnipeg

Seine River

Oak River

Roseau River

Scratching River

Red River

Pembina Hills

St. Joseph

Pembina River

Pembina

H.B.C. Post

North West Angle

Lake of the Woods

Rainy River

Whitemud River

Assiniboine River

MINNESOTA

PARISHES
1	St. Laurent	5	Baie St. Paul	9	St. Charles	13	St. Vital	17	Ste. Anne des Chênes	21	St. Andrew's (South)
2	Portage la Prairie	6	St. Francis Xavier (West)	10	St. James	14	St. Norbert (North)	18	St. John's	22	St. Andrew's (North)
3	High Bluff	7	St. Francis Xavier (East)	11	St. Boniface (West)	15	St. Norbert (South)	19	Kildonan	23	St. Clement
4	Poplar Point	8	Headingly	12	St. Boniface (East)	16	Ste. Agathe	20	St. Paul's	24	St. Peter's

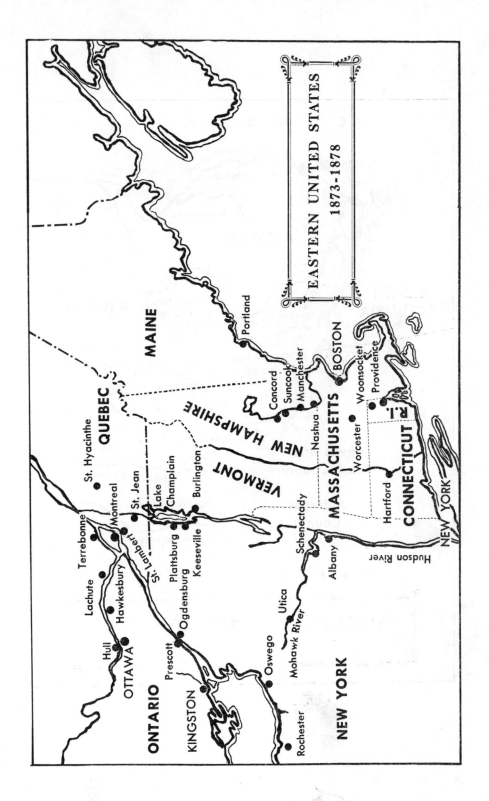

EASTERN UNITED STATES
1873-1878

ONTARIO
QUEBEC
MAINE
NEW HAMPSHIRE
VERMONT
MASSACHUSETTS
CONNECTICUT
R.I.
NEW YORK

St. Hyacinthe
Montreal
St. Jean
Lake Champlain
Burlington
Portland
Concord
Suncook
Manchester
Nashua
Boston
Worcester
Woonsocket
Providence
Hartford
Schenectady
Albany
Terrebonne
Lachute
Hawkesbury
St. Lambert
Plattsburg
Keeseville
Hull
OTTAWA
Prescott
Ogdensburg
KINGSTON
Oswego
Utica
Mohawk River
Rochester
Hudson River

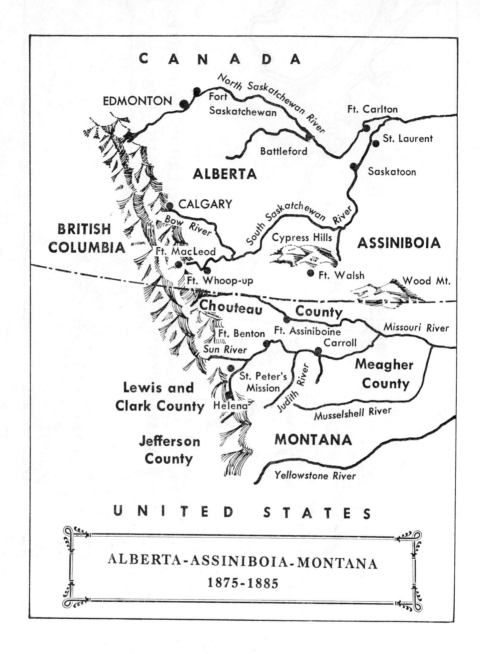

CANADA

EDMONTON
North Saskatchewan River
Fort Saskatchewan
Ft. Carlton
St. Laurent
Battleford
Saskatoon
ALBERTA
CALGARY
South Saskatchewan River
ASSINIBOIA
BRITISH COLUMBIA
Bow River
Cypress Hills
Ft. MacLeod
Ft. Whoop-up
Ft. Walsh
Wood Mt.

Chouteau County
Ft. Benton
Ft. Assiniboine
Carroll
Missouri River
Sun River
Meagher County
Lewis and Clark County
St. Peter's Mission
Judith River
Helena
Jefferson County
Musselshell River
MONTANA
Yellowstone River

UNITED STATES

ALBERTA-ASSINIBOIA-MONTANA
1875-1885

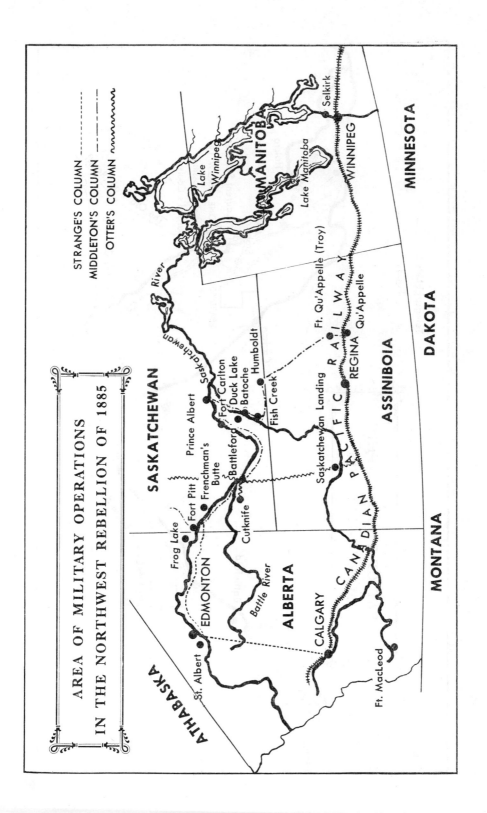

AREA OF MILITARY OPERATIONS
IN THE NORTHWEST REBELLION OF 1885

STRANGE'S COLUMN ----------
MIDDLETON'S COLUMN ----------
OTTER'S COLUMN ~~~~~~~~~~

ATHABASKA

ALBERTA

SASKATCHEWAN

MANITOBA

ASSINIBOIA

MONTANA

DAKOTA

MINNESOTA

St. Albert

EDMONTON

Frog Lake

Fort Pitt

Frenchman's
Butte

Battleford

Cutknife

Battle River

CALGARY

Ft. MacLeod

CANADIAN PACIFIC RAILWAY

Saskatchewan Landing

REGINA   Qu'Appelle

Ft. Qu'Appelle (Troy)

Humboldt

Fish Creek

Batoche

Duck Lake

Fort Carlton

Prince Albert

Saskatchewan

River

Lake
Winnipeg

Lake Manitoba

WINNIPEG

Selkirk

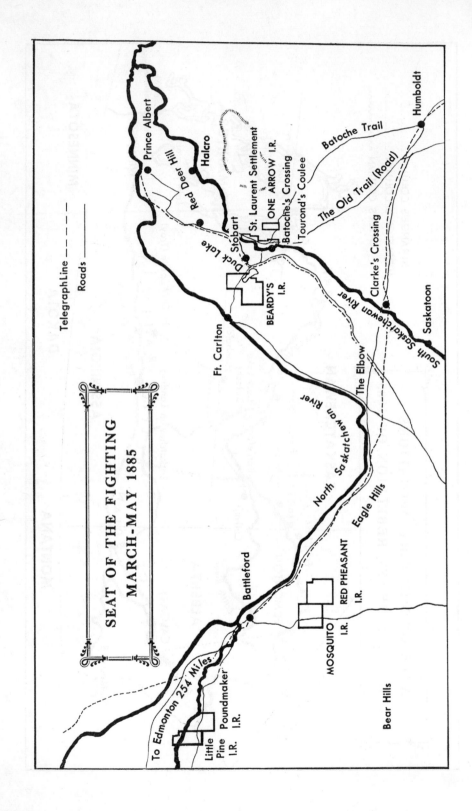

SEAT OF THE FIGHTING
MARCH-MAY 1885

Telegraph Line ----
Roads ——

CHAPTER 1

Family

ON OCTOBER 22, 1844, Julie Lagimodière-Riel's first child was born. The birth took place at ten o'clock in the morning, in a small, one-storied, log house, that had walls plastered on the outside with mud in the métis fashion. The baby was a boy. At four o'clock in the afternoon he was taken from his home, along the banks of the Seine River, to the cathedral at St. Boniface, where he was baptized by the Bishop, Mgr. Norbert Provencher. He was named Louis, after his father.[1]

The baby's mother, Julie Lagimodière,[2] like her son, had been born in the west. But Julie's mother had come from Canada. In 1807, Marie-Anne Gaboury of Maskinongé had married Jean-Baptiste Lagimodière, a young French-Canadian of the same village, who had spent several years in the North-West as a voyageur.[3] It is unlikely that Marie-Anne ever suspected that her husband would return to the west country after his marriage; but no more than a few months passed before Jean-Baptiste announced his intention of going back to the prairies. With her husband, Marie-Anne undertook the long journey, braving the discomforts of travel by canoe, the hardships imposed by the weather, the embarrassments of living with and like the Indians, and even the threat to her life from a jealous Indian whom her husband had taken to wife during his earlier years in the North-West.

From Montreal they went to Fort William, then to Red River, and then to Pembina, where Marie-Anne bore her child, the first white child to be born in wedlock in what is now Manitoba.[4] Later the Lagimodières went to Edmonton where they lived for four years. Following the establishment of a colony at the junction of the Red and Assiniboine rivers by Lord Selkirk, the Lagimodières moved again, this time to a small cabin on the banks of the Assiniboine, about twelve miles from the point where the two rivers join. From November, 1815, until December, 1816, Marie-Anne lived alone. Her husband had undertaken to carry despatches to Lord Selkirk in far-away Montreal. As a reward for these services, the Earl granted Jean-Baptiste a plot of land on the Red River opposite Point Douglas. Here, in 1819, Julie, Marie-Anne's sixth child,

1

was born. When the floods came in 1826, driving away many of the settlers, Marie-Anne pleaded with her husband to return to Canada. But Jean-Baptiste had decided he would never leave the west. The country was in his blood; he would never renounce the free life of the hunter for the confining one of the farmer, nor the limitless prairies for the narrow horizons of a Quebec village. All he did was rebuild his house at the mouth of the Seine, where that stream joined the Red. When Madame Lagimodière was widowed in 1850, she went to live with one of her children. In 1878, she died at the age of ninety-six years.

Julie Lagimodière grew up in the Red River Settlement among the métis. There were few white children for her to meet in the colony, except those of the Scots and the Swiss, and they neither spoke her language nor attended her church. She was devoted to her mother, her sisters and her brothers; but, above all, she was devoted to her church. She possessed much of her mother's fortitude and resignation, and all of her deep, unquestioning religious faith. Indeed, Bishop Provencher was so impressed with her that he hoped she might be led to adopt the life of a religious.[5] In 1843, when the restless young Louis Riel, who had recently come from Canada, sought her hand in marriage, she refused. Should she become a wife or a nun? Her parents favoured the young man's suit; she herself was inclined to the religious life. Seeking direction in prayer, she saw a vision of an old man surrounded by flames whose deep voice commanded her to follow the will of her parents. Convinced that the voice she had heard was the voice of God, she submitted. On January 21, 1843, she was married in the cathedral of St. Boniface by Bishop Provencher, and went to live in a log house not far from the house of her parents. The union resulted in eleven children;[6] the eldest and greatest bore the father's name, Louis. Julie died in 1906, having lived to see her son become, in turn, the founder of a province, a member of the parliament of Canada, an outlaw, an exile and, finally, a victim of the hangman. Always in the background, never to the fore, she was her son's unfailing refuge of comfort and strength in the brightest moments of his success and in the darkest days of his despair. Her religious faith was the rock on which she built her own life, on which she sought to build the lives of her children.

Julie's husband, Louis Riel, like the Lagimodières, was a westerner by birth, upbringing and sympathy. In the absence of positive evidence, it would appear that the Riels were descended from a family of the same name in Brittany, France, where the name under various forms—Réel, Rehel—still exists. According to tradition, one member of the family, a soldier, spent some time in Ireland in the diocese of Limerick, where a son was born. This same son, Jean-Baptiste Riel *dit* l'Irlande, came to

Canada where, in 1700, he received a grant of land from the Seigneuresse of La Valterie.[7]   In 1704 he married one Louise Cottu of La Valterie, and in 1710 received his certificate of naturalization from the Sovereign Council of New France.[8]   In 1798 another Jean-Baptiste Riel, the fourth of this name in Canada, journeyed to the west in the service of the North-West Company.   At Ile-à-la Crosse he married a Franco-Chipewyan métisse by the name of Marguerite Boucher, where another Riel, Louis, was born.   In 1822 the Riel family returned to Lower Canada.   On September 23, at Berthier, Louis Riel was baptized by the Rev. L. Lamothe.   The godparents of the five-year-old boy were Louis Boucher and Adelaide Turenne.[9]

Louis remained in Canada until he reached the age of twenty-one. He attended the local school and learned the trade of carding wool. Then, like his father before him, he resolved to go to the distant North-West.   He entered the service of the Hudson's Bay Company and for several years was stationed at Rainy River.   Returning to Canada, he entered in 1842 the novitiate of the Oblates of Mary Immaculate, a religious order that was to become intimately associated with the history of western Canada—although in 1842 the Oblates were recent arrivals in Canada from France.   But the priesthood was not for Louis. After several months with the Oblates, he yielded to the call of his mother's land and made his way to the colony on the banks of the Red River.   He obtained some land near the Lagimodières.   Here he met Julie Lagimodière and married the reluctant, twenty-four-year-old French-Canadian woman.

II

In 1844, the year Louis, Julie's son, was born, the Red River Settlement was very young.   In the first years of the century, there had been a colony of sorts some miles to the south, where Alexander Henry discovered houses and families of métis.[10]   It was not, however, until 1812 that a settlement was started where the waters of the Assiniboine joined those of the Red.   In that year, Miles Macdonell brought the first of Lord Selkirk's settlers up the valley of the Red.   He selected the junction of the two rivers for the site of the Earl's colony.   Late in 1812, Macdonell planted the first seeds of wheat; in 1813 more grain was sown; in the same year, Peter Fidler began the first surveys, dividing the land into narrow river lots, as in the old province of Quebec.   More settlers arrived, and the colony began to assume the shape of a permanent settlement.

The early days of the Red River Settlement were days of toil and strife. There was the basic problem of food and shelter.   Nothing had been prepared for the settlers, and they found themselves obliged to camp in the open and fish and hunt for their livelihood.[11] During the winter of 1812/13 they were compelled to move south to the métis colony near Pembina, in order to hunt buffalo. They had to hunt or starve. And starve they almost did, for the Scottish settlers were unskilled in the use of snowshoes and sleds, and the prairie winds blew biting cold. The settlers purchased some supplies from the North-West Company at inflated prices, but they obtained more from the métis as charity. Macdonell was angry and a bit discouraged. Reporting to Lord Selkirk in 1813, he wrote, "I have been interfered with & opposed on all sides— the N.W. Co. tampered with my people—the Indians threatened to destroy us—Even some in the employ of the H.B. Co. acted with more hostility than friendship. My situation last Winter was uncomfortable in the extreme."[12]

But this was only the beginning of trouble for the Red River settlers. The North-West Company strongly suspected that the whole Selkirk scheme was no more than a plot on the part of their business rivals to injure the trade of the Canadian company, so they determined to do what they could to thwart the Hudson's Bay Company plans. Macdonell had been warned by the Earl to avoid antagonizing the traders of the North-West Company, but he was not a tactful man. He was stubborn, with a strong sense of loyalty, and he was determined to carry out his duties as the head of the settlers. To avoid another serious food shortage, he issued a proclamation prohibiting the export of pemmican and other provisions from the Settlement.

This order of dubious legality merely convinced the Nor'Westers that their suspicions were well founded. Nothing Macdonell could have done would have affected them more adversely. The whole of the western fur trade was dependent upon maintaining a supply of pemmican for the traders and voyageurs who acquired furs and carried them over half a continent to Fort William and then to Montreal. What made Macdonell's order all the more serious was its timing. Foodstuffs were no longer available from Michigan since the American recovery of Detroit in 1813,[13] and Red River pemmican was indispensable to keep the fur brigades moving from the Saskatchewan to the Lakehead. The Nor'Westers therefore decided they would have to destroy the colony and remove the threat of its continued existence. But they would not do this themselves. They would use the métis.

The métis were the mixed-blood descendants of the French-Canadians who served the explorers and the fur traders and contracted marital alliances with the Indian women in the regions through which they travelled. Marriages à la mode du pays were easily contracted, and as easily dissolved. An Indian woman was not only a valuable help in the Indian trade; she was often necessary for survival itself in the plains and park lands of north-western North America. Métissage in the west had probably begun with the advent of the very first white men in the west, although it was not until the widespread development of the fur trade that the métis began to emerge as a significant group in the country.[14] Many of the voyageurs and traders, after they ended their terms of employment with the fur companies by agreement or desertion, chose to settle down with their Indian wives and their half-breed children and live as hunters or independent traders. This was particularly true after the dissolution of the X.Y. Company in 1805. If these "freemen," as they were called, no longer had obligations to the companies they had served, many retained a sense of loyalty to their old masters, a loyalty that was encouraged by many a "bourgeois" or factor. After all, such loyalties were useful, if only to keep the goodwill of the métis and their Indian relatives, and to ensure a good supply of buffalo meat at company posts.

As the years passed, the mixed-bloods began to develop a sense of community of their own, a sense of identity, a sense of nationality. They were a people apart. Neither Europeans nor Indians, they were an in-between people, one that possessed many of the ingredients of nationality—common origin, common language and an organization distinctly its own. This organization was imposed upon them by the nature of their life and their economy. It was a means of livelihood and of self-defence. It was a semi-military organization with its captains, soldiers and its own self-imposed discipline. There could be no room for a selfish individualism when the métis ran the buffalo or when they were forced to withstand an attack by the Sioux.

This vague and inchoate nationalism was what the Nor'Westers thought to use for their own purposes. They encouraged the métis to think of themselves as different from the white men; they called them the "New Nation"; they talked of the native title to the soil; they subtly suggested that the Selkirk settlers had come to rob them of their heritage. It was intoxicating talk—and dangerous as well. For the métis had no halftones in the register of their vision; there was only black and white, belief and unbelief, truth and untruth. And they did not question what they were told. Led by the half-breed son of a former "Bourgeois," Cuthbert Grant, "Captain General of all the half-breeds in the country," the New Nation determined "to clear their native soil of intruders and assassins."[15] "It must end," wrote Laughlin McLean, "in some sickly work in the long run."[16] And it did. Robert Semple, the new governor who had replaced Miles Macdonell, did not understand the métis; he did not know how to talk to them or manipulate them; his rigid temperament and sense of racial superiority only served to irritate a people who were both proud and sensitive. The "sickly work" that McLean feared was an exchange of shots between Grant's métis and Semple's settlers at Seven Oaks, on June 19, 1816. Semple and twenty of his fellow colonists were killed, while Grant lost only one man. The métis were rewarded for what they had done. Archibald McLeod made complimentary speeches to the New Nation, and Pierre Falcon, the métis versifier, lauded the success of the half-breeds against "the Governor who thought himself an emperor," whose men had come "to pillage our country."[17]

For the moment, the outburst of violence at Seven Oaks put an end to the colony. But only temporarily. Lord Selkirk recruited soldiers from the Swiss regiments that had been recently disbanded in Canada after the War of 1812, and with them he set out for the North-West. He arrested the North-West Company partners at Fort William and later went on to Red River. The settlers had been driven out, it is true, but they had gone only a few miles down the river and were ready to return under the Earl's leadership. They were nothing if not courageous— perhaps they were merely stubborn. The lots surveyed by Peter Fidler were once more allocated to the various settlers (one of whom was Jean-Baptiste Lagimodière), and sites were selected for a church and a school. Selkirk also planned public utilities on the grand scale. There was to be an experimental farm, as well as roads, mills and bridges. Selkirk remained in the Settlement for three months and during this time established the colony on a stronger foundation that ever before. The results must have seemed pitifully small for the expenditure of so much effort, money and lives; but the Earl was doing what he wanted most to do, and he was building a greater structure than he or his heirs realized.

Five years after Seven Oaks, the North-West Company passed out of existence. In 1821 the two great fur companies, the North-West Company and the Hudson's Bay Company, whose rivalry had dotted with trading posts the Canadian North-West from the Great Lakes to the Pacific, from the Red River to the Arctic, were amalgamated. But it was not really an amalgamation of equals. The struggle with the English company had driven the Canadian company to the wall. The long haul from Montreal, the expenses of the court proceedings against Lord Selkirk, the vigorous counter-strokes by the Hudson's Bay Company[18] and the discontent among the Nor'Westers themselves had undermined the company. When Edward Ellice approached the Hudson's Bay Company in 1819, he did so not only because this course had been suggested to him by the Colonial Secretary, Lord Bathurst, but, as he said himself, "from obvious considerations of interest."[19] Selkirk would have nothing to do with Ellice's proposals, nor with the organization which had so strenuously resisted the establishment of his colony and so remorselessly harried him in the court room. But Selkirk had not long to live, and a year after the Earl's death the Hudson's Bay Company absorbed its defeated rival. Ellice thought that he had driven a good bargain for his partners, but many Nor'Westers ended their lives broken in spirit and in pocket.

To the Red River Settlement, the union of the fur companies brought peace but not much prosperity. The union also brought about a profound change in the nature of the colony. A considerable number of employees of the two companies were thrown out of work. Some returned to Scotland or to Canada, according to their family ties and interests, but the majority simply settled down at Red River. There was every reason why they should. The country, the faces and the mode of life were familiar. There was no need to readjust to a society and an environment that had become strange after long absence. Most of the company servants had married either Indian or métis women, and to abandon them and their children was either too callous or too inconvenient. Moreover, there were lands to be had for the asking. It had been a condition of the concession to Lord Selkirk in 1811 that one-tenth of the area granted should be reserved for any "persons being or having been in the service or employ of the said Governor and Company for a term of not less than three years."[20] So Red River became the favourite place of settlement of retired or discharged company servants and their half-breed progeny. In 1821 the first group of these arrived, conveyed to the colony at the expense of the Hudson's Bay Company. In 1822 the number was less, but in 1823 it increased considerably. According to Sir George Simpson, no fewer than two hundred clerks and employees left the western posts that year for the colony.[21] The process of immigration continued every year. The immigrants included not only the lower-grade employees, but also those whom Simpson called "the commissioned gentlemen." Soon Red River, rather than Canada or Scotland, became the accepted place of retirement for company servants.

The colony grew, and the people spoke French or English according to the father's place of origin. When Nicholas Garry visited Red River in 1821, he found only 419 people.[22] Within ten years this number had increased beyond 2,000 and, by 1840, it was well in excess of 4,000.[23] This increase, it should be noted, took place at a time when various people had left the area. The Swiss and the de Meurons, who had been induced to settle in the colony by the Hudson's Bay Company and by Lord Selkirk, had decided that the floods and the grasshoppers were more than they could bear, and they had abandoned their farms to seek more congenial regions in the United States. Between 1849 and 1856 there was a further loss of European and Canadian families, believed by Henry Youle Hind to number 102.[24] These losses only served to emphasize the altered nature of the settlement. Red River was no longer a Scottish colony with a few French-Canadians on the periphery; it was a colony of mixed-bloods. This fact was amply borne out by the first federal census in 1871 which enumerated the elements of the population: French métis, 5,720; English-speaking half-breeds, 4,080; white settlers, 1,600.[25]

Although the two half-breed groups had much in common, there were strong differences between them. The language of their fathers was obviously different: but there were other differences—religion and temperament—differences emphasized by the fact that each group tended to live in its own region in the colony. The Scots and English-speaking half-breeds lived in the parishes north of the river junction in Kildonan and St. Andrews, and westward along the Assiniboine in St. John's and St. James; the French-Canadians and French-speaking métis lived south of St. Boniface, in St. Vital, St. Norbert, and on the Assiniboine west of St. James in St. François Xavier. This geographical separation was assisted in part by the clergy, who came to the Settlement after Bishop Plessis of Quebec sent Father Provencher to Red River in 1818 at the request of Lord Selkirk. Each religious denomination, Roman Catholic, Anglican and Presbyterian, sought to isolate its own parishioners in order to minister more effectively to their spiritual needs.

One effect of the missions was to emphasize more strongly the paternal cultures of the two mixed-blood groups. Both the half-breeds and the métis were drawn away from the cultures of their Indian mothers—the greatest bond of unity between them—towards those of their fathers. With an emphasis upon cultural differences, there followed an emphasis on the historic aspirations and prejudices of the cultural groups to which their fathers had belonged.

There is no doubt that the missionaries did a great deal towards fixing the attitudes of the groups to which they ministered. The Scots, all staunch Presbyterians despite their exposure for many years to Anglican ministrations within the Settlement—it was that or nothing until the arrival of the Reverend John Black in 1851—regarded work and thrift as cardinal virtues. So, too, had their fathers before them. Theirs was the Calvinist ethic—no frivolity among the Scots, no improvidence, no open house with relays of fiddlers playing all through the night; but instead, industry and moral rectitude; for amusements, literary and debating clubs, and funerals. Overriding everything was "a fine ideal of duty and a vivid sense of the over-ruling Will."[26]

The English-speaking half-breeds were mostly of Scottish origin. They did not fit snugly into the pattern of the Selkirk settlers at Kildonan, but were, after all, the sons of their mothers. But they approached the pattern sufficiently to win the approval of the Scots, who were content that others should try to follow the Calvinistic path they themselves trod with such deliberation and sense of virtue. John McLean was prepared to write: "Very few resort to the plains, unless for the purpose of trafficking the produce of their farms for the produce of the chase; and it is said that they frequently return home better supplied with meat than the hunters themselves."[27]

It was, instead, the French métis who resorted to the plains. There was nothing Calvinistic about them. They saw no virtue in work for the sake of work; why should a man grub a living out of the soil when he could earn his way hunting, catching gold-eyes, catfish or even sturgeon, or carrying goods for the Hudson's Bay Company? Not that hunting was an unrewarding occupation. There was a good market for meat, and one Scot was willing to concede:

No one who ever saw one of these plains hunters come in to Fort Garry, after the season's work on the Saskatchewan, could fail to see that he was a person in exceedingly comfortable material circumstances. In his train he had any number of carts (with ponies for each and to spare) and these were laden with the choicest viands in the shape of buffalo meat, marrow-fat, beaver-tail, etc., while he also had a goodly supply of furs that would bring handsome prices.[28]

The real fault, in the eyes of their critics, was that the French métis were frivolous, reckless and vain. "A half-breed able to exhibit a fine horse, and gay cariole," wrote Alexander Ross, "is in his glory; this is at once the height of his ambition, and his ruin. Possessed of these, the thriftless fellow's habitation goes to ruin; he is never at home, but driving and caricoling [sic] in all places, and every opportunity; blustering and bantering every one he meets."[29]

Different as these men might be in ethnic background, temperament and language, they all had one thing in common: dislike of change. They did not want to face new problems and new adjustments. They sought no more struggles and wrenchings. They were still too close to the basic fundamentals of wresting their living from a grudging land and an inhospitable climate, still too close to the floods and the plagues and the knife-edge of famine. They were, moreover, isolated from the outer world: from Europe by a long sea voyage; from the United States by a long trek over the Minnesota prairie; from Canada by the barren wilderness of rocks and trees and muskegs lying between the western frontier of Upper Canada and the valley of the Red River. This isolation made them appear reserved, wary and at times suspicious of strangers approaching the Settlement. The Red River community, French and

Scottish, was a static rather than a creative one.   It was one in which
men, whether they spoke English or French, whether they attended
cathedral or kirk, grew up and embraced life as they saw it, not as they
wished it to be.   There was nothing in Red River to seize their minds
or stir their imaginations.   There were only the familiar local problems,
and these, without exception, were concerned with the mechanics of
day-to-day living.   The Red River people were a free people, but they
were not an articulate one; they were a dogmatic people despising
abstract speculations; the life they lived was a simple one, uncomplicated
rather than primitive.

The administration of the colony, too, was simple in the extreme.   In
the earliest days of its existence the Red River Settlement was ruled by a
Governor appointed by Lord Selkirk.   After the Earl's death, the colony
remained the property of the Douglas family, although in actual fact the
responsibilities of caring for it were taken over by the Hudson's Bay
Company.   In 1836, however, the sixth Earl of Selkirk surrendered the
territory granted to his father, and the Red River Settlement reverted to
the jurisdiction of the Hudson's Bay Company.   This change of ownership made very little difference to the settlers.   The Company carried
on the traditional forms of government, appointing a local governor and
naming a council to assist him.   Although primarily filled with men
whose interests coincided with those of the Company, this body included
other elements of the population.   The two main religious denominations,
Roman Catholic and Anglican, were given representation; so, too, were
the English-speaking half-breeds.[30]   Only in 1853 was the first French-
speaking métis given a seat on the Council of Assiniboia; but in the years
that followed both the half-breeds and the métis were given more
substantial recognition in the matter of appointments.

The powers of the governor and council were strictly limited.   None
of their measures had any effect fifty miles beyond the junction of the
Red and Assiniboine rivers, that is, outside the limits of what became
known as Assiniboia; nor could the council infringe upon the powers of
the Governor of Rupert's Land, who held court at Norway House.
Nevertheless, the Governor and Council of Assiniboia adopted many
measures of a purely local nature, dealing with such matters of importance
to the community as roads, surveys, animals, fires and sale of liquor.
In 1837, a General Court was established and placed under a Scottish
Canadian, Adam Thom, and several judicial districts were organized to
function under three magistrates.   There was no organized police force,
although constables were engaged from time to time; but except on a few
notable occasions the absence of an armed force was of little consequence.
The people generally were law-abiding, and the faithful heeded the

admonitions of their priests, nuns, ministers and pastors. "Civilization" had not yet brought to Red River dishonesty and unscrupulousness and the crimes of premeditated violence of a later period. If a local settler should occasionally drink himself into a stupor, it was easier, certainly cheaper, and probably better, to allow him to sleep it off at home or in the field than to thrust him into the local gaol.

III

Life at Red River was not entirely idyllic. The colony was not without political heart-burnings, nor were relations between the Hudson's Bay Company and the settlers without friction. The great source of trouble was the vexatious question of the Company's trading monopoly. From the outset this had been recognized as a potential cause of contention, if only because of the economic stagnation of the colony and the presence of American traders on the frontier. The Americans not only had goods for sale but provided a market for furs or foodstuffs, so the settlers were prepared to buy and sell quietly across the boundary. Trade with the Americans began as early as 1819, when the settlers were compelled to go to Wisconsin to obtain seed grain. In 1820 a contract for cattle was offered to a merchant in Prairie du Chien. He was unable to fulfil his part of the bargain when the animals starved to death during the winter; but another trader, Joseph Rolette, a former Nor'Wester, took advantage of the situation to drive a few cows to Kildonan in 1821, where they were purchased "with great avidity."[31] Other American merchants did likewise.

The Hudson's Bay Company officials looked with a wary eye upon such proceedings. For the moment, however, there was nothing that they could do in the face of instructions from London that they "would not suffer the fur trade to oppose or oppress the Settlement, and if it be attempted, the expense of redressing the evil must and will fall on the fur trade as in Justice it ought."[32] The anxiety of the London office that the local governors should avoid irritating the settlers was illustrated by the reduction to four per cent of the seven and a half per cent revenue tax upon imports imposed by the Council of Assiniboia in 1835.

There was irritation in any case. The settlers disliked even the four per cent tax. They liked even less the constant reiteration by Company officials of the statement that whatever concessions might be made about other articles of trade, fur was and would remain a Company monopoly. Inevitably the settlers turned to smuggling. The risks were not particularly great, if the common routes were avoided and travelling was done at night, and the inducements of higher prices offered by the Americans at Pembina were considerable. Inevitably the Company replied with a more active espionage system, with more frequent searches of carts moving to the south, and with the confiscation of all peltries and skins found in private hands. What concerned the Hudson's Bay Company was not so much the quantity of furs reaching American hands as the fact that the métis were managing to get hold of the finest and the lightest furs from the Indians and were sending them south in return for American products.[33]

Finally, in 1844, Governor Christie of Assiniboia decided to take more emphatic measures to end the illicit trade, which was increasing in significance daily or nightly. He would forbid the use of the Hudson's Bay Company's ships for importing goods by any settler who refused to sign a declaration that he had "neither directly nor indirectly trafficked in furs." He would even go further. He would order all letters leaving the colony to be sent to Fort Garry with the sender's name clearly written on the outside; should the sender be suspected of dealing in furs, his letters might be opened and their contents examined and, if necessary, the letters stopped.

This was more than most of the settlers were prepared to accept. Andrew McDermot, one of the leading businessmen of Red River, and James Sinclair, an active, intelligent half-breed who sought to take over the leadership of the half-breeds from Cuthbert Grant, now a docile tool of the Company, frankly refused to obey Christie's orders, and then compounded their defiance by ostentatiously purchasing goods from American traders in Pembina. "Over and above the direct results of their own operations," wrote Sir George Simpson, "the example of these two persons has proved to be peculiarly pernicious, inasmuch as their superior standing and comparative intelligence gave considerable weight to their opinions."[34] The Company authorities answered this challenge to their authority and dignity by neglecting to renew Sinclair's and McDermot's contracts for freighting goods, and by imposing a special duty of twenty per cent on goods imported for trade. To spare the legitimate importers, whose activities were not offensive to the Company, licences were to be had exempting the holder from the tax, provided that he would give an undertaking to stay out of the fur business, and stating that he was importing goods for his own personal use and not for resale. New land deeds were also drawn up to include the stipulation that there should be no infringement of the Company's "exclusive rights, powers, privileges and immunities of commerce, trade and traffic."[35]

Measures such as these were unpopular among the whites, the half-breeds and the métis. All of them were, to a greater or lesser extent, engaged in a trade the Company was determined to stamp out. Therefore Sinclair and a number of half-breeds demanded from the Hudson's Bay Company a clarification of their status and their rights in the colony. When the Governor's reply proved unsatisfactory, the half-breeds drew up a petition to the British government in London. The métis, acting on the advice of one of their missionaries, the Reverend Georges Belcourt, did likewise.[36] Both the English and French petitions were then taken to England by Sinclair, and presented to the Colonial Secretary on behalf of the people of Red River by A. K. Isbister, a London lawyer who had been born in the Saskatchewan country who never forgot his half-breed origin. But the Red River petitions were lost in the endless corridors of departmental delay, or forgotten in the files of official indifference. No action was taken by the Imperial authorities to redress the settlers' complaints other than to send a regiment of infantry to the colony for two years, to ensure that there would be no disorder.

The petitions were sent to London in 1846. Three years later the whole question of the Company's monopoly was solved by direct action on the part of the inhabitants of Red River. Guillaume Sayer and three other mixed-bloods were caught and charged with illicit trading in furs. Before they could be brought to trial, however, the métis and half-breeds decided to intervene. Every one of them felt that his interests coincided with those of the men under charge. A deputation and a threat were sent to the Recorder of the Court, Adam Thom. Thom was not intimidated, but he yielded as far as to allow Sayer's counsel, James Sinclair, to select his own jurors. In the end the jury returned a verdict of guilty accompanied by a strong recommendation for mercy. When this recommendation was supported by the Hudson's Bay Company factor at Fort Garry, John Ballenden, Thom dismissed Sayer with an admonition. Technically the Company's monopoly had been upheld, and law and order had been vindicated. But there was no one in the colony who believed it. To the métis, the absence of any punishment meant only one thing, that the monopoly could no longer be enforced through the courts. Sayer's release was greeted with shouts of triumph: "Le commerce est libre—Vive la liberté."[37]

They were right. The Company had, in reality, lost the battle to hold its privileged position in the matter of trade. There was still the statement in the Charter, still the regulations in the book of rules, but so far as the Red River Settlement was concerned the monopoly was as meaningless as it was ineffective. Every year more and more carts made their way south to the trade centres in Minnesota.

IV

If the half-breed, James Sinclair, emerges as the principal leader in the struggle of the people of Red River with the Hudson's Bay Company, certainly those next in importance are the Abbé Belcourt[38] and Louis

Riel.   The former, when he arrived from Lower Canada, entered whole-heartedly into the agitation against the Company.   He gained the confidence of the French-speaking métis by identifying himself with their aspirations and serving as their political as well as their spiritual adviser. But if Belcourt was the guide, the counsellor, the father confessor of the métis protesters, the man of action, the orator, the political leader was the husband of Julie Lagimodière.   He was an obvious choice.   Had he not received a schooling in Quebec?   Had he not once trained with the Oblates?   This alone would have placed him above his fellows, but more than that he possessed the dynamism that belongs to those to whom leadership seems to come naturally.

Unfortunately it is not clear how far Riel had a hand in the petition of 1846.   It was Belcourt who advised the métis to prepare it; it was Belcourt who drafted it.   It is known, however, that one of the names on the document was that of "Louis Rielle."   It is known that Riel was the leader of the band of métis who took direct action to free the Abbé Belcourt in 1848, when the priest was charged with being a trafficker in furs, and that Riel carried him in triumph to St. Boniface.[39]   It is known, too, that it was Riel who formed the vigilance committee of métis who acted in a similar manner in the case of Guillaume Sayer.   On this occasion Louis gathered together a group of his compatriots, men like his brother-in-law Benjamin Lagimodière, Urbain Delorme, Pascal Breland and François Bruneau, and then discussed with them what they should do.   Naturally they turned to Belcourt, who, although he had been removed from Red River by Bishop Provencher, was still nearby with his beloved métis at Pembina.   From Belcourt, Riel and the others obtained a statement that the Hudson's Bay Company Charter was invalid, and that resistance to the Company's monopoly was in no way illegal.   "I desire peace and advise it," he wrote to Riel, "but if men, irritated by such abuses of power, unite to maintain a right which is more real than that which is offered in opposition to them, and to support those of a similar mind who are insulted and unjustly robbed, the only people who would be to blame would be those attracted by the abuse of their pretended power."[40]   The métis were a logical people, even if sometimes they carried logic to dangerous ends.   With them there were no subtleties, no shades of right and wrong.   Belcourt's statement was all they needed.   They would defend what they believed to be their rights; and how else did one defend one's rights except by arms?

The Sayer trial had been fixed by the recorder, Adam Thom, for Ascension Day, May 17, in the hope that the French-speaking inhabitants of the colony would devote themselves to their religious observances at St. Boniface rather than attend the court room at Fort Garry.[41]   This was a poor dodge, if ever it was intended as such. Riel had already read Belcourt's message to the métis after Mass on the previous Sunday, and on the day of the trial his voice could be heard at the church door urging the departing congregation to free Sayer and to "come armed and fully prepared to assert their rights."[42] Crossing the river in boats provided by James Sinclair, the métis arrived *en masse* at Fort Garry. As they milled about the court house, shouting and firing volleys into the air, a "complaint" was presented to the court demanding that "all prosecutions against individuals for trading in furs be suspended" and declaring that "the people . . . are determined to trade in furs until such time as Her Majesty shall issue a proclamation to the contrary."[43] There is no doubt that the threatening attitude of the half-breeds and métis had an intimidating effect. Adam Thom might remain on the bench, apparently undismayed—even those who questioned his judgment never questioned his courage—but at least one of his fellow magistrates, Hugh Poleson, "was seized with a panic in his body and limbs" and "sneaked out through the crowd; mounted his horse and fled at full speed."[44] When Sayer was released it was Riel and the métis who shouted loudest. They had acted deliberately, and they had gained their end.

Emboldened by their success, the métis leaders kept up their agitation. This time they directed their attacks upon the recorder. They wanted a judge who would and could speak both languages. It was Thom's misfortune that he had denounced the *Patriotes* in 1837 while living in Lower Canada, and his reputation as a Francophobe was well known through the colony. The demand of the métis for a bilingual judge was not an unreasonable one, and the métis pressed their case upon Sir George Simpson, the Governor of Rupert's Land, demanding Thom's removal from his office. A petition was prepared to this effect and signed by ten métis, one of whom was "Louis Rielle."[45] Simpson was quite ready to return a soft answer. He wanted to calm the agitation and avoid any kind of political trouble in the Settlement. He therefore persuaded Thom to abstain from acting as recorder for the time being, hoping that the storm clouds would blow over, people would forget and Thom could resume his duties at a later date. But the métis did not forget, and as soon as Thom reappeared on the bench there were protests from Riel and others. Thom was not immediately removed, but whenever he sat in judgment he did so by the grace of Riel and the métis.[46] It was a situation that could not last, and when the London office finally ordered Thom to step down to become clerk of the court over which he had presided, the unrepentant Scot resigned his appointment and made his way back to Canada. When a new recorder was appointed, he was F. G. Johnson, a man who was familiar with both languages used in the Settlement, a *persona grata* to the métis.

With the passing of Adam Thom, the excitement in the Settlement began to diminish. Nevertheless there was no doubt that further concessions were in the offing. Alarmed at the situation which had developed in the colony, Sir George Simpson had asked the Bishop of St. Boniface for his advice. Should any métis be appointed to the Council of Assiniboia, and who should they be? The request embarrassed Provencher. But he was prepared to admit that, even if it were probably true that few if any métis had been qualified for council appointments at an earlier date, by the mid-nineteenth century there were several who were worthy of consideration.[47] Sir George Simpson therefore recommended to the Governor and Committee of the Hudson's Bay Company in London the appointment of six mixed-bloods to the Council, and then permitted knowledge of this recommendation to trickle through the Red River Settlement. Perhaps more than anything else Simpson's actions brought peace to the colony. Peace remained, even if François Bruneau did not receive a Council appointment until 1853; even if it was four years before he was joined by Maximilien Genthon, Salomon Hamelin and Pascal Breland. Louis Riel was not appointed—perhaps because of his relentless pursuit of Adam Thom; perhaps because he was too outspoken, too ardent an advocate of métis rights; perhaps because he was looked upon as too independent, too firm to be easily moulded to the will of the Governor, or too restless a spirit to become a man of substance. Whatever the reason, neither Bishop Provencher nor Sir George Simpson saw fit to advance his name for any of the government appointments.[48]

The Sayer trial marked the high point in the career of Louis Riel. On other occasions he appeared briefly in the public eye—for instance, in March, 1857, when he presided over a meeting addressed by one William Kennedy in favour of annexation to Canada;[49] in September, 1861, when he protested against the anti-Catholic bias of the *Nor'Wester*.[50] But with his victories over Thom, Riel and the métis subsided into an attitude of complacent satisfaction with things as they were. They had their freedom to trade in furs; they had their representatives in the Council of Assiniboia; they had their representatives on the bench and in the surveyor's office. They did not seek any more, so Louis spent the years that remained to him with fruitless projects, such as establishing a textile mill in Red River.

Riel had been trained in Quebec as a wool carder. He had not been long in the Settlement when he sought to interest the Hudson's Bay Company in establishing a fulling mill in the community. John Ballenden, the Company factor at Fort Garry, was interested, and a small mill was erected about 1847 on Riel's farm. The mill seems never to have functioned, and it brought no financial return to the miller. Apparently Riel received no rent for the use of his property; his share of the proceeds was to have come from his miller's fee. Accordingly, in 1850, he sent a petition to the Council of Assiniboia complaining of the inactivity of the mill and blaming it upon Ballenden's failure to carry out a promise that the Company would purchase no cloth that had not been properly cleansed and thickened, "which would have kept the mill employed."[51]   He asked for a subsidy from the Council in order to keep the mill open and available for use, but his request was rejected.   Then Riel decided to work the mill himself, and in 1852 he wrote again to the Governor and Council explaining that "your fulling mill has not been employed once since five years, and as there is no appearance of more encouragement for the future" he would be willing to purchase most of the machinery and re-erect the mill on the Seine where he proposed to build a water-mill.[52]   The Council debated the matter and at their meeting in March, 1853, it was agreed to accept Riel's offer and sell the mill for fifteen pounds.[53]   Tradition has it that Riel devised the new mill to card wool and also to grind grain, and that he dug a canal about ten or twelve miles in length from the Rivière à la Graisse to the Seine in order to ensure an adequate supply of water.[54]

This was scarcely finished when Riel began to think in terms of another mill, this time a textile mill.   He attempted to interest some of his friends in the project and enlisted the support of Fisher, Charles Larance and Pierre Gladu.   In the summer of 1857, he went to Montreal to acquire the necessary machinery and to learn something of his new trade.   He had the encouragement of the new Bishop of St. Boniface, Monseigneur Alexandre Taché; through Taché, Riel obtained financial assistance from Madame Masson, the seigneuresse of Terrebonne.[55]   In the spring of 1858, he returned to Red River filled with enthusiasm.   His ecclesiastical patron was probably less enthusiastic, but he was hopeful and wrote in May, 1858, that Riel had purchased a "magnificent" machine for only £200.[56]   But the machinery was so bulky that it would require thirty-three Red River carts to transport it and a new and costly building to house it.   Both would require money, and money was hard to come by in a frontier community like Red River.   So the new textile mill never produced cloth, and Louis Riel *dit* l'Irlande ended his life doing odd jobs for the Hudson's Bay Company and helping about the cathedral of St. Boniface.

Riel remained a figure of significance in the community until his death in 1864.   But he was a man with a past rather than a future, a man with political potential which for some reason or other was never fully realized.   Always he was a man who loved his family, his people and the country he had made his own.   This was the man whom the boy Louis Riel knew as his father.

CHAPTER 2

Education

LOUIS RIEL was brought up among his own people, the métis, on the east side of the Red River not far from St. Boniface. As a young métis he was exposed to the two powerful factors in métis life, the growing sense of nationality and the all-embracing influence of the Roman Catholic Church. Both of these played a part in moulding the mind and shaping the thoughts of Riel. Race and religion were never very far away, or far apart.

Some of what follows must, of necessity, be no more than historical speculation. It is difficult, if not impossible, to produce documentary evidence for all the assumptions that the biographer must make. And yet there are occasions when the imagination leads one closer to the truth than the document does. Is it unreasonable, for instance, to assume that, as a five-year-old boy, Louis must have applauded, as any boy would have applauded, the dramatic part his father played in the struggle for freedom of trade in Red River? He must have listened eagerly to the tales of métis exploits; have heard Pierre Falcon singing his song of the victory over Semple; have watched the departure and return of the buffalo hunters, with their prancing horses and polished guns. He must have counted the Red River carts, as they started off for St. Paul, and envied the freighters, with their black corduroy pants, their blue coats and brass buttons, their red sashes and their white shirts with the fancy bosoms.[1] He must have known excitement when he heard the stories of how the métis had battled the Sioux on the plains and won. He could hardly have been a boy and not done these things.

In spite of the failure of his father to secure political recognition for himself, as the boy grew older he must have felt a sense of pride in the emergence of the métis as a strong group in the Red River community, a group which was developing its own bourgeoisie, its own leaders, a group whose voice was being heard and respected in the Settlement. Without a doubt Louis shared in the social life of the métis, in the family parties, the feasts of galettes, tikameg (whitefish), buffalo steaks and boiled tea, in the annual migration to the nearby lakes to hunt the Canada goose during the autumn. Perhaps he watched, even if he did not take part in,

Louis Riel, Sr.

Louis Riel, about 1858

Julie Lagimodière-Riel

Louis Riel, about 1868

Louis Riel, about 1866

the night-long dances and the political gatherings on the church steps after Mass.   Perhaps he asked his father or his cousins about the organization of the buffalo hunters, about his own race, their sensitiveness, their myths, their depressions and their exaltations.   Because Louis Riel was always a thoughtful boy, proud, introspective, just a little aloof, these things would have interested him.

The dominating factor of his boyhood seems to have been his religion. For this his mother, the woman who might have been a nun but for her obedience to the will of her parents, was responsible.   And Louis Riel, it should never be forgotten, was particularly close to his mother.   He was her first and oldest child, but the fact that the next two children, Elie and Philomène, died in early childhood, and that the fourth child was a girl rather than another boy, must have made Louis that much more precious to his mother.   If Louis was his father's pride, he was his mother's whole life.   From his mother he learned his first words, not the affectionate diminutive names a child applies to his parents, but the names of Jesus, Mary and Joseph.[2]   Among the few childhood recollections that Louis committed to paper in his later years were those associated with his church, his first confession to Father Bermond when he was seven years of age, his preparation for confirmation by Father LeFloch and his first communion at the cathedral on March 25, 1857. "The first time I received the Holy Eucharist I was trembling," he wrote to Bishop Taché, "but, with the respect that I felt for my adorations, I also felt feelings of love rise in my heart.   The priest had opened to me the road of my aspirations towards God."[3]   In the same letter he also wrote:

My first years were perfumed with the sweetest scents of the faith, for my beloved father would permit no one to speak evil in my presence. Family prayers, the rosary were always in my eyes and ears.   And they are as much part of my nature as the air I breathe.   The calm reflective features of my mother, her eyes constantly turned towards heaven, her respect, her attention, her devotion to her religious obligations always left upon me the deepest impression of her good example.

As a child Louis never failed to make the sign of the cross and to repeat his prayers every night.   When he did anything of which he was not certain, he would run to his mother to see if it had been all right.   The story is told that on one occasion at school one of Louis's playmates snatched his cap and threatened him.   His temper quickly aroused, Louis advanced towards his challenger, then drew back saying: "I shall ask my mother's permission to fight you; if she says yes, we shall meet again."[4]

With such strong parental and religious influences in the home, it was natural that the Riel family should have been very closely knit.   If any one quality stood out among the Riels, it was their deep affection for one another. It is impossible to read the correspondence of theirs that has survived without sensing this fully. And the deaths which inevitably broke the family circle were, for Louis, occasions of the deepest grief, bordering almost upon morbidity.

Louis Riel's first schooling came from his parents, but when he was seven years of age he was sent to the school run by the Grey Sisters in St. Boniface.[5] The Riel family gave up their house about this time, and for a short period lived in cramped quarters in the Bishop's house until they were able to obtain accommodation from Prosper Ducharme. This was only a temporary uprooting while Riel's father was engaged in the construction of his new mill on the Seine.[6] Eventually the family returned to the old property, next door to Julie's mother, Marie-Anne Lagimodière. As Louis progressed in his studies, he was transferred to the school run by the Christian Brothers.[7] This was an important step, for it brought him, for the first time, under the direction of men teachers. It removed his education from the deeply religious but unworldly atmosphere that had marked his schooling in his earliest years.

The Bishop, Monseigneur Taché, had for some years been concerned over the state of secular education in the Red River Settlement. Following his consecration as Bishop in 1853, one of the first tasks to which he turned his attention was that of providing good schooling for boys. It was true that the Grey Sisters had a flourishing school for girls, to which boys might be admitted. It was attended by children from Red River, both Catholic and non-Catholic, but for some reason few métis boys ever attended it. In 1851, Bishop Taché wrote to Bishop Bourget of Montreal, "The education of the boys has been badly neglected among our Catholics at Red River: the fact is all the more painful because our separated brethren have always shown the way." Then he put his finger on what he believed was the real trouble, "The métis do not like to be governed by women, and this probably explains why their children do not go to school."[8] Taché wanted a few teaching brothers from Canada, and in 1854 to his great satisfaction three Christian Brothers arrived at Red River. They established a school in the Bishop's house. Subsequently a new building was constructed, known at various times as "the college," "the old college" and "Provencher Academy."[9]

It was to the Bishop's house that Riel went to school, for the new building was not ready for occupation until 1858. He appears to have been a good student. In September, 1857, he began the study of Latin under Father LeFloch.[10] The schoolroom was in the library, a room so small that after the pupils were seated—there were only four of them— poor Father LeFloch, if he wished to sit down, had to go into a neighbouring room.[11]   Riel's progress and piety attracted the attention of the Bishop who visited the schoolroom regularly, knew the pupils by name, examined their notebooks and watched them at work and at play.[12]   He was anxious to find potential priests among the métis, and in 1857 he had made arrangements with several of the colleges in Quebec to take any candidates whom he might think sufficiently worthy to send them. In the spring of 1858, he announced that four métis boys had been chosen to go to Canada: Louis Riel, Daniel McDougall, Louis Schmidt and Joseph Nolin.   But Nolin's parents would not let him leave the Settlement.   On June 1, the other métis boys assembled at St. Boniface.   They received the Bishop's blessing and bade farewell to their parents and to their friends.   Louis's mother was there, with his sister, Sara, to whom he had been most attached as a child.   Sara later became the religious her mother wanted to be.   For them the occasion was an exciting but sorrowful one.   All three knew that this was not an ordinary parting, for weeks, or even months, but that it would be for years.   And it would be the first time that Louis had ever been away from home.   When he returned he would be a man.   He might even be wearing a soutane.

II

Louis Riel had not reached his fourteenth birthday when he set out for Montreal on June 1, 1858.   At that age he was able to enjoy to the full the experience of a journey that took him over fifteen hundred miles from the banks of the Seine to those of the great St. Lawrence.   The first part of the journey was to be by ox-cart, along with métis tripmen on their way to St. Paul.   There were two people to watch over the boys and assist them on their way, the Reverend Sister Valade, Superior of the Grey Nuns at St. Boniface, who was on her way to Montreal to find new recruits for the western missions, and an old Canadian, Granger by name, whom Taché had asked to go along with the party.[13]

The first few days of the journey seemed slow and tedious.   The Red River trains plodded along leisurely in single file, an ox harnessed to each cart, with a métis tripman in charge of each group of three carts. Fifteen or twenty miles a day was the limit.   Between St. Boniface and Pembina, the country offered little in the way of scenery that differed from familiar scenery of the region around the junction of the Red, the Assiniboine and the Seine rivers.   To the west, there was the seemingly endless prairie, with its rich black earth covered with the coarse rich grasses that nourished both the buffalo and the grasshopper.   To the east, on the horizon, there were the trees that extended to Lake of the Woods, poplars, pines, cedars and the red willows that the Indians called *quawpemug*, whose inner bark could be smoked like tobacco.   And all along the trail, never very distant from it, flowed the sluggish, muddy Red River, taking its name from the colour of its waters. It was summer, and the soil was dry. Clouds of dust enveloped the long line of creaking Red River carts as they slowly made their way southwards. From Pembina, they cut in towards the east, to take the "wood road" in order to avoid, if possible, any encounter with Sioux Indians wandering on the plains. It was a lonely journey, for there were no buildings and no human habitation to be seen until they reached the ferry over the Mississippi at what is now Crookston, Minnesota.

Here, on the banks of the river, Louis met his father. The latter was on his way back to Red River with the machinery for the textile mill which he had purchased in Montreal. It was a moment charged with deep emotion for both father and son, for if Louis revered his mother, he dearly loved his father. Louis Schmidt, who lacked the ability to write in any other than the simplest and baldest fashion, was moved to say, "The encounter of father and son was very touching. And, it was to be their last here on earth."[14] Louis Riel did not know it, but he was never to see his father again.

The ox-cart train was on the road for twenty-eight days before it finally reached St. Paul. Here was the first surprise for the three métis boys, who had never seen anything larger than Fort Garry and St. Boniface. The capital of the territory of Minnesota, although it was still in 1858 no more than a raw, lusty frontier town, appeared a great city to Louis Riel and his companions. Here, for instance, were steamboats, a mode of transport they had heard about but never seen. On one of these boats they embarked for the next stage of their journey to Prairie du Chien. Every day seemed to bring new experiences, each piling upon the other until the cumulative effect was overwhelming. At Prairie du Chien, Sister Valade and her charges climbed into a train and continued their journey to Chicago, then on to Detroit, and finally into Upper Canada. At Hamilton they caught their first glimpse of Lake Ontario, "What a beautiful city; what a magnificent view," wrote Schmidt. Here Sister Valade bought the boys some oranges, the first they had ever tasted. Another new sensation! At first Schmidt did not like the bittersweet taste, but Riel and McDougall liked them, and soon they were eating oranges in such quantities that Schmidt became ill. At Toronto they passed the night at a convent and then they were off to Montreal.

The long journey—it had taken five weeks to accomplish—ended on July 5 with the arrival of Sister Valade and the three métis boys in Montreal. It was evening and they all hurried to the convent of the Grey Sisters near St. Antoine Market. The boys were tired and perhaps a little frightened. Everything seemed so strange, so foreign, so crowded and noisy. They felt dwarfed by everything around them. The following day, July 6, they were told where they would be sent. McDougall was to attend the college at Nicolet, where Father LaFlèche was teaching; Schmidt would continue his journey to St. Hyacinthe; Louis Riel would remain in Montreal, to be placed under the charge of the Gentlemen of St. Sulpice.

III

The College of Montreal, *le petit séminaire*, was the oldest of the colleges on Montreal island.[16]   It had been founded in 1767 by M. Curateau de la Blaiserie, a Sulpician priest and curé of the parish of Longue Pointe, for the purpose of educating young boys for the priesthood.   The college itself wàs an act of faith and defiance, a protest against the assimilation policy of the first years of the British domination, and a means of maintaining French culture and the Roman Catholic faith under a Protestant government.   Eight years later the college, then called St. Raphael's, was moved to the Chateau de Vaudreuil on St. Paul Street, in the lower town.   Here it remained until the destruction of the Chateau by fire in 1803.   From 1804 to 1862 the college occupied a site on St. Paul and McGill Streets.   But this location had certain disadvantages and, acting upon the advice of the Abbé Casault, the founder of Laval University, the Sulpicians looked about for new ground upon which to establish their college.   Several years before, in 1845, the Jesuits had been offered a site on Mount Royal for their College of St. Mary, but they did not take up the offer, and the land was made available to the Sulpicians.   Here, in 1854, the Gentlemen of St. Sulpice began the construction of a new building.   Three years later, the building, only partially completed, opened its doors to the students in theology. Those following the regular course of studies continued to attend the old college until 1862.

   The life of a young seminarian attending the College of Montreal was not an easy one.   Discipline was strict and the routine was marked by frugality and austerity.   Only occasionally, at the great festivals, was the regimen relaxed; on All Saints Day, Christmas, New Year's, Easter and Pentecost, butter was added to the morning meal of barley porridge, and meat pie or ham replaced the seemingly endless boiled beef.   On St. Raphael's day and on St. John the Baptist's day, the boys received a small glass of wine, coffee or tea, and perhaps a choice of desserts.   This last, if nothing more, must have fixed these dates, the days of the patron saints of the college and of French Canada, in the minds of the boys attending the school.   At the noon and evening meals, pupils in residence at the college were required to read edifying passages from a book selected

by the director.   This was preceded by a few passages of scripture and
followed by a short biographical sketch of the saint whose festival would
be celebrated on the morrow.

Although no uniform was prescribed after 1840, the boys generally
wore a costume consisting of navy blue pants, a kind of Prince Albert
coat of the same material which extended to the knees, a light blue belt,
and a round cap bearing the monogram of the college.   Until 1862, when
the old college was closed, every boy looked after his own laundry.
Each Saturday, after supper, the boys were entitled to a weekly bath or
foot bath.   Daily attendance at Mass was required after breakfast,
before classes began.

The course of studies was that of the ordinary French classical college.
It occupied eight years, called Latin, Syntax, Method, Versification,
Belles-Lettres, Rhetoric and Philosophy.   The subjects studied included
religious instruction, Latin, Greek, French, English, mathematics,
philosophy, and the elements of physics, chemistry, astronomy and
botany.   The emphasis was thus upon the humanistic studies, with only
a cursory nod in the direction of the sciences.   Each pupil's day was full.
With frequent examinations, both oral and written, there was little time
for idle dreaming.   It seemed a long struggle for the young boy, but the
reward at the end was the classical baccalaureate.

When Louis Riel entered the college as a boarding student in September, 1858, he went, not to the new college on Sherbrooke Street with its
round towers that recalled the earlier days of the Ancien Régime, which
as yet housed only a few theological students, but to the old, four-storied,
stone building on St. Paul and McGill Streets.   It was a forbidding
structure enclosed within a high stone wall.   On the west side there was
a playground with some poplar trees; but there were no organized sports,
and very little time for games and play.   There was, indeed, no contact
with the outside world.   The boys seldom left the grounds of the college,
except in the vacation period, and all their activities were carried on
under the vigilant eyes of the black-robed instructors, who dominated
their lives both within and outside the classroom.   The director of the
college at this time was Mr. Pierre Paul Denis, pss.   It was Mr. Denis
who had agreed to accept Louis Riel at Bishop Taché's request some
months before and to charge no fees for his education.[17]   In 1859, Mr.
Denis was followed as Director by Mr. Charles Octave Lenoir-Rolland,
pss, who held this appointment until 1871.   He it was, therefore, who
presided over the college during the greater part of Riel's residence there
as a student.   Riel himself left no comments upon the personality of the
director, or upon his relations with him; but one of Riel's contemporaries,
Joseph Dubuc, described Mr. Lenoir-Rolland as "a good, friendly man, as

tender as a mother, but strict in the observance of regulations, just and impartial for all."[18] Among the other teachers through whose hands Riel passed were Pierre Deguire, Jules Claude Delavigne (who acted as as Louis Riel's confessor), Daniel Lefebvre, Jean Moyen, Jacques Palatin and Leon Alfred Senterre.

Riel entered the second year (Syntax.) There were thirty-seven other boys in the class. Despite the fact that Louis, a shy, awkward métis from the country beyond, an unsophisticated lonely boy, had received his preliminary training in the inadequate quarters, with the inadequate facilities then available at St. Boniface, he was able to hold his own with those who had been more fortunate. His success was a tribute to the patience and skill of his first teachers, and especially the Reverend LaFlèche, and the Reverend LeFloch. One of the first college reports, that of October 8, 1858, showed that Riel stood twenty-fourth in his class. Three weeks later, Louis had improved his position to thirteenth. His reports, it must be admitted, show considerable fluctuation from week to week but, generally speaking, he was to be found high in the lower half of the class. There were frequent "good enough" comments on his work, but very few as poor as "passable" or "mediocre."[19]

In the following year, 1859/60, there was a noticeable improvement in the quality of his work and in his standing. He was now better adjusted to his surroundings, and his native ability began to make itself evident in his competition with his fellows. He was, moreover, an intent scholar and he devoted himself to his studies. During this year he moved, generally, between third and ninth in his class. On one occasion, in the presentation of a Latin composition on January 13, 1860, he came second, tying with Eustache Prud'homme; then, several weeks later, he stood first. There were no "passable" or "mediocre" reports any more; instead there were numerous "very good" and even the "perfect" comments so eagerly sought by the better students in the school.

Riel's achievements in his year of Method were carried into his third and fourth years, despite a serious interruption in the routine of the college. In December, 1861, the old college was requisitioned by the British military authorities to house a regiment of infantry sent to Canada as part of the reinforcements for the Canadian garrison. The regiment had been sent in view of the belligerent attitude of the United States following the *Trent* affair in November. The building on Sherbrooke Street was still not ready in January, 1862, when the pupils returned, but there was no place else for them to go. They were, therefore, installed in a wing in the east side: the wing reserved for the seminary. The chapel was unfinished; even the windows in the building

were not yet all in place.   Both boys and instructors suffered dreadfully
from the cold and from the drafts that seemed to blow everywhere
through the long corridors and underneath the doors.   As before, Riel
sometimes led his class; sometimes he came second or third; more often
he stood fourth, fifth or sixth.   His conduct drew praise from his instructors and his work was frequently "very good" or "perfect."   In every
way he seemed to conform to the pattern of the good, if not exceptional,
student; although on one occasion his teacher noted on the weekly
report, after Riel had submitted a theme in French, "the subject of his
composition was the death song of a Scandinavian king confined in a
prison filled with snakes."[20]   It seemed to indicate a peculiar twist of
mind, not usually associated with a youth bent upon a religious life.

These were perhaps Riel's happiest years at the College of Montréal.
He excelled in Belles-Lettres and Rhetoric, and he enjoyed the opportunities that were offered to express himself on all manner of topics.   It
was about this time, too, that he took to writing poetry.   One of his
schoolfellows wrote of him, "Sometimes he cultivated the Muses, or
sought to bestride Pegasus, but I must confess at once that this illustrious
steed proved rather too stubborn, and he was never able to ride him in a
skilful manner, that is to say, Louis Riel never was able to produce even
a short piece of poetry bearing the mark of good style or sound criti-
cism."[21]   A harsh judgment perhaps, but not an untruthful one.   The
solemn dignity of the college, its atmosphere of piety and devotion, struck
a responsive chord in him.   In his later years he spoke with great respect
of "the enlightened and pious" men under whom he had studied, and in
particular of the influence over him of his confessor, Mr. Delavigne, "one
of the wisest spiritual directors in the world."[22]   On one occasion he
wrote, "The seven years I spent in that excellent institution inculcated
good principles in me, so that my spirit was filled to overflowing with
them."[23]

Riel's success as a student was equalled by that of his relations with
his fellow students.   At least this would seem to be the gist from the
limited evidence that is available.   Eustache Prud'homme, one of Louis's
classmates, wrote in 1870, "During his entire course of studies, he knew
how to win the esteem and friendship of his companions; without doubt
he was one of the quickest and best students that there were in the
class."[24]   He admitted that Louis had a keen sense of pride, and a
sarcastic tongue when provoked, but he asserted that the young métis
"gained respect in conversation by his calm and dignified cheerfulness.
He knew to perfection the art of charming people by his amazing fluency
of speech."   Another contemporary, J. O. Mousseau, wrote that Riel
was "liked by his teachers, admired by his schoolfellows, filled with a

gentle and sincere piety," and that he won the respect of his comrades "who saw in him an example to follow." Because he was serious, he played few games and took his recreation by walking in the garden. However, "sometimes when he did happen to play ball, he would suddenly leave off the game without saying a word whenever he saw that his contemporaries were cheating." If Louis disliked cheating, he liked bullying even less. According to Mousseau, "nothing irritated him as much as an abuse of strength against the weak,"[25] and on one occasion he took sides against several of his schoolmates in defence of a young Irish boy in his own class who was being picked on by the others.

If his school days were happy days so, too, were those of the weeks of vacation. For the most part these were spent in company with his friend and former schoolmate, Louis Schmidt; sometimes at Boucherville, at the home of the Tachés; sometimes at Terrebonne, with the Masson family who had taken so strong an interest in Louis's father, and in the two métis boys whom the Bishop had recommended; or at Chateauguay, with the Grey Sisters, where Riel and Schmidt admired the beautiful lawns where the Calvary stood, lawns of a greenness never seen in the prairie grass to which they had been accustomed.[26] On one occasion they underwent the thrilling experience of running the rapids of the St. Lawrence at Sault St. Louis. It recalled similar experiences to Schmidt who had been born on the Saskatchewan, but to Riel it was something new; and he was exhilarated by the sound of the rushing water, by the white, churning, foaming waves dashing over and alongside the rocks, by the sense of danger and by the feeling of confidence in the skill of the pilot. On another occasion the two boys, joined by their comrade, Daniel McDougall, witnessed the celebrations that accompanied the visit of H.R.H. Edward, Prince of Wales, to Canada in 1860.[27] In 1861 these happy summer days together came to an end. Schmidt and McDougall both returned to the Red River Settlement, and Louis Riel, alone of the four boys originally selected by the Bishop of St. Boniface to prepare for the priesthood, remained in Canada to carry on his studies.

In 1863, Riel entered his first year of Philosophy. As before, his results were academically adequate. His report for 1864, after all his examinations had been written, read: "Conduct, very good; Application, very good; Success, very good." He was now nineteen years of age, going on twenty. He was ready to enter his final year of Philosophy. Graduation was only a few months away. Everything seemed to be in his favour, a good intelligence, a charming personality, a strong physique and a good appearance. He was, according to one of his friends, "a fine looking man" almost six feet in height, with strong curly hair, high forehead, bushy arch-shaped eyebrows, deep set, penetrating eyes, prominent cheekbones and full lips. His shoulders, too, were broad. Almost everyone who knew him wrote of the charm of his appearance as well as that of his personality.[28]

But there were other traits in Riel's character that did not win such outspoken praise: his pride, his quick temper, his inclination towards broodiness. He was too ready to argue with his teachers whenever he thought their orders unreasonable or arbitrary. Moreover, in arguments with his schoolfellows, he was not prepared to brook their contradictions. "To offer an opinion contrary to his was to irritate him," wrote Mousseau. "He did not understand that everyone could not share his views, so much did he believe in his personal infallibility."[29] Pride was Louis's greatest weakness. It was pride that pushed him into exaggerations, into positions of extremes, from which he could not withdraw, to which, in the end, he was to fall victim. He lacked the humility necessary to become a good priest.

Nor was Riel's academic career wholly without its sombre tones. Louis had always been a sensitive and a brooding boy, and when, in February, 1864, he learned of the death of his father in Red River, the blow seemed doubly severe because he was so far from his home, his mother, his brothers and sisters. The lonely boy abandoned himself to his sorrow. So deep was his depression that his religious advisors urged him not to write to his mother until he was more completely master of himself. And so it was that he wrote first to Madame Masson on February 20 to inform her of "the blow that God has dealt our family."[30] Then, on February 23 he could hold himself no longer and wrote to his mother: "My dear papa always gave us an example to follow, the resignation that the holy Virgin has granted to us all at such an unhappy moment is also the source from which I can draw the courage that I need so much." As he wrote he became more and more lost in his grief: "Papa, dear papa, you will care for us still in heaven above . . . we shall pray for you, pray for you. . . . Dear mama, pardon me, I yield too readily to my sorrow. Let us have courage and faith in God."[31] In March he wrote again to his mother, asking her to tell him all her sorrows, worries, everything "for now I have the right to suffer with you." He ended his letter on a hopeful note, telling his mother that he had passed his examinations with good marks—"St. Joseph helped me most certainly"—and urging her to pray for the Gentlemen of St. Sulpice who "are indeed true fathers."[32]

But if this letter suggests a lessening of the intensity of Louis's grief, there was an underlying note of melancholic dejection, a preoccupation

with his own loneliness, in one of his poems that dates from this period
of his life:[33]

> In the midst of the crowd, rolling and restless,
> When a man is seen, a man with pensive look
> And air of sadness and nobility,
> Others throw him a glance of suspicion
> They whisper to one another
> "Brother, who is that fellow?"
> But the attention that he momentarily evokes
> Is limited to a vague uneasiness, nothing more.
> He wanders, lonely, his heart full of sadness.
> He suffers.
> The emptiness in his heart is filled only with sighs,
> Alone with his sorrow, an exile from all pleasures,
> In pain he lives out his days overflowing with bitterness.

Riel took a long time to get over the shock of his father's death.
Perhaps he let it prey too much upon his mind; perhaps he could not
help it, for his father and his mother had meant so much to him.   In
spite of the satisfactory marks he continued to make in his examinations,
there was a change in his attitude towards his work which worried his
instructors, a certain nervousness, a restlessness, a rebelliousness, a lack
of stability.   They began to question whether he really had a sense of
religious vocation after all.

And Louis seems to have wondered much the same thing.   For in
spite of his success in the examination in December, 1864, and the fact
that he had only six months more to go to complete his course, he went
to see Mr. John Atkinson, Madame Masson's agent at Terrebonne, about
the possibilities of entering a commercial career.   Atkinson reported
Riel's visit to Madame Masson, telling her that her métis protégé had
been to see him "respecting his future prospects in life."   "He informed
me," Atkinson wrote, "that it was his intention, if approved by his
friends, to remain in Montreal for some years, and he was undecided
whether to take a profession or enter a store.   I told him that I was under
the impression that he would enter the Church.   He told me no, that
his tastes led him into the world as he hoped at some future day to be
able to assist in settling his young brothers and sisters."[34]

Then suddenly, in March, 1865, four months before the end of the
academic year, Riel quit the College of Montreal.   There is no evidence
to show that this was the result of long contemplation, of days spent in
the chapel in prayer, of hours spent with his confessor.   It seems almost
to have been a sudden whim or caprice, without real thought of the future.
It would almost seem that he became completely obsessed with the weight
of his new responsibility as head of the family, and yielded to the nagging

anxieties of what he would do with his life. Clearly he had been unhappy and restless for some months, ever since the death of his father. Before he had been well; now he complained of ill-health, and he absented himself from class. Before he had accepted the restrictive regulations of the college; now he complained of them. He asked that he be allowed to continue his schooling as a day pupil rather than as a boarder, and that he be allowed to live with the Grey Sisters.

Mr. Lenoir-Rolland, pss, the Director of the College, would not grant Riel's request. He believed that if Riel lived outside the college it would only further unsettle him. In the end he yielded, and Louis went to take up residence at the convent. The Sisters had their regulations, too, but they could not enforce them as effectively as could the priests at the college, and Louis began to come and go as he pleased. Filled with alarm, the Sisters complained to Mr. Lenoir-Rolland that Riel not only would not do what he was told, but that he would stay away from the convent, not even returning to sleep there.[35] Then came more frequent absences from classes at the college; first one, then two, and then several in a row. Riel endeavoured to explain these absences by pointing out that he was obliged to spend some time in town looking for employment when he should graduate; he would do better in the future. But his promises were not kept, and finally he was told that he could no longer remain at the college "owing to his continual infractions of the rules of the house." There were no recriminations on either side. When Mr. Lenoir-Rolland wrote to Bishop Taché to explain Riel's withdrawal from the college, he remarked, "we have no regret for having given him his education. It is true that we would have been happier if we had been able to return to you, in his person, a good missionary. But God does not seem to have called him to that estate. I am very much afraid that the poor boy was not worthy of it. In any case it is a thousand times better that he should be an ordinary Christian than become a bad priest."[36]

IV

It was a strange and unfamiliar world in which Riel found himself when the doors of the College of Montreal were closed behind him on March 8, 1865. It was a world of intellectual ferment, of religious strife and political controversy. French Canada had become aware of itself. French-Canadians were enjoying an intoxicating sense of pride in their historic past. They had resented Lord Durham's jibe that they were a people without a culture. Now François Garneau was stirring their imaginations with his heroic portrayal of the history of New France; and Octave Crémazie was providing them with patriotic songs. The visit to

Quebec in 1855 of the French corvette *Capricieuse* had given a fillip to the patriotic idea. It had started a legend that for the first time in almost a century New France was once more the cultural child of mother France.

The revived interest in cultural nationalism was not the only feature of the intellectual climate of mid-nineteenth century Quebec. There were other forces at work, ultramontanism and liberalism. Ignace Bourget, the saintly Bishop of Montreal, was the soul and inspiration of the first. It was Bourget who, because he sympathized with the *Patriotes* during the Rebellion of 1837/38, was able to give to ultramontanism a nationalistic quality which marked it as different from its counterpart in Europe. To Bourget the preservation of the Roman Catholic faith and the survival of French Canada were mutually dependent upon each other. Let a French-Canadian lose his language and he would, all too often, lose his faith as well. Race and religion: they could not be separated. Thus Canadian ultramontanism, with its emphasis upon the supremacy of the Church over the State, emphasized equally the defence of French-Canadian culture and the national idea.

In opposition to the *Ultras* were the *Rouges*, led by men like L. A. Dessaulles, Joseph Doutre, Arthur Buies and Eric Dorion, who were no less nationalist than the *Ultras*, but who talked of political liberalism, of republicanism and of the subordination of the Church to the State. Their ideas were advanced through the medium of the *Institut Canadien* in Montreal, an organization which had been established in order to provide an intellectual centre for young French-Canadian graduates of the classical colleges. Between the *Rouges* and the *Ultras* there could be no compromise, no common meeting ground, not even on the ground of a common allegiance to a common national ideal. The *Ultras*, supported by the publication in 1864 of Pius IX's *Syllabus of Errors*, and the *Rouges*, critical of the religious orders and supporting non-sectarian schools, engaged in hostilities for over a quarter of a century. It lasted until the victory of the former, following the Guibord case in 1875, a victory the *Institut Canadien* did not long survive.

Another issue which filled the columns of the newspapers during these same years was the political future of the provinces of British North America. Alexander Galt had made the adoption of the federation of British North America as part of the Conservative party programme the price of his entering George Cartier's cabinet in 1858. It was the same year that Louis Riel went to Montreal to study. As federal union moved from the mere expression of an idea to actual negotiations between the provinces at Charlottetown and Quebec, questions were raised with regard to the place of French Canada in such a union. Nationalists of all colours began to question the motives of the confederates. George Cartier and Hector Langevin might protest that the scheme evolved at Quebec in 1864 provided the necessary guarantees for the survival of French Canada as a cultural entity, but there were many who doubted whether the guarantees really guaranteed very much. The debate in the Canadian legislature in 1865 was long and, on occasions, bitter. And the recriminations became more bitter when the provisions to protect the rights of the English minority in Quebec were not matched by similar provisions for the French-Canadian minority in Ontario.[37]

In the cross currents of these controversies the young Louis Riel must have been tossed to and fro. His nationalistic and romantic bent would have turned him towards the anti-confederates; but his strong clerical upbringing would have directed his sympathies towards the Church. For the moment the Church, and particularly the Sulpicians, were inclined to give a restrained and somewhat cautious support to confederation, if for no other reason than the fact that the most inveterate opponents of the union were a small group of anti-clericals in the *Institut Canadien*.[38] There were no clear-cut lines. Everything was muddling and confusing. It was all rather frightening.

There was, however, nothing to show that Louis was alarmed or daunted by what he found outside the walls of the college in 1865. He went to live at Mile End village, St. Jean Baptiste, with his aunt, Mrs. John Lee—his father's sister Lucie had married a Montrealer of Irish origin some years before—and here he remained for some months.[39] He was still depressed by his father's death. But he rapidly gained confidence and began to talk politics. Here was something which interested him almost as much as religion. There had been little chance to talk politics in the College of Montreal where even newspapers were not allowed; but there had been a few occasions when some of the pupils spoke of what was happening outside, and all had been able to share the excitement and enthusiasm when George Cartier had been welcomed to the college in 1860, to the accents of "O Canada, my land, my love." Perhaps that was why Louis had written to Cartier on the death of his father in 1864, and why he approached him again early in 1865 seeking an interview. But the interview, if it ever took place (and there is no evidence to show that it did) led to nothing, and some time elapsed before Louis was able to find a place for himself. Meanwhile he talked more and more about politics. Some of it sounded rather like that of the *Rouges*, except that it was a métis republic that Louis was thinking of rather than a French-Canadian republic.

Sometimes his talk was less coherent. When Father Vanderberghe came to see him in July, 1865, it was about the fur trade that Louis spoke, about how he had obtained a large sum of money from a stranger to invest in furs, and how he would go into the fur trade on his own. Vanderberghe was not impressed. Nor was he impressed by Riel's "fashionable" appearance and his shaggy, uncut hair.[40] "This poor boy arouses my pity," he wrote to Bishop Taché. "He is off to make his fortune, but I am afraid that he is getting beyond his depth."[41]

Riel had written several verses to George Cartier lauding his stand and urging him to "work for us who are your brothers, crush every obstacle before you, defeat your enemies and their noxious schemes, close your ears to the vulgar spite of those who are carried away by their own foolish ideas. . . ."[42] But it was in the law office of Cartier's great opponent, Rodolphe LaFlamme, that Riel found employment.[43] LaFlamme was a strong nationalist, a strong anti-clerical and a strong anti-confederate. It hardly seems to have been the kind of atmosphere in which Riel, the clerical and the conservative, could have thrived. In any event, it was soon obvious to all that Riel was not cut out to be a lawyer. He was too intolerant of the law's formalities, too impatient of its subtleties and too resentful of the contradictions that court work involved. Too frequently he quit his office to carry his thoughts, if not his brief, to the slopes of Mount Royal, from which he could look at the clear blue sky and the broad waters of the St. Lawrence. His thoughts may have turned towards the plains and rivers of Assiniboia; more probably they were on the face and form of the young girl whom he hoped some day to marry. But if he learned little law from LaFlamme, he may well have absorbed some of LaFlamme's ideas. Not that he could have shared LaFlamme's anti-clericalism—his religious training had made too deep an impression for that—but he could well have been influenced by LaFlamme's enthusiasm for politics, his national sympathies and his opposition to confederation.

Louis spent a little over a year in Montreal, between the time he left school and the day he decided to return to the west. This decision was, apparently, the result of the disappointment he suffered in a love affair. Some time during his years in Montreal, the young Riel met and fell in love with a young woman, Marie Julie Guernon, the daughter of Joseph Guernon and Louise Euphémie Bourque, who were neighbours of the Lees. The lovers did not inform Marie's parents of what had happened, but they secretly concluded a marriage contract on June 12, 1866, before the notary, A. C. Décary of Montreal.[45] When the bans were subsequently published in the Church of the Holy Infant Jesus, Mile End, St. Louis, Marie's parents raised such objections to their daughter marrying a métis that the match was broken off; and Louis Riel, angry and disappointed, shook the dust of Montreal from his feet.[46]

According to his former schoolmate, the companion with whom he had travelled east, Riel went first to Chicago, where he lived with the Canadian poet Louis Fréchette and wrote verses in the style of Alphonse de Lamartine.[47] Unfortunately no letters survive from this period of Louis's life. All that can be offered in corroboration of Schmidt's statement is the fact that there was a colony of expatriate French-Canadians in Chicago, and that Fréchette (who was of the same generation as Louis Riel and who, like Riel, was a strong romantic) was the voice of this group and the author of some violent diatribes against English Canada.[48] It was the kind of atmosphere in which Riel would have been at home and in which he could have indulged his inclinations towards authorship. But it would not have been the place for him to earn his living. And this he was obliged to do. Even if he did stay with Fréchette—and this may be open to question in the absence of further evidence—his stay could not have been a long one. According to one source, he worked briefly for Ed Langevin in St. Paul; according to another, he was employed for a while by Gilbert Lachance.[49] All that can be stated with assurance is that Riel left St. Anthony early in July, 1868, for St. Joseph. From here he went on, by steamer, to St. Boniface, where he arrived on July 28. "It was early in the morning," he wrote, "when I saw my birthplace again; a Sunday, before sunrise. It was a beautiful day. I saw my very dear mother, brothers and sisters that very same day."[50]

Louis Riel was home again. But he was not wearing a soutane. He was almost twenty-four years of age, educated, clever, imbued with a strong sense of pride in himself and in his own people, and unemployed. It was an explosive mixture.

CHAPTER 3

Red River

T HE RED RIVER COLONY to which Louis Riel returned in July, 1868, was not the colony he had left ten years before. There had been many changes: changes in the physical aspect of the colony, and even more important changes in the colony's economy and political attitudes. The old cathedral at St. Boniface that had been built by Bishop Provencher had gone; it had burnt to the ground in December, 1861, and had been replaced by a new one, built by Bishop Taché. The house in which Riel had learned the rudiments of Latin before setting out for Montreal had also been reconstructed. Only the statue of the Holy Virgin above the door was still the same.[1] There was now a new village across the river from St. Boniface; it was called for a short time McDermotstown but, by 1868, it was known as Winnipeg. When Louis Riel was a boy, only Andrew McDermot and his son-in-law, A. G. B. Bannatyne, had storehouses there; by 1862, Henry McKenney had built a large two-storied wooden building, known locally as the "Noah's Ark," "at a spot where the Assiniboine and Red River tracks met close to the boundary of the Hudson Bay Company's land reserves."[2] McKenney had been followed by another merchant, William Drever. Other buildings followed: John Schultz's brick drug store, Henry McDermot's grist mill, John Kennedy's gun shop, Archibald Wright's harness shop, H. S. Donaldson's bookstore, Henri Coutu's butcher shop, James Ashdown's tin shop, Ryder Larsen's photography gallery, and Tom Lusted's carriage shop. In addition there were two churches, a school run by the Sisters of Charity, two saloons, Hugh O'Lone's and Onésime Monchamp's, Dutch George Emmerling's hotel, Charles Garrett's Garrett House, and other buildings. There were new houses, too, belonging to the McKenneys, the Birds, the Rosses, the Logans, the Bannatynes, the Drevers, the McKays, the McDermots, the Schultzs and others. Winnipeg was a growing lusty place, with frame buildings, roads sticky and muddy or dry and dirty according to the weather, métis tripmen, boatmen, buffalo hunters, Yankee adventurers and Canadian traders, miners, and army deserters from Fort Totten, all filling the streets, the saloons and the night with their shouting, roistering and fighting.[3]

There was also a newspaper; this was something new. In 1859, two Englishmen, William Buckingham and William Coldwell, arrived from Canada by way of St. Paul. With them they brought a press, boxes of type and bales of paper. On December 28, the first newspaper to appear in the Canadian North-West, the *Nor'Wester*, made its appearance. According to the prospectus, "Its projectors come hither to hold to no set of men, influenced by no narrow prejudices shackled by no mean antipathies. Their journal will be the vehicle of news and for the pertinent discussion of local questions; governed only by a desire to promote local interests, and a determination to keep aloof from every entangling alliance which might mar its usefulness at home and abroad."[4] In fewer words, the aim of the newspaper was to attack local institutions, the Hudson's Bay Company in particular. In 1864 the controlling interest in the *Nor'Wester* was bought by Dr. John Schultz, who turned the editorial duties over to James Ross, the half-breed son of the sheriff of Assiniboia. In 1868, Schultz sold out to Dr. Walter Bown, a Canadian who, between editorials, practised dentistry in the settlement.

Dr. John Christian Schultz was one of the new figures Riel saw in Red River. Schultz had been born in 1840 at Amherstburg, Upper Canada, of Danish and Irish descent. He had been educated at the universities in Toronto and Kingston. After a brief visit to the North-West in 1861, he had decided to make his home in the Red River Settlement. Here, he thought, was a field suitable for his talents; for Schultz, a tall, powerfully built man, over six feet in height, had both ambition and an alert mind. In the opinion of one of his contemporaries, he possessed "in a large degree the spirit of adventure that has helped make Britain, Great Britain."[5] Those who knew him intimately spoke of his shrewdness— some might call it unscrupulousness—and his ruthlessness.[6] There is no doubt that he was a determined man, with strong convictions and the strength of will to carry his plans through to a conclusion: and his plans did not include the maintenance of Red River as a half-breed community or a Hudson's Bay Company preserve. By temperament, Schultz was born to lead; by his political aggressiveness, by Masonic affiliations,[7] he was bound to come into conflict with the native population, at least with those who spoke French and wished only to be left alone. From the standpoint of the métis, Schultz was a man to be not only hated but to be feared.

Dr. Schultz was not without supporters in the colony. Since Riel had left St. Boniface ten years before, a number of Canadians had come to settle in Assiniboia. Unlike the Americans, who made their way to Red River to seek adventure or sell liquor, the Canadians came to take up land. They came to stay. Many of them were the overflow of that great western migration from Canada to Wisconsin, Michigan and Minnesota, which took place during the mid-nineteenth century.[8] Some of the new settlers established themselves in Kildonan among the old Selkirk settlers, others moved up the Assiniboine to the comparatively unoccupied area about Portage la Prairie. A few of them were traders who came to take advantage of the quickening tempo of economic life in Red River, and these settled in Winnipeg. All of them were strongly in favour of the annexation of Red River to Canada, strongly opposed to the Hudson's Bay Company, and supremely indifferent to the half-breed population. It was to Dr. Schultz that they looked for leadership, and it was at McKenney's, and later at Schultz's store in Winnipeg, that they foregathered to ridicule the paternal institutions, of the colony,[9] to discuss the leading articles written by Ross or Bown in the *Nor'Wester*, and to drink toasts in Demarara rum to the absorption of the North-West by Canada.[10]

If the native settlers, the half-breeds, the métis and the Scottish settlers were disposed to look beyond the horizons of Assiniboia, it was southwards that they looked, as they watched the departure of trains of Red River carts towards Pembina and St. Paul. In 1843, when Joseph Rolette had started a regular service between Fort Garry and St. Paul, he found that half a dozen carts were sufficient for his purposes. By 1858 the number had grown to 600. In 1865, on one trip alone, Norbert Welsh travelled with a train of 300 carts[11]; and by 1869 some 2,500 Red River carts lunged and screeched their ungreased way behind the ponderous ox-teams that hauled them along the road to St. Paul. Even the Hudson's Bay Company had taken to using the St. Paul route, and Fort Garry acquired significance as a distributing point for the interior. Every year saw more and more York boats sailing down the Red River towards Lake Winnipeg, bound for the Saskatchewan posts and bearing their cargoes of pemmican and flour. Then, in 1859, the merchants of St. Paul launched the first steamboat, the *Anson Northrup*, "a lumbering old pine-basket, which you have to handle as gingerly as a hamper of eggs," on the Red River.[12] Her career was brief, but she showed the way for the others that followed, like the *International* (1862) and the *Selkirk* (1871). Hard on the stern paddles of the river steamboats were the driving wheels of the railway engines. In 1858, Riel had not embarked in a train until he had reached Prairie du Chien. Now the railway ran as far north as St. Cloud, and the Northern Pacific had received a charter from Congress to build a line from Duluth to Puget Sound. [13]

The years spent by Riel in Montreal had, in fact, been the years that had breached the walls isolating Red River. More and more the

Settlement was becoming, economically at least, the northern extension of Minnesota. Canada was far away; Great Britain was even more remote. Americans were talking openly of annexing the Company's territories to the United States. And even in Red River the editor of the *Nor'Wester* wrote:

It cannot be denied that of late a feeling in favour of the U.S.A. has been gaining ground among the inhabitants of this Settlement . . . The constant intercourse is creating sympathies which 'ere long might result in a demand for annexation . . . a route from the Canadian side of the Line should be opened at once. . . . We are indebted to the Yankees for the only route that there is to and from this country for ordinary commercial purposes.[14]

In another issue he wrote, with some asperity, "We speak advised when we say that the people of Red River are becoming indifferent to the British connection. They care very little for it. They would bear a severance without regret."[15]

II

If the people of Red River were turning their faces to the south, those in Minnesota had their eyes directed to the north. The annexation of neighbouring territories was no new phenomenon in American history. Sometimes it occurred peacefully, sometimes by purchase, sometimes by threats, sometimes by force of arms. Florida, Louisiana, California, Texas, Oregon had been added to the American union by methods which, if open to question on moral grounds, were at least unquestioned owing to their effectiveness. But the idea of annexation had not been limited to the south and west. There was also a drive towards the north. If this movement has been given less emphasis by American historians, it may be because the movement failed, and because Americans have been prone to equate importance with success.[16]

The northward drive of the United States had, indeed, begun as early as the year 1775, when Richard Montgomery and Benedict Arnold marched their troops into Canada in an effort to make Quebec the fourteenth colony in the American union. The invasion of Upper Canada in 1812 was another phase of the same desire to encompass the whole of North America within one single political entity. The failure of the American armies to achieve their purpose during the War of 1812/1814 diverted American expansionism towards the west and south; not until the middle of the century did the northward drive begin again. American frontiers had, by this time, reached the Rio Grande and the Pacific Ocean, but there was still room to the north, and the forty-ninth parallel was not the kind of barrier to discourage either immigrants or soldiers. Moreover, the northern regions were beginning to look attractive. First, there were the gold discoveries in the Fraser and the Cariboo; then there was talk of gold in the valley of the Saskatchewan; above all there were the fertile black-loamed farmlands of the Red River valley. In 1861, William Seward, President Lincoln's Secretary of State, revealed his great northern vision, in which he saw St. Paul emerging as the seat of power in North America.[17] This was heady stuff, particularly for the Minnesotans. Small wonder that Charles Adams declared that the effect of Seward's speech was "much like intoxication."[18] The newspapers took up the cry. They were filled with articles on annexation and showed a hypocritical concern for the welfare of the people of Red River.

Although the cause of annexation was advocated in other regions of the northern United States, notably in Chicago and in Detroit, the real centre of the agitation was St. Paul. This community was, by now, the *entrepôt* of the North-West trade, British as well as American, and it saw in its own future the fulfilment of Seward's dream. In St. Paul everyone was an annexationist: the merchants, because they felt that annexation would provide them with still greater opportunities to expand a trade already estimated at between one and two million dollars, not the inflated paper dollars of the 1960's but the solid gold dollars of the 1860's; the railwaymen, because annexation seemed to offer opportunities for new railway lines into the British territories to the north, which would take the carriage of goods and passengers away from the slower and more cumbersome steamers; the politicians, because they saw in annexation a sure and easy way to obtain votes. Annexation was a political matter; and so it was the politicians who took the lead in pressing it upon the United States government. Of these, the principal exponent was the former governor of Minnesota and a member of the Senate of the United States, Alexander Ramsey. Echoing Ramsey's demands in Washington were those other apostles of expansionism, Senators Zachariah Chandler and Joseph Howard of Michigan, and General N. P. Banks of Massachusetts.

Of all advocates of the annexation of the North-West, no man worked harder to bring it about than James Wickes Taylor. For years by his own personal charm, Taylor persuaded western Canadians he was their closest friend, and he did everything possible to bring Western Canada into the maw of the United States.[19] United States' treasury representative, American consul, railway lobbyist, undercover agent, he moved in and out of the history of Manitoba for a quarter of a century, never abandoning hope that he might live to see the end of British and Canadian rule in the west.

It was in 1859 that Taylor was first appointed special agent of the
United States Treasury and sent to report on the situation in the Red
River Settlement.   In his early accounts he expressed the view that the
colony was ripe for American occupation, preferably by peaceful means;
but, if war should come, Minnesota could readily and easily "hold,
occupy, and possess" the entire Red River Valley as far as Lake Winnipeg.[20]   Taylor kept a close eye on the editorial columns of the *Nor'Wester*,
and every indication of pro-American sentiment was reported to
Washington.   Taylor sent his reports not only to the Capitol, but also he
wrote consistently to Governor Henry Sibley and Alexander Ramsey of
Minnesota, providing them with the ideas and data that they put
forward in the legislative buildings both in St. Paul and Washington.
In 1866, General Banks introduced a bill in the House of Representatives
for "the admission of the States of Nova Scotia, New Brunswick, Canada
East, Canada West" and for the organization of the Territories of
Selkirk, Saskatchewan and Columbia.   The voice that advocated this
insolent proposal was that of the noisy representative from Massachusetts, but the hand that wrote it was the hand of the personable and
attractive James Taylor.[21]   Banks's bill was not pressed owing to the
"demonstrations against the measure in Canada."[22]   The bill was not,
however, out of harmony with the views and ideas of the Secretary of
State; and this is shown by Seward's statement to a Boston audience in
1867, "I know that Nature designs that this whole continent, not merely
these thirty-six states, shall be sooner or later, within the magic circle of
the American union."[23]

It would appear that the real meaning of the Banks's bill was less a
desire to acquire the whole of Canada—although this proposal was
constantly advanced after the close of the Civil War as a means by which
Great Britain might pay the *Alabama* claims—than the hope of securing
the British North-West for the benefit of American railway builders.
There was no doubt that they, as well as the land seekers and the
politicians, had a real interest in the future of the North-West.   As early
as 1824 there had been talk of building a wagon road across the continent
to the Pacific.   In 1832, S. W. Dexter of Ann Arbor suggested the
construction of a railway from New York to the Columbia and, in 1845,
Asa Whitney proposed to build it.   For years the promoters of the
railway scheme argued the economic, political and military advantages
of such a line; finally, in 1864, Congress granted a charter and a large area
of land to the Northern Pacific.   The railway company lacked the money
to build the line, so its promoters sought to enlist the assistance of the
financial genius, Jay Cooke.   At first reluctant, Cooke became convinced
of the financial possibilities of a railway that might draw upon the

resources of the British as well as the American North-West.   In 1865, he undertook to dispose of the bonds of the proposed transcontinental railway company.[24]

The most serious problem, as far as the Northern Pacific was concerned, was the fact the British controlled the land north of the 49th parallel.   As long as the British were there, the Northern Pacific would be unable to eliminate competing lines, especially as the Canadians were already talking of building their own railway across the continent from Canada West to British Columbia.   It was in the interest of Cooke and the Northern Pacific to do what they could to erase all possibilities of competition, and the best way to do this would be to do away with the political boundary between the Hudson's Bay Territories and the United States.   To assist this worthy cause, Cooke hired James Taylor as his pressing agent and lobbyist.   After all, Taylor had many useful contacts in government circles in Washington.   And Taylor, with his mania for annexation, saw no inconsistency in using his official position while acting as Cooke's agent.   It hardly appears to be an ethical arrangement, but Taylor saw no conflict of interests in his two jobs, and he served his two masters with diligence and sincerity.[25]

Continuing his efforts, Taylor wrote in 1867 to the Assistant Secretary of the United States Treasury.   He argued that "the voluntary annexation of British America is nearer than we have supposed" and urged reconsideration of Banks's bill:

I firmly believe, if the bill referred to was placed among the laws of the United States, as a standing proposition for the consideration of Great Britain and the Provinces, that the state of public sentiment over the border . . . would soon be irresistible.   We have only to deposit an "open basket" (to use an illustration the New York *Evening Post* applied to this bill) under the tree, and the ripe fruit will speedily fall.

To show how ripe the fruit was, he contended that "West of the Great Lakes . . . the European population does not exceed 30,000, nine-tenths of whom desire annexation to the United States."[26]   It was an estimate based on wishful thinking, but Taylor never allowed accurate statistics to becloud his hopes.

A year later Taylor persuaded the Minnesota Legislature to adopt three resolutions which were sent to Washington.   One of these urged the United States to insist upon Great Britain holding a referendum in the North-West before settling the future of the territories, and another declared: "the legislature of Minnesota would rejoice to be assured that the accession of North-West British America to the United States, accompanied by the construction of the Northern Pacific railroad, are regarded by Great Britain and Canada as satisfactory provisions of a treaty which shall remove all grounds of controversy between the respective countries."[27]

This was the kind of thing that delighted Ramsey; he returned to the floor of the Senate suggesting, as terms of the proposed treaty, the payment of six million dollars to the Hudson's Bay Company, the organization of three new territories and the construction of a transcontinental railway line. If this were done, he maintained, Congress would "determine the destiny of northwest British America." Ramsey was backed by the committee on the Pacific Railway which put forward, as its clinching argument, the assurance that the construction of such a railway would inevitably result in "the British possessions west of the 91st meridian" becoming "so Americanized in interests and feeling that they will in effect be severed from the new dominion, and the question of their annexation will be but a question of time."[28]

This time element alarmed the people of Canada. They did not share Taylor's, or Ramsey's or Banks's enthusiasm for incorporation in the powerful, truculent, aggressive country to the south. They, too, were aggressive and expansionist in their own way, and they did not want the North-West to go the way of California or Oregon. They knew what to expect from the United States. After all, Canada had considerable experience of its sometimes unscrupulous neighbour, and Canadians knew that Americans would always take advantage of their strength and position. If the American threat hovering over the North-West were to be dissipated, it would have to be done by the Canadians themselves. Canada would have to establish a firm grasp on the Company's territories.

In 1846, Sir Richard Bonnycastle in his book *Canada and the Canadians* had referred to the discovery of coal on the Pacific and urged the construction of an "iron belt" to the Pacific across the lands of the Hudson's Bay Company.[29] Shortly afterwards, Lt. H. M. Synge suggested the building of a transcontinental railway as an unemployment relief measure and a means of sparing the North-West the fate of California. During the 1850's several railway companies were chartered. None of these projects got beyond the blueprint stage; in 1857, however, something positive seemed to be imminent. In that year the British government appointed a Select Committee to "consider the State of those British Possessions in North America which are under the Administration of the Hudson's Bay Company, or over which they possess a Licence to Trade." The Company's efforts to play down the North-West as a potential area for colonization and settlement carried little conviction, and in the end the British government expressed its willingness to cede to Canada certain portions of the Company's territories, such as the Red River and Saskatchewan valleys, "on equitable principles."[30] This was a departure from the government's earlier policy of defending the inviolability of the Hudson's Bay Company Charter, and the Canadians saw in it an opportunity to build their dykes in the Red River valley before the Americans could flood the region with settlers and propaganda.

Negotiations with officials of the Colonial Office and the Hudson's Bay Company did not proceed smoothly or rapidly. The Canadian government was never very friendly towards the Company and its charter. Canadians liked to think they had been first in the west, and they advanced a claim based upon prior discovery and occupation during the Ancien Régime; they were, in consequence, opposed to paying the Company for land that they argued had always rightfully been theirs. Further delays were imposed by the many political problems at home, unstable ministries, frequent changes of government, the possibility of British North American union and, after 1860, the question of Canada's attitude towards the two parties fighting a Civil War in the United States. The only progress made was the despatch of several exploring parties led by Captain John Palliser, S. J. Dawson and Professor H. Y. Hind, and the purchase of materials for a transcontinental telegraph. Sometimes people like the Governor-General, Sir Edmund Head, expressed the view that it might be better if the Imperial authorities should themselves establish a crown colony in the North-West. But no one listened. The British did not want the responsibility, and the Canadians desired the region for themselves.

It was not until after the passage of the British North America Act in 1867 and the formation of the first federal cabinet that the North-West question was taken up seriously. In April, 1868, negotiations with the Colonial office were resumed. The Canadians, although still disposed to be difficult, were more disposed to yield to British pressure and accept the principle of compensation. The Company, too, yielded to pressure from the same source and reluctantly agreed to dispose of its rights and privileges, under the famous charter of Charles II, for a token cash payment of £300,000 (Ramsey would have given them four times as much, and with considerably less haggling), a land allocation equal to one-twentieth of the land in the area to be opened for colonization, a promise not to impose restrictions against the Company's trade and the purchase of the materials for the neglected telegraph line. It was a victory for Canada; certainly the compensation was pitifully small for an area extending from the Great Lakes to the Rockies and from the 49th parallel to the Arctic. Nevertheless, the niggardly attitude of the Canadian government, its determination to take as much as possible and give as little as practicable, left a legacy of ill-will among Company servants in Great Britain and the Territories alike. There was little that Canada could expect from them in the way of co-operation and assistance in facilitating the transfer when it should take place.

Nor was there any reason why Canada should expect help from the people of Red River. In the discussions in London the latter had played no part. Their views had never been considered; even their existence had scarcely been recognized either by Canada, Great Britain or the Hudson's Bay Company.[31] As far as the Dominion was concerned, the government continued to maintain the fiction that the North-West had belonged by right to Canada since the days of the Ancien Régime. The people who lived there were therefore Canadians. How could there be any question of consulting them about their future when they were merely returning to their original allegiance? As far as the Indians were concerned, their title could be extinguished by some treaty arrangements: but the Selkirk settlers, the French métis and the Scotch half-breeds were forgotten or rather simply ignored. So Canada went ahead with its plans for the transfer without attempting to ascertain the climate of opinion in Red River, or even informing, officially, the Governor and Council of Assiniboia of what was being planned in Ottawa for the little colony on the banks of the Red and Assiniboine Rivers.

The date of the transfer was fixed initially for October 1, 1869;[32] that date, however, had to be postponed, and December 1 was finally agreed upon as the day when Canada should take over its new responsibilities in the North-West. In the meantime, what objection could there be to the Canadian parliament adopting an Act for the Temporary Government of Rupert's Land by a Lieutenant-Governor and council, or to the Prime Minister advising the Governor-General to appoint the Honourable William McDougall to fill the Lieutenant-Governor's appointment?

III

In 1869 the Red River Settlement was ripe for a change of administration. It had ceased to be what it had been twelve years before, when the Company's overlordship had been discussed by the Select Committee in London. It was no longer a community that could, with any justice, be described as one in which the people were "without the vexations and the heart-burning of active politics"; one in which "the rivalries that existed were in keeping with their simple life, and had nothing of that fierce element of competition into which the newer civilization was to hurl them";[33] or one in which the contests of life turned on the speed of horses "especially if they were owned in different parts of the colony," or who could be first with the seeding and the harvest, or who could carry the greatest number of bags of wheat, or who could survive longest in the almost endless rounds of the Red River jig. It is true that the people had challenged the Hudson's Bay Company on the question of the Company's trade policy, but they had never tried to replace the Company rule with some other form of administration. They had accepted the Council of Assiniboia without worrying very much about whether it was an elective or appointed body, or whether the Company was really behind the throne of the governor of Assiniboia. They had driven Adam Thom out of the country, not to challenge the jurisdiction of the Quarterly General Court, but because they questioned Thom's impartiality and resented his unilingualism. The local government had seldom had a military force to back up its decrees, but it had seldom needed one. It had succeeded in maintaining its authority largely because the people were prepared to accept it.[34]

The newcomers who had entered the colony within the last ten years felt no sense of loyalty to the Hudson's Bay Company or to the local government in the Settlement. On the contrary, many of them regarded themselves as the advance guard of a new economic and political order. All of them brought in their trunks and valises the political ideas and prejudices of the part of Canada from which they had come. Almost to a man they had come from Canada West or Ontario. They challenged the Company régime, they ridiculed it, they refused to obey its orders, they tore the trappings of dignity from it, bared its nakedness and revealed its puny muscles. The years between 1857 and 1869 were the years of decline in the old order in the Red River Settlement, the years of chaos, and finally the years of the collapse of the local administration.

The most serious challenge to the Hudson's Bay Company rule came from the newspaper, the *Nor'Wester*. The paper's first issue had spoken of "assisting in the work of governmental organization," as if there was no question whatsoever of the need of some new organization.[35] At the outset, editorial comment in the paper was comparatively mild, but after 1860, when James Ross began to write the leading articles, there was a noticeable sharpening in the tone of the editorials. Ross, although he had been born in Red River, had been educated in Canada. He had seen the outside world and had picked up new political ideas. If not really a very able man, he did possess considerable facility with his pen, and under his direction the *Nor'Wester* began to advocate closer trade relations and more intimate ties with Canada. Ross even began to talk about the end of Hudson's Bay Company rule in the North-West, and the possibility of a crown colony being established in the Company's territories. "It requires neither acuteness nor hostility on our part," he wrote, to see that for things to continue as they were was "*simply impossible.*"[36] As months passed, the *Nor'Wester* became more insistent upon change; an elective council was needed;[37] perhaps annexation to the United States was the answer to the colony's requirements.[38]

In 1862 the Sioux Massacre in the United States, and the withdrawal of the Indians to British territory, provided Ross with new material for his agitation.   At the very gates of Fort Garry, there were Indians who had been killing white men to the south.   How could the feeble government of the Company protect the Settlement and the settlers?   A stronger political body was needed.   The Governor of Rupert's Land thought a few soldiers would meet the needs of the Settlement.   He therefore prepared a petition to be sent to the imperial authorities asking for the despatch of regular troops to Red River.   But Ross would not print Governor Dallas's petition on the presses of the *Nor'Wester*; instead he substituted a petition drafted by himself to which he appended, to Dallas's request for troops, an expression of dissatisfaction with the administration of the Hudson's Bay Company and a request for a complete change of government.[39]   Both petitions were hawked about the Settlement in search of signatures; and both obtained them in considerable numbers.   Dallas was much concerned about Ross's success, for he wrote to the Bishop of St. Boniface protesting the good will of the Company towards the people generally.   He declared that the opposition of Ross and the *Nor'Wester* was no more than "the offspring of a few discontented individuals of no weight and with little stake in the country" who had "brought unfair influence to bear in obtaining the signatures of illiterate, ignorant and young people incapable of comprehending the meaning of the document to which their names are affixed."[40]   It is of little moment to discuss whether Dallas was right or not.   The very fact that Ross was as successful as he was indicates the extent of the split that had developed within the ranks of the local population.   Surely it would have been better had the Governor and his Council not been so prompt in dismissing Ross from his two appointments as sheriff and postmaster.[41]   Such action seemed to savour too much of vindictiveness and only gave the belligerent editor more ammunition with which to attack the Company.

That Ross did not have the wholehearted support of the people is clear from the meetings that followed the battle of the petitions.   At one meeting held in the parish of St. James, old Louis Riel made one of his infrequent appearances during the last years of his life, in order to declare: "Mr. Ross is a deceiver and a misleader of the people for he says that dissatisfaction with the Company's rule is universal, whereas the truth is among my people there is no such dissatisfaction."[42]   It must have sounded odd to hear the man who had defied the Company in the days of Sayer's trial defending it twelve years later.   But Riel's intervention is significant. It showed better than anything else the fact that the métis, the largest single group in the colony, were not prepared to march along the road down which Ross and his Canadian sympathizers were trying to lead the people of Red River. That Riel correctly interpreted the views of the majority of the population is shown by a letter written by Bishop Taché to Governor Dallas. The Bishop stated that in his opinion and in the opinion "of the immense majority of the people" a change of government would be "a real disaster"; the country was not ready for a change, and for the time being the Company "does all that can be reasonably expected for this Settlement."[43]

Late in 1862 another episode occurred that became a *cause célèbre* in Red River. In December, the Reverend Owen Corbett was arrested on a charge of endeavouring to procure an abortion for a servant girl whom he had allegedly seduced. It was a coincidence that Corbett was an outspoken advocate of annexation to Canada and that he had signed James Ross's petition rather than Dallas's; but it was enough of a coincidence to convince his friends that he was being made the victim of political persecution. There is no need to dwell upon the details of this unsavoury business.[44] It is sufficient to note that Corbett was given a fair trial—John Schultz admitted as much[45]—and that his sentence was a lenient one. More significant is the fact that Corbett's friends prepared a petition for his release from prison. When this was refused, a crowd of sympathizers led by one James Stewart, the schoolmaster from St. James, broke down the prison door and released the inmate. Stewart in turn was arrested. Then he too was forcibly released by a number of men led by two of Stewart's friends, William Hallett and John Bourke, both English half-breeds, the former being Captain of the English-speaking half-breeds in their expeditions to the plains.[46] On both occasions the law had been set aside and the law-makers intimidated, for neither Corbett nor Stewart was re-arrested. When the matter was discussed by the Council of Assiniboia at its meeting on April 28, the four magistrates of the Settlement, Robert McBeath, François Bruneau, Thomas Sinclair and William Cowan, excused their weakness by pointing out the absence of any armed force at the disposal of the civil power;[47] they would have been more perspicacious had they noted the growing lawlessness that now characterized the Settlement, and the breakdown of that respect for law, without which no administration can function, even with force at its command.

Up to this time the leader of the agitation against the Company had been James Ross, the half-breed son of the early historian of the Red River Settlement. He had gone further in his demands than had his predecessors, Sinclair or Riel, but he really had little of a positive nature to offer with regard to the future of the North-West, except perhaps the suggestion that it become a crown colony. That he enjoyed as much success as he did was due, in part at least, to the general dislike with which the people of Red River viewed the Governor of Rupert's Land, Alexander Dallas, who had taken over in 1862 from Sir George Simpson. Dallas not only lacked Sir George's administrative skill, but, understanding neither his own role nor the temper of the people of Red River as Sir George had done, he was disposed to push himself forward, to interfere in local matters, to play a more obvious part in the affairs of Assiniboia than Simpson had ever ventured to do. He had none of Simpson's tact, nor did he have the advice of experienced men like Pelly and Colvile to guide him. Unlike Simpson, Dallas was disposed to stand up to any opposition in Red River rather than let it rumble on, unnoticed.[48]

However, from 1864, when John Schultz took over control of the *Nor'Wester*, the agitation and the agitators became more positive, more provocative, more emphatically Canadian. Schultz's aim was annexation to Canada, and to that end he worked unremittingly. And he had the material with which to work, since Ross had prepared the way. It did not need Schultz to expose the weakness of Company rule, to stir the dormant waters of political thought, to raise doubts about the security of the Company's land titles or to create a general feeling of discontent within the Settlement. All that Schultz had to do was to take advantage of what Ross had done and to keep pressing forward to the overthrow of the Company régime. It should be remembered that Schultz and the Canadian Party, of which he became the acknowledged head, were not taking an unreasonable stand when they contended that the existing régime had ceased to meet the needs of the Settlement. A commercial company could not hope to govern indefinitely a colony in an age that was becoming increasingly democratic. It could offer no defence against American infiltration; the fate of Oregon was proof of that.

The atmosphere of Red River was changing, and this was clear to all. It was obvious to A. G. B. Bannatyne, a local settler, when he wrote to a friend: "Old Red River is going to the devil faster than ever, and God only knows what is to become of us if the English Government or some other friendly soul does not take us by the hand."[49] It was obvious to Lord Wharncliffe, a casual visitor, when he stated in the House of Lords, that there was "an absolute want of government in the Red River Settlement."[50] In 1866 a young Montrealer, Thomas Spence by name, endeavoured to hold a mass meeting in Winnipeg "for the purpose of memorializing the Imperial Government praying to be received into and become part of the Grand Confederation of British North America."

The meeting ended in a wild confusion of shouting, jostling, and breaking of bottles, all to the background music of "Come, Landlord, Fill the Flowing Bowl."[51]   The *Nor'Wester* reported the meeting as if it had been a serious expression of colonial opinion, and in Canada, where the Canadians read excerpts from the *Nor'Wester* in the Toronto *Globe*, they came to believe that the people of Red River were living under an intolerable tyranny, waiting only for Canada to come and free them. It was a pretty picture, this picture of the Canadian St. George slaying the Hudson's Bay dragon.   But it was an imaginary one.

By this time the *Nor'Wester* was in full battle array against the Hudson's Bay Company.   On February 6, 1866, reflecting the views of its owner, the paper insisted that the Canadian Government "buy out the Hudson's Bay Company's rights to rule over the North-West," adding that "thousands of ambitious young Canadians are already settling in Minnesota only awaiting the throwing open of the Red River lands to settlement."   Similar articles appeared regularly in the *Nor'Wester* during the remainder of that newspaper's existence.   Scarcely a week passed without some charge or other being hurled at the Company, or some admonition to Upper Canada to come and people the promised land west of the Great Lakes.   This was the way the Americans had acquired Texas and Oregon; Canada could well afford to take a leaf from the American book.   In 1868, Schultz severed his connection with the news-paper; but its new owner, Dr. Bown, one of twenty Canadians who came to the Red River Settlement in 1867, merely continued the Canadian Party line.   Like Schultz, Bown knew that the *Nor'Wester* did "not meet with the approbation of all parties," but he lashed out at "the sneaking, cowardly, mean and contemptible misrepresentation of some of our opponents."   He declared his own stand in a single sentence: "We believe that this Territory belongs to Canada."[52]

IV

The 1860's were not only years of political agitation, they were also years of drought, distress and sometimes of famine.   "Dry, Dry," wrote Samuel Taylor in 1863, "the Weather was never seen, people say, so long without rain, it Thunders often and yet no rain . . . it gets very rain like sometimes but it clears off and there is no rain."[53] With the drought came declining crop yields, the closing of the grist mills, the virtual cessation of water transport, a slowing down of the economic tempo of the Settle-ment.   All this was bad enough: but there were the grasshoppers as well.

There had been previous grasshopper plagues in Manitoba, but the plague that afflicted the colony in 1867/68 seemed to be worse than anything experienced before. In the autumn of 1867, Father Lestanc in St. Boniface remarked on the "devastation caused by the grasshoppers" and "the consternation in the hearts of our poor métis." Never had anybody ever seen so many of the "voracious insects" within the limits of Red River. The grasshoppers: "were as snow in the air and as flakes of snow upon the ground. They penetrated into the parlours and kitchens, bed chambers and bedding, pots, pans, kettles, ovens, boots and coat pockets. One scarcely dared to open one's mouth. On the rivers they floated like scum, or were piled two feet deep on the banks where they rotted and stunk like carrion."[54] In the spring conditions were even worse. Everything green was devoured, and the colony faced starvation. What made the situation particularly bad was the fact that the buffalo hunters "instead of furnishing their large share of provisions, arrived starving from the usual hunting grounds."[55] The buffalo had apparently disappeared from the plains that were within reach of the Red River hunters. The rabbits, too, had gone, no one knew where. Even the fisheries were a partial failure. The Reverend George Young wrote to a friend, "I have heard of one family last week who had killed and eaten their house cat, and others in the distance have eaten their horses."[56] The distress was appalling. Efforts were made to provide relief for the starving settlers. The Council of Assiniboia voted £1,600, part of which was earmarked for seed grain for the following year. Public subscriptions were opened in Canada, Great Britain, and the United States. In London, the Hudson's Bay Company raised £2,850 for relief purposes. A Central Relief Committee was established in the colony, and local committees were set up in each of the parishes, and an inventory of needy families was prepared. According to the Committee's report, no less than 2,342 people were considered to be in need of "immediate" help.[57]

The Canadian government thought to relieve the situation by building a road from Fort Garry to Lake of the Woods. Steps were already under way to build a road-water route from Lake Superior to the west, and a road to Fort Garry would see the completion of the project. Thus the Red River settlers would have their relief, and the Canadians would have their road. This road would be of great advantage when the colony should become part of Canada. The Canadians had no doubt that this was not far distant, even if they had not yet settled the final terms with the British government and the Hudson's Bay Company. Accordingly, in the autumn of 1868, John A. Snow and a small party of Canadians arrived in Red River, sent there by the Hon. William Mc-Dougall, the Canadian Minister of Public Works. Oddly enough McDougall had not taken the trouble to ask the permission of the

Hudson's Bay Company before sending a work party into the Company's territories. It is not clear whether this was simply an oversight or actually deliberate. If the latter, it may be regarded as an ungracious assertion of the traditional Canadian view that the Hudson's Bay Company had never had a good title to the country: if the former, it was inexcusable in a Minister of the Crown. The Company protested, but allowed the road work to proceed.[58] Snow, at least, did make some effort to observe the proprieties by asking the Governor of Assiniboia, William Mactavish, for permission to go ahead with the road project. This request was made orally, and Mactavish gave his permission in the same way, wondering whether or not he was acting within his authority.

Snow began the initial survey at Oak Point (later Ste. Anne des Chênes) where there was a small métis settlement. Subsequently charges were made that he underpaid his men and that he overcharged them for the provisions he issued in lieu of wages;[59] whether these charges are true or not, it is clear that Snow's party was welcomed in the Settlement when it first arrived. Although Snow never employed more than forty men, and did not provide much in the way of relief,[60] half a loaf was better than none, and a little extra money in the Settlement was felt to be a good thing.

What made Snow unpopular was not any failure on his part in the management of his men and his supplies, but the fact that he and the Canadians with him, men like Charles Mair, his paymaster, chose to associate with John Schultz and the aggressive Canadian minority in Winnipeg.[61] Yet it was natural that they should do so. After all, Snow and his men were from Ontario; they were enthusiastic about the possibilities of a large-scale immigration to the North-West; and they were oblivious to, or ignorant of, the traditional attitudes, habits and sensitivities of the people of Red River.

Charles Mair was the greatest offender in this respect. He had been born in the village of Lanark near Perth and had studied at Queen's University. He wrote poetry and, in 1868, had published a volume of poems that had attracted considerable attention. He was a friend of the Minister of Public Works, and it was through McDougall's intervention that he was appointed paymaster of the road crew. Mair seems to have been attracted to Schultz from the outset. After a short stay at Dutch George's hotel, he went to live with Schultz. "The change was comfortable, I assure you," he wrote to his brother, "from the racket of a motley crowd of half-breeds, playing billiards and drinking, to the quiet and solid comfort of a home."[62] His intimate association with Schultz was sufficient to make him suspect in the Settlement, particularly among the métis; it did not improve matters that Schultz should have been the agent for the road party and the man through whom supplies were issued.

To compound this aggravation, Mair wrote a series of letters to his brother in Perth describing his journey and the beauties of the Red River valley. Ostensibly they were private letters; but there seems little doubt but that Mair expected them to be printed. And printed they were, first in the *Perth Courier* and then in the Toronto *Globe*. It was unfortunate that, while talking in glowing terms about the land and its fertility, Mair should have made slighting remarks about the morals of the women of the colony, the half-breed women. He suggested that the real explanation for the destitution in the colony was the fact that the half-breeds were on "their beam ends" simply because they "will hunt buffaloes, drive ox-carts . . . do anything but farm." Mair suffered for his rude and distasteful remarks when he was horse-whipped by Mrs. Bannatyne;[63] but the damage had been done, and the growing animosity of the métis spilled over on everyone who came from Canada. Even then Mair might have been forgiven: after all, he had come to the Settlement with letters of introduction to Bishop Taché.[64] But he sought no advice from those who could have helped him most, and he continued to send communications to the newspaper stressing the attractiveness of the country for Canadian immigrants—"Minnesota is *sand* compared to this." The Canadian farmer, dissatisfied with the tree-grown or rocky land in Ontario, was urged to come to Red River at once. He should: "bring with him provisions to subsist his family for at least one year. He should also bring his seed grain (spring wheat), a Pittsburgh plough with movable point, harrow teeth, and a combined mower and reaper, or, better still, one of Marsh's Harvesters, and a separate mower." On arrival in Red River: "he could find Canadian friends to advise and assist him, in Dr. Schultz and others, and he would have no difficulty in selecting a farm. There is no Hobson's choice about it—'this or none.' The cake is 700 miles long and 400 miles wide with plenty of elbow room."[65]

Statements such as these seemed to give colour to the mutterings that were growing in volume throughout the Settlement. They implied that the Canadians wanted to swamp the old settlers with immigrants, with democratic, anti-clerical, anti-French, anti-half-breed immigrants. What would happen to the old settlers, to their lands, to their simple economy, to their easy-going live and let-live bi-culturalism? At least Schultz knew what to expect from the anticipated explosion of immigration. "I shall buy heavily in Montreal and ship at once and still hope to be back in time," he wrote from Toronto in March, 1869. He added: "It does one's heart good down here . . . to hear the Honourable Hudson's Bay Company racked up—all classes write in cursing the monopoly that keeps that great country from Canada. And if the Company *had* a body to kick, many a Canadian shoe would be battered in the service."[66]

V

This was the Red River Settlement to which Louis Riel returned in 1868: a land bare of grain fields, overrun with locusts; a land in which a large part of the population was on short rations; a land filled with suspicion, and fear; a land rent by political divisions, lacking an effective administration and coveted both by Canada and by the United States; a land in which the people wondered what their political and economic future would be—and feared the worst. How different it all was from 1858.

For the moment there was not much that Riel could do about it. He had been away for ten years and had much to learn about the happenings in the interval. Turning to his old school companion, Louis Schmidt, he invited him to live with him at St. Vital.[67] Everybody was talking politics in the Settlement, and the conversations of the two young men "naturally turned to the changes which were being prepared for our country." They made plans but did nothing about them. "As we knew nothing definite yet about the intentions of the Canadian government we had to wait upon events," wrote Schmidt, "quite resolved, however, to take part in public affairs when the time should be ripe."[68] But the months could not be passed in fruitless talk, and when Schmidt finally received some money for his services during the Sioux troubles of several years earlier, he purchased a few Red River carts and joined the long trains to St. Cloud. Riel remained at home. He wrote a sharp protest to *Le Nouveau Monde* against the "falsehoods" that Charles Mair had been spreading in Ontario, advising Mair to stick to his poetry, "for in that way his writings would make up in rhyme what they lack in reason."[69] But in his own mind Louis was wondering if, like Schmidt, he should not try to secure some kind of employment. Perhaps he ought to go back to St. Paul.[70] There seemed nothing for him to do in Red River.

CHAPTER 4

Provisional Government

I

A S THE DAYS grew warmer, the winter snows of 1868 melted into the dirty slushy spring of 1869. The frozen streets of Winnipeg softened into thick and clinging mud, but there was no relaxation of the frosts of political tension. The grasshopper plague might be over, or at least less devastating, but there was no indication that the plague of doubts and apprehensions would recede. The people of Red River were now certain of one thing: the Hudson's Bay Company was going to sell its territorial rights to the Dominion of Canada. The shareholders of the Company might shout "treachery" when they heard for the first time the details of the arrangement with Canada; but they knew that in the end they would accept the terms agreed upon by the Company's negotiators. This they did in April, 1869.[1] All that remained was for the Colonial Office to rewrite the terms in language which would conform to the Address from the Parliament of Canada. The long-drawn-out business would be completed before the end of the year. No one thought to inform the people of the Red River Settlement how the Canadians were going to take over the colony; or what was going to be done to extinguish the aboriginal title to the soil; or what would happen to the old land patents; or to those who had no patents at all; or what was to be the nature of the institutions the colony was to receive; or what was to be done about the political rights of the people; or about the schools, or about any of the many things that agitated the minds of those who lived at Red River.

Only the Canadians in the colony seemed to be certain about the future. They were sure that they were on the winning side. Some of them probably hoped they might receive some political recognition for their long advocacy of Canadian annexation. The only fly in the Canadian ointment was the possibility that, for a brief period at least, the Canadians were likely to be outvoted in any new democratic legislature. This was an idea that had not occurred to them earlier; but it was something to be thought about and acted upon. Accordingly, John Schultz wrote to J. McDougall, brother of the man whom everyone

54

expected to become the first Lieutenant-Governor of the new province, or territory, of Red River, warning him that:

The greatest danger from the Hudson Bay influence will be in *giving the franchise to our people at once.* Theoretically fair and even necessary it is fraught with very great dangers till our people feel the change and we get an immigration of Canadians on Canadian principles. Our people will be satisfied with simply the local town and country self-government and to have *No Elective Choice Whatever Over the Necessary Officers for these Positions.*[2]

Bown echoed his master's voice and the *Nor'Wester,* that hypocritical exponent of democracy in Red River, cautiously asked, "Are we ready at this moment for the Elective Franchise? Who are our electors?"[3] Small wonder the people of the Settlement, and the métis in particular, regarded the Canadians with distrust and Dr. Schultz with hatred and fear. Was this not simply another way of telling them that they would be excluded from political preferment?

The Canadians not only had their eyes on the political jobs, they had their eyes on the vacant lands too. There was good land in the Settlement—Mair had written frequently on this subject—and it was to be had for the taking. Certainly men like Schultz and Mair were not likely to lose any opportunity to turn an honest or dishonest dollar when the Canadian immigrants would come pouring into the country. Good land close to the river and the centres of population would demand good prices. There is evidence that not only did Schultz and Mair speculate in lands, but that Snow and other government employees did likewise.[4] The staking of land-claims, even if the claims did not infringe upon existing rights of ownership, was enough to nourish the cancer of suspicion that was growing throughout the body of the population of Red River.

It was the staking of lands that, in fact, led the métis to take the first steps in their resistance to Canada. During the month of June, Mair and Snow, accompanied by William Hallett, who, despite his half-breed origin, was thoroughly on the side of the Canadian Party, visited St. Norbert. They began to look over the area and to pace out lots. It is questionable whether they ever trespassed upon private property, but their actions were watched by the local métis with some alarm. The association of Mair and Snow with the hated Schultz was enough to prompt the métis to warn them to leave the vicinity. The hostility of the métis was plain enough, so Mair and his friends quickly departed. But their very appearance had frightened the métis and on July 5, a number of them met together at St. Norbert and asked Baptiste Tourond and Jean-Baptiste Lépine to organize a patrol to keep a wary eye on the neighbourhood and see that "no stranger should establish himself on the

lands" in the métis parishes along the Red and Assiniboine rivers.⁵   The
patrol was apparently effective, and several "strangers" visiting the
region were persuaded by threats and warnings that, if they wanted to
take up lands, they had better do so south and not north of the Rivière
Sale.

Such precautions, if they met the need of the moment, did not provide
any permanent solution for the other problems which every day bulked
larger in the minds of the native inhabitants.   The métis were still
confused, uncertain and without a real leader.   They talked a lot, and
would continue to do so, but they had evolved no clear-cut plan of action.
On July 24, a curious notice appeared in the *Nor'Wester*; it was an
invitation, ostensibly signed by such well-known métis and half-breed
leaders as Pascal Breland, Joseph Genthon, William Dease and William
Hallett, asking the native peoples of the Settlement to meet at the court
house at Fort Garry.   The meeting was held on July 29, and the court
house was filled to overflowing.   Dease, although he was only one of the
signatories, was clearly the moving spirit of the meeting.   But Dease
was not trusted by the French métis.   Although his mother was French-
speaking, and Dease himself was often looked upon as a French métis,
he was suspected of being in Dr. Schultz's pay,⁶ and the French métis
would not follow him.   At the Fort Garry meeting he demanded that
the £300,000 to be paid by Canada to the Hudson's Bay Company be
divided among the original owners of the soil: that meant the Indian
and mixed-blood population of the Territories.   It was an argument
that struck a familiar chord.   It stirred memories of the days of the
North-West Company when the Nor-Westers had stressed the idea of a
half-breed share in the aboriginal title to the soil and had used this idea
with much effect against Lord Selkirk's settlers.   Most of Dease's
listeners were disposed to agree with his demand; but they were not
prepared to go along with him when he proposed that the métis and
half-breeds should back up their claim by force and seize the Hudson's
Bay Company property in Red River.   Among those who spoke against
the latter suggestion were John Bruce and Louis Riel.⁷   The meeting fell
flat, much to the satisfaction of the Abbé Ritchot of St. Norbert, who was
convinced that Schultz had been prompting Dease and Hallett behind
the scenes in the hope of directing métis animosity away from Canada
towards the Hudson's Bay Company.   The only effect of the meeting,
he wrote, was to put "the métis on their guard."⁸

In actual fact it was Ritchot himself who was on guard.   For it was
Ritchot, more than any other person, who was watching events and
guiding the thoughts of the people to whom he ministered in his parish
at St. Norbert.   Twenty years earlier it had been a priest, the Abbé

Belcourt, to whom the métis had turned for counsel; now it was to the Abbé Ritchot that they looked. If the combination of Belcourt and the elder Riel brought freedom of trade to the people of the Red River Settlement, the combination of Ritchot and the younger Riel brought about the formation of the province of Manitoba.

Late in the summer of 1869 the tempo of political events in the colony began to accelerate. The immediate occasion for this change was the action of the Minister of Public Works, William McDougall, in sending surveyors to Red River to lay out lots for the prospective settlers whom Schultz and Mair had said were banging on the doors of the colony clamouring for entrance. John Stoughton Dennis and his crew arrived in the Settlement in August. Their instructions were clear enough. They were not to disturb existing holdings. On this occasion the Canadian government had remembered to ask the permission of the Hudson's Bay Company, and Dennis made a point of speaking to the Governor of Assiniboia, William Mactavish, and of visiting the Bishop's palace in St. Boniface. However, neither in Fort Garry nor in St. Boniface did Dennis receive a very warm welcome. Mactavish considered the whole project ill-conceived and dangerous. He anticipated that "as soon as the survey commences, the half-breeds and Indians will come forward and assert their right to the land, and possibly stop work till their claim is satisfied."[9] In St. Boniface, the administrator of the diocese, the Reverend J. M. Lestanc—Bishop Taché had left the Settlement to attend the Œcumenical Council in Rome—merely promised to repeat Dennis's explanation of his instructions in church the following Sunday.[10]

Lestanc had been coldly correct; but one of his fellow priests, Georges Dugast, felt that Dennis had not been completely honest in his dealings with Lestanc and Mactavish. The surveyor, he claimed, had not been consistent and was not to be trusted.[11] Dugast was well aware of the temper of the métis and sympathized with them. Only a few days earlier he had written to Bishop Taché to tell him that the people of the Settlement did not like the way in which the transfer had been brought about and were openly saying that "if the Canadian government believes it has the right to give us as prey to the adventurers from Upper Canada, it will find out that it is wrong."[12] There was the rub: Dennis had identified himself, like Snow and Mair before him, with the detested "adventurers" from Upper Canada; he had become one of Schultz's gang. Dugast wrote to Taché that Dennis "came to Red River with Schultz. He lodges at his place. He is English from Toronto. I think he will try to do us a bad turn. His purpose, as I see it, is to pick out the best places for the new colonists when they come from Upper Canada next spring or even this autumn."[13]

Thus Dennis gained nothing for his pains. He was contaminated by his association with Dr. Schultz; and to the nostrils of métis this smelled bad. In the end Lestanc said nothing in church on the Sunday. Instead, after Mass, the young Louis Riel harangued the crowd and told them that the proposed surveys were a threat to the land holdings of all the métis people.[14]

Dennis wrote in haste to Ottawa to inform the Minister of "the considerable degree of irritation" existing among "the native population in view of the surveys and settlements being made" and particularly among the French métis who "have gone so far as to threaten violence should the surveys be attempted to be made."[15] These warnings, however, were ignored, and Dennis was ordered to "proceed with the survey on the plan proposed."[16] But Dennis had sense enough not to try to continue his surveys from Oak Point, as originally planned. He moved his men south to the unoccupied areas with the object of working north from Pembina. In this way he would, for the time being at least, be out of sight of the people of the French parishes along the Red River.

Gradually the mutterings, discussions and watchful patrols of the spring and summer were translated into more meaningful action. Slowly a métis leader emerged, the eloquent, personable and energetic young métis Louis Riel. Here, at last, was a man who had the attributes of leadership, who could fill the shoes that Dease would have liked to fill. Politics must always be associated with a heroic name, just as religion must always be associated with a god. Only in this way do politics and religion cease to be purely abstract matters, and become concrete, comprehensible and humanized. Riel possessed a heroic name, for the memory of Louis's father and the shouts of *Le commerce est libre* had never been forgotten in the parishes along the Red River. Moreover, he was a devout man, of a mystical turn of mind. This, too, was an asset among a simple, deeply religious, unsophisticated people.

Of Louis Riel's activities during these weeks of early autumn, 1869, little evidence is to be found. However, it would appear from notes preserved by the Abbé Ritchot, that "a young man"—unquestionably Louis Riel—had taken the initiative among the métis, or among those of the métis who were sufficiently concerned, to persuade the people to do something more than organize patrols to watch for possible claim-jumpers. He convinced some of them that a central committee for the whole colony should be formed, and that the métis should choose from among themselves a small number of men who would be prepared to meet together to "consider the state of the country and see if there were not some means at least of making a clear protest against the injustice and injuries done the country by Canada."[17]   The men were elected, two from each parish,[18] and with Riel acting as their secretary, they assembled from time to time at Ritchot's presbytery in St. Norbert.   Ritchot was content to remain in the background, to watch and advise.   He was a secretive man who liked the role of "grey eminence" that history cast for him.   He was unlike Dugast at St. Boniface, quick to speak and say too much, and while he kept Dugast well informed, he did not tell him everything.   Thus Dugast was able to report to the Bishop on September 4 only that he had been to St. Norbert and found the métis planning something, he was not quite sure what, but something that would prevent the Canadian governor from coming into the country.[19]   Nor was Lestanc completely in Ritchot's confidence.   "I do not know too much about what is in the heads of our métis," he wrote to Taché, "but I should not be surprised that the end result will be a ridiculous mess."[20] Thus Lestanc merely urged his clergy to observe neutrality in the political events of Settlement life, and he preserved a neutral attitude himself.[21]

For the moment all was quiet.   Still at work on his road, Snow was having troubles, not with the métis but with some of the workmen he had brought from Ontario, notably one by the name of Thomas Scott.[22] McDougall, whose appointment as Lieutenant-Governor had frightened the métis, had not appeared on the frontier as yet, and there were no signs of Dennis and the surveyors.   But it was a short-lived calm. When the survey team, driving north from Pembina towards the Assiniboine, finally reached the area of settlement and started running their lines over the "hay privilege"—the land to the rear of the long river farms on which each farmer cut his hay—which belonged to André Nault, a group of métis, led by Louis Riel and Baptiste Tourond, quickly appeared on the scene.   There was no violence.   The métis simply stood on the chain while Riel declared that the territory south of the Assiniboine belonged to the people of Red River and not to Canada, and that the métis would not allow the survey to proceed any farther.   This was no unplanned, impulsive act.   The métis knew what they were doing, and they had been on the watch for just such trespasses or encroachments ever since Mair's encounter with Tourond in June.   Dennis went to Fort Garry to complain to the magistrate, Dr. Cowan, and the Governor, William Mactavish.   When Riel was asked for an explanation of the métis action, all he did was advance the argument which he was to din into the ears of the people of Red River for the next eight months.   The argument was that the Canadian government "had no right to make surveys on the Territory without the express permission of the people of the Settlement."[23]   From this position he would not budge.

II

The surveyors were stopped on October 11. The very same day a party of men from Canada was watching a group of half-breeds loading the wagons and carts that met the railway train at St. Cloud. The Canadians were looking forward to the journey to Pembina and an early arrival at Fort Garry. The senior member of the group was a heavy-built man, with a drooping moustache and an air of authority about him. His name was William McDougall. He was the former Minister of Public Works in Ottawa, but as the Lieutenant-Governor designate of Canada's most recent territorial acquisition, he was on his way to take over his functions on the day the transfer of the Hudson's Bay Company territories should be officially announced, December 1. With him was a mild-mannered man, J. A. N. Provencher, the nephew of the former Bishop of St. Boniface, and a stiff, brusque, military man, Captain D. R. Cameron, son-in-law of one of McDougall's cabinet colleagues in Ottawa, Sir Charles Tupper. Both Provencher and Cameron were on their way to Red River in anticipation of appointments as members of McDougall's council. The first Canadian administration was not to be a democratic one. It was to be the administration that Dr. Schultz had urged upon McDougall's brother in April.

McDougall knew that all was not well in Red River. What he did not know was how strong the feelings were against him, and how widespread the exaggerated stories that were current, of his cheating the Indians during the Manitoulin treaty negotiations and his insulting Bishop Taché in Ottawa.[24] The reports he did hear from the Settlement he was inclined to dismiss as alarmist and of little substance. Perhaps he might learn something definite from his colleague Joseph Howe, who had paid a hurried visit to Red River in the autumn and was on his way back to Ottawa. He and Howe met at Fort Abercrombie. Unfortunately their encounter was short. Yet Howe had something to tell McDougall. He had spent only a very few days in the Settlement, but he had learned that the Canadian Party was not held in high esteem by the settlers, white or mixed-blood. He had studiously avoided becoming entangled with Schultz, and he tried to win the goodwill of both Mactavish and Lestanc. He had even attempted to get in touch with Louis Riel. But the day he met McDougall was a dirty one; each man was anxious to avoid uncomfortable delays on the prairies and to get on with his journey. There was only the briefest exchange of courtesies. Then both men were on their respective ways, McDougall carrying with him a promise from Howe to write in detail, later.[25]

The news of McDougall's approach gave a sense of urgency to the plans forming in Riel's mind, plans concerning the colony's relations with Canada. But still many métis were inclined to hesitate. Some of them enjoyed a comfortable position in society; they did not want it disturbed. Some, like Salomon Hamelin, Roger Goulet and Pascal Breland, were members of the Council of Assiniboia; they saw no reason for a change. Some, like Dease, had thrown in their lot with Schultz; they were actively opposed to Riel. Even within the small circle of those who met with Riel at Ritchot's presbytery, there were some who considered it would be useless to try to stand in the path of political union with Canada. Probably because he did not have the whole-hearted support he needed, Riel postponed to a more propitious moment the mass meeting which he had planned to hold in September. During the interval he worked hard to convince the faint-hearted, appealing to their sense of nationality and stimulating their fears of John Schultz. Finally, by mid-October, Riel felt confident enough to call his meeting.

By this time there were plenty of men in the Settlement ready to throw their weight behind any métis movement: the voyageurs of the Portage La Loche, and the York and Saskatchewan boat brigades. Their work season had come to an end, and they had returned to Red River. They were rough, tough men, prepared to fight with their fists and their guns, and ready not to think too much before they struck, or afterwards. Moreover, they were tied to the fur trade, and it is very probable that they knew what the senior Hudson's Bay Company servants had been saying about the transfer of the Company's territories to Canada. They were the stuff out of which revolutions were made, even if they were not the stuff to make revolutions. All they wanted was a leader to follow. On October 16, they met at St. Norbert to adapt the traditional métis organization for the annual buffalo hunt to the political needs of the moment. They elected as their president an ill-educated, weak man, named John Bruce, and as their secretary, Louis Riel. Bruce may appear to have been a most unlikely choice; but his name had been put forward by Louis Riel.[26] Everyone knew that Bruce would be only a figurehead and that it was Riel who possessed the necessary education, sense of mission and power to direct that Bruce lacked. Riel had been secretary of the earlier committee and probably felt that, in view of the short time he had been back in the Settlement, it would be better for him to continue in a subordinate role, at least for the time being.

During the next week the executive of the métis "National Committee," as the new organization was known, met frequently both at St. Norbert and St. Vital. It adopted resolutions providing for the codification of "the natural, wise and just laws of the prairie"; for the publication of these laws and their explanation to the people by Louis Riel; for the organization of a military force with captains and soldiers. On October 20, when the Committee learned that among the various items of McDougall's baggage there were several cases of rifles with which he proposed to arm a force to preserve peace and order in the colony, "several captains" and their men were despatched to meet the man "with the title of governor of the country from a foreign power." On the following day Riel and several of his councillors went to St. Norbert to discuss this latest development with the Abbé Ritchot and the Abbé Dugast. As they talked they were joined by a number of armed men, each one armed, according to Ritchot, "with a musket, a revolver, a powder horn, and a bag of cartridges, with a dirk or hunting knife." The outcome of this conference was a short, curt communication to McDougall.   It read:[27]

> Dated at St. Norbert, Red River, this 21st day of October, 1869.
> Sir,
>   The National Committee of the Métis of Red River orders William McDougall not to enter the Territory of the North West without special permission of the above-mentioned committee.
>   By order of the President, John Bruce.
>   LOUIS RIEL, *Secretary.*

While this document was being drafted, the métis soldiers rubbed their hands and shuffled about in the snow, for winter had come early and the day was very cold. Some of them kept themselves warm by erecting a barrier just north of the point where the road from Pembina crossed the Rivière Sale.[28]

There was no real secrecy about these hostile preparations, and the news soon flew through the parishes that Bruce and Riel were planning to defy the governor who had been sent by Canada. The more moderate métis were alarmed. They shared the general uneasiness the Canadian Party had inspired, but they did not want to take up arms and were fearful of the consequences. Such action looked too much like rebellion. Could they put the brake upon the more aggressive left-wing elements within the National Committee? Some, at least, were prepared to try. On October 24—it was a Sunday—after Mass, the conservative and radical groups met at St. Norbert. The arguments between them grew bitter, and it looked as if they might come to blows. Reluctant as he was openly to take sides in the dispute, the Abbé Ritchot felt compelled to intervene and still the troubled waters of political controversy. They were all in agreement, he said, that Canada had not treated the colony with respect; they all agreed that a protest should be made; the only real point of disagreement was the form the protest should take. As tempers subsided, Ritchot managed to persuade the conservative element to remain neutral; they need not follow Riel and the National Committee; they need only refrain from actively opposing him. In this way no one would be forced to do anything against his will; Ritchot even hinted that his own sympathies were with the conservatives and neutrality.[29] It was cleverly done and was a good political lesson for Riel. For the most part the conservative métis remained throughout the period of the resistance simple spectators of Riel's success.

The next day, October 25, Riel and Bruce were summoned to appear before the Council of Assiniboia. Ineffective and virtually moribund as it was, the Council was still the legal government of Red River, and it would remain so until the official transfer of the Hudson's Bay Company territories to Canada. Governor Mactavish did not attend the session. He was ill—too ill indeed to play any significant role in the events that followed[30]—and the chair was taken by Judge John Black. It is significant that none of the métis members, with the sole exception of William Dease, was present. The chairman expressed the Council's hope that the rumours which had reached him of the plans of the French métis to prevent the Hon. William McDougall from entering the Settlement were without foundation. But Riel quickly removed whatever scales may have been over their eyes. The métis were, Riel said, "perfectly satisfied with the present Government and wanted no other"; they "objected to any Government coming from Canada without their being consulted in the matter"; they "would never admit any Governor no matter by whom he might be appointed, if not by the Hudson's Bay Company, unless Delegates were previously sent, with whom they might negotiate as to the terms and conditions under which they would acknowledge him"; they were "uneducated and only half civilized and felt that if a large immigration were to take place they would probably be crowded out of a country which they claimed as their own"; they believed they were acting "not only for their own good, but for the good of the whole Settlement"; they did not feel that they were breaking any law, but were "simply acting in defence of their own liberty"; they "did not anticipate any opposition from their English-speaking fellow countrymen, and only wished them to join and aid in securing their common rights." It was a long and rambling discussion, but Riel left no doubts in the minds of the members of the Council when he declared that the métis were "determined to prevent Mr. McDougall from coming into the Settlement at all hazards."[31]

The Council members did their best to persuade Riel that his ideas were "erroneous" and that his proposed course of action would be attended with "disastrous consequences" to the half-breeds and the

Settlement generally. But Riel was adamant. He would not be diverted from the course he had mapped out. He had never liked to be contradicted, and he did not like it now. All he would agree to do—and this he did with ill grace—was to promise to tell his supporters what the members of the Council had said. After Riel and Bruce had departed, the councillors discussed what course of action they should adopt. They had no military force at their disposal, and to try to raise one might precipitate a civil war that would be certain to involve the Indians as well. Finally, at A. G. B. Bannatyne's suggestion, it was decided to ask William Dease and Roger Goulet "to collect immediately as many of the more respectable of the French community as they could and with them proceed to the camp of the party who intend to intercept Governor McDougall and endeavour if possible to procure their peaceable dispersion." The members of the Council may well have believed that Dease and Goulet could muster sufficient opposition to Riel to prevent him from acting as he had said he would do. If they did, it was because they did not know that Dease had no following among the French métis and that Goulet preferred to adopt Ritchot's advice and not take sides in the dispute.

Dease did his best. Apparently he had some money at his disposal, and he tried to purchase support both by arguments and by gifts. He even went as far as to enlist the services of the disreputable Georges Racette, a man feared and hated by almost everybody in the Settlement, in the hope of intimidating some of Riel's supporters.[32] But when the two groups met at St. Norbert on October 27, there was no doubt in anybody's mind which group was the stronger. The meeting was a triumph for Riel and, incidentally, for Ritchot as well. When the Council of Assiniboia reconvened on October 30, Judge Black reported that "Mr. Dease's mission had entirely failed in producing the desired result."[33] There was nothing more the Council could do. It adjourned, and never met again in its capacity as the governing body of the District of Assiniboia.

On the same day, October 30, McDougall and his party arrived at the frontier village of Pembina. They were now only 70 miles from Fort Garry; but McDougall was never to complete his journey. When he reached the American customs post he was given a note by a métis courier. It was Riel's order not to enter the British North-West without the permission of the métis. He read it and in an outburst of anger "addressed the messengers in contemptuous and insulting language."[34] He would ignore the order—after all what was this métis committee? He would set his feet on British soil and move as far north as the Hudson's Bay Company post, two miles inside British territory. Yet McDougall was none too confident, for he left his wife and several members of his company behind. Provencher decided to go farther, and not long afterwards Cameron decided to do the same. But neither man succeeded in reaching Fort Garry. Provencher had the advantage of bearing a name familiar to every métis in the Settlement, but neither the hoped-for magic of his name nor his appeal to the Abbé Ritchot could get him past the barrier at St. Norbert. Captain Cameron tried to force his way through with a mixture of bluff and bravado. But Cameron's peremptory order to "remove that blasted fence" merely annoyed the métis guards. In the end both Provencher and the discomfited captain were conducted back to Pembina by an escort of métis horsemen.[35]

Almost to the hour, McDougall was faced with a similar humiliation. On November 2, a métis patrol, commanded by Ambroise Lépine, visited the Hudson's Bay Company post and ordered McDougall to leave the country. He produced his commission as governor, but to no avail. He demanded to know who had sent this imperious order, but Lépine merely replied, in the language of the buffalo hunt, "the government." What else could McDougall do but obey? As he crossed the boundary line he heard the words "you must not return beyond this line."[36]

III

By now Riel's actions were beginning to reveal a consistent pattern. He had no intention of committing an act of rebellion against the crown. Despite the arrival in the Settlement, on August 13, of a plausible, well-educated, French-speaking consul from the United States, Oscar Malmros, who was prepared to do more for his country than was required by the strictly diplomatic nature of his duty, and the none too casual visits of the Minnesota intriguer, Enos Stutsman, at no time does it appear that Riel ever seriously contemplated throwing himself into the arms of the Americans. As early as October, he had declared "in the name of the métis population of Red River" that "they are loyal subjects of Her Majesty the Queen of England."[37] He adhered to this course throughout the disturbances of 1869/1870. His note to McDougall did not prohibit the Lieutenant-Governor from ever entering Red River. It simply made his entry conditional upon his receiving the permission of the métis committee. Riel's statement to the Council of Assiniboia on October 25 was an elaboration of the same point: the métis would not admit McDougall or any other governor unless "the terms and conditions" of Red River's entry into the Canadian confederation were the result of free negotiation between the colony and Canada. Riel's purpose was, therefore, in some way to delay the establishment of any kind of Canadian administration in the country until the Canadian

government should do what it should have done in the first place, that is,
provide officially the assurances that the people demanded, assurances
with regard to their economic and political security—and their religious
security too, for Riel still remained the devout Catholic of his student
days.

Although he never left positive proof of this, there seems little doubt
that Riel's thoughts must, on occasions, have returned to the arguments
he had heard so frequently in those days in Montreal in 1865 and 1866,
when Taschereau and Dorion and LaFlamme were expressing their fears
as to what confederation would do to the French minority.   The situation that had confronted Quebec in 1865 confronted Red River in 1869.
How much more cogent those arguments would seem when applied to a
small group like the métis and the half-breeds of Red River.   He would
make no mistake.   He would not refuse outright to enter confederation,
but he would do it only on terms that would be satisfactory to the little
colony with which he had so completely identified himself.

If negotiation with Canada was Riel's first aim, his second was to
achieve negotiation with the support of the whole mixed-blood population
behind him.   He did not want or expect the French métis to have to
carry the whole burden of political resistance by themselves.   He would
have a far more telling argument in Ottawa if he could show that both
the English-speaking and the French-speaking peoples of Red River
were of one mind in regard to the transfer of their country to Canada.
It was for this reason that in the autumn Riel visited several of the
English parishes explaining what he hoped to do.   Early in October, he
and Bruce attended a meeting of the English half-breeds in the home of
Thomas Sinclair, a half-breed member of the Council of Assiniboia.   He
endeavoured to persuade those present that they should make common
cause with their French brethren.   But the English half-breeds kept
aloof.   They preferred to wait and see.   This cautious approach to the
political crisis annoyed Riel.   Ritchot could find no other explanation
for it than the fact that the Protestant clergy were, for the most part,
men from Canada, with a greater concern for the interests of Canada
than for the welfare of the people of Red River.[38]   Nevertheless, if the
English half-breeds were disposed to follow a noncommittal course, it
did not mean they were hostile to the métis movement.   Half-breeds and
métis were blood brothers, sons of the prairie.[39]

The same day that the métis patrols were escorting McDougall back to
Pembina, Louis Riel and a number of his followers took possession of Fort
Garry.   It was with difficulty that Riel persuaded the métis to act with
such imagination.[40]   However, Riel now had at St. Norbert men in such
numbers that he needed both the accommodation and the provisions

Fort Garry could provide. Some two hundred had taken the oath on October 20-21, and by November 1 there were over four hundred on the muster roll.[41] But if the seizure of Fort Garry would provide the answer to the practical problem of maintaining a large armed force, there were even more important political advantages to accrue from such a step. The fort not only had solid defence works supported by cannon, but it was situated at the very heart of the colony, the centre from which all roads radiated to the north, south and west. With active patrolling, it would be possible for whoever controlled the fort to limit all movement within the Red River Settlement. What would happen to the métis movement should McDougall or the Canadians decide to take the fort?[42] And, too, how could one measure the prestige value that would attach to so decisive a move?

The actual deed proved to be unexpectedly easy. No bloodshed was involved. The Hudson's Bay Company had neither the troops to man the guns nor the opportunity to enlist a force,[43] for Riel's decision had been taken only at the last moment and the news had not yet had a chance to infiltrate the Settlement. Just before leaving St. Norbert, Riel and the Abbé Ritchot erected a wooden cross near the barricade,[44] a symbol of their belief in divine support. Then Riel set off, with his small party of men, for Fort Garry. Others followed, in groups of varying numbers, all casually making towards the fort as if they were bound there on no urgent business. Then they slipped quietly through the governor's private entrance, until there were about 120 of them inside the walls. When challenged by Dr. Cowan as to what their business was, Riel simply replied that they had come to "guard the fort." "Against whom?" inquired Cowan. "Against a danger," was Riel's reply, "which I have reason to believe threatens it; but which I cannot explain to you at present."[45] Nor would he say anything more, except to agree not to molest any persons or disturb private property within the fort. There was nothing for Cowan or Governor Mactavish to do. They could have found no more than a handful of men to help them, and as Cowan ruefully remarked, the men most sympathetic to the Company were the very ones to be found among the ranks of Riel's soldiery.

The chances were small that McDougall would now be able to take over the administration of Red River. It would have been better for his reputation and his peace of mind if he had left Pembina and returned to Ottawa. To oust Riel and the métis would require a military force, and McDougall had no hope of persuading the Canadian authorities to undertake a winter campaign over the wild, inhospitable land that lay between Ontario and the Red River valley. His alternative lay in persuading the local people themselves to take up arms and overthrow the métis régime. This might well end in a civil war, but it was the course McDougall was induced to try.

Firmly established in Fort Garry, with his patrols watching the roads and his men checking every item of baggage and confiscating every musket as it was brought into the colony, Riel now felt free to follow the policy he had mapped out for himself. He would resume his efforts to get the backing of the English-speaking settlers. In this way he would thwart any plans the Canadians might have of overthrowing him by force, and he would be in a much stronger position to talk terms with the government of Canada. Accordingly, on November 6, he issued a proclamation[46] stating:

The President and Representatives of the French-speaking population of Rupert's Land in Council (the Invaders of our rights being now expelled) already aware of your sympathy, do extend the hand of friendship to you, our friendly fellow inhabitants; and in so doing invite you to send twelve Representatives from the following places [and here were the names of eleven parishes, with two representatives being allotted to the "town of Winnipeg"] in order to form one body with the above Council, consisting of twelve members, to consider the present political state of this Country, and to adopt such measures as may be deemed best for the future welfare of the same.

The immediate reaction on the part of the English-speaking parishes was one of reticent curiosity. The English half-breeds and the Selkirk settlers felt that Riel was inclined to move too quickly and too far, and that the seizure of the fort and some of his other actions were "uncalled for in their cause."[47] At the same time they could see no real objection to meeting with the métis and discussing the situation with them. Accordingly, the English parishes accepted Riel's invitation, elected their representatives and sent them to Fort Garry.

Riel had, in fact, moved rather too promptly in calling a convention of the people of Red River. He was not really ready to meet the English-speaking delegates in conference. Moreover, the English half-breeds had taken no steps to organize along the lines of the métis National Committee and had no obvious leader. Nor had they given much consideration to the problems imposed by the transfer; and Riel had not thought to prepare a proper agenda or a clear-cut programme to put before the men who assembled to the firing of a *feu de joie* and salvos of cannon fire in the Court House at Fort Garry on November 16. Because of this lack of preliminary preparation and the general ignorance of the rules of parliamentary procedure, the meeting quickly degenerated into a series of verbal exchanges between Louis Riel and James Ross, the

Scottish half-breed from Kildonan, who had formerly edited the *Nor'-Wester* and who was the only member of the convention who equalled Riel in education and debating skill. Unfortunately they argued, not about the important things, but about details. The English did not like Riel's parade of military power; the French thought it was no more than the proper accompaniment of a dignified ceremony. The English wanted to elect a new chairman and a new secretary for the sessions; the French would accept none other than Bruce and Riel until there should be some measure of agreement between the two groups upon questions of fundamental policy. The English objected to the interference with McDougall; the French argued that their action was necessary to prevent the Canadians from taking over the government of the colony. Then, to add to the general confusion, a proclamation drafted by the Governor of Assiniboia at McDougall's request, was introduced into the debate. After reciting what he characterized as the "unlawful acts" committed by the métis, Mactavish urged "those engaged in them, before they are irretrievably and hopelessly involved, immediately to disperse themselves and peaceably to depart to their habitations or to their lawful business, under the pains and penalties of the law." He concluded his admonition with the words: "You are dealing with a crisis out of which may come incalculable good or immeasurable evil; and, with all the weight of my official authority and all the influence of my individual position, let me finally charge you to adopt only such means as are lawful and constitutional, rational and safe."[48] At once Ross took the view that no further debate was necessary and that the métis were in a state of rebellion. Angry, Riel jumped to his feet. "If we are rebels," he cried:

we are rebels against the Company that sold us, and is ready to hand us over, and against Canada that wants to buy us. We are not in rebellion against the British supremacy which has still not given its approval for the final transfer of the country. . . . Moreover, we are true to our native land. We are protecting it against the dangers that threaten it. We want the people of Red River to be a free people. Let us help one another. We are all brothers and relations, says Mr. Ross, and it is true. Let us not separate. See what Mr. Mactavish says. He says that out of this meeting and its decision may come incalculable good. Let us unite. The evil that he fears will not take place. See how he speaks. Is it surprising? His children are half-breeds like ourselves.[49]

It was a good reply. It displayed an understanding of the psychology of the people to whom Riel was speaking, a thorough understanding of their prejudices and their loyalties, of their distrust of Canada, their devotion to Great Britain and their common heritage as mixed-bloods. It revealed Riel to be not only a man of resolution but an able politician as well.   In his report to the Bishop, Lestanc noted with a touch of pride, "Everybody I have seen agrees in saying that L. Riel surpassed himself in the preliminary debates, and that he flattened Js. Ross to his own and everybody else's satisfaction."[50]

At this point the convention adjourned to permit the General Quarterly Court to use the Court House.   In the meantime, a great deal of discussion took place in the English parishes about what had gone on in the convention, and about the now obvious cleavage between the two language groups within the Settlement.   Bannatyne and Alexander Begg were disappointed at the turn of events.   They represented the moderate English group which took the view that if the colonists were to secure consideration for what they regarded as their rights, métis and English half-breeds and old settlers would have to stand together.   Thus far they believed Riel was right.   The problem was how to bridge the gap between the more obdurate among the English and their French-speaking counterparts.   For the French seemed determined to obtain a statement of the English will to co-operate before they would discuss the nature of the rights they wished Canada to guarantee; and the English appeared equally adamant upon obtaining a statement of the rights before they would agree to collaborate.

Riel, too, must have been doing some furious thinking during these several days: not so much about matters of political principle as about the practical problems of how he was going to continue to pay and feed his soldiers.   Thus, when the convention reconvened on November 23, he still did not have any new proposals to put before the members: hence the same fruitless argument, the same emphasis on scoring debating points, the same failure to make any progress towards unity.   Finally, on the night of November 23, Riel came to a firm decision; he would suggest the formation of a provisional government that would replace the dying Council of Assiniboia.   In this way he would be able to forestall any Canadian argument that McDougall's government was the only practical alternative to that of the Hudson's Bay Company, and he would construct the political machinery with which to engineer negotiations with Canada, either by the métis alone or by the united colony, should such union be achieved.   Whether the provisional government was Riel's own idea, or whether it was whispered in his ear by Enos Stutsman during the latter's visit to Fort Garry on November 22, is not known.   Perhaps it may have come from Ritchot or Dugast.   In any event the idea commended itself to Riel.   To his surprise he found that his own supporters in the National Committee were rather half-hearted about it; and he was obliged to argue half the night in order to get them to agree to it.   "It was unbelievable," he said, "the opposition I have to overcome. What they feared most was the appearance of a rebellion against the Queen. It was only by dint of showing them and telling them that we are remaining faithful to the Queen, that the Government of Assiniboia had been so weakened as a result of the sale that it no longer had the power necessary to protect us, that if it had anything at all it was only the name."[51] By sheer perseverance he gained the acquiescence of his followers, and when, next day, James Ross repeated the familiar demand that the French should reveal their plans, Riel replied: "You know perfectly well what we want. We want what every French parish wants. And they want to form a provisional government for our protection and to treat with Canada. We invite you to join in it in all sincerity. This government will be made up equally of French and English. And it will be only provisional in nature."[52] This proposal came as a complete surprise to Ross and to the English-speaking members of the convention. They did not know what to make of it. And so they asked for an adjournment to consult their constituents.

There is no doubt that Riel had shaken the English group within the convention by the boldness of his proposal. Once more he had seized the initiative, directing policy rather than being directed by it. The English could accept or reject his idea of a provisional government; in either case he would go ahead with his plans to negotiate with Canada, and Schultz and his friends would be left out in the cold.

In the English parishes everybody was discussing Riel's proposal, but very few liked it. There seemed to be something vaguely illegal about the plan. However, just as the métis had been divided earlier, so too were the English-speaking settlers. Some of them were for rejecting the suggestion outright and withdrawing from the convention; others felt it would be a great misfortune if the French and English should be unable to find grounds on which they could co-operate. To fail to close the breach between them would be, in fact, to play the political game as the Canadian Party wanted it played. Without unity among all elements of the old settlers, there would be little chance of Canada giving a serious hearing to the demands put forward from Red River. For this reason a small group of level-headed English-speaking settlers—including Dr. Bird, a native of the Settlement and a member of the convention for St. Paul's, together with W. B. O'Donoghue, the Irish American who represented St. Boniface, and A. G. B. Bannatyne and Alexander Begg—put forward the suggestion that the Council of Assiniboia be permitted to continue as the legislative body of the Settlement, while a new council, an executive council, should be elected, "whose duties would be to treat with the Canadian government as to the terms on which this country should be annexed to Canada."[53] On November 27, they put this

counter-proposal before Louis Riel.   And to back up their arguments
they brought along with them Oscar Malmros, the American consul,
who apparently had no compunctions about abandoning the neutrality
imposed by his diplomatic status and dabbling in local politics. Although
the proposal would have yielded almost everything Louis Riel wanted
while preserving the fiction of legal government by the Council of
Assiniboia, it was a compromise.   And compromise was a word not to be
found in Riel's vocabulary.   Finally, towards evening, he gave in.   Yes,
he would accept the compromise if he could be sure that the English
parishes would support it and that they would join forces with the
French "on equal terms" in order to lay "the claims of the people before
Canada."[54]   Three days later, on November 30, he changed his mind.

IV

Meanwhile the Canadians had been at work to frustrate Riel's plans.
They had tried, without success, to convince the English parishes in the
Settlement that they should not send representatives to the convention
when Riel issued his invitation on November 6.   Then they purloined a
copy of Governor Mactavish's proclamation and hurried it into print on
November 17, before the convention met.   A special edition of the
Nor'Wester was run off carrying what purported to be a petition from
"the friends of Canada" to Mactavish, demanding that he issue an order
to the métis to disperse, and printing a truncated edition of the Governor's reply.   "It was really amusing," wrote Begg, "to see the little
editor of the *Nor'Wester* hopping about from door to door on the evening
of the 17th November, distributing the 'extras' with his own hands.
'There', he roared, as he pitched in a few copies of his 'Loyalty
Triumphant' at one door, 'see what we have done'; and at the next house,
'We'll show you now, what we can do.' "[55]   When the convention
revealed a split between the French and the English, Schultz endeavoured
to get up a petition to unseat the representatives from Winnipeg (one of
whom was Henry McKenney who had brought a suit against Schultz
some years before) in order to ensure the election of a member of the
Canadian Party.[56]   None of these efforts seemed to yield much return,
but the Canadians were not discouraged.   They still had their trump
card, William McDougall, at Pembina, and it would be only a few days
more before his commission as Lieutenant-Governor would come into
effect.

   In spite of Riel's patrols, the Canadians were in constant communication with McDougall, and that hapless man, unfortunately, was too much
disposed to listen to them.   Both Snow and Mair urged him "on no
account" to leave Pembina, and they told him "the English have not

risen because they have not been called upon by the authorities, otherwise they would have risen."[57] They told him that he had only to issue his proclamation on December 1 and the great part of the English-speaking element in Red River would flock to his standard. If only McDougall would stick it out for a few more days, Riel would find himself outside the law. Any action taken then to disperse the métis and overthrow Riel's National Committee would be perfectly legal and would have behind it the full sanction of legally established authority. There were moments when McDougall wondered whether Canada would, in fact, go through with the transfer on the date set,[58] but he thrust these thoughts from his mind; they neither suited his own inclinations nor coincided with the advice he was receiving from Red River. When December 1 came, he took the decisive step. With a few of his supporters he recrossed the frontier, and on British territory read a proclamation, which he had drafted in the Queen's name, stating that the North-West was now Canadian territory and that he held the commission of Lieutenant-Governor thereof. It was bitterly cold, and when the proclamation had been read, the shivering company hurried back to such meagre comforts as were to be found in the none too friendly atmosphere of Pembina.[59]

A copy of the proclamation had been sent in advance to Winnipeg. Additional copies were printed and scattered throughout the Settlement. The door of Dr. Schultz's house was "literally covered with them."[60] Copies were also sent to the English-speaking members of the convention. This, for sure, would put a dent in Riel's plans to unite the two language groups within the Settlement. And it did. For the moment Riel wondered if the document might not be genuine: but, genuine or not, he would not withdraw now and allow McDougall to come into the colony just to establish Schultz and the others in the seats of authority. If this happened, there would be no chance of securing any concessions from Canada. Rightly or wrongly, this is what Riel believed. He believed, too, that the English members of the convention would not now support the compromise that Bannatyne and Dr. Bird had drawn up, which he had accepted on November 27. That is why Riel withdrew his promise. But he was willing to make another effort to win English support. He told Ross on December 1, when the convention reconvened, "If Mr. McDougall is really our Governor today, our chances are better than ever. He has no more to do than prove to us his desire to treat us well. If he guarantees our rights, I am one of those who will go to meet him in order to escort him as far as the seat of his government."[61] When Ross asked what demands were to be made of McDougall, the French adjourned to prepare a draft list of rights. It was something that Riel should have anticipated, and which, had he been a man of more political experience, he would probably have done earlier.

Two hours later the convention met again. The List of Rights which Riel presented to the delegates was by no means an unreasonable one.[62] It was very much what one might have expected, given a knowledge of the circumstances at Red River. There were demands for the right of the people of Red River to elect their own legislature; for the appropriation of public lands for the building of schools, roads and other public works; the payment by Canada for four years of the expenses of public administration, official status for both the French and English languages in the courts and legislature, the confirmation of all existing "privileges, customs and usages" and "full and fair" representation in the Parliament of Canada. Several demands, such as the election of sheriffs and magistrates, the power of the legislature to override the executive with a two-thirds majority, and the inapplicability of all federal legislation unless sanctioned by the people of Red River, betrayed an ignorance of the nature of the Canadian federation; and the request for the construction of a railway line "to connect Winnipeg by rail with the nearest line of railroad," in the United States, suggests the hand of James Taylor. The one unexpected omission was the absence of any references to denominational or bilingual schools. There was very little in the list with which Ross or any other English-speaking member of the convention could quibble. The one bone of contention was the demand that William McDougall should not be admitted into the colony until he should give his personal guarantee that these demands would be granted, or promise to secure the necessary consent from Ottawa. It was upon this rock that the earlier sessions of the convention had foundered; and it was the same rock that wrecked the convention and brought about the collapse of Riel's initial efforts to secure a united political front in Red River. His face blazing with choler, Riel shouted to the English members of the convention, "Go, return peacefully to your farms. Stay in the arms of your wives. Give this example to your children. But watch us act. We are going ahead to work and obtain the guarantee of our rights and yours. You will come to share them in the end."[63]

Schultz and his friends had succeeded. With McDougall's proclamation they had forced open the breach between the French and English in Red River. They had defeated Riel's (and Bannatyne's) efforts to bring about an effective collaboration between the two racial groups. They had brought about the dissolution of the convention. But they had not succeeded in overthrowing Riel. This, they hoped, would be their next victory; and the means they proposed was a commission prepared by William McDougall appointing J. S. Dennis, the surveyor "Lieutenant and Conservator of the Peace" in Rupert's Land, with authority to "raise, organize, arm, equip and provision a sufficient force" to "attack, arrest, disarm or disperse the . . . armed men so unlawfully assembled and disturbing the public peace; and for that purpose and with the force aforesaid to assault, fire upon, pull down or break into any fort, house, stronghold, or other place in which the said armed men may be found."[64] With this commission and an armed force, the Canadians would be able to attack Riel with impunity; and Schultz asked Dennis if he might be allowed to raise a force of surveyors and road men and attack Fort Garry at night. But Dennis was never as hopeful or as enthusiastic as Schultz. His military career during the Fenian Raids had not revealed him to be a man of ruthless decision, and he would take no action until he had raised a "sufficient" force. But this he was never able to do. The Canadians in Red River were willing to pen their names to his muster roll; but the great bulk of the Red River population would not join him, "cowardly dastards that they are," wrote one of the Canadians.[65]

As soon as he learned of Dennis's efforts to raise a military force, and particularly his enlistment of Indians, Riel acted with the very decision and despatch Dennis lacked. He closed the office of the *Nor'Wester*, mustered all the men he could find, cleared the shops of Winnipeg of guns and ammunition, and prepared to meet attack. He believed that the Canadians would stop at nothing. And if they were prepared to use force, then he would meet force with force. But no attack developed. Without the necessary men Dennis retired to Lower Fort Garry, 20 miles below the centre of the Settlement. At the same time, he instructed Schultz and the group of Canadians gathered in Winnipeg to do the same before the shooting started.[66]

Schultz had in his warehouse a stock of Canadian government pork that had been consigned to him and which he would not abandon to the métis. He probably knew that Riel needed supplies to feed his men, and he might have wondered whether Dennis might not need it too. In any event, he paid no attention to what he regarded as Dennis's craven counsel; he remained in Winnipeg, his house occupied by a garrison of forty-eight Canadians. Whether this decision was prompted by bravery or by lack of judgment is for the reader to decide. It should be remembered that Schultz had nothing but contempt for the métis, and he was not the kind of man who would retreat, like a beaten dog before his master. Neither was Riel the kind of a man who could brook opposition, or one who would yield to an act of defiance, especially from one he hated as much as he hated Schultz. Accordingly, Riel marched his soldiers from Fort Garry to Winnipeg. He surrounded Schultz's house with his men and then unlimbered two cannon. The Reverend George Young and A. G. B. Bannatyne intervened on Schultz's behalf, begging Riel to allow the Canadians to retire without the bloodshed that would follow an exchange of gunfire. But their appeals fell on deaf ears. Riel was determined upon a showdown with John Schultz, and he gave the Canadians fifteen minutes to surrender.[67] He meant war and the Canadians now knew it. They surrendered, with no other understanding than the promise that their lives would be spared. Chastened in spirit, they marched to Fort Garry, escorted by the armed métis, and entered the cold, cheerless cells in the bastions of the fort.

Riel's bloodless victory put an end to the Canadian Party's appeal to force. Discouraged by his failure, and by the imprisonment of Schultz, Dennis left Red River for Canada. On December 13, McDougall decided to write to Riel; when he received no answer, he, too, decided to go back to Ottawa. He knew by then the enormity of his blunder, that he had been misled and that Canada had not, in fact, accepted the transfer of the Hudson's Bay Company territories on December 1. He knew that the Company had indeed signed the deed of transfer on November 19, but that one week later, on November 27, the Governor-General of Canada had informed the Colonial Office in London that "Canada cannot accept transfer unless quiet possession can be given."[68] He knew that the ground had been cut from under his feet. The proclamations he had uttered in the Queen's name were spurious documents with no legal authority whatever. Yet their effect had been to give the finishing blow to the Council of Assiniboia. Not that Canada's refusal to complete the deal with the Hudson's Bay Company gave any lawful basis to Riel's government, but it did leave the Provisional Government the only effective administration within the boundaries of the District of Assiniboia. Sir John A. Macdonald in Ottawa had feared that such might be the outcome of McDougall's ill-advised action. He had written to the Lieutenant-Governor designate, although too late to prevent the issuing of the Proclamation: "An assumption of the Government by you, of course, puts an end to that of the Hudson's Bay Company's authorities. . . . There would then be, if you were not admitted into the country, no legal Government existing and anarchy must follow. In such a case . . . it is quite open by the law of nations for the inhabitants to form a Government *ex necessitate*, for the protection of life and property. . . ."[69]

Schultz and his supporters had been captured on December 7. The next day, Riel emphasized the strength his success had given him by issuing a proclamation of his own. This document, issued in the name of "the people of Rupert's Land and the North-West," set out, in terms vaguely reminiscent of the American Declaration of Independence, the reasons for the métis opposition to Canada. It concluded by offering "to enter into such negotiations with the Canadian Government as may be favourable for the good government and prosperity of this people."[70] Then, on December 10, Riel and Lépine and O'Donoghue hoisted the flag of the provisional government on the big flag pole in the centre of the square at Fort Garry. It was a white flag with a fleur-de-lis. Bannatyne and Governor Mactavish watched the ceremony from the Governor's house. As the men shouted and fired their guns, Mactavish muttered, almost as if to himself, "Oh the fools! the fools!"[71] But to Riel there seemed to be nothing foolish about it. Seventeen days later, John Bruce resigned as president, and Louis Riel became president of the provisional government in name as well as in fact. Louis Schmidt, Riel's old schoolmate, became secretary.

Riel's star was in the ascendant. From a discontented young man without an apparent future in Red River, he had become within six months the head of the colony's only effective government. He had removed the threat of civil war. He failed in only one thing; he had not yet constructed a wide and solid foundation for his gimcrack government. It still rested solely on métis support; it was still, in essence, the National Committee of October. Nevertheless he was ready to go ahead with his purpose, to negotiate the terms that would see the entrance of Red River into the Canadian confederation.

CHAPTER 5

Donald A. Smith

T HE STARTLING EVENTS which occurred in the Red River
Settlement during the autumn and early winter of 1869 attracted
considerable attention in the United States. Even before the Canadian
government had learned of the rebuff to the Canadian appointed
Lieutenant-Governor, the people of Minnesota were laughing at accounts
of McDougall's discomfiture and the métis occupation of Fort Garry.
It all sounded rather like the story of Texas with McDougall cast in the
role of Santa Anna. On November 9 a highly coloured version of what
was happening in Red River—it was probably written by Enos Stutsman
—appeared in the St. Paul *Press*, concluding with the words, "Nothing
short of a very liberal government, independence, or annexation to the
United States will satisfy the people."[1] Certainly this would have
satisfied Stutsman. To assist in bringing about the annexation of Red
River he travelled to the Settlement, holding conferences with the métis
leaders,[2] talking with American sympathizers at Dutch George's or at
O'Lone's Red Saloon,[3] discussing the situation with Oscar Malmros or
Henry Robinson or H. S. Donaldson,[4] and writing tendentious letters to
St. Paul and Washington.[5] Stutsman seems to have been something of a
privileged character, for he had a pass through the métis lines at St.
Norbert and he moved to and fro between Pembina and Fort Garry.

Stutsman and the other Americans interested in the fate of Red River
undoubtedly felt that time was on their side. They knew that for many
years the people of the Settlement had carried their products to St. Paul
and made their purchases there; that Minnesota had provided the
principal means of entry to and egress from the colony; that Minnesotans
had furnished the Red River settlers with their steamboat and their mail
service. Minnesota was nearby and very real; Canada was remote and
thought of largely as the home of men like Schultz and Mair. They
knew as well that the outbreak of trouble in Red River had almost
inevitably been followed by looking towards the United States on the part
of the local people. Father Lestanc wrote to Taché on October 23 that
this was the case, and that public "indignation" against Canada had led

78

to the development of pro-annexationist sympathies within the colony.[6] To foster this sympathetic disposition towards the United States, Stutsman and his friends decided to establish a newspaper in Winnipeg in order to take the place of the now defunct *Nor'Wester*. Riel had apparently made it clear that he would have no objection to such a course, provided the journal would not be hostile to the Provisional Government. Accordingly the printing machinery of the *Nor'Wester* was purchased and the first issue of the paper appeared on Friday, January 7, 1870. The editor was Henry M. Robinson, an American journalist living in Winnipeg, and the name of the paper was *The New Nation*. The choice of name was obviously intended to appeal to the métis sense of nationality; but it is clear that *The New Nation* was not the organ of the Provisional Government. Riel did not exercise any control over the paper or its policy, at least not until March when Robinson was forced out of the editor's chair and his place was taken by a Canadian, Thomas Spence. For three months *The New Nation* reported the events in Red River in details which delight the historian; at the same time it never omitted an opportunity to press for annexation in its editorial columns. The very first issue set the policy from which the paper never deviated:

. . . the United States Republic offers us today that system of Government which would best promote order and progress in our midst and open up rapidly a country of magnificent resources. But in our present dependent position what we need in that direction, and hence we will hold it to be our duty to advocate, Independence for the people of Red River as a present cure for public ills. Our annexation to the States will follow in time and bring with it the advantage this land so much requires.[7]

In Minnesota itself the overthrow of the Hudson's Bay Company régime and the failure of Canada to establish its authority were greeted with unconcealed enthusiasm. In Pembina there was an active pro-annexation group which included men like Joseph Rolette, Jr., the U.S. Customs officer, Charles Cavelier, the postmaster, and, for a brief period, a French-Canadian by the name of Joseph Lemay.[8] These men had many contacts among the métis in Red River, for the métis, like the Indians, tended to be an international people in the sense that they crossed and recrossed the frontier at Pembina without hindrance. There had always been close ties of blood and interest between the métis of Red River and those of northern Minnesota. Moreover, as the knowledge of the events in Red River became widespread, adventurers of all kinds began to move to Pembina, to foregather in the Robber's Rest or the Ragged Edge Saloon, to drink raw whiskey, boast of their physical prowess, and enlist in any filibustering expedition that might be organized to seize the British territory to the north.   These were rough, lawless characters, the unemployed riff-raff of the American frontier.   These were the men the Canadian observer W. F. Sanford saw on his journey through Minnesota and Dakota in November, 1869, gathering in St. Paul and St. Cloud.[9]   They were the men the editor of the *New York Times* had in mind when he said that the people of Red River "may draw aid and comfort of a very practical kind from the bold adventurous element which forms so large a proportion of our frontier population. . . ."[10] Elsewhere in Minnesota less shady characters were using their influence towards the same end.   On November 24, Ignatius Donnelly, "the voice of Minnesota" and one-time Lieutenant-Governor, addressed a meeting of the St. Paul Chamber of Commerce poking fun at Canada's efforts to establish a "ludicrous and burlesque aristocracy" in Red River, declaring that the expansion of the United States into the Red and Saskatchewan valleys must come about inevitably through "geographical necessities." He added, "If the revolutionists of Red River are encouraged and sustained by the avowed sympathy of the American people, we may within a few years, perhaps months, see the Stars and Stripes wave from Fort Garry, from the waters of Puget Sound, and along the shores of Vancouver."[11]   Senator Ramsey, too, was politically and vocally active. A few days after Donnelly's speech he introduced a resolution into Congress asking for a full report from the State Department on the situation in the Red River Settlement.[12]   This agreed to, with Banks and Chandler he renewed their demand for the construction of a railway line that would bring Red River into the communications empire of the Northern Pacific.   Once it was tied economically to the United States, the colony would soon seek political union with Minnesota as a matter of course.

The State Department in Washington had been well informed about the developments on the frontier of Minnesota.   Both Malmros, the consul at Winnipeg, and Taylor—who for the moment held no official appointment—kept the mails filled with their despatches.   As early as September 11, Malmros had written to the Hon. J. C. B. Davis, the Acting Secretary of State, suggesting that "in case of insurrection" the people of Red River could probably raise "a small regularly armed force of say 1,000" which "would form a nucleus around which volunteers from the North Western States might collect. . . ."   He protested that he had always been circumspect in his public statements, wary of compromising the United States, but that "by conversing on the causes of success or failure of revolution in other countries, I have indirectly endeavoured to prevent mistakes and ill-considered movement on the part of this people."[13] On November 6, Malmros urged the United States on no account to allow Canadian troops to be sent through American territory, assuring Mr. Davis that "should this revolution be successful it may, I think, be safely predicted that in less than two years time all the British colonies on this continent will apply for admission into the Union."[14] In order to ensure that the "revolution" would be successful, he pointed out to Washington on January 15: "it is to be feared . . . that on account of their poverty the French half-breeds will not be able to hold out much longer unless they obtain pecuniary aid from abroad. The sum of about $25,000 promptly sent would materially aid and I think secure the success of the independence movement."[15] When writing to his friends in Minnesota, Malmros was much less reticent in his financial demands. "I am convinced," he informed Ramsey, "that $100,000 would make the annexation movement a success."[16] Finally, in March, Malmros raised the question of a *de facto* recognition of the Provisional Government.[17] Small wonder that after the publication of his indiscretions Malmros felt it advisable to leave the Settlement. His further services would only have embarrassed the federal authorities in the United States.

Taylor, however, was a man of a different stamp. He was discretion itself. After reading Taylor's letters from the west, the Secretary of State, the notorious expansionist Hamilton Fish, appointed him "special agent" of the State Department—euphemism for a spy—with instructions to investigate the troubles in Red River and keep the United States government advised on all developments. From December, until his appointment in April as consul in Winnipeg, and indeed for some time afterwards, Taylor sent numerous and detailed despatches to Washington. There is much of value to the historian in these letters. They reveal Taylor as an astute observer and a man of balanced judgment, but they are always coloured by their writer's obsession with the idea of annexation and twisted by his association with Jay Cooke and the Northern Pacific. It cannot be doubted that Taylor's and Malmros's communications were taken seriously in Washington. Indeed, Fish was sufficiently interested to cause inquiries to be made by the United States ambassador in London regarding the alleged pro-American sympathies of the Hudson's Bay Company. "I am convinced," wrote the Deputy Governor of the Company in January, "that the government at Washington feels a much greater interest in this Red River affair than anyone supposes, and the settlement may possibly take a very different turn from what we supposed two months ago."[18]

II

It seems surprising, in view of the excitement in the United States, that Sir John A. Macdonald and the Canadian government should have viewed the disturbances in the Red River Settlement with such apparent equanimity. The Canadian press had not ignored what was happening during the summer of 1869, and Macdonald and his colleagues had been informed that the negotiations between Canada and the Hudson's Bay Company had aroused the misgivings of the old settlers in the colony. In 1868 the Anglican Bishop of Rupert's Land had offered his services to the government of Canada to help smooth the way for Canadian rule.[19] Mactavish, too, had warned the Canadian authorities that they would find governing the North-West no easy task.[20] On his way to Rome, Bishop Taché had a few words with Sir George Cartier, only to find himself treated with the same smiling courtesy and the same blank indifference as the others.[21] There was nothing that Ottawa wanted to know about the North-West or its problems.

It was not like Sir John A. Macdonald to brush aside these warnings without some queries on his part. Certainly matters relating to the North-West bulked large in his correspondence during 1869. Perhaps he had so many more urgent problems, urgent at least because they were much nearer than those from the land beyond the Great Lakes; perhaps he had begun to drink again, heavily, and could not clearly distinguish the clouds gathering upon the western horizon. Had he not dealt with those western problems when he drafted the Act for the Temporary Government of Rupert's Land? McDougall's government was not to be a permanent thing; it was intended only as a means of bridging the gap between the rule of the Hudson's Bay Company and that of Canada—no more than an excuse to give McDougall a chance to size up the situation and make recommendations for something more permanent. Yet Macdonald wondered, when he watched McDougall board his train for St. Paul, whether the new Lieutenant-Governor might not run into trouble. "It will require considerable management to keep those wild people quiet," he wrote.[22]

The trouble proved to be much worse than he ever anticipated. As he received reports from the North-West, he became more and more impatient. Schultz, Mair, Dennis, Snow—those friends and employees of McDougall's Department of Public Works—had all been "indiscreet" and "offensive." He picked up his pen and wrote sharply to the Governor, "You must bridle those gentlemen or they will be a continual source of disquiet to you."[23] If from Ottawa he could recognize the deleterious influence of these men, why could not McDougall who was right on the spot? It was unfortunate that the mails were so slow and that his own replies always seemed to arrive too late at Pembina. Meanwhile Macdonald was learning something of the complex nature of the western problem, of the various influences at work within and outside the Red River Settlement: the strength of métis nationalism, the activities of the Canadian Party, the indifferent attitude of the Hudson's Bay Company, the role of Ritchot and Dugast, the intrigues of Stutsman. Something had to be done. This something was the cancellation of the transfer; the issuance of a proclamation on December 6 promising an amnesty to all who would lay down their arms and desist from further illegal action; the despatch of the Very Reverend Jean-Baptiste Thibault and Colonel Charles de Salaberry to Red River, to explain the true intentions of the Canadian government and to remove from the minds of the métis and the half-breeds all possible fears and suspicions of Mc-Dougall. Macdonald may well have congratulated himself on his selection of emissaries. Thibault had served as a missionary for over thirty-six years in Red River, and de Salaberry had been a popular member of the Canadian government exploring expedition of 1857/58. Theirs would be a mission of goodwill. There would be no question of negotiating with Riel. Thibault and de Salaberry would persuade, not bargain.

In the meantime, Donald A. Smith, the chief representative of the Hudson's Bay Company in Canada, called upon the Prime Minister and assured him of the loyal co-operation of the officers of the Company "to restore and maintain order throughout the territory."[24] Impressed with Smith's appearance and calm determination, the Prime Minister resolved to send him to Red River as a "Special Commissioner, to enquire into and report upon the causes and extent of the armed obstruction offered at the Red River . . . to the peaceful ingress of the Hon. Wm. Mc-Dougall," and to "explain to the inhabitants the principles on which the Government of Canada intends to govern the country, and to remove any misapprehensions that may exist on the subject. Also to take such steps, in concert with Mr. McDougall and Governor Mactavish, as may seem most proper for effecting the peaceable transfer of the country and the government from the Hudson's Bay authorities to the Government of the Dominion."[25] These instructions were dated December 10. They did not, in fact, go much beyond those given to Thibault and de Salaberry. But two days later Smith was approached privately by the Prime Minister and was given authority to buy off some of the leaders of the disturbances with offers of money or employment.[26]

III

Riel had spent the Christmas season worrying, and just a little apprehensive about the future. He was still anxious to secure the support of the English-speaking settlers, but he seemed unable to convince them of his determination to stick to the Provisional Government or that the best chance for both racial troups to obtain concessions from Canada was to be found in united action. He was anxious, too, about the activities of the Americans who never seemed to lose an opportunity of pressing for annexation; about the Fenian proclivities of W. B. O'Donoghue whom he had taken into his council; about the movements of those who sympathized with the Canadians and had helped some of the prisoners to escape;[27] about the revival of opposition in the métis ranks in the persons of Charles Nolin and Pierre Léveillé;[28] and about the growing shortage of funds.

The last was the problem most easily solved. All that was necessary was to seize the funds of the Hudson's Bay Company; and this Riel did on December 22, after Governor Mactavish had refused to give him a loan.[29] The other problems were more difficult. Nevertheless, there were some steps that he could take. He would avoid any move which might suggest hostility to the British connection, and he could approach individuals among the English-speaking settlers, men like James Ross, William and Robert Tait, James Bannatyne and John Fraser,[30] who might be persuaded to give him their open support. On December 24, he visited Kildonan where he talked to William Fraser. He told Fraser that "the French still desired the English and Scotch to join them—twelve English councillors and twelve French—these twenty-four to elect a Governor or President from amongst their own number." Fraser, with true Scottish caution, answered only that "he would state the matter to his people." Disgruntled, Riel replied that if the English-speaking people would not join the French "the latter would force it on them in time." Then he returned to the fort. It was the night before Christmas, so he paid his men with the monies taken from the Hudson's Bay Company. When Mass was sung at the cathedral that midnight, few of the métis soldiers were in attendance—they had gone to Dutch George's to spend their pay and had become roaring drunk.[31]

It was on the day before Christmas when Grand Vicar Thibault and his companion reached Pembina. To their surprise they found themselves objects of suspicion and distrust. Acting on the advice of Provencher and Cameron, who had stayed behind after McDougall's departure, de Salaberry remained at Pembina while Thibault went on towards St. Boniface. As the priest travelled north, a courier hurried ahead of him bearing a letter to Riel from Stutsman suggesting that if there was to be any conference with the Canadian commissioners, it should be held at the frontier.   The letter warned the young métis leader that if Thibault and de Salaberry "are permitted free communication with your people they will give you trouble.   Inasmuch as Father Thibault comes in an official capacity, he should be regarded as an official and *not* as a minister of Christ."[32]

Christmas day brought to Louis Riel the news of Grand Vicar Thibault's arrival in the Settlement.   Riel had no intention of molesting the priest, but he did think it the better part of discretion to go to St. Norbert to meet Thibault, and, incidentally, to discuss the situation with the Abbé Ritchot.   Thibault reached St. Norbert late that night.   Not until the next day did he explain to Riel what he and de Salaberry had been instructed to do.   At Thibault's request, Riel agreed to allow de Salaberry to join him.   It was not, however, until January 5 that the Canadian officer reached Fort Garry.   Meanwhile, Thibault took up his residence in the Bishop's house at St. Boniface.   But he was not allowed to move freely among the people, and his papers, including his commission and the Governor-General's promise of an amnesty, were taken from him by Riel.

It had not taken the métis leader long to judge the stature of the two Canadian commissioners.   Thibault had been too long a missionary to the métis not to sympathize with the hopes and aspirations of the people to whom he had ministered.   Exposed as he was to the influence of the Abbé Dugast and the Abbé Giroux, while a guest in the Bishop's house, it was only a matter of days until he was won over to the métis point of view.   His companion, de Salaberry, the bearer of a name deeply engraved on the historical record of Canadian military achievement, was a pleasant, amiable but ineffective man.   He could not do much harm to Riel unless it were true, as Malmros had hinted to Washington, that he had been provided with a "corruption fund" to buy Riel's supporters.[33] Riel watched him closely enough to make certain that he did not wander unaccompanied throughout the Settlement.   Finally, on January 5, Riel invited the two commissioners to speak to the métis council.   With his abundant personal charm, he told the Grand Vicar that he was sorry to see that their documents gave them no authority to negotiate, but that he would gladly hear what they might have to say.   With equal grace Thibault replied:

Since you have done us the honour of hearing us, we will commence, by telling you that we are in truth, bearers of good news; and we are enabled to assure you, that the intentions of the Government, who have sent us, are altogether those of peace and good will.   It desires to respect your persons and your rights; to labour for the improvement of your country, by making a road in order to communicate more easily with Canada. It admits that it may have been mistaken in its choice of employees, whose extravagant conduct may possibly have compromised it in this territory; but, it strongly condemns the arbitrary acts of such employees as have wantonly abused its confidence.[34]

Thibault went on in this strain for some time, and the métis listened with the same respect they would have given to one of Thibault's sermons. Then Riel thanked him "very courteously," made a few vague references to their mutual desire for a settlement and promised to "look into the matter with his council." He even whispered into de Salaberry's ear, as he was quitting the room, "Colonel, don't be in a hurry to leave, I think of charging you with a commission, which can't but be agreeable to you." Riel did not reveal the nature of this commission. But he knew in his own mind what he intended to do. He would use both Thibault and de Salaberry for his own purposes; he would enlist their services in winning back men like Nolin and Léveillé and all those faint-hearted ones whose numbers seemed to be increasing daily. The two commissioners would help him close the métis ranks once again.

At this point Donald A. Smith arrived at Fort Garry. Much more astute than either Thibault or de Salaberry, he had left his documents at Pembina in Provencher's care and with his brother-in-law, Richard Hardisty, travelled as a simple Hudson's Bay Company employee to the Settlement. When he reached the fort he went to see Riel, explained his association with the Company, and hinted that he held a Canadian government commission. Riel endeavoured to get him to take an oath to do nothing to undermine the Provisional Government "legally established"; but Smith side-stepped this commitment by agreeing only to do nothing to upset the government "legal or illegal as it might be" without first notifying Riel.[35] It was an equivocal statement; but Riel accepted it and allowed Smith to take up his quarters in the fort. This was the first encounter between the two men, each one carefully trying to take the measure of the other. What Riel did not know at first was that it was Smith, rather than de Salaberry, who had the government's money to spend, and that he would distribute it carefully among those métis whom he felt would carry weight amongst their fellows. In 1874, Smith told the Select Committee that he had spent £500 among the métis "whose assistance had been absolutely necessary in my position as Canadian Commissioner in 1869 and 1870." The outcome was exactly what Smith and Macdonald had hoped for. Some of the leading métis withdrew their support from the Provisional Government, and drew about themselves those already disposed to hold aloof from political action. According to métis tradition, Smith even tried to bribe Riel but without success. There is no evidence from Riel that such an effort was ever made; and all that Smith wrote was the cryptic statement in his report, "On January 6 I saw Riel and soon came to the conclusion that no good could arise from entering into any negotiations with his Council."[36]

Louis Riel was very much concerned with the re-appearance of a breach within the ranks of the French métis. On January 1, he went to Oak Point. In this region of the Red River Settlement Charles Nolin's influence was greatest,[37] and Nolin had walked out of Riel's council and had returned home on December 24.[38] Despite their kinship to Riel, the Nolins, according to Father Lestanc, had "almost always wavered in their support" of the métis movement.[39] Here and elsewhere Riel was prepared to protest his moderation and to declare that he wished nothing more than an arrangement with Canada that would secure half-breed rights and privileges. "Proper terms" were the words used by Alexander Begg in his *Journal* to describe Riel's object.[40] One thing he was not prepared to do, and that was to stand by and see what he had already accomplished undone. He believed that his cause was righteous, and that it would be fatal to the people of Red River if they allowed the Canadians to obtain a secure footing in the colony before the necessary guarantees had been extracted from Ottawa. But if things were to continue as they were going, he feared that he would find himself deprived of the support of the English-speaking half-breeds and a goodly number of his own people.

He would have to do something to re-establish his ascendancy over the community. Yet he would have to work carefully. As soon as he realized Donald Smith was a Canadian emissary, he recognized that Smith, rather than Thibault, was the man he had to fear. He therefore placed Smith under guard and demanded to see his credentials. When Smith replied that he had left them at Pembina, Riel offered to send one of his men to accompany Richard Hardisty and bring them to Fort Garry. He had made up his mind that he must see if Smith had really been given the authority to negotiate with the people of Red River. Until he knew this he was determined not to allow Smith the opportunity to speak to the council. He planned to intercept Hardisty, seize the papers, read them and bring them to the fort himself. Mactavish, however, divined what was in Riel's mind and hurriedly sent three half-breeds, including Pierre Léveillé, to follow hard upon Hardisty's heels.[41] Thus it was Léveillé who intercepted Hardisty rather than Riel. Nevertheless, on the return journey, Riel and Ritchot made an effort to gain possession of Smith's papers at St. Norbert. But to Riel's surprise he found himself looking down the barrel of Léveillé's pistol, while Ritchot was pushed irreverently aside and told "not to interfere any further with matters unconnected with his spiritual duties." There was nothing to be done but to make the best of it. Riel returned with Léveillé and Hardisty and the others to Red River, to see the documents he had hoped to obtain for his own private study turned over to the Canadian Commissioner. When Smith proposed that there should be a mass meeting of the people of Red River, where the documents should be given a public hearing, rather than a meeting of the council of the Provisional Government, Riel felt that he had no choice but to agree.

For the moment Riel had been outmanœuvred. He had acted indiscreetly and rather stupidly when he tried to seize Smith's papers, and he felt his humiliation keenly. Smith had been able to side-step giving recognition to the Provisional Government for a second time, and he would be able to put the Canadian case directly before the people of the Settlement. As Riel thought of this, anger welled inside him. At three o'clock in the morning he strode into Smith's room. Perhaps he intended to arrest Smith, perhaps merely berate him. If so, he changed his mind. He gave Smith a rather lame excuse for the intrusion and abruptly departed.[42]

IV

The meeting which Smith had proposed was arranged for January 19. It was a bright and sunny day, but it was cold, so cold the thermometer stood twenty degrees below zero. Even so, many people of the Settlement gathered in the square at the Fort. A thousand of them came— from the north, from Kildonan, St. Andrew's and Headingly; from the south, from St. Vital and St. Norbert; from St. Boniface and from St. James. Finally Riel and Smith appeared; the one, twenty-five years of age, inexperienced, visionary, unsure of himself; the other, twice as old, confident, a master of business and of men: for one, fate held only poverty and the scaffold; for the other, great wealth, a peerage and the highest diplomatic post as his country's gift. Both men took their places on the gallery of the large stone building which faced the south gate opposite the open square—for the court house would not hold the crowd. With them were other dignitaries of the Settlement, the Anglican Bishop, the curé of St. Norbert, and the Canadian commissioners, Grand Vicar Thibault and Colonel de Salaberry.

On a motion by Louis Riel, seconded by Pierre Léveillé, Thomas Bunn, the English half-breed from St. Clement's, who had been a member of the first convention, was chosen chairman. Judge Black was elected secretary, and Riel himself agreed to act as French interpreter. Smith began by demanding the lowering of the métis flag. But when he sensed that a large number of his audience was not yet ready for such a step, he said no more. Admittedly he had won or purchased a good deal of support, but he could not proceed too far or too quickly, and he had the political intuition to know just how far he could go and when he must stop. Then he began a short address. He disassociated himself from McDougall and identified himself with the Red River community by pointing out that he was married to a half-breed woman and was related to many of the English half-breeds present on the square. He declared that he would be ready to resign from the Hudson's Bay Company should it be necessary for the good of the Settlement. Much of this was said with tongue-in-cheek, but Smith was out to win friends and not to make enemies. Having created an atmosphere favourable to himself, he started to read the various documents in his possession; his commission, his instructions, letters to McDougall and to Mactavish, all of which were designed to show that Canada was the embodiment of good will, and that the Canadian government had nothing but the very best of intentions towards the North-West.

The meeting lasted five hours, and the listeners shuffled about in the crisp, crackling snow, stamped their feet and swung their arms as they huddled beneath their blue capotes. There was no controversy to excite their spirits or warm their blood. It was all straightforward, rather monotonous and repetitive. Riel himself made few interjections; he confined himself to doing the translations while Smith did the talking. Then, just as the meeting was about to adjourn, for there were more papers to be read on the morrow, a voice—it was John Burke's, the Burke who had joined William Hallett in releasing Corbett and Stewart from gaol back in 1863—demanded the release of the prisoners taken from "Fort Schultz." "Not just now," cried Riel. Other voices shouted: "Yes, yes." It was a tense moment. But Riel had the men with the muskets, even if there were some of dubious loyalty among them, and with the appearance of his soldiers from the background of the fort, the hecklers subsided and the meeting was adjourned until the next day.[43]

On January 20, an even larger number gathered in the square at Fort Garry. The temperature was the same, but in some way the atmosphere of the meeting had changed. Riel seemed to be stronger than before and Smith weaker. It was hard to explain. Someone had been at work among the people. And that someone was Father Lestanc at the cathedral, who had been assisted by Thibault and de Salaberry.[44] The clergy had been alarmed at Smith's policy of using the commercial power of the Hudson's Bay Company, as well as government money, for political purposes. They desired not so much to support Riel as to avoid a situation which might lead to civil strife or bloodshed within the Red River Settlement.   They were prepared to do what they could to calm the malcontents and persuade them that a united Settlement would achieve more than one divided against itself.[45]

The second meeting opened on a conciliatory note.   Judge Black, it is true, refused to serve as secretary, but A. G. B. Bannatyne was willing to act in his place.   What was more significant was John Burke's apology to the gathering for his intervention the previous day.   He claimed that "the sentiments were not his own, but what were put into him by another party to say."[46]   Almost everybody then agreed that "during the present doubtful state of affairs" it would be premature to allow the Canadians complete freedom in the Settlement.   Father Lestanc stepped forward and said, "We have been good friends to this day in the whole Settlement; and I want to certify here that we will be good friends tonight."[47]   This was greeted with cheers.   Smith then resumed the reading of his official documents, including the Governor-General's letter to Mactavish, that closed with the words: "And the inhabitants of Rupert's Land, of all classes and persuasions, may rest assured that Her Majesty's Government has no intention of interfering with, or setting aside, or allow others to interfere with the religions, the rights or franchises hitherto enjoyed, or to which they may hereafter prove themselves equal";[48] and Joseph Howe's letter of December 7 to McDougall telling him to assure the people of Red River that Canada would respect "all their civil and religious liberties"; that "all their properties, rights and privileges of every kind as enjoyed under the government of the Hudson's Bay Company will be continued"; that "in granting titles to land now occupied by the settlers, the most liberal policy will be pursued," that local people would be appointed to the Council; and that McDougall's government was "merely provisional and temporary."[49]   These and other documents were greeted with cheers, not always because they were understood, but because cheering helped to keep people warm in the subzero weather.

Then Riel came forward.   On January 19, he had kept himself in the background, if only because of his uncertainty as to whether he could control the meeting.   Now he was much more self-assured.   He was beginning to realize the Canadian had lost ground, that Smith no longer held the attention of the meeting, that the people were bored with the constant repetition of Canadian goodwill without any positive suggestions how to translate that goodwill into action.   He therefore proposed, with Bannatyne's support, that twenty representatives should be elected by the English-speaking population to meet with twenty representatives of the French population, on Tuesday, January 25, at noon, in the Court House, "with the object of considering the subject of Mr. Smith's commission, and to decide what would be best for the welfare of the country." It was apparently an innocuous suggestion, but its adoption once more gave Riel a chance to direct the course of events and keep Smith in the background. Riel's proposal was carried with cheers; then more cheers followed for Father Lestanc, Bishop Machray, Father Ritchot and for Louis Riel and the commissioners. At that moment, from the audience, a voice shouted: "That resolution seems to cast doubt on Mr. Smith's commission. We do not doubt it." This did not bother Riel. "We accept the commission as genuine and are merely to consider what is to be done under it," he replied. He was now at ease and completely in control of himself and of the situation. After platitudinous speeches by Father Ritchot and Bishop Machray, Riel cried in a manner that could scarcely hide his satisfaction:

Before this assembly breaks up, I cannot but express my feelings however briefly. I came here with fear. We are not yet enemies [loud cheers] but we came very near being so. As soon as we understood each other, we joined in demanding what our English fellow-subjects in common with us believe to be our just rights [loud cheers]. I am not afraid to say "our rights," for we all have rights [renewed cheers]. We claim no half-rights, mind you, but all the rights we are entitled to. Those rights will be set forth by our representatives, and what is more, Gentlemen, we will get them [loud cheers].[50]

As the meeting adjourned, men threw their caps into the air and shook each others' hands. They shouted and cheered. All of them believed that the crisis was over. They had not wanted to fight Canada or each other. They merely wanted to be sure that the Canadian government meant well towards them. They had heard these assurances; all they would have to do now would be to outline their rights as they saw them and arrive at some firm understanding with the representatives of the Dominion. That was all. Even Riel was infected with the general feeling of goodwill, and on January 22 most of his soldiers were sent home. Only a small guard was retained at Fort Garry.[51]

V

The elections were held. On January 26, the new convention met, one day later than had been planned. On the surface it seemed as if the goodwill of the 20th still prevailed. But behind the scenes there had been a great deal of intrigue and bitter rivalry. In Winnipeg the pro-American element had packed the nomination meeting and had elected the American editor of *The New Nation* chairman of what they chose to call a "primary." Then they nominated Alfred Scott, a bartender in

O'Lone's Red Saloon.   A. G. B. Bannatyne's name was also put forward, but by a show of hands Scott was elected.   Immediately there were protests that this was not a proper election, no more than a nomination meeting, that both candidates would have to be voted upon later in a proper fashion.   These protests, however, were drowned in shouts and catcalls and demands for adjournment.[52]   Even more significant than the victory of the Americans over the old settlers—for that is what the success of Alfred Scott amounted to—was the electoral battle between Charles Nolin and Louis Riel.   Despite the efforts of Fathers Lestanc and Thibault,[53] Charles Nolin had not yielded to Riel, and he had remained the rallying point for the anti-Riel métis, including the Léveillés, the Charettes, the Deases and the Hamelins.   In the end, Nolin managed to win three seats out of the twenty contested, those gained by George Klyne, Thomas Harrison and Charles Nolin himself. He almost gained another in St. Charles, where John Grant disputed Baptiste Beauchemin's election.[54]   Nevertheless these were three seats that Riel did not wish to concede.   They broke the solid front with which he had hoped to confront the English delegates.   However, if he lost at Oak Point, Riel gained at St. François Xavier, where both Pierre Léveillé and François Dauphinais were defeated.   In St. Boniface, W. B. O'Donoghue and Louis Schmidt had both won seats; and in St. Vital, Louis Riel himself had been elected without difficulty.   In the English-speaking parishes, no less than five members of the November convention were returned, including James Ross, Dr. Bird and Thomas Bunn; a Canadian from Portage la Prairie, Kenneth Mackenzie, was elected for St. Mary's.

Although irritated at Nolin's success, Riel opened the session of the new convention of forty in a conciliatory manner.   It was he who nominated Judge Black as chairman of the assembly, despite the fact that the judge was no friend of his.   He likewise agreed without opposition to the suggestion that the old List of Rights, which had been drawn up on December 1, should be discarded because it had not been adequately considered, and that a new list should be prepared by a committee especially appointed for the purpose that contained three French-speaking and three English-speaking members selected from "natives of the country."[55]   Riel himself consented to serve on the committee, along with James Ross, Charles Nolin and three others.

The task confronting the six men was formidable.   It was virtually the task of preparing a constitution for the Red River Settlement. However, by January 29, they had completed their work and the new List or Bill of Rights was presented to the convention.   In some ways it resembled the previous list; but there were several changes that engendered some argument from those who had assembled at Fort Garry. There was the familiar demand for improved railway communication between the Settlement and St. Paul; but now there was also a demand for "steam communication" between Red River and Lake Superior "within five years." Here was open recognition of the fact that if the Settlement was to become part of Canada it could not, indefinitely, depend on the United States for its communications. There were demands for monetary appropriations for schools, roads and bridges; for no direct taxation so long as the region did not possess provincial status; for all the institutions and privileges appropriate to provincial status when the "exceptional" period of territorial status should come to an end; for the "common" usage of French and English in the courts and in the legislature; for promises that "all the properties, rights and privileges as hitherto enjoyed by us, be respected and that the recognition and arrangement of local customs, usages and privileges be made under the control of the Local Legislature"; that the local legislature should have "full control of all the lands inside a circumference having Upper Fort Garry as a centre, and that the radius of this circumference be the number of miles that the American line is distant from Fort Garry"; that the franchise should be granted to every man in the colony of twenty-one years of age or over and to any other householder after a three years' residence in the country; that the territory should have two members in the federal parliament and one in the Senate; and that the people of Red River should in no way be held responsible for the payment of any of the £300,000 promised by Canada to the Hudson's Bay Company. Through-out the list one could see Riel's anxiety to protect the lands, the local customs, the usages and languages of the people of his native country. Here would be solid guarantees against a too violent change once the country should become part of Canada.[56]

For several days the convention of forty debated the List, clause by clause. The scrutiny of the members was searching, but their discussion was not acrimonious, at least not until February 3 when Riel proposed, by way of amendment, that the convention should demand provincial status immediately, and not leave this status to the discretion of the Canadian government to concede at some future date. In this way, he felt, the people would gain a more secure hold on their rights and privileges and would be able to turn to their own advantage local control over public lands and natural resources. But this suggestion was more than the members of the convention were prepared to accept. When the question was put to a vote, Riel lost. It was a temporary rebuff. Then he failed a second time to carry a majority of the members of the convention with him, when he proposed there should be a clause setting aside the bargain concluded between Canada and the Hudson's Bay Company for the transfer of the North-West, and substituting for it a new agreement between Canada and the Red River Settlement. Two reverses, one following on the heels of the other, were more than Riel's temper could stand, particularly when both suggestions had been defeated by Nolin's small group voting with the English-speaking delegates. With great warmth, Riel cried, as he strode up and down the room, "The devil take it; we must win. The vote may go as it likes; but the measure, which has now been defeated, must be carried. It is a shame to have lost it; and it was a greater shame, because it was lost by those traitors." He jabbed his finger in the direction of Nolin, Klyne and Harrison.[57] Nolin jumped to his feet to shout indignantly. "I was not sent here, Mr. Riel, to vote at your dictation. I came here to vote according to my conscience. While there are some things for which we blame the Company, there is a good deal for which we must thank them. I do not exculpate the Company altogether; but I say that, in time of need, we have often been indebted to them for assistance and kindness." Controlling himself with difficulty, Riel replied: "While I say this matter must be carried, I do not wish to speak disrespectfully of the convention. But I say it will be carried at a subsequent stage." Yielding to his anger, he continued, "You must remember that there is a Provisional Government, and, though this measure has been lost by the voice of the convention, I have friends enough, who are determined to add it to the list, on their own responsibility." Turning to the three French delegates, he cried in a threatening manner: "as for you, Charles Nolin, Tom Harrison and George Klyne—two of you relatives of my own—as for you, your influence, as public men, is finished in this country. Look at the position in which you have placed yourselves. You have lost your influence forever." Nolin, his face flushed and his voice trembling, shouted, "You, Mr. Riel, did what you could to prevent my coming here, and failed; and, if it suited my purpose to come back again, I would come at the call of my parish in spite of you."[58] The meeting broke up in confusion. It was just as well. An adjournment would give time for tempers to cool. But not for several years would relations between Riel and Nolin warm to the point of cordiality.

In a belligerent frame of mind and determined to prove to everybody including himself that he was still the leader of the government, Riel hoisted a new Provisional Government flag "much larger than the first one."[59] Then he turned to deal with those he believed responsible for what he regarded as a deliberate challenge to his authority. In Riel's opinion, and in those of Lestanc and Ritchot, the Hudson's Bay Company was at the bottom of Léveillé's and Nolin's activities. The Company had taken a number of métis and half-breeds into their employ and Riel was convinced that Smith and Mactavish and Dr. Cowan were directing the opposition from the background.⁶⁰ Accordingly he went to Mactavish's sick room, abused the former Governor of Assiniboia and placed guards about his house. Dr. Cowan was arrested and was placed in the same prison room with William Hallett. When Bannatyne refused to stay away from Fort Garry, he too was placed behind locked doors, regardless of the fact that he, more than any other English-speaking settler, had shown a willingness to collaborate with Riel and to support the Provisional Government.⁶¹ Then Riel looked for Charles Nolin. But Nolin knew what to expect and was carefully guarded by his brothers. When several of Riel's men attempted to seize Charles, Duncan Nolin drew his pistol. One of Riel's soldiers levelled his carbine. Fortunately, both weapons misfired. "It was the hand of God," wrote Father Giroux, Riel's old classmate, who was now chaplain to his soldiers, that prevented bloodshed, and prevented an outbreak of fighting between the two métis factions.⁶²

For a brief period it looked as if the work of the past weeks would be undone, and that Riel's petulance would destroy his positive achievement. Some of the English delegates were, indeed, disposed to abandon the convention and have no more to do with Riel and with the radical wing of the métis;⁶³ but calmer wills prevailed, and on February 7 the convention met again with both sides fully represented. Their purpose was to find out if the Canadian commissioners were really in a position to guarantee the rights outlined in the List that had been accepted by the convention. After listening to Thibault and de Salaberry, the members could appreciate what Riel had known for several weeks—that the two French Canadians were no more than messengers of peace and had no authority at all. But Smith was not in the same category. Clearly he had been given some power; the question was, how much?

As before, the meeting of February 7 was dominated by the clash between Louis Riel and Donald Smith. On the one hand, there was the métis leader, trying to prove that Smith had no power to concede any of the métis demands; on the other, was the resourceful Scotsman trying to cover the deficiencies in his commission and anxious to bring his mission to a successful conclusion. For each thrust of Riel, Smith appeared to have a parry. But the métis had the better of the exchange. From the outset Riel made it quite clear that he, for one, was not satisfied "with what Mr. Smith thinks, but what he can guarantee." "I want some certainty," he continued, "and not merely an expression of opinion on what we desire. We are now in a position to make demands. How far is the Commissioner in a position to guarantee them on behalf of the

Canadian Government?" When Ross suggested that Smith might be asked to comment upon the List of Rights, clause by clause, Riel interjected: "I would like to hear from Mr. Smith first, whether, without going into details, Mr. Smith can say that he is in a position to grant us what we want. Is he, as Commissioner, able to guarantee one single article on the List?" Smith tried to avoid a direct negative by replying, "While I might have power in regard to some of the articles, to assure you, so far as assurance can be given to anything which has not yet occurred, I could not, at the same time, do so equally in regard to the whole." Again Riel pressed his question. This time Smith answered, "I believe that the nature of my commission is such that I can give assurances, full assurances, so far as any such guarantee can be given, that the Government of the Dominion would so place the right guarantee before Parliament that it would be granted." Riel interrupted him. "So you cannot guarantee us even a single article in that List?" He was right, but Smith would not admit it. The commissioner replied again, "I believe my powers to be sufficient to admit of my guaranteeing, so far as anything can be guaranteed which is not yet passed by Parliament, certain articles in this List." The sparring continued. Finally Riel stopped. "You are embarrassed." He said to Smith: "I see you are a gentleman, and do not wish to press you. I see that the Canadian Government has not given you all the confidence which they ought to have put in your hands. At the same time, we will hear your opinion, although we are satisfied you cannot grant us, nor guarantee us anything by the nature of your Commission."[64]

One by one the articles of the List of Rights was brought forward. To each one Smith gave an answer marked by characteristic caution. To some he said that he could give "explicit assurances"; to others he would only promise the "utmost deference" and "full and substantial justice." Riel could afford to be magnanimous and to refrain from discussion and controversy. He had gained his point. And he knew what his next step would be. He was scarcely surprised when, at the end of the session, Smith, on behalf of the other Canadian commissioners and the Canadian government, declared that he was authorized "to offer a very cordial reception to the delegates who might be sent from this country to Canada." "I, myself, feel every confidence," he continued, "that the result will be such as will be entirely satisfactory to the people of the North-West. It is, I know, the desire of the Canadian Government that it should be so."[65] On the following day the convention accepted the Canadian invitation. It was, after all, what Riel had wanted and what he had worked for.

Thus far Riel had achieved all he had set out to do. He had forced

Canada to agree to negotiation, and he had done so with the support of the majority of the people of Red River, English- and French-speaking alike. Now, he felt, was the time to nail his leadership to this firm foundation. He would revive the proposal of a Provisional Government that had failed to obtain widespread support in December. He had sound arguments to bolster his case. Who would administer the colony in the weeks that must follow the despatch of the delegates to Ottawa and the arrival of Canadian authority? McDougall had killed the Council of Assiniboia, and Macdonald's refusal to go through with the transfer had prevented the establishment of any other government. There was, in actual fact, no governmental authority in Red River at all. Riel put this suggestion up to the convention: "We have arrived at that point, or very near it, where we must consider the nature of the Convention. Notwithstanding our differences of opinion, we have been friendly to this point. But we are yet in a loose, unsatisfactory way. It is now necessary for us to place ourselves in a more suitable position. We must have a more fixed existence before proceeding much farther."[66] After a few more vague generalities, Riel came to the point. A permanent executive, a Provisional Government, was needed if only because the dissolution of the convention would "leave open a gap in which all our people may be engulfed and in the angry waves of the flood which might sweep over the Settlement, we may find reason for regret that a wiser course had not been adopted when it lay in our power." And this gap would be all the more dangerous should there be any truth in the rumours, circulating among the members of the convention of forty, that the Canadians were planning an armed rising in Portage la Prairie.

The debate was not an acrimonious one, but it dragged on throughout February 8 and 9. The English-speaking delegates could not rid themselves of nagging doubts as to whether the course Riel proposed was strictly constitutional. Riel became annoyed. "The Provisional Government is an actual fact," he declared. "Why not recognize it? You have, in reality, practically recognized it by your acts in this Convention. It has accomplished some good. Help it do more." Still the English delegates hesitated. Then the suggestion was put forward that the whole matter might be put to Governor Mactavish. This was agreed to, and John Sutherland and John Fraser of Kildonan, accompanied by Ambroise Lépine and Xavier Pagée, went to see the weak dying man who had held the title of Governor of Assiniboia since 1864. On their return to the convention hall, Sutherland reported that Mactavish had said: "Form a Government, for God's sake, and restore peace and order in the Settlement."[67] It did not matter that Mactavish had also said that he would not delegate his power as Governor to anyone. He had given his blessing to a Provisional Government and the English delegates were ready to fall in line with Riel. With one change the committee which had drafted the List of Rights was asked to take on the task of drafting a constitution for the Provisional Government.[68]

On the afternoon of the 10th, the committee submitted its recommendations to the convention. It was proposed that there should be an elected council of twenty-four members, twelve from the English- and twelve from the French-speaking population. There should also be an executive comprising a president, two secretaries, one French and the other English, and a treasurer. The General Quarterly Court and the Petty courts would continue their sittings as before, except that William Dease would be replaced by Norbert Larance as a justice of the peace. The appointments would be filled as follows: President, Louis Riel; secretaries, Thomas Bunn and Louis Schmidt; treasurer, W. B. O'Donoghue; Chief Justice, James Ross. The previous appointments of Dr. Bird as Coroner, Henry McKenney as Sheriff, and A. G. B. Bannatyne as postmaster were confirmed. There was some discussion about Riel's appointment, and Ross proposed that he should be one of the delegates to Ottawa. But Riel was determined to accept nothing less than the presidency. When some of the English representatives began to talk about consulting their constituents, Riel in a typical speech remarked:

I know you are bound by your people; but why did you not say so when you were organizing the Committee? What was the use of appointing the Committee if you could not act? That Committee gave the English people all the officers but one or two. But it is an organization without a head. . . . If it is your duty to go back, go; and if you do not come again, why your people can stay as they are. As for us we will work as we have done . . . we will do, not our work alone, but your work. . . . If you do not come back, we will look upon what has been done as nothing at all. We will make out a new Bill of Rights, form a Provisional Government and try to make it obeyed.

Then, in a burst of passion, he added: "On my life I will say so, if the prejudices of your people are to prevail, they may do so, but it will be in my blood." Even if the words did not convey much meaning, Riel's manner did. Everyone feared that he would act alone as he had in December, and that the work of the Convention would be ruined. It was hardly worth while to dispute Riel's claims. When Xavier Pagée moved that the report of the committee be accepted with Riel's name added as president, his motion carried without a dissenting voice, although three of the English members, including Judge Black, did not vote.[69] Charles Nolin had agreed to support the establishment of the

Provisional Government, provided Mactavish, Cowan and Bannatyne should be released.   Now satisfied with his victory, Riel not only gave orders for the release of the three men, he promised to release the Canadians and others still languishing in Fort Garry.

It was almost eleven o'clock at night before the debate on the Provisional Government was completed, and the first news of its successful conclusion reached Winnipeg with the booming of the cannon from the fort.   Then into the town poured the members of the convention and the soldiers of Riel's garrison.   That night, Thursday, February 10, was stormy with wind and snow flurries, but nobody noticed or cared very much.   *The New Nation* reported that "the town welcomed the announcement by a grand display of fireworks and the general and continued discharge of small arms."[70]   What made it all the more exciting was that the fireworks belonged to Dr. Schultz and had been gathered in his warehouse to celebrate the establishment of McDougall's government. The yelling and the shooting continued for many hours, for everyone was filled with enthusiasm, good will, soft feelings and hard liquor.   Alexander Begg wrote in his diary, with less circumspection than the editor of *The New Nation* had used, "a regular drunk commenced in which everyone seemed to join" and "which was kept up till about four o'clock in the morning."[71]

Louis Riel did not join in the festivities in Winnipeg.   But he did take "a good horn of brandy" with Mr. Bannatyne, when the latter was released from custody.[72]   Both men had, after all, some reason to celebrate.

CHAPTER 6

Thomas Scott

ONE GROUP in the Red River Settlement did not greet the formation of the Provisional Government with shouts of alcoholic joy, the Canadians. These were the men who had supported John Schultz and had taken their ideas from the *Nor'Wester*. They had backed William McDougall and had participated in Colonel Dennis's military comedy in December. They always seemed to be in the minority and on the losing side. Even Donald A. Smith had not been able to help them. Their principal leaders were still in prison at Fort Garry, suffering the cold misery of isolation and close confinement. Fifty-six of them had known the humiliation of surrender to Louis Riel back in December. They had been marched between two files of armed métis from Winnipeg to Fort Garry, and had been crowded, all of them, into three small rooms in a building inside the walls of the fort. The first two or three days had been the worst. There had been only pemmican to eat and water to drink; and there was the added distress of watching, through the iron grill in the window, the hoisting of the flag of the Provisional Government.[1] This last act seemed to make their defeat final.

However, as the days passed, conditions began to improve. On the 11th, some of the prisoners were moved to the common gaol outside the walls of the fort.[2] If they could not see their friends, at least there were more frequent visits from Archdeacon McLean and from the Methodist minister, the Reverend George Young. Moreover, food parcels from Mrs. Drever and others came often enough to be encouraging. On the 13th, Riel himself came to see the prisoners and to leave them a number of Canadian newspapers.[3] The lack of exercise was perhaps the worst feature of the imprisonment; but, if we may believe one of the prisoners, Henry Woodington, on December 24 they were permitted to send out for a fiddle "and have a stag dance" in which the métis guards joined.[4] On Christmas day there was roast beef, plum pudding and cakes, and another dance to help pass the day. From time to time various prisoners were taken to see Riel who endeavoured to persuade them to take an oath to obey the Provisional Government, or to leave the country and not return in arms against it. On January 4, nine of the prisoners were released after accepting these terms.[5] But there was a small group among them who remained adamant in their opposition. They would never give in to Riel; they would never take an oath to obey him. They would take advantage of any opportunity, should one arise, to overthrow him.

Riel's imprisonment of the men who were taken on December 7 may appear to have been an irresponsible and an arbitrary act. But in Riel's opinion the maintenance of peace in the Settlement depended almost entirely upon keeping the Canadians quiet. The English-speaking settlers might not actively support him, but they would not take up arms against him. The Canadians would never hesitate to do so. Riel was determined that there should be no further attempts to raise an armed force to prevent the people of Red River from settling their affairs with Canada in the manner that seemed best to them. Riel's views regarding the Canadians were not his alone; his refusal to release the prisoners when Burke demanded it on January 19 had received the general approval of the mass meeting of the Settlement. To most of the settlers, as to Riel, the release of the prisoners at that time would have been as hazardous as it would have been premature.

Nevertheless there was still a fair-sized body of Canadians and sympathizers at large in Red River. In particular they were to be found in the vicinity of Portage la Prairie and in the parishes of Poplar Point and High Bluff along the Assiniboine. For the moment they were leaderless. Schultz and Mair were both in prison, and Colonel Dennis had returned to Canada on December 15 after issuing orders to the "loyal party" in the Settlement "to cease from further action under the appeal to arms made by me."[6] There were potential leaders, like Captain Webb, Milner Hart and A. C. Boulton, all members of Dennis's survey crew; but they were unwilling to act on their own initiative. Thus, while some of the more belligerent among the Canadians might mutter threats against Louis Riel, and talk about getting up a military force to release the prisoners from Riel's fort, the majority were apparently prepared to join in the election of representatives to the Fort Garry convention, and thus, indirectly, to participate in the formation of the Provisional Government.

Then came the jail breaks of January. The first serious break occurred on January 9. It was a Sunday and several men with small knives managed to cut away the wooden casing from two windows and to remove the iron bars. In the dark, when the sentries were being changed—a proceeding which took place in the guard room owing to the cold—they managed to crawl out of the windows and climb the palisade around the building.   Others followed when the attention of the guards was diverted from the windows by a great deal of yelling and shouting inside the gaol.   Twelve of the inmates managed to get out; among them were Charles Mair and Thomas Scott.   Immediately they struck out in various directions over the plains and through the snow banks towards Portage la Prairie.   Most of them suffered bitterly from the cold— W. F. Hyman had his feet badly frozen—and several were recaptured. Mair, however, made his way to William Drever's house in Winnipeg, where he took a quick drink of a warming stimulant and obtained a few heavy clothes.[7] Thomas Scott, with Henry Woodington and George Parker, one of Snow's work party, attempted to steal some horses. When their efforts failed they trudged bravely through the snow until they reached Headingly where they found sympathy and shelter.[8]   From Headingly to Portage la Prairie was not a long journey.   On January 15, Scott and the others reached the Portage settlement where they felt they were safe from Riel's horsemen.

Meanwhile John Schultz, who had planned to escape earlier, succeeded in getting away on January 23.   Using a pocket knife smuggled into him by his wife, he cut his buffalo robe into small strips and then wound them together to form a rope.   As he let himself down from the window, the rope snapped and Schultz fell to the ground.   Despite the pain he suffered from the fall, he eluded his guards, climbed over the wall of the fort and made his way as far as Robert MacBeth's house in Kildonan. MacBeth and Schultz had not always seen eye to eye in matters of politics, for MacBeth was a member of the abused Council of Assiniboia, but the highlander would not shut his door against his opponent, and Schultz was permitted to hide upstairs while Riel's men searched throughout the parish for the one they feared most.[9]   Their failure to find him was interpreted by Schultz's greater admirer, the Reverend George Young, as evidence of divine good will; for there were many who were convinced that had Schultz been captured he would have been shot.[10]   When the excitement died down, Schultz quietly made his way down the river to St. Andrew's, about ten miles north of Fort Garry.

With Schultz, Scott and Mair at large there was bound to be trouble for Riel, and trouble developed both at the Portage and in the lower settlement.   According to Boulton, Thomas Scott's "graphic" stories of his imprisonment and escape excited sympathy among the people of the Portage for the prisoners still in Fort Garry.   Talk was heard about the possibilities of a relief expedition being arranged to secure the release of Riel's captives.   Boulton had tried to discourage such talk when he had heard it earlier to avoid any action on the part of the Canadians that might interfere with the work of the Canadian Commissioners.   But on this occasion, Scott and his friends kept their plans quiet, and they only let Boulton into the secret after the decision to move against Fort Garry had been firmly taken. Boulton did not like the project, but he felt it would be better if he were to go along with the Portage party, if only to restrain them from some foolish and precipitate action.[11]

The whole project bore the mark of haste and lack of thought. But there was plenty of enthusiasm. Though they lacked arms, transport and provisions, a small number of Canadians set out for Fort Garry, intent upon attacking the fort, overthrowing Riel and releasing their comrades. It was a fool-hardy venture, and Boulton must have realized it. The Portage men picked up a few additional supporters at Poplar Point and High Bluff, and by the time they reached Headingly they numbered a little over one hundred.[12] Here they were delayed by a blizzard that raged for forty-eight hours and by the admonitions of two members of the convention, Kenneth Mackenzie and F. T. Lonsdale. Boulton, too, delayed matters when he resigned as commander because he disapproved of so desperate a scheme. However, when the members of the party agreed that they would attempt no more than the release of the prisoners, Boulton consented once again to act as leader.[13] As soon as the storm abated and their course of action had been agreed upon, the Portage party sent runners to drum up support in other parts of the Red River Settlement. William Gaddy, an English half-breed, was sent to Dease to obtain the support of the anti-Riel métis. John Taylor, one of the few members of the convention who supported the counter-movement, went to get in touch with Schultz and inform him that Boulton's command would join him at Kildonan.

II

On February 10, the day the Provisional Government received its noisy and spirituous welcome, Louis Riel had given a promise to the members of the convention that the Canadian prisoners would be released.[14] Once he had obtained the backing of the English-speaking settlers, there was little he would have to fear from the few Canadians in Red River, particularly if he could persuade them not to break the peace. It was in accordance with this undertaking that Riel released William Hallett and several others on February 12. But the gaol delivery proved to be slower than many of the English settlers would have liked, for Riel was still determined to make each prisoner give his word of honour not to try to overthrow the Provisional Government.

As the rumours of the Portage movement began to sift through the snow-drifts between the Assiniboine settlement and Fort Garry, the more stable element in the community became concerned with the unhappy results a hostile demonstration might have at this point. For this reason Lonsdale and Mackenzie hastened to Headingly to do what they could to persuade Boulton's men to hold themselves in check. Lonsdale returned to Fort Garry on the 12th with the alarming news that the Portage men were determined to go ahead with their plans to rescue the prisoners if they were not immediately released.[15] The next day John Grant came in with the same information. Riel explained the reason for the delay and finally, in order to accelerate matters, Miss Victoria McVicar, a Canadian visitor in the Settlement, and A. G. B. Bannatyne undertook to convince the prisoners that the oath that Riel had demanded was nothing more than a promise to keep the peace.[16] Whether it was owing to the charms of Miss McVicar or the sweet reasonableness of Bannatyne matters little, the prisoners, including the most stubborn of them, agreed to sign the oath and were released. James Farquharson, Dr. Schultz's father-in-law, was even "pushed out of the Fort" without an oath for, as Riel declared, Farquharson having already broken his word twice, his oath was not worth witnessing.[17] Thus, by evening on the 15th, the cells of Fort Garry were vacant for the first time in several months, and "everyone appeared relieved that peace seemed once more certain."[18]

But peace was by no means certain, as the president of the Provisional Government and the people of Red River were soon to learn. The Portage party had continued with its plans. The fact is that the men behind the counter-movement from Portage la Prairie—men like Charles Mair, Thomas Scott, Murdoch McLeod and the old Chelsea pensioner, Michael Power—wanted to do more than hasten a gaol delivery. They resented the domination of the Settlement by Louis Riel and the métis, and they were determined to overthrow the Provisional Government. It was they who carried the Portage party along in spite of the half-hearted leadership of Major Boulton. On the night of the 14th, Boulton's men began their march through the "cold but not unpleasant" night to Winnipeg. Here they quietly surrounded the house of Henri Coutu— where Riel frequently slept at nights—while Scott and Boulton entered it to seize the person of the métis chieftain. But Riel was not there, and after apologies and explanations to Coutu, the Portage men proceeded their way to Kildonan.[19]

In the meantime Dr. Schultz had been active up and down the Scottish parishes. He had argued against the convention and against the Provisional Government, and now he was busy enlisting supporters, both white and Indian, with which to bolster Boulton's party. The arrival of Taylor was a source of great encouragement and, on the 15th, Schultz set out for Kildonan at the head of several hundred men and a small cannon drawn by four oxen.[20] Schultz's powerful voice, personality and magnificent physique dominated the scene. It even overrode the weaknesses of the military plan. Here was the man to take command; not the weak and vacillating Boulton. And Schultz's men had imbibed something of his spirit. As they marched, they sang their own words to the tune of the old Jacobite song "Hey, Johnny Cope."[21]

> If ye're nae waking we'll nae wait,
> For we'll take the fort this morning.

"They were enraged," wrote Boulton, "at the insincerity of Riel." But Boulton, as ever, was plagued with anxiety, "fearing that a conflict was inevitable."[22]

There were, however, factors at work which were to defeat the counter-movement. Schultz and Boulton had counted on the support of the anti-Riel métis, the English-speaking half-breeds and the Scottish settlers. The anti-Riel métis failed them when Boulton's messenger, William Gaddy, was caught with several others at Dease's house on February 14. Dease himself escaped through a rear window.[23] But Riel was anxious to conciliate Dease, and on the 15th and 16th he sent two letters to him appealing to him to close the métis ranks and to support the Provisional Government.[24] Dease took Riel at his word and on the 18th subscribed to the oath of allegiance. As for the English-speaking settlers, they were still disposed, as they had been when Dennis appealed to them, to remain aloof and watch events. There were some who would have agreed with the opinion of one Selkirk settler who said, "We don't want any officials from Canada to make laws for us, and what is more we won't have them."[25] But most settlers would have agreed with James McKay when he wrote, "I cannot take up arms against my own people, nor can I against the Governor."[26] The dominant attitude was one of neutrality, particularly among the older men, although some of the younger ones were willing to join Schultz for the sake of adventure.[27] The Protestant clergy, too, actively urged moderation among the hot-heads who had hoisted over the Kildonan schoolhouse a large red ensign with the Union Jack and the inscription "God Save the Queen" embroidered on it, and who were commandeering provisions and making last-minute preparations for attacking Fort Garry. These clerical counsels were so effective in dampening the belligerent ardour of many of Schultz's men that one disgruntled "loyalist," probably Charles Mair, wrote in disgust to the *Globe*:

The Protestant clergy are for "peace, peace, when there is no peace" and to that cause and that cause alone, must be attributed the failure [of the movement] . . . if the Reverend Quartette had quietly studied their sermons, or in their closets offered a prayer for our success instead of going through the ranks discouraging our men, we would ere this have had the proud satisfaction of seeing "the flag that braved a thousand years" floating over Fort Garry, and not be disgraced by that symbol of Jesuitical Fenianism that now hangs on the flag staff.[28]

Thus far none of the disturbances in Red River had resulted in bloodshed. It was unfortunate, therefore, that on the 16th a frightened young métis, Norbert Parisien, who had been taken prisoner the previous day in the belief that he was a spy, should, while attempting to escape, have shot and mortally wounded Hugh Sutherland,[29] the son of one of the members of the convention. Parisien himself was seized, brutally beaten and died some days later.[30]

This episode had a sobering effect upon the Canadians. According to Charles Mair, "a panic began" with young Sutherland's mother and other women from Kildonan, "crying and beseeching the men from the lower parishes to separate or they would all be murdered, kneeling and clasping them round their legs and imploring, and they and the clergy urging Boulton and his men from Portage not to start a civil war."[31] When a conciliatory note from Louis Riel arrived at Kildonan the same day, stating that "war, horrible civil war" would only lead to "the destruction of this country" and protesting that all that "the prisoners are out" and "they have all sworn to keep the peace," Schultz's "noble little army" began to disintegrate. It broke up all the more rapidly when the men recalled that Louis Riel had been telling only the truth when he wrote to them: "Mr. William Mactavish has asked you for the sake of God to form and complete the Provisional Government. Your representatives have joined us on that ground. Who will now come and destroy the Red River Settlement?" The Portage party likewise lost its stomach for fighting and turned to consider how best to return home. Boulton urged his followers to "accept the hospitality of our friends in the English settlements until excitement had somewhat quieted down, when we could return singly" to Portage la Prairie. But Michael Power argued that "we had come down like brave men" and that "we should go back like brave men, in a body."[33] Murdoch McLeod even threatened Boulton and told him to his face "to be a man and go right on."[34] There would be no truckling to Louis Riel. The Portage men would be bold, even if boldness were the lesser part of discretion. Accordingly, the Portage men tied up their blankets and their buffalo robes, packed what food remained and, after securing a number of sleighs, set out upon the road leading through Winnipeg to the Portage. It did not deter them that this road would lead them within a few hundred yards of Fort Garry.

In the meantime there had been great excitement inside the walls of the fort. Although he had gone about releasing the prisoners in his own good time, extracting a promise of peaceful conduct from each, Riel was greatly alarmed by the mustering of the Canadians at Kildonan and their efforts to win over William Dease. He believed that it could mean only one thing, an assault upon the fort, the overthrow of the Provisional Government and very probably his own imprisonment if not his death. Every man available was therefore ordered to report to the fort and guards were posted at strategic points both in and about Fort Garry. As the reporter of *The New Nation* described the scene: "Men were gathering in hot haste. Cannons mounted, grape and canister laid in order. Five hundred men and more, we are informed, were told off to man the bastions, ramparts, etc. Shot and shell were piled around promiscuously. Everything that could be done, was done to make a bold stand to strike terror into the hearts of *les anglais*."[35] In Winnipeg shops were closed and women and children were removed to less dangerous locations. O'Donoghue and a number of métis soldiers scoured the town for arms and powder. When Bannatyne refused to yield the keys to his magazine, they tore it apart "and such a clean sweep made of its contents that not a solitary keg was left to the disgusted proprietor."[36]

Then, at the height of the excitement, about eleven o'clock on the morning of February 18, a number of sleighs bearing armed men were seen approaching in the distance. Suddenly they veered to the west off the main road just north of Winnipeg. Were they planning to surround the fort or to put in an attack from the west flank? A group of horsemen led by Lépine and O'Donoghue raced out the north gate to the cheers and yells of the métis soldiers lining the walls of the fort. They "plunged through the snowdrifts," wrote a contemporary observer, "in a manner which justified the appellation long since received by the Red River hunters that they are among the best horsemen in the world."[37] Behind the horsemen struggled a group of some fifty men on foot. Everybody watched intently from the fort and from Winnipeg; and everybody watched with apprehension as guns were raised and hammers were cocked. But Boulton had given orders that "on no account" should any member of his party fire a shot;[38] and when O'Donoghue ordered the Portage men to drive to Fort Garry, they complied. Once inside the gates they were disarmed—forty-eight of them—and shoved into the cells so lately vacated by the prisoners whom they had planned to release. Among them were Major Boulton, Thomas Scott, Murdoch McLeod, George Parker and John Taylor.[39] Charles Mair had been more careful. He had decided to follow another road back to Portage la Prairie.

Whether the arrest of the Portage party was actually ordered by Louis Riel, or whether it was an impulsive action on the part of O'Donoghue and Lépine and an excited and ill-disciplined group of métis soldiers, is not clear.[40] For the moment Riel may have hoped to get his hands on John Schultz. He had been galled by Schultz's escape and was inclined to blame him for every attempt to overthrow the Provisional Government. But Schultz, like Mair, knew that he was a marked man, and had kept out of sight. While the métis were riding the length and breadth of the Red River Settlement searching for the missing doctor, Schultz was, in fact, on his way back to Canada, travelling by snowshoe and sleigh despite his injury, accompanied by the English half-breed, Joseph Monkman. But Riel did not know this for some weeks. Undoubtedly he was disappointed when Schultz's tall form and bearded face were not to be found among the prisoners. But, having taken the Portage men prisoners, he was prepared to make the most of what had been done.   The one course from which Riel never deviated was building a strong government in the colony to negotiate with Canada. He had wanted to unite, not to split, the Settlement. But here were Schultz and the Canadians constantly trying to cause trouble and sow the seeds of dissension. They were the trouble makers, these newcomers who had tried to hurry the establishment of Canadian rule, who had backed McDougall and had twice tried to cause rebellion in Red River. They needed to be taught a lesson. Someone should be punished.

That someone was to be Major Boulton. On the day of his capture Boulton was condemned to death by a métis court-martial. It took only a matter of minutes, and Riel went to the door of Boulton's room, opened it, and without entering the room said: "Major Boulton, you prepare to die tomorrow at twelve o'clock." Boulton replied, "Very well." Riel withdrew, leaving the soldier alone. It was all done very quietly and very calmly, too quietly for Riel. Not long afterwards Riel returned. He wanted to know more about the Portage party, and what Boulton's purpose had been "in coming down with the force." He likewise wanted to know what Boulton and Thomas Scott had intended to do with him had they caught him at Henri Coutu's. Then, after a few more questions, he turned to leave. "You wish to see Archdeacon McLean? I will allow him to come,"[41] said Riel.

The news of Boulton's impending execution spread like a dark threatening cloud over the whole Settlement. There was scarcely a man of English or Scotch extraction who did not feel a sense of foreboding.[42] The Archdeacon, Bishop Machray and Father Lestanc and others, including Mr. and Mrs. Sutherland, the parents of the young man who had so recently lost his life at the hands of the terrified Parisien, visited

Riel and pleaded for the condemned man. Miss Victoria McVicar came to throw herself dramatically on her knees crying "Mercy, mercy, mercy!"[43] James Ross and Oscar Malmros added their voices to the others; and Pierre Delorme, one of the French representatives for Pointe Coupée, went home saying that he "would not return to the Fort in a hurry."

If Riel was moved by these appeals—and there is evidence to show he was deeply affected by the visit of the Sutherlands[44]—the most effective voice was that of Donald A. Smith. On the 19th, Smith went to see Riel and to reason with him long and earnestly. Smith's approach to the métis leader was not emotional. By now he had divined what Riel's hopes and ambitions were, and he argued that Boulton's execution would have no other effect than that of permanently dividing the Settlement just at the time when Riel had finally brought about its union in the Provisional Government. Riel listened carefully. This was language he understood. Finally he spoke up. He admitted the validity of Smith's arguments, but he also saw in the situation, which he had created by the threat to Boulton, an opportunity to use Smith himself to restore order and to reinforce the authority of the Provisional Government. "Hitherto I have been deaf to all entreaties, and in now granting you this man's life, may I ask you a favour?" he asked. "Anything," replied Smith, "that in honour I can do." Riel continued, "Canada has dis-united us, will you use your influence to reunite us? You can do so, and without this it must be war—bloody civil war!" Smith felt himself being pushed into a corner, but replied that he would give his "whole heart to effect a peaceable union of the country with Canada." "We want only our just rights as British subjects, and we want the English to join us simply to obtain these," said Riel. "Then," remarked Smith, "I shall at once see them and induce them to go on with the election of delegates for that purpose." Riel pressed his advantage. "If you can do this," he said to Smith, "war will be avoided. Not only the lives but the liberty of all the prisoners will be secured, for on your success depends the lives of all the Canadians in the country."[45] Immediately afterwards Riel went to the prison and told Archdeacon McLean that he had agreed to spare Boulton's life and that after the election of the new legislature all the prisoners would be released. McLean rushed to give Boulton the welcome news. Shortly after the Archdeacon had left, Riel himself knocked on Boulton's door and entered, a lantern in his hand. Boulton had fallen asleep and was surprised to see the métis leader in the room. Riel looked at the Canadian. "Major Boulton," he said, "I have come to see you. I have come to shake you by the hand, and to make a proposition to you. I perceive that you are a man of ability, that you are a leader. The English people, they have no leader. Will you join my government, and be their leader?"[46]   Boulton was taken aback by the offer but, when he had recovered himself, he told Riel if the métis chief would release all the prisoners and allow him to go back to the Portage to consult his friends, he "would consider his proposition seriously." Riel turned and left the room. "That night," wrote Boulton, "the chains were moved from my limbs."[47]   Prison discipline generally was relaxed, and the prisoners were allowed to have provisions brought to them by their friends.

Again Riel had secured a tactical, political triumph. He had ridden the storm of threatened rebellion against his authority. He had forced the man whom Sir John A. Macdonald had sent from Canada to quiet "those wild people" in the Red River valley to join him in closing the ranks of the Settlement by giving his personal backing to the Provisional Government. He had, admittedly, come close to the brink of disaster, but in the end he had turned the crisis to his own advantage and, as he believed, to the advantage of the colony itself. But the strain had been a severe one. He was not a man of war, and war, "bloody civil war," had been a very near thing. He was, moreover, a lonely man with few confidants other than the taciturn priest at St. Norbert, an intense and restless being. It is not too surprising that he should have taken ill at Henri Coutu's on the morning of the 24th with what was called "an attack of brain fever."[48]   At this distance and without medical evidence, it is difficult to determine how serious the attack was; but it was serious enough, in any event, for Coutu to call the priests from St. Boniface, and to notify Riel's family at St. Vital. As she had done when he was a little boy at the farm on the Seine, Riel's mother came to his bedside to look after the son of whom she was so very proud. Perhaps the rest and quiet and the touch of his mother's hand was all Louis required. By the 27th, he felt well enough to return to the business of government. There were so many problems demanding immediate attention—the election, the despatch of the delegates to Canada, the scarcity of food and money in the Settlement, the disposal of the prisoners in the cells of Fort Garry, as well as the threats of an attack by the Sioux Indians, and the gnawing uncertainty of the whereabouts of the leaders of the Canadian rising, of Charles Mair and, above all, of John Schultz.

III

The prisoners: what was to be done about them? There was no doubt in Smith's mind or in Archdeacon McLean's mind that Riel had promised to release them as soon as the new Provisional Government was firmly established. Such a promise would have fitted the pattern of Riel's thinking, and this was what he had done before. Throughout his life Riel tended to follow the same course, especially when it had enjoyed success on a previous occasion. But when he made this promise Riel neglected to take into consideration the attitude of his own followers. Without his soldiery at Fort Garry, he would never have gained or held his position as head of the Provisional Government; in the final analysis, the success of his movement depended upon their loyalty and their continued support. This was one reason why Riel needed a wider basis for his government and why he strove to obtain it. But the métis soldiers were not a disciplined body;[49] they followed their leader not because they had to but because they wanted to. They would forsake him as soon as his actions failed to satisfy them. And so Riel had to keep on the good side of his men or suffer the consequences. During the last days of February, in the excitement and tension of a civil war that always seemed to threaten but never develop, Riel's men were edgy and unruly, and all the more so when Riel was ill in bed. And the new batch of prisoners contained several men who were truculent and aggressive and difficult to handle—particularly after they learned of the reprieve granted to Major Boulton.

Of the new prisoners, Thomas Scott was unquestionably the leader in the absence of Schultz. Boulton, the man who had led the Portage party, had lost the respect of his men, for they believed him lacking in fortitude and determination. It was Boulton's fate that his common sense was equated with cowardice, and Scott's misfortune that his pugnacity was mistaken for courage. Scott had come to Ontario from northern Ireland some seven years before. He lived for a while in Hastings county and served briefly with the Sterling Company of the Hastings Battalion of Rifles. According to his company commander he was "the finest looking man in the battalion . . . about six feet two inches in height and twenty-five years of age . . . an Orangeman, loyal to the backbone."[50] In 1869, he joined John Snow's work party in Red River. Although his militia captain had thought highly of him and referred to him as "gentlemanly," Scott soon revealed other qualities, qualities likely to emerge under frontier conditions, recklessness, stubbornness and lawlessness. Perhaps it would be fairer to say that Scott was a man prepared to stand up for what he believed to be his rights and prepared to flout authority in order to secure them. His leadership of the road workers' strike in July, 1869, and his attempts to hurl his employer, Snow, into the river[51] illustrate the pugnacious side, the dominant side, of his character. Out of work, he drifted into Winnipeg where he drank and fought,[52] and where he came under the influence of John Schultz. Here were two men who understood each other; the one was a man whom Schultz could use, the other a man whom Scott could serve. Scott therefore threw in his lot with Schultz and was one of those who gathered in Winnipeg to defend the supplies of pork which were in the doctor's possession. On December 6, the day before the surrender of the men in Schultz's house, Scott was taken prisoner by the métis along with Alexander McArthur.[53] The métis believed the two men had left Schultz's with the object of assassinating the leaders of the French National Committee.[54] It is more likely they were trying to escape to the lower settlement to communicate with Dennis. In an event they were recognized as Schultz's men and imprisoned.

Scott was in prison only a month. He was one of those who escaped with Woodington, Mair and Parker on the night of January 9. He had played a leading role in rousing the people of Portage la Prairie to the desperate venture, described by Sir John A. Macdonald as "foolish" and "criminal,"[55] that ended in surrender on February 18.

Again in prison, Scott and one of his companions, Murdoch McLeod, set out to make life miserable for their captors. They hurled insults at the métis and jostled and threatened them on every possible occasion. Finally, on February 28, after an altercation with Scott, the métis guards grabbed him and, in spite of his great strength, dragged him outside, with the intention either of killing him or giving him a severe beating. It was only the timely arrival of one of Riel's councillors that saved him. Scott was then ordered to be returned to his cell. The following day Riel, informed of the altercation on the 28th, went to see if he could calm the guards who were surly and resentful. He went also to visit Scott to try to persuade him to be more tractable lest his continual provocation lead to bloodshed. Scott merely "sneered" at Riel and "made fun of" the métis leader.[56] He had nothing but contempt for all mixed-bloods and to his sense of racial superiority he added the narrow bigotry of the Ulster Orangeman. The yelling and the cursing began all over again, and Scott was, in consequence, put in irons.[57] For a man like Riel, who even as a schoolboy had been noted for an inability to brook opposition, Scott's actions were both irritating and provocative: to a man like Scott, narrow, ignorant and lacking discretion at a time when passions were aroused, Boulton's reprieve and Riel's admonitions were signs of timidity. Both men misunderstood each other, and as Riel yielded to the demands of his followers that Scott must be punished, Scott was crying: "The métis are a pack of cowards. They will not dare to shoot me."[58]

It was a dangerous challenge at any time. It was doubly dangerous when feelings were raw and tempers were rising. On March 3, the métis called a court-martial to try Scott for "insubordination." This was the way they handled problems of a similar nature on the prairie.

It was the buffalo hunters' method, the formation of an *ad hoc* tribunal. All the men comprising the court-martial were familiar with the law of the prairie. The presiding officer was Ambroise Lépine. With him sat Janvier Ritchot, André Nault, Joseph Delorme, Elzéar Lagimodière, Elzéar Goulet and Baptiste Lépine. The clerk of the court was Joseph Nolin, the young man whom Bishop Taché had chosen to go to Quebec with Riel and Schmidt, but whose parents would not let go so far from home.

The court met in the evening. Scott was not called in for the preliminary hearing. Several witnesses were examined, including Riel himself, and two of the guards, Joseph Delorme and Edmund Turner, the latter the son of an Irish pensioner in the Settlement. Nolin took the oath from the witnesses, each of whom told how Scott had rebelled against the Provisional Government, how he had struck a captain of the guard and how he had assaulted the person of Louis Riel. Finally, Scott was brought to the court room. Riel asked Nolin to read what had taken place, and when Nolin excused himself from doing so on the ground that his notes were inadequate, Riel himself explained in English the evidence that had been given. It is not clear whether Scott asked to examine any of the witnesses or not; Nolin's memory on this point was defective and Nolin was the only eye-witness to give any details about the trial. At this point Janvier Ritchot moved that the death penalty be invoked. André Nault seconded the motion, and both Goulet and Delorme agreed with them. Baptiste Lépine, however, was opposed to the imposition of so harsh a penalty, and Lagimodière suggested that it would be quite sufficient to send Scott out of the country. Ambroise Lépine, the president of the court, said only that, since the majority favoured death, that would be the penalty imposed. Scott had listened to this exchange of views wondering what was being said. Then Riel turned to translate the court's decision to him. The shackles were removed from the prisoner and he was taken back to his room where pen and ink were provided him on Riel's instructions.[59]

The Reverend George Young, the Methodist minister, was returning home from an appointment in the country when he encountered one of the métis guards who asked him to go to the fort. He went immediately to Scott's cold, fireless room. The prisoner was in a daze. He could not bring himself to believe that what he had seen had taken place and that what he had heard was really true. Perhaps it was only a threat. "I believe they are bad enough," he said to Young, "but I can hardly think that they dare do it."[60] Young felt much the same way but decided to see Riel. He failed to secure an interview that night, but early the next morning he went about the Settlement, calling upon people who were friendly with Riel to ask them to use their influence with the métis leader should he really be determined upon so drastic a course. No one would believe Riel had anything more in mind than to put a scare into the prisoners. It was the Boulton business all over again. Finally Young went to see Donald A. Smith, who consented to go to remonstrate with Riel. But even Smith was a little skeptical of Young's alarm and promised to see Riel after Young himself had a talk with him first. Admitted to Riel's presence, Young pleaded for Scott. But Riel was emphatic in his reply: "He is a very bad man, and has insulted my guards and has hindered some from making peace; so I must make an example to impress others and lead them to respect my government, and will take him first, and then, if necessary, others will follow."[61] When Young found he could make no impression on Riel, he sent immediately for Smith, and "paralyzed with horror" went to console the worried but still incredulous young man in his cell.

Taking Father Lestanc with him, Smith went to Riel's office. When the priest spoke up on Scott's behalf, Riel cut him short with, "My Reverend Père, you know exactly how the matter stands," and then turning to Smith he went into a lengthy explanation of how Scott had been a "troublesome character" ever since he had come to Red River; of how he had been "the ringleader in a rising against Mr. Snow"; how he had "risen against the Provisional Government" in December; how he had "again been taken in arms" and despite the promise that the prisoners' lives and liberties would be respected, he had been "incorrigible and quite incapable of appreciating the clemency with which he had been treated"; how he was "rough and abusive to the guards" and "insulting to him, Mr. Riel"; and how "his example had been productive of the very worst effects on the other prisoners who had become insubordinate to such an extent that it was difficult to withhold the guards from retaliating." Smith argued with Riel. He pointed out that the "one great merit" claimed for the insurrection "was that, so far, it had been bloodless, except in one sad instance which all were willing to look upon as an accident," and he implored Riel "not now to strain it, to burden it with what would be considered a horrible crime." Riel exclaimed sharply, "We must make Canada respect us." This was, after all has been said, the real motive behind the execution. There were more arguments, more entreaties, more protests, but Riel would not withdraw from his stand. To him the carrying out of the decision of the court-martial had now become a matter of prestige. He closed the interview by saying: "I have done three good things since I commenced, I have spared Boulton's life at your instance, and I do not regret it, for he is a fine fellow; I pardoned Gaddy, and he showed his gratitude by escaping out of the bastion, but I do not grudge him his miserable life, and now I shall shoot Scott." Lépine, who had just entered the room, said merely, "He must die." There was no further discussion. Riel then turned to Father Lestanc and suggested that he might offer a prayer for the condemned man. But Smith did not wait to hear it.[62]

At the appointed hour, on March 4, Elzéar Goulet and André Nault went to Scott's room. Scott was given permission to say good-bye to the other prisoners, all of whom were silent now. With the Reverend George Young at his side, he marched down the outside stairway and through the gate. As he walked, he turned to Young and muttered, "This is horrible! This is cold-blooded murder!"[63] Only then did he realize that the episode he had regarded as only a meaningless comedy was going to end in an equally meaningless tragedy. At Young's request, Scott was allowed a few minutes of prayer. With Scott in the centre, the party moved down the stairs, Young having his arm around the prisoner to keep him from falling forward; then a white bandage was adjusted over the prisoner's eyes. Frantically the clergyman appealed to the captain of the guard, André Nault, and to W. B. O'Donoghue who was standing nearby. Could there not be, say, a day's stay of execution? But O'Donoghue merely said: "It is very far gone." He did nothing.[64] Nor did any of the crowd of morbidly curious people who stood about, silently watching. On a given signal the rifles were raised. Only four of them fired. Scott sank to the ground and the blood from his chest ran slowly into the snow upon which he lay. He was still moving when one of the firing squad stepped forward and, with his revolver, delivered the *coup de grâce*.[65] It was just noon, and the sun shone brightly over the fort.

Riel had been standing somewhere in the background watching with the others. Then he stepped forward and in a sharp tone of voice ordered the crowd to disperse. As he stood there the inert, blood-stained body was placed in a rough board coffin and was carried by several métis guards inside the walls of Fort Garry.

V

Probably no action of Louis Riel excited as much controversy and as much strong feeling as the execution of Thomas Scott. No act of his is harder to explain. There are some who argue that it was an impulsive act of vengeance on the part of the métis, that Riel was virtually forced to agree to the execution owing to the pressure upon him of his own men. It has been said that Riel himself was threatened unless he agreed to the death of Scott. There are others who take the view that the execution was a deliberate act of policy. The latter was certainly the explanation offered by Riel himself.   And it probably fits the circumstances better than the former, if only because the métis, if quickly moved to anger, were not a people given to bloodshed.   The division within the court-martial itself suggests that the pressures on Riel were not so irresistible as to force him into an action against his better judgment.   Moreover, Riel several times attempted to explain what lay behind his act.   In a memorandum which he sent to L. R. Masson in 1872, he said that the shooting was necessary, not because the métis soldiers insisted upon it, but because it was essential "to intimidate the conspirators."   Even though the Portage people had, following Boulton's reprieve, agreed to recognize the Provisional Government, they made it clear they were only waiting for another opportunity to overthrow that government "as soon as they were able to do so."[66]   It should be remembered that Riel's delegates had not yet left for Ottawa to negotiate the terms of Red River's entry into Confederation, and that Riel was anxious and deter-mined to prevent anything from interfering with this part of his policy. It had been his *idée maîtresse* from the very beginning of the rising.   If it was necessary to spill the blood of a malcontent, one who had not only refused to co-operate with the other settlers, but had even appealed to force in an effort to disrupt the arrangements the Provisional Government was making to obtain concessions from Canada, then that blood would be spilled.   It was as simple as that.   Moreover, there was the desire to impress.   Underneath all his assertiveness, Riel suffered from a feeling of insecurity.   Neither he nor his government were taken seriously enough by the Canadians in the Red River Settlement, or by those in Canada.   Perhaps an execution would show them that he meant business. "We wanted to be sure that our attitude was taken seriously," Riel wrote to Masson.[67]

The execution of Scott was a political act: and, as such, it was a political blunder.   It may have been followed, as it assuredly was, by a lessening of tension and by a period of calm, but it was not a healthy calm.   The English-speaking parishes were stunned by the news of Scott's death.   They would co-operate with the Provisional Government for the sake of the Settlement which they all loved; but there could be no warmth, no sincere affection in their co-operation, no real unity of spirit. Riel gained his immediate end; but in the long run he opened a breach between the French- and English-speaking elements of the population of Red River which has never been entirely closed.   If henceforth little love was lost between them, it was because there was little love to lose. Elsewhere in Canada the Scott affair stripped from the underlying bitter-ness, of race and religion, the veneer of co-operation with which it had been covered by Confederation in 1867.   In the years to come, both Scott and Riel ceased to be men, human beings with human frailties; they became political symbols, political slogans, around which men rallied and for which they argued and fought with little knowledge of the real strengths and weaknesses of the men whose names they bandied to and fro.

By one unfortunate error of judgment—this is what the execution of Scott amounted to—and by one unnecessary deed of bloodshed—for the Provisional Government was an accomplished fact—Louis Riel set his foot upon the path which led not to glory but to the gibbet.

CHAPTER 7

Bishop Taché

ON MARCH 8, four days after the shooting of Thomas Scott, Bishop Alexandre Taché arrived at St. Norbert. The next day, in company with Father Lestanc, the Abbé Ritchot, Angus McKay and a crowd of people, the Bishop drove to St. Boniface.[1] He went first to the church to pray, and then to the stone building that bore the rather pretentious title of the Bishop's palace.

In the previous autumn, Bishop Taché had gone to Rome to attend the Œcumenical Council. Before leaving Canada he had intimated that, despite the snub he had received from Sir George Cartier,[2] he would be willing to return should there be any need for his services. When the need arose and Taché was asked to return, he did so willingly. After stopping briefly in England, where he had a conversation with Sir Stafford Northcote, the Governor of the Hudson's Bay Company,[3] he set sail for North America. On his arrival at Portland, he received a letter from Cartier asking him to come at once to Ottawa. In the Canadian capital, Taché found Sir George in a penitent mood and ready to confess all the errors of omission and commission of the Canadian authorities in Red River. The Bishop was introduced to various members of the cabinet, and with them he discussed all the aspects of the Red River troubles as he knew them from the letters that he had received regularly from Lestanc, Dugast and others at St. Boniface. Then he set out for Red River on February 17 armed with the Governor-General's Proclamation of December 6, which Smith had not published at Red River, and with letters from Joseph Howe and Sir John A. Macdonald—the latter stating: "If the Company's Government is restored not only will there be a general amnesty granted, but in case the Company should claim the payment for such stores, the Canadian Government will stand between the insurgents and all harm."[4]

The arrival of another Canadian commissioner in Red River—there had already been three of them—even if that commissioner was the beloved Bishop of St. Boniface, was not looked upon with great favour by Louis Riel. He would not give him official welcome; he would not even go to meet him. When the Bishop arrived at St. Boniface, Riel remarked wryly: "It is not Bishop Taché who is passing . . . it is Canada."[5]   It would not be diplomatic, in a community where so many of his own followers were devout Catholics, for Riel to try to restrict the Bishop's movements as he had done those of Donald A. Smith, but he was prepared to place a military guard at the Bishop's door.[6]   He had had previous experience of Canadian commissioners and of their efforts to undermine his authority by creating a division within the métis ranks; and the presence of Angus McKay, one of Riel's métis opponents, in the Bishop's suite did not seem to augur well for the future.   Would the Bishop, as Canada's representative, try to do the same thing that Smith had done?   A guard would at least be a measure of precaution.   It would also be a measure of precaution to arrest Nolin and Hamelin and Grant and McKay, all men who had been influenced by Smith and who had led the métis opposition to Riel in February.[7]   If he did nothing else, Riel would be able to keep the Bishop from communicating with the unreliable elements among the métis and also note those who came and went from the Bishop's house.   In any event, whatever powers the Canadian government might have bestowed upon Taché, Riel was determined that he would not deviate from the course he had laid out for himself.   The Provisional Government was now a fact, and the task it set for itself would be carried out, to the end.

II

Meanwhile arrangements had been completed for the election of the new Council of the Provisional Government which had been agreed upon February 10.   Early in March *The New Nation* carried the following announcement:

> A meeting of the Council of the Provisional Government of Rupert's Land is hereby ordered to be held at Fort Garry, on Wednesday, 9th inst.
> By order of the President.

LOUIS SCHMIDT
Assistant Secretary

On the day appointed, some nineteen of the twenty-four members of the Council gathered at the fort.   Most of the French-speaking members had been elected before as members of the convention, but more than half of the English-speaking members were new men, new in the sense that they were elected for the first time, including A. G. B. Bannatyne and William Fraser, both of whom had supported Louis Riel, and John Norquay, the English half-breed who was later to become premier of Manitoba.[8]   Although there was not full representation, Riel went ahead with the meeting and delivered an address marked by moderation and

conciliation.   He declared his faith in the good will of the majority of
the people of Red River, and he pointed out with pride that as a result
of the work of the convention "the people generally now have, for the
first time in the history of this land, a voice in the direction of public
affairs."   His appeals for co-operation and unity were punctuated with
cheers:

. . . now that we have come together once more, I believe we are actuated
by such feelings as will lead to a thorough union.   We have come here to
decide on that which we believe to be our duty, and will do it honestly.
We are here as the public authority.   We are here to act in that capacity.
. . . There are, I know, some differences between the residents of different
localities—and perhaps the easiest way to dispose of them would be that
each side should concede something.   A spirit of concession, I think,
ought to be manifested on both sides; and if it is, we will be cordial and
united.   If we were so united—as was said long ago—the people of Red
River could make their own terms with Canada.

Riel was ringing the changes on the old familiar theme, the union of the
Settlement and negotiations with Canada.   There was, therefore, no
mention of the execution of Scott, no more than a hint of trouble from
the Portage.   Oddly enough nobody wanted to conjure up the ghost of
the dead Irishman.   It would return to walk the stages of Canadian
history soon enough.   Probably Riel was desperately anxious to forget
the whole sordid business and regretted the deed immediately the rifles
had been fired.   He continued his speech with references to the three
Canadian commissioners, and to the arrival of the fourth, Bishop Taché:

We have had already three commissioners from the Dominion; and now,
perhaps, we have another come amongst us in the person of His Lordship
the Bishop of St. Boniface, one who is generally beloved and esteemed
in the land, and to whose mission, I doubt not, the highest attention
will be paid.   For my part, I would certainly like to see, in the person of
His Lordship, a Commissioner invested with full power to give us what
we want.   But we have to be careful; for we do not know what that
power is; and we must not rush blindly into the hands of any commissioners.   Let us act prudently—that is all I urge; if we do so, we
will be safe enough.[9]

Riel's remarks were well received by the members of the Council who
heard them; and the Council adjourned until March 15.

    Following this meeting of the Council, Taché went to see Riel in the
fort.   It would be best to have a clear understanding with the métis
president.   Lépine and O'Donoghue were with Riel, the one deeply
concerned about the question of an amnesty, the other anxious about the
Bishop's attitude towards American annexation.   The little gathering
in Riel's room on March 11 was both critical and decisive.   When the
Bishop emerged the crisis had passed.   Although he had known nothing

of the Portage rising, and the shooting of Scott had yet to occur when Taché was in Ottawa, the Bishop sincerely believed that the promised amnesty included everything which had happened or might happen prior to his arrival in the Settlement. He had, in fact, raised this very question of bloodshed while talking with the Canadian ministers. For this reason he gave Riel and Lépine categorical assurances that an amnesty would be granted them covering all adventures and mis-adventures of the Red River rising. He told them, too, that they should go ahead with their plans to send a delegation to Ottawa and that the delegates would be well received by the Canadian authorities. In reply, to O'Donoghue's disgust, Riel protested his own loyalty to the British Crown and denied that he had ever any intention of rebelling against the Queen; his aim had always been "to arrive at an understanding with the Canadian authorities before entering Confederation."[10] Several days later he took positive steps to prove his loyalty by taking over *The New Nation* as the Provisional Government newspaper. He altered the tone of its editorial comment, and removed its American, pro-annexationist editor, H. N. Robinson, replacing him by Thomas Spence, a Canadian and former member of the convention for the parish of St. Peters.'[11] These actions, combined with the precipitate departure of the American consul from Winnipeg following the publication of his despatches to Washington, greatly reduced the influence of the American group within the Settlement.

To all intents and purposes, Louis Riel and the Bishop of St. Boniface had been completely reconciled, but it was a surface reconciliation only. Deep in his heart the Bishop was hurt by the obvious indications of Riel's lack of trust in him, and the relations between the two men were never as warm as they had been in the days when Taché watched the young métis boy studying his Latin under Father LeFloch and chose him to be one of those for whom he had arranged an education in Lower Canada. When the Bishop removed Giroux as chaplain to Riel's soldiers, as part of his policy of political neutrality, Riel began to wonder whether the Bishop was his real friend or one against whom he should be on his guard. It was a suspicion which ate deeply into him, one from which, throughout his life, he could not escape. For the present, however, the relations between them were correct, and when Taché preached in the cathedral on Sunday, March 13, to a congregation that filled the pews and crowded the aisles, Riel was among those who listened while the Bishop appealed for unity within Red River and declared that Canada would "do all that was just to the people of the country." Like the others he was deeply affected; and like a few, he wept.[12]

On the afternoon of the 15th, the Council met again.   On this occasion the Bishop was present.   It was the stormiest day of the whole winter. While the wind howled and the snowdrifts built up against the walls of the fort, the men in the council chamber listened to the quiet voice of Taché as he repeated what he had been told in Ottawa, read Howe's telegram that the terms of the List of Rights drafted by the convention in February were "in the main satisfactory."   The telegram asked that the delegates from Red River should go to Ottawa "to settle the details," and it told them of Howe's denunciation in parliament of McDougall's blunders at Pembina.[13]   Then, almost as if it were an afterthought instead of the carefully planned manœuvre which it was, he paused and asked Riel "as an act of grace" to release half the prisoners.   Riel jumped to his feet and, amid loud cheers, replied: "I have great pleasure in stating, in response to His Lordship's request, that one-half of the prisoners will be liberated this evening—and the other half will be set at liberty as soon as we have heard from a certain quarter to which some of the prisoners belong.   This I do out of respect for the assembly." He kept his word.   That night seventeen of the prisoners were released. On the next day, others were released, including Major Boulton who had once been condemned to die for leading the Portage men in their ill-fated expedition of mid-February.   Then Riel spoke about the possibilities of reinstating the Hudson's Bay Company as a commercial body, and of conducting the Provisional Government "on as near the footing of the late government as possible," saying that he would willingly give up his place as President as soon as a proper governor should come from Canada.[14]

In its subsequent meetings the Council returned to constitutional matters.   There were two motions to be discussed at length and passed, one censuring "the Government of England, the Canadian Government and the Hudson's Bay Company" for having ignored "our rights as British subjects when they entered into arrangements on the subject of the transfer of the Government of the North-West without consulting the wishes of the people of the North-West Territory," and the other expressing "the loyalty of the people of the North-West towards the Crown of England" despite the "insults and sufferings" borne by the people of Red River and "provided the rights and properties, usages and customs of the people be respected."   These motions disposed of, the Council established a committee to look into the constitution of the "Provisional Government of Rupert's Land and the North-West Territory."   Riel quietly accepted the suggestion.   "The resolution is a very important one," he said.   "Before beginning, it is necessary, of course, to have some bounds.   We are only a Provisional body, but it seems to me that it would be well to show, in the way proposed, what are the aims of the present Government."[15]   He made no effort to outline the aims or give guidance to the committee.   For the moment he had other responsibilities, and he was quite prepared to allow the members of the Council to spend their time in discussing non-controversial constitutional details.

III

The real business absorbing Riel's attention during these days was preparing the delegates for the journey to Ottawa.   As early as February 11, immediately following the establishment of the Provisional Government, Riel had appointed three men—a priest, a judge and a bartender—to carry out the important negotiations with Canada.   The priest, naturally enough, was his friend and confessor, Abbé Ritchot; the judge was John Black, the Recorder of Red River; and the bartender was Alfred H. Scott, who had worked in O'Lone's Red Saloon.   Each of the three was expected to represent an element of the population: the French, the English and the American.[16]   There was some delay over the departure of the delegates, occasioned partly by the events following the counter-movement led by Schultz and Boulton, and partly by the reluctance of Judge Black to accept appointment by Louis Riel.   Eventually, however, these problems were worked out, and on March 22 the three delegates each received a commission from Thomas Bunn, the Secretary of the Provisional Government, authorizing him "to proceed to the city of Ottawa, and lay before the Dominion Government the accompanying list of propositions and conditions, as the terms upon which the people of Assiniboia will consent to enter into confederation with the other Provinces of the Dominion."   With this commission came a letter of instructions, also signed by Bunn, and a list of the "terms and conditions" referred to in the commission.   Some of the latter were to be regarded as "peremptory," others were to be left to the discretion of the delegates who would "bear in mind that, as you carry with you the full confidence of this people, it is expected that in the exercise of this liberty, you will do your utmost to secure their rights and privileges, which have hitherto been ignored."   The final instruction to the delegates was to remind them that they were "not empowered to conclude finally any arrangements with the Canadian Government; but that any negotiations, entered into between you and the said Government, must first have the approval of and be ratified by the Provisional Government, before Assiniboia will become a province of the Confederation."   Riel was determined that there would be no doubts about the delegates going to Ottawa as the delegates of the Provisional Government, and no argument about the Provisional Government not possessing the final say about the entry of the country into the Canadian federation. There would be no dictation from Ottawa. This was more than Smith had contemplated when he had invited the convention to send delegates to Ottawa, but it was no less than Riel was determined to have.

On the 23rd, Ritchot and Scott set out for Canada, and on the following day Judge Black left Red River in company with Major Boulton. Two weeks later James Wickes Taylor set out for Ottawa. He was going to keep an eye on negotiations in the Canada capital and report and advise the authorities in Washington.

The "terms and conditions" with which the delegates were furnished on March 22 were not those that had been agreed to by the convention and that had been commented upon by Donald A. Smith in February. The situation had changed since that time. By March the Provisional Government had been organized; it had been accepted by the population; it had met in session to hear Bishop Taché. The convention of forty had no authority save that of a mass meeting in Fort Garry. Now there was a *de facto* government that rested on the basis of popular consent and popular participation. It had a proper executive and the formal framework that the previous body had lacked. This was how Riel saw it, and Riel, too, had been thwarted by the convention in his efforts to have provincial status included in the List of Rights. He was, therefore, prepared to ignore the earlier list and ready to prepare a new list bearing the imprimatur of the Provisional Government, a list which insisted upon provincial status. But he was not quite ready to refer the matter to the Council. Taking advantage of their preoccupation with the nature of their own organization and the reasons for their own existence, Riel referred the question of a List of Rights to his own Executive. Dominating this small group, which included Bunn, O'Donoghue and Schmidt, Riel was able to impose his own will and introduce several new demands into the old List of Rights,[17] as well as reword most of the clauses as Donald A. Smith had seen them. Thus it was that the first clause of the revised list insisted "the territories, heretofore known as Rupert's Land and North-West, shall not enter into the Confederation of the Dominion, except as a province, to be styled and known as the Province of Assiniboia, and with all the rights and privileges common to the different provinces of the Dominion." There were also the demands for additional representation in the House of Commons and the Senate, for a bilingual lieutenant-governor, for uninterrupted steam communication between Fort Garry and Lake Superior, and for an amnesty for all members of the Provisional Government "or any of those acting under them" for "any of the actions which led to the present negotiations."[18]

The new List of Rights indicated a greater appreciation on Riel's part of the realities of the political situation. It also indicated a lessening of his dependence on American advice and a widening of his understanding of the nature of the Canadian federal system. Riel had made himself familiar with the British North America Act during the earlier discussions,[19] and by March he was better equipped to discuss the problems of provincial status than he had been at an earlier period.

It is, indeed, interesting to follow the change that had occurred in Riel during the months since October. At the outset he had been no more than the moving spirit, and probably not even that in comparison with Father Ritchot, of the métis National Committee. His one interest and one concern at that time was to secure for the métis the lands and privileges that he felt were theirs by virtue of their Indian origin. Then, as he grasped the necessity of giving a wider basis to his movement by bringing within its compass the English-speaking people of Red River, he found himself obliged to extend his demands to include those which would take care of the special interests and concerns of the group to which he was appealing. Finally, he began to see Red River as not merely an agglomeration of French- and English-speaking half-breeds but as a political entity with an ethos of its own, as a province within the union of provinces comprising Canada. As he grew in political stature, it was essential, even inevitable, that the emphasis in his "terms and conditions" should alter. And it did.

But Riel was not alone in his concern for the future welfare of the North-West. Bishop Taché was also concerned. Despite the maturing of Riel as a political leader, he was still not as familiar as the Bishop with the realities of Canadian political life. Taché knew that Riel was intent upon altering the List of Rights, and he wondered just what changes Riel was anxious to make, and whether he would be sure to insist upon that all-important matter of denominational schools. He picked up his pen and wrote to Ritchot: "While I trace these lines the Bill of Rights to be asked from Canada is being revised at Fort Garry. What will be the result of this work? By whom will it be done? I do not know! I only know that it is an extremely important question. . . . I need not tell you that an immense responsibility is attached to your momentous mission. You perfectly understand this responsibility."[20] On the 22nd, he wrote to Riel asking him for a copy of the List of Rights.[21] Riel had not thought of including anything in his demands about a separate school system. Schools in Red River were and always had been denominational schools. There never was a public school system. What funds had been devoted to education by the Council of Assiniboia had been divided among the Roman Catholics and the Anglicans. Riel had received his education in a denominational school in Montreal and had little knowledge of the controversies over sectarian and public schools that had marked the history of Upper Canada. But the Bishop knew the problem, and he knew what would happen should there be a large influx of Protestant Ontarians into the new province once it became a part of Canada. And even if he had been disposed to forget—which was most unlikely—he had been reminded when he received a letter from Joseph Lemay, a French Canadian at Pembina, who wrote to Bishop Taché on March 12 expressing his opposition to the annexationist efforts of Stutsman and Rolette, and declared that the Americans had three gods: "Money, women and public schools."[22] Red River, said Lemay, should be able to obtain far more concessions and religious freedom from Canada than it could ever hope to obtain from the United States.

It is true that there is no definite evidence proving that Taché modified Riel's List of Rights—evidence that would leave no room for doubt in any skeptic's mind. But the inference seems clear enough. Riel, Ritchot, Dugast and O'Donoghue had a hand in drafting the first List of Rights, and perhaps the second and third. None of them had thought of the school issue or, if he had thought of it, had inserted a demand for separate schools in any of the three Lists. The only new figure in the story is Taché. More than any of the others, he was alive to the importance of making some provision for the existing schools in the Settlement. If Taché himself did not draft the changes that were made, then he must certainly have inspired or suggested them. This is all the more obvious when it is remembered that only Ritchot carried the List containing this demand with him to Ottawa.[23]

In the final, or fourth List of Rights, there were only two major changes. The first change was a spelling out of the nature of the constitution of the new province. It was to have a legislative Assembly, a responsible ministry, a senate and a lieutenant-governor, just like Quebec. The second change was the demand that "the schools be separate, and that the public money for schools be distributed among the different religious denominations in proportion to their respective populations according to the system in the Province of Quebec."[24] The other clauses were reworded, but they remained substantially the same as those of the third List.

If Ritchot carried with him the hopes of Louis Riel and Bishop Taché for the future province of Manitoba, he also carried with him a warning from the Bishop not to let his zeal for justice to the métis and the people of Red River carry him to extremes. "The evils which threaten us," wrote Taché:

are perhaps greater than those which were meant to be avoided! This is why I entreat you to do all in your power to effect an arrangement with Canada. It is our only plank of safety! It is our only hope! To obtain this let me tell you; there should not be any absolute will. You have your own opinions. Very well; but on the other hand, others have theirs also. It is hard to say that in all cases they are less sincere and less well inspired . . . I know how sincere you are! If anything could cause me uneasiness, it would be an excess of sincerity.[25]

IV

Once the delegates were safely embarked on their journey to Canada, Louis Riel felt free to resolve the problems that still clamoured for his attention. The métis had made pretty free with the goods and property of the Hudson's Bay Company since they had occupied Fort Garry on November 2, and the Company had replied by refusing to issue more bills of change. But spring was coming. The voyageurs would be off again to man the York boats on the Saskatchewan; the tripmen would be driving their Red River carts to St. Cloud; the winterers would be gathering at Fort Garry to dispose of their furs. It was essential that some effort should be made to get the machinery of trade moving once again. It was even more essential to clarify the relation between the Company and the Provisional Government. There were no bills of exchange, nor was there any gold and silver in the Settlement. Money, if necessary for trade and commerce, was equally necessary for the maintenance of government and administration. Riel therefore approached William Mactavish, the senior Hudson's Bay Company official in the Settlement. Despite the urgency of the situation, Riel was able to argue from a position of strength, for he still possessed the military force that the Company lacked. On March 28 he presented Mactavish with what amounted to an ultimatum:[26] the Company would formally recognize the Provisional Government; the Company would lend £3,000 to the Provisional Government; should the negotiations with Canada fall through, there would be a supplementary loan of £2,000; the Company would provide some £4,000 worth of provisions and supplies for "military" purposes; the Company would resume its issue of bills, and trade would be carried on in the customary manner. In return, Riel promised to return Fort Garry and its supplies to the Company and to ensure that there would be no more trouble either at that post or at any other posts in the interior.

It was a hard bargain and Mactavish was reluctant to agree to it. But Riel knew that public opinion was on his side. He knew that it would only be necessary to reveal the fact that he had made an approach to the Company, and that he had asked them to reopen the trade, to convince people that any delays were the responsibility of the Hudson's Bay Company and not that of the Provisional Government. It would be easy enough to make it appear that the soulless corporation, which had sold Red River to Canada, was showing once more its hostility to the people of the Settlement. Even if Mactavish had had the physical stamina to resist Riel's forceful diplomacy, it is doubtful if he would have gone to the extent of antagonizing the métis by refusing to accede to Riel's demands. He therefore accepted what he knew he could not refuse. This point gained, Riel then despatched a circular letter to the métis of the plains outlining the achievements of the Provisional Government and urging them to preserve "order and peace."[27] At the same time Patrice Breland was sent to the interior to carry word of the government's arrangements with the Hudson's Bay Company.[28] Breland was told to do everything possible to calm the fears of the métis and Indians, and to discourage any hostile actions which might be contemplated against the Company's forts. Then, on April 8, Riel turned over the keys of Fort Garry to the officials of the Company, reserving for himself and for the Provisional Government only such accommodation as was considered absolutely necessary. *The New Nation* recorded the event with satisfaction:

The negotiations between the Hudson's Bay Company and the Government were concluded on Wednesday last, when the documents were signed and the Company allowed to resume its business. Some of the buildings heretofore occupied by the Government were given up for its requirements. The regular business of the Company will now be resumed as heretofore, without delay. This, together with the anticipated lively spring trade, will make good times for all.[29]

On the 9th, the Company issued its first bill of exchange on London, and Company employees began to take an inventory of the goods restored to their possession. On the same day, Riel issued a Proclamation—it was "a kind of chant of victory"[30]—announcing the removal of all restrictions on movement within the Settlement; the resumption of trade by the Hudson's Bay Company; and an amnesty to all "who will submit to the Provisional Government." "Let us remain united and we shall be happy," wrote Riel. "With strength of unity we shall attain prosperity." But if there was a note of jubilation in the proclamation, there was also a note of warning. Let no one forget the divisions and dissensions of the past: "In order to prevent similar calamities, the Government will treat with all the severity of the law those who dare again to compromise the public security. It is ready to act against the disorder of parties as well as against that of individuals. But let us hope rather that extreme measures will be unknown and that the lessons of the past will guide us in the future."[31]

There was really little need for Riel to have inserted any threats in his proclamation. He had no reason to fear another outbreak on the part of the Canadians in the Settlement. The representative of the Portage had declared in the Council meeting of March 9 that any rumours of trouble brewing in his district were "utterly without foundation." "Except in one instance, we have done our utmost to keep the peace," he stated. "We feel that we are in duty bound to come under the Provisional Government, and are now on perfectly good terms with all the people of Red River."[32] From time to time rumours reached Fort Garry of restlessness among the Canadians,[33] but with their leaders, men like Dr. Schultz and Charles Mair, out of the Settlement, and other discontented Canadians leaving it daily,[34] there was not much likelihood of any attempt at organized resistance. If the Canadians were unhappy at the turn of events in Red River, for the most part they kept quiet and bided their time. As for the native settlers, many of the métis were returning to their former occupations as voyageurs, tripmen and hunters; and the Scotch and the English-speaking half-breeds were watching the rapidly disappearing snow, wondering about the possibilities of floods on the rivers, wondering when they could get on the land again. If any of them thought seriously about politics, it was merely to note with approval Riel's action in hoisting the Union Jack over Fort Garry on April 20, and in posting André Nault to guard it against O'Donoghue's efforts to have it removed.[35]

Even the members of the Council had lost their zest for politics. It had been an interesting occupation during the winter but not now when spring was at hand. Thus the members who had, with Riel's blessing, undertaken to revise the Constitution of the Provisional Government on March 18, did little more than adopt the name of "The Legislative Assembly of Assiniboia" and talk vaguely about setting up a "senate," before they accepted with alacrity Riel's suggestion that in place of debating each afternoon the ill-prepared suggestions the committee had drafted in the forenoon, they should adjourn and let the committee have sufficient time to draft a complete constitution.[36] On March 24, the following oath was administered to Riel as president of the Provisional Government:

I, Louis Riel, do hereby solemnly swear that I will faithfully fulfil, to the best of my ability, my duties as President of the Provisional Government, proclaimed on the 24th November, 1869, and also all the duties which may become connected with the office of President of the Provisional Government of Assiniboia, as they may hereafter be defined by the voice of the people.[37]

Oaths were also administered to each member of the Assembly and to James Ross as Chief Justice. After some desultory discussion of the

proposal that the "hay privilege" should be converted to simple ownership, the Assembly adjourned on March 26 in a spirit of good will and
satisfaction.

V

If life within the Red River Settlement was at last returning to normal,
Riel continued to be plagued with problems and anxieties.   He never
seemed to enjoy peace of mind.   In the first place, there was Lépine and
his inability to get along with his men.   A large, slow-speaking man,
Lépine had somehow developed into a military martinet.   Perhaps he
was too good a soldier to command men who were prepared to submit to
leadership but not to discipline.   On March 25, there was a minor
mutiny against him, and a number of métis soldiers went back to their
homes.   Lépine did the same thing, and he returned to Fort Garry only
after Riel's solicitation.[38]   Then there were the tales circulating throughout the Settlement, started by those who disliked or were jealous of
Riel—tales of his vanity, of his overbearing manner, of his living at ease
while his poor mother was starving.   Even those who were his friends
disliked it when they heard he had appropriated for his own use the
furniture that McDougall had sent to Red River for the use of the
Lieutenant-Governor.   "They say," wrote Alexander Begg in his diary,
"Riel's quarters are magnificent with McDougall's furniture."[39]   This
was too much for most of the Red River settlers to whom "putting on
airs" was the sure road to disfavour.   Perhaps this was one reason why
Riel made the gesture of raising the Union Jack.   Such a gesture would
gain the support of at least the English-speaking settlers.

Riel had other worries too.   There were those persistent reports that
his old enemy Schultz was doing everything he could to whip up feeling
in Ontario against him; that Ritchot and Scott had been arrested in
Canada on a charge of murder; that the Canadian Government was
preparing a military expedition for the purpose of overthrowing the
Provisional Government and establishing Canadian rule by force.   Riel
began seriously to question the honesty of Macdonald, Cartier and Howe.
He began to wonder, too, how far he could trust Bishop Taché's
assurances that an amnesty would be granted for past offences.   Was
there anyone in whom he could place his faith?   Perhaps he had been a
bit hasty in so completely cutting himself off from the possibilities of
American help.   Thus, when William R. Marshall, the ex-governor of
Minnesota, arrived in Red River to look over the situation on behalf of
Jay Cooke and the Northern Pacific, he was not given the short shrift
that had been accorded the Canadian, Arthur Rankin, who had
approached Riel early in March with another railway scheme.[40]   Riel

treated Marshall with respect, talked with him, even left with him the impression that there was perfect accord in the ranks of the Provisional Government and that he, the President, and O'Donoghue, while prepared to go through with the arrangements with Canada, were not disposed to slam the door upon American annexation. The Marshall party returned to the United States as quietly as they had come, leaving as a record of their visit the following description of Riel, "a fine physique, of active temperament, a great worker, and I think is able to endure a great deal." The letter continued:

He is a large man, with a high forehead (not broad) of very winning persuasive manners; and in his whole bearing, energy and ready decision are prominent characteristics:—and in this fact, lies his great powers— for I should not give him credit for great profundity, yet he is sagacious, and I think thoroughly patriotic and no less thoroughly incorruptible. In his intercourse with us, he was very diplomatic and noncommittal.[41]

Of course Riel was noncommittal, even if Marshall wanted to believe him to be "secretly" in favour of annexation to the United States. He had made his bed and he would lie in it; he would go through with the marriage with Canada and would not dally with the United States.

When the Legislative Assembly resumed its session towards the end of April, there was more trouble in store for the harassed president. Hardly had the delegates left for Ottawa than stories were heard that changes had been made in the List of Rights that the convention had prepared in February.[42] Just what these changes were, no one seemed to know. There was the rumour too that the delegates had been told to insist that the new province should be known as Manitoba, not as Assiniboia. Riel knew both of these rumours were true, that a new List had been drawn up without the Assembly being consulted or informed, and that he had written to Ritchot suggesting the name Manitoba rather than Assiniboia, since the latter might be confused with the small district that had been administered by the Hudson's Bay Company.[43] He realized, too, that he would have to make this known some day to the Assembly; but he did not look forward to doing it. For the first few days of the session he said very little. He allowed the members to argue about the hay privilege and to talk about the constitution. Finally he took the plunge. He admitted to the Assembly that the List of Rights had, in truth, been modified. It was a confession that he had acted upon his own authority, that he had ignored the other members of the legislature.

The confession was received with cold disapproval. Riel tried to defend his action, and he renewed his appeals for unity. He pointed out that Schultz and his supporters were trying to stir up trouble in Ontario; that they were making capital out of any and every division within the

Settlement; that they were arguing conditions had changed within the Settlement since February and that the Red River delegates should be barred from Ottawa. "It is true there has been a change," he told the Assembly:

but it is, I think, one for the better, as the terms proposed in the long run could more easily be assented to, than those agreed on in the Convention. Some changes were found to be necessary, by the Executive, and they had to be quickly decided on, as the Commissioners were expected in Canada, and the people here were anxious to see them starting to Ottawa. Hence the manner of making the alterations. But I would like to place them before the House, so that Hon. members can judge for themselves. Hon. Mr. Bunn, the Secretary, was with us while the alterations were being made, and so limited was our time for the work that we had to work day and night in order to finish and enable the Commissioners to start at the time they did.

The members were not moved. Riel continued:

The Commissioners, of course, had certain powers in regard to these demands, but before anything was finally settled, they were instructed that the approval of the Legislative Assembly of this country was necessary; so that, while complying with circumstances we had at the same time a saving clause that the ratification of the action of our Commissioners depended altogether on the will of the Legislature of this country.[44]

It was as good a defence as he could make. But it was not one to remove the soreness that the English-speaking members felt at being ignored by the Executive. Riel must have realized this and, anxious to avoid further irritation, he accepted with good grace the disapproval of the Assembly and the defeat of his proposal to establish a senate as part of the legislative machinery of the colony. The session was not, however, a lost effort. The Assembly debated and adopted a series of practical measures dealing with the administration of justice, customs duties, the number and duties of constables, intestate estates, postal regulations, fires, hay privilege, liquor laws, trade and roads. All these were very practical measures that resembled in many ways the kind of legislation that had issued from the old Council of Assiniboia during the days of the Hudson's Bay Company. But there was a sense of tension in the relations between the Assembly and the Executive; and when the Assembly adjourned on May 9 there were no shouts, no demonstrations, no expressions of satisfaction, no platitudes. No date was even set for the next session. Riel merely remarked that "in the event of anything official coming from the Commissioners in Canada he might call a special session of the Legislature."[45]

Riel knew that his prestige among the English-speaking settlers had slipped and that his hold on the Settlement was accordingly much weaker.   He knew, too, that his own position was more vulnerable than it had been for several months.   Most of his soldiers had been paid off.[46] They had been, for the most part, Hudson's Bay Company men, and they were returning to their seasonal jobs again, now that spring had arrived in the west.   As far as Captain Gay's small force of horsemen was concerned,[47] it was little more than a police force.   There might be some help forthcoming from the métis on the plains, should it really be true that Canadian troops were on their way to Red River.   But such help was not likely to be effective, if only because the winterers had taken no part in the events at Fort Garry, and the other métis bands were too remote to yield readily to the personal spell of Riel, especially in view of the opposition of Pascal Breland, the son-in-law of Cuthbert Grant.[48] Riel knew, whether he wanted to admit it or not, that he was in no position to offer military opposition to Canada.   His only hope lay in Taché's promises.   The question was, how reliable were they?

On May 13, the first of the clouds on the political horizon began to lift. This was the news that Ritchot and Scott, the two Red River delegates, had been released from custody and the charges against them dropped.[49] Two weeks later the sky looked even brighter.   Ritchot reported that the negotiations had been brought to a successful conclusion, "matters are going well for our poor but brave people of Red River," he wrote to Taché.[50]   There were no further details, and Riel wrote impatiently to Ritchot complaining that the Provisional Government had received no official notification of the passing of the Manitoba Act by the Canadian Parliament, and that he had received nothing to calm the "suspicions" and "fears" engendered in the Settlement by the military preparations under way in Canada.[51]

When Riel wrote this letter, Ritchot was already on his way back to Red River.   On June 17, when the steamer *International* docked at Fort Garry, the dark bearded priest, who had played so important a role in the Red River rising from its inception to the conclusion of arrangements with Canada, stepped ashore.   From the first house north of the frontier, all the way to Fort Garry, every family living along the river had, on recognizing the priest's soutane, rushed to the water's edge waving and welcoming him home again.   At Fort Garry there was a large crowd to greet the returning delegate.   To the front was Riel who led Ritchot to the fort, while twenty-one guns boomed their noisy and smoky salute from the walls.[52]   Bunn and Schmidt hurriedly penned instructions to the members of the Assembly to convene again at the fort on the 23rd. Everybody was excited.   Everybody wanted to hear what had happened at Ottawa, and what the future held for the settlers living along the banks of the Red and the Assiniboine rivers.   And none more so than Louis Riel.

CHAPTER 8

Manitoba

EVENTS IN RED RIVER had not aroused much public interest or comment in Canada, at least not until the shooting of Thomas Scott. The general reaction to William McDougall's discomfiture at Pembina had been one of mild amusement or derisive satisfaction. The English-language newspapers were inclined to be scornful of the attempts of a handful of French métis to stand in the way of the new Dominion of Canada, but few of them had much regard for the unfortunate Lieutenant-Governor who had deserted one political party but had never been wholly welcome in the other. Even the members of McDougall's entourage at Pembina never really liked the man. His aide-de-camp, Captain Cameron, wrote several times to the Prime Minister to complain of the Governor's discourtesy;[1] McDougall reciprocated with letters asking Sir John A. Macdonald: "For God's sake, don't send me any more captains with glass eyes."[2] In Ottawa, members of the cabinet learned of McDougall's mishaps with despair. In a letter to Sir John Rose, Macdonald complained that between them McDougall and Dennis "have done their utmost to destroy our chance of an amicable settlement with those wild people, and now the probability is that our Commissioners will fail and that we must be left to the exhibition of force next spring."[3] Even the opposition newspapers, such as the Toronto *Globe*, which fluctuated between its traditional dislike and distrust of French Canada and its traditional disposition to blame Sir John A. Macdonald for all the ills of the country, was inclined to share the government's view.

The news of the death of Scott brought about a change. Immediately there was an outburst of indignation in English-speaking Canada. The *Globe* in Toronto and the *Herald* in Montreal published the first account of the trial and execution of the young Ontario Orangeman on March 26, 1870. Three days later Edward Blake, the rising hope of the Liberal Party, asked for an official statement from Macdonald in Parliament. For the moment there was still none of the shrill frenzy that was to mark the tone of press and politics several weeks later. As days passed, however, racial feelings in Ontario and Quebec grew sorer under the whip-lash of political agitation.

In Ontario the prod was furnished by a small group of men who, in 1868, had found a common bond of sympathy in their determination to "advance the interests" of their native land and to build up "a strong and powerful community" in Canada.[4] Among them were George T. Denison and William A. Foster of Toronto, Charles Mair of Lanark, and Robert Haliburton of Halifax. This group, known later by the slogan "Canada First," had strongly favoured the acquisition of the North-West by Canada, and its members followed events in Red River with an interest scarcely shared by Canadians in the Maritimes, Quebec, or even Ontario. This interest was stimulated by the knowledge that the United States had its eyes on the west, and by the conviction that the North-West was Canada's natural hinterland, with Canadian associations going back beyond the English régime to the days of La Vérendrye. They were interested, too, because one of their members, Mair, had joined Snow's work crew and was about to make the journey to the Hudson's Bay Company territories. Anxious to publicize a region Canadians generally knew very little about—and the little that they did was based on the misrepresentations of the great fur company—the members of the group arranged with George Brown of the Toronto *Globe* for Mair to write a series of letters giving an account of the territory and its suitability for Canadian settlement. During the months he spent in Red River, Mair not only wrote regularly to the *Globe* and to the *Gazette*, he also kept up a personal correspondence with Denison and with "Canada First."[5] Moreover, he told Schultz about the group and about its aims. In March, 1869, when Schultz paid a visit to Ontario, he carried with him a letter of introduction from Mair to Denison. Denison found Schultz a man after his own heart. He was, therefore, warmly welcomed "into our ranks," wrote Denison.[6] When he returned to Red River, he knew he had behind him all the resources of a small but influential secret organization of men whose views he shared and who would be able to mould public opinion along the lines he desired. Denison and his friends were enlarged as a group by several significant additions, including George Kingsmill, the editor of the *Toronto Daily Telegraph*, and Joseph E. McDougall, the brother of the Lieutenant-Governor designate. As might well be expected, they were "keenly aroused" by the imprisonment of Schultz and Mair in Fort Garry in December. But for some reason which Denison could never quite understand, the general public had remained apathetic and indifferent. The man in the street shared the view held by members of the Cabinet— that the Canadians were largely to blame for their own misfortunes, and that McDougall had been ill-advised and indiscreet. They therefore showed small sympathy for the men who languished in Fort Garry from

December until February. Then the news came that Thomas Scott, "a loyal Ontario man," and an Orangeman, had been put to death by the French-Catholic métis.

This was just the kind of news that Denison and "Canada First" needed. "Foster and I, who had been consulting almost daily," wrote Denison, "were much depressed at the apathy of the public, but when we heard that Schultz and Mair, as well as Dr. Lynch,[7] were all on the way to Ontario, and that Scott had been murdered, it was seen at once that there was an opportunity by giving a public reception to the loyal refugees, to draw attention to the matter, and by denouncing the murder of Scott, to arouse the indignation of the people, and foment a public opinion that would force the Government to send up an armed expedition to restore order."[8] At once the propaganda machine began to move. The *Daily Telegraph* came out in mourning for Scott, and a series of inflammatory editorials written by Foster and published by Kingsmill at once attracted attention. Public interest replaced public indifference. Alexander Mackenzie, the Liberal leader at Ottawa, took up the cries of "murder" and "treachery" and demanded that there should be no intercourse with the "traitors" from Red River.[9] In the background the *Globe* and the other English language newspapers began to beat the war drums of vengeance and retribution.

In the meantime Schultz and Mair, the one accompanied by Joseph Monkman and the other by John Setter, were on their way to Canada. They had managed to elude Riel's soldiers after the collapse of the February rising. Travelling by snowshoe in the coldest month of the year and following different routes—Schultz by way of the Winnipeg River and Duluth; Mair by the White Mud and the plains—they reached safety in St. Paul, Minnesota. Here they sent their telegrams to Canada, and set out by train for Toronto.

To his surprise, Denison found some of his colleagues reluctant to take advantage of this opportunity to make political capital out of the return of the "refugees." They were afraid that a public demonstration might attract too few persons to be of any use, and they counselled delay "until the refugees had gone to Ottawa, and had laid their case before the Government."[10] But Denison would have none of this. He declared that Schultz, Mair and the others had "risked their lives in obedience to a proclamation in the Queen's name, calling upon them to take up arms on her behalf; that there were only a few Ontario men, seventy in number, in that remote and inaccessible region, surrounded by half savages, besieged until supplies gave out." He went on to point out that "they had escaped and were coming to their own province to tell of their wrongs, to ask assistance to relieve the intolerable condition of their comrades in the Red River Settlement." He asked, "Is there any Ontario man who will not hold out a hand of welcome to these men? Any man who hesitates is no true Canadian. I repudiate him as a countryman of mine." It was strong stuff, but the public liked it. Small wonder that Denison wrote, "I soon had the whole meeting with me."[11]

The agitation began to have its inevitably intoxicating effect. When, on April 6, Schultz, Mair and another Canadian from Red River, Dr. Joseph Lynch, arrived in Toronto with the two half-breed guides, Monkman and Setter, there was a large crowd at the railway station to greet them and escort them to the Queen's Hotel. In the evening they went to St. Lawrence Hall, where it had been planned to hold a large meeting to allow the refugees to tell their stories to the public. But the building would not hold the crowds who gathered to see and hear the men who attempted to overthrow Louis Riel. The demonstrators abandoned the building and set off to hold their meeting in the open area in front of the City Hall. There were over five thousand people present, and according to the *Globe* it was "one of the most enthusiastic meetings" held in Toronto "for many a day."[12] The Mayor, S. B. Harman, shouted to the crowd that the names "of those gallant men who stood up for British supremacy in Red River . . . would live in history, and be handed down side by side with those who led the gallant charge at Balaclava to uphold the dignity of Britain against the greatest odds that could be brought against them." It mattered very little to the Mayor or to his listeners that neither Schultz nor Mair had done much in the way of charging the enemy. In another historically inept comparison— "the same power which had been able to make itself felt at Lucknow and Delhi would be sufficient to put down that miserable creature who attempts to usurp authority at Fort Garry, and establish again the supremacy and glory of the British flag"—supported by a biblical allusion: "with a strong trust in Him who said 'Vengeance is mine, I will repay,' " His Worship declared that the meeting would "show to our statesmen and rulers" that the people of Toronto "were prepared to uphold British supremacy on this continent." Setter demanded that "Riel and his followers should be punished." Then Charles Mair took the platform to give an impression of the Red River people and the country in which they lived. As Mair spoke the attention of the audience began to wander. This was not the blood and thunder that they had come to see and hear.

When Schultz stood up, the atmosphere changed. The tension increased—due partly to his magnificent appearance; partly also to the way he struck out against his enemies. The situation at Fort Garry,

Schultz said, "was simply this, that the Fenian flag floated from its flag staff.   The rebels hold high revelry within its walls, and Canadians lay in dungeons within it."

Here was the secret of Schultz's success.   He knew what his audience wanted; he could play upon their prejudices.   There was no need to beat about the bush, no need to produce well-reasoned, well-balanced arguments, just go straight to the point.   "It was from Ontario this movement to add Red River to the Dominion commenced; it was in Ontario this expression of indignation was expressed; and it was to Ontario the Territory   properly   belonged."[13]   Schultz's   speech   was   trenchant, provocative, stimulating and inflammatory.   It was just what Denison and his friends wanted; and it was followed by the enthusiastic adoption of a series of resolutions endorsing the actions of the Canadians in Red River, calling for decisive measures to suppress the revolt and declaring that: "it would be a gross injustice to the loyal inhabitants of Red River, humiliating to our national honour, and contrary to all British traditions for our Government to receive, or treat with the emissaries of those who have robbed, imprisoned, and murdered loyal Canadians, whose only fault was zeal for British institutions, whose only crime was devotion to the old flag."[14]

The same evening and during the next day Denison and Foster were closeted with Schultz and Mair to consider plans to incite agitation elsewhere in Ontario.   It was agreed that a deputation should be sent at once to Ottawa, and that local demonstrations should be organized at various towns along the railway line, at Cobourg, Belleville and Prescott. Everything worked out as planned, except that the people of Belleville— it was a well-known Orange town—demanded that Mair and Setter should stay behind to address a great public meeting there.   But the atmosphere in Ottawa was decidedly chilly.   Here Riel's Quebec friends still had some influence with Macdonald's colleague, Sir George Cartier, and the members of the government had their ears tuned, not only to the agitation in Ontario, but to the protests that the agitation had aroused in Quebec.   As the English-language newspapers had raised their sights from events in Red River to fire their salvos at the Roman Catholic Church and at French Canada generally, the French Canadians had replied in kind against Ontario and its Orange Order.   There were votes to be counted in Quebec as well as in Ontario, and Denison reported with disgust that "on our arrival in Ottawa we found that the Government were not at all friendly to the loyal men, and were not desirous of doing anything that we had been advocating."   Even Denison's threat to withdraw his political support from Macdonald did not change the Prime Minister's reluctance to act with precipitation.   In Denison's opinion, Macdonald was following the familiar tactic "of neglecting his friends and buying up his enemies."[15]   But Denison was being unfair to Macdonald.   The fact was that the Cabinet was divided, and Cartier had talked of resigning if matters were pressed to extremes.   And Cartier's support was something neither Macdonald nor the Conservatives could afford to lose.[16]

Rebuffed by the Prime Minister, the "loyalists" turned to the Governor-General, Sir John Young.   Denison drafted a formal protest which was signed by Dr. Lynch, reciting the story of the imprisonment of the Canadians and the death of Thomas Scott.   It denounced Ritchot and A. H. Scott as "among the first organizers and promoters of the outbreak" and "supporters and associates of Mr. Riel and his faction" and declared that both of them had been present "at the time of the murder" of "one of our loyal subjects."   This indicated the strategy that Denison resolved to adopt.   The Red River delegates were to be arrested and charged with murder.   While Denison, Schultz and Lynch were in Ottawa, Foster and Hugh Scott, the brother of the unfortunate Thomas, applied for a warrant from the police magistrate in Toronto for the arrest of Ritchot and A. H. Scott on a charge of aiding and abetting in the murder of Thomas Scott.   The warrant was then sent to the chief of police in Ottawa.   When Riel's delegates arrived in the city, they found themselves arrested like common criminals.

II

It was on March 24 that the Abbé Ritchot, with Alfred Scott and Colonel de Salaberry, set out from St. Norbert.   They reached Pembina on the 25th and, on the following day, were joined by Judge Black, Major Boulton and J. A. N. Provencher.   It was an odd group of individuals that was bound for Ottawa.   Each man in his own way had played a part in the Red River drama: Black represented the old order of the Hudson's Bay Company; Ritchot was one of the leading figures of the métis rising; Scott was an annexationist; Provencher had been one of McDougall's party; and Boulton one of Dennis's party.   De Salaberry had been one of the commissioners sent by the Canadian Government to pacify the Settlement.   Now they were all journeying to Canada, with Black, Ritchot and Scott empowered by Riel to make an agreement with Canada to bring Red River into the Canadian federation, not on Canadian terms but on those determined by the Provisional Government of Assiniboia.

The journey was a slow one.   Horse and sleigh were the only means of transportation.   Finally, on April 6—the day Schultz was inciting the crowd in front of the City Hall in Toronto—Ritchot and his companions

reached St. Cloud in Minnesota, where they took the train.   Black and
the others travelled to Detroit and Toronto, but Ritchot and Scott
journeyed to Buffalo and Rome, south of Lake Ontario.   They then
turned north to reach the St. Lawrence at Ogdensburg just opposite
Prescott, where they arrived on April 11.   Here they were met by
Gilbert McMicken of the Canadian Secret Service, who had been sent
by Sir John A. Macdonald to conduct the Red River delegates to Ottawa.

On April 12, the day following his arrival in the Canadian capital,
Ritchot went to see Sir George Cartier.   He was courteously received and
assured that the government would pay little heed to "the outcry of a
certain group of men who were only seeking to create trouble for the
Government."[17]   Cartier gave no undertaking as to what he and Macdonald proposed to do about the demands of the Red River delegates:
nor did Ritchot ask for any.   He preferred to wait until he had been
joined by his colleague, Judge Black.[18]

Cartier seems to have felt that the agitation led by Denison and his
friends would be of short duration and would soon dissipate itself.   He
therefore told Ritchot that he thought it advisable to postpone discussions for a few days, at least until the uproar in Ontario had subsided.
Other French Canadians gave Ritchot the same advice, always holding
out to him the promise of a satisfactory settlement.   But Ritchot was
not as sanguine as the Canadians.   He was suspicious by nature, and he
had heard a report that his co-delegate, Alfred Scott, had already been
taken into custody, and that a warrant had been issued for his own arrest.
The next day his worst fears were realized.   Several of his friends, including Major Futvoye, Sir George's secretary, informed him that the
police were looking for him, and they suggested it would be well for him to
give himself up.   Bail was readily found, and on the 14th Ritchot and
Scott were arraigned in an Ottawa court room.   The presiding judge
quickly decided that the magistrate who had issued the warrant in
Toronto had no jurisdiction in Ottawa, and he ordered the release of both
men.   However this possibility had been foreseen by the members of
"Canada First."   Hugh Scott had come to Ottawa to apply for a new
warrant, should one be necessary,[19] and almost immediately, before they
had had time to leave the court room, Ritchot and Scott were re-arrested
on the new warrant.   Nine days later the case was brought before
Magistrate O'Gara.   Meanwhile Ritchot had sent a strong letter to the
Governor-General protesting the violation of his diplomatic immunity
as a delegate of the Provisional Government of Assiniboia.[20]   There was
not much the Governor-General could do, or the Canadian government
for that matter, since the information had been sworn by a private party.
But the Canadian authorities did retain the services of Hon. J. H

Cameron as counsel for the two delegates, and they hastened to assure the British Government that they had in no way been party to the arrest.[21] It was all done very quietly behind the scenes, and when the case came before the court, the crown prosecutor declined to proceed for lack of any evidence to support the charge. The two men were released and, as they left the court room, they were greeted enthusiastically by a large crowd of French and Irish Canadian sympathizers. But Ritchot wanted no demonstration. He returned quietly and very indignantly to his room at the Bishop's Palace.[22]

During the interval, Ritchot and Black had held several interviews with Sir George Cartier and Sir John A. Macdonald. They were always treated "with politeness" but received nothing from the Canadian authorities that could be construed as a formal recognition of their official status as representatives of the *de facto* régime in Red River. This annoyed Ritchot. On April 22, the Abbé wrote privately to Joseph Howe, and on the 23rd all three delegates wrote officially requesting the opening of formal negotiations.[23] Two days later Ritchot and Black spent considerable time with Cartier and Macdonald. The priest was still ruffled by his arrest and was formal and abrupt in his manner. He complained that he had been in Ottawa for a fortnight and nothing had been accomplished. In particular he had received no official recognition. Cartier tried to mollify him by pointing out the very fact that the delegates had been received by the Prime Minister was tantamount to official recognition, but Ritchot wanted something on paper, something that he could show to the members of the Provisional Government in Fort Garry. He then asked about the amnesty Bishop Taché had promised, and demanded an explanation of the rumours that Ottawa was planning to send a military expedition to Red River. He then made it clear that the Provisional Government would accept nothing less than provincial status for the Red River colony. Judge Black might be inclined to compromise; but he, Ritchot, would insist strongly upon all of these points.[24]

By the time this meeting was over, both Macdonald and Cartier realized they would have no easy time with the Red River delegates. Back in February Macdonald had written to Sir John Young, "Everything looks well for a delegation coming to Ottawa, including the redoubtable Riel. If we once get him here, he is a gone coon."[25] But Ritchot was no "gone coon." Judge Black could be persuaded, and Scott preferred the bar at the Russell Hotel to the negotiation table in Cartier's office, Ritchot, however, was dedicated and stubborn. He was not to be swayed from his line of duty by mere politeness or impressed by high rank. With Louis Riel's help he had launched the métis movement and, like Riel, he was determined to erect the barriers he believed necessary for the protection of native peoples of the Settlement against the influx of immigrants which would inevitably follow the entry of Red River into Confederation.[26] There would be some hard bargaining before the negotiations would be concluded; and if Ritchot was to yield to the Canadians, it would only be in return for major concessions on the part of Canada.

Ritchot gained his first demand, official recognition, on April 26, when Howe replied to the delegates' letter of the 22nd with a formal invitation to open negotiations with the Prime Minister.[27] Then followed other victories; provincial status was conceded by Macdonald, and then separate schools. When it came to the demand for provincial control of public lands, the Prime Minister refused. This, he declared, would remain a matter for the federal government. By way of compromise, Ritchot demanded that a special area of land be set aside for the mixed-blood population as a recognition of their aboriginal title. Macdonald offered 200,000 acres. Ritchot refused. He wanted 3,000,000 acres. For several days the bickering and arguing went on, and Macdonald finally agreed to 1,400,000.[28] This obdurate priest was enough to drive a man to drink; and, on the 28th, Sir John took to the bottle, leaving Cartier to settle the problem of whether or not Portage la Prairie should be included within the boundaries of the new province.[29] By May 4, sufficient progress had been made for the Manitoba Bill to be introduced into the Canadian House of Commons for the first reading. On that day Ritchot telegraphed to Thomas Bunn to tell him that the Bill was "satisfactory" and that the delegates were "confident of amicable and acceptable arrangements."[30]

Ritchot was being just a little premature in his satisfaction. There were several rough spots yet to be ironed out. There was still the question of the amnesty which Ritchot was pressing upon a not very sympathetic Governor-General.[31] Would this demanding cleric never appreciate the difficulties the government had to face? Did he not realize that the newspapers of Ontario were clamouring for a punitive expedition and demanding that there should be no truck with "rebels" and no intercourse with "murderers"? Would he not accept the Governor's proclamation of December 6 as sufficient, and not keep asking for a new document which would only cause political embarrassment to the Conservative party? Macdonald could do no more than he had already done. Sir Clinton Murdoch, the special representative sent by an anxious Imperial government to Ottawa to keep an eye on developments, verbally assured Ritchot that there was nothing the Queen desired more than the re-establishment of peace and "to pass the sponge" over what had taken place at Fort Garry.[32]

When the full text of the bill became available on May 6—this was the day set for the second reading—Ritchot put forward several more demands. But Cartier would make no changes now. He pointed out that any modifications would probably imperil the passage of the bill and that any little problems that remained to be cleared up could be dealt with by order-in-council. On May 4, Macdonald had written to the Governor-General, "The Bill affecting Red River . . . will pass without any serious opposition."[33] But it was not Macdonald who piloted the bill through the second and third readings. On the 6th, waiting for the debate to begin, he was seized with an illness that almost took his life.[34] It was Cartier who had to take on the responsibility that would otherwise have been Macdonald's. Perhaps because of Macdonald's illness, and fear that the old leader was dying, the House of Commons did not respond to Mackenzie's efforts to ridicule the creation of a province of little more than 1,000 square miles, with its population of 15,000 as something out of *Gulliver's Travels*, or to McDougall's efforts to make something out of the shooting of Scott. Macdonald's prediction proved true. A subdued House of Commons passed the Manitoba Bill, 120 votes to 11. On May 12, the Bill received the Royal Assent.

The Abbé Ritchot had watched the proceedings from the gallery. When the last opposition amendment was defeated, and the bill was passed by the House of Commons, he returned to the Bishop's Palace and wrote to Taché: "We have only to say that we have done what we could for the welfare and advantage of the people of the new province of Manitoba. We have spent about seventy-five hours in discussion with Sir George and Sir Joseph [Howe?] to conclude this important business; both gentlemen were delegated by the ministry to hear us. . . ."[35] To Bunn he sent a telegram: "The Manitoba Act is sanctioned. It is satisfactory."[36]

But Ritchot was not yet ready to return home. He had "several matters of detail" to settle first. There were those pressing questions about the amnesty, and about the government's intentions with regard to the military force being prepared for service in the North-West. On May 18, Ritchot wrote to Cartier: "The questions raised by the 19th clause of our instructions are of the highest importance, I trust Sir, and the past is my warrant for the future, that you will be able to secure us, before our departure, all the guarantees promised by Sir John and you in relation to these highly important questions."[37] On the following day, Cartier took Ritchot with him to Rideau Hall. The Governor-General declared that the people of Red River had "nothing to fear," once more referring to his Proclamation of December 6. When Ritchot reminded His Excellency that "I had never been willing to accept that proclamation as sufficient to satisfy our population" the Governor-General replied that a document from Great Britain would be forthcoming soon and that in any case it would arrive before the Governor in Red River.[38] This was all the satisfaction Ritchot could get out of Sir John Young, and Cartier's letter of May 23 was no more satisfactory. Cartier merely wrote reminding Ritchot of the interview with the Governor-General "at which I was present," and during which "His Excellency was pleased to state the liberal policy which the Government proposed to follow in relation to the persons for whom you are interesting yourself. . . ."[39] With this letter he sent a draft petition to the Queen which he asked Ritchot to sign. This was, Cartier assured the priest, "a mere matter of form . . . a means of bringing the negotiations for a proclamation of amnesty to a successful close." "If the Government had not wished to support it," said Sir George, "they would not have drafted it." Ritchot signed the document and it was forwarded to Young for despatch to London.[40] For several days, from May 15 to May 28, Ritchot continued to importune Cartier. He was nothing if not persistent. But he did not receive anything in black and white, only the same assurances that he had heard time and again, interspersed with admonitions to "be quiet and not rack my head about anything; that the men with whom I was dealing knew something about business."[41] Cartier was becoming impatient with these pressing solicitations. In order to rid himself of this troublesome priest, he told him, in answer to a query as to "who was to govern the country, pending the arrival of the Lieutenant-Governor," "let Mr. Riel continue to maintain order and govern the country, as he has done up to the present moment."[42]

It was the same with the military expedition. The suggestion that troops might be sent to Red River had been mulled over by the members of the government for months. As early as August, 1869, G. T. Denison had written to Mair to say he had heard that his own name had been mentioned in connection with "a corps of Mounted Rifles which it was thought might be necessary to organize for the protection of the Red River Territory as well as for the maintenance of order in it."[43] It was only a rumour, and McDougall went to Pembina with the rifles but not the riflemen. At the end of October, McDougall wrote to Macdonald urging the despatch of a military force. A week later, with complete disregard for the political realities of the situation, he suggested that Canadian troops might be concentrated in Minnesota.[44] Others, like Colonel G. J. Wolseley, were also talking about a military expedition. Macdonald, while agreeing with the idea of a show of force in Red River, had in mind not Canadian but Imperial troops. However, for the moment at least, the Imperial authorities were indisposed to allow British soldiers to be used to relieve the Canadian government of the political problems they had contracted. Not until March 5 did London agree to Macdonald's proposal, and then only "if reasonable terms were given to the Roman Catholic settlers" and if the Canadian government would complete the terms of the transfer with the Hudson's Bay Company "simultaneous" with the movement of the troops.[45] Obviously there was to be no coercion.

Unfortunately, owing to the excitement over the sad fate of Thomas Scott, the military expedition became entangled with the political controversy that surrounded the unfortunate event. Ontario demanded that soldiers be sent to the West at once; Quebec demanded that the military expedition be abandoned altogether. Taché had told Howe on March 11 that the despatch of troops to Red River would inevitably hinder the work of pacifying the Settlement;[46] but Denison and other Canada First men were loud in their protests that to abandon the expedition would be a sign of weakness and vacillation. In the exchange of opinions, no doubt the Canada First group had louder voices, more emotional appeals and stronger political influence. They spread, where they did not start, stories of how poor Scott had not been killed outright by the firing squad but had died a terrible death of pain and suffering in his coffin;[47] of how some Canadians had dipped their handkerchiefs in the blood of the dying man, while one had managed to secure a small vial of his blood.[48] John Schultz managed to secure a piece of rope which he alleged had been used to bind Scott's wrists, and he sent it to Denison with the instructions: "Use it at Indignation meetings and then present it to the Master of the Orange Lodge, or make any disposition you may choose to make of it, as say, sending it to Cartier . . . with a request that Riel's hands be tied with it before he is hung."[49] Tactics such as these, supplemented by stories and rumours, most of which were either exaggerations or without substance, added fuel to the fire that Canada First had lighted in Ontario. What security, demanded Denison, could there be for Canadians in Red River, after the murder of Scott and the official recognition of his murderers by the federal government, if the military expedition should be withdrawn?[50] Inflammatory placards in large type were posted on fences and walls throughout Toronto: "Shall French rebels rule our Dominion?" "Orangemen, is Brother Scott forgotten already?" "Men of Ontario, shall Scott's blood cry in vain for vengeance?" Schultz suggested that a movement should be started for the erection of a monument to Scott in Winnipeg. "I think," he wrote, "if matters started in Toronto and circulars were sent to the wardens of every Ontario county that subscriptions limited to one penny would do the whole business well." He also urged Denison to keep up the pressure, "It will be well not to let the matter die out altogether. Mair is at Montreal—Setter at Bath—Garratt and McArthur left here today for Toronto. Garratt is going to lecture and get up emigration—Good idea—Lynch and I go to Montreal tonight."[51] There were to be more meetings in Kingston, Hamilton and Brantford.

An agitation of this nature could not be ignored or shrugged off as merely the excitement of the moment. Neither Denison nor Schultz would let it subside, and the government had to remember that there was another election coming. Regardless of what Cartier might say or think, Macdonald and the other Ontario members of the Cabinet had to do something to satisfy the agitators, and the latter had made it clear that they would be content with nothing less than the use of force against the "rebels." And so there was a compromise. To satisfy Cartier and the French Canadians, the government agreed to negotiate with Ritchot, Black and Scott; and to mollify the aroused electorate in Ontario, the military expedition was organized. But it would not be a punitive expedition. Wolseley and the troops would, as the Governor-General put it in his speech closing Parliament on May 11: "go forth on an errand of peace, and will serve as an assurance to the inhabitants of the Red River Settlement and the numerous Indian tribes that occupy the North-West, that they have a place in the regard and counsels of England, and may rely upon the impartial protection of the British sceptre."[52] With this Ritchot had to be content.

There is no doubt that Cartier and the French-Canadians who told Ritchot that they "approve the sending of an expedition" honestly believed Wolseley's battalions were bound for the west on nothing more than a minor police action, and that there would be no cause for any alarms in Red River. There is no doubt, either, that Cartier was sincere in the assurances he gave Ritchot in connection with the amnesty. But it is equally beyond doubt that Cartier overestimated his own strength in the Canadian Cabinet, as much as he underestimated the impact that the agitation in Ontario would make upon his colleagues, even upon the Governor-General. When he penned a lengthy memorandum to Sir John Young on June 8, outlining the events in Red River, analyzing the causes of the métis disturbances and recommending that an amnesty should be granted by the Queen that would "except no one,"[53] he believed it would be forthcoming. He did not know that, when Young forwarded this memorandum to the Colonial Office, he carefully robbed it of its force by drawing Granville's attention to the fact that, while it was

Louis Riel and his Associates, 1869

Top Row CHARLES LAROCQUE, PIERRE DELORME, THOMAS BUNN, XAVIER PAGÉE, AMBROISE LÉPINE, BAPTISTE TOUROND, THOMAS SPENCE

Centre Row PIERRE POITRAS, JOHN BRUCE, LOUIS RIEL, W. B. O'DONOGHUE, FRANÇOIS DAUPHINAIS

Front Row H. F. O'LONE, PAUL PROULX

Thomas Scott

"entitled to all the consideration due to the writer's long experience and high political standing in British North America," it was "not to be regarded as a Minute of Council nor as the expression of the opinion of the united Cabinet."[54] Nor was he aware that the Governor-General was prepared to follow up this memorandum with a petition from Dr. Lynch in which it was stated that an amnesty would be "injudicious, impolitic and dangerous" if it were to include the leaders of the rebellion, and threatened that those "who have seen their comrade and fellow prisoner led out and butchered in cold blood" might "in that wild spirit of justice called vengeance take the life of Riel or some other of the leaders."[55] Nor did he know that the Governor-General would forward Lynch's petition to London without any explanation regarding its authorship or any qualifications such as he had seen fit to append to Cartier's recommendations.[56] These were things that Cartier did not realize when Ritchot finally turned his face towards Red River early in June. His last words to the priest were still words of confidence, "You are too particular, you have as much as you can desire, and you will see that Riel will be satisfied."[57]

III

On Friday, June 17, Ritchot arrived back in Fort Garry. Almost immediately he was in conference with Louis Riel. Riel had been alarmed at the long delays, at the stories of soldiers thirsting for vengeance and at the absence of any formal document announcing a general amnesty. He was anxious, too, to hear the details of the Manitoba Act. Ritchot repeated the assurances he had heard so frequently in Ottawa: the military expedition was a friendly one; the amnesty would soon be forthcoming from the Queen in England. Riel professed himself satisfied. On the 18th, Ritchot wrote to Cartier that the Manitoba Act had been "well received" and that Louis Riel, just as Cartier had predicted, was "satisfied with it." He then promised that the new Lieutenant-Governor would meet with "a cordial and sympathetic reception" and suggested that it might be well to hasten his arrival by sending him to Fort Garry by way of St. Paul. If necessary, the Provisional Government would send someone "as far as Ottawa to meet him." Then he added:

The setting out of the troops before arrangements were completed is displeasing to the people; however, the explanations which I have given on this point, and the assurances they are coming for a pacific and useful purpose satisfies them. We have even a wish to send a certain number of half-breeds to meet them, in order to introduce them within the country. I am convinced that all will go well, provided always that the amnesty reaches us in good season[58].

Word quickly spread through the Settlement that Riel was happy about the results of the negotiations, and Alexander Begg noted in his journal: "A general feeling of satisfaction is felt at the successful result of Père Ritchot's mission to Canada—and now there is little fear of any further trouble existing here."[59]

On June 24, one week to the day after Ritchot's return, the Legislative Assembly of Assiniboia met in Fort Garry. It was a warm and sultry day, and the mosquitoes were "very bad," particularly at night. But mosquitoes or no mosquitoes, the members were anxious to hear Ritchot's official statement. Riel, as president of the session, spoke only briefly. He congratulated Ritchot and his associates "on the issue of their labours, performed under circumstances of danger such as only the protecting arm of Heaven could bring them through with safety."[60] Then Ritchot took the floor. He spoke in French, and Louis Riel translated his remarks into English. He told the Assembly that he and his fellow delegates had been well treated, even if they had been subjected to certain "indignities." He assured the members the Canadian government had given formal recognition to the delegation from the North-West. He outlined the steps by which an understanding had been arrived at, and he discussed the main terms of the Manitoba Act. Finally he turned to the question of the amnesty; it was a question vital to more than one man who sat in the council room that late afternoon. Ritchot declared categorically that he had insisted upon the amnesty as a *sine qua non* of any agreement; but that the Canadian government had been compelled to admit that, because it would have no authority over the people of Red River until the official proclamation of the transfer on July 15, the amnesty would have to be a matter for the British Crown rather than the Canadian authorities. He told them of his talks with the Governor-General and with the British special representative, Sir Clinton Murdoch; and then he concluded his speech with some kind remarks about the people of Canada:

I found them very kind, generous and fair, and they did not, as a rule, take the same view of matters which some papers had done. They looked at the occurrences of last winter in the proper light; and, while censuring where they thought it deserved, they did not blame the people, and they thought they were in peculiar circumstances. And, as to the action of the Government, it was felt that as it had been attacked, and had to defend itself, no other set of men could, perhaps, have done less under the circumstances.[61]

Ritchot's speech was greeted with cheers. But those who cheered probably did not realize that Ritchot's experience of Canadians had been

limited almost entirely to those of French and Irish origin. He knew
little of the climate of opinion in Ontario.

   Then Riel asked the Assembly to express its views on the Manitoba
Act.   There was no need for any long discussion about it.   When Louis
Schmidt moved that "the Legislative Assembly of this country do now,
in the name of the people, accept the Manitoba Act," Pierre Poitras
quickly seconded the motion. As it was carried, *The New Nation*
reported, the members cheered enthusiastically. Then there was a
motion "that we welcome the new Governor on his arrival."   It, too,
was carried with cheers. Finally Riel closed the session with these
words:

We must not expect to exhaust the subject.   If we have the happiness
soon to meet the new Lieutenant-Governor, we will have time and
opportunity enough to express our feelings.   For the present let me say
only one thing—I congratulate the people of the North-West on the
happy issue of their undertakings.   I congratulate them on having trust
enough in the Crown of England to believe that ultimately they would
obtain their rights.   I must, too, congratulate the country on passing
from under this provisional rule to one of a more permanent and satisfactory character.   From all that can be learned, also, there is great room
for congratulation in the selection of Lieutenant-Governor which has
been made.   For myself, it will be my duty and pleasure, more than any
other, to bid the new governor welcome on his arrival.   I would like to
be the first to pay him the respect due to his position as Representative
of the Crown.   Something yet remains to be done.   Many people are
yet anxious and doubtful.   Let us still pursue the work in which we have
been lately engaged, the cultivation of peace and friendship, and doing
what can be done to convince these people that we never designed to
wrong them but that what has been done was as much in their interest
as our own.[62]

That evening Begg noted in his journal, "This 24th day of June therefore
is the turning point in the affairs of the Settlement."   Others preferred
to mark the significance of the day in another fashion, as is shown by
Begg's subsequent entry, "Some of the members of the Legislative
Assembly got drunk tonight at George Emmerling's in honour of the
occasion."[63]

   Riel was pleased with himself, and he had reason to be.   A novice in
the game of politics, he had played his role with strength and with not a
little skill.   He had achieved nearly everything he had set out to do.
He held the uncritical adoration of his supporters and the grudging
respect of most of his opponents.   He had brought a new province into
being, the Province of Manitoba.   It was in no hypocritical vein that
he wrote to Bannatyne: "We will bring in Red River a responsible
government.   Such a young country having gained and possessing such

a complete franchise. . . . You are right, better days will come, because nothing violent can last, because every man is under the intelligent care of the Might from above."[64]   Greater men than he had seen the hand of God in their personal achievements.

The Bishop of St. Boniface, however, was less enthusiastic than Riel. He was perturbed that Ritchot had brought back with him no piece of paper, only verbal assurances of an amnesty.   Priests and lawyers have a tendency to insist on the utmost to which they are legally entitled— perhaps because of their awareness of man's fundamental dishonesty. In Taché's case this was probably because of his knowledge of the ease with which politicians can make promises and then forget them.   Taché firmly believed he had been given the power to promise an amnesty in the name of the Canadian government when he had been in Ottawa conferring with Cartier.   Now Ritchot was telling him that the amnesty was beyond the power of the Canadian government to grant, that it was a matter for London, not for Ottawa.   This contradiction would have to be straightened out, if only that Taché might clear himself of any charges of deliberate misrepresentation on his part.   And so, before the echoes of the cheers with which the Assembly had greeted the Manitoba Act had died away, the Bishop was preparing to return to Canada to see if he could not get something in writing about the amnesty, and to do what he could to ensure the establishment of civil government before Wolseley's troops reached Fort Garry.

On his arrival in Ottawa, Taché went immediately to see Sir George Cartier.   According to the Bishop, Cartier verified everything that Ritchot had said.   The Canadian minister repeated, "The thing has not changed.   We are waiting for the proclamation every day, and if you remain for a few weeks, it will arrive before you leave."[65]   Then he urged Taché to come with him to see Sir John Young at Niagara.   Along with A. G. Archibald, the Lieutenant-Governor elect who was on his way to be sworn in to his new office, Cartier and Taché travelled to Prescott where they took the steamer bound for Toronto.   At Kingston, Cartier received disturbing news.   There was "great excitement" in Toronto and the people were planning "to insult" Cartier because he was travelling "with the traitor, Bishop Taché."   Cartier was prepared to go ahead; but Taché wanted to avoid violence and agreed to stop at Oswego and travel by train to Buffalo.   Cartier was relieved.   He "looked uneasy," said Taché, and "told me indignation meetings had taken place in Toronto and had given His Excellency a good deal of uneasiness."[66]

Both Sir John Young and Sir George had every reason to be uneasy. John Schultz had heard that the Bishop and the minister were on their way to Niagara and had told Denison.[67]   Immediately Denison went to work. He went to see Lieutenant-Colonel Durie, the District Adjutant-General, and told him that if he were planning to muster a guard of honour to protect Sir George and Taché and to "intimidate" the people of Toronto, then "we would take possession of the armoury that night, and that we would have ten men to his one, and if anyone in Toronto wanted to fight it out, we were ready to fight it out on the streets." When Durie accused Denison of threatening revolution, the latter replied, "Yes, I know I am, and we can make it one. A half a continent is at stake, and it is a stake worth fighting for."[68]

But Denison found that threats were sufficient. Placards were posted everywhere, and a huge meeting was arranged to be held in St. Lawrence Hall. Strong words were used, and Cartier was denounced as a rebel. Denison himself shouted to the enthusiastic audience:

Bishop Taché had offered to place the Governor-General in possession of British territory. Was our Governor-General to receive possession of the North-West Territory from him? No! There were young men from Ontario under that splendid officer Colonel Wolseley who would place the Queen's Representative in power in that country in spite of Bishop Taché and without his assistance. We will have that country in spite of traitors in the Cabinet, and in spite of a rebel Minister of Militia.

He continued, "Cartier was a traitor in 1837. He was often called a loyal man, but we could buy all their loyalty at the same price of putting our necks under their heels and petting them continually."[69] Then several resolutions were adopted declaring that any effort to abandon the military expedition "now on its way to Fort Garry to establish law and order" would be "an act of supreme folly, an abdication of authority, destructive of all confidence in the protection afforded to loyal subjects by a constitutional Government—a death-blow to our national honour. . . ."[70]

Was it wholly surprising, when Taché rejoined Cartier in Hamilton, that the Governor-General appeared rather reluctant to talk about the amnesty or about the military expedition? He had had his fill of both these subjects in his interviews with Ritchot, and now here was another black-robed priest knocking on his door. Although he could not afford to admit it, he had no sympathy with them or with their impossible demands for an amnesty. Thus, when Taché waited upon him, Young treated the Bishop with a chilliness bordering upon discourtesy. "Here is my proclamation," he said, pointing to the familiar document which he had signed on December 6, "it covers the whole case." Then he added, "See Sir George Cartier; he knows my views upon the subject, and he will tell you all."[71] Returning to Cartier, Taché pointed out the

inadequacy of the Proclamation of December 6 and the need for something more, especially in view of newspaper reports that there would be no
amnesty after all.   But Cartier had done all that he could do; there was
nothing he could add to what he had already told Ritchot.   Despite the
Governor-General's statement, Cartier did not, in fact, know what Sir
John Young's views really were.

Even Taché's efforts to hurry Archibald's arrival in Red River ahead
of the troops were nullified by the agitators.   The Bishop soon found
that there would be no chance of having the expedition cancelled—not
that he really felt that this would be desirable.   On the contrary, he was
disposed to favour the posting of an Imperial garrison at Red River if
only as a means of discouraging acts of personal vengeance.[72]   But what
he did hope to get was an agreement on the part of the Canadian government to send the Lieutenant-Governor to Red River by the quickest
possible route through the United States.   This, however, was politically
inadvisable.   Archibald had to reach Fort Garry by way of Canada.
All that could be done would be for Taché to persuade Archibald to
travel to the North-West Angle of Lake of the Woods and there meet a
métis delegation who would hurry him into the Settlement by way of
Mr. Snow's road.   "Do not worry," he wrote to Riel, "time and faith
will bring us all we desire, and more, although it is not possible to
mention it at this time owing to the hot-headedness of certain people."[73]

IV

In Red River Riel was waiting and watching.   He was very anxious.
Everything seemed to be confusing and uncertain.   On the one hand,
there were Ritchot and Taché both claiming that an amnesty had been
promised and that it would be forthcoming before the arrival of the
soldiers; on the other, there were the constant reports in the Ontario
newspapers that there would be no amnesty. At his shoulder,
O'Donoghue was continually telling Riel that he could not rely on any
of the promises that had been made to him, that no reliance could be
placed in anything that a Canadian politician said, that when the troops
arrived they would take over the country and hang the ringleaders of the
rising.[74]   Could even O'Donoghue be trusted?   Was he not simply
trying, like Stutsman, to create a situation which would appear to justify
American intervention?

The trouble was there were just a few grains of truth in what
O'Donoghue was saying.   Fred Denison, one of Wolseley's staff, wrote
to his brother in July, "If Riel stays in the country he is more plucky
than I take him to be, it will be a risky business for him.   There are
some here I am told who threaten to deal him the direst vengeance."[75]

He added, if an amnesty is granted "it will be only one more example that it pays much better in this country to be a rebel than to be loyal." Riel knew, too, that there were Canadians in the Settlement, those who had been quiescent since the shooting of Scott, who entertained "the hope that as soon as the troops arrive, martial law will be proclaimed, to be followed by the hanging of a few of the French party."[76] Always there was this threat to his life. Even some of his enemies among the French métis were becoming vocal again.[77] Schultz and Mair were both on their way back to the Settlement. "We are now in a position to revive the *Nor'Wester*," wrote Schultz from Thunder Bay to his friend George Denison, "and to print moral sentiments or anything you damn please."[78]

For a short time Riel toyed with the idea of resistance.[79] He could fight it out along the banks of the Winnipeg River or in the wilds of Lake of the Woods. All he would need would be a small number of determined men. But where could he find the determined men? Neither the Scotch nor the English half-breeds would fight. And the fighting men among the métis were on the plains or on the rivers to the north. No, he would not fight. He would follow Cartier's advice that "the Canadian half-breeds must show themselves more loyal than any."[80] He would be "the first to welcome" Archibald, and he would invite the settlers to prepare a reception for him. O'Donoghue and the Americans might object; they might call him names, but he would "watch them closely."[81] On July 22, he personally superintended the printing and circulation of a proclamation which had been issued by Colonel Wolseley declaring that the military expedition was "one of peace," that the troops represented "no party either in Religion or Politics" and that "equal protection" would be given "to the lives and property of all races and of all creeds."[82] This was what Ritchot had said and what Howe had told Taché. On the 24th, he wrote to the Bishop, "We are making preparations for the arrival of the Governor. We shall endeavour to show him as many horsemen as possible." Then he added, "How severe a task have you not imposed upon yourself in going to that wicked Ottawa. . . . The only consolation to be found is to be a Christian, and to believe that no real harm can happen us so long as God is on our side."[83]

During the next few weeks Riel's actions were marked by indecision. He did not seem to know what to do. He would make a plan of how he should receive the Governor, and then he would abandon it at the slightest show of opposition. He even neglected to send the promised escort to meet Archibald at the North-West Angle. "He is played out and has no friends," wrote one of the Americans in Winnipeg to Enos Stutsman. "His day is gone, and if he does attempt to do anything, he will have to

rely on himself."[84] He would indeed. The precarious union of the
Settlement seemed to be breaking up while he waited. Even some of his
own followers appeared inclined towards O'Donoghue. Riel knew that
the troops were approaching. He knew when they were at Rainy Lake;
when they reached Lake of the Woods; when they entered the Winnipeg
River. Outwardly calm but inwardly harassed he wondered what was
going to happen. Was there any truth in the rumours that his own life
was in danger? Where was the amnesty? Where was Lieutenant-
Governor Archibald? Where was Bishop Taché?

Finally, on August 23, the Bishop returned to St. Boniface. Immediately Riel and several members of his council hurried across the river.
Did the Bishop have any news about the amnesty? "I represented to
them that there was not the slightest danger to them," said Taché later,
"that my conversations with the civil and military authorities had
convinced me that there was not the slighest danger, in fact that the
19th clause of the articles submitted by Father Ritchot and the other
delegates had been accepted."[85] While they were still talking, a messenger arrived to tell Riel that the troops had reached the mouth of the
Red River at Lake Winnipeg. Taché could hardly believe it. What
had happened to Archibald, and what about the plans to establish the
civil government before they reached Fort Garry? Then came another
messenger. The troops were even closer; they had passed the Stone
Fort only twenty miles away.

The evening of the 23rd was one of extreme anxiety for Riel.[86] He
met some of his councillors. He talked briefly and discursively with
them and with Marc Girard, and Joseph Royal, and with his old schoolmate, Joseph Dubuc, who had come to Red River during the summer at
the request of Bishop Taché. But he did no more than suggest that those
of his council who had any papers or effects in the fort should remove
them. Then, posting a few guards at the gate to prevent the Canadians
from trying to seize the fort in advance of the arrival of the troops, he
went out with several companions to see what he could for himself.
There was not much to be seen. It was raining heavily and it was with
difficulty that Riel kept his own companions within view. Finally, in
the vicinity of Seven Oaks, where the métis had gained their victory over
Semple in 1816, he saw the flickering lights of Wolseley's campfires. He
pushed a little closer; close enough to see the fires themselves. The
horses were snorting continually, and Riel became apprehensive lest his
presence be discovered. Then he returned to the fort about 1 A.M.
He threw off his wet overcoat and moccasins, drew his blankets around
him and went to sleep. At dawn he awoke and ordered a breakfast of

cold meat. He was hungry. But the cold, the lack of sleep and the anxiety left him feeling lifeless and weary.

Colonel Wolseley had planned to reach Fort Garry on the 23rd.[87] He did not manage to do this owing to the heavy, drenching rain that made progress much too slow for the impatient commander. As a matter of fact, the whole expedition had been marked by delays. First there had been the vacillation of the Minister of Militia; then the trouble with the Americans at Sault Ste. Marie; and the time lost in building a road from Prince Arthur's Landing to Lake Shebandowan; and the many portages, and the muskegs, and the insects and the dysentery. And now, only six miles from Fort Garry, this torrential rain, and the "sea of deep clinging mud" which covered the plain. It would, at least, cloak his advance from métis spies. Perhaps he could take the fort by surprise the next day. On the 24th, the troops—they were British regulars, men of the 60th Rifles—clambered into their boats and rowed up the Red River as far as Point Douglas. Now they were only two miles from the fort. They could see the dull, shabby town of Winnipeg and behind it, through the mist, the grey walls of Fort Garry. Struggling through the mud, they continued their advance. Why were there no cheering crowds to welcome them? What did that wily Riel have up his sleeve? Every moment they expected the guns from Fort Garry, which they could now see quite clearly, to open fire upon them. Finally Wolseley sent several officers to reconnoitre. They returned with the news that "Riel had bolted and that the fort gates were open." "It was a sad disappointment to all ranks," wrote Wolseley, who seems to have forgotten that his was a mission of peace. "Personally, I was glad that Riel did not come out and surrender, as he at one time said he would, for I could not then have hanged him as I might have done had I taken him prisoner when in arms against his sovereign."[88]

It was true. Riel had fled. A horseman, a Hudson's Bay Company man, had ridden hard that morning from Kildonan. He had rushed into Riel's room and had cried, "For the love of God, clear out, the troops are only two miles from the city and you are going to be lynched."[89] As he looked over the prairie Riel could just see the hazy figures of the riflemen as they moved forward through the mist. This, then, was how it was to end. There would be no need for him to clean the breakfast dishes; no need to hoist the British flag; no need to tune the instruments of Father Dugast's band from the school at St. Boniface . . . only the need to save his life from the vengeance of his enemies. He was filled with anger and with bitterness. Accompanied by O'Donoghue and two of his supporters, he slipped through the gate of the fort, crossed the Red River, and went straight to the Bishop's house. "You have left the

Fort," said Taché in surprise. "Yes," replied Riel, "we have fled because it appears that we have been deceived." "Why?" asked the Bishop. Riel answered, "Because no later than last evening we were told by Your Lordship that there was no fear. . . . Rather than run the risk of being killed or murdered we prefer to leave the fort. . . ."[90] Then he turned and walked out while Taché stood gazing at Wolseley's soldiers as they rushed into Fort Garry, ran up the Union Jack and fired a salute from the cannon on the square.[91]

With his two companions, Riel set out for St. Vital, where his mother lived. As he cast a glance behind him at the cheering figures in Fort Garry, he said quietly, "No matter what happens now, the rights of the métis are assured by the Manitoba Act; that is what I wanted—My mission is finished."[92]

CHAPTER 9

O'Donoghue

WHEN he left Bishop Taché's house in St. Boniface with O'Donoghue and Lépine, it was Louis Riel's intention to go first to St. Vital to see his mother. But he could not remain long at St. Vital. His life was in danger and he would have to leave almost immediately for Pembina. Only in the United States would he be able to find shelter and safety. He could stay there with friends until the storm blew over.

Louis Riel's flight to the United States was marked by one mishap after another. During the first night, while the three fugitives slept, their horses wandered away, and in the morning they had to resume the journey on foot. Then, believing they would make better progress on the west side of the river, they ripped apart a rail fence, bound the logs together with strips torn from their clothing, and with this makeshift raft reached the other side. But in the process Riel lost one of his shoes and he had to continue barefoot.[1] In this forlorn condition—their clothing in shreds, their feet swollen, cold, hungry and thoroughly miserable— they finally reached Louis Bottineau's house on August 27. Here they were offered hospitality and the loan of some horses. But Riel wanted to go farther. He would accept only a pair of shoes. Then he continued his flight, guided through the woods by Antoine Gladu of St. Joseph's.[2]

At last he reached the Reverend Father LeFloch's house. Here he knew he would find rest and sustenance with the man at whose feet he had learned the rudiments of Latin in those far-off days of 1857 and 1858. Gladu then hurried back to St. Norbert to tell Louis's sister Sara, the nun at St. Norbert, of her brother's safe arrival. Riel was "very tired," said Gladu, but he was not "depressed," only "worried" about the future. No, he would not return to the Settlement before the arrival of the Lieutenant-Governor, "nor before matters are arranged. . . ."[3] At St. Vital, Julie Lagimodière prayed for her son: "my poor boy—my little Louis! He is everything to me, he is my life." "Only a mother's heart can understand how much she loves you,"[4] wrote Sara to her brother.

On September 6, Bishop Taché wrote to his former protégé. He told Riel of the unsatisfactory state of affairs in the Settlement and urged him to be calm and patient.   Archibald had arrived without the promised amnesty; it would be better for the former president of the Provisional Government, for his family and for the métis, if he remained where he was.   "Too much haste can lead to disaster . . . time alone will help us; patience then, God will surely not abandon us."[5]   Louis replied at once.   He was patient: he would be careful.   "My life belongs to God," he wrote.   "Let Him do what He wishes with it."[6]   But he was afraid. There were "assassins" skulking in the vicinity; they were probably "some of Schultz's followers."   "If they catch me, please pray for my soul," he begged the Bishop.[7]   For the time being he was prepared to stay at Father LeFloch's house, although from time to time he slept elsewhere in order to foil his would-be murderers.   Perhaps because he was afraid, he turned to his religion for strength.   It always meant so much to him when he was a boy; perhaps in recent months he had been disposed to rely too much on his faith in himself and not enough on his faith in God.   So he made a retreat while living with LeFloch.   The priest wrote to the Bishop, "I have been very pleased with him.   I shall even say that I admire him.   Sometimes his pride takes over, but he is easily calmed.   He is now in an excellent state of mind.   He does not want to start anything, he will await developments. . . ."[8]

But LeFloch was too much impressed by Riel's show of piety, sincere as it may have been.   The period of religious surrender would pass, and politics would again become Riel's dominant passion.   He once had a sip of political power, and its effects had been intoxicating.   It was not Riel's temperament to remain patient very long—especially as he was surrounded by an excited and excitable group of métis, anxious to avenge the wrongs done their chief; and with O'Donoghue at Pembina, trying hard to keep the political pot boiling, and encouraging the métis there to look to him, rather than to Riel, for leadership.   Riel had already quarrelled with the young Irishman during the summer and did not trust him.   He suspected O'Donoghue of being less interested in the métis and more in promoting American annexation,[9] and believed that O'Donoghue would do everything he could to undermine Riel's leadership while posing as the defender of métis rights.   Even during the flight from Fort Garry when both of them were fugitives, the two men had quarrelled, and O'Donoghue had gone straight to Pembina to join Stutsman and Rolette, while Riel had gone to St. Joseph's.   Riel was not unaware of O'Donoghue's intrigues for the leadership of the métis, and of his references to Riel as a coward and a traitor.   When they met at Charles Grant's, O'Donoghue hurled the charge in Riel's face and struck him a blow, challenging him to fight.[10]

II

Far more serious than O'Donoghue's intrigues were the reports that reached Riel from Red River. It was clear that the situation in Red River was not a happy one. With the leaders of the Provisional Government in flight, and the other members of the Provisional Legislature anxious to remain in obscurity, no organized government of any kind existed in the colony when Wolseley's troops entered Fort Garry. Wolseley himself had been given no civil powers, since everyone had expected that Archibald would already be in the Settlement by the time the soldiers got there. Unwilling to impose martial law, Wolseley asked Donald A. Smith, as the representative of the Hudson's Bay Company, to assume responsibility until the Governor's arrival and act as a *de facto* Governor. Smith did so with reluctance.[11] When Archibald finally appeared on September 2, Smith surrendered his powers to the Lieutenant-Governor. "I yield up my responsibilities with pleasure," Smith declared. "Yes," replied the Governor, "I really do not anticipate much pleasure on my own account."[12]

The first few weeks after Riel's flight were weeks of lawlessness and debauchery. The soldiers in Red River, particularly in Winnipeg, released from the enforced sobriety of the semi-military, semi-voyageur life they had led since they left Collingwood in May, broke loose. They flocked to Monchamp's and Dutch George's saloons. They were joined by the voyageurs and the civilians who had followed in their wake. Soon the streets were filled with quarrelling, fighting men in all stages of drunkenness. The Reverend George Young, who watched with a disapproving eye, wrote: "It was most distressing for me to see, on that first night especially, so many of these men—soldiers, voyageurs and Indians—who had abstained from all intoxicants so advantageously to themselves and the entire force, now so crazed with the vile stuff they were buying at very high rates from these abominable rum-shops, as to be actually rolling and fighting in the miry mudholes of Winnipeg."[13]

By organizing a strong picket, it was possible for Wolseley to quiet the regulars, but he had no control over the civilians, Canadians bent upon revenge, men from Ontario who were moved by racial and religious bigotry. When the militia battalions took over from the British regulars, a period of bullying and maltreating the métis started that was little short of deliberate persecution. A number of militiamen had enlisted for no other reason than to revenge the death of Scott—this had been the effect of Denison's and Schultz's agitation. They looked with bitterness on all half-breeds as men who had imprisoned and murdered their countrymen. According to Lieutenant-Governor Archibald:

With some (I cannot say how many) of the volunteers who went up, a desire to avenge the murder of Scott was one of the inducements to enlist. Some of them openly stated that they had taken a vow before leaving home to pay off all scores by shooting down any Frenchman that was in any way connected with that event. The great bulk of the French population having been, one way or other, concerned in the troubles, the feeling gradually grew to be one of intense dislike towards the whole race, which was heartily reciprocated by the French.[14]

The Governor tried to calm the excited spirits on both sides by following a policy that was both moderate and conciliatory; and when the initial excesses were over, the majority of the English-speaking settlers were prepared to support him and to look to the future rather than back to the past. But there was a small minority, led by John Schultz, who could neither forget the defeats of the past months nor regard their former enemies with forbearance. This minority, active, aggressive, relentless, caused Archibald to write in confidence to the Prime Minister, Sir John A. Macdonald: "Unfortunately there is a frightful spirit of bigotry among a small but noisy section of our people. The main body of the people have no such feeling—they would be only too happy to return to the original state of good neighbourhood with each other; but it is otherwise with the people I speak of, who really talk and seem to feel as if the French half-breeds should be wiped off the face of the globe."[15]

On September 13, one of Riel's most active supporters, Elzéar Goulet, ventured into the streets of Winnipeg. He was a brother of Roger Goulet, a highly respected half-breed who had been a magistrate under the Hudson's Bay Company and a member of the Council of Assiniboia. But he had been a member of the court-martial that had condemned Thomas Scott. It was not long before he was recognized and pointed out to several soldiers who happened to be nearby. Two soldiers and one of the civilians took after Goulet who immediately turned and ran for his life. Reaching the bank of the river he plunged in to swim to St. Boniface. Stones were hurled at him from the shore. It may have been that Goulet was a poor swimmer; more likely it was that he was hit on the head with a rock. In any event, Goulet sank beneath the waters and drowned.[16] The next day his body was recovered from the muddy river and buried. In the absence of the coroner, an investigation was carried out by two magistrates, Robert MacBeth and Salomon Hamelin. They heard the evidence—although with some difficulty, because of Hamelin's unfamiliarity with English and MacBeth's inadequate knowledge of French—but they managed to fix the responsibility.

Feelings were, however, running high in Winnipeg, and it was considered advisable not to make any arrests or proceed with any prosecution.[17]

There were other deaths, beatings and threats.   François Guillemette, who had administered the *coup de grâce* to Scott, was killed near Pembina by persons never identified but believed by the métis to be vengeful Canadians; Bob O'Lone, part owner of the Red Saloon, was killed in a bar-room brawl; James Tanner was killed when his horses were startled by an object hurled at them in the dark; André Nault was beaten and left for dead.   Father Kavanaugh, who had actually been very critical of Louis Riel,[18] barely escaped assassination at the White Horse Plains. Thomas Spence, who had edited *The New Nation* after it had been taken from American hands, was also assaulted.   Riel himself was too carefully guarded by his friends to be caught, but a warrant had been issued by Donald A. Smith, while acting as *de facto* Governor, and there were plenty of men who were willing to serve it, especially after John Schultz's father-in-law offered a reward of twenty pounds for Riel's capture.[19] Like Taché the métis looked upon these as "sombre days" in Red River.[20]

More than anything else, it was the death of Elzéar Goulet that aroused the exasperated métis.[21]   And it was to them that O'Donoghue addressed his crafty appeals.   He had much in his favour.   Was it not O'Donoghue who had urged them to resist Wolseley when his troops were struggling through the water wilderness of Lake of the Woods?   Was it not O'Donoghue who had warned Riel not to believe the promises of Taché and Ritchot; was it not O'Donoghue who had prophesied the treachery of the Canadian government?   But first he would try to work through Riel; and he and Lépine therefore conferred with Riel at the latter's hiding place at Pointe-à-Michel near St. Joseph's.   Between them they agreed to call a meeting at St. Norbert.[22]   It had been here, almost a year earlier, that the National Committee had been organized.   Perhaps the Committee might be revived and steps taken to defend the métis from the persecution they were suffering at the hands of the victorious Canadians.

The meeting was held on September 17 and was attended by some forty French half-breeds.[23]   Riel acted as president and as usual took the lead.   He condemned the "perfidious treachery" of the Canadian government; its arrest of the Red River delegates, after expressly inviting them to go to Ottawa; its failure to implement the promises that had been made to Taché and Ritchot; and the many "outrages" committed against "our unoffending people."   Then Riel and O'Donoghue drew up a "Memorial and Petition."   It was to be sent to the President of the United States.[24]   Perhaps the Americans would help the métis.   The petition asked the President to intercede with the Queen on their behalf, in the hope that an investigation might be made "into the extent and nature of our grievances" and that "full reparation be made for all these violated pledges and the injury and damages resulting to us therefrom."[25]

Thus far all were in agreement. But O'Donoghue did not want merely to enlist President Grant's assistance in redressing the grievances of a group of French half-breeds. He had always been an annexationist, and he wanted to use this opportunity to turn the discontent of the métis into a demand for the incorporation of Manitoba into the United States. By introducing the annexation issue, he was hurling a challenge at Louis Riel who had, from the outset, protested his loyalty to the Queen and who had thrown in his lot with Canada when he had sent the delegation of Ritchot, Black and Scott to Ottawa. As before, Riel opposed the idea of American annexation. He did not feel that the American métis were any better off than those in Manitoba, and he would have nothing to do with O'Donoghue's proposals. There was nothing wrong with the Act passed by the Canadian parliament in May. All that was lacking was the amnesty that might still be forthcoming. When O'Donoghue argued, Riel turned upon his former colleague, his face livid with anger, and told him that "he had only been required in the late trouble for the sake of his G—d d—d tongue."[26] On this note of hostility the two men parted company. Riel had carried the métis with him. It had been a close thing. O'Donoghue had no followers, but he still had many sympathizers. If the métis had remained loyal to Riel, it was not because they were convinced that he was right; but because he was Louis Riel, the son of his father. He was one of themselves; O'Donoghue was not.

Knowing that Taché would soon learn of the meeting at St. Norbert—for such a gathering could not be kept a secret—Father LeFloch felt it necessary to tell the Bishop that Riel had adopted a moderate rather than a belligerent attitude. "I can assure you that he [Riel] has no great taste for war," wrote LeFloch, "I find him very reasonable and very reserved." It was true that the métis at Pembina were uneasy and were talking in more alarming terms than those of St. Joseph's, but "they do not want to act without Riel."[27] The real source of trouble was that "firebrand" O'Donoghue. "In his pride he would like to lead Riel," declared LeFloch, "but Riel through pride will not be led." Several days later LeFloch wrote again, "Riel is not without anxiety about O'Donoghue; he is afraid he is going to look for a band of Fenians to raise trouble in the country."[28]

But it was not to the Fenians that O'Donoghue was looking this time. From St. Norbert he had gone back to Pembina; and there, with the help of Stutsman and others, he decided to revise the "Memorial and Petition" which the métis had discussed on the 17th.[29]   The meeting had selected him as the obvious person to carry the Memorial to President Grant, and here was an opportunity to insert a few demands for annexation. It would not need much more than the alteration of a few words here and there, and the addition of a paragraph asking that the people of Red River:

be permitted peacefully to enjoy a Government of our own choosing, or to change our allegiance for political and commercial reasons to some other Government of our choice, and being thoroughly satisfied that neither peace nor prosperity can exist in our country, under a Government which has by its bad faith forfeited all claim upon the confidence of our people . . . and considering further the vast extent of barren and impassable territory that separates us from the Dominion of Canada, we again earnestly appeal to Your Excellency . . . to take all such steps as Your Excellency may deem appropriate and proper, to enable us to enjoy the blessings of life, liberty, property, and the pursuit of happiness, under a Government of our own choice, or in union with a people with whom we think that we can enjoy these blessings.[30]

With the new version of the "Memorial and Petition" (of which Louis Riel was unaware), O'Donoghue set out for the capital of the United States.   In St. Paul he was warmly welcomed.   So warmly, in fact, that it was not until December that he reached Washington.[31] On October 25, he had written to Taché, pointing out that he had the sympathy of all parties and "the influence of all that is influential in this State (Minnesota)" and expressing his hope "that your Lordship will not interfere."[32] With the assistance of Senator Ramsey, O'Donoghue conferred with those ardent advocates of annexation, Banks and Chandler.   This was grist to the mill which they had been grinding for months.   Finally, on January 28, 1871, O'Donoghue was admitted to the presence of the President of the United States.   Grant received him "very kindly" and "listened attentively" but no more.   He was not convinced by O'Donoghue's oratorical efforts that the people of the new Province of Manitoba were yearning to become part of the American union.   Therefore he merely assured the former Christian Brother that, although he was not disinterested in the possibility of annexation, he did not regard the métis movement which O'Donoghue claimed to be leading "as a ripe disposition of a majority sufficiently large to guarantee unanimity of allegiance to a new government."[33]

III

Following the meeting at St. Norbert, Louis Riel returned to St. Joseph, not because he wanted to but because he was urged to do so.[34]   He had found the whole experience a stimulating one, and he had lost some of his earlier resignation. He had a chance to think about the wrongs that had been done him, and he wrote to Bishop Taché in a manner that hardly bore out Father LeFloch's reports of his submissive attitude. He enlarged upon the bad faith of the Canadians, declared that he had been "tricked" and that it could hardly be expected of him to show much enthusiasm about the new Lieutenant-Governor while the "assassins" of Elzéar Goulet were still allowed to walk the streets of Winnipeg. "If we talk this way to you," he said to the Bishop, "it is for no other reason than to tell you what we think, when we see all the efforts that Your Lordship is making to pacify us and to excuse the shameful actions of Canada."[35] Nevertheless LeFloch still had considerable influence over his former pupil. It was not long before Riel settled down again, particularly after the departure of O'Donoghue. Both he and Ambroise Lépine gave their assurances to the priest that it was far from their wish or their desire ever "to cause any trouble."[36]

Both the provincial and federal authorities at this time were in agreement on one thing. It would be best for Riel to remain quiet and not to become involved in politics in any way. Out of sight of his opponents in Red River, it would not be long before he would be out of their minds. And time would be the healer of all wounds.[37] Riel's friends really believed that time was on the side of conciliation. And conciliation was the policy that the tall Nova Scotian, Archibald, was trying to carry out. But with the best will in the world, Archibald could not please everybody. He could appeal to the large body of moderate opinion within the province, but he could not win over those who held their strong opinions strongly. He could not reconcile Riel's demands for an amnesty with Schultz's demands for vengeance. And yet he made the effort.

Several weeks after his arrival at Fort Garry, Governor Archibald felt that he was sufficiently familiar with the problems and the personalities of the province to organize a government. His first appointments to his Council were those of Alfred Boyd, a merchant of Winnipeg who had been a member of the Convention of Forty, and Marc Amable Girard, a young French-Canadian from Varennes near Montreal, who had recently arrived in the Settlement. This was followed by the organization of a provincial police force under Captain François Villiers of the Quebec Battalion of Militia, and the appointment of several magistrates. In each instance, Archibald took care to preserve the bi-racial aspect of the province and to maintain a strict balance between the French- and English-speaking population. The next step was to take a census. The province was divided into five sections with an English and a French enumerator in each. The census disclosed that there were 11,963 people in the province, of whom 558 were Indians, 5,757 French métis, 4,083

English half-breeds, and 1,565 whites. Of the last group, 747 were native to the country and 294 were found to have been born in Canada.[38] The outcome of the census was most annoying to Schultz, who called the whole proceeding a "farce," and wrote to his friend Denison, "Riel is *actually* down in the census roll."[39]   But there seems to be little question of the fairness of the census, for the figures of the English and the French enumerators are so much alike, that any small discrepancies between them are of little significance.   On the basis of the count, the province was divided into twenty-four electoral districts and writs were issued for the first provincial election in the history of Manitoba.   At the same time, plans were made for the election of Manitoba's four members to the federal parliament in Ottawa.

Louis Riel watched these developments in his native province with a growing interest.   Politics was in his blood,[40] and it was not like Riel to remain long aloof from them, particularly after his appetite had been whetted by the meeting at St. Norbert on September 17.   Where would the métis find a leader?   They were, as Riel knew, disheartened and dispirited as a result of the collapse of the Provisional Government. And they needed leadership if they were going to stand up to Schultz and his supporters.   Since Riel was not available, perhaps Joseph Dubuc would lead the métis.   As early as January, 1870, Riel had written to his old schoolmate from the College of Montreal to ask him if he would come to Red River.[41]   In April he had repeated the invitation.[42]   When Ritchot went east to negotiate with the Canadian authorities, he renewed Riel's appeals.   Dubuc finally agreed to go to Manitoba, and he joined Ritchot on the latter's return journey in June.   For several weeks Dubuc had lived with Riel at Fort Garry and had then moved to the Bishop's palace.[43]   Other French-Canadians also made their way to Red River later, men like Girard, Joseph Royal and Alphonse LaRivière, but it was to Dubuc in particular that Riel looked to assist his people.[44]   At first Dubuc was reluctant to step into Riel's shoes.   He was not a métis; he was not a native of the country; and he wanted to see Riel take his proper place in the legislative councils of the province.   More-over, the métis themselves wanted Riel back again, a fact of which Dubuc was well aware.   Early in November, Paul Proulx, André Nault and several other métis from St. Vital sent a letter to Riel asking him to offer himself as a candidate in the provincial election.[45]   This request was of a nature to appeal to the métis leader, but Riel rejected it.   He had learned from other sources that Sir George Cartier had expressed the hope that he would, for the present, stay out of active political life.   Hoping for much from Cartier, Riel felt that it would be advisable to avoid giving any possible embarrassment to Sir George.[46]   Even after further

requests—from the métis of St. Norbert, Pointe Coupée and St. Vital—
on November 27 that he run for the legislature,[47] Riel returned a negative
answer. He appreciated the invitation, but regretted that he could
not accept it.[48]

Riel's friends were both relieved and pleased. Father Giroux, who
had been chaplain to Riel's soldiers, wrote to his former chief, "Although
all your friends here would like to see you taking your part in the debates
in the legislature . . . for grave reasons, they approve your generous
decision."[49] Joseph Royal hastened to tell him that Cartier wanted to
remind him of the example of the leaders of the rebellion of 1837 who,
like Cartier himself, had submitted to a voluntary exile and later had
been able to return to their country and enter public life without any
stain or blot upon their names.[50]

But if Riel did not run in the provincial election, this did not mean he
was wholly unconcerned about the outcome. When, early in January, he
heard from Joseph Lemay that seventeen of the new members were
"friendly" to himself "and the principles" he had advanced,[51] Riel was
overjoyed. It was with real satisfaction that he wrote to Taché about
the success "of a good number of honest men, our friends" and the
defeat of "the worst enemies of the country." He was particularly
pleased with the defeat of John Schultz in Winnipeg by Donald A.
Smith.[52] To Riel this was but natural justice; to Schultz's friend,
Denison, it was incomprehensible. "Why the devil did you not elect
Dr. Schultz for Winnipeg," he wrote to Charles Mair, "it means uphill
work for loyal Canadians, British Canadians, for years to come."[53]

The provincial election, if hardly a justification of Riel's actions
during 1869, was indeed a victory for the moderates and the old settlers;
in particular it was a marked defeat for the Canadians. At least half of
the new members had taken part in the events of 1869/70 as members
of the two conventions. Among them were both secretaries of the
Provisional Government, Louis Schmidt and Thomas Bunn. Some of
the new members—men like Dubuc, Royal, Girard and Lemay—were
newcomers to Manitoba politics, as were several of the old settlers like
J. H. McTavish and Angus McKay. But most of them were sympathetic
to Riel and favoured the promulgation of an amnesty. In St. Vital,
where Riel would most likely have been a candidate, André Beauchemin,
who had been one of Louis's colleagues as far back as the days of the
National Métis Committee, was elected. The results of the election of
the Legislative Assembly were reflected in Archibald's appointments to
the Legislative Council, which included both François Dauphinais and
Salomon Hamelin, French métis; James McKay, a Scotch half-breed;
Donald Gunn, a Scottish naturalist and historian who had been a

member of both conventions; and Colin Inkster, a Hudson's Bay Company man.   Only two seats went to the newcomers, and these were not men associated with the party of which Schultz was the acknowledged leader.   To Fred Denison, one of Schultz's associates and a member of the Ontario Battalion of Militia, the new government was the work of Bishop Taché and Lieutenant-Governor Archibald, the latter being the tool "of his master in Ottawa, Sir George Cartier."[54]

The federal election results were, perhaps, less satisfactory from the standpoint of the métis.   Pierre Delorme, one of the horsemen who had captured Major Boulton and the Portage party, was elected for the District of Provencher, but Angus McKay only managed a tie vote with Schultz's friend and co-agitator, Dr. Lynch, in Marquette. Donald A. Smith was successful in Selkirk; but in Lisgar, Dr. Schultz gained an easy victory over Colin Inkster, who had run with the backing of the Hudson's Bay Company.

But Riel was not interested in the federal election.   The hardships of the flight from Fort Garry, the constant fears of assassination which preyed upon his mind,[55] the strains and stresses of an uncertain future, the delays in the promulgation of the amnesty, the worry about the maintenance of his mother and sisters and brothers: everything seemed to catch up with him at once, until he could no longer bear the double burden of anxiety and misfortune.   In February he fell ill, seriously ill. For several weeks those about him despaired of his life.[56]   Louis had wanted to keep word of his illness from his mother, in order to spare her the alarm and worry that such news would bring.   But he could not keep it from his sister Sara, and it was she who told Louis's mother.   "Poor mother," she wrote, "a single thought, that of her son—to go to care for him was the only thing that mattered."[57]   He was her eldest, her firstborn, her dearest.   Under her care Louis gradually improved, but the illness seemed to drag on for a long time.

It was April before Riel began to think of leaving St. Joseph's to return to his home at St. Vital.   He knew that he could not remain much longer at Father LeFloch's house.   He had his mother, his sisters and his brothers to think about; he could not leave them dependent on his friends indefinitely.   Expenses were always heavy, and even if the Grey Nuns had been willing to take Henriette, Eulalie and Octavie into the girls' boarding school at St. Boniface,[58] there were still the two boys, Joseph and "Louis' spoiled boy," Alexandre.[59]   Dubuc, too, felt that it would be well for Louis to return to his home, if only for his mother's sake.[60]   But Louis was still weak, and it was not until early in May that he was in a condition fit to make the voyage north.[61]

On May 3, Riel arrived quietly at St. Vital, thin and weak from his long illness. He did not want to give publicity to his movements, for he could never shake the haunting fear that vengeful Orangemen were always seeking him to have his life. But within several days his friends, even some of his former adversaries, were calling to see him at St. Vital "in crowds."[62] It resembled more a victor's than a vanquished's return. Only Marc Girard seemed to sound a sour note when he warned Bishop Taché that Riel's presence at St. Vital was "extremely imprudent and dangerous" and that it might well revive demands for his arrest.[63] But Girard was never one of Riel's warmest adherents, and Dubuc was disposed to look upon him as a "blockhead" who was interested only in his own career and was anxious to appease the English. To Riel Dubuc wrote in great confidence, "We are strong, in relation to the English we are extremely strong."[64]

Riel did not share Dubuc's enthusiasm. He felt much too uneasy about the attitude of the militiamen and the Ontario immigrants, and about the revival of the Scott affair in Ontario during the provincial election in that province, to make himself conspicuous. He therefore kept close to his own home, and as long as he remained quiet no effort was made to serve a warrant of arrest upon him. This self-imposed inactivity was galling to Riel now that he fully recovered his health; but his better judgment prevailed. To Dubuc he wrote that he would like "to be in a position to do something" but that he would "remain neutral a little while longer."[65] Not until September, when Bishop Taché was elevated to the Archbishopric of St. Boniface, did Riel make any public appearance; and then only to read a short speech of congratulation.

Meanwhile the new provincial legislature had assembled and had been prorogued. The first session was held in a house purchased from A. G. B. Bannatyne. Joseph Royal was chosen speaker, and Henry J. Clarke, a Montreal lawyer whom Cartier had prevailed upon to go to Red River, acted as premier.[66] The proceedings were conducted in both English and French. There were no bitter recriminations, no attempts to fight the battles of the past on the floor of the legislature. Under Archibald's guidance the members devoted themselves to discussing and passing laws with regard to courts, police, surveys, roads, real estate, noxious weeds, Sabbath observance and schools, very much as the Council of Assiniboia and the Legislative Assembly of the provisional régime, had done. At the same time the federal authorities were active in their efforts to remove potential sources of grievance by negotiating a treaty with the Indians, and appropriating 1,400,000 acres of undivided land to be allotted to the half-breeds in accordance with the Manitoba Act. And there were also the payments made to compensate those who had suffered losses during the troubles of 1869/70. Of the several claims put forward, the largest was that of Dr. Schultz, who asked for no less than $65,000 including $10,000 balm for his imprisonment by Riel.[67] All of this gave rise to the rather bitter little jingle that ran through the Settlement:[68]

> To John Schultz, honour and money, plenty;
> To friend fools, Scaffolds or pockets empty.

IV

While Riel had been convalescing from his long illness, his former colleague and now his enemy, William O'Donoghue, had been continuing his efforts to bring about American intervention in the affairs of Manitoba. President U. S. Grant had disappointed him, and so he had turned to John O'Neill and J. J. Donnelly, two of the Fenian leaders who had just been released from imprisonment for violating American neutrality with an invasion of Canada in 1870. With O'Neill's assistance, O'Donoghue was able to press his case before the governing body of the Fenian Brotherhood in New York. He descanted upon the wrongs suffered by the people of Red River at the hands of the brutal British, the hostility of the Manitobans to all Canadians and their eagerness to rise against their overlords. With a little help from outside they could overthrow Canadian rule. But the Brotherhood had heard all these arguments before. They had believed them then, and had tried two invasions of Canada in 1866 and 1870, without success and without any assistance from the people whom they were proposing to free. They had enough of raids into Canada which did not bring either Canadians or Americans rushing to their standards. They promised O'Donoghue their prayers, but not their dollars or their arms. Several months later O'Donoghue tried again. He put up to the Brotherhood a complete plan for the liberation of "the down-trodden people of Manitoba."[69] O'Neill gave him every possible support. But neither O'Donoghue's eloquence nor O'Neill's backing could persuade the Brotherhood to embark on any more futile military ventures, at least not without the open and acknowledged support of the American government.

But if O'Donoghue did not win over the Brotherhood as an organization, he did manage to gain the adherence of several of its leading figures. Of these, the chief was John O'Neill. Together O'Donoghue and O'Neill set out to raise funds and recruit men for the army of Manitoban liberation. They managed to secure a good supply of breech-loading rifles,[70] but that was about the limit of their success. The Irish republicans had no stomach for fighting, and even the unemployed Irish navvies from the Northern Pacific seem to have been reluctant to throw in their lot with O'Donoghue and O'Neill. When Gilbert McMicken, the Canadian secret agent, passed through Minnesota on his way to Manitoba, he reported that the former member of the Provisional Government could muster no more than seventy men at Pembina.[71]

Such a limited and inadequate response to his appeals did not discourage O'Donoghue. He had placed his main reliance not so much on the Americans as on the métis themselves. He believed that he still enjoyed great prestige among them and that with their assistance he could create a situation in Manitoba that would attract or compel the United States government to intervene. Even if the métis were still disposed to look to Riel, they were, he knew, despondent, unhappy, resentful and sullen. They were ripe for rebellion and were ready to overthrow the Canadians who had cheated and then bullied them. He would only have to appeal to their sense of national consciousness, as Riel had done in 1869 and Cuthbert Grant had done in 1816. He would promise them independence. He sat down in Pembina and, on September 15, drafted his Constitution for the Republic of Rupert's Land. There would be a president—he named himself for that post—and a council of ten members, five of whom would be appointed by the people of the country, and five chosen "by the immigrants who shall come in," that is, the Americans. There would be new courts established, over which W. B. O'Donoghue would preside as Chief Justice; and a military defence force, of which W. B. O'Donoghue would be "the commander-in-chief."[72]

On October 5, all was ready. In the early hours of the morning O'Donoghue and O'Neill with some thirty-five men crept stealthily out of Pembina. They were anxious not to arouse the suspicions of the American frontier guard which had been stationed there since the events of the previous year. They crossed the river and then rushed into the small Hudson's Bay trading post on British territory. The Company trader was made prisoner and the post formally occupied in the name of the Provisional Government of Red River. Almost two years before, William McDougall, the Canadian Lieutenant-Governor elect of Assiniboia, had crossed the same river, stood on the same spot and taken possession of the same land in the name of the Queen of England.

O'Donoghue was no more successful than McDougall. Although his men occupied the Hudson's Bay post for several hours, no métis horsemen appeared on the horizon, only Captain Lloyd Wheaton and a detachment of American soldiers. The "Fenians" scattered in all directions. However, within a short period of time all the leaders and most of the invaders had been captured. O'Donoghue attempted to seek safety by striking out for the north; but by an ironic turn of fate, he was taken prisoner by two French métis and turned over to the American authorities. The raid was over the very day it began. The invaders were in jail.

In the meantime the Manitoban authorities were taking steps to resist the attack that everybody believed would be much more serious than it turned out to be. O'Donoghue had never bothered to keep his plans secret. For months there had been rumours that O'Donoghue was on his way back to Red River, sometimes with the families of Irish immigrants, sometimes with a Fenian army. "Everybody had the news from someone who had learned it from someone else who had seen him," wrote Father Proulx, "but this someone else, no one ever seems to have seen himself."[73] He had written freely to Bishop Taché,[74] and he had taken pains to circulate stories that he had no less than one thousand men behind him.[75] Apprised by McMicken and by his scouts of the mustering of O'Donoghue's men at Pembina, the Lieutenant-Governor drafted a proclamation on October 3 (it was issued on the 4th) calling upon all loyal men in the various parishes throughout the province to enroll themselves "irrespective of race or religion, or of past difficulties" and "to rally round the flag of our common country" to resist the "band of lawless men calling themselves Fenians" who had "assembled on the frontier of the United States at or near Pembina" for the purpose of making "a raid into the province" and committing "acts of depredation, pillage and robbery, and other outrages upon the persons and property of our loving subjects, the inhabitants of this province."[76] Several companies were mobilized and equipped on the 5th, the actual day of the invasion, and shortly before dusk a small force of 80 soldiers and 120 volunteers set out under the command of Major A. G. Irvine to defend the province against the Irish-American filibusters. The rain had been falling heavily, and the troops wallowed in mud. Nevertheless they pushed ahead, reaching St. Norbert on the 6th, and Ste. Agathe on the 7th. By this time they were convinced that the raid had collapsed and that there would be no second attempt. So they turned around and trudged home again.[77]

In retrospect the whole episode smacks of comic opera. Yet it was not as fantastic or absurd as it might appear at first glance. O'Donoghue may have failed to organize his force properly and to co-ordinate his efforts with those of the métis: but he did know there were many métis who were hostile to Canada and who sympathized with his schemes to appeal to the United States; and he knew, too, that the métis had been holding meetings among themselves to discuss what they should do. What O'Donoghue did not know was the stand that Louis Riel would take on the issue. He had no means of knowing that on September 23, two weeks before the raiders crossed the frontier, Louis Riel had assured Bishop Taché that he was in no way associated with O'Donoghue's movement.   He admitted that he had not yet made up his mind exactly what he would do, but he said openly and without hesitation: "You know perfectly well that my life is not safe.   I may go in the front and fight against the Fenians, and I am sure to be killed by those behind me. So I am at a loss [to know] what I can do, but you can rest assured there is not the slightest danger of me or any one of my friends going with the Fenians.   We dislike the Fenians, for they are condemned by our church, and you may be assured I will have nothing to do with them."[78]

Three days after his meeting with Archbishop Taché, Riel called a meeting at St. Vital of the principal métis leaders of the Settlement.[79] Among those who responded were Ambroise Lépine, Baptiste Tourond, Elzéar de Lagimodière, André Nault, Pierre Parenteau and others.   One by one they discussed the questions that Riel brought forward.   Had the Canadian government fulfilled its pledges?   Would it honour its undertakings in the future?   Was O'Donoghue really coming?   What did he propose to do?   And "what conduct must we follow respecting him and respecting Canada?"

It was this last question that aroused the greatest amount of interest and discussion.   It seems clear, if only by inference, that there was some division among the métis as to the course that should be followed. But there was no doubt what Riel had in mind.   To him the most important thing was that the métis should act as a group.   Unity was essential.   And there was no doubt that Riel had no intention of playing second fiddle to O'Donoghue.   What could the Irishman offer him? Riel's one hope lay with Cartier and the Canadian government, and Riel knew it.   Only from Canada could come the amnesty he wanted so much.   So he directed the discussion to secure a resolution that none of métis leaders would accept an invitation to join O'Donoghue "without an express permission of our Association."   Then he moved:

that every one of the members of this meeting get in touch with the representatives of the people and the influential persons of the various parishes, to bring the métis, in an unanimous manner, as much as possible, to pronounce themselves in favour of the advantages already possessed by the Manitoba Bill, and not to allow themselves to be carried away by the contingencies farther than to ask, loyally and with moderation, the accomplishment of the clauses and of the things guaranteed by our arrangements with Canada.[80]

It was just as Riel had foreseen.   On the night of the 2nd, O'Donoghue sent a message to the métis parishes asking Riel, Lépine, Nault, Tourond and the other principal métis leaders to join him.   Out of curiosity and in order to "see what O'Donoghue wants" and "whether he is strong," André Nault and Baptiste Lépine set out for Pembina. Before they had returned, Archibald's proclamation appeared, and Riel expressed his satisfaction with it. Here was an opportunity for him to prove the loyalty that had so frequently been questioned by his enemies. He would muster the métis in support of the government and place Ottawa under an obligation to him. The idea appealed to him, and when the métis leaders met again at Riel's on the morning of October 5, it was agreed, twelve votes to one, that the métis should unite their forces with those of the Manitoba government. Only Baptiste Tourond held aloof. He had been ill-treated in Winnipeg and could not bring himself to go any further than to advocate complete neutrality.[81]

On October 6 another meeting was held at St. Vital to hear the reports from Nault and Lépine. On this occasion Riel and the other métis leaders were joined by Hon. François Dauphinais and Angus McKay, both members of the provincial legislature. The two scouts told the gathering that they had seen O'Donoghue and had talked with him, and that he had told them of his plans and solicited their assistance. But there was no question of any of the métis yielding to his blandishments. They would follow Riel's lead, and all the more readily when strongly endorsed by Dauphinais and McKay. It was therefore agreed that meetings should be conducted by those present in their own parishes and the opinion of the central committee made widely known. In every instance, where local meetings were held during October 6—at the White Horse Plains, St. Boniface, Pointe du Chêne, Ste. Agathe, Pointe Coupée, St. Norbert, St. Vital—the people voted to assist the government and to form local companies of horsemen under the command of Pascal Breland, Ambroise Lépine, Charles Nolin, Louis Morin, Pierre Delorme, Pierre Parenteau and Louis Riel as their respective captains.[82]

The provincial government had been much concerned about the attitude of the métis in the event of a Fenian invasion. Archibald knew well how the French half-breeds felt. He wondered if any of them would be attracted to the side of O'Donoghue, or whether they would show their appreciation of his conciliatory efforts to forget their grievances and animosities against Canada, and support him. Should they throw in their lot with the Fenians, the situation would be desperate, for a series of friendly French parishes to the south of Winnipeg would give the invaders an easy road into the heart of the Settlement, right to Fort Garry itself. And Fort Garry was still the key to the province, just as it had been when Riel seized the fort in November, 1869. Accordingly, the Lieutenant-Governor asked Donald A. Smith and J. H. McTavish, the latter a well-known Roman Catholic and member of the Legislative Assembly, to go to St. Boniface.[83]   Archbishop Taché was away—he had gone to Ottawa to see about the long-delayed amnesty—but the two men talked with Father Dugast and asked him to use his influence with the métis.   Dugast then went to see Archibald— he rather liked being involved in political matters—and pointed out that if the government was to win métis support, it must first win the support of Louis Riel.   He was the important man.   The best way to influence Riel would be through his friend and adviser, the Abbé Ritchot.   It was therefore Archibald who sent for Ritchot and who prevailed upon the priest to do everything he could to persuade Riel to use his influence "to direct his compatriots, in the present state of affairs, and to prevent them from taking a false course."[84]

Ritchot, like Dugast, saw in the Governor's request an opportunity to help Riel in his long struggle for recognition.   He pointed out that Riel could hardly act openly without "some guarantee that his action will be looked upon with favour by Your Excellency."   Archibald recognized the justice of the remark and assured Ritchot that "Should Mr. Riel come forward as suggested, he need be under no apprehension that his liberty shall be interfered with in any way."   He added the significant words, "the co-operation of the French half-breeds and their leaders in the support of the Crown, under the present circumstances, will be very welcome and cannot be looked upon otherwise than as entitling them to most favourable consideration."[85]   When Riel learned of these assurances on October 5, he no longer hesitated.   It was for this reason that he took the lead at the métis meeting on the same day which voted to come out in favour of the provincial authorities.

Following the organization of the several métis companies on October 6 and 7, Riel wrote to the Lieutenant-Governor to tell him what had been done and to offer him the services of the métis horsemen.   "Your Excellency may rest assured," he wrote with complete candour, "that without being enthusiastic, we have been devoted.   So long as our services continue to be required, you may rely on us."[86]   Archibald was glad of the offer.   He had learned that one of the guns in Fort Garry had been spiked, apparently by a Fenian sympathizer in the garrison; and he shared the general belief that O'Donoghue would not rest content with one effort to cross the frontier.   Even Major Irvine, having heard "from the front" that "the Fenians intend making a raid between this and tomorrow night," sent a panic note to Archibald at 3.30 A.M. on the morning of the 8th appealing for "reinforcement *at once; 150 men.*"[87] Accordingly, when Joseph Royal, the speaker of the Legislative Assembly, and the Hon. Marc Girard asked Archibald if he would go with them to St. Boniface to review some 200 métis troops ready to offer their services to the Crown, he readily agreed to do so.   In a time of emergency one need not enquire too closely into the sources of help.   Taking with him Captain Macdonald, who commanded at Fort Garry in the absence of Major Irvine, the Lieutenant-Governor crossed the river and went to St. Boniface on the forenoon of Sunday, October 8.   He saw the métis, clad in their traditional blue coats and hoods, armed with muskets and rifles.   He listened while they fired a salute of welcome, and they gave him the customary cheers.   Then he met their leaders and shook hands with them.   Girard was careful not to mention Louis Riel's name;[88] but Archibald was never in any doubts about the identity of the man to whom he spoke.   After thanking the métis for their response, he asked them to provide a mounted patrol to keep an eye on any movements along the frontier.   During the next few days some fifty métis horsemen, commanded by Pascal Breland and Joseph Royal, scouted the prairies between the Assiniboine River and Pembina.   But it soon became clear the "Fenians" had shot their feeble bolt.   There was nothing more to fear.

When word spread throughout the country that the Lieutenant-Governor had not only met and talked with, but had actually shaken hands with, Louis Riel, there was an outburst of indignation on the part of those who were forever confusing their bigotry with patriotism. Charles Mair, who refused to believe that the métis were not secretly supporting O'Donoghue,[89] regardless of their public professions, wrote belligerently from Perth, "If bloodshed must come, let it rest upon the head of those who brew it.   We shall not flinch in the hour of danger, and if the French half-breeds assist the Irish they have wrung their death knell.   We shall make clean work of it this time. . . ."[90] Edward Harrison, an Ontario volunteer from Belleville, urged Denison to keep up the momentum of the agitation "until it crushes the Enemy beneath it."   By keeping the matter alive in the newspapers, "the feelings of the people of Ontario can be so moulded as to bring about a most desireable end . . . which is the *recall* (nothing less) of Archibald from the Governorship of Manitobah [*sic*]."[91]   Everywhere in Ontario abuse was heaped upon the head of the man from Nova Scotia.

In Manitoba, with few exceptions, the people felt that the Lieutenant-Governor had handled the "Fenian" incident in a satisfactory manner. Resolutions were adopted in both houses of the legislature that endorsed Archibald's policy of "forbearance and fair play towards all classes of the people."   The resolutions expressed joy that "irrespective of race and creed" the inhabitants, French and English, had "showed a spirit of patriotism and union becoming the owners of a common country and the sharers of a common destiny."[92]   "It seems to me," wrote Archibald rather testily to Joseph Howe in Ottawa, "that the people here must be allowed to be judges of how to manage their own affairs" without any help from Ontario. "If they are to be responsible to the people of other Provinces, the members should be elected there." Then he added sarcastically that, if responsible government had no more place in Canadian life, "it should be your business, in dealing with these men, to erect not hustings but gallows . . . unless you expect to 'gather grapes of thorns or figs of thistles' you can hardly hope to carry on responsible Government by inflicting death penalties on the leaders of the majority of the electors."[93]

Although he was discreet enough not to show himself in Winnipeg, Riel began to move about more freely in the French-speaking parishes, and he visited St. Boniface more frequently. There were really very few in Manitoba who thought about hanging Riel or any métis leaders. On December 8, when a number of the métis and French-Canadians resolved to form a local branch of the St. Jean Baptiste Society, Riel not only attended the meeting; he even allowed his name to stand for the office of first vice-president. The other officers were all his friends: Joseph Royal, the president; Elzéar Lagimodière and Charles Nolin, vice-presidents; Louis Schmidt, secretary; and Father Dugast, chaplain.[94] It was almost like the days of the first Provisional Government, except that O'Donoghue was no longer with him. The ex-treasurer was wandering about Minnesota looking for a job as a schoolteacher, and talking about another attempt against Red River the following summer. "If it is God's will," wrote Father Proulx, "he will be responsible for another fiasco."[95]

CHAPTER 10

Member of Parliament

I N SPITE of Lieutenant-Governor Archibald's protests to Joseph Howe, Manitoba's affairs were apparently not merely the concern of the Province of Manitoba alone. From the day the news of Thomas Scott's execution reached Ontario, Manitoba's politics became the business of both Ontario and Quebec. The agitation that had been directed, if not provoked, by Denison and Schultz was never allowed to subside, and feelings against Riel were not permitted to subside. Neither Sir George Cartier nor Sir John A. Macdonald expected that the debate over the events of 1869/70 would be so prolonged or bitter. They had been sincere in their promises to Taché and to Ritchot, and they hoped only that Riel would remain quiet long enough for the recollections of his actions in March, 1870, to be submerged by more immediate and more important political problems.

But it seemed as if neither Riel's enemies nor his friends would allow the Scott affair to be forgotten. To the Liberal Party in Ontario the affair was too important a political issue to be neglected. Accordingly, Edward Blake tried to force through the Ontario legislature a motion demanding that the "murderers" of Scott be brought to justice. It was hardly within the competence of the provincial legislature to adopt a resolution tantamount to a censure of the federal government; and Sandfield Macdonald sought to turn it aside by arguing that the Scott affair was a matter for the federal and not the provincial authorities of Ontario. Blake knew this as well as Macdonald, but he persisted with his resolution, if only to prod the Orangemen into anti-Conservative action by suggesting that the Tories were running Manitoba "in the French and rebel interest."[1] It was also good politics to argue that as long as Sir John A. Macdonald "retained power at Ottawa," Riel and his associates would remain "in the same position in the North-West."[2] Ogle Gowan and D'Arcy Boulton, both leading figures in the Orange Order as well as in the Conservative party, might deplore this attempt to "make political capital out of our Brother's murder by arousing the passions of Orangemen on the eve of a general election against a government that has no power whatever to deal with the crime. . . ."[3] But

Blake and Mackenzie knew their people; there is no doubt that Sandfield Macdonald's opposition to Blake's motion played an important part in the defeat of the provincial government in the spring of 1871.

Even after he won his election, Blake would not let matters rest. He proposed another resolution urging the apprehension and punishment of Scott's "murderers," and he offered a $5,000 reward to any person bringing about their arrest and conviction.[4] If nothing else, this resolution and reward would be a perpetual embarrassment to the Conservatives in Ottawa.

The significance of Blake's manœuvres was not lost on the astute old gentleman who held the senior cabinet post in the capital of Canada. He had become Prime Minister in 1867. It was now 1871. A few more months and he would have to risk his political future and his party's in a general election. He had no intention, if he could avoid it, of suffering the fate of his namesake Sandfield Macdonald. Everything seemed to point to a Conservative victory: peace had been achieved with the United States, albeit at the sacrifice of the Canadian fisheries; British Columbia had been added to the Canadian federation; there was every chance of starting work on a transcontinental railway that would link the Pacific with the Atlantic provinces of Canada. "I am, as you may fancy," he wrote to Sir John Rose in London, "exceedingly desirous of carrying the elections again. . . . Confederation is only yet in the gristle and it will require five years more before it hardens into bone."[5]

Macdonald's one anxiety was that annoying man, Louis Riel. Would he never keep out of sight? Why had Lieutenant-Governor Archibald been so indiscreet as to appear in public with the métis leader and shake his hand? Surely the business of arranging métis support against the Fenians could have been done quietly and without undue publicity. Now there was that humourless, dedicated Edward Blake trying to turn the people of Ontario against the Conservatives over the death of some obscure Orangeman in Red River. Blake's reward would be certain to tempt someone into seizing Riel and then bringing him into a court-room on a charge of murder. Then there would be an outbreak of racial feeling in Quebec. Macdonald's main purpose was to achieve unity in the new federation, and this could not be achieved with Ontario and Quebec at each other's throats over the Scott–Riel affair. For this reason, Macdonald resolved to do what he could to get Riel out of Manitoba, beyond the reach of any man whose cupidity or desire for revenge would induce him to seek out the métis leader and arrest him.

It had been Sir George Cartier's wish, as expressed to Joseph Royal, that Riel should submit to a voluntary exile, not of several months but of several years.[6] To Riel's friends in Manitoba the only just solution

Louis Riel, Member of Parliament, about 1873

Louis Riel, about 1875

Marguerite Riel, Wife of Louis Riel

seemed to be in the implementation of the promise of the amnesty, not in asking Riel to return once more to the United States. In particular Archbishop Taché was hurt and annoyed that no steps had been taken by Cartier or the Ottawa government to carry out the promises that had been made to him and Ritchot during the spring and summer of 1870. He felt he had been placed in an impossible position by the federal authorities. In May, 1871, he wrote to Sir George, "I assure you that I am deeply afflicted. I have spared neither pain, nor fatigue, nor expense, nor humiliation to re-establish order and peace, and it has come to this, that I am to receive from my people the cruel reproach that I have shamefully deceived them."[7] When he received no satisfaction from Cartier, Taché packed his bags and set out once more for Ottawa. Perhaps by personal contact he might obtain a reply that would not only assure Riel's safety but also vindicate the Archbishop's honour.

In Ottawa, Taché soon learned that political considerations had over-ridden those of simple justice. Sir John A. Macdonald was quite prepared to talk frankly to the Archbishop as a man of the world, to admit that the delays in granting the amnesty were prompted by factors that were political in nature. When Taché talked about the amnesty, the Prime Minister merely pointed out that it was not politically feasible to grant the amnesty. Sir John never denied that he had promised an amnesty; he simply took the view that "No government could stand that would endeavour to procure the amnesty"[8] and that the government should stand, while Confederation was still "in the gristle," was more important to the country than the inconveniences suffered by Louis Riel or the embarrassments experienced by the Archbishop. Instead of an amnesty, Macdonald was prepared to talk about the ways and means of persuading Riel to leave the country "for a while." Taché was quite willing to admit the force of the Prime Minister's arguments, but in conversation with Cartier he could not but point out that it would be "extremely difficult" for him to approach Riel, especially in view of the deception that had been practised on him with regard to the amnesty. But Cartier supported Macdonald's arguments. Could Taché do nothing to persuade Riel to leave Manitoba? "You must remember," replied Taché, "that this man is poor; his mother is a widow with four young girls and three young boys, and she has no means of support especially when her eldest son is away. He himself has only his labour for his support, and I do not think it is fair to ask him to leave his home without some compensation or some means of travelling." "That is true," replied Sir George, "we will see about that."[9] After further consultation with Cartier and with the Archbishop, Macdonald wrote privately to Taché, sending him a bank draft for $1,000, "for the individual that we have talked about," suggesting that the money be paid to him periodically rather than in one lump sum, "otherwise the money would be wasted and our embarrassment begin again." He stipulated that the money should be paid over twelve months.[10]

It was no secret why the federal government wanted Riel out of sight. Both Cartier and Macdonald admitted to the Archbishop that, should Riel remain in Manitoba and take an active part in public life, the Liberals would seize upon this and use it to belabour the Conservatives in the forthcoming federal election. Cartier went a step further. He suggested that the voluntary withdrawl of Riel would make it easier for the government to gain "a larger support in the elections, and . . . thus be better able to procure the amnesty."[11]

Lieutenant-Governor Archibald was also anxious to see Riel leave the province. Only a few days after the métis leader had fled from Fort Garry, he had expressed the view that even if Riel, Lépine and O'Donoghue were amnestied "they ought not to come in for some considerable time, till the feeling about them blows over. Their presence here would be a continuous temptation to outrage, and nobody could say when a thing of the kind would quit if once begun. Their own interests, therefore, and the interests of the whole Province alike, concur in keeping them away in the meantime."[12] It was true that Archibald had been glad enough to see Riel, Lépine and their soldiers at the time of the Fenian threat. But once that danger had passed, the old problems reasserted themselves with all the unpleasant possibilities that Archibald feared so much. Perhaps some vindictive "loyalist" might try to serve a warrant to the former president of the Provisional Government; perhaps Riel would resist; perhaps there would be bloodshed; perhaps the métis might be so incensed that civil strife would break out. "I had learned privately, through the instrumentality of the police," wrote Archibald to Sir George Cartier, "that immediately after the arrival of the telegraphic news" of Blake's offer of a reward for Riel's apprehension "meetings were held in each French parish on the subject, and that there was but one feeling among the people on the subject. They determined that the parties against whom the rewards were directed should remain in the country, and that the people should protect them by armed force against any attempt to arrest them. I fear very much that had the attempt been made it would have led to bloodshed." The danger lay not so much with the old English-speaking settlers, continued Archibald, as with "the small band of lawless men, idlers and roughs who infest the taverns of Winnipeg. These men have no influence except for mischief, but they might light a flame it would be hard to extinguish."[13]

These apprehensions were not without some justification. This seemed to be shown on December 8, when several men armed with revolvers forced their way into Riel's house at St. Vital. It happened on the night Louis had gone to St. Boniface to assist Royal and the others to organize the local branch of the St. Jean Baptiste Society. But the armed men threatened Marie, Riel's sister. They turned the house upside down searching for their victim. It is likely that they were half drunk; certainly their conduct was offensive and insulting. Janvier Ritchot and Paul Proulx arrived in time to see them depart but were unable to identify them by name. However the métis hastened to warn Riel of what had happened and to provide him with an armed escort.[14] Riel's mother appealed to the authorities for protection, but no arrests were made. All that remained to the métis was a sense of grievance and persecution, as well as a conviction on Riel's part that his life was in danger.

Thus, when Taché returned to St. Boniface with Cartier's suggestion and Macdonald's bank draft, he found both Riel and Lépine not unwilling to comply with the government's request that they go into exile. It was a bitter pill for Riel to swallow. He had been promised an amnesty; he had administered the country for several months with Cartier's consent; he had rallied his people to support the government in an emergency. For this he was being driven from his home; his name was being reviled; his life threatened; and now he was being asked to accept a voluntary exile for political reasons. He pointed out to Taché that $1,000 would not go very far towards keeping him and Lépine in the United States and supporting their families at the same time. It was not an unreasonable argument. With Archibald's assistance, Taché persuaded Donald A. Smith to add another £600 to Macdonald's gift.[15] On February 16, 1872, the Archbishop handed the money over to Riel and Lépine, reserving $800 to take care of the two families. "Go," he said to both men:

disappear for a time; do not leave even a pretext to those who are assailing you so unjustly. They want to accomplish evil ends, to disturb the country, to ruin it if possible, and with that view they gladly make use of the pretext that you are here. Deprive them of that pretext. . . . Shew once again that your patriotism is not confined within the narrow limits of personal advantages, but that on the contrary you are capable of forgetting self when good is to be done.[16]

In the darkness, on February 23, Louis Riel and Ambroise Lépine slipped out of St. Vital. They travelled not by public stage but by private carriage for fear of detection. With them went several policemen furnished by Louis de Plainval. They were to protect the fugitives from all the dangers of the night.

II

But Riel's exile, if it brought peace of mind to Sir John A. Macdonald—
and made it possible for the Prime Minister to face a wrathful Ontario
electorate with the disclaimer, "Where is Riel?   God knows; I wish I
could lay my hands on him"[17]—brought no tranquillity to the métis
leader himself.   After a brief stop at St. Joseph's on February 25, Riel
and Lépine continued their journey to St. Paul where they arrived on
March 2.   Several days later Riel wrote to Joseph Dubuc to ask him to
tell his mother of their safe arrival and to pay his respects to the Archbishop.[18]   For the present, he told Dubuc, he and Lépine were putting
up at the Montreal House on 79 Minnesota Road in St. Paul.

There was not much for the two men to do.   Riel, at least, could turn
his hand to writing.   He began the compilation of a memorandum on
the Scott Affair and on the organization of the Provisional Government
which had been requested by his friend, Rodrigue Masson, in Ottawa.
Riel had brought a number of his private papers with him to refresh his
memory for this very purpose.   He did not expect to be interrupted in
his work.   There seemed little reason for him to fear pursuit; in any
event he had taken the precaution of hiding his identity under the name
of Louis Bissonette[19] and of avoiding walking in public places where he
might be recognized.   It was therefore an alarming experience when he
caught sight of his enemies, Dr. Schultz and Dr. Bown, the former editor
of the *Nor'Wester*, in St. Paul.   Why were they there?   Had they
followed him deliberately?   It was even more alarming when he learned
that Schultz had approached W. Devlin on March 17 and offered him
fifty dollars in cash and one thousand dollars "to be paid by the Government of Ontario" to steal Riel's papers.   Devlin had talked over the offer
with his friend John Mager of St. Boniface, and both men went before a
magistrate, swore an affidavit about Schultz's offer and then took it to
Riel.[20]   Schultz had been thwarted for the moment.   But Riel was now
more fearful than ever.   He wondered if he might not be safer among his
own people on the Red River than in this unfamiliar city where every
man was a stranger, and every stranger a potential enemy.   If he could
get a job in Red River, he would return there quietly, Macdonald or
no Macdonald.[21]

For the present he continued to work on his memorandum for Masson.
It would occupy the time, and it might be of some use.   He wrote an
historical account, beginning with the first meeting of the convention
and continuing the story to the execution of Scott, which he argued
was "inevitable" simply because "it was necessary to intimidate the
conspirators, isolate Schultz by silencing the dissensions among our own

people which encouraged him, and to command the attention of Canada."
Perhaps it was a poor defence, but it was a position from which Riel
never withdrew.   On April 4, he put the whole thing together and sent it
to Masson, with the comment, "Lower Canada . . . is our whole
support . . . it is the land of our fathers."[22]

Meanwhile, Joseph Royal, on his way to Canada, visited Riel at
St. Paul.   He reported that he found Riel in "good health" and "adding
a little weight," but Lépine was "bored to death."   What worried
Royal was Riel's obvious state of fear.   "He believes himself more in
danger here than at Red River," Royal wrote to Taché.[23]   He was
keeping out of sight, seeing no one and never daring to go out at nights.
Even though Schultz had left St. Paul, Riel was afraid there would be
others in town who would do anything to get their hands on Blake's
$5,000.   Nor did it help Riel's peace of mind to learn that Schultz's
return to Manitoba had been followed by a new outbreak of lawlessness
on the part of his supporters, by attacks upon the persons of Pierre
Léveillé and Maxime Lépine, and by the burning of effigies of Riel and
Archibald (paid for by Dr. Schultz) in the streets of Winnipeg.[24]   All
the rioters were doing was celebrating their victory over the Lieutenant-
Governor, for Archibald had announced his intention of retiring at an
early date.   But when de Plainval attempted to tear down the remnants
of the burning effigies, he was threatened by the "loyal" mob and
unmercifully attacked in Schultz's little newspaper, *The Liberal*.[25]
When he heard about these things, Riel left his room in the hotel and
moved to the house of Louis Demeules where, he wrote Taché, "I
feel . . . rather less uneasiness than before."[26]   But this new sense of
security was not of long duration.   On April 28, he and Lépine over-
heard two men discussing what steps they should take to earn the $5,000
offered by the Ontario government "for the so-called murderers of
Scott."[27]   So they fled to Breckenridge.   Even here the two métis
leaders believed themselves in danger of assassination.   In the end,
Lépine returned to Manitoba.   Riel, lonely and anxious, decided to
return to St. Paul.   On May 19, he wrote to the Archbishop, "I am
uneasy.   I place myself in the hands of God."[28]

In Lépine's absence, Riel felt more isolated and exposed and homesick
than he had felt before.   Only the letters from his friends, from Taché
and from Dubuc, seemed to sustain his spirit.   Every day he looked for
the envelope bearing Dubuc's handwriting; for Dubuc's letters were
filled with talk about politics, about the métis and about his mother.
Moreover, there was the stimulating suggestion that Dubuc had put
forward, even before Riel had left St. Vital, that the ex-president of the

Provisional Government might allow his name to go before the elec-torate.[29]   In April, Dubuc brought it up again in one of his letters. This time the suggestion was positive.   "They are going to elect you for the county of Provencher," he had written.[30]   The idea was really Dubuc's, but he had discussed the proposal with the Abbé Ritchot who had approved.   It was true that Joseph Lemay had notions of running in the next federal election; but Lemay was quite willing to stand aside in favour of his friend Riel.   Louis Riel thought over the idea of letting his name go before the electorate.   The more he thought about it the more he liked it.   And yet a few doubts lingered in his mind.   "You tell me that people want to elect me to the Commons," he wrote to Dubuc, "but let us be serious for once . . . is it a serious proposal? As far as I am concerned, I am serious.   And I repeat to you that I should like to be elected to the Commons, and to the Local house if there is not federal law forbidding it."[31]

Archbishop Taché was less enthusiastic about Riel becoming a candi-date for parliament than was Dubuc.   He understood the practical implications of such a course.   He knew that the members of the Canadian cabinet would view the suggestion with disfavour, if only because they had taken such pains to get Riel out of the country during the very period of the general election.   He feared, too, that Riel's candidature would divide rather than unite the métis; for there were still some métis who were not disposed to follow Riel's leadership.   The Lieutenant-Governor was appalled at the idea.   He hurried to tell Taché that it would be nothing less than "madness" and that Riel "would probably be either expelled or shot."[32]   But like Riel, Dubuc was stubborn.   He maintained, both to Riel and to Taché, that his proposal was a serious one, and that Riel would most certainly allow his name to be nominated.   He was right about Riel.   Riel was prepared to run. His only hesitation arose when he heard that the Conservative party was anxious to put up Dubuc himself as a candidate.   How could he run then, Riel asked, when the "man whom I most respect in Manitoba" was likely to oppose him?[33]

But it was not Dubuc who had ideas of running for Parliament.   It was the Provincial Attorney-General, Henry J. Clarke.   A Roman Catholic and a friend of Sir George Cartier, Clarke had made a deliberate effort to cultivate the good will of the métis.   The federal election seemed to offer to him an opportunity to ask of the métis some return for his patronage.   But Clarke would have no chance of success should Louis Riel decide to offer himself as a candidate.   In the latter part of June, Riel left St. Paul and went to St. Joseph on the Canadian frontier.[34] From here he made frequent trips into Manitoba, and these trips convinced him that he should abandon his exile and return to public life. This decision put an end to any chances of election that Clarke might have had; all the more so when Riel began to campaign actively in the French parishes, even in the regions in which the influence of Charles Nolin, Riel's one-time adversary, was paramount. Finally Dubuc, Royal, de Plainval and Clarke met to discuss the course to be adopted in Provencher. Clarke declared that he would run in the election, even against Riel. Riel, he argued, would only be a source of embarrassment to "our friends in Ottawa." He would do far better to remain in hiding, at least until the election was over. Against Clarke, Dubuc maintained that Riel's presence in the Canadian capital would in no way "be prejudicial to Manitoba," and he suggested that Clarke should try his fortune in some constituency other than Provencher. Angry and stubborn, Clarke declared that it "was not just a matter of beating Riel, it was to beat . . . the fool who would not listen to his best friends." Riel, shouted Clarke, would be killed if ever he went to Ottawa. "It was absurd to hear that from a sensible man," wrote Dubuc to Riel.[35]

On Sunday, August 18, Riel and Clarke faced each other on the political platform at St. Norbert. It was a bitter encounter, more bitter than the one that had taken place some days before. Clarke was quick-tempered like his adversary, and he allowed his anger to get the better of him. He denounced Riel in terms scarcely calculated to win him support in a region where Riel had always enjoyed his greatest strength By way of contrast, Riel managed to control himself. He appeared "calm and very dignified" and won the sympathy of nearly all his listeners. According to the French-language newspaper in St. Boniface, *Le Métis*, which reported the Clarke–Riel encounter, Riel, even though some "of his devoted friends here and elsewhere" believe he "is returning to public life too soon," had resolved to take his chances, and was asking "only to be heard."[36] And he was heard, as he went from parish to parish, followed by resolutions asking him to represent them in the parliament of Canada. The métis wanted him as their member; they wanted him to go to Ottawa to justify himself and themselves before the people of Canada;[37] they wanted him to obtain the fulfilment of the terms upon which they had agreed to enter Confederation. As Clarke saw his chances of political glory receding, he became more and more violent. Finally, at Oak Point, he challenged Riel to a duel. What a situation, wrote the editor of *Le Métis*, with the Provincial Attorney-General trying to win political arguments with a revolver. He added, "the people will see that M. Riel has other arguments to support his candidature."[38]

Louis Riel was not, after all, elected to parliament in 1872. Early in September, Sir George Cartier was defeated in Montreal East by an

alliance of Liberals, anti-clericals and ultramontane "nationalists."[39]
Hurriedly Sir John A. Macdonald sent a telegram to the Lieutenant-
Governor: "Get Sir George elected in your Province—do not, however,
allow late Provisional [President] to resign in his favour."[40] Archibald,
who was awaiting the arrival of his successor, felt that despite the latter
part of Macdonald's telegram the only county in which Cartier's election
could be assured would be Provencher.   Here would be a chance not only
to elect Macdonald's principal French-Canadian associate, but also to
rid the government of the embarrassment of a victory by Riel.   At once
he wrote to Taché, "now or never—do not let the chance, which will
never recur, be lost.   Could you see me today."[41]   Both men were in
complete agreement.   Here was the opportunity "to bind Sir George
so tightly that he could not help doing even more afterwards than he
had done towards the amnesty."[42]   It should not be surprising that Riel
was not so easily persuaded as Taché.   If he were to withdraw from the
election, he would do so on his own terms.   Sir George would have to
pledge himself to secure the fulfilment of the promise regarding the
half-breed lands that was still in abeyance.   He asked nothing for himself: the amnesty he was prepared to leave to Cartier's good will.   This
condition was telegraphed to Macdonald who replied that he thought
"the constituency ought to elect Sir George promptly and without
stipulation," adding "they could safely confide in promises which, being
already made, can gain no strength in repetition."[43]   Cartier promised
he would willingly do all he could "to meet the wishes of the parties."[44]

On the nomination day, September 14, the Returning Officer opened
the meeting at St. Vital.   Riel's name was put forward by Pierre
Delorme, Joseph Royal and Joseph Lemay.   Clarke was nominated by
George Klyne and Joseph Hamelin.   Both men then declined the
nominations—Clarke had already yielded to Archibald's pressure—then
Sir George Cartier was nominated by Pierre Delorme, seconded by
André Beauchemin.   There were no other nominations and Cartier was
declared elected by acclamation.   Riel then congratulated the electors
upon their moderation and good judgment and, accompanied by his
supporters, returned to St. Norbert with a cavalcade of flags.[45]   Meanwhile a telegram of congratulation was sent to Cartier.   It was signed
by Louis Riel and Ambroise Lépine.[46]

In the opinion of Archibishop Taché and Lieutenant-Governor
Archibald, Riel's withdrawal of his nomination in Provencher had placed
the Canadian cabinet minister under a deep obligation to the métis
leader.   Macdonald, however, preferred to look upon it in a different
light.   Both Riel and Clarke, in his view, had resigned in order to secure
a cabinet minister for representative, thus acquiring for the province a

direct voice in the Cabinet. Of what use would this voice be if it were not raised on behalf of the electors? Even Macdonald admitted as much when he wrote, "Sir George agrees with me . . . it will be his interest to secure the approbation of his constituents, and he can be of more service to them than any other man."[47] What more could this mean, than obtaining the long-awaited and much-promised amnesty?

The election in Provencher had been accompanied by nothing more demonstrative than an outburst of cheering. Elsewhere in Manitoba the general election was marked by violence and lawlessness. De Plainval had armed his men in anticipation of trouble. Even so, a number of Canadians in Winnipeg, urged on by a rabble-rousing lawyer by the name of F. E. Cornish, who harangued the crowd upon the misdeeds of Archibald and all his French and Hudson's Bay Company supporters, crossed the river to St. Boniface and attacked the polling booth. When Donald A. Smith endeavoured to quiet them, he was driven off with a barrage of mud and worse. Then the rioters vented their spleen upon the two newspapers, *The Manitoban* and *Le Métis*. Schultz was gleeful, for he hated both newspapers. On the 23rd, he wrote to John Gunn, "The Governor and his faction are still and have been badly scared." Then he described the state of the *Manitoban* office as one of "a perfect pandemonium of printers' ink—windows smashed—press ditto. The *Métis* office as near as I can hear went bodily out of the window, and it will be some time before Jean Baptiste can express his grievances in print." Nor could Schultz avoid a few personal references: "Clarke made himself exceedingly scarce on Thursday and a party who went to his boarding house to ride him on a rail failed to find him. Donald A. escaped miraculously from a shower of stones and axe handles and has not been visible since. Plainval's head is still badly swollen and his stick or baton of office is in the hand of Tom White as a trophy of the day."[48]

III

During the next few months Riel remained quietly at home. He was waiting for the repayment of the debt he felt Cartier owed him. He knew that Archibald's term of office was almost at an end, and he knew that his successor would probably be neither as sympathetic nor as helpful as the Nova Scotian. The amnesty would have to come soon, and it would have to be Cartier who would get it. But Riel did not know that Cartier was ill—too ill even to meet his cabinet colleagues. He was well enough only to board the vessel that would take him to England where he hoped to find health, but where he was to die.[49]

Early in December the new Lieutenant-Governor, Alexander Morris, arrived in Manitoba. Macdonald had assured the Archbishop that he would find Morris "a very prudent man."[50] Scarcely had the Lieutenant-Governor put his foot in his office than his prudence was put to the test. On December 3, an attempt was made to arrest Louis Riel. Riel escaped. On January 3, he and Lépine addressed a lengthy letter to Morris summarizing the whole situation from the métis point of view.[51] Morris made no comment upon it. He merely forwarded the document to Ottawa.

Meanwhile Rodrigue Masson, Riel's friend in Ottawa, had taken steps to assist the métis leader. He had received Riel's memorandum and resolved to do what he could to bring about an amnesty. In Cartier's absence, he approached Hector Langevin, now the leading French-Canadian minister. Langevin took up the question with Sir John A. Macdonald.[52] But it was the same old story. Macdonald would not touch the amnesty for political reasons; and political reasons were speaking with a loud voice that winter of 1872/73. Macdonald's Conservative party had emerged with only a small majority from the electoral contest of 1872. Indeed, it was only by virtue of his victories in the Western and in the Maritime Provinces that he was back in power at all. He had lost seats in Ontario—partly over the Riel–Scott issue— and he had barely held his own in Quebec. How could he be expected to weaken his position still further by becoming involved in this explosive amnesty question. The return of Ritchot to Ottawa with his peremptory demands for an amnesty did not add to Macdonald's good temper, or his willingness to listen to arguments from Masson and Langevin about that fellow, Riel. There was nothing he would or could say that he had not said before. So he merely repeated the familiar argument: the amnesty was an Imperial responsibility, not one for the Canadian government. But Macdonald could not shrug off Ritchot with these excuses. The importunate priest had come personally to Ottawa. He talked to Langevin, to Masson, to Macdonald and to the new Governor-General, Lord Dufferin.[53] But he accomplished nothing. Macdonald was much too busy and concerned about the growing threats of the Liberal Opposition inside the House of Commons, with finding answers to the Liberal charges that Macdonald and Cartier had asked for and accepted financial assistance during the last election from Sir Hugh Allan in return for a contract to build the new transcontinental railway. How could Macdonald worry himself about Riel and Lépine, and the métis of Manitoba, with the fate of his government hanging in the balance? How much more strident sounded the voices of Huntingdon, Dorion and Blake, than those of Ritchot or Taché or Riel. And where would he ever find another man like Cartier to help him?

Macdonald's absorption in political tactics in Ottawa, and his failure to do anything for Riel, led Riel's friends to put the métis leader forward once again as a candidate for parliament. Not that the idea had ever left Riel's mind. In a moment of exaltation, Riel's friend and former associate in the Provisional Government, André Beauchemin, had offered to resign his seat of St. Vital and allow Riel to run for the provincial legislature. He had, in fact, actually handed his resignation to the Lieutenant-Governor; but he had worded it in such a way as to make it clear that he was resigning "in favour of Mr. Louis Riel."[54] When he was told that his resignation would have to be without condition, he had second thoughts and did not press the matter. He was, in fact, coming around to Royal's views that Riel's election would achieve no positive benefit for the province and might lead to further outbreaks of disorder.[55] But Riel was more interested in federal than in provincial politics. When, after the death of Sir George Cartier, Robert Cunningham, the member for Marquette (Manitoba), telegraphed Taché suggesting that Riel should again offer himself for parliament,[56] Riel seized upon the idea. He was annoyed at Macdonald's indifference towards Ritchot and at the apparent impossibility of holding the Prime Minister to any of the promises given, as he believed, in all sincerity in 1870. He would have to plead his own cause in parliament. With Cartier dead, there was none other upon whom he could rely.

If Riel liked the idea of running for parliament, there were those of his friends who regarded it with apprehension. In Ottawa, Sir John A. Macdonald spoke to Marc Girard, whom he had named to the Council of the North-West Territories in January, 1873, about "the thorny question" of Riel's candidature in Provencher. Girard told the Prime Minister that Riel "would certainly be elected." Macdonald professed to be unconcerned about whether such an eventuality would take place or not, but he expressed his fear that, should Riel come to Ottawa to take his seat, he would most certainly be arrested or murdered. "No one would rejoice more than I," wrote Girard to Taché, "to see him [Riel] in a position that would enable him to defend and protect the people he loves, but I am afraid he will not be allowed to attain it."[57] Royal wrote in a less sanctimonious strain. "If Riel is elected he cannot come to Ottawa: and besides, if he does come, he will be assassinated."[58] Rather more subtle, but equally convincing, was Masson's suggestion that it was Macdonald's wish that Riel should not run "before the proclamation of the amnesty."[59]

But if there were those who would have been happier to see Riel stay out of active politics, the very same men were quite prepared to admit that, should Riel choose to run, there would be none who could defeat him.   When it became clear that among those who were openly backing Riel there were some of the old settlers—men like Bannatyne, J. H. Mc-Tavish and Robert Cunningham—the possibility of election by acclamation became a distinct probability.   Only John Bruce opposed Riel, but he carried no weight at all.[60]   And why should Riel not run for parliament asked *Le Métis*?   Had not both Louis-Joseph Papineau and William Lyon Mackenzie sat as members of the House of Commons after the rebellions in Upper and Lower Canada in 1837?[61]

In June, Riel began to campaign actively for the by-election in Provencher.   As soon as Morris learned of this, he sent word to Macdonald, "Riel's defeat will be very difficult to effect, even if possible. What line do you wish taken?"[62]   For the moment there was no line at all to be taken.[63]   Perhaps Royal, Girard and some of the French-Canadians in St. Boniface would be able to dissuade Riel from accepting the nomination.   There was still plenty of time before the election. But as the weeks passed, Riel showed no disposition to abandon his declared intention of running for parliament.   Each day he grew in strength physically and politically.   He grew bolder and appeared more frequently in public, at Mass in the Cathedral and at meetings of the St. Jean Baptiste Society in St. Boniface.   On June 29, he joined in the parade which marched to the Cathedral and presented Archbishop Taché with the Society's compliments, declaring "The French-Canadian métis extending their hand to their brothers the French Canadians, wish to continue here the good work that the noble and generous province of Quebec has carried on for so long a time."[64]

In July a formal invitation came to Riel to allow his name to go before the electors of Provencher.   The invitation was extended by Royal and Girard, as well as by Dubuc and LaRivière; they were ready to climb on the Riel band wagon, once they had realized that nothing would stop Riel from running or winning his election.   Riel was grateful.   He thanked Dubuc and the others for their support, calling them his "strong arm" against all his adversaries.[65]   They might not be métis, but they were French-Canadians, and it was to French Canada that Riel now looked for encouragement and assistance.   From English Canada, from Ontario, the métis could expect nothing but abuse and, in the end, submergence and extinction.   To the métis, Ontario was typified by Schultz and his supporters, hostile, Protestant and Orange.   Taché and Dubuc were the personification of Quebec, friendly, Catholic and French.   Still waiting for instructions, Morris telegraphed in August to Ottawa, stating that Riel's election was a certainty.   "What do you advise?" he asked.[66]   But Ottawa was in as much of a quandary as

Winnipeg. The only answer Morris received was "cannot suggest any way of avoiding evil."[67]

Everything was going well for Louis Riel, perhaps too well. Henry Clarke and William Dease both attempted to drum up an opposition to Riel, accusing him of cowardice for never putting foot in Winnipeg.[68] But with Donald A. Smith said to be supporting him, as well as John McTavish, Bannatyne, Dubuc and Royal, Riel was supremely confident —so confident that when Father Forget-Despatis told him that the authorities in Ottawa were looking with a chilly eye upon his candidature, he lost his temper and declared that he had given up his seat once before at the request of the federal government, this time he would do it for nobody.[69] He even announced his intention of going into Winnipeg with a force of métis at his back and defying his opponents to arrest him. It took Cunningham to calm him down and to convince him of the foolhardiness of such an action.[70] Father Forget-Despatis, who was looking after the diocese in Taché's absence, became more and more worried. Unlike Ritchot and Lestanc, he was a very gentle and cautious man. He wondered how it was all going to end. He poured out his worries to Taché: "Cunningham is encouraging him [Riel] too much to believe that everything is going well in Ottawa; and that once there he will be able to plead his own cause and re-establish his reputation in everybody's opinion."[71]

As it happened, Father Forget-Despatis was right. Riel was too confident. His opponents might be quite incapable of beating him in a fair election, but they still had a weapon they could use effectively against him: the charge that he had participated in the "murder" of Thomas Scott. On September 14, several Canadians met in the office of F. E. Cornish to discuss how they might collect the reward that was still being offered by the Ontario government. They sent for William Farmer, who had been taken prisoner with Boulton's Portage party on February 18, 1870, and who harboured an inveterate hatred of the métis leader. Farmer was their man. He would swear out the information necessary to obtain a warrant for Riel's arrest. Pressed by Cornish and Henry Clarke,[72] Dr. H. J. O'Donnell, the magistrate, issued the necessary warrant. The warrant was then turned over to two constables, John Kerr and John Ingraham, who with an interpreter, Léon Dupont, set out to find Riel. It was raining heavily when they crossed the river and took the road to St. Vital, so heavily that they were obliged to give up their struggle with the mud and the darkness to spend the night in a métis farmhouse.

On the following morning, the two constables found, to their chagrin, that Riel could not be located. However there was still Lépine, Riel's one-time Adjutant-General and companion in exile. At Lépine's farm they found Lépine playing with a small child on his knee, just after eating his breakfast. For a moment Lépine contemplated resistance. He was a man of tremendous strength—"a clout from his fist would have been like the kick of a mule," wrote one of the constables[73]—and he had a pistol in his bedroom. Nevertheless he yielded quietly, and taking leave of his weeping wife and child, he went with his captors. By the time Kerr's party reached the old cable ferry over the Red River at St. Boniface, there was a menacing crowd on hand. The ferryman, a métis, refused to take them on board his ferry. However, when he was told that he too would be arrested, he gave in, and Lépine was taken across the river and lodged in one of the bastions of Fort Garry.[74] Several weeks passed before a case was made out against him, and it was exactly one month later, on October 14, when Lépine was committed to stand trial in the November Assizes. On November 15, a True Bill was found against him. But the case was postponed until the question of the jurisdiction of the court could be settled and, on December 22, Lépine returned home on bail of $8,000 provided by the French-Canadian and métis community. Not until February 14, 1874, was Lépine once more called upon to take his stand in the prisoner's dock and undergo trial for his life.

Meanwhile Louis Riel had gone into hiding. He had heard from A. G. B. Bannatyne of the issue of the warrant[75] and had taken refuge in the woods at Vermette's Point across the river from St. Norbert.[76] He was carefully guarded by several of his friends. Despite every effort made to find him—searches were made of the homes of his relatives and friends including those of Robert Cunningham, A. G. B. Bannatyne and Father Ritchot—he was never found.

The arrest of Lépine and the threat to Riel aroused strong feeling among the French métis throughout the whole of the province. On September 20, 1873, Le Métis published an outspoken letter of protest by Riel against Lépine's arrest, declaring it a violation of the good faith of the government. On Monday 22, a large meeting was held at St. Boniface to consider "the unanimous action" to be taken by all the half-breeds of the several French-speaking parishes.[77] Dubuc, LaRivière, Girard and Royal were there, and so were those who had been Riel's opponents during the days of the Provisional Government—Father Kavanaugh, William Dease and Charles Nolin—as well as representatives of the sympathetic English-speaking population, such as Bannatyne and Cunningham. Strongly-worded resolutions were adopted, and Royal declared that he would resign from the provincial legislature should his friends want him to do so. With the assistance of Cunningham, Bannatyne, McTavish and Smith, the resolutions were put into more suitable form, and a deputation was sent to interview Lieutenant-Governor Morris. Morris had asked the members of his cabinet to join him, but only Clarke was there. Girard, Cunningham, Dubuc and Ritchot argued the case for Riel and Lépine. "They kept me two hours this afternoon," wrote Morris to Macdonald.[78] But Morris could do nothing and could promise nothing. He did not even admit what privately he wrote to the Prime Minister: "My sympathies have been strongly with the mixed population. . . . If the supporters of Riel had remained quiet, and if they do now, it is a question whether it would not be best to secure an amnesty."[79]

In Ottawa the news of Lépine's arrest came as one more cause for embarrassment. Langevin had hastened to telegraph Taché disclaiming any federal responsibility for O'Donnell's action in issuing the warrant.[80] There was nothing that the Macdonald government wanted to see less than a revival of the Riel–Scott affair. The whole thing, Langevin was convinced, had been a political manoeuvre on the part of the Liberal party. Even without knowing the facts, Macdonald was astute enough to suspect that the arrest had been engineered by F. E. Cornish; and Cornish, as Langevin wrote, "is not our friend."[81] Whether it was a political dodge or not made no difference as far as the attitude of Ottawa towards the amnesty was concerned. If anything, it made it more difficult than ever for Langevin and Masson to press the amnesty on Sir John Macdonald.

Nevertheless the arrest of Lépine did not prevent Riel from continuing as a candidate for election in Provencher. It had come as a shock to him and to the whole French-speaking community that it should have been Dr. O'Donnell, of all people, who should have issued the warrant, for O'Donnell had always been looked upon as more than mildly sympathetic with the métis point of view.[82] It was even a greater disappointment when a second warrant for Riel was issued by a French-Canadian, Judge Louis Betournay.[83] Riel had been certain that the federal government would never let matters go as far as to permit his arrest and trial. There had been too many promises, too many assurances, too many indications of a positive nature to let him believe that Macdonald would condone or encourage such an act. So he decided to wait while Taché took the matter up with Macdonald. Perhaps all that worried Sir John was that once elected he, Riel, would join the opposition Liberal forces; perhaps it would be well to assure the Prime Minister that once elected he would join the Conservative caucus as a supporter of the government. Perhaps Taché would make this clear to Macdonald. Thus, during these trying days, he did not become discouraged. Rather he remained, as Father Proulx found him, "calm and cool before the fury of his enemies."[84]   Indeed his hopes seemed to be buoyed up by the successive postponements of Lépine's trial.   He would still have a chance of being elected and going to Ottawa to plead his own and Lépine's cause before parliament.

Nomination day was fast approaching.   On October 11, *Le Métis* published an editorial urging "the electors of Provencher county" to elect "Louis Riel, head of the French population of Manitoba," by acclamation.   Nominations were to take place at Baptiste Tourond's at St. Norbert on the 13th.   On that day some 450 to 500 métis gathered at Tourond's.   They were determined to allow no other nominations to be made except that of their chief, Riel, for there was still some talk that Clarke might come forward at the last moment.   Pierre Delorme put forward Riel's name, and the nomination was supported by Bannatyne, Tourond, Lemay, Nolin and others.   When other nominations were called for, there was silence; and when the polls closed Riel was declared elected by acclamation.   Expecting that Riel would attend the nomination meeting, several armed men drove to St. Norbert hoping to seize the métis leader.   But Riel had remained in hiding, and an encounter that must certainly have led to bloodshed aroused nothing more than a few muttered oaths and threatening gestures.   The métis then dispersed, Riel's principal supporters adjourning to Ritchot's rectory to celebrate the victory of their leader.   While they were there, the police arrived and searched the church and convent as well as Ritchot's house.   But they could not find Riel.[85]   He was still sheltering in Vermette's haystack on the other side of the Red River.   This was on the 13th.   On the next day, Judge Betournay ordered Lépine to stand trial on the charge of murder.

It had been decided by Riel's friends that as soon as the election was over he would go to Ottawa.   The necessary funds to defray his expenses had been raised, Dubuc, Royal, Bannatyne and McTavish being among the contributors.   The Archbishop, still in central Canada, sent one hundred dollars for "poor Louis."[86]   Even Charles Nolin, who had been one of Riel's opponents, made a contribution to the fund for Riel.[87]   Everything was planned in advance. Someone would have to accompany the métis leader to make all arrangements for tickets and rooms: above all, Louis' journey must be kept a secret and he must not show himself for fear of recognition.   He was to avoid using his own name.   Dubuc suggested "an ordinary name like Pierre David, Jean Dubois, etc."[88]   On arrival in Montreal, he would put himself in touch with the Archbishop or Robert Cunningham, or one of the French-Canadians, Alphonse Desjardins or Dr. E. P. Lachapelle, who had taken up his cause in

Quebec.   At first it was thought that Alphonse LaRivière might accompany Riel,[89] but when it was found that Joseph Tassé, a young Canadian journalist, was returning to Montreal, it was decided that Riel should accompany him.   They would go to Duluth and there board an American steamer for Milwaukee.   From there they would travel by train to Albany or Troy.   From either of these cities it would be only a short journey to Montreal or Terrebonne.[90]

Riel left St. Vital on October 21.   During the first part of the journey he travelled in company with Maxime Lépine and Quintal Pagé, both of whom were sent by Riel's friends to act as guides and bodyguards. When they reached the United States they met Tassé.   Lépine and Pagé returned home while Riel and his Canadian companion pursued their uneventful way to Montreal.

CHAPTER 11

Outlaw

IT WAS FIFTEEN YEARS since Louis Riel had made his first journey to Canada in 1858. Many changes had occurred in the meantime. Then, the Red River Settlement was still part of the Hudson's Bay Company territories; the economy of the country was dominated by fur traders and buffalo hunters; immigration from Canada was no more than a small trickle; and those Americans who made their way into the colony were either traders or deserters from the United States Army. By 1873 the old order had all but disappeared. Red River had become a province of the new Dominion of Canada, and immigrants were pouring into the valley. The surveys were being pushed ahead, and Manitoba was taking on something of the aspect, in architecture, speech and attitude, of the neighbouring Province of Ontario. New industries appeared, lumbering, banking, brick-making and flour milling. Winnipeg had not existed in 1858; by 1873 it had acquired a population of over 3,000. The old families of the earlier years, the Bannatynes, the McDermots, the Sutherlands and the Rosses, were almost submerged by the new arrivals, the Ashdowns, the Luxtons, the Stobarts, the Cornishes and the McArthurs.[1] Neither the Red River cart nor the York boat had entirely disappeared from the Manitoba scene; but there were now steamboats and the prospect of a transcontinental railway line with a branch to Pembina. In only five years the S.S. *Selkirk* would arrive with a flatboat bearing "The Countess of Dufferin," the first locomotive to enter the Canadian North-West.

The territory to the south had also changed. From a raw frontier community entering statehood in 1858, Minnesota had developed into an expanding political unit with a population of 500,000. Everywhere, over the Minnesota prairies, new railways were pushing their steel tentacles northward and westward. In 1870, the year Wolseley struggled over the Dawson route to Fort Garry, a railway line was completed between St. Paul and Duluth; and the next year the main line of the St. Paul and Pacific reached the Red River at Breckenridge. During the same time the Northern Pacific extended its line from Duluth to Moorhead on the same river. By 1873 another line was driving north towards Pembina.[2]

196

As the railways advanced, the old means of communication and the old economic activities became less and less significant. Even the steamboat was no more than a passing phase in the life of the people on both sides of the frontier. When Louis Riel set out for Montreal in October, 1873, he did not travel, as he had done in 1858, with the métis tripmen and their long line of Red River carts. Instead he joined Tassé at Glendon Station and boarded a Northern Pacific railway train for Duluth.

Louis Riel, too, had changed. From a timid, deeply religious, young métis visiting the outside world for the first time, he had become an experienced politician, the founder of a province and a member of the Parliament of Canada. He had crowded much into those fifteen years.

II

When Riel arrived in Montreal he was tired and depressed. For three years he had not known what it was to feel safe and secure. First there had been Wolseley's vengeful soldiery; then Schultz's vindictiveness; then Clarke's jealousy; and now Farmer's hatred. In Ontario the Orange fanatics had never ceased to demand his head. He had listened to promises, repeated many times over, that he would be amnestied; he had even been furnished with money from the public purse to ease his voluntary exile. But the future remained as uncertain as it had been in 1870. Perhaps he had relied too much on others. Perhaps he himself could persuade the government and the people of Canada that his course had been just. Perhaps he could make them see that public honour was at stake when pledges made to him were not honoured.

In Montreal Riel was met by Honoré Mercier, then member of parliament for Rouville in the province of Quebec.[3] Mercier had taken up Riel's cause as that of French Canada at large. Riel also met Alphonse Desjardins, the owner of the newspaper *Le Nouveau Monde* (a newspaper popularly believed to have been inspired by Bishop Bourget) on whose staff Joseph Royal had been employed before going to Red River. *Le Nouveau Monde* was strongly "nationalist" in tone, and it had, from the beginning of the troubles in Red River, opened its columns to Father Dugast and other supporters of the métis movement. Between them Mercier and Desjardins arranged for Riel to go at once to Ottawa to take his seat in the Commons Chamber as the member for Provencher. On the day appointed, the three men met in Hubert Paré's house in Hull; then they crossed the river to the hill on which stood the grey, stone, gothic structure that housed the Parliament of Canada. But Riel lost his courage. He could not go through with it. How could he be sure there were no men awaiting him to seize him and turn him over to the

Ontario authorities? So instead of signing the roll and taking his seat, he fled to Montreal.[4]

Dubuc had advised Riel to make Montreal his headquarters. It seemed to be the logical place; not only were there friends in Montreal who would look after him and conceal him from his enemies, but Montreal was near enough to the United States to make possible a quick flight out of Canada should circumstances demand it. In view of Riel's obvious ill-health and jittery state of mind, it was agreed the best thing for him to do would be to take refuge with the Oblate Fathers at Plattsburg on the shores of Lake Champlain. Plattsburg would be a convenient resting-place as it was no more than 70 miles from Montreal. Its proximity to the French-Canadian lumbering community of Keeseville might help remove some of the strangeness that Riel had found so oppressive in St. Paul. At Christmas, Riel was visited at Plattsburg by Fathers Lacombe and Poulin.[5] He still felt and looked poorly; and he was bored with inactivity. In a letter to Taché written on January 1, he told the Archbishop that he was anxious to resume political life again as soon as possible. He had heard that Sir John Macdonald had been forced to accept the inevitability of defeat over the Pacific railway scandal and that the Liberal leader, the honest but unimaginative Alexander Mackenzie, had become Prime Minister. Riel did not know that Mackenzie had made up his mind to dissolve parliament, although he suspected as much and asked for Taché's "help and blessing" in the next election. But he still felt sorry for himself. "May heaven have pity upon me," he wrote, "for I am poor and lonely."[6]

Some of his loneliness was, however, eased by a visit to Keeseville early in January. It was the first of a number of visits to a village and a household in which he was to find love and affection as the months passed. Riel wrote to his mother that the curé, whose name was Fabien Barnabé, "has his good mother with him; they have been very attentive to me," and had given him three scapulars for Mrs. Riel, Eulalie and Octavie, and "a beautiful little heart for my dear little sister, Henriette."[7] Louis did not mention the fact that the priest also had his sister, Evelina, with him—perhaps because his visit was only a short one, perhaps because his mind was more upon himself than upon others. In any event, Louis's visit was pleasing to the Barnabé family. "I have decided to write to you," Father Barnabé wrote later to Riel, "to tell you just how lively is the memory of your visit. Scarcely a day passes by without your name receiving an honourable mention. We think of you, we talk about you, we feel for you as one would for a devoted friend, a loved brother. You are one of the family."[8]

By mid-January Louis had decided he was well enough to go back to

Montreal. A return to politics was imperative. On January 7 the writs
for the new general election had been issued, and the voting was to take
place in February. He could afford to delay no longer. He had, moreover, completed a long memoire on the amnesty question for Desjardins,
and he wanted to see it published in *Le Nouveau Monde*.[9] The housekeeper
at the priests' establishment in Plattsburg was sorry to see him go. She
had sympathized with the sad-looking man who had spent several weeks
with the Oblates. "He was very lonely," she wrote to Riel's mother,
"and I would go and see him in his room to cheer him and pass away his
time . . . he would always talk about his folks, his mother and his little
sister, Henriette."[10]

Returning to Canada, Riel went first to live with his relatives, the
Lees, in St. Jean Baptiste, where he had spent several months after
leaving school in 1865. He was still not in robust health, but seems to
have improved under his aunt's care.[11] Later he moved into Montreal
where Desjardins was prepared to give him hospitality at his own house
at 758 Dorchester Street, just behind the Bishop's Palace. These
arrangements had been made by Dr. Lachapelle, who assured Riel that
no one could possibly suspect him there. "Under the name of David,"
wrote Lachapelle, "you can live quietly while observing at first hand the
movements of public opinion here, and thus put yourself in the position
of knowing and appreciating the ground on which you will have to fight
on taking your seat in Ottawa."[12] It would be all the better, too, as
Desjardins was a member of parliament. Besides defending Riel in
Le Nouveau Monde he could give Riel sound political advice as to how to
handle himself once he was in the House of Commons. Riel was anxious
and excited by the thought of returning to the centre of the political stage.
He had been encouraged by a visit to Bishop Bourget who looked upon
him as "the instrument of providence."[13] He was convinced, as he wrote
to Taché in St. Boniface, that God was on the side of the métis.[14]

Once a new general election had been decided on by Alexander Mackenzie, the spectre of Riel's participation arose to haunt the ministry.
Just as Cartier had before him, Antoine Dorion, the principal French-
Canadian minister in the new Liberal administration, hoped that Riel
would refrain from running as a candidate in Provencher. It was at least
worth the effort to try to convince Archbishop Taché to intercede with
the métis leader and persuade him to remain quiet. It was even more
essential to the Liberals than to the Conservatives that Riel should not
run, especially since Riel had chosen to identify himself with the ultramontane wing of the latter party. Accordingly Dorion sent a telegram
to the Lieutenant-Governor, Alexander Morris, asking him to tell Taché
that "in order to avoid excitement, Riel should not be a candidate."[15]

The Archbishop was extremely annoyed—annoyed that Morris should have sent his secretary to give him the contents of Dorion's message instead of coming himself, and annoyed that once again a federal cabinet minister should ask him to do political dirty work for the government without even hinting that the promised amnesty would be forthcoming as a *quid pro quo*.   He replied huffily to Dorion:

The whole Province of Quebec ask you to do an act of justice on behalf of men who have been shamefully deceived, and the only answer is to request me to manage so that their leader shall not receive a proof of the respect and confidence of his fellow countrymen.   This man is within two or three hours' journey of Montreal, and an eight days' journey from me, and I am to take steps to induce him to hide himself and to continue with his family in misery!   What is to be offered to Mr. Riel as a recompense for the sacrifices which he is called upon to make?   Misery, exile, or a jail if he returns to his native land.   There is no other alternative. . . . For four years I have been made use of, nominally for the good of the people whom I love, as an instrument to deceive that same people. . . . Allow me to tell you that now, more than ever, my interference in the direction requested (unless there were certain compensation) would to me be productive of pain and difficulty.   I cannot act unless, I repeat, I have something certain to offer.   If you knew all the indignities to which our poor people have been subjected, you would not be annoyed at my experiencing the painful feelings which I do.[16]

Taché, therefore, would not interfere.   He had had enough of politicians and their promises.   He had gone to Ottawa late in 1873 to talk to Langevin, Robitaille and Masson; after the fall of Macdonald's government he had approached Dorion and Letellier.[17]   But he could extract nothing definite from any of them.   He had, therefore, made up his mind to publish the whole story in pamphlet form.[18]   This was the only course left to him—an appeal to public opinion above the heads of government chiefs.   If his pamphlet had no other effect it would at least show the métis and the people of Red River what the Archbishop had done and how he himself had been the victim of assurances and promises that were, apparently, never to be fulfilled.   Dorion turned to Father Lacombe hoping that he might be willing to pull the hot chestnuts that Taché would not touch.   But Lacombe, too, refused.   He was no more anxious to become involved than the Archbishop.[19]

If Dorion found difficulty in finding someone willing to dissuade Riel from running in the election, Riel found many who were willing to encourage him to do that very thing.   From Ottawa and Red River he received optimistic missives expressing the hope that he would go ahead with his original plans.[20]   Indeed, it would have been impossible to have prevented him from doing so.   He had made up his mind to run; and he

had made up his mind that this time, after his election, he would not
falter when it came to taking his seat in parliament, even if it should
mean his death.[21]

Riel's victory in Provencher in February, 1874, was not won by
acclamation. Riel's opponents, with Liberal support,[22] managed to
persuade Joseph Hamelin to let his name be put up as a candidate.
Hamelin was the son of a former member of the Council of Assiniboia,
and he had taken no part in the troubles of 1869/70. It was understood
that Hamelin was not likely to draw many votes from St. Norbert, but
it was hoped that he would receive support in those regions in which the
anti-Riel faction of the earlier period was still strong, along with sufficient
votes elsewhere to carry the day. But Hamelin really had no chance of
election, especially with the whole weight of the French-Canadian
community in St. Boniface backing Louis Riel. *Le Métis* damned him
as a man "without patriotism" and with "little enough pride in his own
reputation."[23] He was accused of conniving in attempts to have the
names of Riel's supporters removed from the electoral rolls in Ste.
Agathe. Finally, when the votes were counted, it was found that
although Hamelin did win a narrow majority in Ste. Agathe, he was
swamped in the other parishes of the constituency. For the second time
Louis Riel had been elected to represent the Provencher county in
parliament.[24] In the other Manitoba constituencies those men who had
been elected in 1873 retained their seats. Riel's friend, Robert Cunningham, was returned for Marquette, and D. A. Smith and John Schultz
were elected in Selkirk and Lisgar respectively. "We are pleased with
the results," wrote Dubuc to Riel.[25]

As soon as he learned of his re-election, Riel made arrangements to go
to Ottawa. Travelling quietly to Hull, he endeavoured to secure an
appointment with Antoine Dorion. But Dorion would not see him.[26]
The minister was afraid that if it should become public knowledge that
he was negotiating with the ex-president of the Provisional Government,
it would place both himself and the Liberal party in an impossible
position; particularly because his chief, Alexander Mackenzie, had
campaigned during the general election on an anti-Riel platform,
roundly accusing Macdonald of having promised an amnesty. There
was, in fact, no difference in the attitude the Liberals adopted towards
Riel, now that they were in power, and the attitude of the Conservatives
when they had held office.

After returning to consult with friends in Montreal, Riel went back
to Hull on March 25. In a letter written the next day, Dr. Lachapelle
asked Desjardins to urge upon Riel the necessity of caution in all his
actions: "Let our friend have the patience to await an opportune moment

to make his entry into the House, and let everything be well prepared for all eventualities."[27]   He suggested that should Riel "for one reason or another" find it inadvisable to remain in Ottawa, he should come back to Montreal and take up residence with Dr. Durocher or with himself. A doctor's house, said Lachapelle, was a public place, and the presence of a stranger would not be likely to attract very much attention.

The plans were made and the day selected.   It was March, a cold day, with the snow still on the ground, cold enough to make the wearing of heavy coats and wraps a common enough sight on the streets of Ottawa.[28] In the afternoon several figures crossed the Ottawa River from Hull and walked towards the buildings whose stone towers and metal spires dominated the city.   Two of the men entered a side door and walked towards the office of the Clerk of the House, Alfred Patrick.   One of these men, Romuald Fiset, the member for Rimouski and a former schoolmate of Riel's, asked Patrick if he would swear in a new member.   It was a routine action, and Patrick paid little attention to what was going on. He did not even inquire the name of the new member, and noted only that he wore "a heavy whisker, not exactly black."[29]   He administered the oath of allegiance and listened indifferently as the reply came, "I do swear that I will be faithful and bear true allegiance to Her Majesty Queen Victoria."   Patrick then produced the roll which the two men proceeded to sign.   Then they turned to leave.   "I did not pay particular attention," said Patrick later, "and did not look at the roll until they were leaving the room.   To my astonishment I saw the name 'Louis Riel.'   I looked up suddenly and saw them going out of the door.   Riel was making a low bow to me."   Fiset and Riel then left the building hurriedly, and Patrick, scarcely yet recovered from his astonishment, rushed along the hallway to inform the incredulous Minister of Justice of what had happened.   Louis Riel, in spite of the efforts and plans of his enemies to secure his arrest, had actually entered the parliament buildings and had signed the register as the member for Provencher.

There was great excitement in the Canadian capital, and the session on the evening of March 30 opened in an atmosphere of expectancy.   Would Louis Riel be present or not?   Would he rise in his place to defend his actions?   But it was not Riel who held the floor.   It was Riel's two friends, J. O. Mousseau and Rodrigue Masson.   Mousseau sought to justify the rising of 1869/70 and demanded the promulgation of a general amnesty.   Masson, too, spoke on Riel's behalf.   But the motion for an amnesty was defeated, and Mackenzie Bowell, the Orange leader from Belleville, Ontario, proposed that the House should take evidence that would establish the exact status of Riel.   On the next day Henry J. Clarke, once the friend of the métis and now the bitter enemy of Riel, appeared before the House of Commons bearing the indictment against Riel for murder and declaring that he was a fugitive from justice. How, asked Joseph Cauchon, could Riel be a fugitive when he had come to Ottawa and had signed the members' roll? This was just what Bowell had expected, and at once he moved that "Louis Riel be ordered to attend the House tomorrow."[30]

The next day the galleries were filled with curious onlookers wondering and watching what was going to happen. The Governor-General's wife, Lady Dufferin, went to the House, as she wrote in her *Journal*, "expecting to see Riel take his seat. There was great excitement outside."[31] The streets and lobbies of the parliament buildings were crowded with detectives. Would Riel emerge from his hiding-place? Would he attempt to take his seat? There were cases of mistaken identity, and several unsuspecting individuals were arrested by over-zealous constables. The faces of the darker-skinned members were closely scanned and compared with photographs of the métis leader.[32] But there was no sign of Riel. Both his friends and his enemies were disappointed. All that happened was the adoption of a motion to adjourn for a week.

In the interval the French-Canadian members of the House went into caucus, regardless of party, to establish their solidarity on the question of the amnesty. Public meetings were held in order to protest complete sympathy with the métis leader and the determination of the French-Canadian population to protect him from arrest. When the House reconvened, Louis Riel still made no appearance. It had been agreed that a Select Committee should be appointed to "enquire into the causes of the difficulties which existed in the North-West in 1869 and 1870, and into those which have retarded the granting of the amnesty announced in the Proclamation issued by the late Governor General of Canada, Sir John Young. . . ."[33] But Mackenzie Bowell refused to wait until its deliberations had been completed and its report issued. He was determined to force the issue. He moved that "Louis Riel, having fled from justice and having failed to obey an Order of this House that he should attend in his place, Thursday, the 9th day of April, 1874, be expelled this House."[34] The seconder was John Schultz.

The debate that followed was marked by strong emotion. The Prime Minister, Alexander Mackenzie, much as he might have wished to side-step the issue, had no choice but repeat his earlier stand that Scott's death was a crime against humanity, justice and law. Again Riel's friends sprang to his defence. Again Mousseau came up with an amendment in favour of an amnesty. This motion had already been defeated, and there was no chance that it would be successful a second time.

Desjardins, who hoped to persuade some of the English-speaking members of the House to support a delaying action until the Select Committee should make its report, felt that Mousseau's motion was a political blunder.   There was no possibility of ever getting Dorion and the French-Canadian Liberals to support a motion to which Mackenzie was so adamantly opposed.   Archbishop Taché, too, felt that Mousseau had been "too direct" and that his action had been "inopportune."[35]   The result was that Mousseau's motion merely closed the Liberal ranks, and the amnesty suggestion was defeated with the French-speaking Liberals voting against it.   When a motion was put to stay proceedings to await the Committee's report, it too was defeated.   There was no doubt now that Bowell's motion for expulsion would carry without difficulty.   The English members had the greater numerical strength and, by a majority of fifty-six votes, Riel was expelled from the House of Commons.   "So Riel has been thrown out!   What a sad business," wrote Father Lacombe to the Archbishop of St. Boniface.[36]   The Prime Minister saw it differently.   It "was a mistake," he wrote to Alexander Morris in Winnipeg, that Manitoba should ever have been made a province and that Riel should ever have become a member of parliament, if only because his expulsion would be sure to arouse the métis "and exercise a harmful influence with the Indians with whom they are intimate."[37]

III

Despite his early resolutions, Louis Riel had not remained to follow the course of the debate.   He was in too great fear for his life to stay longer in his hiding-place in Hull.   There were too many policemen about, and Blake's $5,000 was no small inducement to the weak-hearted or to the unscrupulous to betray his whereabouts and turn him over to the Ontario authorities.   Thus, immediately after signing the roll on March 30, he slipped away in the gathering dusk and hurried towards Montreal.   Travelling all night, he managed to reach L'Abord à Plouffe by 4 A.M. the next morning.   Here he went at once to the house of Venance Lemay, a friend of Sir George Cartier, to whom he had a letter of introduction.   But Lemay hesitated to take him in.   Mme. Lemay was a Scottish Canadian from Glengarry in Ontario, and her husband felt that she might be suspicious of the bearded stranger.   He suggested to Riel that he should push on towards the city itself, and perhaps take refuge with Lemay's son.   But the son, too, was not disposed to take the risk of sheltering the métis chief.   Perhaps the safest place, after all, would be Alphonse Desjardins' house, where Riel had stopped before.   But Desjardins' house was no longer a secure refuge.   A neighbour, a certain Mr. Austin, had become suspicious of the identity of Desjardin's guest and had started to ask rather embarrassing questions.[38] Riel began to wonder if, perhaps, he might not return to the west. Accordingly, after a short visit to St. Hyacinthe, where he met Honoré Mercier and several other supporters,[39] Riel went on to spend a few days with Father Barnabé, and then continued his journey towards St. Paul, Minnesota.

It was on May 19 that Riel reached the capital of Minnesota. He went to stay with a French-Canadian, a certain Dubeau who lived alone "in an attractive cottage, with his wife."[40] He was prepared to remain, at least briefly, in St. Paul, although it was clearly his intention to return, if at all feasible, to Manitoba. On May 27 he sent a letter to his friend, Dubuc. It was an optimistic letter despite the developments in Ottawa. Riel could not but feel a sense of pride when he recalled that: "in the autumn of '69 we began the defence of our rights with only a handful of men; that a few months later half the colony was on our side; that by March, 1870, the whole colony actively endorsed what we were doing; that eight months after the beginning of the struggle, we obtained the concession of all our rights by a treaty which became law." The métis leader also expressed his pleasure with the publicity which his *Mémoire* was receiving, and told Dubuc, "The fact is that our cause is making progress. . . . I can almost say it, our cause is shaking the Canadian Confederation from one end of the country to the other. It is gaining strength daily."[41] If there was any cloud on the horizon, it seemed to be only in Manitoba, where French influence was declining and where the proposed provincial redistribution bill would reduce the number of French-speaking members in the legislature.

Riel's expulsion from the House of Commons made vacant the parliamentary seat of Provencher county. But neither Riel nor his friends were prepared to sit idly by and allow the by-election to go by default. They were convinced that Riel should run again, and win, and thus strengthen his case in the minds of the general public with this additional proof of the loyalty of his constituents. Dr. Lachapelle had already written to Dubuc in Winnipeg to assure him that Riel's Montreal friends were thoroughly pleased with the métis leader. They were willing to give him not only "moral" but also "material" support to help him win his election. As practical evidence of their good will, Lachapelle sent a postal order of $100 "that our friend has asked me to send to his mother."[42]

There was much to encourage Riel and his friends. There seemed to be something in the nature of a shift in public feeling towards the métis chief and the events of 1869/70. Riel's *Mémoire*, published by Desjardins in *Le Nouveau Monde* in February, had excited considerable discussion among the newspapers of Quebec, both French and English. *Le National* and *La Minerve* both demanded the promulgation of the amnesty, blaming the delays upon the Liberals; the *Herald*, while condemning the execution of Scott, struck out at the government for its negligence and its shameful reluctance to carry out promises that should never have been made; even the *Witness* was moved sufficiently to call for an enquiry into the truth of Riel's allegations. The interest aroused by Riel's pamphlet was excited further by Taché's publication of his brochure, *The Amnesty*, at the beginning of April. This was followed not long afterwards by the revelations of witnesses before the Select Committee appointed by the House of Commons. The Committee began its sittings on April 10, and every day until May 21 document after document, sworn statement after sworn statement seemed to build up an impressive volume of proof that promises had been made to the effect that an amnesty would be granted—promises that had never been carried out. Taché, Ritchot, Archibald, Girard, Royal and others took the stand and poured their testimony into the ears of the committee members.[43] Sir John A. Macdonald endeavoured to excuse himself by insisting that he had never recognized the Red River delegates. He said he had never given any undertaking to use the good offices of the government to secure an amnesty from the Imperial authorities. He was certain his colleague, Sir George Cartier, who was dead, had never done so either. Nevertheless Cartier's secretary, Major Futvoye, and Cartier's own letters and memoranda supported the testimony of Taché and Ritchot. After listening to Macdonald, Taché could not restrain himself. He wrote to his old friend, Monseigneur LaFlèche, who at one time had been a member of the Council of Assiniboia before becoming Bishop of Three Rivers: "The Rt. Honourable John A. Macdonald lied (excuse the word) like a trooper."[44] Every day the press in Quebec published the depositions of the various witnesses. The Ontario newspapers, too, gave considerable space to the sessions of the committee. Papers like the *Globe* were anxious to emphasize those parts of the evidence that involved Macdonald and his colleagues in what their editors regarded as questionable dealings with priests and half-breeds, and to play down those statements that suggested the Red River troubles had some moral justification behind them.

Despite an interest in the question of his re-election in Provencher Riel did not return to Manitoba. Dubuc felt that it would be better if he were to stay in the United States until he could return as a free man.[45] The case of Ambroise Lépine was still pending, and other arrests had been made on the same charge of murder, including those of André Nault and

Elzéar Lagimodière. Riel himself had heard disturbing news, news that might or might not be significant, but which revived all his old fears. He had been recognized while in St. Paul, and Dr. Schultz had been seen not far away in the town of Moorhead.[46] Although he had been scarcely more than two weeks in St. Paul, Riel hurried back to the eastern United States. There he might feel safe, particularly with his friends in Keeseville. When Desjardins wrote to Riel on June 13, to tell him that Antoine Dorion was leaving politics to become chief justice of Quebec and that the minister's place was being taken by Felix Geoffrion,[47] Riel was already on his way east. Louis had no definite plans, except perhaps to take part in the celebrations of St. Jean Baptiste Day in Montreal. He would simply wait to see what Desjardins, Lachapelle, Fiset and others could do towards accelerating the granting of the amnesty. They could do little. Desjardins noted with some disgust: "Fournier, Geoffrion, and even Langevin, they are all, in my opinion, just food for the Orangemen or the Grits of Upper Canada. If the good Lord really is to have mercy upon our dying race . . . He will have to raise up a few men who will drive out these more or less nonentities who call themselves our leaders."[48]

If the métis cause seemed to be making little headway at Ottawa, it seemed to be going reasonably well in Manitoba. Riel was delighted when he learned in July that Henry J. Clarke's government in Manitoba had been defeated over the redistribution bill and that the new ministry, headed by Marc Girard as premier, contained his friend Joseph Dubuc as Attorney-General.[49] There seemed to be no reason why Riel should not win his seat again in Provencher. A special "Manitoba" Committee had been formed in Montreal to assist Riel in every way it could. This committee, which included in addition to Desjardins and Lachapelle such well-known ultramontane and "nationalist" Conservatives as Louis Taillon, Onésime Loranger, Sévère Rivard and François Trudel, was prepared to agitate the métis cause on every possible occasion. To them the cause of the French half-breeds and the French-Canadians was one and the same.[50] Riel himself was in fine fettle, according to Dr. Lachapelle. There was only one thing that gave him cause for concern, and that was Riel's homesickness, his anxiety to return to Red River. Much as Riel liked and admired his Quebec friends, they wearied him a little with their importunities, and he wanted to see his mother and the familiar scenes of his boyhood. He was a little worried because he had heard rumours that some of his former backers in Red River were not as strong in his support as they had once been. Perhaps they needed to be reminded that there must be no compromise, that they must all remain united.

The rumours were true. Some of Riel's friends had begun seriously to question if anything was to be gained by continuing to return Riel to parliament when he could never take his seat. They wondered if it might not be better for him to wait until the amnesty should be granted. It was, indeed, a return to the policy that Cartier had urged with so little success in the months after the flight from Fort Garry. Joseph Royal was one of those who wondered. He had written to Montreal expressing doubts about the political advisability of running Riel in Provencher again.[51] Girard, too, had weakened in his support of Riel and roused suspicions that he was interested only in his own future.[52] LaRivière too. But most serious of all, Archbishop Taché was inclined to take the view that Riel ought to withdraw from active political life for the time being.[53] Such a wavering in support of what Desjardins and his associates believed to be a truly "national" cause met with their strong disapprobation, and also with the disapproval of Louis Riel, who wrote to Dubuc to ensure his support at least: "With me in the federal Parliament and you in the local Ministry, if we follow the same ideals, we shall be useful to one another, there is no doubt about it."[54] Then Riel wrote to Father Dugast to enlist the support of the clergy. At the same time, Lachapelle sent a postal order for fifty dollars to Father Ritchot asking him to use it as Riel's election deposit, assuring him that it would only "chill the sympathies" of those people in Quebec, who were "so ardent for the métis cause" if Louis Riel should be dropped as a candidate in Provencher, simply because he had not yet received the justice due him in the form of the amnesty.[55] To lend further support to Riel, Rodrigue Masson paid a hurried visit to Manitoba towards the end of August.[56]

To some extent at least, it was as a result of the strong support he received from the ultramontane Conservatives of Quebec that Louis Riel was the sole candidate whose name was put forward when nominations were called for at Pierre Delorme's house on September 3.[57] None of the other men who had talked of running, or whose names had been suggested as possible candidates, was prepared to enter the lists against Riel, Dr. W. R. Bown, Alphonse LaRivière, L. O. Bourget or Joseph Tassé. Riel's election in September, 1874, was by acclamation, just as it had been the year before.

Riel was grateful to the métis for their unswerving loyalty and to Joseph Dubuc and Father Ritchot for the efforts that they had put forth on his behalf. They had organized the meetings; they had used their influence. But the Archbishop, although he had urged LaRivière not to run, had not raised his voice for Riel. Riel was hurt by Taché's apparent indifference, and he was also a little alarmed. He felt that the Archbishop was weakening the cause by compromising when he should be

standing firm.   If Taché should continue this course it would mean only
one thing, that the two men, instead of supporting each other, would be
in opposition.   The métis people would have to choose between them.

This may have been the reason why Riel, when the election was over,
unburdened himself not to Taché, but to Ritchot.   He wrote to tell
Ritchot that the election results had been "well received" in Quebec,
and that the Conservative Opposition in Ottawa would, in consequence,
feel strengthened and encouraged.   "Actually the Opposition is not
very strong in Ottawa," he wrote, "but with a strong issue such as the
amnesty" it would be able "to influence considerably the action of the
Ministry there."[58]   Riel was now thoroughly imbued with the interpretation that Desjardins, Lachapelle and the French-Canadians had
given to the métis rising in 1869/70.   It was a matter of French rather
than half-breed survival.   Riel was convinced that his re-election was
something more than just the vindication of his own personal stand.   It
was the symbol of something far more significant; it was the answer of
French Catholic Canada to Orange Ontario; it was the assertion of the
principle of equality of the two races in all Canada.   He therefore urged
that there should be no more bowing to political threats, no more tem-
porizing with bigotry, no more compromising with fanaticism.   If
Ontario wanted to battle it out on the field of race and religion, French
Canada would accept the challenge and would abandon the meaningless
struggles of political parties.   All men who spoke French and accepted
the Roman Catholic faith would unite to safeguard French influence in
Manitoba and the North-West.   To defend Riel would be to defend
French culture and the Catholic Church on the prairies.   This was how
Riel wrote to Ritchot.   His views did not originate with himself.   They
were not the views that had inspired him in the summer of 1869.   But
they were the views his friends held, and with justification, once the local
issues of Red River had become inextricably confused with the traditional
rivalries of the French and English in Canada.

Riel did not attempt to take his seat in parliament following his
re-election in September of 1874.   He paid visits to Three Rivers and to
Quebec where he had a brief audience with Cardinal Taschereau.[59]   Then
his thoughts again turned to the west.   In November he went as far as
St. Paul,[60] but he did not remain there.   A few days later he was on his
way back, passing through Chicago en route to the eastern United States.
Here he would find his warm friends, Father Barnabé at Keeseville and
Abbé J.-B. Evariste Richer, one-time missionary in Manitoba, now at
Suncook in New Hampshire.   A few miles to the south of Suncook was
Nashua, where Father Milette, a friend of Richer's, was the incumbent.

The best place would be Keeseville. It was within easy reach of Montreal, and he could travel there without much expense or loss of time whenever the political situation should necessitate such a journey.

IV

In the meantime Riel's former lieutenant, Ambroise Lépine, had finally been brought to trial. Alexander Mackenzie's government had been as little disposed as its Conservative predecessor to hurry matters along, and the trial had been postponed several times owing to the unwillingness of Judge Betournay and Judge McKeagney to rule upon the question of the Court's jurisdiction over crimes committed in the territory before it became part of Canada. It was not until E. B. Wood was appointed Chief Justice of the province that the question was settled and Lépine's case was proceeded with. The case for the Crown was in the hands of Francis E. Cornish and Stewart Macdonald; the defence was the responsibility of Adolphe Chapleau and Joseph Royal. At the previous hearings, Dubuc had shared the defence with his colleague, Royal; but the intensity of feeling aroused in Quebec by the treatment of Riel induced Chapleau to accept the invitation extended by Royal and Desjardins to defend Riel's colleague as a matter of duty to his own race and people.[61] Chapleau was not only a prominent Conservative politician; he was considered to be one of the best criminal lawyers in Canada. With gratitude and optimism Desjardins and his friends gathered at Bonaventure Station in Montreal to bid godspeed to Chapleau as he set out for Manitoba on September 27.[62] In his hands would rest not only the fate of the giant métis who had commanded Riel's soldiers during the months of the resistance but the hopes of French-Canadians throughout the whole of Canada.

The trial began on October 13, just one year after Lépine's arrest, and it continued until November 2.[63] The Crown produced a large number of witnesses, including several men who had been Riel's prisoners at Fort Garry. But the real strength of the prosecution rested on the evidence of three métis, John Bruce, Joseph Nolin and François Charette. Bruce's bias was obvious. He claimed that Lépine had said, some days before the execution of Thomas Scott, "We will release the prisoners before long, but we will put a couple to death before releasing them."[64] Nolin identified Lépine as the president of the métis court-martial.[65] Charette claimed that Lépine had given Guillmette the revolver which had delivered the *coup de grâce*.[66] In reply, the defence was able to point out that the bulk of the Crown's witnesses could not say positively that Lépine had been present at the shooting of Scott. The main burden of Chapleau's defence was based on the argument that the Provisional

Government had been a *de facto* government, and that the métis court-martial derived its authority from this fact. He also argued that the court, then trying Lépine, did not have the right to do so, since it had no jurisdiction to try offences committed in the Hudson's Bay Company's territories prior to the admission of Red River to the Canadian federation. But the Chief Justice would not accept the latter argument, and would not permit Chapleau to introduce as evidence the private letters of Cartier and Macdonald upon which he relied to prove that the Canadian government had given formal recognition to the delegates of the Provisional Government as a *de facto* government.

From the reports of the trial that are available, the whole proceeding seems to have been conducted with remarkably little care for the normal rules of evidence. It also seems clear that both Royal and Chapleau neglected to make the most of their opportunities during the periods of cross-examination. The explanation for this may rest in the fact that neither Royal nor Chapleau was fully at home in the English language. The brilliancy of Chapleau's address to the jury, if it was appreciated by six French-speaking jurors, must have been more or less lost on the others; and Royal's address in English was not the equal of that given by Cornish in the same language. Chapleau may have been, as Royal later assured Rodrigue Masson, "admirable, in tact, devotion and eloquence."[67] But in the end the jury returned the verdict of "guilty with a recommendation for mercy." The decision, as Royal admitted, was given by a jury that could not have been improved upon from the standpoint of the defence. Chief Justice Wood imposed the sentence. It was the sentence of death.[68]

The conviction of Lépine was followed by an outburst of indignation in the province of Quebec. *Le Nouveau Monde* declared that the French-Canadian ministers in the Liberal cabinet should immediately secure an amnesty or resign their appointments. This was echoed by other newspapers in the province. When Chapleau returned to Montreal on November 14, he was greeted as a national hero. From all parts of the country petitions poured into the offices of the federal cabinet ministers. The Archbishop and six Bishops of Quebec added their prayers to that of Taché in a demand for a pardon. The Quebec legislature, prompted by Adolphe Chapleau and François Trudel, passed a unanimous resolution asking the Governor-General to grant an amnesty to Lépine and Riel.

Alexander Mackenzie felt he was caught in a cleft stick. It mattered little how he wriggled. If he granted the amnesty, he must offend the province he relied on for support; if he did not grant it, he would alienate the other province. And yet do something he must. Like Macdonald before him, he sought to throw the responsibility from his own shoulders to those of the Imperial government.   It was not up to the federal cabinet to grant the amnesty; it was up to the Colonial Secretary and the British government.   When he said this he admitted quite frankly to the Governor-General that he did so because of "the obvious embarrassments attending the settlement of a controversy . . . so seriously complicated by the vehement international antagonism which they have excited in this country."[69]

Lord Dufferin, the Governor-General, had been in Canada long enough to appreciate the nature of Mackenzie's problem. "This is the most thorny business I have ever had to deal with," he told the Colonial Secretary, "thanks to the imbecility of almost everyone who has hitherto meddled with it."[70]   Nevertheless he grasped the nettle that neither Macdonald nor Mackenzie wanted to touch, and in a long despatch to London he reviewed the whole story of the amnesty, concluding with the decision to commute, upon his own authority, the death sentence which Chief Justice Wood had passed upon Ambroise Lépine.   Dufferin would not admit there was any validity to the argument that Riel's government had even a *quasi*-legal basis as a *de facto* administration, or that Taché had any real authority to make the promises he gave to Riel and others. But he was impressed with the demonstration of métis loyalty during the "Fenian" troubles, and he admitted that he could not shake his doubts that once Lieutenant-Governor Archibald had "put arms in the hands of a subject, and . . . invited him to risk his life with the full knowledge that the individual in question is amenable to the law for crimes previously committed, the executive is any longer in a position to pursue that person thus dealt with, as a felon."[71]   The Colonial Secretary was happy to see this problem—which had aroused public feeling in England as well as in Canada—so conveniently solved.   He fully approved Dufferin's assumption of responsibility for a decision that would be as embarrassing to the British as to the Canadian cabinet.   His one amendment was a suggestion that to the commutation of the death sentence should be added forfeiture of political rights.   Accordingly, on January 15, two weeks before he was to be hanged, Lépine received the news that his sentence of death had been reduced to two years' imprisonment and permanent deprivation of his political rights.[72]

There still remained the question of what was to be done about Louis Riel.   He had not given himself up to arrest; nor had he attempted to take his seat in parliament.   And the warrant for his arrest was still waiting to be executed.   As long as Riel was at large, there could be no permanent settlement of the North-West question.   When parliament met in February, 1875, Mackenzie was ready to come to grips with Riel. On the 11th, he introduced a motion that:

a full amnesty should be granted to all persons concerned in the North-West troubles for all acts committed by them during the said troubles, saving only L. Riel, A. D. Lépine and W. B. O'Donoghue. That in the opinion of this House, it would be proper . . . that a like amnesty should be granted to L. Riel and A. D. Lépine conditional on five years banishment from Her Majesty's Dominions.[73]

O'Donoghue was excluded from the amnesty because of the part he had taken in the Fenian raid in 1872. In his speech Mackenzie did not retreat from his stand condemning Riel and the métis rising, but he argued that since the Conservatives had promised an amnesty, the Liberal government was morally obliged to honour the promises made. It was a clever speech. It threw the blame on the Opposition, and yet conceded what so many French-Canadians were demanding. Both Mackenzie Bowell and Sir John A. Macdonald rose to protest that no such promises had ever been made by the previous government; but the French Conservatives refuted their leader's argument. Masson and Mousseau demanded an unqualified pardon without the banishment which carried with it the implication that Riel and Lépine were criminals. But Mousseau's motion was lost. On the evening of February 12, Mackenzie's proposal of banishment for five years received the approval of the House of Commons on a straight party vote, 126 to 50.[74]

It was a poor sort of amnesty. It removed the threat of hanging; but it gave Riel only the freedom of the outlaw. For five years he would be a man without a country.

CHAPTER 12

Fugitive

IN APRIL, 1840, Ignace Bourget became the second Bishop of Montreal. More than any other churchman, Bourget left his mark upon the history of Canada during the years of the nineteenth century. Born in 1799 and educated at the Seminary of Quebec, he was ordained in 1822. From the early years of his priesthood, he took a lead in what was called the "New School" in Quebec, a school noted for its devotional piety, its zeal for Papal authority and its emphasis on the alliance of nationality and religion. The "New School," or Ultramontane Movement as it is often called, should not be confused with the Ultramontane Movement in Europe. Ultramontanism in Canada was essentially Canadian in character. Never in Canada, not even in the days of the Ancien Régime, was Gallicanism a serious force in the relations of church and state. Canadians had been too well tutored by Bishop Laval and the Jesuits to think in terms of a national Canadian church. Yet Canadian Ultramontanism had its "national" character, "national" in the sense that French Canada was not to be thought of separate from the Catholic faith. The two stood side by side, and each strengthened the other. This was, of course, the direct outcome of the defeat of French arms and the cession of Canada by France to Great Britain in 1763. Confronting an alien authority which wanted to assimilate the French-Canadians culturally and religiously, church and nation stood shoulder to shoulder in self-defence.

Montreal, because of its numerous and wealthy English-speaking population, rather than Quebec, experienced the most serious tensions of race and religion during the nineteenth century. In consequence, it is not surprising that Montreal should have showed greater hospitality to Canadian Ultramontanism than did the provincial capital where the stresses were fewer and the strains less severe. If the "nationalist" movements of 1837/38 and 1871/72 drew most of their support from Montreal and its environs, it was because the clergy of Quebec were less willing than their Montreal brethren—except for the Sulpicians—to throw their weight behind the *Patriote* agitation. Bourget, who in 1837 became coadjutor Bishop, openly sympathized with the followers of

214

Papineau. From the day he succeeded to the See of Montreal, he became a leader in the resistance of French-Canadians to all efforts on the part of the British government and governors to de-nationalize them along the lines recommended by the Earl of Durham in his famous Report.[1] As Bishop, Bourget brought many new religious orders to Canada from France; he initiated the construction of a new cathedral for Montreal patterned on St. Peter's in Rome; he replaced the French liturgy with the Roman liturgy in his diocese; and he encouraged the formation of the Papal Zouaves who went to Italy in 1868 to defend the temporal power of the Papacy against the assaults of Garibaldi. Bourget's right hand man was Mgr. Louis LaFlèche, the one-time missionary to Red River and, since 1867, Bishop of Three Rivers. But perhaps his greatest and most influential supporters were the members of the Society of Jesus whom Bourget brought back to Canada in 1842, eighty-two years after the English authorities had forbidden recruiting for the Society in Canada.

In opposition to Bourget and the "New School" there were the *Rouges*, a small body of radical anti-clericals, including Joseph Doutre and Rodolphe LaFlamme. In opposition, too, were the moderate, liberal churchmen such as Elzéar-Alexandre Taschereau, Cardinal Archbishop of Quebec. No distinction could be drawn between Bourget and Taschereau on the question of their allegiance to His Holiness. The French-Canadian clergy, whether they followed the lead of Montreal or that of Quebec, were *Ultras* in the sense that they all looked to Rome. The difference between them was one of degree rather than one of kind.

Nevertheless there were differences. One of these was in the political affiliations of the two schools of ecclesiastical thought. Generally speaking, the Ultramontane clergy were supporters of the Conservative party. Taschereau and Laval University were believed to be politically sympathetic to the Liberals.[2] Admittedly this is an over-simplification of the situation, for there were differences between the Conservatives in the quality of their churchmanship. George Cartier, for instance, was not an Ultramontane, while Sir Hector Langevin was. If the *Ultras* were disposed to give their votes to Conservative candidates, it did not mean that they always approved the stand taken by that party, either the stand taken by the Conservative party in the dispute with New Brunswick over the establishment of separate schools, or the reluctance of Sir John A. Macdonald to grant an amnesty to Louis Riel. In the broad sense, however, it is true to say that the alliance of the *Ultras* with political conservatism was a very real one in the early years of Confederation. Prominent Ultramontane laymen like Joseph Royal, E. L. de

Bellefeuille, F. X. A. Trudel, Alphonse Desjardins, Rodrigue Masson, Charles Boucher de Boucherville and others were strong Conservatives. Such Ultramontane newspapers as *Le Nouveau Monde, Le Courrier des Trois Rivières, Le Courrier du Canada* and *Le Franc Parleur* gave editorial support to the party led by Macdonald and Cartier. It was with this Ultramontane Conservative group that Louis Riel associated himself after his election to parliament and his journey to Montreal in October of 1873.

Riel had always been deeply moved by religion. He had been brought up in a devout atmosphere by a devout mother; he had been educated under the watchful eye of the Bishop of St. Boniface and the Gentlemen of St. Sulpice. It had been hoped that he would take holy orders. If Riel toyed with Liberalism while associated with LaFlamme and Fréchette, this association, if it existed, was of such brief duration that it left no deep impress on his mind. During 1869/70 in Red River, Louis Riel sought and followed the directions of his clerical adviser, the Abbé Ritchot. When he returned to Montreal he gravitated naturally towards the clerical group, towards the Ultramontanes. As one of them, he became imbued with their ideals of religion and race. He began to see himself as God's chosen instrument for the regeneration of his people, the métis. This was not a hypocritical attitude, and there was nothing deceitful about it. Riel believed in all sincerity that it was his duty to protect the métis—and through them the whole body of French-speaking people in Canada—against the assaults of the anti-Catholic, Orange, English population which dominated Canada by the sheer weight of its numbers.

This sense of mission was the controlling factor in Louis Riel's life during the years that remained to him. And it was greatly stimulated by Riel's meetings with Bishop Bourget. The métis leader paid a visit to the venerable Ignace early in January, 1874, and each man seems to have made an abiding impression on the other.[3] This was the first of several encounters between the two men, and the later meetings only deepened the impression the first made. When Bourget told Riel that he had a mission in life, he used words Riel never forgot. Time and again Louis thought about them and brooded upon them. God's grace was with him. He would fulfil God's will. The French-Canadian race would triumph over its adversaries. And there were those other words of Bourget's: "May your faith increase in strength in order that you may never be intimidated by the difficulties which your present life necessarily offers in whatever situation you may find yourself."[4] These, too, were words Riel always remembered.

II

When Riel left St. Paul in November, 1874, he went not to Montreal but to Washington. Father Barnabé had written to Edmond Mallet urging him to take up Riel's cause with Congress, and deploring the divisive effect of Canadian party politics on the people of French Canada. There was only one man, he believed, "who can withdraw our dear province from this state of humiliation, it is our dear friend—and how? by the complete triumph of his cause. Let us unite our feeble efforts to hasten, if possible, this desired moment."[5] He wrote again, this time to Riel, sending the métis leader funds and telling him of the fall of Marc Girard's government in Manitoba. "The Bismarckian spirit is everywhere," he said, "and I am afraid that it constitutes an obstacle to our dearest wishes."[6]

In Washington, Riel spent some time with Mallet, a Franco-American who had been born in Montreal, but who had gone to the United States while still a small boy. It came as something of a shock to Mallet, when he returned to his native land at the age of twenty-four, to find himself almost isolated from his own people, for he had forgotten much of the language and most of the traditions of French Canada; so, with no wish to be regarded as an outsider, Mallet set out to identify himself with his own people.[7] The evidence is uncertain, but it is not unlikely that Mallet, when he went to Montreal in June of 1874 to attend the great St. Jean Baptiste celebration of that year, met the métis leader. Mallet seems to have been deeply affected by the story of Riel's struggle for recognition, and he was prepared to assist the cause of the French halfbreeds in Western Canada. However, there was little that Mallet was able to do to help Louis Riel in Washington, and Riel with no employment to absorb his time and energies in the American capital, found time heavy upon his hands. More and more he devoted himself to his religious duties; more and more he bent his mind to the mysteries of his religious faith. "On the 18th of December, 1874," he said at a later date:

while I was seated on the top of a mountain near Washington . . . the same spirit who showed himself to Moses in the midst of the burning cloud appeared to me in the same manner. I was stupefied. I was confused. He said to me 'Rise up, Louis David Riel, you have a mission to fulfil'. Stretching out my arms and bowing my head, I received this heavenly message.[8]

The trip to Washington yielded nothing more than visions, so Riel turned his face northwards. Towards the end of December, he went to Worcester in Massachusetts, where the parish priest was Father Primeau, whose cousin was the curé of Boucherville in Quebec province. Worcester was the centre of an emigrant French-Canadian population, and Riel felt happier here than he had in Washington—happier because he could hear and speak his own tongue, and happier because in Worcester he found himself the centre of attraction. The Franco-Americans had taken up the cause of the métis and were demanding an amnesty both for Riel and Ambroise Lépine. When he was invited to take the platform at a protest meeting, Riel accepted with alacrity. It gave him the sense of power he loved so well. He recited the story of the negotiations in Ottawa, of the promises made and never carried out, of the shifting attitudes of the Conservative and Liberal politicians to suit their respective party needs. But there were hopes for the future. "Justice will triumph over oppression," Riel declared. "The sound of Lépine's and Nault's chains have aroused the sympathies of every French Canadian and every Catholic. The time must pass when those who have defended their liberty and their homes should suffer hanging. The amnesty will be granted to us." Then he appealed to his audience to strengthen the numbers of the French-speaking population of Western Canada, to pack up their belongings and emigrate to Manitoba. "Come, come to our land," he cried. "The métis extend the hand of welcome, come work on our soil, and assure the victory of the French-Canadian nationality in the vast territory of the North-West."[9] It was a strongly emotional speech he made on this occasion, and it was interrupted by frequent bursts of applause. Riel relished the enthusiasm his remarks had engendered. Yet he must have been disappointed when, in the days that followed, the enthusiasm quickly evaporated, and the efforts of Charles Lalime and others to drum up emigrants for the Canadian North-West should have been so poorly rewarded.[10]

After his visit to Worcester, Riel went to Suncook in New Hampshire to stay with Father Richer. From here he wrote to Bishop Bourget. He was about to undertake a novena and wished for Bourget's prayers.[11] But he needed more than pious blessings, so he wrote to the Cardinal Archbishop of Quebec.

Riel had paid a visit to Cardinal Taschereau the previous September, but he had failed to arouse in Taschereau's heart the same warm, uncritical response that he had received from Bishop Bourget. Taschereau, a more liberal as well as a more careful and discreet prelate than his Montreal colleague, had held aloof from the agitation that had engulfed the person of Louis Riel, just as he had stood aside from the efforts of the Ultramontanes to establish a Catholic political party in Canada.[12] Riel knew these things. He knew, above all, that his own support came from only one wing of clerical opinion, and he was anxious to see if he could enlist the strength of the liberal wing of the church.

If he could bring Taschereau and Bourget together in support of his cause, how much stronger he would be.   And how much stronger, too, would be the voices of French-Canadians when they shouted in unison for the amnesty.   "I hope, my lord," he wrote in his letter to the Cardinal, "that I shall often have the consolation of finding in you the inspiration which I need to continue the religious and national struggle upon which I have been engaged for five years, because our enemies have forced it upon me, and that I hope to carry on as much through a sense of honour as of duty."   He continued:

Since the Bishops of Lower Canada are willing to come to our aid, as they are already doing with their influence, to rescue us from the fury of our enemies, and since for some time to come it is certain that Upper Canada will try to crush the little group of métis, and because our safeguard, after Heaven will always be the province of Quebec, my lord, when I am freer than I am today, I shall venture to pay my respects to you in the capital of Quebec.   Your beneficial influence and the influence of your city will weigh heavily in our favour, in these critical times.[13]

It was a heavy-handed letter, and it evoked no response from Taschereau. Unlike Bourget, the Cardinal did not ask Riel to come and see him again. Thus, when a warm invitation came from Barnabé to "come and see our beautiful sky, contemplate our beautiful mountains, our splendid countryside,"[14] Riel accepted it and went to live with the Barnabé family at Keeseville.   It was the nearest thing to returning to his own home, if only because of the sincere affection he received from the priest's mother and sister, and because of the genuine sympathy the priest himself always showed towards the French-speaking people of Manitoba.   At Keeseville, Riel could always find something more than shelter and charity.   He could find love and freedom to talk politics or indulge his bent towards religious mysticism.

Louis was still at Keeseville when he learned of the commutation of the death sentence passed upon Lépine and his own sentence of exile. If he was happy that his friend's life had been spared, Riel was desolate at the thought that now he, himself, was a man without a country.   Riel never really believed that Lépine would hang, nor did he ever imagine that the amnesty, when it should come, would take the form of banishment.   However, there it was, and Riel felt he had little choice but to draw closer to the bosom of the faith in which his mother had raised him. In February, when he wrote to Ritchot, whom he had lately neglected, he showed a flash of the defiance of earlier days when he declared, "I look upon it as a consolation, I would even say that it is in one sense a promise of success for our cause and for me to learn that my outlawry has begun by being proclaimed at St. Norbert."   His enemies might think that they had dealt him a "fatal blow"; what they did not realize was that it had been delivered just at a time when God "has begun to bless me." Then the letter lost its punch as Riel subsided into Christian submission. He would not return to Canada; he would wait to learn from God what he should do and where he should go. "My confessors," he wrote, "allow me to approach the holy table almost every day. I try to strengthen myself; I try to build up my moral resistance with obedience, and with the peace of the strong. And I am not worried. My anxiety is only for those who are dear to me and for our cause. And my hope is greater than ever." If he were expelled from parliament, he would not run in Provencher; if he were to run at all, it might be "in some constituency in Quebec," as Ritchot had once suggested.[15]

The expulsion that Riel anticipated was not long coming. There was some dispute among the members of the House of Commons as to whether Riel could legally be made an outlaw by the simple process of declaring him one. Sir John A. Macdonald expressed this view. But there was very little disagreement that Riel's seat, Provencher, should be declared vacant. Only the well-known *Ultras* in the Conservative party were prepared to continue the argument. However, when the vote was taken on February 24, no more than sixteen members of parliament were willing to support Riel against the 141 who would have nothing to do with him. Among the former were the ex-Conservative ministers, Masson, Mousseau, Robitaille, and Riel's friends from Montreal, Aldéric Ouimet and Alphonse Desjardins. Among those who hoped never to see him again were the Prime Minister, Alexander Mackenzie, and the Liberal ministers, Geoffrion, Fournier and LaFlamme. And, of course, John Christian Schultz.[16]

Although the act of expulsion was greeted with indifference by Riel, his friends saw no reason why they should relax their efforts on his behalf. Despite the rebuffs they had suffered,[17] Desjardins and Lachapelle once more took up cudgels for Riel in order to remove the stain of outlaw from his name.[18] Bishop Bourget, too, refused to abandon him,[19] and in April he signified his willingness to grant Riel another interview.[20] Once more Desjardins' house was placed at Riel's disposal, and in mid-April Riel slipped quietly across the frontier into Canada. He knew the penalty of recognition, but he felt reasonably secure in the loyalty of his compatriots and in the conviction that, with a provincial election in the offing, neither political party would relish his arrest.[21] Although he was careful, Riel did not take any special precautions to avoid detection. He travelled by daylight and openly walked the streets of Montreal.[22]

While in this city he prepared a manifesto to "The Métis Nation and the French-Canadian People."[23] In it he acknowledged his indebtedness

to men like Bishop Bourget, Masson, Desjardins and others, and
expressed his gratitude to his own people for their loyalty.   The manifesto was neither a strong nor a stirring document, but weak and
compromising.   There was no appeal to arms, no call to action, only an
acceptance of what had happened, a pious hope that time would see
the triumph of those things to which he had devoted his life.   It almost
seemed as if Riel had lost the self-confidence that was so marked a
feature of his leadership during those tumultuous months in Red River.
This was how it appeared to Father Thibault, who wrote to Taché on
April 28 that Riel "behaved very well here; but he has the appearance
of a man overwhelmed by boredom."[24]   It was not really boredom.   It
was submission to the counsels of his religious advisers.   Or so it
seemed.

From Montreal, Riel returned to the United States to spend a few
weeks with Father Barnabé at Keeseville.[25]   Then he went to Suncook.[26]
Then back again to Keeseville.[27]   Despite the concern of his friends for
his health,[28] he would not remain in one place very long.   So he left
Keeseville for Worcester.   Every journey cost money, and Riel was
completely dependent upon the charity of his friends.   But he would not
stay still.   On July 12, he wrote to tell his mother that he might go to
St. Joseph to see her.[29]   To Ritchot, three days later, he wrote that his
plans included a journey to Pembina and then a return to Canada before
the sitting of parliament.[30]   There was even talk that he might go to
Europe for reasons of health.[31]   Nevertheless, there is no evidence to
show that any of these proposed trips ever got beyond the talking stage.
All we know is that Riel was in Montreal in September[32] and that he
spent some time in Keeseville in October, when Edmond Mallet once
more offered him the hospitality of his home in Washington.[33]

Wherever Riel spent the summer and autumn of 1875, he spent it
brooding over his past and his future.   The one was dark with persecution, the other bright with promise.   Not political promise, but religious
promise.   He had been stimulated by a letter from Bourget.   When he
wrote to his mother in July, he had not even mentioned the Provencher
by-election—A. G. B. Bannatyne had won the métis leader's old seat—
indeed, he had not mentioned politics of any kind.   He merely urged his
friends in Red River, and their children with them, to "pray that God
may preserve the little métis nation, and cause it to grow . . . and
remain faithful to its mission."   "During the five years that I must pass
in exile," he wrote, "I have only this to say to the métis,—remain métis,
become more métis than ever."[34]

If this letter is another indication of Riel's new and unfamiliar submissive attitude, it is also evidence of his growing obsession with the

idea of his religious mission.   His inspiration, and the sheet anchor of his
hopes, was to assist the cause of French culture and the Catholic faith.
And all the more so when Bishop Bourget told him:

I have the deep conviction that you will receive in this world, and sooner
than you think, the reward for all your mental sacrifices, a thousand times
more crushing than the sacrifices of material and visible life.   But God,
who has always led you and assisted you up to the present time, will not
abandon you in the darkest hours of your life.   For He has given you a
mission which you must fulfil in all respects.[35]

Riel never parted with this letter.   He carried it with him every day,
next to his heart, and he placed it at the head of his bed every night.[36]
In December, after he had gone to Washington, he replied to Bourget
that he would accept the challenge; he would be the willing instrument
of the Holy Spirit.   He would build up the métis as a people deeply
devoted to God and to the service of His church.   Riel's one request of
Bourget was that the Bishop would solicit the blessing of His Holiness
on the mixed-blood population of North America.   For himself, he asked
nothing except a prayer "for my friend A. D. Lépine, for André Nault,
Elzéar de Lagimodière, for all the other métis chiefs; for the family of my
father, for my own household, and all those who are dear to me."[37]

Perhaps it was because he had given up the old aggressiveness that Riel
when he visited Washington failed to make much of an impact on the
people he met, neither on President Grant nor on Senator Oliver Morton
of Indiana.[38]   He seemed nervous and ill-at-ease with strangers, and
much happier when attending Mass or praying in one of the churches of
the city.   Mallet found his conduct exemplary.[39]   His deportment was
commendable; he neither smoked nor drank, and he ate sparingly; he was
clean and neat about his dress and person.   But he preferred to keep to
himself, praying much and taking Communion as frequently as possible.
When he talked, he preferred to talk about religion and about the task
which God had given him.

As the weeks passed, Mallet began to wonder about his guest.
Proximity must have rubbed some of the glamour from Riel's shoulders.
He seemed to be too insistent on the divine sanction behind his mission.
"I could not follow him in all his ways of thinking and in all his plans,"
wrote Mallet, "and I would tell him that God's providence worked
through natural means, except in very exceptional cases."[40]   On
December 6, Riel attended the opening of Congress by President Grant
and left the Capital in a state of extreme excitement.   Two days later,
on December 8, in St. Patrick's Church, he was seized with "a joy so
intense, that to hide my face from my neighbours," he was obliged to
cover it "with my handkerchief, and hold it with my hands over my

mouth and cheeks." This was followed almost immediately by a sensation of extreme depression, "a great sorrow of the soul." With an effort, Riel tried to suppress his weeping, but his sobs sounded loud in the silence of the church. "My pain was as intense as my joy," Riel later described it.[41] The seizure passed. But Mallet doubted if he could any longer harbour a man whose actions and discourse were becoming more and more irrational.[42] Accordingly, he arranged for Riel to return to the parish house at Worcester. Perhaps Father Primeau would be able to calm him.

Primeau likewise could do nothing for or with Riel. He talked and argued with the métis but to no avail. Riel was convinced he was a prophet and that he had a message he should proclaim to the world. Finally Primeau passed him to Father Richer at Suncook. He was very depressed when he did so, and when he wrote to Mallet he said of Louis Riel, "In my view nothing but a miracle will restore him to his normal state . . . very probably his role is finished. . . . May God lead him to an honourable and Christian end.[43]

By this time Louis Riel seems to have had little control over his actions. At one moment he believed himself called upon to regenerate the whole world; at another he saw himself as one of a trilogy, including the Count de Chambord of France, Don Carlos of Spain and himself. These aberrations were not continuous. But the idea of his mission was. Another letter from Bourget on January 2 confirmed Riel in his conviction that God's mercy and aid would keep him from turning aside "from the road that Divine Providence has traced for you."[44] Louis's communications with Archbishop Taché and the Abbé Ritchot[45] reveal a mysticism and self-abasement that must have appeared very strange to the two clergymen who had known him in his younger and extrovert days. A letter to Taché, written on January 8, was particularly revealing. It suggested a strong sense of guilt on Riel's part that his pride and youthful follies should have diverted him from the religious life that Taché had offered him when the Bishop had sent him to the College of Montreal.

Father Richer felt that he was in no better position than Mallet or Primeau to handle a man who was obviously ill. So Riel was turned over to Barnabé, who only a fortnight earlier had written to Mallet inquiring about Riel's health and whereabouts.[46] To his distress—for he loved Riel—Barnabé could do little. He therefore wrote to Riel's Montreal relations, the Lees. John Lee hurried to Keeseville, and to his horror he found his poor nephew spending his nights crying and shouting and filling the whole Barnabé household with terror.[47] There was nobody who could take care of him, for Barnabé's mother was too frightened to go near the métis. Lee, however, with the assistance of a friend from

Worcester, took Riel with him and set out for Montreal. On the train, Louis made bellowing noises like a bull, and shouted at the top of his voice to the amused or frightened passengers, "Don't laugh. I am a prophet! I am a prophet!" At St. Lambert, Lee obtained a carriage to convey himself and his embarrassing charge over the ice to Montreal. This would avoid any confusion and trouble that might arise at Bonaventure station. As the carriage mounted the hill leading from the river bank, passing the little church that Montgolfier built in 1773 on the site of Marguerite Bourgeoys' chapel of Notre Dame de Bon Secours, Riel had to be restrained forcibly from hurling himself out of the carriage in order to enter the building. Finally, and fortunately without mishap, the carriage reached the Lees' house in St. Jean Baptiste.[48]

Louis Riel remained with the Lees for several months. During the first few weeks he kept up his crying and his bellowing. Then, gradually, he began to grow calm. He was carefully guarded from anything that might irritate or excite him, and to those who saw him he seemed to be restored to a normal state of mind. So satisfactory did his improvement in health appear to be, John Lee acceded to his nephew's request to be permitted to attend the parish church. Unfortunately, he was not ready for the stimulation the Mass and sermon gave him. While the curé was preaching, Riel jumped to his feet to argue with him, only to find himself seized and hurried out of the building. He made no resistance, but it was clear to the Lees that they could not risk a repetition of this occurrence. From time to time the old symptoms reappeared. Riel would become violent; he would tear his clothes and the bed coverings; he would demand to be allowed to go to church, to proclaim his mission; he would deny that he was ill, and would shout in a loud voice, as he had done at Suncook and at Keeseville, that he was a "prophet."

John Lee wondered if Louis would ever recover from his mental illness without medical assistance. So he turned to Riel's old friend, Dr. E. P. Lachapelle.[49] With Lachapelle's assistance, Riel was taken quietly to the Hospital of St. Jean de Dieu at Longue Pointe, where he was admitted as a patient, number 565, under the name of Louis R. David, on March 6, 1876.

III

Riel was received at the hospital by Dr. Henry Howard. "He had the appearance of a gentleman, frank and honourable," wrote Howard, "and judging from his appearance I would never have supposed that he was guilty of the crime of which he was accused. At that moment I felt great pity for him; and I thought that his friends ought to have done something better for him than to send him to a lunatic asylum." Howard went towards him to shake hands. "I am happy to see you, Mr. David," said the doctor, "I am Dr. Howard." Riel looked up, surprised. "Why do you call me David?" he asked, "My name is Louis Riel." Putting his hand in his pocket, he extracted a small book of prayers, and opening it at the first page, handed it to Dr. Howard, saying, "Look at my name there, Louis David Riel, written by the hand of my beloved sister." Immediately one of the nuns seized the book and tore the page from it. "You are known here only under the name of Mr. David," she said sharply. Riel was seized with anger. "For several minutes I never saw a man in such a temper," wrote Howard at a later date.[50]

During his stay at Longue Pointe, Riel seems to have alternated between periods of unreason and lucidity. He wrote several times to Bishop Bourget, referring always to his "mission." On occasions he spoke sensibly and clearly; at other times his letters were filled with a religious exaltation as meaningless as it must have been distressing to the venerable Bishop. Sometimes Riel spoke harshly of those who sought to help him: Sister Ste. Thérèse was the "image of the house of Austria"; Dr. Howard "the image of . . . Protestant Prussia"; Dr. Lachapelle "the image of the blackest liberalism; it is he who represents Bismark."[51] Sometimes he declared he had both Jewish and gentile blood in his veins, the one from his Indian ancestors, the other from his French forebears.[52] On one occasion he sent Bourget a letter from the hospital chaplain, Father Prud'homme, asserting that he, Riel, was perfectly sane, and that the effect of his imprisonment in St. Jean de Dieu would be to "enchain the Holy Spirit which is in him."[53]

Louis did not remain in Montreal very long—not because he made any noticeable improvement in health, but because the Reverend Sisters, who were responsible for the hospital's administration, feared they might become the victims of violence should the Orangemen discover Riel's presence. Riel himself suffered from the obsession that he was going to be assassinated and begged "for the love of God, try to get me out of here."[54] Dr. Howard began to fear that Riel might commit suicide if he remained any longer at Longue Pointe. It is doubtful if any of these apprehensions were really justified, but there is no questioning the fact of their existence, or the relief with which both the Sisters and Dr. Howard welcomed Riel's removal from Montreal to Quebec City in mid-May.

The transfer of Louis Riel to the asylum at Beauport was made in comparative secrecy. Even the records of the Hospital St. Jean de Dieu were falsified to cover the move. An entry was made dating the transfer January 15, 1877, when in fact it took place on May 19. Dr. Lachapelle had examined Riel on the 15th and had certified that the métis was suffering from a mental derangement requiring constant surveillance and treatment of a kind that could only be obtained at Beauport.[55] With the assistance of Adolphe Chapleau, the move was made at public expense. On the 19th, accompanied by Chapleau, Mousseau and Doctors Lachapelle and Deschamps, Riel set out for the docks in Montreal. He did not want to go and struggled with his friends. His uncle, John Lee, stood on the pier, out of sight, watching. "It was pitiful to see," he wrote.[56] The next day the vessel bearing Riel reached Quebec City, and the poor man was admitted to the mental hospital at Beauport under the name of Louis Larochelle. He remained there until his release on January 23, 1878.

It is difficult to obtain satisfactory evidence of the true nature of Riel's illness. Politicians, alienists and historians have held and argued their contradictory views.[57] In the 1870's and 1880's the study of mental illness was in its infancy, and those who saw or attended Riel during these years were seldom able to give an unbiased or scientific explanation of the case. To the present-day layman, it would appear that the stresses of the years between 1870 and 1876 were too strong for Riel's nervous system. His elevation to the presidency of the Provisional Government, his flight from Fort Garry, his election to parliament, his fears for his life, his outlawry, his destitution, his over-all sense of persecution and his religious mania—all these imposed a heavy strain on a mind insufficiently equipped to cope with them. When the circumstances are considered, it hardly seems surprising that Riel collapsed. It is even less surprising when we recall the morbid melancholy that he suffered following his father's death, and the hallucinations he experienced in 1865 when he imagined he was a French Jew from Marseilles who had been substituted for the real Louis Riel when the latter had been drowned.[58] Neither by heredity nor by training was he strong enough to withstand the blows fate dealt him. With a mind already disposed towards exaggerations—both political and religious—a prolonged strain or shock of a mental or moral nature was bound to result in the breakdown that Riel was so obviously suffering when he was admitted to the hospitals at Longue Pointe and Beauport in 1876.

In both institutions Riel was apparently subject to periods of violent and irrational actions. He would break the ornaments and candles on the chapel altar;[59] he would run through the corridors stark naked;[60] he would strike and struggle with his guards.[61] But most of his time seems to have been spent brooding on his mission, developing his religious and political ideas, and scribbling notes describing his visions and divine revelations. He called himself "Louis David Riel, Prophet, Infallible Pontiff, and Priest-King." The name David had been added as an indication that he had placed himself under the patronage of the Saint of the same name. As he thought and brooded, he became convinced of the sinfulness and the forthcoming destruction of the old world, and the hope and future of the new. He saw Canada as God's chosen country and the French-Canadians as his chosen people. The Holy See, he came to believe, would be transferred from Rome to Montreal, where it would remain for the next 457 years, after which it would be transferred to Manitoba and be situated at St. Vital, between St. Boniface and St. Norbert.[62] From scribblings on subjects such as these, he turned to verse, verses attacking or poking fun at his enemies, Ontario, the Orangemen, the Liberals, the Conservatives, even those who had been his friends and those of whom he was now suspicious, men like Dubuc, Girard and Royal. Then his verses would take a religious bent. And sometimes his voice was that of the human soul longing for freedom, as when he wrote in October, 1876:[63]

> J'ai passé la Sainte Anne
> En prison dans Beauport.
> Mais la main profane
> Qui me tient, se fait tort,
> Mon Protecteur plane
> Sur moi; lui seul est fort.

From time to time Riel received visits from his friends. Almost invariably they went away discouraged. A mental hospital is never a cheerful place at best; but the figure of Riel, sick, unbalanced, with shadows on his mind, filled everyone with pity. "Poor Riel," wrote Father Lacombe to Rodrigue Masson on May 1, "I feel so sorry for him. He is worse than ever."[64] John Lee found him "indifferent and taciturn" at Beauport, and "more melancholy than at Longue Pointe."[65] In July, Riel forbade Father Bolduc, the hospital chaplain, to celebrate Mass "because you have closed the church to me and have refused to obey me: I who command you in the name of the Holy Spirit."[66] "It would be difficult to find a man more foolish and more stubborn," wrote Bolduc to Archbishop Taché.[67]

Nevertheless rest and time had their healing effects. The visions became fewer and the sense of persecution less marked. Gradually Riel began to recover his health; and so he was allowed a considerable degree of personal liberty. He was not only permitted to obtain books from outside—works of history apparently interested him[68]—but to visit friends like the Vincelettes in Quebec and to travel about the surrounding countryside. On one of these occasions he met the young Wilfrid Laurier, already a power in the Liberal party. Laurier was much surprised by the vigour and the strong personality of the former métis leader, and found him both fluent and well-informed. When, however, the conversation turned to matters of religion, "Riel's deep-set eyes lit up, and he launched into an excited and jumbled harangue, boasting vaguely of the great mission for the further revelation of God's will which a heavenly vision had urged him to undertake."[69]

By the latter part of 1877, Riel was well on the road to recovery. But he had continually to avoid becoming involved in controversy, particularly religious or political controversy. His physicians emphasized the need for care.[70] Dr. François Roy, the Superintendent of the Beauport hospital, said later that when Riel was discharged he was cured "more or less."[71] Now that he had recovered, Riel was grateful for what had been done for him. Although during his stay at St. Jean de Dieu he had accused Dr. Lachapelle of trying to poison him,[72] on February 9, 1878, Riel wrote:

I am more obliged to you than ever. I thank you for all the trouble you have taken to help me when I was unable to look after myself. I am extremely grateful for everything you did for me during the great trials to which it pleased God to subject me. My generous friend, Dr. Roy, told me, when I recovered, that you, more than anyone else, had taken the trouble to have me moved from Longue Pointe to Beauport. I thank you all the more because it was in the latter asylum that I had the good fortune to recover my senses. I was treated there as charitably as any lunatic could be.[73]

IV

When Riel left Beauport, he went to Keeseville to see the friends who had been so loyal to him in 1875 and 1876.[74] He had been warned to avoid excitement, to live in the open air and to take good care of his health.[75] Thus his mind was set on farming. When he resumed his correspondence with Archbishop Taché and the Abbé Ritchot, he told them both of his intention to move to the western United States, Nebraska by choice, where the climate would suit him, and where he could settle down to a normal, quiet life, far enough away from Manitoba to avoid being caught up in the eddies of its political life. Both of Riel's letters were marked by restraint and by a pathetically obvious desire to follow the advice which had been given to him: "I thank God for having humiliated me and for having brought me to understand what human glory is; how quickly it passes; and how vain it is for him who having for a little while captured the attention of men, suddenly feels the hand of God weighing upon him. . . . I am doing all in my power to be submissive and resigned."[76] To Ritchot he wrote, "My prayers and sufferings do not count for much, but such as they are, I have never ceased to offer them to God, through our Lord and our Lady of Good Help, in order that it may please God to bring about the early triumph of his holy church in the world and our cause in the North-West."[77] Riel might intend to avoid all reference to politics and religion; he might try to follow his doctor's advice to remain quiet; but somehow both subjects kept popping into his mind and into his correspondence. It was difficult to put into practice the humility that his confessors were always urging upon him. Nevertheless he was trying, and trying hard, to give himself a new practical aim in life. If he could become absorbed in that, he could leave his mission to those better qualified than himself to carry it out.

But if to become a farmer was his aim, it was too early to put in seed; and, in any event, he did not have the money to buy a farm unless he could sell some of his property in Manitoba.[78] Meanwhile, was there nothing he could do to help himself? Was he going to be obliged, once more, to live on charity? His friends rallied around him, and Barnabé assured him that there would be no need for him to worry about money. "I am once more your treasurer," he told Riel.[79] Thus, for a short time, Riel remained at Keeseville; then he went to Glenn's Falls;[80] then he came back again to Keeseville; then he went off to New York to see if he could not find some employment that would make it possible for him to support himself, perhaps even to support a family. This would give him that stability of purpose about which his confessors and advisers spoke so frequently.

It was Louis's misfortune, however, that his training and experience were not of a nature to equip him for life in a large city; and as his failures to find employment mounted, he began to lose both his health and his faith in himself. The brightest portions of his days were the letters from Keeseville. These were always filled with words of homely suggestion: "Can you get a little good milk for yourself? with difficulty I would think! Ah, if you were not so far away from us, how many times we could send you some milk from our own little cow";[81] and words of encouragement: "There must be a better position for you than a journalist in New York";[82] and words of advice: "It would be better for you to apply yourself to some study . . . that of law. You could be introduced as a clerk into one of the first offices in New York."[83] However Riel found neither employment nor peace of mind in New York. He did not feel well, and he could not shake off his desire to go back to the west. On October 12, Father Barnabé wrote to Major Mallet, "Mr. Riel is not so well at present." There was no question of a return of his former afflictions; Barnabé felt that it was nothing that a few days' rest would not cure. "His mind shows the most perfect lucidity; the greatest agility. One could truthfully say that he had never had a breakdown, if one never knew anything of his past," wrote Barnabé.[84]

If Riel's illness had been diagnosed, it would probably have revealed itself as simple homesickness. It had been a long time since he had seen the buff-green prairies, the brown waters of the Red River, the mud-coated log houses of his own people; a long time since he had experienced the dry, cold winters, the short-lived springs, the hot, sunny summers of the west; a long time since he had seen his mother, his brothers and his sisters, and the men who had followed him in 1869 and 1870. It was no longer of Nebraska that he spoke now—that had been no more than a passing fancy. It was of Minnesota, of St. Joseph, of Pembina, and even of Manitoba that he was thinking. As his thoughts returned to the scenes of his successes and failures, almost inevitably the idea of his mission revived. He could not keep it bottled up forever. And Barnabé did not help him with his talk about Bishop Ireland's plans for colonizing the west with Catholic immigrants from the crowded industrial centres of the east. From Barnabé, Riel learned about Ireland's proposed Catholic Colonization Bureau, and of Barnabé's own thoughts of settling young Catholic orphan boys in a special colony and training them to be farmers. Barnabé himself had caught something of Riel's idea of mission, and he felt that it was his duty "to work for the prosperity of my compatriots and help them preserve their faith by assisting them to become farmers."[85]

Barnabé's proposals were, however, never carried into effect. Riel went to St. Paul and had an interview with Bishop Ireland; but the Bishop was not prepared to avail himself of Louis's services.[86] Perhaps he was disposed to be wary of a man with so unstable a history; perhaps he did not share Riel's ideas or his enthusiasms; perhaps he feared that Riel would become more involved in politics than in colonizing. Riel therefore left St. Paul and went to Pembina. When Father Payette in St. Paul wrote an answer to Barnabé's letters, he urged Barnabé to give up any ideas of leaving his parish in Keeseville. "Think about it seriously," said Father Payette, "I am very much afraid that you will regret such a move . . . life is difficult here."[87] Whether because of the cool tone of Payette's letter, or because of his concern over the health of his sister, Evelina,[88] Father Barnabé apparently accepted the advice offered him, and he took no steps to move to Minnesota or to join Louis Riel in his work with the métis in the United States.

V

Father Barnabé was not the only one who was worried about Evelina. His concern was shared by Louis Riel. Except for Marie Guernon, Louis does not appear to have paid much attention to women during his youth and early manhood. He had been too busy leading a political movement to look closely at the dark-eyed métis girls of St. Vital and St. Norbert. If he had been moved to pity by the appeals of the women who had interceded on behalf of Major Boulton in February of 1870, it was to the appeals of Mrs. Sutherland rather than those of Miss Mc-Vicar that he yielded.[89] But Riel had been touched by Evelina's kindness during those first visits with the Barnabés, and when the two young people were thrown together after Riel's release from Beauport, the compassion of the one and the gratitude of the other united in a mutual love. To the métis, harried and worried, the slight, blonde, pious and affectionate Evelina must have seemed like a ministering angel; to the quiet, protected, convent-educated, young woman, the handsome, cultivated Riel, with his adventurous past and his history of persecution, must have appeared a story-book hero. Father Barnabé did not discourage the romance that developed between his sister and his guest. Perhaps he was not even aware of it, although he frequently spoke of Evelina in his letters to Riel. In any event, before Riel left Keeseville, he and Evelina became engaged to be married. The engagement, however, remained a secret between them.[90]

While in New York, and after he set out for St. Paul, Riel wrote regularly to his betrothed. His first and only love letters, these have not been found, if indeed they are still in existence. Fortunately several of Evelina's letters are extant, and through these the reader can follow the course of Louis's love affair. On October 4, Evelina wrote sending Louis bits of family gossip, telling him that she was learning the songs he had sent her, and concluding, "my last thoughts are of God and of you. It is almost ten o'clock, and I cannot go to bed without saying to you, my own dear Louis . . . I love and embrace you."[91] Later in October she wrote again. It was Louis's birthday, and Evelina sent to him her very best wishes that "the Sovereign Master of all things permit, if it be His will in the course of your 35th year, the realization of all your projects." "Pray for me, too," she added, "the one who must accompany you along the road of life. Pray—I ask you—that I may be a worthy companion and that I shall know how to do it well." Inside her letter she enclosed a few dried flowers, "the emblem of my true and sincere love."[92] In January she acknowledged Louis's letter from Pembina and his gift of "a little Jesus," telling him of the emptiness his absence left in her heart.[93]

Then Evelina fell ill, and for weeks there were no letters. From time to time Louis wrote to her telling her of his plans and sending her little snippets of his verse. They were verses to touch her heart, and verses to make her laugh. For these she was grateful; but her fiancé's letters came at intervals that were too widely spaced to satisfy a woman who was in love. With the return of spring, with its green leaves and its bright flowers, Evelina felt ever so much better. She was filled with the happy memories of what life in Keeseville had been like when Louis was at her side. "Last spring I saw you so often working around the house . . . this year you are very far away from us . . . but in thought we are always near you," she wrote. "I often go and sit under the lilacs, which are ready to bloom. I hasten to gather a few flowers to send you. I am carried back to the days we were so happy, both of us seated on the same bench." Inevitably she wrote of their life in the days that lay ahead of them. "Dear Louis, you tell me in one of your letters that you are making all arrangements to come and get me soon. . . . I must be honest, if you were coming to get me, I would only be an embarrassment to you; however, it is useless to tell you that, and I am sure of it too, you will come and get me, so that we can have our own home. . . ."[94] She did have a few doubts about her fitness for life in the west, for Louis had told her that he was going to live in that part of the country rather than return to settle down in the east; but they were doubts that she expected Louis to brush impatiently aside. "I am afraid that you will repent your choice, for it seems to me that I do not possess the qualities that you wish in a wife. I am a humble woman, not a very courageous one, and I shall not be suited to the high position that I should have to occupy if you are successful. Pray that God will put into my heart the virtues that I must have to be a perfect Christian and a worthy helpmate."[95] In this last letter Evelina enclosed "the first flower of the season." It was a sprig from a laurel tree—the symbol of success.

But for Louis there was no success. He had no home for Evelina and no money to bring her to him. Abruptly he broke off the correspondence. Perhaps she was right. She was not suited to the hardships that any wife of his must inevitably face. Thus Riel's romance came to an end. He had only time and energy for the basic task of nourishing his own body. There was no place in his life for lilacs—or laurels.

CHAPTER 13

American Citizen

I T WAS a changed west to which Riel returned in 1878, different from
the west he had ever known before. On both sides of the frontier,
settlers had poured into the new lands, bringing with them new social
attitudes, new economic activities, new political ideas, bringing about
the very changes that Riel and his supporters had anticipated and feared.
More significant, probably, than any other single factor was the railway.
With the laying of the steel rails, the day of the Red River cart was over,
and with it the freighting business upon which so many métis had relied
for a living.   With the coming of the railway the day of the buffalo hunt,
too, was at an end.

The American railway lines opened up the buffalo range, and an orgy
of hunting and killing followed.   Everybody wanted to kill buffalo—not
that people really needed or wanted the skins or were prepared to take
the trouble to cure them.   Thousands of the animals were shot for their
tongues alone.   What made the slaughter all the more dreadful was the
replacement of the old-fashioned musket by the new breech-loading rifle
with its superior range and greater accuracy.   Of the utter wastefulness
of the buffalo hunt there is no lack of evidence.   1875/76 saw the last
of the great southern herd;[1] and by 1883 the northern herd had been so
decimated by indiscriminate slaughter that only a few small bands of
straggling animals were to be found.[2]   The old west, the west of the
Indian and the buffalo was, with dramatic suddenness, on its way to
becoming no more than an historical memory, although few métis or even
white men at that time were prepared to admit it.

There were many changes, too, in Manitoba.   Winnipeg had absorbed
Fort Garry, and near the site of the old Hudson's Bay Company fort
just north of the international boundary, a new aggressive community
had grown up since 1874 which bore the name of the American essayist,
Emerson.   From nothing it had become a town of 2,000 by 1880, and
its people dreamed of the day when it would become Manitoba's largest
city.   Meanwhile settlers were filling the vacant land of the province,
not merely Ontarians but Icelanders and Germans.   New homes were
built, new farms were ploughed, new machinery was imported, new

233

varieties of grain were planted, new methods of milling were adopted. The province grew in numbers and increased in prosperity.

But the new prosperity did not touch the métis population. Most of the half-breeds still clung to ways that were familiar no matter how obsolete they might appear in the eyes of the newcomers. They did no more than grub a living from the soil; they depended for their livelihood on the buffalo hunt and the fur trade. They could not see that both were almost at an end, as far as Red River was concerned. After 1870, when Manitoba became part of Canada, they continued in the old ways. The old habits of thought and action were still strong. When the excitement of the rising of 1869/70 subsided, the annual migration to the plains began again, and every year hundreds of métis left the valley of the Red to travel further across the prairies in search of buffalo hides and meat. The clergy, who knew what the new conditions meant for their flocks, endeavoured to persuade the métis to adapt themselves to the changes that time was bringing about. With the métis on the plains, it was inevitable that the Ontarians, the Scandinavians and the Germans—the "bona fide" settlers—would take over the lands once regarded by the native population as theirs. When Father Lacombe complained in 1878 of those "ineffable winterings" which every year drew so many half-breeds from Red River,[3] he was simply reiterating the words of other missionaries who had written in a similar strain since 1870.[4]

Few of the winterers were ready to recognize the inevitable. They were unable or unwilling to settle down and compete with the newcomers as agriculturalists. They were hunters and would remain hunters as long as God would allow the buffalo to roam. And as hunters, there was no place for them in a land sprouting farms and fences. As early as 1872, Father LeFloch expressed his fear that many of the winterers would remain on the plains.[5] In 1873, he wrote that his predictions had been true. Not only had few of the winterers come back to Red River, but others were now leaving to join their kindred.[6] "The mission of St. Joseph is falling into dust," he wrote sadly. "There are no longer any more than forty families here. The Norwegians and Germans are taking everything."[7]

Louis Riel's delegates, when they went to Ottawa in 1870, had tried at length and with great persistence to protect the half-breed peoples of Red River. The reward of their efforts had been the concession, by a reluctant Macdonald, of 1,400,000 acres of land to be set aside for the half-breed people in order to extinguish their "Indian" title. But this undertaking, like the promise of an amnesty, had been slow to be fulfilled. At first the federal government, giving a literal interpretation to the 31st section of the Manitoba Act, had included only the children and not the families in the grant; three years later, in 1873, the initial allotments were made on the basis of 190 acres to each child. In 1874, provision was made for the heads of families with grants of 160 acres or $160.00 in money scrip. Two years later it was decided the heads of families would be entitled to scrip only.

Generous as these grants may appear, they did little to help the métis; only the land speculators made any real profit from them. Taking advantage of the ignorance and inexperience of the mixed-blood population, speculators and profiteers were able to obtain, usually for only a fraction of their worth, the scrip certificates the government had issued. Often a few dollars and a few drinks of whisky were sufficient to induce a half-breed to part with his claim to a quarter-section of land in Manitoba. Many of the métis, resenting the persecutions of the first years of Confederation, their traditions tied to the hunt or the fur trade, unable to compete economically or in social prestige with the newcomers, were easy victims for unscrupulous white men. Like the buffalo, the métis were becoming an anachronism in the age that opened with the railway.[8] They left Red River, many of them, to live for a few more years the life they knew and liked, some on the banks of the Saskatchewan and others in the valley of the Missouri.

II

In the autumn of 1878, Louis Riel had said good-bye to Barnabé and his sister Evelina at Keeseville and set out for the mid-west. He was anxious to see his family, and so he went from St. Paul to Pembina. Here he was visited by several of the Red River métis who had been his supporters in the days of the resistance. Here, too, he encountered the French-Canadian, Joseph Dubuc, whom he had invited to Red River and who had been his political adviser during his several election campaigns in Manitoba. Dubuc had now entered federal politics and had been elected in September, 1878, as the member for Riel's old constituency, Provencher, in the election which had seen the defeat of the Liberals and the return of Sir John A. Macdonald and the Conservative Party to power.[9] Dubuc descended from the train at St. Vincent, in January of 1879, on his way to Ottawa to attend the opening of parliament, and he was met at the station by Louis Riel driving a horse and cutter. Together they drove to the hotel at Pembina, where Ambroise and Maxime Lépine were waiting along with several other French métis. Riel was anxious to learn everything he could about the political problems in Manitoba: the fall of Girard's government; Royal's efforts to maintain the principle of duality in the Manitoba government and his proposals for the introduction of party politics on federal lines; the métis land grant; the amnesty.   Dubuc later wrote that Riel became "excited" during the discussion and spoke of the need for adopting "bold" measures.   But the métis leader spoke only in generalities and did not come to grips with any of the issues.[10]

Then they talked about Riel's stay in Longue Pointe and Beauport. Apparently there was no disposition on Louis's part to try to conceal it. "The fact is well known," he said to Dubuc.   "It is useless to try to hide it."[11]   However, when Dubuc raised the question of whether Riel had, in actual fact, been mentally ill, or whether he had merely pretended to be, Riel looked at him sharply and asked him what he meant.   Dubuc explained, "All your friends know that you have been confined in an asylum; but the general opinion among them is that you did not suffer from any mental derangement, that you never were a mad man.   They believe two things; either that the government had you arrested and confined in order to take revenge for your obstinate resistance, or that you yourself simulated madness."   Riel gave a long sigh, and looked up much relieved.   Dubuc had not made up his words.   They were perfectly true.   The majority of the métis in Red River had put no stock in the stories of Riel's madness.   They believed—and still believe— that he was perfectly sane.   Riel was glad to be assured.   Just as Dubuc was leaving, Riel turned to him and said:

Your remark of an hour ago is true.   What is believed about my stay in the asylum is true, at least in one of the alternatives.   No, I was not confined through vengeance or as a result of persecution; but I did pretend to be mad.   I succeeded so well that everybody believed that I really was mad.   And why did I do it?   Because I had held the two governments of England and Canada in check for twelve months, the governments of those countries wanted to see me dead.   But because I was still alive in spite of their efforts and those of their police to arrest me, I had had myself elected: therefore they took the revenge they sought against me on my people, by refusing them their rights and by persecuting them.   Seeing this, I said to myself, they are still afraid of me; but if I should disappear, or if I should lose my mind, their relentless persecution may be relaxed. A poor fool would be pitied, his past overlooked.   Then my enemies would probably cease persecuting my people.   I believed that the idea was worth trying and I resolved to put it into effect. . . . There you now have the key to and explanation of the whole business.[12]

The two Lépines looked on with approval and admiration.   They drank in every word of Riel's statement.   They believed what he said. Dubuc, however, was not so sure.   On January 21, before he resumed his journey to Ottawa, he wrote to Archbishop Taché, "I saw Louis for some time.   He is well, and just as he was before.   He constantly alluded to his stay in the asylums and to his madness.   He is, however, in good health, full of energy and enthusiasm as usual."[13] One month later, after he had had time to think over the significance of Riel's remarks, he wrote again to the Archbishop, "He tried, in a speech lasting half an hour . . . to make me understand that his madness had been simulated and that that was part of his plan. . . . When I heard him express these ideas in an inspired and prophetic tone of voice, I understood that he was still a bit touched in the head."[14] Several weeks later Dubuc wrote to Riel. He said nothing about the question of Riel's real or pretended madness. He merely sent Riel some parliamentary documents which the métis had requested and expressed hopes for Riel's continued good health.[15]

Perhaps the most significant thing to emerge from Riel's meeting with Dubuc was the métis leader's rejection of the proposal that his friends should once more take up the question of an amnesty and press for a complete pardon for him. This was what Romuald Fiset had in mind for the new session of parliament. But Riel had replied, "I am not a murderer. I have not committed any crime. I have no need of a pardon." If there was any need for an amnesty, it was for those who had attacked the Provisional Government. He would not, however, object to an amnesty; it would at least restore to Lépine the civil rights of which he had been deprived, but as for himself, "I don't care about it. I do not even wish to take advantage of it to return to Manitoba. I want to stay here, on the frontier, a living and perpetual protest against England for its ill-intentioned proceedings against me."[16] For the moment Riel was dramatizing himself and rather enjoying his martyrdom.

During several months Louis did what he threatened to do. He stayed just south of the frontier, at St. Joseph, with his friend Norman Gingras, receiving visits from his associates and his relatives. On April 7, he informed Dubuc that he had a visit from his mother and his brother-in-law, Lavallé, Octavie and her youngest child. The visit "filled me with joy," he wrote,[17] but he made no attempt to go back to St. Vital with them. His exile still had another year to run; and in spite of his apparent unconcern about the amnesty, he still rather hoped for one and wondered if Fiset and Dubuc would be able to do anything for him.

Finally it became clear to Riel that nothing was to be expected from the government in Ottawa, and he began to think of leaving St. Joseph. He had written a few verses, notably a stinging attack on Sir John A. Macdonald which appeared in print after his death;[18] but unpublished verses buttered no bread, and Riel was forced to resume his travels. It was natural that he should join one of the métis bands wintering on the prairies.   In December a report appeared in one of the Montana news-papers that Riel had passed through Fort Benton, on the Missouri, on his way to Fort Assiniboine, on the Big Bend of the Milk River, where he was "awaiting the termination of his exile."[19]   It was a hard winter, that winter of 1879/80, one of extreme cold and heavy snow.   Buffalo were few and far distant, the métis horses were thin and ill-nourished, and the hunt was not a profitable one.   Lépine had planned to join Riel at Fort Assiniboine but seems to have missed him.   Finally the métis moved south towards the Judith Basin.[20]   They moved as a group, maintaining their traditional organization with their councillors, their captains and their military discipline.   This organization the métis had evolved for their own protection against the Indians and for the prosecu-tion of the buffalo hunt; this same organization had made it possible for Louis Riel to seize power in Red River and defy the Canadian government in 1869/70.

During the next three years, Louis Riel remained on the plains with the métis, moving from place to place, as the seasons changed, within the general limits of the Milk and the Missouri valleys.   He traded with the Indians, purchasing supplies in Fort Benton;[21] he chopped wood for sale near Carroll;[22] he acted as an interpreter and as an intermediary between the whites, the métis and the Indians.[23]   His companions and associates were Red River refugees, Cree Indians from the Canadian North-West, and Sioux and Nez Percés from Dakota and Montana, as well as the many wolfers, horse thieves, hunters, whisky traders and outlaws who made up the shifting, brawling, hard-drinking population of the American west.   Riel was accepted as one of them.   Sometimes his name appeared in the Montana newspapers; sometimes it appeared in the confidential reports of the North-West Mounted Police.[24]   The fact that he was in frequent touch with the Canadian Indians, who were spending their winters near the Big Bend of the Milk River, was always a source of alarm to the Canadian authorities, who wondered what he was doing and feared his actions would be hostile to the interests of the Canadian government.

While he was with the métis band near Carroll, Louis met and married a young métisse, Marguerite Monet *dit* Bellehumeur.   Not much is known about her, except that she was dark-skinned, small, quiet, obedient, gentle, without education and inclined to be tubercular.   It was not a marriage arising from strong passion or profound love.   There is no depth of feeling in Riel's letters to his wife, nor in the verses he wrote to her.   Very probably he was lonely, and the little métis girl, who worshipped the ground on which he walked, gave him the comfort and the adulation he desired.   He could never see Evelina adapting herself to

life in a métis encampment or finding herself at home in the rough and
often lawless communities of Montana. The contrast between Carroll
and Keeseville was too great.

Riel's marriage took place in 1881.[25] The marriage was prairie-fashion,
"according to the common law," and was naturally a source of concern
to a man with Louis's religious background. When a missionary
appeared, Father Joseph Damiani, S.J., the couple went through a
religious ceremony on March 6, 1882.[26] Two months later a son was
born to Riel and Marguerite.[27] They gave him the name of Jean. The
next year, on September 17, 1883, a second child was born. She was
called Marie Angélique.

Evelina Barnabé was hurt and angry. Through an American newspaper report she learned of Louis's marriage. Hoping the report was
untrue, she wrote to Louis's sister, Henriette.[28] She could not believe
Louis would abandon her, even though he had not answered her letters.
Then she wrote to Louis.[29] Could he really be guilty of such "infamy"?
She begged him to write and tell her if the report was true: "If you do
not do so you will bring on yourself the greatest curses God can utter,
for having destroyed forever the future of one who has only one regret
if such is the case, of having known and loved you." It was a hard letter
for Louis to answer. He had deserted Evelina, and he had married
Marguerite Monet. He could not thrust out of his mind the memory
of all the kindnesses he had received from the family in Keeseville. It
hurt him all the more to learn that Father Barnabé was seriously ill—for
he knew that Evelina would need him more than ever. But what had
been done could not be undone, and he set himself the task of answering
Evelina's letter. Draft after draft he scribbled, trying to find proper
words. But they would not come to him. He tried to argue that
Evelina's efforts to keep the engagement secret had discouraged him;
perhaps she was ashamed of him; and what could he conclude from her
statement that she would not marry until he could provide her with a
suitable home? "I concluded that my affectionate letters had ceased to
be agreeable to you. You wanted indifferent letters. I could not write
that way. I cut short my correspondence. After several months I left
Pembina and came to Montana, without ever ceasing to pray for my
good friends in Keeseville."[30] Beyond that point he never seemed to be
able to continue. Whether he ever sent a reply to his former fiancee is
uncertain. And yet he did not forget her. He always kept her letters.

If Evelina's letter had caused Louis some embarrassment, one written
by his sister Sara, who had joined the Grey Nuns and was at the time
living at Ile à la Crosse, must have done something towards easing his
distress. Sara wrote to her new sister-in-law with all the warm and

gentle affection that marked her life. Louis read the letter to Marguerite, for she could not read it herself:

Only a month ago I learned that my beloved brother had united his life to yours, and that the sacred bonds of marriage have made you my dear sister-in-law. I want to assure you of my tender and deep love; henceforth your troubles are my troubles, your joys will be my joys, your hopes my hopes, and your happiness will make me happy. Live happily together, my beloved sister, for your husband has all that is necessary to make you happy, and since heaven has condescended to give you a son, consecrate him to the sacred heart of Jesus, acknowledge him to the Holy Virgin, that the first name that the little angel may speak will be the holy name of Jesus. Oh my well beloved sister, watch over his innocence; embrace this dear, this loveable little nephew for me.[31]

Having married, and fathered a child, Louis now felt bound to the country in which his son had been born and to the people whose fortunes were now his. He could, if he wished, return to Manitoba since the term of his exile was at an end; but he did not choose to do so. On March 16, 1883, at Fort Benton, Riel appeared before Judge S. Wade in the District court of the Territory of Montana. After establishing that he had been a resident of the United States since January 24, 1878, and had lived in Montana the requisite period of at least one year, and had "behaved as a man of good moral character, attached to the principles of the Constitution of the United States and well disposed to the good order and happiness of the same," Riel was "admitted and declared to be a citizen of the United States of America."[32]

It was thus as an American citizen that Louis Riel paid a visit to Manitoba in the summer of 1883. This was the first time he had set foot in St. Vital since his departure ten years previously, after the arrest of his friend Ambroise Lépine. Now he had nothing to fear. His banishment was over, and he no longer owed any allegiance to Canada. He was a free man; free to come back to visit the scenes of his childhood, to see his mother and to dispose of his property in the Red River valley, as well as the properties of other Red River métis who had abandoned the country as he had done and were now living in Montana. No longer was he pursued by the police. Instead it was the newspaper reporters who sought him out after he attended Mass in St. Boniface cathedral on June 24 and his presence became generally known in Winnipeg. The Winnipeg *Free Press* found him to be a little corpulent, and wearing a reddish brown beard.[33] The *Daily Sun* referred to his dark, curly hair, his prominent well-shaped nose and his expressive mouth.[34] As in his younger days, it was his eyes that seem to have attracted the most attention. The *Sun* reporter described him as "a man of extraordinary

self-possession, but when relating some stirring fact or exciting remini-
scence, his eyes danced and glistened in a manner that riveted attention."
Riel was not very anxious to talk to the reporters, but he yielded to
their importunities and spoke with them about the future of the French
language in Manitoba, about the problems of the métis and, in particular, about the events leading to the founding of Manitoba. "I am
more and more convinced every day," he said, "that without a single
exception, I did right. Of course, I do not mean to say my conduct was
perfect on all occasions, because every man is liable to make trifling
mistakes, but had I the same thing to go through again, I would do
exactly the same . . . and I have always believed that I acted honestly,
and the time will come when the people of Canada will see and acknowledge it."[35] How could he realize that the next two years would give
him the chance to prove his words?

It was a happy occasion, this visit to St. Vital in 1883. Riel was able
to talk with his mother, with his grandmother, Marie-Anne Gaboury-
Lagimodière, and with his friends. Several times he was the guest of
Joseph Dubuc. But there was something missing. Too many of the
métis who had been his warmest friends and closest associates were gone.
Lépine had gone; his one time secretary, Louis Schmidt, had gone; the
Touronds had moved to the Saskatchewan, and so too had Pierre
Parenteau; Charles Nolin, his cousin, but never a true friend, had also
moved; André Nault was still living on the farm from which the surveyors
had been expelled in October, 1869, but both his sons had taken themselves to the west. And the métis who had remained were all too poor
to purchase the properties Riel had hoped to sell. On July 14, Louis
wrote to his wife, "It is already a month since I left the mission. I wish
to return. I am weary. But money is so scarce that I can sell nothing.
There is a financial crisis in Manitoba and lands are selling cheap, rather
they are not selling at all. I think that I shall arrange to leave next
week."[36]

Riel returned to Montana as poor as he had come, but he carried with
him a few ideas and a few disturbing thoughts. Napoléon Nault, old
André's son, had come back to Red River to take part in the eating,
drinking and dancing that accompanied the marriage of Riel's favourite
sister, Henriette, to Jean-Marie Poitras on July 12. He had talked to
Louis Riel.[37] He had told Riel of the agitation of the métis in the
Saskatchewan district, of their concern for their lands and for their
rights, and of the silence that had greeted their petitions. There were a
good many things for Louis to think about . . . and they all brought
back the idea of his mission.

III

Despite the instructions he had received on his discharge from Beauport that he should live quietly and avoid undue excitement, Louis Riel had never abandoned the notion that he had a special mission in life. Among the papers he carried with him wherever he went, Bishop Bourget's letters were carefully preserved; and Barnabé's talk about Catholic colonies in the North-West had reminded him of these letters. His departure from the Eastern United States for the west had been inspired, in part at least, by a vague ill-defined missionary intent, which could always be found, somewhere, in the background of his actions. From time to time he talked loosely of a confederation of all the native peoples, both Indian and métis, living between the Saskatchewan and the Missouri.[38] But the Indians did not respond, and so he turned to the people whom he knew best, the métis.

He had every reason to be alarmed about their future. He knew little about those who had gone to the Saskatchewan; but the métis in the Missouri were, if anything, worse off than they had been in Manitoba. The American whites had little use for them, and referred to them as the "breeds" and "the coyote French." In the words of the frontiersman, the half-breed was "the meanest creature that walks." "He is never equal in courage to his father. . . . He surpasses his mother in dishonesty and treachery."[39] The Red River mixed-blood had generally a stronger sense of identity, a more highly developed culture and a stronger moral background that his American counterpart; but among the American whites this only made him more suspect. The Americans believed the Canadian half-breeds to be the source of nearly all the ammunition traded to the Sioux Indians. "A half-breed camp," wrote the editor of the *Benton Weekly Record* in 1879, "is nearly as great an attraction for hostile Indians as a herd of buffalo is to a pack of famishing wolves, and while the half-breeds are permitted to roam at will, the hostiles will never want for ammunition or whiskey, or cease to prowl on the outskirts of civilization and rob the white settlers of life and property." The American half-breed at least possessed the virtue of being an American citizen; but the Canadian métis was a foreigner. There was "no reason" why they should:

enjoy more privileges than are allowed white families who are not permitted to reside upon Indian reservations, much less to carry on an illicit trade with hostile savages. These Canadian half-breeds pay no taxes; they produce nothing but discord, violence and bloodshed wherever they are permitted to locate. They are a worthless, brutal race of the lowest species of humanity, without one redeeming trait to commend them to the sympathy or protection of any Government.[40]

This was a judgment harsher than anything passed by Charles Mair or John Schultz.

There is no doubt that the Red River métis—whatever he may have been like while living at St. Vital or St. Norbert or St. François Xavier— once he was uprooted from his own country, deprived of the traditional supports of his morals and morale, slipped all too easily and all too quickly into impoverishment, despondency and degradation. The old standards and the old values seemed to have lost their meaning in the new world of immigration, settlement and economic competition. Riel himself wrote harshly of the métis, blaming most of their problems on over-indulgence in cheap whisky, rum flavoured with "painkiller," or alcohol diluted with Florida water. "The half-breed is a man who has a strong passion for intoxicating drinks. He spends most of his earnings in whisky. If he is a mere hunter on the prairie, liquor is one of the principal causes which makes him poor and prevents him from settling. If he is trying to settle, the use of spirituous liquors empties his purse and makes him sink more rapidly into poverty, and poverty drives him away from his little farm." Describing a scene at Fort Hawley, near Wilder's Landing on the Missouri, he told of one whisky trader who sold 2,000 gallons of whisky during the winter months to a camp of some fifteen families.

He traded whisky so freely that the half-breed women . . . used to go in number and get drunk at his saloon. On one occasion ten or twelve of those miserable and degraded females were seen paying treats at the counter, and striking the bar with their fists. They were boasting of having money to pay. At the same time pieces of silver, precious and necessary to buy the bread and clothes for their poor children, rolled and rang on the shop table. When they left the saloon they could hardly walk. They were crying and falling on the road. Oh! I would be glad if public opinion would, in some way, take up that matter and help sheriffs to act in such cases as these.[41]

It was a horrible and disgusting experience to a man who had been brought up in the sober atmosphere of a religious home, and who, during the days he had commanded in Red River, had tried to impose a self-denying ordinance upon the men who served him as soldiers.

If Riel was to help the métis in Montana, two things were necessary. He would have to give his support to the efforts of the Jesuit missionaries to persuade the métis to settle down; the métis would have to accept the fact that, if nothing else, the disappearance of the buffalo rendered the abandonment of nomadism absolutely essential. He would also have to bring about the curtailment of the indiscriminate sale of liquor to the mixed-blood population. Riel recalled that he had tried to meet the problem of nomadism in Manitoba by obtaining a large half-breed grant.   Perhaps it would be worth while trying the same approach in Montana.   Accordingly, he wrote to General Miles, whose troops were deployed to deal with any hostilities from the Sioux, asking that "a special reservation" should be established in Montana "for the half-breeds."   He told Miles that the half-breeds were finding it increasingly difficult to make a living "and owing to our present limited means and want of experience in economy, we cannot compete with the majority of our countrymen."[42]   Once the reserve was established, Riel suggested, the whisky traders should be forbidden to enter it; and public money should be appropriated for the purchase of agricultural implements, seed grain and for the erection of schools.   It was, in brief, a demand that the half-breeds should receive as much consideration as the Indians under the treaties.   This petition was drafted in August, 1880, while Riel was with a band of some eighty métis families living in the Judith Basin.

But Miles was a soldier.   He had no authority to make land grants and set up special reserves for the métis.   After all, the métis were not Indians, and did not want to be regarded as such.   What was more, many of them were aliens from Canada, with no claims whatsoever on the generosity of the United States government.

Failing in his effort to obtain a land reserve, Riel was in no way deterred in his efforts to curb the liquor traffic.   He decided to prosecute one Simon Pepin, a métis, who was acting as an agent for C. A. Broadwater and Company.   Pepin had been one of those trading liquor to the métis and the Indians at Wilder's Landing.   In March and again in April, 1882, Riel reported Pepin's activities to Deputy Marshal John Biedler.[43]   But Riel's charges did not worry Pepin.   Colonel C. A. Broadwater was a power in the Democratic party,[44] and Pepin told Riel that he had nothing to fear from Biedler "since money and favors had easily secured his friendliness to the Company."[45]   Pepin's confidence seemed to be thoroughly justified when no action followed Riel's complaints.   Finally, in June, Riel took the matter up with the United States Marshal, Alexander C. Botkin, threatening to carry it even further should it continue to be ignored at the lower levels of administration. Subsequently Riel had a personal interview with Botkin.   "As I had not at that time been educated up to the practice that may be called the eclectic enforcement of the laws—that is to say the custom of punishing some offenders and protecting others in a monopoly of law breaking," wrote Botkin at a later date, "I encouraged him to procure the necessary evidence and promised my co-operation."[46]   With Botkin's help, Riel was appointed a special deputy marshal.[47]

Armed with authority and backed by Botkin, Riel went ahead with his plans for prosecuting Pepin.   However when the case came to the courts in the spring of 1883, it was thrown out on the grounds that the métis were not Indians, and that legal restrictions on the sale of liquor to the red men did not apply to them.   The métis could continue to drink like white men.   Pepin therefore had done nothing wrong, and he was free to resume his nefarious activities.   Riel, who had thrown all his slender resources into the case against Pepin, emerged from it discouraged and penniless.[48]

Riel's attack on Broadwater's agent had thrust him, willy-nilly, into the turmoil of party politics.   In 1864, Montana had become a Territory, and although the first Governor, who was appointed by President U. S. Grant, was a strong Republican, the Democratic party had succeeded in winning the Territorial seat in Congress.   The Democratic hold over Montana tightened with the years, particularly after the nomination of Martin Maginnis, whose electoral success in 1872 was repeated with monotonous regularity in 1874, 1876, 1878 and 1880.   In 1882, Maginnis was once more seeking the votes of the people of the Territory.   He was confident of success, for behind him there were the big business interests of C. A. Broadwater and H. D. Hauser; the Irish population led by Sheriff J. J. Healy and the one-time Fenian, J. J. Donnelly; the copper kings, W. A. Clarke and Marcus Daly; as well as the Mormons.   It was a formidable and practically unbeatable combination.

Riel, however, had chosen to ally himself with the Republicans. Neither Riel nor Botkin ever said so, but it is most likely that Botkin, put forward as the Republican candidate against Maginnis, had taken advantage of Riel's anxiety to help the métis by encouraging him to support the Republican party.   Once having taken issue with the Democrat, C. A. Broadwater—he had attacked this company first in 1881 for cheating and demoralizing the métis[49]—he had no choice but to throw in his lot with those who were hoping to unseat Maginnis.   The Republicans were prepared to welcome Riel to their ranks, if only because they recognized that he was a power among the half-breed population—and the half-breeds, because they were not Indians, were eligible to vote.   The Democrats, too, made a bid for Louis's support, hoping that a chat with Maginnis might persuade Riel of the direction in which his best interests lay.   But Riel had made his choice.   He could not stomach a man who was looked upon as a tool of C. A. Broadwater. He wrote to the Hon. Martin Maginnis, "Some of your good friends and supporters have had the idea that I might vote for you, with a number of half-breed voters.   But I doubt very much if such will be the case." The Democrats, Riel maintained, had never done anything for the half-breeds; on the contrary, they had cheated them "in a scandalous manner" and had never offered to give them protection against the Indian horse thieves who infested the country. He added:

I know Broadwater and Company's feelings and opinions about half-breeds. The influence of that firm in army circles is simply immense. I am sure they have misrepresented those people in Washington, and I have good reason to believe that you have also endorsed those interested and false opinions. As to Mr. Botkin, I think that he is disposed and willing to protect the best interest of every American citizen regardless of race and color, and therefore I have offered him my support, and he shall have it.[50]

The election was held on Tuesday, November 7. It was a heated and dirty affair. At first both parties claimed victory;[51] then the charges and the counter-charges began.[52] In Rocky Point, ten men were accused of having cast 720 votes for Maginnis; and in Lewis and Clarke county, where the half-breed vote gave a majority to Botkin, Louis Riel was accused of voting unqualified voters. In Meagher county, the regions not dominated by Fort Maginnis went Republican; while in Choteau and Missoula, Maginnis's majority was a substantial one. Broadly speaking, the soldiers, the railway workers and the Irishmen voted for Maginnis. The old settlers were said to have been the mainstay of Botkin's support. But they were apparently in the minority, for Maginnis kept his seat in Congress.

Politics in nineteenth-century Montana were not for the thin-skinned and the squeamish. The charges hurled against Louis Riel were no worse than those that were tossed about indiscriminately every two years by both political parties. But Riel did not like being called a renegade, a rebel, a man who had sold his vote and the votes of his half-breed supporters to the highest bidder. To clear his name, he wrote to the *Helena Weekly Herald*.[53] In a long letter he went over the old story of 1869/70, arguing that the Republican party had shown sympathy even then for the Red River métis. He was no renegade. "British rule does not suit me and I have chosen this country as my adopted land." Were those Americans who took up arms against George III to be called renegades and rebels? As for selling his vote, he declared, "My vote is not for sale. Besides the Republican Party have never offered me any money. They have acted with me honourably and I have voted for them honestly." Then he dealt with the charge that he had "compelled" the half-breeds to vote against Maginnis. There was no need for compulsion, he wrote, since what he had done was to inform them of the resolution of the Republican Club of Choteau County "to use their influence in favour of the American half-breeds whenever they saw them in danger of being treated unjustly and to help them fairly to get justice as any other citizen." Then he took a swipe at Broadwater:

Since I have denounced to the authorities a company of sutlers for their wild trade; since I have chosen to vote for the Republican candidates, although in one case, I am altogether on the side of the law against the lawbreakers, and although, in the other case, I am exercising my rights as a citizen in a constitutional and legitimate manner, there are some who, more anxious to speak than to speak well, come out and say: "See what a perturbator is that man! How turbulent he is!"

The weekly papers at Fort Benton and Helena took up Riel's case. The latter, strong in its loyalty to the Republican party, defended Riel by arguing that the Red River half-breeds, whose votes were regarded as illegal merely because they had voted for Botkin, were the very people whom the Democrats had so assiduously cultivated prior to the election. If the half-breeds were citizens when they voted Democrat, they could not now be disfranchised because they had voted Republican.[54] In reply, the *Benton Record* declared that the métis were simply Riel's protégés, that they voted as he had instructed them; and that even if they had subscribed to an oath that they were entitled to vote, they still had not taken the oath of allegiance.[55] Throughout the winter of 1882/83, recriminations followed recriminations. Botkin instituted a series of legal actions against the Democrats for padding the ballot boxes, and in so doing aroused the wrath of his opponents who declared through the *Benton Weekly Record* that "at the proper and not very far distant time they will show that gentleman that two can play at his little game."[56]

Just what this threat meant became apparent in May, 1883. Sheriff John Healy, one-time whisky trader who had been chased out of Fort Whoop-up by the North-West Mounted Police, and Democratic ward heeler in Choteau county,[57] arrested Louis Riel on a bench warrant for complicity in the election frauds. "Riel is the leader of a lot of British half-breeds," wrote the editor of the *Benton Weekly Record* sourly.

At Rocky Point last election he tried to vote almost all of them, but was prevented, and he then went to Carroll and opened polls at two o'clock in the afternoon and voted all of them. They were British subjects and had refused to swear allegiance to the United States. Mr. Healy found him at work on a ranch above Sun River and took him completely by surprise. Riel is a hard citizen and the Territory can much better afford to board him than to have him at large.[58]

Riel did not, however, remain in gaol. According to the *Record*, he "either scared some Republican into going on his bail bond by threatening to tell what he knows of campaign iniquities," or the sheriff took "pity on the miserable condition of the poor wretch and let him out on personal recognizance."[59]

In September, Riel's case came before the Montana courts. The charge was that he had induced Urbain Delorme and Jerome St. Matt to vote in the election of the previous year, knowing that they had not yet declared their intention of becoming American citizens. The Helena and Fort Benton newspapers indulged in the customary wordy battles. Their descriptions of Riel were at such variance that it would be difficult for the stranger to realize they were speaking of the same man. Riel, whom the Republican *Helena Weekly Herald* described as "a gentleman and scholar, a worthy and desirable friend" and "an American citizen with as full rights and infinitely more character than his persecutors,"[60] was called by the Democratic paper in Fort Benton "a low scoundrel whose fox-like cunning has alone kept him out of jail for these many years" and "as much a gentleman as Sitting Bull and as much a scholar as the famous wild Australian children."[61] The newspapers of the day were nothing if not outspoken and blindly partisan when it came to party politics. It is not a mere coincidence that the man who effected Riel's arrest was one of the managers of the *Benton Record* and a close friend of both Maginnis and Broadwater.

No decision was handed down in September in the case of *The People against Louis Riel*. It was held over until the spring session of the court. On April 16, 1884, the case was tried before Judge Wade. Riel was defended by H. P. Rolfe of Helena. Both the judge and the defending attorney were staunch Republicans, and the case itself had a strong political flavour. By this time, however, the charge against Riel had served its purpose, and the Democrats did not seek to press it. It was therefore dismissed by the District Attorney on the grounds that there was "not a shadow of evidence against Riel."[62] The Benton *Record* noted the fact of the dismissal but made no comment upon it.[63]

IV

It was in the spring of 1883 that Louis Riel, for the first time since going to Montana, succeeded in obtaining permanent employment. He became a schoolteacher at St. Peter's Mission on the Sun River. The mission had been established as early as 1862, but it had never enjoyed much success. The Jesuits who were in charge of it persisted, and in 1878 the Reverend Fathers Damiani and Prando were assigned to it. Damiani took over responsibility for the Indians and the half-breeds living between the Milk and the Missouri rivers, and Prando devoted his attention to the Blackfoot Indians on their reserve on the Sun River. In spite of the opposition of the Indian agent and the lethargy of the Indians themselves, a substantial building was erected, and a residential school was opened for boys. In 1884, the Ursulines opened a school for girls.[64] Hoping to attract the half-breeds to settle down rather than roam the plains, the Jesuits offered the post of schoolteacher to their recognized leader, Louis Riel. It was an appointment which appealed to Riel. The mission would serve as a magnet for settlement, and it would draw the métis now that the buffalo had virtually disappeared from the prairies. The settlement would be the first step in the rehabilitation of métis.

Riel settled at St. Peter's prior to his visit to Winnipeg in June, 1883.[65] He returned to St. Peter's late in July. But teaching was not the kind of life he found greatly to his liking. It seemed slow, irksome and much too quiet. He was forced to live in confined quarters, sharing a small house with one James Swan, and the hours were dreadfully long. But teaching was just what he needed after the excitement of the recent months. Besides, it afforded him a home, a small salary and a means of bringing up his own children in a religious atmosphere. Teaching also appealed to his own bent towards religion, and it gave him the opportunity to talk with his clerical associates and discuss matters of faith with them, as he had been accustomed to do when he had lived with Father Barnabé. It was probably because he had something to which he could cling and devote his attention, that the news of his sister Sara's fatal illness[66] did not lead him into the same state of melancholy he had fallen into when, as a boy, he had heard of the death of his father. Each day was much the same. He would teach his classes, deal with the petty problems of the daily life of the boys, write his verses and talk to anyone who would listen to him about his plans for the rehabilitation of the métis.[67] He was a good teacher and was well liked. At least this inference is to be drawn from a letter he received from one Mrs. M. Murphy who wrote, "Many heartfelt thanks from a devoted mother for all the kindnesses you have shown my little children, with many kind wishes to yourself and family."[68] There was satisfaction to be derived from letters like this. But Louis was restless, and he was bored. On June 3, he wrote to one of the Jesuits:

I have not been well for two weeks. My health suffers from the fatiguing regularity of having to look after children from 6 in the morning until 8 at night, on Sunday as well as on the days of the week. I am interested in the progress of the children and in the welfare of the school. I have its success at heart. And in consequence I try to do my best. I do not know if my work is worth very much; but I do it conscientiously. I do not get enough rest.[69]

Riel wrote this letter on Saturday. The next day, Sunday, he went to Mass, but he did not remain until the benediction. Visitors had arrived and wanted to see him. They were visitors from Canada, from the Saskatchewan valley, Gabriel Dumont, Moise Ouellette, Michel Dumas and James Isbister. They had travelled nearly 700 miles, and they had come to seek his advice on how they should go about obtaining their rights. For the Canadian government would pay no attention to them, and they needed help.

Here was an opportunity for Riel to free himself from the shackles of academic tedium. Here was the opportunity to do what he most liked to do. But he hesitated. He would not give his answer at once; he would have to have twenty-four hours to think over what he had been told. Yet, in his own mind, he must have known what his answer was going to be. The words of Bishop Bourget had cut deeply into his memory. Could he deny the mission that God had given him? More than once he had talked about his mission with his confessor, Father Eberschweiler. Eberschweiler had never really understood the meaning of Bourget's words, and he had required Louis "as penitence in the confessional" to write to Bourget for an explanation of what had really been meant by those words "you have a mission which you must fulfil in every respect."[70] But Bourget's reply had never arrived, and now the métis invitation was in his hands. Was not that the reply?

On June 5, Riel told Dumont what he proposed to do. He did not do it verbally, but he committed his reply to writing. He recalled that the Canadian government owed him a land grant under the 31st section of the Manitoba Act; he would be glad to return with Dumont and the others to the Saskatchewan valley; he would make his own claims upon the federal authorities, and in so doing would assist his métis brethren to obtain their rights. Once he had achieved these things, he would return to Montana where he still hoped to "unite" and "direct" the vote of the Montana half-breeds "so as to make it profitable for themselves and useful to their friends." He would go to Canada; but he would "come back here some time in September."[71]

As soon as Louis made up his mind, Marguerite began to pack up the few pitiful possessions that belonged to the Riel family. She never questioned her duty or Louis's decision. Five days later they set out on the long journey from the Sun River to the Saskatchewan. Dumont had brought a small wagon of his own, and Ouellette and Isbister, "an express drawn by two horses."[72] As the cavalcade passed through the little town of Sun River, Louis Riel paused to talk with the editor of the local newspaper. The journey to Canada, Riel told him, was prompted only by a desire to help his own people "as much as lays in his power," after which "be it much or little," he "will return to Montana." The editor, oddly enough, had been a soldier with Colonel Wolseley just fourteen years earlier, when the military expedition from Canada had driven Riel into exile in the United States. "It was queer to sit and talk to this man," wrote the editor, "and remember how as a drummer boy of fifteen we longed to spill his blood." Nevertheless he wished Riel "success in his mission."[73]

As the little party of half-breeds drew near Fort Benton, they encountered Father Eberschweiler. The priest did what he could to dissuade Riel from returning to Canada, urging him to return to the school at St. Peter's mission and warning him that his journey would probably end in bloodshed and defeat. But to no avail. Riel replied, "Father Eberschweiler, you are a good man, but you have not been obliged to endure the many injustices. . . . I intend to go through with the revolt."[74]

CHAPTER 14

North Saskatchewan

EIGHTEEN EIGHTY-FOUR! This was a year of crisis for the peoples of the North-West Territories of Canada, Indian, half-breed and white. The troubles of 1869/70, if they had done nothing else—and they had led to the formation of the Province of Manitoba—had brought to the attention of the federal authorities at Ottawa the necessity of making some provision for the administration of the territories so recently acquired from the Hudson's Bay Company. In particular, the troubles had emphasized the urgency of extinguishing whatever claims the aboriginal peoples might have had to the soil of the territory surrendered. A grant of 1,400,000 acres had been promised the métis of Manitoba. But there still remained the problem of the métis of the North-West and, above all, of the Indians.

The Indian nations of the west had, long before the transfer of the Hudson's Bay Company territories, undergone a profound change in their economy as a result of their contact with the white men. The horse and musket had made the plains' tribesmen more effective hunters and more devastating warriors than ever before, as well as enlarging the areas over which they roamed. It was not, however, until after 1870 that the Indians began to encounter the full force of white immigration into lands they looked upon as their own. Once Company rule was at an end, it would not be long before white settlers would begin making their way into the prairies, before they would begin their ranching and their farming, before occupying the traditional hunting grounds of the Indians. If Canada was to avoid the bloodshed that had accompanied the opening of the American west, it would be incumbent upon the government to take steps not only to extinguish the Indian title but also to prepare the Indian peoples for the tremendous changes that must soon and inevitably follow.

There were even more urgent reasons for prompt attention to the Indian problem in Western Canada. The appearance of the free traders had undermined the traditional price structure of the Hudson's Bay Company, and had introduced an element of uncertainty into the relations of the white men and the Indians. It had also led to the re-introduction of alcohol as a major article of Indian trade. Whisky and rum had never totally disappeared from the western prairies after the union of the Hudson's Bay Company and the North-West Company in 1821.[1] But drunkenness, debauchery and demoralization had been nowhere as extensive as after the free traders from Red River and Fort Benton spread over the southern prairies. At no time had the Red River traders any scruples about using alcohol when trading with the natives, but they never possessed the same aggressiveness and ruthlessness when dealing with the Indians as the Montanans. Led by the Irishman, John J. Healy, and the half-breed, Joseph Kipp, American traders crossed the Canadian frontier into what is now southern Alberta, building their forts on Canadian territory, Whoop-up, Slideout, Standoff, Whisky Gap and others, pouring their liquor down the throats of the thirsty red men, and introducing a period of lawlessness and anarchy that recalled the worst days of the competition between the North-West and Hudson's Bay Companies. The Montanans traded with the Indians, tricked them, robbed them of their horses, furs and women, and all with a few drinks of raw alcohol coloured with chewing tobacco and spiced with Jamaica ginger. Behind the traders were the financiers, the proprietors of I. G. Baker and Company and T. C. Power and Company, who encouraged the free traders and furnished them with goods and credit.[2]

Canadian and British observers were horrified with what they saw in Western Canada during the early 1870's. Colonel Robertson Ross and Captain W. F. Butler and others reported on the adverse effects of the nefarious liquor traffic, and they enlarged on the alcoholic orgies, the drunken brawls, the murders, the degradation and the lawlessness that had accompanied the Americans into Canada.[3] Humanity, if not economic and patriotic self-interest, demanded that something should be done to establish law and order in the prairie land to the east of the Rocky Mountains. Acting with a decisiveness he rarely displayed when dealing with the problems of the North-West, Sir John A. Macdonald introduced a bill to establish "a Police Force in the North-West Territories" in 1873. The force he contemplated was to be a semi-military one, and it was to be placed under the command of a British army officer, Captain G. A. French. The massacre of a band of Assiniboine Indians in the Cypress Hills by a group of Fort Benton traders hastened the organization of this force—known as The North-West Mounted Police—and its despatch to the western plains. One division was sent to Northern Alberta and the other, and more important group, to the southern territory. This last group, under the command of J. F. Macleod, lost no time in dealing with the whisky traders. Those who were caught found their furs confiscated, their liquor dumped and themselves thrown into prison. Those who furtively escaped poured their alcohol into various creeks and slipped quietly over the frontier to Montana to engage in other pursuits. In spite of the noisy protests and belligerent threats from Fort Benton, as far as Canada was concerned, the days of the "wild west" were over. Once the Mounted Police took the profits out of the whisky trade, it simply disappeared, much to the relief of the federal authorities and to the gratification of the Indian chiefs who were well aware of what "bad men and whisky" were doing to them. "The Police have protected us as the feathers of the bird protect it from the frosts of the winter," said the Blackfoot chief, Crowfoot.[4]

The suppression of the liquor trade was only the first step. The next was the conclusion of a series of treaties between the plains Indians and the Canadian government. Between 1871 and 1877, no less than seven treaties were negotiated with the Cree, Ojibway, Chipewyan, Saulteaux, Assiniboine and Blackfoot Indians living between Lake of the Woods and the Rocky Mountains. Broadly speaking, the seven treaties were all similar, even if there were local variations. In every instance, the Indian nation concerned agreed to surrender all proprietory claims in the regions defined within the treaty, receiving in return promises of reserved areas for their own use, financial annuities and practical assistance to help them adapt themselves to an agricultural economy.

Compared with their kindred in the United States, the Canadian Indians received less, both in the amount of their annuities and in the size of their reserved lands. The Canadian Indians accepted these lesser terms because of a compensating factor—honesty and justice in the administration of the Indian treaties in Canada. It should not be forgotten, too, that in Canada the law-enforcing agency, the Mounted Police, preceded rather than followed the arrival of the white settlers. There was no need for vigilantes in Canada, no need for a man to carry a rifle or a revolver for his own protection. A tradition of fair dealing with the Indians had been established by the Hudson's Bay Company and the Mounted Police. In consequence Canadian Indians were prepared to accept the assurances of the Canadian Indian commissioners in good faith.[5]

There is really no easy explanation for the relative peacefulness of the relations between the whites and Indians in Western Canada, especially when viewed alongside the constant fighting and misunderstanding that seemed to accompany the development of the American west. But there was one factor which was emphasized with considerable justice by James W. Taylor, who had by this time returned to Manitoba as United States consul in Winnipeg. In March, 1878, he wrote to Washington:

If an Indian war with all its attendant horrors is avoided, it will be attributable to a circumstance peculiar to the region so long occupied by the Hudson's Bay Company and without parallel in the Western Territories of the United States. I refer to the extensive intermarriage of the English, Scotch and French residents—prominently the officers and employees of the Hudson's Bay Company—with the Indian women, diffusing over the whole country in the lapse of several generations a population of métis or mixed bloods equal in number to the Indians and exerting over their aboriginal kindred a degree of moral and physical control which I find it difficult to illustrate, but which I regard as a happy Providence for the Dominion of Canada[6]

Concluding the Indian treaties may have been relatively easy; implementing them was something else again. For the moment the problem did not appear to be pressing. No wild mass of immigrants was poised on the borders of Manitoba and Ontario waiting for the opening of the Indian lands for settlement. Accordingly, for several years the Indians were able to continue the old ways of life, living on the plains, hunting the buffalo and moving about as the season or the hunt demanded.

The Canadian government did nothing because there was no apparent urgency to deal with the situation. This does not mean that every man in parliament was blind or silent. There were those who from time to time raised the question of placing the Indians on their reserves and of doing something to protect that staple article of Indian diet and Indian economy, the buffalo. During the parliamentary sessions of 1876 and 1877, these matters were brought before the House of Commons, but with no result other than the North-West Council's reference to the suggestion that there should be a closed season on buffalo hunting. In 1877, the Territorial council passed an ordinance prohibiting the use of pounds and the running of buffalo over steep banks. Indiscriminate slaughter merely for tongues and peltries was also forbidden, and a closed season was declared for the period between November and August. But when the Indians and métis raised their voices loud in protest, the ordinance was withdrawn and the buffalo were left to their impending extinction. It came quickly. Within six years of the withdrawal of the ordinance, the Canadian hunt was at an end.

The extermination of the buffalo precipitated the anticipated crisis. If the Canadian authorities acted promptly, even if belatedly, it was probably through fear that the crowding of the Indians—in the Cypress Hills and along the Milk River, in close contact with the rebellious Sioux and the hostile American soldiery—might lead to bloodshed. There was, moreover, the simple motive of humanity. The Canadians had never adopted the American dictum that the only good Indian was a dead one. It was a matter of Christian charity that something should be done to relieve the starvation and misery the Canadian Indians faced in the early 1880's.

The first step was to strengthen the numbers of the Mounted Police; the next step was to rush supplies of beef, flour and bacon to Fort Walsh and Fort Macleod. But these were not enough. In December, 1882, Inspector Norman wrote from Fort Walsh:

There is a great deal of misery in all the camps owing to the old women and children being housed in wretched cotton lodges, which are no protection whatever in cold weather, their clothing is poor and the only means they have of living is the small issue of food they are at present receiving from the Government. I might add for your information . . . I am issuing about 90 sacks of flour per week to these Indians; were a regular issue of flour made, this quantity would last but two days; with regard to meat, I am giving them about a similar allowance, so that they are receiving two days' food to last them for seven days.[7]

Near Fort Assiniboine, Montana, where they had gone in a vain search for buffalo, a number of Canadian Indians were found in a state of extreme destitution. The *Benton Weekly Record* stated that the Crees of Thunder Chief's band of forty lodges "were selling their guns and every other article of value to procure food, while the women were prostituting themselves to save their children from starvation." This camp had been unable to move north to Canada since their horses had been sold or had died. "Demoralization was everywhere evident," wrote the *Record* reporter:

The men were weak and emaciated from hunger, and women and children were sick and covered with rags and filth. The prostitution of the squaws had brought the foulest diseases into the camp, which they had no medical or other means of curing or checking, and several deaths had already occurred from this course alone. The country is entirely destitute of game, large or small, and the only hope these unfortunate wretches can have to save themselves from speedy death is to shake hands with the Sioux and become enemies of the whites".[8]

To relieve situations of this nature, the Canadian government did everything possible to induce the Indians to settle down on their reserves, to convince them that the day of the buffalo hunt was over and that their survival depended on adopting new methods of livelihood. They should take up farming and learn to support themselves. With a patience greatly to their credit, the Mounted Police and the officials of the Indian Department argued, cajoled, and bribed the Indians—they did not threaten them. As the months passed, various bands capitulated to the inevitable. They selected their reserves and then settled down. From time to time rumours of the presence of buffalo in the Cypress Hills would send some of them scurrying back to the buffalo country only to encounter disillusion, disappointment and starvation. But in spite of the delays, the Police persisted. There would be more conferences, more arguments, more bickering, more complaints, more promises. Finally all the Indians were moved away from the American frontier. Fort Walsh was abandoned and by the end of 1883 all the Saskatchewan Indians were north of the main line of the railway. "Thus may be considered solved one of the greatest problems which has had to be encountered for some years past," wrote the Lieutenant-Governor of the North-West Territories, "and the Indian Department has to congratulate itself on so easy a solution of the difficulty of preventing incursions from our side into the neighbouring territory."[9]

In spite of the Governor's assurances, the Indian problem was far from being solved in 1883. There were still many Indians who did not wish to settle down on their reserves, who clung to the old ways and were prepared to hold out against the government's proposals as long as possible. The leader of this group of recalcitrants was the Cree chief, Big Bear. When Big Bear refused, in 1876, to sign his adhesion to Treaty 6 at Fort Pitt, he attracted to his support all the discontented Indians of other bands who thought as he did about the treaties and reserves. Big Bear was a man of ability and resolution. He did not propose to fight the Canadians; rather he hoped to bring about a confederation of the various Indian bands. With the strength that numbers would give him, he would force the Canadian government to concede more favourable terms to the Indians. This idea of an Indian confederation was not a new one with Big Bear. King Phillip, Pontiac, Tecumseh had all dreamed of the same thing and tried to bring it about. But with the exception of the Iroquois league, the Blackfoot confederacy and several other loose confederacies, the Indians had always failed to unite. They were too individualistic to sink their differences in a major union which might better their lot. It is possible that Big Bear developed these ideas after meeting Louis Riel in Montana; for it is known that Canadian Indians, including Big Bear, spent some time in the region of the Milk River and the Musselshell, where Riel was located with a band of half-breeds between 1879 and 1881.[10] Most of the métis were of Cree extraction, and contacts between them and Big Bear's Indians were far from unlikely. Moreover, the reports which reached the Mounted Police that Riel was talking in terms of a native confederation give support to the suggestion that he may well have broached this subject with Big Bear.

But even Big Bear could not hold out indefinitely, and finally, in 1883, he agreed to go north and sign the treaty. Near Battleford he settled down with his principal adherents, Little Pine and Lucky Man, devouring the government rations and steadily avoiding selecting the reserve which was to be his.   He was thinking of his confederation, and he did not propose to yield to the government demands too easily or too quickly. With a spirit of resentment growing among the Indians who had settled on their reserves and learned to their dismay that farming was not yielding them the returns they had been encouraged to expect, tact tempered with firmness on the part of the officials of the Department of Indian Affairs was more essential than ever before.   If firmness was present when the Deputy Superintendent General of Indian Affairs met Big Bear in the summer of 1883, certainly tact was not.   Big Bear was ordered peremptorily to go on his reserve or be cut off from all government rations.   Big Bear took up the challenge.   He did not move.[11]

He had his own reasons for not complying with the government's request—not immediately that is.   He had learned that Poundmaker, one of the foremost Cree chiefs to the treaty, had become very bitter at the way things had worked out.   He was ready to respond to Big Bear's ideas.   In the south there was Piapot; in Alberta, Crowfoot, the head chief of the Blackfoot who, like Big Bear, had spent some time in Montana before going on his reserve.[12]   In December, 1883, the Assistant Commissioner reported: "Big Bear and his followers were loth to settle on a reserve and from what I could gather, and judging from the Indian nature, I am confident these Indians have some project in view as yet undisclosed and it would not surprise me to find that they are making efforts to procure a large gathering from east and west at Battleford or adjacent thereto in the spring, in order to test their powers with the authorities once more."[13]

The Commissioner was right about the situation.   Plans had been made for a large Indian council in June, 1884.   It was to be held on Poundmaker's reserve, and the excuse was to be afforded by holding the annual Thirst Dance at the same time.   Apparently the half-breeds had been informed of what was in the offing, for in May, several weeks before the Indians were to meet, a Saskatchewan métis wrote to Louis Riel in Montana telling him of the political development in Western Canada and adding:

For my part, I have closely watched the people of the North-West, as well as the Indians, and the one cry resounds from all, it is the spark over a barrel of powder.   It is late, but it is the time now more than ever, for we have right and justice on our side.   Do not imagine that you will begin the work when you get here; I tell you it is all done, the thing is decided; it is your presence that is needed. . . . You have no idea how great your influence is, even amongst the Indians.   I know you do not like the men much, but I am certain that it will be the grandest demonstration that has ever taken place. . . . Now, my dear cousin, the closest union exists between the French and English and the Indians, and we have good generals to foster it. . . .[14]

II

As the above letter indicated, the métis and half-breeds were as excited as the Indians. They had never forgotten the thrill of their successful resistance fifteen years earlier, the sense of isolation that had followed the establishment of Canadian authority, the beatings they had received from the Ontarians, the broken promises regarding the amnesty. The delays and alterations in the half-breed land grant, the pressures exerted by the incoming settlers and the new competitive economy into which they were thrust made the old days and the old ways look even more attractive, when viewed in retrospect. Within several months of the establishment of Lieutenant-Governor Archibald's administration, the Red River métis began to leave the old settlement in small numbers, and the tide of emigration continued with increasing volume, particularly during the eighteen-eighties. Some of the immigrants went to the Missouri—among them was Louis Riel's father-in-law—but the bulk of them went to the Canadian North-West where they could still find their kindred living on the prairie or gathered in small communities like those at Qu'Appelle, or St. Albert near Edmonton, or Duck Lake on the South Saskatchewan. This last community was the outgrowth of a buffalo camp headed by Gabriel Dumont, and it bore the name of St. Laurent.[15]

In their new homes, the métis and half-breeds—for there were English-speaking half-breeds as well as French métis among them—resumed the kind of life to which they had been accustomed on the banks of the Red and the Assiniboine, and on the banks of the Seine in Manitoba. Their farms were long, narrow and running to the river, so that each family would have a frontage on the water. For the first few years they hunted buffalo on the plains, accepting the laws of the hunt and chasing the top-heavy beasts whose existence spelled life to the mixed-blood as well as to the Indian.[16] Unlike the Indians, however, the métis were able to settle down on the land, grub a living out of the soil, growing a few potatoes, a little wheat and a little barley. Farming was the same at St. Albert as it was at St. Laurent and Qu'Appelle, although at Lac la Biche fishing in the cold waters of the lake was a substitute for tilling the soil. In all the settlements the directing figure was the missionary who was anxious to win the métis from nomadism and convert him into a pious agriculturalist. But conversion was not easy, and the transition from one economy to the other produced, even among the half-breeds, the same basic uneasiness that it had produced among the Indians. This malaise began to assume more formidable proportions with the development of the neighbouring white settlements at Edmonton, Battleford and Prince Albert.   For here were land-hungry farmers, government officials, surveyors and middlemen, with their laws and their magistrates —all of them, even the well-intentioned ones, misunderstanding the métis and treading on their sensitivities.

The first indication of uneasiness became apparent as early as 1873, when a group of métis and half-breeds from Qu'Appelle sent a petition to Lieutenant-Governor Morris demanding lands "in compensation of our rights to the lands of the country as métis."[17]   The next year, John Mackay raised before the North-West Council similar claims for the English-speaking half-breeds of Prince Albert and the métis of St. Laurent.   Several years later, as the métis colonies were reinforced in strength by malcontents from Manitoba, the agitation began again. In 1878, there were petitions from St. Laurent, St. Albert, Cypress Hills and Prince Albert.   In every instance, the request was for land grants similar to those that had been given to the Manitoba half-breeds under the Manitoba Act.   The Prince Albert petition was typical: "Your petitioners would humbly represent that their rights to a participation in the issue of the half-breed or old settlers' scrip are as valid and binding as those of the half-breeds and old settlers of Manitoba, and are expected by them to be regarded by the Canadian Government as scrupulously as in that Province."[18]   These petitions were prompted in part by the arrival of the Canadian surveyors.   On this occasion the surveyors acted with discretion.   The events at André Nault's were vivid enough in the mind of Colonel Dennis, now Deputy Minister of the Interior, to prompt him to instruct his men that, in all cases where half-breed settlements had been formed along the rivers, the lands occupied were to be surveyed according to existing lines on the river lot principle. No attempt was to be made to impose the new rectangular survey on the people concerned.   During 1877 and 1878, special surveys were made at Prince Albert and St. Laurent in accordance with these instructions.

Meanwhile the members of the Council of the North-West Territories were bending their minds to the petitions they had received.   Giving some thought to the various memorials, the Council adopted a series of resolutions opposing the grant by the federal government of negotiable scrip, although the Council recognized that the failure to follow the Manitoba example would unquestionably lead to "general dissatisfaction among the half-breeds . . . unless they receive some like consideration." The Council suggested by way of solution the granting of "non-transferable location tickets" for 160 acres to every half-breed head of a family and to every half-breed child resident in the North-West Territories at the time of the transfer of the country to Canada.   In order to avert "the great destitution with which they are threatened, owing to the imminent early extinction of the buffalo" aid in the form of "agricultural implements and seeds" should be given to all families who were prepared to settle down.[19]

Recalling his own misjudgments and misfortunes in 1869, and anxious to avoid any repetition in the Territories of what had occurred in Manitoba, Colonel Dennis was disposed to endorse the recommendations of the Council of the North-West Territories, and in a long memorandum to the Minister of the Interior, Sir John A. Macdonald, he pointed out that "the state of affairs in the Territories in relation to the Indians and half-breeds" called for "the serious consideration of the Government." Dennis opposed the granting of scrip "for the reason that the half-breed, having no idea whatsoever of thrift, or of the necessity of making provision for the future by locating his scrip and securing the land for the benefit of his family, would, as our experience in Manitoba proves beyond all doubt, sell the scrip for whatever he could get for it, which in most cases would be a mere trifle." Dennis suggested that special inducements should be given to the half-breeds to enable them "to settle on land and learn to farm—especially to raise cattle." In addition, he recommended the establishment of industrial schools, the expense of which would be "trifling" he assured Macdonald, "as compared with the value of the results which would be obtained from them."[20]

Believing that it would be advisable to obtain the opinion of the Archbishop of St. Boniface, he sent a copy of his memorandum to Taché.[21] Before sending a reply to Dennis, Taché asked Angus McKay, the Scottish half-breed who had been a member of Charles Nolin's group in opposition to Riel in 1870, for his views on Dennis's recommendations. McKay was indignant. He did not like Dennis's lumping the Indians and the half-breeds together. He denied the charge that the métis were unthrifty, indolent or helpless. They wanted no industrial schools, and they needed no instructor to tell them how to farm or raise cows. What they did want was "recognition as a civilized community and British subjects . . . that they be treated as such, and that the Government expunge all stigmas and insults heretofore published in public and official documents, and that the like in future be studiously avoided. . . ."[21] Then McKay outlined the half-breed demands as he saw them: "a liberal land policy as recompense towards the extinguishing of the Indian title to the lands in the North-West"; "encouragement and liberal aid given to the half-breeds for educational purposes"; representation in the Senate of Canada and in the Council of the North-West Territories; a fair share of government appointments and employment; and "exemption from taxation until railroad communication is completed to the Saskatchewan of the North." Finally McKay suggested the recruiting of a cavalry force of about one hundred métis for police purposes. "Being good horsemen and very accurate and quick with fire arms on horseback, and having a perfect knowledge of the country and familiar with the customs, character and languages of the Indians, they would prove to be a most valuable and efficient force and support to the Government in dealing with the Indian tribes in the North-West."[22]

Taché did not send McKay's reply to Dennis. Instead he softened its strident tone and modified its peremptory demands. He warned Dennis of the half-breed sensitivities and their resentment when they were classified with the Indians. Estimating the number of North-West mixed bloods at about 1,200 families, he suggested a series of half-breed reserves, one for each hundred families, in which the lands, while they might pass from one métis or half-breed to another, could not be alienated to white men or taxed until they had passed "into the hands of the third generation *at least*." Aid in farming might be offered but not imposed, and schools should be established under the supervision of the various denominations concerned. Above all, Taché urged that the half-breed question be dealt with promptly. "There is no doubt the difficulties increase with delay," he wrote.[23]

Nothing emerged from either Dennis's recommendations or Taché's suggestions. Meanwhile the petitions continued. There were demands for the extinction of the aboriginal claims by an issue of scrip; demands for exemption from the operations of the Homestead Law; demands for the survey or re-survey in river lots of lands that had been occupied by métis who had settled subsequent to the earlier river lot survey. But the machinery of government moved slowly when it moved at all. There were replies asking for further "explanation"; promises of "careful consideration"; statements that requests embodied matters of policy "for the minister to consider"; even queries from the Minister himself— "how is it that these difficulties recur so often?"—even positive assurances to parliament that "the half-breeds had no grievances whatsoever in relation to their lands or any other matter."[24]

The experiences of previous years, and the recognition in principle by the Dominion Lands Act of 1878 that the métis had rights to lands in the Territories by virtue of their Indian origin, make it difficult to understand or explain the lethargy of the Department of the Interior. Perhaps Sir John A. Macdonald was too absorbed in the task of being Prime Minister of Canada to concern himself much about the administration of the Department of the Interior. His successor in the Department of the Interior in 1883, Sir David Macpherson, was patently unsuited to deal with his responsibilities owing either to age, personal indifference or his seat in the Senate rather than in the House of Commons.

The half-breeds were not merely concerned with their lands, the security of their titles to their lands and the obtaining of scrip as compensation for their aboriginal title. There were other problems, such as language, the inability of the land agents to speak French and the lack of French-speaking magistrates. It was as it had been in the days of Adam Thom in Assiniboia.[25] There was also the delay in appointing métis members to the Council of the North-West Territories. Pascal Breland had been appointed as the métis representative when the Council was first organized in 1872, and Pierre Delorme had been added shortly afterwards. But when the Council was reorganized, following the passing of the North-West Territories Act in 1875, the number of councillors had been cut to three, and none of them was a métis or even an English-speaking half-breed. Perhaps by his appointments—two stipendiary magistrates, Hugh Richardson and Mathew Ryan; and the commanding officer of the Mounted Police, Colonel J. F. Macleod—the then Prime Minister, Alexander Mackenzie, thought to save the government some expense. But the Lieutenant-Governor of Manitoba was much disturbed at the omission of any mixed-blood from the list of appointees. He strongly urged the federal authorities "to obviate any repetition of the McDougall difficulty which on its initiation largely arose from a fear of a *foreign* Council."[26]

When David Laird became Lieutenant-Governor of the North-West Territories in 1877, he wrote to Mackenzie, "It appears to me highly desirable that we should have a local member of the Council—one for some time resident in the Territory and either a French or Scotch half-breed. . . . I find there is a little feeling here that all the present members of the Council are outsiders."[27] Petitions from St. Laurent and St. Albert put forward the same demand, expressing the desire that at least one French métis should be included in any new appointments. In 1879, Father Lestanc expressed his alarm that, at a time when the Indian problem was becoming more and more acute, "there was not a single métis in the administration of the North-West."[28] If by "administration" he meant the service of the Indian Department, he was right; but if he meant the Council, he was in error. Immediately prior to the election of 1878, the Prime Minister had appointed Pascal Breland to the seat he had previously held. But the appointment was meaningless. Breland had had considerable political experience as a member of the Council of Assiniboia; now he was an old man who was not prepared to spend his time travelling from his home in Manitoba to attend council meetings at Battleford miles away in Saskatchewan. Moreover, he had no influence among his own people. Whatever popularity he had gained as a supporter of Louis Riel, Sr., in 1849, had disappeared when he had failed to give a similar support to Louis's son in 1869. His non-participation in the resistance of 1869/70 no doubt commended him to the authorities in Ottawa,[29] but it won him little confidence among the Red River métis who had migrated to the North-West. They could not look to him to protect their rights. Both Mackenzie and Macdonald, however, were satisfied, and they paid no heed to the warning voice of Alexander Morris, "It is a crying shame that the half-breeds have been ignored. It will result in trouble and is most unjust."[30] The situation in the Territories was beginning, more and more, to resemble that of Assiniboia in the late 1860's.

The agitation of the half-breeds and the métis in the North-West Territories, during the ten years between 1873 and 1883, carried little weight in Ottawa. This may be explained, in part at least, by the hope and belief of the authorities that the native population would soon be outnumbered and submerged in the rising population of white settlers. There is also the fact that the mixed-bloods had no recognized leader and no strategic centre of settlement. St. Laurent, St. Albert and Qu'Appelle were all widely separated from one another, and the local leaders, Charles Nolin, Sam Cunningham and John Fisher were not men of great experience, education or political capacity. Their influence, like their reputation, was largely a matter of local prestige. Yet the material was there, in each locality, to be exploited when the right man should come along. The old feelings of nationalism had not been killed by migration from Red River; they were reviving under the stimulus of indifference and neglect. Bishop Grandin of St. Albert saw what was happening and wrote to Sir Hector Langevin in 1884: "the members of the government ought not to ignore the métis. They, as well as the Indians, have their national pride. They like to have attention paid to them and could not be more irritated by the contempt of which they feel themselves, rightly or wrongly, the victims."[31] All they needed now was a leader, a man who would embody this sense of national identity.

III

The Indians and the métis were not alone when they complained of Ottawa's sins of omission. The English-speaking settlers, white as well as half-breed, were likewise unhappy over the developments in the North-West. Not that they had found themselves unable to adjust to the demands of a new culture imposed on them from outside; rather they had not found conditions as easy or as attractive in the North-West Territories as they had been led to believe. Few of the early white settlers were paupers, men who had left Central Canada owing to their inability to make a living for themselves in the settled parts of the country.   Instead they were adventurous types, men with sufficient means to provide themselves with the "outfit" necessary to start upon their homesteads, or better-to-do immigrants proposing to set up as shop-keepers in the towns springing up along the proposed line of the Canadian Pacific Railway.[32]   But the reality which they found did not correspond to the hopes they had held on leaving their old homes.   The farmers did not know how to combat the problems of early frosts and prolonged droughts.   These were not everyday problems, but at times they were of a most severe nature.   Between 1871 and 1881, conditions were relatively favourable for farming; but between 1881 and 1891, both the frosts and the droughts were devastating.   In 1883, the *Report of the Department of Agriculture* stated:

The grain lightly covered did not receive sufficient moisture to vegetate and come up as quickly as that deeper covered, until the showers in June made it spring up rapidly, but it did not ripen equally with that which was deeper covered.   This made an uneven crop, as the dry weather in the latter part of July and August caused it to ripen, all apparently alike; but that which was late in coming up, is shrivelled and injures the general appearance of the whole; and as we have a very unusual frost on the night of the 7th of September, the millers and grain dealers call all the shrivelled grain frozen.[33]

This report referred specifically to southern Manitoba, but it might have applied equally well to other parts of the prairies.   The frost of September was not general over the whole of the west.   Nevertheless the event was of sufficient significance to be used by one large milling house in Montreal to panic the grain market and depress the prices given the farmer for his product.   Prices for wheat went as low as forty cents a bushel, and for oats fifteen cents.[34]   At the same time, there was no corresponding drop in the costs of transportation, or in the prices charged the farmers for their machinery and other articles imported from the rest of Canada.   This was the traditional burden, and the western farmer had to shoulder it throughout the years following the opening of the prairies—this burden of high costs and low returns.

It did not help matters that the settlers were caught in the fever of land speculation, resulting from the construction of the transcontinental railway, and the influx of immigrants from other parts of Canada. During the early eighties, men were gripped with hopes of rapid develop-ments and early riches—until the boom collapsed.   "In almost every locality," reported the Land Commissioner in 1885, "one meets numerous homesteads, once under a fair state of cultivation, but now deserted; the land once tilled being weed grown and less easily cultivated than the virgin prairie; the buildings fast decaying."[35]

There were other factors that caused discontent and disillusionment: the loneliness and the isolation and the hardships that inevitably accompanied unplanned immigration to a new land; debts, poor crops and a perpetual shortage of money. These combined with adverse economic conditions to produce the first of several agrarian protest movements that have been a feature of the history of Western Canada from that day to this. It mattered little that part of the problem was to be found in the settlers' ignorance of the methods of dry farming that were later imported from the western plains of the United States, or in the lack of suitable varieties of quickly maturing wheat, such as were developed in later years. Nor did the farmers always realize that another aspect of their problem was the fact that adequate sources of credit had not been devised for them to obtain the land, the machinery and the stock they needed to make their operations a success. All they could see was the gap between the prices they received at the track and the prices that were obtained by the millers in the east for the produce they had grown. Therefore they laid the blame for their misfortunes on the federal government which tolerated and protected the railway monopoly of the Canadian Pacific, and on the milling companies that amassed the profits.

The farmers drew together for the redress of their grievances. In southern Manitoba, at Manitou, a mass meeting of agriculturalists led to the formation of "The Manitoba and North West Farmers' Protective Union," whose declared object was "to urge the repeal of laws militating against their interest" by bringing the railway monopoly to an end, by the institution of cheaper freight rates and by the removal of restrictions on trade.[36] Similar meetings were held in other parts of the province, at Brandon, Pomeroy, Pilot Mound, Ruttanville and elsewhere, and local branches of the Farmers' Union were formed. Finally, in December, a provincial convention was held in Winnipeg where the representatives of the various farming communities, taking their cue from Louis Riel in 1869/70, drew up a "Bill of Rights" to be presented to the provincial and federal governments.[37] At first supported by men of all parties, the Farmers' Union gradually fell into the hands of the radical elements among its members. The radicals not only talked of taking steps to discourage further immigration to the west until the government remedied their grievances, they even hinted vaguely at taking up arms.

The excitement in Manitoba was a symptom of the times. In the North-West Territories, similar conditions brought about similar reactions, although the remedies suggested were determined by peculiarly local circumstances. Throughout the Territories, regardless of previous party affiliations, the people were dissatisfied both with economic conditions and their position of political tutelage. With the founding of newspapers in various parts of the country—Battleford in 1878 (*Saskatchewan Herald*); Edmonton in 1880 (*Edmonton Bulletin*); Prince Albert in 1882 (*The Prince Albert Times*)—this discontent found means of expression. And strong expression, for the editors of these early papers were men of intelligence, with active pens and few inhibitions. After the introduction of the first elective members to the Council, in 1883, there began a struggle for autonomy which did not end until the Territories were finally granted provincial status in 1905.

Although active protests against the indifference and neglect displayed by the federal government towards the Territories were voiced in Qu'Appelle,[38] Edmonton,[39] and Moose Jaw, the principal and potentially most dangerous opposition came from the people living in the District of Lorne. This region included both Prince Albert and the French-speaking parishes of St. Laurent, and for some years it contained the largest concentration of settlers both half-breed and white. Lorne had been the first to secure representation in the Territorial Council. It was also the region most seriously affected by the economic depression and by the crop failures of the 1880's. In particular, the district had suffered from the federal government's decision that the main line of the Canadian Pacific Railway should be relocated in the southern part of the prairies in order to make use of the Kicking Horse Pass, rather than the original northerly route through the Yellowhead. Not only had the land boom collapsed in Lorne earlier than it had collapsed elsewhere in the Territories, but the immigrants on whose dollars the revival of local prosperity depended were diverted south, along the new route of the railway to the settlements at Moose Jaw, Regina and Calgary. Lorne therefore suffered not only from stagnation but also from frustration and a continual shortage of money. In 1882, a resident of Prince Albert wrote "there is no quantity of money in the settlement . . . and therefore trade is carried on under disadvantageous conditions. Farmers live entirely on credit, and consequently have to pay much higher prices for goods than would be the case if they had cash."[40]

The people of Lorne were not unanimous over how to obtain the redress of local grievances and bring back prosperity. These were days of fierce partisan politics in the Territories, and feelings ran high between parties. But the differences between the political factions were less of principle than of personality. It is hard to find any fundamental difference between the political proposals advanced by Robert Mac-Dowall and those of Dr. A. E. Porter, when they contested the first election for the new seat in the Territorial Council in the summer of 1883. And the *Prince Albert Times*, although supporting MacDowall, recognized that Porter "would no doubt make a very fair representative" but thought him "still a young man who can afford to bide his time when a wider experience and riper judgment would make him a more acceptable candidate than at the present time."[41]   The election went in favour of MacDowall, who had the support, not only of the newspaper and of Lawrence Clarke, the factor of the Hudson's Bay Company in Prince Albert, but also of the majority of the townspeople of Prince Albert and the French métis of St. Laurent.[42]   His principal opponents had been the farmers of the Ridge on the south branch of the Saskatchewan.

One of the objections of the *Times* against Dr. Porter was his association with a group of agrarian extremists in the District, particularly the several members of the Jackson family, one of whom, W. H. Jackson, had for a brief period published a small sheet called *The Voice of the People*, whose violence of expression was even more than Dr. Porter was disposed to tolerate.[43]   The Jacksons had come from Lower Wingham in Ontario, where the father, T. Getting Jackson, had run a general store.[44] One son, William Henry, had been sent to the University of Toronto,[45] where he remained for several years, until the family decided to try its fortunes in Western Canada.   Prince Albert seems to have been selected as their new home for no other reason than the fact that another son, Thomas Jackson, had answered an advertisement that Dr. Porter had inserted in the Ontario press asking for a pharmacist to assist him in his practice at Lorne.   In any event, the family went west in 1881, prior to the general and large immigration from Huron and Bruce counties that followed the completion of the Canadian Pacific Railway in 1885.   The father and his pharmacist son settled in Prince Albert.   William Henry obtained a grant of land and became a farmer, although more inclined towards politics than farming.   Indeed, the whole family held strong political views and were inveterate enemies of the Prime Minister and the Conservative party.[46]   For a brief period, T. G. Jackson acted as correspondent for the *Toronto Globe*; but William Henry was more interested in the western newspapers, and he took as his model Frank Oliver, the outspoken Liberal editor of the *Edmonton Bulletin*.   Closely associated with them, and sharing the views of William Henry and his father, were two other farmers of the neighbourhood: Thomas Scott, a Scottish farmer married to a French métisse who lived south of Prince Albert at the Ridge (Red Deer Hill), and William Miller, Scott's brother-in-law, who lived not far distant.[47]

William Jackson's object was to organize the farmers and mobilize the rural vote in Lorne.   He protested strongly against the inclusion of non-farmers in the membership of the Agricultural Society, formed during 1883 for the purpose of encouraging improved methods of farming and cattle raising. He denounced Charles Adams, who had been the organizer of the Society at Red Deer Hill, as a tool of Lawrence Clarke and the Hudson's Bay Company: "He is either a very simple man or else a wolf in sheep's clothing commissioned to lead us confiding grangers into the political den of Messrs. Clarke and Sproat & Co."[48] That Jackson was stepping on sensitive toes became obvious when Sproat attacked him as a youthful and irresponsible agitator. But Jackson replied with vigour that it was ridiculous to assume the "sole proof of honor lay in their bald heads" or that mental capacity was to be found "in their beards." Then he opposed the suggestion that Clarke should be made a life member of the Society, nominating instead James Treston "because I knew him to be in full sympathy with farming interests, and too honest to be bought, too shrewd to be flattered, too plucky to be frightened by any or all of the oligarchical party, and resolute enough to maintain an equal right to the title Honourable with Mr. L. Clarke."[49] The upshot was Jackson's expulsion from the Society and the return of his fee of one dollar.

But reverses were no deterrent to Jackson. On the contrary, they were grist to his political mill, and they encouraged those who shared his views that nothing could be done through the mediation of men tied to the Conservative party. During the summer of 1883, a Settlers' Union had been formed at Qu'Appelle to demand land reform and the adoption of laws for the benefit of the people of the North-West rather than rich corporations or needy politicians;[50] and the more radical members of the community of Lorne decided to organize a similar body at Prince Albert.

The first steps in this direction were taken on October 16, when a large public meeting of settlers was held at Prince Albert. There was strong talk at this meeting, and John Slater moved that, in view of the government's failure to take any action upon the numerous representations that had been made to Ottawa, the people of Lorne should form a union "for the mutual protection and defence of the rights and liberties which they, as freemen possess in common with their brethren of other and more favoured portions of the Dominion."[51] A committee was then formed, comprising Miller, FitzCochrane, Slater, Thomas Mackay and several others to draft a constitution and suggest by-laws for the proposed Union. Early in January, another meeting was held, this time at St. Catherine's. The December convention of the Manitoba Farmers' Union had attracted considerable attention in the Territories, and the settlers of Lorne were more convinced than ever of the urgent necessity of organized action on their part. The St.

Catherine's meeting therefore appointed a committee, comprising James Isbister, a prominent English half-breed, W. Kennedy and T. Swain, to draft a programme for the Union in co-operation with other committees appointed elsewhere in the District. Towards the end of the month, a general meeting was held at Halcro where the resolutions of the earlier meetings and the committee recommendations were discussed. Another committee was then appointed to draft a petition to be sent to Ottawa. At this meeting, W. H. Jackson, the Secretary of the Union, was asked to see if he could obtain the co-operation of the French métis.[52]

The enlistment of métis support by the Settlers' Union was designed to close the gap in the ranks of those opposed to the federal government. It was a great disappointment to Jackson and others that MacDowall had won the support of the French-speaking half-breeds during the election if 1883, and that Dr. Porter had failed to win a single vote in St. Laurent.[53] It would strengthen the opposition if some alliance between the aggrieved white settlers, the English half-breeds and the French métis could be brought about. After all, the grievances of each group, at least as far as lands and titles were concerned, were substantially the same.

Jackson began his task by approaching the leaders of the métis agitation, Charles Nolin, Maxime Lépine and Michel Dumas. He soon won them over to the idea of collaborating with the English-speaking population.[54] Since the three métis leaders could speak only for themselves, it was decided that Jackson's proposals should be put up to a general meeting of the St. Laurent métis at Abraham Montour's house, Batoche, on March 24. About twenty men attended the meeting, and Gabriel Dumont, who had been won over to Nolin's way of thinking, urged his compatriots to join forces with their English neighbours and prepare a List of Rights which could be combined with the demands of the Settlers' Union and sent to Ottawa. During the discussion some of the more militant métis muttered threats of taking up arms rather than drawing up more petitions. Some, including Napoléon Nault, asked about the possibility of bringing Louis Riel back to act as their adviser and their leader. This idea had never occurred to Nolin or to Dumont, but it was one that caught the imagination of every man present. Another meeting of the métis followed in April. This time it was held in the open air, and in spite of the cold and the discomfort to the men who stamped around in the wet and muddy snow, it lasted four or five hours. A series of resolutions were agreed upon, condemning the composition of the North-West Territories Council, complaining of the failure of the government to answer the earlier petitions, pointing out the government's neglect of the Indians and demanding for the North-West half-breeds concessions similar to those given to the mixed-blood population of Manitoba. There was nothing new in any of these resolutions. They were the same resolutions that had been adopted on previous occasions and embodied in innumerable petitions. By May it was clear that both the French and English groups in the Settlement were prepared to act in unison. Even the *Times* seemed to be on the side of the Union, the editor writing in strong terms about the "insatiable maw of the eastern Leviathian." He added that the significant threat "where they get the information which induces them to believe the people likely to submit tamely much longer we do not know, but we can assure them that they need not look for their friends among the Canadians, half-breeds or Indians, as they are likely soon to be made aware of in a manner at once startling and unpleasant."[55]

But still there was no single dynamic personality in charge of the protest movement in Lorne—no one man acceptable to all three elements of the population and able to lead them to political success. Neither Miller the farmer nor Isbister the English half-breed had the necessary prestige; Jackson was obviously not up to the task, if only because of his youth. The most popular man of them all, Gabriel Dumont, was illiterate and not politically inclined. Charles Nolin, despite the fact that he had been a member of John Norquay's cabinet in Manitoba, was an intriguer and was not trusted by either the whites or the métis.[56] As far as the latter were concerned, they could think only of one name— that of the man who had led the resistance in Red River; who had brought about the union of the French and English half-breeds and the old settlers in the provisional government of Assiniboia; who had compelled the federal government to grant the concessions embodied in the Manitoba Act. But would he be acceptable to the English half-breeds and the whites? Still attached to Riel's memory was the stigma of Thomas Scott's execution; however, that was fourteen years in the past, and in any event Riel had served the term of his exile. Still associated with the Manitoba troubles was the feeling that it was a rebellion; but even rebellion was not such a bad thing according to Frank Oliver, who asked in the *Edmonton Bulletin*: "If it was not by—not threatening, but actual rebellion—and appeals to the British Government for justice, that the people of Ontario gained the rights they enjoy today and freed themselves from a condition precisely similar to that into which the North-West is being rapidly forced, how was it?" He added: "If history is to be taken as a guide, what could be plainer than that without rebellion the people of the North-West need expect nothing, while with rebellion, successful or otherwise, they may reasonably expect to get their rights." And Oliver also referred to Riel when he wrote: "Was it not by armed rebellion coupled with murder, that Manitoba attained the rights she enjoys today from the very men who hold the reins of power at Ottawa?''[57]

On May 6, white and English-speaking half-breeds of the Settlers' Union met at the Lindsay School House under the chairmanship of the half-breed, Andrew Spence. Charles Nolin, Maxime Lépine, Gabriel Dumont, Baptiste Arcand and Baptiste Boyer attended the meeting as the official representatives of the métis council.[58] The grievances of all parties were once more aired and argued. But there was no disagreement. Everybody shared the same feelings of indignation against Ottawa and the indifference displayed by Sir John A. Macdonald and his cabinet ministers towards the North-West Territories. Then came the suggestion that Louis Riel should be consulted. At this point the unanimity of the earlier part of the meeting came to an end. But Andrew Spence, who had already committed himself at the métis meeting in April to support bringing Riel into the North-West Movement, argued strongly on behalf of Riel and succeeded in winning over a fair number of those who, if they had not spoken out against Riel, at least had mental reservations about the advisability of becoming associated with him. The métis had previously thought of sending Nolin and Dumont to Ottawa with the petition, merely diverting them on their journey to visit Riel in Montana to discuss the political strategy with him. But this proposal seemed now to be unduly expensive, and in the end the following resolution was adopted:

We, the French and English natives of the North-West, knowing that Louis Riel made a bargain with the Government of Canada, in 1870, which said bargain is contained mostly in what is known as the "Manitoba Act," have thought it advisable that a delegation be sent to said Louis Riel, and have his assistance to bring all the matters referred to in the above resolutions in a proper shape and form before the Government of Canada, so that our just demands, be granted.[59]

Following the adoption of this resolution, a committee was appointed with William Cromarty as chairman and Louis Schmidt as secretary, to arrange for a delegation to carry the invitation to Louis Riel. Their choice fell on Gabriel Dumont, Michel Dumas and James Isbister, thus ensuring the representation of both the French and English population. There was some talk of Louis Schmidt joining them—after all he had been a prominent member of the provisional government in 1870—but Schmidt was appointed on May 12 to the Land Office in Prince Albert, and he felt it inadvisable to prejudice his appointment by going to Montana.[60] Moïse Ouellette went in Schmidt's place, although without any special mandate from the committee. To raise the necessary funds to assist the delegates, a collection was taken up among those who attended the meeting at the Lindsay School. It was indicative of the new sense of union prevailing in the District of Lorne that one of the "Canadians from Ontario" took "the lead in opening his purse when subscriptions were called for."[61]

If the whites and métis were generally agreed upon the mission to Riel, Mgr. Vital Grandin, Bishop of St. Albert, who was then on his way to Prince Albert, regarded the entire proceedings with some apprehension. "Our poor métis," he wrote to his clergy at St. Albert: "pushed by a certain Charles Nolin, have made a terrible blunder. They have sent a deputation to Louis Riel to bring him back to act as their leader with a view to opposing the government. They would not listen to Father André, nor to the governor, nor to anybody. They are going to compromise everybody, give themselves a bad name, and will be unable in the future to obtain anything from the government."[62]

CHAPTER **15**

Agitator

THE JOURNEY undertaken by the Riel family, Louis, his wife and two children, Jean and Angélique, from St. Peter's Mission to Batoche, was uneventful. Accompanied by the delegates who had been sent to Montana, Dumont, Dumas, Isbister and Ouellette, they bumped their way over the rough, dirt trails, through the hilly country and past the strange flat-topped buttes of Montana towards the Canadian frontier. Then they crossed the buffalo country east of the Cypress Hills, until they reached the grey, muddy waters of the South Saskatchewan River. By the beginning of July—they had been three weeks on the road—the little party reached the steep ravine through which flowed the stream known as Fish Creek. They had left the prairies behind them and had entered the parkland of Saskatchewan, with its clumps of poplars and Manitoba maples and its Saskatoon bushes which would bear their dark blue berries in the autumn. Once across the ravine, they were in the métis country, with its small, square farm houses and its little patches of blue-black earth splashed here and there among the yellow-green, native grasses.

From Fish Creek, or Tourond's Coulée as it was known locally, the road led northward to Batoche. As they approached the village, the travellers could see, on the high ground to the left, the small wooden church of St. Anthony of Padua and, just beyond it, the square two-storied frame presbytery. There were more trees and bushes here than farther south, and the growth became even heavier as the road turned to the left and began to descend towards the river bank. It was here, rather than on the hill where the church stood, that the village of Batoche had been founded. It was not a compact, tidy village, nor one showing many signs of wealth; it was no more than a modest collection of houses and stores that straggled along the road and the river bank where Xavier Letendre *dit* Batoche had a ferry to convey travellers across the river. Most of the buildings were small and built of logs in the métis style, plastered with mud and white-washed on the outside. But there were a few larger buildings. Batoche himself had one; Charles Nolin, Riel's cousin, had

274

another. And it was to Nolin's that the Riels went on their arrival in the métis settlement.

Among his own people, Louis and his wife were received with an enthusiasm as demonstrative as it was genuine. At Tourond's Coulée, they were met by a cavalcade of some fifty wagons.[1] Here were held the first greetings and the first introductions. At Tourond's the Riels spent the night. It was only a short journey the next day to Nolin's house at Batoche, where they spent the next four months. Word quickly spread throughout the whole of the District of Lorne that Riel had arrived at last, and the métis, half-breeds and whites came to see him and to talk with him. "I have been received with open arms by everybody," Louis wrote to his brother Joseph in St. Vital. "The English half-breeds extend the hand of welcome to me. The Upper Canadians declare themselves for me. Several of our former prisoners have invited me to go to see them."[2] Father Vital Fourmond, the parish priest at St. Laurent, declared enthusiastically, "Here is a dedicated man."[3] And Louis Schmidt, Riel's old schoolmate at St. Boniface and former secretary, took up his pen and wrote to Le Manitoba: "It is said that Riel has arrived with his family. May it be his intention to remain permanently in our midst. This man can do nothing but good for his compatriots, and he is the only one who will obtain everybody's support in any kind of a dispute. His is a great name among both the French and English half-breeds, and it is undeniable that his influence, well directed, will be of immense assistance to them."[4] Schmidt obtained temporary leave from his appointment for a few days and hurried to see his old chief. "It was not without emotion," he wrote in his memoirs, "that I saw him again, knowing all the misfortunes he had experienced, he who had been master in his own land to which he now returned as a homeless stranger."[5]

Less enthusiastic was the report written by the Indian Agent at Fort Carlton to the Lieutenant-Governor of the North-West Territories, the Hon. Edgar Dewdney. After reporting Riel's arrival at Batoche, he observed: "It does not appear that sinister motives actuate the half-breeds, though they are so unstable and susceptible to the influence of their leaders that they might be led to the commission of indiscretions which would terminate in acts of a serious nature."[6]

Under the impact of Riel's personality, Schmidt was willing to give up his government post in the land office at Prince Albert. But Riel urged him not to do so, believing his friend would be of more service as a government clerk than as a political agitator.[7] Moreover, Schmidt could write, and from Prince Albert he would be able to send his contributions to Le Manitoba as well as he could from Batoche. Riel felt that

Schmidt made a real contribution to the North-West movement. This is shown by a letter he wrote some time later, stating that the only outside publicity the movement had received in the French-language press was to be found in Schmidt's letters to *Le Manitoba*: "He has rendered us very good service, in that way especially," wrote Riel. "If it had not been for him, I think no news of any importance from Prince Albert would have reached public opinion amongst those who speak and write French."[8]

On July 8, about six days after his arrival, Riel gave his first public address in Saskatchewan. A number of métis assembled at Nolin's house in Batoche to hear the report of the delegates who had been sent to Montana two months before to consult the former president of the provisional government of Assiniboia. Several official papers were read, including the formal reply to Dumont Riel had written on June 5. Then Riel himself was introduced and given a chance to say something about the problem of the North-West as he saw it. For the moment Riel was content to urge unity among both the French and English half-breeds. To him unity was the first essential of success. A purely sectional movement would result only in failure.[9] Remarks such as these were neither exciting nor inflammatory; but from the way in which they were delivered, it was obvious that Riel had lost none of his power to arouse enthusiasm, even with platitudes and generalities.

Three days later, on July 11, Riel, along with Nolin, Maxime Lépine, Gabriel Dumont, Baptiste Boyer and Baptiste Boucher, went to meet the English-speaking settlers at the Lindsay School at Red Deer Hill. This would be a greater test of his political capacity and personal charm than the meeting at Batoche. But there was no need for concern on either score. Riel was greeted with acclaim, several hundred people turning out to see and hear him. Again the documents relating to Riel's return to Canada were read and explained; again Riel was moderate in his views about the situation in the North-West and the needs of the situation. There was little spark in his manner and none in his words. Indeed, some of the other speakers, including Charles Adams, who presided over the meeting, W. H. Jackson, the secretary of the Settlers' Union, and Thomas Scott were more direct and outspoken than the man whose reputation among English-speaking people in the North-West was that of a fire-brand.[10] Thus, with far less trouble than he had ever anticipated, Riel won the support of the malcontents of the Settlers' Union by his calmness and moderation.

English- as well as French-speaking settlers were apparently prepared to accept him and co-ordinate their activities under his direction. Yet there was to be no attempt to amalgamate the Settlers' Union and the

Métis Committee. Each organization was to retain its own identity and continue its own agitation among its own people; but there was to be a central executive committee to draw up the petition to be sent to Ottawa and ensure the maximum co-operation between the two groups. This committee was agreed upon following another joint meeting at Michel Dumas' house at Batoche. Its members included, among others, Andrew Spence, Charles Adams, Thomas Scott, James Isbister, William Cromarty, Joseph Halcrow, John Stevens, Henry Monkman, Gabriel Dumont, Maxime Lépine, Baptiste Boyer, Baptiste Arcand, John Ross, Calixte Tourond, Michel Dumas, Toussaint Lussier, Xavier Batoche, Pierre Gariépy, Baptiste Boucher and Charles Nolin.[11]

Despite the formation of this committee, the most effective co-operation between the French- and English-speaking settlers was achieved by William Henry Jackson who, while remaining secretary of the Settlers' Union, spent considerable time at Batoche closeted with the métis leader. If not formally, at least unofficially, he became Louis Riel's secretary,[12] as well as one of the most active spirits in the North-West movement in the District of Lorne.

Meanwhile a group of men in Prince Albert, headed by the lawyer, W. V. Maclise, had invited Charles Nolin to hold a public meeting in Prince Albert to be addressed by Louis Riel. Nolin replied that the best way would be for them to prepare a formal request and send it directly to Riel.[13] Riel was, in spite of the welcome he had already received, rather reluctant to expose himself to a purely English-speaking and white audience. His recollections of the years following 1870 were still too vivid. Such memories may have been exaggerations of reality, but they were none the less real to Louis merely because they were the product of his fears. There was some justification for Louis's hesitancy. No sooner did Lawrence Clarke hear talk about the possibility of Riel speaking in Prince Albert, than he wrote hurriedly to Father André, the parish priest at Prince Albert, pointing out the strong likelihood of unpleasantness resulting from such a visit and asking the Reverend Father to use his influence to dissuade Riel from accepting the invitation. André was one of the few who had regarded Riel's return with misgivings and who was not impressed by Louis's demonstrations of piety and religious devotion. He was disposed to agree with Clarke, and he wrote to Riel advising him against going to Prince Albert.[14] Riel accepted André's advice and answered to his Prince Albert friends:

I know that as your guest I would be perfectly safe from anything like discourtesy; and with such a respectable body of men as those who have signed the invitation I would feel far above any insult that could be offered me. But for the sake of avoiding even the slightest trouble, in order to allow no germ of division to weaken our basis of action, I beg leave to be excused. Please consent to put off the meeting[15]

The proposal that Riel should speak in Prince Albert was not, however, allowed to rest there.   A petition was circulated asking Riel to reconsider his decision.   It was signed by no fewer than eighty-four people, only four of whom were half-breeds.[16] Confronted with this petition and with André's advice, Riel was in a quandary.   He did not wish to do anything that would alienate the clergy—he wanted their full support for his reform movement—nor did he wish to dampen the enthusiasm of his adherents, some of whom, like Maxime Lépine, were pressing him not to miss so favourable an opportunity to put his case before the white settlers of the District.[17]   The decisive factor in Riel's decision finally to go to Prince Albert was his receipt of a short note from André withdrawing his previous objections and assuring him that he was "the most popular man in the country" and that "with the exception of four or five persons every one awaits you with impatience."[18]   Once he had André's approval, Riel accepted the invitation and went to Prince Albert on July 19 accompanied by both Lépine and Nolin.

The meeting was held in Treston Hall.   It was the largest building available for a public meeting.   William Miller, the farmer from Red Deer Hill, prominent in the organization of the Settlers' Union and in the activities that led to Riel's return to Canada, was chairman.   William Henry Jackson acted as secretary.   Almost the whole community of Prince Albert turned out to see and hear the former president of the Provisional Government of Assiniboia.   Many obviously came out of curiosity, others because they were in sympathy with the cause Riel now represented.   That Louis was nervous seems clear from the newspaper report of his speech.   Nevertheless, he was able to captivate his audience by his personal charm, and his remarks were punctuated with applause.   It was not a brilliant performance.   Undoubtedly he would have been more at home in his own language; even so his speech probably sounded better than it read.   He did not get down to concrete proposals, but he spoke with a moderation that seems to have impressed many of his listeners.

Riel replied to charges which had appeared earlier in the *Prince Albert Times* that he was an alien, an American citizen "of notorious antecedents,"[19] by claiming that, like the members of his audience, he was a human being and was entitled to the rights and privileges of all human beings under a British sovereign who proclaimed as her motto, "Dieu et mon Droit."   He then urged all races in the North-West to drop their differences and unite in a common demand for the redress of their grievances.   He declared that, although he was an American by naturalization, he had, nevertheless, been born in Manitoba and had rights of his own which he intended to press upon the Canadian government.   But there must be

no violence.   He "wished them to understand no trouble would have his
sanction, as he was for peace, believing that the object would be gained
faster if they acted orderly and peaceably."   Referring to the Indian
nations who were then gathering near Fort Carlton, he said they had
been "robbed" of their living "by the advance of civilization," and that
they, like the half-breeds who "could not compete with people from the
East," should be compensated by the federal government.   He struck
several wordy blows at the Territorial administration and concluded by
urging everybody, regardless of race, to work "constantly, peaceably, for
responsible government, struggle till you get what you want."[20]

The meeting was calm, if enthusiastic.   There were few interruptions.
Only one man, Captain Richard Deacon, a one-time volunteer in the Red
River expeditionary force, attempted to cause trouble by shouting that
Riel was a criminal who "up to this time" had succeeded in evading the
consequences of his crime.   But Deacon was thrown out of the meeting,
and when order was restored Miller, Slater, Scott and Jackson all spoke
on Riel's behalf and in favour of the agitation against Ottawa.   Deacon
wrote sourly to the *Prince Albert Times*: "Have the professional agitators
who are running the 'grievance department' forgotten the time when
they used stronger language than mine against Riel?   Why do they now
take him by the hand?   Is the opportunity to create a false impression
throughout the Dominion that we are on the eve of rebellion too precious
to miss?"[21]   André was able to report to the Lieutenant-Governor that
Riel had acted and spoken in a quiet, sensible way, and that he appeared
to have no other object than to help his people by "legitimate and peaceful means."   Analyzing Riel's demands, André suggested to Dewdney
that they were threefold: free title for lands held by the settlers; provincial status for the Districts of Saskatchewan, Assiniboia and Alberta, or
at least representation of the Districts in the federal parliament; and the
amendment of the land laws in a way that would encourage and facilitate
settlement.   Perhaps Riel's agitation would be a good thing, said
André, if only it would keep the people of the District from brooding on
the poor crops and the dull times; in due course it would all die down with
improved economic conditions, and then Riel "whom we regard as a
prodigy today, will be looked upon as no more than a simple human
being."[22]

Riel himself was thoroughly pleased with the results of his trip to
Prince Albert.   "Not long ago I was a humble schoolmaster on the
far away banks of the Missouri," he wrote to his brother and brother-in-
law in Manitoba, "and here I am today in the ranks of the most popular
public men in the Saskatchewan. . . . What has brought all this about?

Dear Joseph, Dear brother-in-law, you know that it is God. I humble my soul to the ground. The Lord has done great things for me. What shall I render to God for the favours he heaps upon me?"[23]

II

There is little doubt that Riel's performance at Prince Albert, perhaps because it was so mild, gave a considerable fillip to the North-West movement among the English-speaking settlers. Hitherto Riel's name had been synonymous among the English, half-breeds as well as whites, with the idea of rebellion. Now Riel's was the voice of moderation. The more strident voices of agitation were those speaking English. Almost immediately after Riel's speech, James Isbister wrote to the *Winnipeg Sun* outlining the grievances of the settlers in the North Saskatchewan region. He pointed out that although he had been one of the first settlers in St. Catherine's he had never yet received his land patent; and that it was the unrelieved indifference of the federal authorities that had prompted the people to ask Riel to return to Canada. If Riel could win the people their rights in Manitoba, perhaps he might do as much for the inhabitants of Saskatchewan.[24] Jackson sent reports to the *Globe* and to the *Mail* in Toronto. At the same time, he visited various parts of the District of Lorne, organizing the activities of the local branches of the Settlers' Union and arguing with the members on behalf of Riel. On July 23, he wrote to Louis:

Today, I shall finish up work in town, and tomorrow start for the Lower Flat, etc. I will try and get out to your place towards the end of the week. Please be working up the petition into shape, and we will get it in neat form before the committee is called to endorse or alter it, as they see fit. . . . There is a big work for us while the petition is waiting an answer, but I think we will be ready for a stiff campaign when an answer does come. A number of trimmers are waiting to see if the current in your favour will last. By the time they are satisfied it will be too late for them to bother us much, if disposed to so do.[25]

Clarke, Sproat and Deacon did what they could to counter Jackson's activities. But the young Ontarian seemed to possess boundless energy. He enlisted the support of Dr. Porter and that of many of his adherents, thus giving more and more of a party colour to the agitation. He gathered statistics to show that the Hudson's Bay Company had depressed both the wages paid to métis freighters and the prices they were offering for supplies. He obtained copies of the federal government's replies to the demands Premier John Norquay had advanced on behalf of Manitoba. What he wanted, he told Riel, was "a clear, concise, logical petition," one which would have the facts and the figures.

Such a document "will strengthen our hands more than a month of speechifying," he wrote. "Any bungling work will earn for us the contempt of the business man."[26]

As an answer to the suggestion that the Conservative party should adopt Riel's programme "under their party name," Jackson issued a manifesto on July 28 giving a clear statement of the objects and purposes of the North-West movement and calling upon the people for their support. Jackson had assembled a number of resolutions, adopted by local branches of the Union, attributing the economic depression to the policies of the Conservative government, and these he embodied in his manifesto. This document, he felt, would serve to clear the minds of the people as to what the Union stood for, but it would also serve as a trial balloon for the petition that would be sent later to Ottawa. After demanding provincial status "with full control over our resources and internal administration, and power to send a just number of representatives to the federal legislature" as "the remedy to the root of the evil," the manifesto went on to explain the role of Riel:

Louis Riel of Manitoba fame has united the half-breed element solidly in our favour. Hitherto it has been used largely as the tool of whatever party happened to be in power in the East, but Riel has warned them against the danger of being separated from the whites by party proposals. The general impression is that Riel has been painted in blacker colours than he deserves; that in regard to his public attitude it is better to accept his services as long as he works for us; while as to his private record it would be well to suspend judgment until his side of the case has been heard, especially as his bearing is frank and straightforward, indicating sincerity of purpose and assurance of his convictions. As long as both elements work on the square, doing justice to each other, there will be no clash, but a marked advance toward our end, i.e. justice in the North-West. . . . It is by force of right that we hope to win our cause and any inconsistency on our part will greatly damage our cause, as it will lose us the moral support of Great Britain and the United States. Restrain any tendency toward the forcible taking charge of our own affairs before we have used all constitutional means.[27]

In the last paragraph of his manifesto, Jackson referred briefly to the Indian problem, declaring that false rumours were being deliberately circulated by the press of the Territories, "seeking a pretext for placing the country under martial law and so goad the people into a false step." Louis Riel, he maintained, "will do more toward pacifying Big Bear than could be accomplished by twenty agents in a month of Sundays."[28]

This reference to the Indians was a significant one, for Big Bear and the disaffected Indians of the North Saskatchewan valley had assembled at Poundmaker's reserve in June to discuss their relations with Canada and to formulate the demands they were going to put to the federal government.   The Indian council had broken up following an encounter between the Indians and the Mounted Police under Crozier;[29] but Big Bear was determined that it should reassemble as soon as possible.[30] And the return of Louis Riel to Canada confirmed him in his intentions. During July, Big Bear and several of the Indian chiefs in the vicinity of Fort Carlton had interviews with Louis Riel or with his representative Baptiste Arcand.[31]   In August, Big Bear met Riel at Jackson's house in Prince Albert.   Jackson's brother, describing the latter interview, said Big Bear complained that the Canadian government had broken the terms of the treaties and asked Riel and his friends if, when they had secured their rights, they would help the Indians obtain theirs.[32]   It was with Riel's assurances of help from the North-West movement (which, incidentally, adopted more liberal treatment for the Indians as one of its objectives) that Big Bear and other Indians met in council at Carlton in August.   The Lieutenant-Governor was frightened at what the Council might bring forth.   "If the half-breeds are in earnest in wishing a redress of their grievances," he wrote to Sir John A. Macdonald, "they will certainly not try to bring it about through the Indians.   What I fear is that the white scoundrels will persuade the half-breeds that they will have a good time if they bring about a row, in which case they certainly would work with the Indians."[33]

When he blamed the outsiders for the Indian agitation, Dewdney was doing less than justice to the sincerity of the Indians and the reality of their grievances.   The Indians needed no outside prodding from the métis or anybody else.   Even a momentary glance at the Indian speeches delivered at the Carlton Council will convince the reader that the Indians had genuine complaints and that their resentment was neither simulated nor without foundation.   At Fort Carlton, Big Bear was particularly eloquent in his denunciation of the lack of good faith displayed by Ottawa in its dealings with the aboriginal population.   The only apparent evidence of outside influence is to be found in the Indian demand that they should be permitted to elect a spokesman every four years who would act as an intermediary between the Indians and the government and who "could make the understanding progress all the time between the Indians and the white man."[34]

As frequently was the case with Indian councils, the Carlton council broke up without any positive result.   But it did witness the partial success of Big Bear's efforts to bring the Indians together, and the inability of the federal government to prevent him from agitating for better terms.   Big Bear had successfully defied all efforts to compel him to settle upon his reserve, and his reputation among the discontented Indians of the Territories had grown accordingly.   Now he had the advice and support of Riel and Jackson.   According to Hayter Reed, the Assistant Indian Commissioner, the whole Indian agitation could be attributed to the subversive influence of Louis Riel.   In a letter to Ottawa he wrote:

Big Bear is an agitator and always has been, and having received the moral support of the half-breed community, he is only too glad to have an opportunity of inciting the Indians to make fresh and exorbitant demands.   There are Indian as well as white agitators and the hard times make one and all, good and bad, only too prone to give any assistance they can towards procuring more from the authorities without having to work for it.   Riel's movement has a great deal to do with the demands of the Indians, and there is no possible doubt but that they, as well as the half-breeds, are beginning to look up to him as one who will be the means of curing all their ills and obtaining for them all they demand.[35]

But the Indian agitation, as far as Riel and Jackson were concerned, was not the main issue.   Their principal interest was the formulation of their own grievances and the presentation of these to the federal authorities—all the more because their opponents were becoming increasingly active.   In July, Jackson reported to Riel that Clarke and Sproat had gone to Battleford.   Whether the visit had as its purpose the influencing of public opinion in that area or not is obscure, although it is curious that from July the *Herald* began to pour scorn upon the North-West movement.   Even more significant was the change of heart on the part of the editor of the *Prince Albert Times*.   From the talk of armed rebellion which characterized the editorials of May, 1884, to the solid support afforded the government in August, the *Times* moved rapidly from the left to the right in its political attitude.   The editor could still write with vigour, but he now turned his fire upon the Jacksons and said no more about federal authorities.   T. G. Jackson, William Jackson's father, was referred to as "an old gentleman who has meandered tolerably decently through an uneventful life without exhibiting any more thoroughly marked characteristic than that of amiable stupidity" who had now, for some reason, "set up as a full blown rebel."   Only "unseemly jocularity," declared the *Times*, could explain the sight of "otherwise apparently sane men in dragging M. Louis Riel to head an agitation meeting in our town."[36]

Far more serious than the opposition of the local newspapers or the local oligarchy, was the growing chilliness of the Roman Catholic clergy. Except for Father Fourmond who, in his simplicity and guilelessness was the last of the clergy to break with Louis Riel, the several missionaries in Prince Albert and St. Laurent had become alarmed at the twist that the agitation seemed to be taking.   In particular, they were concerned that the accusations might be correct and that Riel was encouraging the Indians in their demands.   Louis Schmidt did not believe that Riel was the instigator of the Indian troubles, but even he began to wonder with André and others if Riel were not just too anxious to turn the Indian discontent to the advantage of the North-West movement, so that he and his associates might profit from whatever fear the possibility of an Indian war might inspire in Ottawa.[37]   In his turn, Riel was annoyed at the lack of enthusiasm on the part of the clergy in the District for his movement.   When he spoke to the métis after Mass at St. Anthony's on August 10, his annoyance was plain enough for all to see. On the following Sunday, he and Lépine engaged in a furious altercation with André.   To the priest's astonishment, Riel declared that he was losing faith in the clergy—they were too closely allied with the government—and he questioned not only their infallibility in matters of politics but also in matters of faith.

Then Riel launched into the theme that had been commonplace to his thinking for many years—the establishment of the French métis as a distinct race in North America—declaring that French-Canadian immigrants, when they came to western Canada, should identify themselves not as French-Canadians but as métis.   André could give as well as he could receive in any verbal exchange.   He charged Riel with mixing religion too much with politics, with too much talk of his "divine mission," and with utopian and unrealistic ideas about the métis nation. He even declared that Riel was a "veritable fanatic."[38]   André had never deviated from the position he had taken at the outset, that as long as Riel was reasonable and constitutional, he would not oppose or interfere with him.   But the attitude of non-interference or neutrality was just what irritated Riel.   He did not want the clergy's passive acquiescence; he wanted, and he needed, their active support.   He wanted and needed another Ritchot and another Dugast.   But these were roles André would not and Fourmond could not play.

In the latter part of August, Judge Rouleau and Hayter Reed, the Assistant Indian Commissioner, paid a visit to Prince Albert.   Both were anxious to discover what they could of the developments in Lorne about which so many rumours were circulating throughout the Territories.[39]   Accordingly they went to see Father André.   André was, however, very discreet.   He might oppose Louis Riel in discussion, but this did not mean he was an informer or the tool of the government. He told Rouleau that Riel was acting with moderation and had no evil intentions, and that up to the present he had nothing to say against the métis leader.   When Rouleau suggested that Riel's had been the hand that had manipulated the Indian council at Fort Carlton, and that his had been the voice that Big Bear had echoed in putting forward his demands, André simply denied the allegation. Rouleau was partly, but not wholly convinced. In his report to the Lieutenant-Governor, he said: "Soon after our arrival at Prince Albert, Mr. Reed and I were soon [sic] convinced that the report concerning the Indians and the half-breeds was greatly exaggerated, but still that rumour had some foundation." There was evidence that the Indian chiefs "had interviewed Riel for the purpose of drawing that petition, and that he had agreed to do so, but did not and would not advise them." He added, however, "I would in your place impress the Government with the desirability of settling the question of the half-breeds under the shortest delay possible" if only because "the *patriotic Grits* make use of the agitation to promote their own political ends" and because "by settling that question shortly it would take away the credit to Riel of having obtained that end, and all further grounds for any more agitation."[40]

In the meantime, Riel and Jackson had gone ahead with their plans. They had learned that Sir John A. Macdonald's colleague, Sir Hector Langevin, the Minister of Public Works, proposed to pay a visit to the North-West Territories. This was too good an opportunity to lose. Why not use the occasion to present their grievances in person to a member of the federal Cabinet? It might not make the petition to Ottawa completely unnecessary, but it would, at least, acquaint one member of the government with the complaints of the farmers and the half-breeds. Accordingly, an address was drafted, and a statement of grievances similar to Jackson's manifesto of July was prepared and signed by white settlers, English half-breeds and French métis alike, including among others Spence, Isbister, Adams, Slater, Scott, Stewart, Miller, Jackson, Meyers, Cromarty, Porter, Nolin, Lépine, Monkman and Batoche. Riel, too, resolved to prepare an address for Langevin, but it would be different from that written by Jackson.[41] Riel would appeal to the historical mission of French Canada in the North-West, the achievements of its explorers and its missionaries; he would recall Chapleau's defence of North-West rights during the trial of Ambroise Lépine; and he would identify French Canada with the métis, with their aspirations and their hopes.[42]

But neither Riel's nor Jackson's address reached Sir Hector. There was no railway line north of Regina. The Minister, anxious that his tour should be as non-political as possible, was unwilling to undertake a wearisome wagon journey over the prairies for the sake of exposing himself to the demands of the malcontents of Lorne, no matter whether they spoke French or English. On August 19, he telegraphed Rouleau that he would be unable to go to Prince Albert.[43] Rouleau either forgot or neglected to pass the word to Riel—there was no reason why he should have done so—and for several days the half-breeds diligently watched the roadways, scanning every wagon for a face that might resemble Langevin's. Finally, on August 25, Riel wrote to Jackson, "People at Batoche's place have been paying attention to those who crossed the river there. Yesterday at noon there was no indication whatever that any stranger like the Hon. Sir Hector was expected that way. The general rumour now is that the Minister of Public Works will avoid our District."[44] Both Riel and Jackson were disappointed. Sir Hector had escaped what might have been an embarrassing political commitment; but he could not so easily spare his government. The two men determined to return to their earlier plan of drafting a petition to be sent to Ottawa. Langevin, back in Ottawa, wrote to his Chief, "Riel is still at Prince Albert and is a permanent danger. However, we must take care not to make a martyr of him, and thus increase his popularity. Some concessions to, and good treatment of, the half-breeds will go a long way to settle matters. . . ."[45]

Unquestionably Riel and Jackson had placed too much reliance on the hoped-for meeting with Sir Hector Langevin. Jackson had gathered the material and had put it into the form of an address to the Minister; but this address was not what he and Riel wanted to put into the petition to Ottawa. They had, indeed, been so busy with their agitation, organization and preparations for Langevin that the petition had been neglected, and the executive committee of French and English had never been assembled to discuss the matter. At least one member of the committee was annoyed at the failure to act on the petition. On September 4, James Isbister wrote to Riel accusing him of unnecessary slowness. "You said to me in a letter some time ago that by moderating the movement would make it sure," he wrote. "But you would be surprised perhaps if you saw how many of the English people believe our moderation might be a cause of weakness." Isbister then went on to complain of the delay in drawing up the petition: "I must say we the people of the Ridge, Red Deer Hill, Halcro Settlement and St. Catherine's find you are too slow, or does the delay rest with Mr. Jackson and his people? Yet we are satisfied to think you are doing every good to keep our friends, your people, to work together unimously [sic]. . . ." Then Isbister placed his finger on one development about which Riel had already become very much concerned: the attitude of the Roman Catholic clergy. "We are so glad to find all our friends, the people amongst whom you live, are working well together," he wrote. "Only I must not forget to mention that we Protestants have learnt from very good authority lately, your Clergy are doing their utmost to break the existing unity between the French and English half-breeds."[46]

Here, obviously, was a fence that needed mending. Without a union of the mixed-bloods, French and English, the North-West movement would achieve nothing. It was a matter that Riel would have to take up with Mgr. Vital Grandin, Bishop of St. Albert in Alberta, then about to pay a pastoral visit to St. Laurent.

III

On September 1, Bishop Grandin reached St. Laurent. With him came Amédée Forget of Regina, clerk of the North-West Council and secretary to Lieutenant-Governor Dewdney. Grandin had his ecclesiastical duties to perform, including the administration of confirmation to some eighty children in St. Laurent; Forget was therefore free to move about, to look at the various ferries across the Saskatchewan River and, more profitably, to talk with various métis. According to Charles Nolin, one who heard him, Forget hinted broadly that if the people wished it Riel could probably be appointed a member of the Council of the North-West Territories in place of old Pascal Breland.[47] Such an appointment, Forget said, would provide Riel with the opportunity of doing something for his people and also yield him a salary of $1,000. There is no evidence to show that this proposal ever had the sanction of the Canadian government authorities—it may well have been no more than an idea that had occurred to Forget—but it would not have been out of keeping with the policy the government was disposed to follow. Louis Schmidt had been appointed to the land office; Michel Dumas had been offered a post in the Department of Indian Affairs; and Charles Nolin was encouraged to submit a tender for supplying timber to the government. It looked as if an effort was going to be made to stifle the agitation by buying Louis Riel with an appointment to the Council. In any event this is the way Nolin interpreted Forget's remarks, and he and Lépine hastened to warn Louis of what Forget had in mind. But Riel could not be bought by a seat in the territorial council. "Do you think I would dirty my name by accepting an appointment like that?" he said.[48] Later Nolin suggested that Riel's refusal was no more than a bid for something better. Sergeant Keenan of the North-West Mounted Police, who, along with Sergeant Brooks, had been sent to the region of St. Laurent to keep an eye on the métis agitation, reported that Riel was talking of an appointment to the federal cabinet or to the Canadian Senate.[49]

However it was not Forget but Grandin that Riel wanted to see. When the Bishop had completed the task of blessing the new bell at St. Anthony's church, he accepted an invitation to attend a gathering of the people of the settlement at St. Laurent. In silence the Bishop listened to Riel press his charges that the Catholic clergy had failed to give their full support to the North-West movement, and that, in consequence, a coolness had grown up between the priests and the people. Nolin, Lépine and Dumont echoed Riel's complaints. They accused Grandin of paying too much attention to the prejudices of his clergy and, like Archbishop Taché, of favouring the French-Canadians at the expense of the métis. There was too much talk of submission to authority and not enough of justice. All of them spoke in terms that alarmed even the sympathetic Fourmond by their tenor. Forget declared that they spoke "apparently under great excitement."[50]

Refusing to reply in kind, the Bishop spoke quietly and carefully to an audience that he knew was inclined to be hostile, and his soft answers turned aside Riel's wrath. He told the métis that he and his clergy were being asked to countenance a movement "concerning whose object and means of action" he and they had been "kept in complete ignorance." In spite of his conversations with the métis leader, Riel had never really informed him "as to the course of action they intended to pursue." As a Bishop he had, naturally, a warm feeling for all "his children," and he assured them that the clergy would always be ready to sympathize with their hopes and to assist their cause, but that they could "not approve any secret agitation."[51] The Bishop then gave his blessing to a suggestion that Riel had put forward as a means of closing the breach between the people and the clergy, namely, the formation of a national métis association. He named St. Joseph as the patron of the new body and authorized the celebration of the feast of the Saint as a national holiday for people of Indian extraction. If they wished it, they could inaugurate the new association on September 24.[52]

The above meeting took place on September 5. The next day, Grandin and Forget went to Gabriel's Crossing where they stayed overnight at Joseph Vandal's house. During the evening, Gabriel Dumont arrived and spent some time in conversation with Forget. He told the French-Canadian why the people of the North-West had sent for Riel, and he warned him that any attempt on the part of the police or the government to arrest him would be resisted. "We need him here as our political leader," Dumont said to Forget. "In other matters I am the chief here."[53] He also explained the relations between the métis and the Indians: "They are our relatives and when they are starving they come to us for relief, and we have to feed them. The Government is not doing right by them." He concluded by saying, "We want the Indians fed, our rights recognized, and Mr. Riel as our leader, but we don't desire to create any disturbance." Then he handed a memorandum to Grandin. It was a paper drafted by Louis Riel in answer to the Bishop's complaint of ignorance of what Riel and his friends were helping to achieve. All they were after, wrote Riel, was responsible government, and the same concessions that had been given to the Manitoba half-breeds: the immediate issue of patents; the setting aside of two million acres of land to provide funds for the relief of distress and for the purchase of machinery and seed grain for the métis; that "works and contracts of the Government in the North-West be given as far as practicable, to residents therein, in order to encourage them as they deserve and to increase circulation of cash in the Territories."[54]

On his return to Regina, Forget sent Governor Dewdney a long report of what he had seen and heard at St. Laurent. He also forwarded him a copy, in English, of Riel's memorandum to Bishop Grandin. "The agitation is not at present as noisy as in the beginning," he wrote:

but nonetheless serious, I believe. It comprises nearly all the French and English half-breeds and a number of unprincipled white settlers at Prince Albert. These latter are opponents politically of the present party in power and would delight in causing trouble that might embarrass the present government. Constant communications, most of them of a secret nature, are being kept between these different elements. During the short interval I was there, Mr. Riel received two deputations from Prince Albert, one composed of all English half-breeds and the other of two white settlers. Nothing transpired of what was said or done between them. A couple of days later Mr. Riel, while in conversation with me, said that were it not for his presence there serious complications would already be existing, and added having received that very day a letter from a certain party in Prince Albert reproaching him with being too slow and casting suspicions upon his intentions [obviously a reference to Isbister's letter]. Several Indian chiefs have had interviews with Riel. Three from Qu'Appelle (whether chiefs or not I have been unable to ascertain) came in on the 7th of September, just as we were leaving the South Branch."

Then Forget added the significant words: "Another remarkable feature of the agitation and perhaps the most alarming, considering the religious nature of the half-breeds, is their loss of confidence in their old missionaries, such as Fathers André, Fourmond and Moulin."[55]

After studying Forget's report and the account he had received earlier from Judge Rouleau, Governor Dewdney wrote a lengthy despatch to Sir John A. Macdonald. He told the Prime Minister that "Riel has no good will towards yourself or your Government" and that the métis leader "will make the best of this opportunity to further his own private ends." But he added, "If the half-breed question is arranged this winter, it will settle the whole business; if not, a good force in the North will be necessary."[56]

As the autumn leaves began to shrivel and change from green to yellow and brown, Louis Riel's prestige reached its greatest heights. According to Father Fourmond, the métis looked upon him as "a Joshua, a prophet, even as a saint."[57] He had united both the English and the French half-breeds; he enjoyed widespread support among the white settlers; and now he had closed the breach between the clergy and the people in St. Laurent by his appeal to Grandin. On September 24, a special service was held to inaugurate the new society, the Union Métisse St. Joseph, and Riel was easily the dominating figure. Father Moulin of St. Anthony's celebrated Mass and delivered the sermon, and Father Fourmond of St. Laurent composed a special canticle to add to the solemnity of the occasion. But it was not Moulin's sermon in favour of temperance that the métis came in great numbers to hear, nor Fourmond's canticle, which none but he could sing;[58] it was their chief, it was Louis Riel. And Riel did not disappoint them. There was none of the hesitancy of his earlier speeches now; none of the tired and weary schoolmaster about him. All the old skill and fire had returned. "Now we are established as a nation," he cried. On this occasion, Riel gave a far better sermon than did Moulin, who fumbled his lines by talking of St. John the Baptist instead of St. Joseph. He ended his oration of three-quarters of an hour on the church steps by acclaiming the Pope, the bishops, the clergy and Her Majesty Queen Victoria.[59]

But if Riel believed he had brought about a solid reunion of race and religion in St. Laurent, there were those who had their own doubts about the durability of the union. Father Fourmond might urge his parishioners to add an *Ave* to their prayers each night for Louis Riel, who had done so much for them: but Fourmond's clerical brothers, in particular Fathers André and Végreville, had their private opinions about Riel. Moreover, Bishop Grandin had left the métis settlement with a gnawing question in his mind; instead of being a dedicated leader, might not Riel be "a dangerous man who could cause real trouble?"[60] Archbishop Taché of St. Boniface, who had known Riel since he had been a little boy in St. Vital, who had seen him during his days as president at Fort Garry, wondered whether Riel was following a sound political course when he demanded special land grants or scrip in view of the "sad use that most of our people made of the lands they held in Manitoba."[61]

Meanwhile Riel and Jackson busied themselves with the petition. Riel paid frequent visits to Prince Albert to consult his colleague and enlist the collaboration of Dr. Porter. It was not all smooth sailing. Porter did not approve of Riel's insistence on the métis land grant.[62] Even Jackson questioned its advisability.[63] But Riel would not be shaken from his course. The métis in the Territories would have nothing less than what their kindred in Manitoba had received, even if a large number of those who expected to share in the land grant had already received scrip in the other province and had disposed of it before moving westwards. Finally, in December of 1884, the petition was completed. It was generally well received. "Everything is serene," wrote Jackson to Riel. "Dr. Porter is solid. . . . Spence took a copy down to Mac-Dowall who said he would not sign it but thought it a very good one. . . . I shall take care to leave every committee man in good heart and understanding."[64] The petition was apparently endorsed by the executive committee of French and English, which had been named earlier. On December 16, it was signed by Andrew Spence as chairman of the committee and by W. H. Jackson as secretary, and despatched to the Hon. Adolphe Chapleau as Secretary of State for the Dominion of Canada.[65] There was something in it for everybody: a demand for more liberal treatment of the Indians; demands for a land grant for the half-breeds; for the early issue of patents to those who already occupied their farms; for responsible government; representation in Parliament; control of their own natural resources; reduction of the tariff; vote by ballot; and the construction of a railway to Hudson Bay. There was also a long complaint regarding the treatment accorded Louis Riel in Manitoba, with a harking back to the negotiations with Ottawa and the failure of the Canadian authorities to implement the promise of an amnesty.

Receipt of this document was acknowledged by Chapleau. In his naïveté, Jackson wrote to Riel expressing his belief that this early reply was a "good sign," particularly in view of "the bold tone of my letter, and our audacious assumption that we are not yet in Confederation, an assumption which, it seems to me, they have conceded in their letter. . . . It is evident that they are prepared to communicate with us on something like equal terms."[66] Jackson even began to think about the possibility of sending delegates to Ottawa, as Riel had done fifteen years before in the case of Manitoba.

Now that the petition had been drafted, sent to Ottawa and acknowledged by the federal authorities, the question arose as to whether or not Louis Riel should return to the United States. He had been quite sincere when he had told Dumont, on June 5, that he did not intend to remain permanently in Canada and would go back to Montana. Now it was several months past the date he had set for his return. After all, he had said that he would come to Lorne only to help his people prepare their petition, to give them the benefit of his education and experience. He had done all that had been expected of him. Perhaps it was time for him to think about his own future and that of his wife and family.

CHAPTER 16

Exovedate

I

A LMOST the whole of his life Louis Riel was dependent on the charity and generosity of his friends. To Archbishop Taché he was indebted for his education in Montreal. The support of his friends had sustained him between 1870 and 1875. Following his discharge from Beauport, and after his arrival in Saskatchewan, it was the same story. This time his cousin and former opponent accorded him hospitality—at least until November 8, when Riel and his family quit the Nolin house to go and live with Moïse Ouellette.[1] Only by selling some of his property at St. Vital, by doing a little trading on the Missouri and by teaching school at St. Peter's had he managed to maintain himself between 1879 and 1884.

As he brooded over his misfortunes, Riel could not escape the conclusion that he had been compelled to sacrifice too much. He felt there was owing to him not only his share of the Manitoba half-breed land grant, but some return for his services to Canada in 1870 in bringing Manitoba peacefully into Confederation; for taking the field against the Fenians; for surrendering his parliamentary seat to Sir George Cartier; as well as some compensation for the long years of persecution he had suffered for no other reason than the unwillingness of the government to implement the promise of a general amnesty. "For fifteen years I have been neglecting myself," said Riel in 1885:

My wife and children are without means, while I am working more than any representative in the North-West. Although I am simply a guest of this country—a guest of the half-breeds of the Saskatchewan—although as a simple guest, I worked to better the condition of the people of Saskatchewan at the risk of my life, to better the condition of the people of the North-West, I have never had any pay. It has always been my hope to have a fair living one day.[2]

More and more, as the autumn passed into early winter in 1884, Riel dwelt on his personal grievances and on the words Bourget had written him almost ten years before. Outwardly he remained calm, devoted and deeply religious: inwardly his spirit was agitated and his mind

292

disturbed.   It was difficult for him to contain himself; difficult to accept
with good grace and a submissive spirit the delays, the procrastinations,
the doubts and the opposition that always seemed to be his lot.   He had
worked hard to help put together the petition that had been sent to
Ottawa, and harder still to influence the opinions of the half-breeds and
the whites in favour of the North-West movement.   He had been
angered by the partisan opposition of the *Prince Albert Times* and
annoyed at the indifference displayed generally by the clergy.   He
could not help but compare the weak, if enthusiastic, support of Father
Fourmond, with the strong will and helpful advice of Father Ritchot
in 1869 and 1870.

Then, just as his whole project was beginning to reach completion,
Fourmond produced another petition of his own asking Ottawa to
provide an annual subsidy of $1,000 to support the school run by "The
Faithful Companions of Jesus" at St. Laurent.   Fourmond's petition
would only be an embarrassment; it would detract from his own petition;
it would promote discord among the Catholic French and the Protestant
English half-breeds.[3]   And that was exactly what it did do.   Hearing
of Fourmond's petition, the *Prince Albert Times* denounced the introduction of sectarianism into the North-West movement and blamed the
whole thing on Riel.[4]   In haste Riel informed his English-speaking
supporters that he had nothing to do with Fourmond's petition, that he
disapproved of it, that he favoured equal support for the schools of
Catholics and Protestants.   Thomas Jackson wrote to the *Times*:
"Mr. Riel availed himself of the first opportunity afforded by a public
meeting . . . in which he explained . . . the dangers of arousing the
opposition of those who would otherwise be in sympathy with their
forthcoming demands."[5]

The whole episode soured Louis Riel more than ever on the Catholic
clergy in the District of Lorne.   Not only had they failed to give their
whole-hearted support to his own agitation, but in their own clumsy way
they had seriously embarrassed it.   For this reason, Riel vented his
ill-will on Father Vegreville who, one night late in November, found
himself obliged to seek shelter with Moïse Ouellette at the very house in
which Riel was living.   The métis leader could not restrain himself.
He launched into a bitter tirade against the Canadian government and
against the ecclesiastical authorities of the North-West who seemed to
combine to thwart all his efforts to better the lot of the métis.   Vegreville
would have liked to reply to Riel, but he was taken aback by the intensity
of Riel's attack and frightened by the presence of so many of Riel's
supporters, all of whom seemed to be in a sullen mood.   Not content
with berating Vegreville, Riel went to St. Laurent on December 5, where

he renewed his attack on other members of the clergy, on Fourmond, Touze and Brother Piquet. He said nothing that he had not said before, but he said it with greater vigour and with greater vehemence: the Canadian government had acquired the North-West by illegitimate means; there would have to be a reorganization of both the temporal and the spiritual government of the territories; and he, Louis Riel, had a vocation as a reformer which came to him from God. Alarmed, Vegreville wrote to Taché in St. Boniface, "the present movement is none other than that of 1870; to establish an independent nation of which L. Riel will be the royal autocrat, with his own religion of which he will be the supreme pontiff; and to attain this end all means are justified."[6]

This outburst, one of several to follow, did Riel no good. It may have impressed some of his followers who never questioned his claim to divine inspiration; but it did alarm some of the educated, those of moderate disposition who were content to support Riel, the constitutional leader, but who were not prepared to follow Riel the political and religious zealot. Louis Schmidt, whom Father André informed about Riel's excesses at this time, wrote: "For my part, I do not think that Riel is crazy, but I do think that he is too enthusiastic and too confident in his star. He relies on the fact that he has always been looked upon as a man to be feared; and if he uses only commonplace methods to make himself understood, he thinks he may thereby lose his prestige and appear as an ordinary individual." It was Schmidt's opinion that Riel was acting in the way he was only to impress the ignorant and retain the allegiance of those métis who looked upon him "as a little god."[7]

In spite of his unorthodox ideas and his attacks on individual members of the clergy, Riel faithfully continued to attend Mass and confession and to conduct himself in an edifying manner. When the clergy met to discuss whether he should be excluded from the sacraments, they decided to take no action.[8] It was charitably agreed that Riel's outbursts were the results of his misfortunes and his mental suffering over many years, and that they should, in consequence, be overlooked. At the same time it was also felt that his continued presence in the country was bound to result in increasing embarrassment. Nothing would be more pleasing to the clergy than to hear that the one-time president of the Provisional Government of Assiniboia was ready to return to Montana. Accordingly, when Riel met Father André early in December and made his peace with the church, André promised that he would use whatever influence he possessed to help Riel obtain some financial compensation from the federal government.[9]

It was in fulfilment of this undertaking that André invited D. H. Mac-Dowall, the local representative of the District of Lorne in the Territorial

Council, to join him in a private discussion with Riel. They would go to Batoche, listen to Riel's plaints, hear his arguments and discuss how far it would be possible to meet his demands. On December 22, three days before Christmas, André and MacDowall went to St. Laurent. For several hours the three men talked together. Riel told his visitors that he had come to Canada "at the request of a deputation of three half-breeds . . . to confer with the half-breeds here on the subject of their rights and grievances, and with the intention of eventually returning to Montana." Then he confronted them with the statement that he "had claims of his own against the Government which he hoped to be able to press at the same time as he advocated the claims of the British half-breeds." He argued that he had "advocated a proper and respectful bearing towards the government"—although he admitted that he had become a little "excited" during Forget's visit and had spoken "hastily" of "what he would do if his claims were not satisfied." Then, according to MacDowall's report of the interview to Lieutenant-Governor Dewdney, Riel proceeded to state that "if the Government would consider his personal claims against them and pay him a certain amount in settlement of these claims," he would ensure that his followers would be "satisfied with almost any settlement of their claims for land grants that the Government might be willing to make," and also that he himself would be prepared to go back to the United States. He declared that the government owed him compensation, and that Sir John A. Macdonald had admitted as much when he once authorized the Rev. J. B. Proulx to offer him $35,000. MacDowall considered this demand excessive. "I believe myself," he wrote, "that $3,000 or $5,000 would cart the whole Riel family across the boundary." Summing up his impressions of the interview, MacDowall continued:

He [Riel] appeared to me to be an enthusiast, who had suffered personal losses and who felt as one "hounded" in '70 to '74—that this feeling of injury had grown into a monomania which had been brooded over and which was nourished by his enthusiastic nature, and that the only danger there is in him lies in his enthusiasm which, added to his past history, gives him an immense influence for good or for evil over his ignorant followers, who are joined without reason by the agitator class and those whom they had made discontented.

MacDowall did not foresee any likelihood of serious trouble until the elections in May or June, when "if his demands are not satisfied, he will become excited at the public meetings which will then be held and at which he will meet opposition and there is no knowing where that excitement will end."[10]

MacDowall was the very embodiment of tact during his interview with Louis Riel. He allowed the métis leader to talk but said nothing himself. He would and could in no way compromise the federal government; and in spite of Riel's entreaties and demands, he kept his own counsel. André, who was present, was filled with admiration at the way MacDowall conducted himself. But André, like Riel, was not satisfied with a calm countenance and meaningless phrases. He wanted Riel to leave the North-West, and he wanted every inducement to be given Riel to go. "I think it is really the duty of the government to get Riel out of mischief as soon as possible . . . there has never been any fear of an outbreak, but the presence of that man in the country will be a source of anxiety to the government, and we do not know what may happen at last." André agreed with Riel to the extent of arguing that "he has certainly certain claims against the Government." Quite obviously $100,000 was a ridiculous amount; $35,000 was exorbitant as well; but there should be no quibbling: "Mr. MacDowall and I will make him agree to any conditions, but in duty bound I am obliged to say that it will be better to concede him that amount than to keep him in the country." He continued, "I know that if Riel is satisfied, all the half-breeds will be united in the next election, and, as a man, they will vote for Mr. MacDowall, and we will carry everything before us; so I strongly recommend you to use all your influence at Ottawa to obtain for Riel that sum; if things are settled satisfactorily, we will not hear much of Riel after that, for he desires to go back to Montana."[11]

It was only a matter of waiting for the replies from Ottawa. Perhaps Riel would be given enough to go to the federal capital to plead the case of the North-West settlers in person;[12] perhaps he would go back to Montana and organize the half-breeds there; perhaps he might be able to purchase a newspaper and use its editorials columns to advance the claims and rights of the métis.[13] In the meantime he would stay in the Saskatchewan region where his popularity was still considerable— considerable enough, in any event, for him to be entertained at a banquet organized by Dumont, Lépine, Boyer and others, and presided over by Charles Nolin, at which he received a purse of money collected among the métis of Lorne for his support.[14]

But the days and the weeks went by, and there were no answers. On January 16, Riel went to Prince Albert with Nolin and Lépine. Three weeks had passed, and Riel was anxious to know if there was news from Ottawa. He was becoming impatient; and his impatience was acquiring a sharp edge, for it was whetted by the thought that there might never be an answer at all. On January 21, Father André reiterated his request that the government pay Riel some kind of indemnity and preserve peace within the North-West. "Riel is sincere in his desire to remain quiet and to use his influence among the half-breeds for peace, if he is satisfied," said André; adding, however, that the métis leader was "much pinched just now and requires help greatly." There was no point in worrying about "some paltry thousand dollars when the peace of the country is at stake."[15] A week later, MacDowall wrote very much the same thing to Dewdney: "If red tape can be abolished for one month, I can tell you how to settle the whole of this half-breed row at the expense of some $6,000. Get the Government to give you full power as commissioner, and I can have all cut and dried, but I must have $5,000 for Riel, one thousand more or less will do the rest."[16]

As January came to an end and February began, Riel and his friends commenced to show signs of considerable exasperation. Charles Nolin, to whom MacDowall had lent money to enable him to submit a tender for wooden poles for the government telegraph line, was forced by his colleagues to withdraw the tender. On February 2, MacDowall telegraphed Dewdney: "Riel and leading half-breeds have been here to hear intention of Government respecting Breed matter—great discontent at no reply to representation. Nolin and Lépine have been compelled by Riel's supporters to withdraw tender for telegraph poles on Battleford line at great personal sacrifice. . . . I anticipate no immediate danger but urge Government to declare intention immediately."[17] André, too, returned to the charge with a letter reporting "great indignation" on the part of the half-breeds at the "Government's silence," and expressing the priest's alarm lest "such excitement might easily lead them to extreme acts."[18] At the same time the correspondent of *Le Manitoba* informed his newspaper from Prince Albert that the government would be well advised to accelerate a declaration of its policy, if only because people in Lorne were beginning "to hear rather bold, if not imprudent speeches" from some of the métis leaders.[19]

In spite of these warnings, the authorities at Ottawa seemed deaf to all appeals from the North-West. To Sir John A. Macdonald, Riel's demand for money appeared to be blackmail, a cynical attempt "to extract money from the public purse."[20] Accordingly the cabinet merely agreed on the early appointment of a commission of three members to make a census of the métis of the North-West. "Government has decided to investigate claims of half-breeds," Dewdney was informed on February 4, "and with that view has directed enumeration of those who did not participate in grant under Manitoba Act."[21] Such a message was cold comfort to the discontented métis. Not only had they heard vague promises like this before, ever since 1878, but many of them had, in fact, come from Manitoba where they had already received scrip and had disposed of it.   More particularly, there was nothing in the message for Riel—not a word about his own claims, which had been included in the petition forwarded by Spence and Jackson, and pressed both by MacDowall and André.   When the message from Ottawa was passed on to Charles Nolin—Dewdney thus deliberately slighted Riel— Louis cried out in anger: "In forty days Ottawa will have my reply."[22]

Angry though he may have been, Riel knew that the government's telegram would have to be made known to the people.   Accordingly, on February 24, a public meeting was held in the church of St. Anthony in Batoche.   Father Moulin had removed the Blessed Sacrament from the altar, so the building could be used for public purposes.   Ostensibly the object of the meeting was simply to read the telegram and discuss it. But the real object was to decide the future of Louis Riel himself. Neither Fathers André nor Touze were present at the gathering, only Fourmond, still one of Riel's supporters, and Father Moulin.   Father Vegreville also attended, having been asked by Inspector S. Gagnon, the officer commanding the Mounted Police at Prince Albert, to take him to Batoche.   When Gagnon reached St. Anthony's, it was made clear to him that his presence, although not expressly forbidden, was not welcome. The policeman did not, therefore, attempt to force his way in.[23]

Behind the walls of the church, Riel broke into one of his characteristic attacks on the federal government, its illegal theft of the west from the people, its unwillingness to recognize the métis grievances and to grant the concessions they demanded.   Then he changed his tone.   In a quiet voice he announced that his work in Saskatchewan was done.   He had helped draft the petition.   The petition had been answered.   A govern- ment commission would be appointed.   Now he must return to Montana. He could do no more in Canada.   In fact his presence was clearly a hindrance, a drag on the North-West movement, since the Canadian government would not treat with him, a foreigner, nor recognize him as the intermediary between the people of Saskatchewan and the Prime Minister in Ottawa.   However, when he proposed to go back to the United States, the church was filled with shouts of "No! No!"   And among those who cried loudest were Nolin and Fourmond.   One old métis rose and said, "If you leave, nephew, we will go with you."   When the shouting subsided, Riel asked quietly, "But the consequences?" Almost to a man the métis answered, "We will accept them."[24]   An English-speaking delegate from Prince Albert rose and added his voice to the métis demand that Riel stay in the country and continue to act as their political head.   Then Fourmond, with what Louis Schmidt called "an incomprehensible enthusiasm," closed the meeting by praising Riel for his patriotism.[25]

There is some doubt how far Louis Riel was sincere when he offered to return to the United States. Charles Nolin, a hostile witness, later declared that Riel never really intended to leave the Saskatchewan and that he engineered this demonstration on his own behalf.[26] Schmidt was disposed to take much the same view, writing to Archbishop Taché that it was Riel's personal claque that carried the métis in the demand that Riel stay in the North-West.[27] On the other hand, there is some evidence to suggest that Riel did have notions of leaving the country. Father Vegreville, likewise no warm partisan of Riel, wrote to Taché on February 19, telling him Riel had made arrangements with Louis Marion to drive him to Winnipeg in mid-March—probably, suggested Vegreville, to see the Archbishop. "The fact is that he is extremely poor and lives by charity," wrote the priest.[28]

In any event, whether by design or genuinely moved by the demonstration of loyalty on the part of his people, Riel declared that he would not leave Saskatchewan. Several days later he spoke to a group of English-speaking half-breeds at the Halcro Settlement in the vicinity of Prince Albert. He was supported by a number of his French-speaking compatriots, some of whom were armed. But there was no need for Riel to be afraid. The English half-breeds showed the same strong feelings of hero worship for Riel as did the French-speaking métis. The one surprising announcement was made by W. H. Jackson who, after delivering himself of a strongly worded and much applauded attack on the federal government, suddenly announced his withdrawal as secretary of the Settlers' Union and his decision to devote himself to the salvation of his soul.[29]

II

Of the various qualities Louis Riel possessed when he arrived in the District of Lorne, his striking appearance, his intelligent countenance, his searching eyes, his personal magnetism and his halo of martyrdom, the quality that appealed most to the people among whom he lived was his sense of religious vocation. From his boyhood Riel had been something of a religious mystic. It was this side of his character that had been uppermost during the months of his illness at Longue Pointe and Beauport; it was this aspect of his nature that had made him so susceptible to the words of the saintly Bishop Bourget; and it was this same mysticism and religiosity that so impressed the people of the Saskatchewan valley. The métis, wrote Bishop Grandin in September, 1884, "spoke to me of Riel with an extraordinary enthusiasm. For them he was a saint; I would say rather a kind of God. . . ."[30]

If Riel's pietism and mysticism appealed to the métis, it did not make the same impression on the Roman Catholic clergy, who looked with some apprehension on the unreasoning adulation with which Riel was regarded. The clergy was all the more apprehensive when this was coupled with with an equally unreasoning acceptance by the métis of Riel's insistence upon the divine nature of his mission in the North-West.   As the doubts of the clergy grew, so too did the strength of the métis affection increase. The French half-breeds, with few exceptions, never challenged Riel; but they did question the clergy, and they wondered whether the coolness of so many of the priests towards Riel was not a matter of jealousy, an unconscious manifestation of the white man's sense of racial superiority over the half-breed.[31]

Riel himself derived great satisfaction from the loyalty he found everywhere being demonstrated by the people whose cause he had made his own.   Almost daily he grew more and more pietistic.   His speeches were sprinkled with religious allusions, and his actions were marked by a mysticism which left a deep imprint upon the impressionable and superstitious natures of the métis.   Louis Schmidt wrote in the spring of 1885, "He shows himself to the people, devout, mystical, full of pious affectations which lead a great number of people to believe that he is nothing less than a saint."[32]   On one occasion, at the wedding of Marie Ouellette and Joseph Bremner on November 24, Riel insisted that a vacant place be left at the wedding table to commemorate the presence of Jesus Christ at the marriage of Cana.   And while the guests danced, drank and sang their songs, Riel spent his time upstairs deep in prayer.[33] Some of the métis thought that Riel's conduct on this occasion was "a little odd," but most of them were merely confirmed in their belief that Riel was more righteous than the clergy, "none of whom had ever had this good idea, even when they attended a wedding."[34]   According to Charles Nolin, Riel spoke to him almost from the moment of his arrival, of matters religious, of the decline of Rome and the presence of the Holy Spirit in Bishop Bourget, of many of the heterodox ideas that had been the mark of his illness.   Philippe Garnot, who became his secretary in March, likewise bore testimony of the manner in which Riel seemed to use his religious experiences to twist the world of reality into a world as he wished it to be.[35]   On January 7, Superintendent Crozier informed Lieutenant-Governor Dewdney that "of late he [Riel] has appeared in the role of a religious reformer . . . he has influenced even in that direction people proverbial for their regard for the teachings of their Church and clergy, proving his influence which he might use with embarrassing results."[36]

With Riel taking upon himself the role of religious reformer, the founder of a métis national church, the breach between the Church and the métis chieftain became even wider. The clergy knew they were losing ground among their parishioners; every argument with Riel only seemed to impress the métis the more with his virtues. It was useless to try to convince him of his errors, either political or doctrinal; every attempt was blocked by his spiritual egoism and the inward certainty that his role in the North-West had divine sanction behind it. As he stimulated the métis with talk of their nationality,[37] of their future as a nation, of the possibility of a métis republic—"He excited the pride and ambition of the métis," wrote Philippe Garnot[38]—he told them that the Catholic missionaries were men of a nationality different from their own, that they were Canadians who had sold out to Canada. He made it clear to Grandin that neither he nor the métis would again give blind obedience to the Church.[39] He spoke in terms of an ecclesiastical reorganization in which the clergy would return to the traditions of work and poverty, in which there would be no hierarchy, in which all clergymen would be known simply as "servants of God." Then he began to talk about the spoilation of Rome by "the brigand king" Victor Emmanuel II of Italy, and of the transference of the papacy to Canada. "I am," he said, "a prophet of the new world."[40]

This abiding conviction that God was directing his thoughts and actions induced Riel to take the steps he did in that fateful month of March, 1885. With God's help, how could he do wrong? In the earlier months of the agitation, during 1884, there had been occasional murmurs that stronger measures than petitions and speeches should be adopted. Nolin, among others, had hinted vaguely at taking up arms.[41] But Riel and Jackson had held to a course that was thoroughly legal and constitutional. By the end of February, 1885, however, Riel had come around to Nolin's way of talking. He was not yet thinking in terms of actual rebellion—rather, he was thinking of his own political strategy in 1869/70. His past success blinded him to the weakness of his present position. He forgot that in 1869 the North-West was not yet part of the Dominion, whereas in 1885 it was. He forgot, too, that in 1885 there was a railway line from central Canada, and that the protection afforded by the isolation of 1869 had disappeared. He seemed mesmerized by the memories of the Manitoba resistance. If the course he had followed in 1884 had proved itself inadequate, it was because he had been too mild—because he had not followed the pattern that had been successful in the past, because he had not remembered the lessons of his own history. If the Canadian government would not listen to his petitions, might they not be roused as they had been before, were he to revive the old traditional organization of the métis buffalo hunt, with its council, its captains and its soldiers? The answer to the North-West question might be the revival of the old Provisional Government and the conducting of formal negotiations with Ottawa on a basis of equality. But before there could be equality, the métis would have to have an armed force.

Accordingly, on March 1, following the meeting at which he was urged to stay in the Saskatchewan valley, Riel spoke from the steps of the church at St. Laurent. He told those present that since they wanted to keep him he would adopt new and possibly more promising tactics in dealing with Ottawa. Obviously the hitherto peaceful agitation had achieved nothing; more satisfactory results might be forthcoming if the métis were "to bare their teeth." Perhaps they should make a show of force. "For," said Riel, "I have only to lift my finger and you will see a vast multitude of nations rushing here who are only awaiting the signal on my part."[42] The next day he went to Prince Albert. With him went Napoléon Nault and Damase Carrière. Riel was excited, and he wanted to see Father André. Despite his dislike of André and his disagreements with the clergy, he still wanted ecclesiastical approval. He told André, "You must give me permission to proclaim a provisional government before twelve o'clock tonight."[43] André would have nothing to do with such a wild scheme. Like Bishop Grandin, he stood for the principle of authority, and he had just managed to extract a promise from Charles Nolin to take no part in any violence the métis might be planning.[44] At first Riel was polite, even obsequious. Then his anger got the better of him, and after a short sharp dispute he was shown the door.

The métis leader was beside himself with rage. He was already suffering from a severe emotional strain,[45] and André's opposition had no other effect than that of confirming Riel in his decision to go ahead with his plans for a provisional government. He therefore held a meeting of several followers and persuaded them to sign a resolution to do everything necessary "to save our souls by compelling ourselves night and day to live righteously in all things and in all places" and "to save our country from evil government by taking up arms if necessary."[46] Then, with the signatures of Gabriel Dumont, Pierre Gariépy, John Ross, Moïse Ouellette, Napoléon Nault and several others, he went with Dumont to see Nolin. Nolin, however, had given his promise to André; moreover, he was a man far more belligerent in speech than in action. The idea of committing himself to a promise so drastic as that of taking up arms terrified him. He temporized and suggested to Riel that if he wanted to fight for the glory of God and for the salvation of the métis, it would be better to think in terms of prayer than in terms of guns. Perhaps it would be a good thing to make a novena—nine days of public prayers in the chapels of the métis parishes—to go to confession and communion, and then, at the end of the nine days, to consult one's own conscience as to what should be done. Such a proposal held no merit in Riel's eyes. Nevertheless, the following day he agreed. A novena would commence on March 10 and would continue until March 19, when the feast of the patron saint of the métis, St. Joseph, would be celebrated.[47]

Such a turn in events was greeted with satisfaction by the clergy. They all agreed that the novena would provide time for the hot heads to cool. They could use these days to remind the métis of their obligations to the church. At first the response to the novena was sufficiently favourable to encourage Vegreville to write to Bishop Grandin on March 12 that it was "certain" that there would be no "revolt." Riel, said Vegreville, had at long last decided to follow the directions of the clergy.[48] Unfortunately both Vegreville and Fourmond, who also wrote in a similar strain, were unduly optimistic. They noted the assiduity of Nolin and the piety of W. H. Jackson. They would have been better advised to have noted that Riel himself did not turn up at Mass until Sunday the 15th. On that day the church of St. Laurent was filled. Riel, Lépine, Dumont, Carrière and all the more warlike métis leaders were there. Father Fourmond preached a sermon in which he condemned resistance to properly constituted authority, and he ended by threatening to withhold the sacraments from any métis who should take part in an armed rising. Riel listened to Fourmond's remarks with growing irritation. At this last threat he remonstrated with Fourmond. "You have transformed the pulpit of truth into the pulpit of falsehood, politics, and discord," he cried, "by daring to threaten with the refusal of the sacraments all those who would take up arms for the defence of their most sacred rights."[49]

Father Fourmond still hoped that the novena would ease the situation, but after Riel's demonstration on the 15th, it was a most pious kind of hope. The fact is that Fourmond never had a very deep understanding of politics or the nature of men. He was always surprised at the turn of events. Riel and Dumont then set out to collect their supporters, urging them to gather at St. Laurent on the 19th, the last day of the novena. They were to bring their guns with them, so that they might fire a *feu de joie* in honour of the baptism of the Methodist, W. H. Jackson, who was to be received into the Roman Catholic Church that day.[50]

The change in Riel during these early weeks of March was no secret to the Canadian authorities in Regina. Riel had been too outspoken to have expected the Mounted Police to remain in ignorance of what he was saying and doing. On March 10, Inspector Gagnon informed Superintendent Crozier at Prince Albert that the half-breeds were "excited" and were "preparing arms."[51]   The next day Crozier passed this information on to Commissioner Irvine at Regina with the added warning that the métis were talking of attacking Fort Carlton, that they were refusing to carry freight for or take employment from the government and that they were "getting arms ready."[52]   The cause of the excitement was, he pointed out, the federal government's refusal to negotiate with Riel on the grounds that he was an alien.   As a precautionary measure, Crozier undertook to reinforce the Mounted Police at Fort Carlton.   Dewdney forwarded the warnings to Ottawa with the remark, "If the half-breeds mean business the sooner they are put down the better.   They are like Indians, when they gather and get excited it is difficult to handle them, but if they are taken unawares there is little difficulty in arresting the leader."[53]   On the 14th, Crozier warned the Commissioner that a rebellion was "liable to break out any moment";[54] and on the 15th Irvine was authorized to take a force of one hundred men and move north to the troubled area as soon as possible.[55]   Irvine was thus en route for Prince Albert while Riel and Dumont were riding around the District of Lorne urging the métis to go to Batoche on the 19th.

Following his outburst on the 15th, Riel went to Vandal's house on the 16th where, according to Garnot, he played "the prophet."[56]   Then he went to Tourond's at Fish Creek, where he spent the night of the 17th. On the morning of the 18th, he set out for Batoche accompanied by a number of métis horsemen.   About eight miles from his destination he stopped for lunch at Baptiste Rocheleau's place.[57]   Here he encountered Dr. John Willoughby, a physician of Saskatoon, who had accompanied a half-breed, Norbert Welsh, to Batoche and was returning home.   Riel showed no signs of hostility to Willoughby; instead he wanted to talk and boast of how the métis were going "to strike a blow to gain their rights."[58]   He talked about his return from Montana and about the many petitions that had been sent to the government.   He declared that he could, if he so desired, bring hordes of half-breeds and Indians from the United States to support him.   He also talked about reforming the government and filling it with "God-fearing men," and about opening the west to various races, Poles, Bavarians, Italians, Germans, Irish and others.   But he could wait no longer for the federal government.   "The time had come now," said Riel, ". . . to rule this country or perish in the attempt."[59]

Continuing towards Batoche, Riel and his supporters—there were some sixty to seventy with him—stopped at a small store belonging to the Kerr brothers.   By this time Riel was clearly under the influence of a strong emotional excitement, a combination of fear, anger and desire for revenge.   He had just learned that Lawrence Clarke, while travelling from Regina to Prince Albert, had told a group of métis, including Napoléon Nault and Michel Dumas, who had asked him for news about the government's plans with regard to redressing their grievances, that the answer was on the way, in the form of 500 Mounted Police who would suppress the whole half-breed agitation.[60] Either Clarke was guilty of deliberate exaggeration—he was obviously referring to Irvine's force—or he was misunderstood by the métis who themselves exaggerated his remarks. However, the credulous métis believed the worst and hurried to tell the terrible news to Riel. Thus, when the shouting, angry mob reached Kerr's store and found several government officials there, including the Indian agent from Fort Carlton and his interpreter, they took them prisoners,[61] and hurried with them towards Batoche. When the métis reached St. Anthony's, Riel rushed to the door of the presbytery to ask Moulin for the use of the church for a meeting. Moulin refused to allow the building to be used for secular purposes whose object he feared, and cried out against Riel's forthright course in taking possession of the church regardless of his protests. Riel merely brushed the priest aside. "Look at him," he said, "he is a Protestant!"[62] Then turning to his followers, Riel shouted "Rome is fallen." When Moulin stood his ground and accused him of heresy, Riel, furious at the priest's opposition, cried, "Take him away! take him away!"[63] With his supporters he took over the church and turned to the serious business of getting their approval to form a provisional government; he had done the same thing at St. Norbert years before, but at that time he had the blessing of the priest. "Providence," he told them, "which has foreseen this miraculous movement, has prepared this church to serve as our stronghold. St. Anthony's is going to become celebrated in history as the birthplace of the emancipation of the North-West."[64]

The métis did not remain long at St. Anthony's. They hurried on towards Batoche, taking their prisoners with them. When they reached the Walters and Baker store, Riel entered and said to the proprietor, "Well, Mr. Walters, it has commenced." Then he demanded all the arms and ammunition that Walters had in his possession. Walters would not hand them over; he wanted to be paid for them. Riel promised that, if he succeeded in his plans, he would be able to pay for everything; if he failed, the federal government would pay for anything he had taken. "It would be all right either way," Riel assured Walters. When Walters remained obdurate, Riel's men simply helped themselves and made the hapless storekeeper a prisoner.[65] The prisoners were then placed upstairs under guard, and Riel and Dumont despatched parties of men to cut the telegraph line to Prince Albert. All these provocative actions were the work of an organized and aggressive minority. It is doubtful if very many métis in the District of Lorne knew what was happening. If they did know of it, they thought not in terms of rebellion but in terms of a threatening demonstration to give dramatic emphasis to their point of view.

Meanwhile Louis Riel, with W. H. Jackson and several métis, continued their ride to St. Laurent. Since the announcement of his conversion, Jackson had remained with Riel, completely under the spell of Riel's personality. Jackson was in no sense a prisoner, and he wrote to his mother giving his reasons for adopting his new faith, inviting his friends to come and see him, and announcing his intention of remaining at Batoche "at least until after my admission to the Church."[66] It was about ten o'clock when they reached Fourmond's presbytery. By this time Riel was in a state of exaltation. "A Provisional Government has been established," he told Fourmond, "we already have five prisoners. Old Rome has fallen. There is a new Pope in the person of Mgr. Bourget. You will be the first priest of the new religion and henceforth you will obey me." "Never," replied the priest. But Riel was in no mood to tolerate opposition; he threatened Fourmond and the other priests who were present, "If you do not obey, your churches will remain, perhaps, but they will be empty."[67] Poor Fourmond scarcely knew what to do. All he could think to do to quiet Riel was to proceed with Jackson's baptism, in spite of the fact that it was to have been the highlight of the ceremonies on the morrow. Accordingly Fourmond performed the baptism, and Riel, his belligerency evaporating almost as quickly as it had developed, signed the register with the name, "Louis 'David' Riel."[68]

Meanwhile men were gathering at Batoche. Many of them came in answer to the appeal to witness Jackson's baptism; others came to protect their leader from the threat of arrest which appeared to hang over his head ever since Clarke had uttered his careless threats on the 17th. There was, therefore, a large number of armed métis—many of them carried only shot guns—at Batoche on the 19th. It was the final day of the novena. At St. Laurent the congregation was composed largely of women whom Father Fourmond urged to say their rosaries daily during the threatening state of affairs in the settlement. At St. Anthony's, Father Moulin celebrated Mass and urged calmness and caution upon those who were present. But neither Riel nor Dumont were interested in Moulin and his ineffective sermonizing. They were determined to push forward with their plans. On the 19th, they formed the Provisional Government about which they had talked at Moulin's church the previous day. There was no election. Riel and Dumont picked the officers, and as they were named they were approved by the

Louis Riel, about 1884

Charles Nolin

shouting mob of métis.   Pierre Parenteau was chosen president, Philippe
Garnot became secretary, and Gabriel Dumont was chosen Adjutant-
General.   Those who were named as councillors included Baptiste
Boyer, Donald Ross, Damase Carrière, Ambroise Jobin, Norbert
Delorme, Moïse Ouellette, Baptiste Parenteau, David Tourond, Pierre
Gariépy, Maxime Lépine, Albert Monkman and Baptiste Boucher.
Riel remained aloof.   To be a member of the council did not fit his role
as prophet.   But he did make his own special contribution by giving the
new body a name.   Each man was called an *exovede*, and the council
itself the *Exovedate*.   Both words were synthetic Latin by construction
and meant "those picked from the flock."[69]
    Riel had acted with initiative, albeit with precipitation and without
considering the consequences.   He believed in his star and believed, too,
that with his Provisional Government and his prisoners—hostages he
called them—he could force the hands of Sir John A. Macdonald as he had
done in 1870.   But he felt that his future success, like that of the past,
would depend on his maintaining complete unanimity among his own
people, and upon his receiving the backing of the English-speaking half-
breeds.   Above all, he could tolerate no traitors among the métis, no
fouling of his own nest with treason.   However on March 19 he did not
have the unanimity that he felt to be essential.   And he knew it.

III

If Riel had not achieved the solidarity in Saskatchewan that he had
achieved in Manitoba, it was largely because of his rupture with the
Catholic Church.   Despite the enthusiasms of Fourmond, Riel had
never convinced the stronger-minded and more influential members of
the clergy that they should give him their unqualified support.   His
heterodoxy had alarmed them, and the drift towards violence frightened
them.   These alarms and fears were communicated to their parishioners.
The religious sentiments of the métis, and their traditional acceptance
of the moral direction of the missionaries, could not be erased completely
from their minds, even though their hearts responded to Riel's appeal to
their métis blood and to their sense of nationalism.   Always in the background there remained the old attachment to the church, causing doubts
and sapping the strength of their enthusiasm for Riel and his policy of
direct action.   This inner conflict between their admiration for Riel and
their loyalty to their church not only confused many of the métis, it did
much to weaken the unity that was essential for Riel's success in the
spring of 1885.
    It was the person of Charles Nolin around whom the Catholic clergy
hoped to gather a group of "loyal" métis.   Nolin had been one of the

more belligerent promoters of the North-West Movement, but he had been won over to a pacific attitude as a result of pressure from Father André. Nolin had been the Church's instrument in applying a brake to Riel's headlong course towards an armed rising when he put forward the suggestion of a novena in the early part of March. The clergy must have appreciated the fact that Nolin lacked Riel's personal magnetism. But there was always the chance that his prestige as a one-time provincial cabinet minister and his piety and submission might attract a sufficient number of métis to save the New Nation from the catastrophe which Grandin and André feared would be the result if a recourse were had to rebellion. On March 15, Nolin and the clergy agreed that a division must be made in the métis ranks; and on the 16th, Nolin solicited the help of William Boyer in this effort. Riel was well aware of Nolin's defection and felt that he had no choice but to strike a blow at his clerical enemies by seizing Nolin as a prisoner. Accordingly, no sooner was the novena ended and the Provisional Government proclaimed, than Nolin was arrested and brought up for trial along with Louis Marion and William Boyer, two other métis who had refused to take up arms at Riel's request.[70] This was the first task to which the Exovedate addressed itself after its formation on the 19th. The trial itself was brief and Nolin, as the ringleader of the opposition, was sentenced to death. According to Philippe Garnot, Riel "made a long speech accusing Ch. Nolin of treason and said that an example was necessary and that it was essential that Nolin should be condemned to death."[71] Riel, however, did not press for an immediate execution of sentence; he knew his man, and he wanted to leave a way open to force the hands of the clergy by granting Nolin his life in return for clerical approval, or at least clerical neutrality during the days to follow. Nolin, badly frightened and encouraged by Lépine, made his submission and agreed to support Riel. So, too, did Louis Marion. Boyer was discharged.[72]

Riel's policy of intimidation had the effect of removing the obvious opposition and of defeating the clergy's effort to build up a "loyalist" resistance. But it did no more than restore the appearance of solidarity to the North-West Movement among the métis. There were still others who wished to remain aloof. Throughout the rebellion, threats, arrests and trials had to be resorted to by the Exovedate to encourage the hesitant and prod the reluctant.[73] Even so there were some métis, among them even a relative of Gabriel Dumont, who took a firm stand against armed violence.[74] There were many others, such as Maxime Lépine and Philippe Garnot, who stated later, and with sincerity, that they had never contemplated war against Canada; that they had thought only in terms of an armed demonstration. Lépine declared that it had always been his hope that Riel would accept a seat in the Council of the North-West Territories and work there on behalf of the métis and the half-breeds.[75]

After securing the professed if scarcely enthusiastic adherence of Nolin, the Exovedate turned its attention to the question of what to do next. The step to follow might have been predicted by any person familiar with the events of 1869/70. There was no strong strategic centre in the District of Lorne similar to Fort Garry in Assiniboia; but there was Fort Carlton, the Hudson's Bay Company post, not far away on the south bank of the North Saskatchewan River. It was useless from the standpoint of military defence, if only because it was open and exposed to the high ground to the east; but it was a depot with various supplies which Dumont would need to maintain his forces in the field, whether there was to be any fighting or not. Riel, however, wanted to seize Fort Carlton without fighting. He did not want to become involved in bloodshed; for casualties would do more than anything else to weaken his support. The more outspoken and aggressive among his followers, such as Gabriel Dumont, were anxious to enlist the Indians as soon as possible, but Riel still believed that the Prime Minister, Sir John A. Macdonald, would yield to the threat of war rather than risk its possibility. In the end a compromise was agreed upon. A motion by Boucher, seconded by Carrière, was adopted by the Exovedate that "we desire to effect the capture of the fort without spilling any blood, and the greater our force the more certain of attaining our object, but in case we are compelled to fight, justice compels that we should take up arms. . . ."[76]

Meanwhile Superintendent Crozier, having been warned of developments at Batoche and St. Laurent by Father Paquette,[77] had made preparations to resist an attack upon Fort Carlton. He had appealed to the civilians in Prince Albert to strengthen his small garrison of mounted policemen. In 1879, during the months Sitting Bull's Sioux Indians were encamped in the southern Territories, two volunteer companies had been organized in Prince Albert by Colonel Osborne Smith, the officer commanding the militia in Winnipeg.[78] These companies were subsequently disbanded; but Crozier asked one of the former officers, Captain H. S. Moore, to be prepared to reorganize the force and come to his assistance. Several companies were then formed, one of which, under Moore himself, set out for Fort Carlton on March 20.[79]

Unwilling to precipitate hostilities—if only because he knew that Commissioner Irvine was marching north with police reinforcements—Crozier agreed to let Thomas McKay, a well-known Scottish half-breed who was a member of Moore's volunteers, go with a local merchant, Hillyard Mitchell, to talk to Riel. Mitchell had already spoken to Riel at Batoche on March 19 and had listened to the métis leader while he had ranted about his own grievances and those of the métis. He heard Riel boast that he would bring Sir John A. Macdonald to his knees.[80] Mitchell claimed that he had tried to reason with Riel, but to little effect; Riel declared that he was determined to gain possession of Fort Carlton. On March 21, McKay and Mitchell set out on their mission of peace. As they approached the Walters and Baker store they were halted by métis sentries. Then, with Gariépy acting as their guide, they continued to Riel's headquarters at Norbert Delorme's house, a small building not far from St. Anthony's church. Here the Exovedate was in council session. Mitchell introduced McKay to Riel. When McKay commented on the "great excitement," Riel replied, "there is no excitement at all; it was simply that the people were trying to redress their grievances, as they had asked repeatedly for their rights, that they had decided to make a demonstration." McKay ventured to suggest that it was "a dangerous thing to resort to arms." But Riel merely answered that he had been waiting "fifteen long years" and that his people "had been imposed upon" and that "it was time now, after they had waited patiently, that their rights should be given." Then Riel turned on McKay and accused him, as a half-breed, of failing to do anything to forward the rights of his own people. From a quiet and polite man, he became an angry, excited demagogue, shouting at McKay in a loud voice, "You don't know what we are after—it is blood, blood, we want blood; it is a war of extermination, everybody that is against us is to be driven out of the country. There are two curses in this country—the Government and the Hudson's Bay Company."[81] In his anger Riel talked of arresting McKay and of placing him on trial for his life. Then he regained control of himself, and his temper moderated. He apologized and told McKay that he was "sorry" McKay "was against him, that he would be glad to have me with them, and that it was not too late to join them yet."[82] No, he would not go and discuss the situation with Crozier; he was afraid he would be taken prisoner. But he would send two of his men to carry a message to the Superintendent of the Mounted Police at Fort Carlton.

The two men selected to bear Riel's despatch were Nolin and Lépine. They were given a letter which Riel addressed to "Major" Crozier, in which he demanded the unconditional surrender of Fort Carlton. In return he promised to set Crozier and his men free "on your parole of honour to keep the peace." Should Crozier refuse to surrender, the police would be attacked "when to-morrow, the Lord's Day, is over." Once the shooting started, there would begin "a war of extermination upon all those who have shown themselves hostile to our rights."

"Major, we respect you," Riel's letter continued. "Let the cause of humanity be a consolation to you for the reverses which the governmental misconduct has brought upon you." The postscript to this amazing document was addressed to Nolin and Lépine. It said:

If Major Crozier accedes to the conditions of surrender, let him use the following formula, and no other: "Because I love my neighbour as myself, for the sake of God, and to prevent bloodshed, and principally the war of extermination which threatens the country, I agree to the above conditions of surrender." If the Major uses this formula and signs it, inform him that we will receive him and his men, Monday.[83]

While he was engaged in negotiations with Crozier, Riel was also endeavouring to secure the adhesion of the English-speaking half-breeds. This he needed almost as much as he required solidarity among the French métis. He was very anxious about the English half-breed attitude towards his plans to take Fort Carlton. The English half-breeds were none too pleased with the new developments. They had not bargained for rebellion. They were disturbed at the turn that events had taken, and they did not look with approval on any recourse to violent methods. At the same time, they could scarcely be expected to take up arms against Riel and engage in a fratricidal war. Accordingly, when news reached the English half-breed communities lying between St. Laurent and Prince Albert that the whites were mustering militia in Prince Albert and that the French métis were under arms at Batoche, the English-speaking half-breeds gathered hurriedly at their old meeting place at the Lindsay School. The meeting took place on March 20 under the chairmanship of Thomas Scott. The decision taken by those who attended was to send a delegation comprising Scott, Hugh Ross, and William Paquin to Batoche "to see what steps might be taken for the settlers . . . to protect themselves."[84] There was no hostility towards Riel or enthusiasm for the government; when the meeting closed the members broke up with cheers for the delegates and cheers for the métis leader.[85]

On March 21, the day following, the same day that McKay and Mitchell went to see Riel, the English half-breed delegation went to Batoche. The delegation was well received by Riel who greeted Scott with, "I hope you have come to make peace to save bloodshed." Riel reminded Scott that the answer to their petitions had been an increased force of Mounted Police to suppress the agitation—"to wipe them out" were Riel's words.[86] But when the métis leader asked the English half-breeds to join him, the latter professed their opposition to an armed rising and their desire to remain neutral.[87]

Neutrality was not the role Riel had in mind for his English-speaking supporters. He wanted their active co-operation and their actual participation in his policy of armed demonstration. Above all, he wanted their aid in the capture of Fort Carlton. Neutrality would be of greater assistance to Crozier than to Riel; it would deprive the latter of the men he required, whereas Crozier would have little need of further manpower once Irvine had reached Prince Albert and the Canadian militia had been mustered. Accordingly Riel wrote a letter for Scott and his companions to take back to their constituents. In the letter he reminded them of the years of indifference on the part of Ottawa, the years of neglect; of the high-handed way the government had answered their requests; of the "Government spoliation and usurpation of the rights and liberties of all classes of men, except their resident oppressors, the Hudson's Bay Company, and the land speculators." "Let us all be firm in the support of right," he pleaded, "humane and courageous, if in him to fight, just and equitable in our views; thus God and man will be with us, and we will be successful."[88]

On the 22nd there were meetings of the English settlers both at the Ridge and at St. Catherine's. Crozier was anxious to prevent the half-breeds from going over to Riel's side, and he asked the Reverend Edward Matheson, a native of Kildonan and Anglican priest at Prince Albert, to attend the meetings and use his influence against Riel.[89] Scott was present at both meetings; he read Riel's letter and urged those present to press for the return of the militia to Prince Albert and the laying down of arms by settlers and half-breeds. If there was to be any fighting, why not let the Mounted Police and the métis do it? The role of the English half-breeds, Scott argued, should be to keep the Indians quiet and avoid taking sides in the dispute. Neutrality was the course that suited the English half-breeds best; and it was a course in which Matheson was obliged to acquiesce. Yet there was no doubting the fact that the half-breeds felt there was much to be said for Riel. As one of them put it, the English half-breeds "sympathized very strongly with the French half-breeds, as being acquainted with them and many of them near relations."[90] The outcome of the meetings of the 22nd was, therefore, the adoption of a series of resolutions which stated that "the members of this meeting continue to sympathize, as they have always done, with the French half-breeds in their desire to obtain their legal rights, by all constitutional means," but expressed disapproval "of the resort to arms or the rising of the Indians and wish to remain neutral."[91]

Riel knew perfectly well that neutrality on the part of the English-speaking half-breeds would greatly weaken his own position. Yet he would have to move carefully; he could not gain their support by berating or threatening them. The policy he had used against Nolin could not be used against Scott. He would have to plead and cajole. So Riel wrote again, thanking the half-breeds for their sympathy and agreeing that "situated as you are, it is difficult for you to approve immediately of our bold but just uprising." Nevertheless, he reminded them once more of the iniquities of Ottawa and the danger of an Indian war. Again he appealed to the bond of blood: "Gentlemen, please do not remain neutral. For the love of God help us to save the Saskatchewan. . . . If we are well united our union will cause the Police to come out of Carlton as the hen's heat causes the chicken to come out of the shell. A strong union between the French and English half-breeds is the only guarantee that there will be no bloodshed."[92]

Again the English half-breeds met in council. As before, the meeting was at the Lindsay School. Again the Reverend Edward Matheson and William Craig did what they could to steer the meeting in the direction that would give the greatest comfort to Crozier. Again the members expressed their warm sympathy for Riel and the métis. And again they decided in favour of neutrality, little realizing what they were doing to Riel. Scott wrote to Riel, "At a meeting held at the Lindsay School tonight, which was largely attended, the voice of every man was with you, and we have taken steps which I think will have a tendency to stop bloodshed and hasten a treaty. We will communicate with you inside of forty-eight hours after you get this. Notify us of any step, if any is liable to take place."[93]

The nature of Scott's plans revealed themselves the following day when another meeting was held. This was on March 24. A large number of settlers turned out, and Charles Nolin and Albert Monkman arrived with a band of twenty métis horsemen for the purposes of enrolling recruits if any could be found.[94] Scott presided over the meeting and produced a petition he had drafted earlier which already bore a number of signatures. This document urged the government to take prompt steps to redress the grievances of the people of the North-West, offering as the only choices open to the authorities a treaty with the métis and half-breeds or a war with them.[95] The petition was circulated among those present, and when the meeting broke up there were no fewer than 455 signatures appended to it. It was unlikely that the idea of another petition would appeal very much to Riel, now that he had committed himself to a more violent course of action; but to the English half-breeds there was the hope, faint as it might seem, that the obvious community of interests between the English half-breeds and the métis, and the large number of signatures on the petition, would impress

Lieutenant-Governor Dewdney, perhaps even Sir John A. Macdonald. And while there was such a hope, there should be no hasty action which would lead to bloodshed.   In the hope of deterring Louis from moving too quickly, James Isbister and George Sanderson were asked to take a copy of the petition to Batoche.   At the same time, William Miller and Charles Adams were given another copy to take to Superintendent Crozier.[96]

Unfortunately the petition was barren of results.   Before the delegations could get either to Batoche or to Fort Carlton, Crozier and Dumont met near Duck Lake on March 26.   Shots were fired; the snow was spotted with the bodies of policemen and métis alike.   The bloodshed, which the English half-breeds feared, and which Riel had threatened, but really did not want, had begun.

CHAPTER 17

The North-West Rebellion

THE ENGAGEMENT at Duck Lake on March 26, 1885, was a chance encounter and not a premeditated one. It was not planned beforehand, either by Louis Riel or by Superintendent Crozier. The Exovedate had, admittedly, talked about occupying Fort Carlton, but no preparations had been made for doing so, other than sending Nolin and Lépine to demand Crozier's surrender on March 21. And Crozier, while refusing to surrender, had done no more than sit firm at Carlton awaiting the arrival of his superior officer, Colonel A. G. Irvine, who was expected on March 26 with a reinforcement of 100 men. Each side seemed to be waiting for the other to make the first move.

The event that precipitated the trouble was Crozier's decision, on March 25, to send a detachment of men under Sergeant Stewart and Thomas McKay to get "some provisions and flour" from Stobart and Eden's store at Duck Lake.[1] It does not seem to have entered into his calculations that the métis might attempt to stop him. In the early hours of the morning of the 26th, with a handful of Mounted Policemen and a number of sleighs, Stewart set out to fulfil his mission. Nearing Duck Lake he encountered a group of métis. There was a certain amount of shoving, a great deal of shouting of threats and much brandishing of rifles. Gabriel Dumont accused McKay of betraying his own race by supporting the Mounted Police; some métis even attempted to seize the bridles of the police horses; but there was no shooting. In the end Stewart decided nothing was to be gained by trying to force the issue, so he and his men turned about and made their way back to Fort Carlton. It was a journey of about fourteen miles. As they neared the gates of the fort, they could see Crozier mustering his men and preparing to march to their relief.

The Mounted Police Superintendent had been pushed into taking action both by his own men and by the Prince Albert Volunteers. They had learned from a scout whom Stewart had sent to Crozier that the métis had intercepted the police, and they wondered at Crozier's hesitation whether he should attempt to enforce the majesty of the law or await the arrival of Irvine. The latter would have been the wiser

315

course, particularly after Stewart's safe return to Carlton.   But Crozier himself was an impatient man.   He felt all too keenly any slight to "the Force," and he yielded to the prodding of Lawrence Clarke and others to put the métis in their place.   Vague mutterings of cowardice implied a charge no man of Crozier's temperament could tolerate.   The "fall-in" was sounded, every available team was harnessed, the seven-pounder muzzle-loading gun recently brought from Battleford was placed on a sleigh, and the little force, joined by Stewart's detachment, set out for Duck Lake.   Later Commissioner Irvine wrote critically that Crozier's "better judgement was overruled by the impetuosity displayed both by the police and volunteers."[2]

The métis, too, had been interested in the supplies at Duck Lake. Dumont had partially ransacked Stobart's store on the 25th and was still hovering about the neighbourhood on the 26th.   During the night he had captured two volunteers, who had been posting Crozier's proclamation promising protection to any métis who had been forced into rebellion and was willing to give himself up;[3] and on the morning of the 26th, he encountered Stewart's party while the latter was still several miles from its destination.   When Stewart finally turned around, Dumont was elated.   Word was sent to Batoche, and shortly afterwards Riel himself arrived at Duck Lake with a number of armed métis and several Indians from the Beardy and One Arrow reserves.   With him he brought his prisoners who, like those taken by Dumont, were now confined in Hillyard Mitchell's house.[4]   In all, about 300 métis collected at Duck Lake.[5]   Early in the afternoon—Dumont says the métis had scarcely let their horses out to eat—a startled shout was heard, "Here come the police!"[6]   Immediately there was a scramble and every man grabbed his gun and rushed to find his horse.   Within a few minutes there was a wild dash westwards along the Carlton trail.

It was not Gabriel Dumont's intention to meet Superintendent Crozier's Mounted Police and volunteers in a headlong charge.   This was not the way the métis or the Indians fought in Western Canada. Instead, as soon as Dumont's men reached a suitable place in which they could find cover, they dismounted, tethered their horses and crept forward, protected by low ground on each side of the road and by the trees and shrubs in the vicinity.   Crozier's scouts, however, observed the métis movement and hurried back to inform the police commander. Crozier therefore ordered his own men to halt and to form a barricade across the road with their wagons.   Believing that the métis wished to parley, he went forward with his interpreter, an English half-breed, Joseph McKay, to talk with an Indian and Isidore Dumont, Gabriel's brother, who approached along the roadway.   As the parley began, the

Indian made a grab for the interpreter's rifle. McKay struggled with his assailant, attempting to keep the Indian between himself and Dumont who was carrying a rifle. Crozier, aware of the fact that the métis were trying to circle his own force, and convinced that the parley was a waste of time, gave the order to fire. McKay therefore whipped a pistol from his belt, shot the Indian and, with a quick movement, turned his gun upon Isidore Dumont before Dumont could make use of his own weapon. Then, with Crozier, McKay rushed back to the barricade.[7] Immediately Louis Riel, who had watched the parley from horseback, shouted orders to the métis, in the name of the Father, Son and Holy Ghost, to return the fire of the police.[8] The shooting became general. Blood trickled down Crozier's face when he was grazed by one of the first métis shots.

Despite the fact that Crozier's men had unlimbered their little cannon and brought it into action, it gave them no advantage over their opponents. The métis enjoyed a superiority both of numbers and of cover; and even if their weapons were generally inferior to those in the hands of Crozier's men, their position—in a log cabin on the one flank, and a wooded depression on the other—gave them a chance to pour a hot and well-directed fire into the crowded ranks of the red-coated police and the volunteers from Prince Albert. One of the Mounted Policemen wrote later:

We had a lively time of it for about one-half hour. The bullets fell like hail. We were catched in a nice trap and flanked on three sides. They were on our right, left, and in front of us. We were nearly as badly hemmed in as the noble six hundred. . . . When the battle started and we seen the position that the enemy had, and the box we were in there were not one of us expected to get back alive. Again I tell you that it was very unpleasant to hear the bullets rattling, trying hard to dodge them.[9]

For a while Crozier held his own, but he knew he was virtually at the mercy of his opponents. After thirty minutes of firing, he gave the order to retire. In spite of the appalling confusion of yelling men, plunging, terrified horses and tangled harness, the police and militia managed to hitch the horses to the wagons and to extricate themselves from what was a very critical position. The police delayed long enough to pick up their own casualties, but the dead militiamen were left behind in the snow.

What might have happened to Crozier's men had the métis mounted their horses and pursued the straggling column may be left to the imagination; but at the point when the retreat might have been transformed into an annihilation, Riel stayed his men. Louis had watched the battle from the back of his horse, grasping a large crucifix which he had taken from one of the churches in the métis settlement, and he had witnessed enough fighting. There had been, he declared, "already . . . too much bloodshed."[10] There had indeed. The little government force of ninety-nine men had lost twelve of its number killed, and another eleven were wounded, among them were a nephew of Sir Francis Hincks, at one time a Canadian Minister of Finance, a nephew of Joseph Howe, the Nova Scotian statesman, and a cousin of the Liberal party leader, Alexander Mackenzie. The métis lost five men, including Gabriel Dumont's brother, Isidore. Dumont himself was slightly wounded in the head.[11]

Returning with the victorious métis to Duck Lake, Riel assembled his men in two ranks and shouted, "Give three cheers, Hurrah for Gabriel Dumont! Thank God who gave you so valiant a leader."[12] While the bodies of the métis dead were being laid out in a nearby house, Riel accompanied a wounded prisoner to Mitchell's quarters where he turned him over to the care of the other prisoners. He seemed "elated at his victory," one of the prisoners said later, and he talked loudly about the half-breed claims, about the Canadians having no business in the country, which belonged to the métis and the Indians, and about "the new church" of which he was the founder.[13] Then he and his followers spent the rest of the day in prayer for the souls of those who had lost their lives in the fighting.[14]

The métis success at Duck Lake was even greater than Riel or Dumont immediately appreciated. Colonel Irvine, who reached Fort Carlton only minutes after Crozier's defeated column dragged its way through the gates of the stockade, decided that Fort Carlton was untenable from the military standpoint. Not only was it isolated from the nearest white settlement at Prince Albert, but it was dominated by the high ground behind it. Moreover, the Prince Albert Volunteers, who had marched out of the fort with such confidence, if not cockiness, were now alarmed about the fate of their families in Prince Albert, should there be a general Indian rising. They wanted to go home; they did not wish to remain at Fort Carlton fighting off a métis attack. Accordingly, on the night of March 27/28, Irvine and Crozier, with as many supplies as they could salvage, set out for Prince Albert. Some loose hay, scattered about the floor as the men were stuffing mattresses for the wounded, caught fire, and the walls were burning as the long train of police and civilian teams pulled up the steep hill and began the trek for Prince Albert.[15] Irvine placed his horsemen in advance and on the flanks to protect the column; but it is hardly likely that they would have been of much protection had Riel permitted Dumont to carry out the plan to ambush Crozier which Dumont had in mind. "We could have killed a lot of them," said Dumont, "but Riel, who was always restraining us, formally opposed the idea."[16]   Late in the afternoon of March 28, Irvine's column reached Prince Albert.   Here they found the inhabitants in a state of panic.   Here, too, they found Charles Nolin.   Nolin had been looking for a chance to desert the métis, and when Riel and Dumont dashed off to meet Crozier, Nolin seized a horse and cutter and fled to the north.   He had tried to persuade Maxime Lépine to join him.   But Lépine, although he would do nothing to stop Nolin, chose to remain with his own people.   To his chagrin, Nolin found himself looked upon with suspicion by the people of Prince Albert.   He was promptly placed in detention where he remained until the close of the rebellion.[17]

Several days later Riel and the métis decided to return to Batoche. They had surveyed the half-burned ruins of Fort Carlton and had ransacked the various buildings of Duck Lake.   They saw no reason for remaining at either place.   On March 31, the Exovedate met at Duck Lake, and on a motion by Dumont which was seconded by Lépine it was resolved to return to St. Anthony's, "there firmly to await the 315 police-men who are marching, it appears, against us."[18]   So they recrossed the South Saskatchewan River and took up their old quarters at Batoche.

Riel was now riding the crest of his popularity.   The métis had never expected so easy a victory.   Many of them had joined him with reluc-tance, or under pressure, and few of them—with the exception of a hard core of belligerents—had really wanted to fight against the Canadian government.   But they had fought and they had won.   Everything had seemed to work in their favour.   Who but God could have delivered Crozier into Dumont's hands at Duck Lake?   The métis faith in Riel's divine mission was more firmly established than ever.   Who would now challenge his claim to be a prophet?   Certainly not the members of the Exovedate who met in council and adopted the resolution:

That the Canadian half-breed Exovedate acknowledges Louis David Riel as a prophet in the service of Jesus Christ and Son of God and only Redeemer of the world; a prophet at the feet of Mary Immaculate, under the visible and most consoling safeguard of St. Joseph, the beloved patron of the half-breeds—the patron of the universal Church; as a prophet, the humble imitator in many things of St. John the Baptist, the glorious patron of the French Canadians and the French Canadian half-breeds.

The resolution was carried unanimously, although there was one doubting Thomas, Moïse Ouellette, who said "if after a time his views changed, he would record his vote."[19]   In his journal, that strange mixture of visions and fears which Riel kept during March and April, the métis leader wrote, "Oh Jesus, Mary, Joseph and John the Baptist, change the bad will of Moïse Ouellette; let him reject gracefully and willingly his Romish

propensities.   Pray God to nullify his heart and let him embrace entirely
the celestial reforms of Divine Worship and reject all those things that
the religion of Rome has inculcated in the hearts of all the nations of
the Globe."[20]

II

Despite the fact that blood had been shed at Duck Lake, Louis Riel still
believed there might be some active support for his movement from the
English-speaking half-breeds.   He hoped they might regard the unfortunate event as one forced on him by the Mounted Police.   His principal
difficulty for the moment was how to get in touch with any potential
supporters who had not yet joined his ranks.   However, on March 27,
the day after Duck Lake, one of the prisoners, Thomas Sanderson,
offered to carry a message to Superintendent Crozier asking him to come
and pick up the bodies of the dead volunteers who had been left behind
when Crozier's column had retreated to Fort Carlton.   Sanderson
promised to return "and give myself up again as a prisoner."[21]   To Riel
this seemed to offer an opportunity to communicate with those who had
backed the agitation, at least up to the formation of the Provisional
Government, and to place his case before them once more.

Accordingly, at Riel's request, the Exovedate was assembled, and a
formal motion was adopted to the effect that one of the prisoners should
be released to bear a message to Crozier, promising him safe conduct to
Duck Lake for the purpose of recovering the bodies of his soldiers; at the
same time, the Exovedate suggested that one of the physicians in Prince
Albert, Dr. Bain or Dr. Porter, might be asked to come to Batoche to
look after one of the wounded volunteers.[22]   Riel agreed.   He therefore
wrote a letter addressed to Crozier, which he handed to Sanderson, at the
same time asking Sanderson to "tell the people (the volunteers) that he
did not wish to fight them, that he wished them to remain neutral and
afterwards help him establish a government."[23]   The letter to Crozier
read, in part, as follows:

A calamity has fallen upon the country yesterday.   You are responsible
for it before God and man.   Your men cannot claim that their intentions
were peaceable since they were bringing along cannons.   And they fired
many shots first.   God has been pleased to grant us the victory; and as
our movement is to save our lives, our victory is good; and we offer it
to the Almighty.   Major, we are Christians in war as in peace.   We
write you in the name of God and of humanity to come and take away
your dead, whom we respect. . . .[24]

Then he went to see another prisoner, Harold Ross, and asked him if he
would get in touch with a doctor in Prince Albert.[25]

When Sanderson finally located Crozier, he found himself regarded with considerable suspicion. Crozier immediately arrested him as a spy or collaborator. However, the volunteers felt very bitter about the abandonment of their dead comrades and took Sanderson's assurances at their face value. They protested vigorously to Crozier and finally obtained Sanderson's release and permission for two settlers, William Drain and Thomas Jackson, to go to Duck Lake on their mission of mercy.[26] Jackson was particularly anxious to go because he wanted to see Riel. He was worried about his brother, of whom he had heard little since his baptism on March 18, and that little had suggested that William Henry was suffering from a mental breakdown. He hoped, if possible, to persuade Riel to allow him to take his brother back to Prince Albert with him.

Jackson's interviews with Riel did not, however, bring about William's return with his brother. Instead, Riel sought to use Thomas Jackson for his own purposes. He expressed "great sorrow" to Jackson at the blood which had been shed at Duck Lake and blamed the whole unfortunate business on the Mounted Police. He defended the métis part in the battle as a simple matter of self-defence, a right which belonged to any man when attacked. Then he asked Jackson if he would carry a letter to the people of Prince Albert and call a meeting of the inhabitants to discuss it. Jackson felt obliged to agree, and Riel wrote his letter. It was an appeal to his erstwhile sympathizers for their continued help and assistance.

If the Police could be isolated from the people of Prince Albert, we would make them surrender easily enough, I think, we would keep them as hostages, until we have a fair treaty with the Dominion. Join us without endorsing our taking up arms, if you feel too much repugnance to do it, but send us delegates to meet ours. We will discuss the conditions of our entering into Confederation as a province.

It was almost as if he was living in the world of 1870! The letter continued:

The emigrants as well as the natives have a clear case against the Hudson's Bay Company. Do not strengthen her monstrous monopoly by helping along her shrewd miserable schemes, at the present crisis. If you leave the H.B. Company and the Mounted Police to fight their own disputes, you will see how far we will go to uproot her influence from the Saskatchewan. Let us unite on those interests which are common to the English and French half-breeds, and to the emigrants and we will celebrate our peace and our success on the 24th of May.

Then came a threat, a threat of American intervention—was his mind returning to O'Donoghue and the Fenians? "But if we cannot unite, the struggle will grow. Indians will come in from all quarters, and many people will cross the line early in the Spring, and perhaps our difficulties will end on an American fourth of July."[27]

Jackson took the letter with him, but he did not make it public. He even claimed at Riel's trial that he had destroyed it.[28] Nor did he call a meeting to discuss neutrality or co-operation with the métis. He knew that his own position was suspect and that he would have to walk warily in view of the participation of his family in the activities of the Settlers' Union.

Several days later, Jackson proposed to return to Batoche. On April 1, Toussaint Lussier, a métis who had deserted Riel, told him that William Jackson's mental condition was becoming worse. Thomas Jackson therefore asked Irvine for permission to go to the métis settlement to try, once more, to convince Riel to let his brother go. Irvine at first refused—he wondered if Jackson was acting as Riel's spy—but he finally yielded to the tearful solicitations of Jackson's mother. Thomas then hurried, first to Carlton, then to Duck Lake and finally to Batoche. The métis made no effort to interfere with him; after all they had been long aware of the sympathy of the Jacksons for the métis movement. But Riel had grown suspicious. Perhaps Thomas Jackson was Irvine's spy. He would not agree to any proposal that the younger Jackson should leave the métis settlement—there was, in fact, no evidence to show that William Henry had any desire to do so; nor would he allow Thomas Jackson himself to go back to Prince Albert. "Mr. Jackson is too neutral to be allowed to go," said Riel to the members of his council. He did not place Thomas under close confinement until May 3; but he did keep him under watch and would not allow him to leave Batoche or to communicate with any of the prisoners.[29]

III

By this time Riel had pretty well given up hope of any assistance from the whites and English half-breeds who had supported the agitation at an earlier period. However events did suggest that he might obtain help of an active kind from the Indians. The red men were familiar with Louis's sympathy for them. They had listened to him expound his idea of a half-breed Indian confederacy in the North-West when he had been encamped in Montana with Ambroise Lépine in 1879.[30] They had sought him out in 1884, when he returned to the Saskatchewan, and asked his advice as to how best to obtain redress of their grievances.[31] In January, 1885, Superintendent Crozier had written to the Indian Commissioner that although there was no evidence of any definite understanding between the Indians and the métis, nevertheless there were "undoubtedly bands and individuals among other bands who look to

Riel and the half-breeds as their champions, and who, I think have promised to join or act with them as they bid."[32] There is no doubt, too, that Riel was anxious to maintain touch with the Indians, and that métis runners to various Indian bands did what they could to build up Riel's prestige, to convince the Indians what they themselves had come to believe, that Riel was a prophet and that he was in communication with heaven.

Thus, when word circulated among the Indians that the métis, under Riel's leadership, had actually met and defeated the Mounted Police in battle, the more belligerent tribesmen were ready to follow the métis example. At Battleford, Indians from the Poundmaker and Little Pine reserves broke into the stores and buildings in the town, pillaging them and driving the terrified white inhabitants into the shelter of the Mounted Police stockade. The Stonies of the Eagle Hills killed their farm instructor and established a soldiers' lodge in anticipation of setting out on the warpath. Farther west, up the North Saskatchewan River, Big Bear's Crees, led by the war chief, Wandering Spirit, murdered the Indian agent and several white men including two priests at Frog Lake, and then started off to take Fort Pitt. Elsewhere, at the Bears' Hills, at Lac la Biche and at Green Lake, excited Indians attacked government stores and spread terror throughout the white settlements of the North-West Territories.[33]

It was to these Indians and the various bands of métis who were settled along the North Saskatchewan and in the Qu'Appelle valleys that Riel sent his messengers during the month of April, 1885. To all of them he gave an account of the métis success at Duck Lake, and from all of them he requested help and assistance. "We have the pleasure to let you know that on the 26th of last month, God has given us a victory over the Mounted Police," he wrote to the French half-breeds of Qu'Appelle, "Yourselves, dear relatives, be courageous; do what you can. If it is not done yet, take the stores, the provisions, the ammunition."[34] To the Indians and métis at Battleford he wrote, "The police have attacked us, we met them and God gave us the victory. . . . Bless God with us for the success he has kindly granted us. Rise: face the enemy, and if you can do so, take Battleford—destroy it—save all the goods and provisions and come to us."[35] To the métis farther west he wrote in a similar vein:

Be ready for everything. Take the Indians with you. Gather them from every side. Take all the ammunition you can, whatsoever storehouses it may be in. Murmur, growl, and threaten. Stir up the Indians. Render the police of Fort Pitt and Battleford powerless. . . . Implore St. Joseph, for he is powerful with God. Commend yourselves to the powerful intercession of St. John the Baptist, the glorious patron of the Canadians and half-breeds."[36]

If Riel anticipated that the intervention of the Indians would strengthen his case in Canada, he must have been sadly disappointed. The prospect of an Indian war might terrify the local white settlers, but it merely hardened the will of the Canadians to fight. All over Canada there were expressions of horror and anger, of a determination to have done with Riel and all his works. That there might possibly be mitigating circumstances, that both the métis and the Indians might have legitimate grievances crying for remedy, was overlooked in the demand for vengeance against those who had slaughtered white men in cold blood. Riel might hopefully believe that the Canadian government would answer the threat of an Indian war by sending commissioners as they had done in 1870; but Canadians knew that troops rather than emissaries would be sent to the North-West in 1885.

Even before the news of Duck Lake had reached Ottawa, the Canadian Prime Minister had decided that force should be used to suppress the incipient rising in the North-West. On March 19, Irvine had been ordered to send reinforcements to strengthen the Mounted Police in the Saskatchewan valley; and on March 23, Major-General Middleton, the General Officer Commanding the Canadian Militia, had been ordered to proceed to Winnipeg. Instructions were also issued for the mobilization of various Canadian militia units; and on March 25, a company of the 90th Winnipeg Rifles set out for Troy. Then came the word of Riel's victory over the Mounted Police. What Sir John A. Macdonald had at first regarded simply as a riot[37] was taking on the proportions of an armed rebellion, and troops from almost every province of the country were mustered to form Canada's first truly national army.[38] The citizen soldiers were clamouring to be enrolled;[39] and before the rising in the North-West was at an end, almost 8,000 Canadians had enlisted for active service against the métis and the Indians.

General Middleton's plan of campaign was simple in the extreme. He would assemble a force at Fort Qu'Appelle and then move north directly against Riel's headquarters at Batoche. At the same time, another force under the command of Major-General T. B. Strange would march from Calgary to Edmonton and then strike Big Bear in the rear by moving eastwards along the North Saskatchewan River. As soon as Middleton had taken Batoche, the two columns would join forces to strike at the Indian threat from Poundmaker and his allies. For the present, Middleton was not disposed to pay much attention to Battleford. He merely ordered Lieutenant-Colonel Herchmer to hurry north with a handful of Mounted Police from Regina. But Herchmer knew his force would in no way intimidate the Crees and Stonies who were threatening Battleford, and he did not carry out his orders. Subsequently Middleton modified his plan and ordered a third column of troops to be formed under the command of Lieutenant-Colonel William Otter and sent to relieve the pressure on the people cooped up in the Mounted Police barracks on the Battle River.

The commanding general was a ponderous man, both physically and mentally. Like so many regular British officers, he had little faith either in the efficiency or the fighting qualities of his citizen soldiers. He was also a cautious man, and he moved slowly with great deliberation. After assembling a force comprising a total strength of 402 men and a wagon train of 120 vehicles,[40] he set out from Fort Qu'Appelle on April 6. The weather was cold, and there was a strong wind blowing, with flurries of sleet and hail. "I am afraid the dress of my Aide-de-camp and myself would have astonished if not horrified an Aldershot General and his Aide-de-camp," the general wrote in his account of the campaign. "We were both clad in short buffalo skin coats, staff pantaloons, fur service caps, and long English shooting boots, with jack spurs. Swords were worn under, and revolvers over, our coats. The men and officers were in the regular British uniform, supplemented with snow boots, fur caps and gloves, and most of them with hideous red comforters round their necks."[41] By April 13, the troops had reached Humboldt. A week later they were at Clarke's Crossing on the South Saskatchewan River. They had covered over 180 miles in two weeks and were now only 35 miles from Batoche. Having received reinforcements while on the way, Middleton's column now numbered 800 men.

For some reason—the explanation offered by Middleton that Riel had men on both sides of the river scarcely seems adequate—the general now divided his force. He sent almost half his troops to the west side of the river under the command of Lord Melgund, his Chief-of-Staff. The crossing was a laborious matter since there were only two cable ferries available to move both men and horses. On April 23, the two columns, separated from each other by the South Saskatchewan, and incapable of supporting or reinforcing each other except by means of a scow, or even of communicating with each other except by flag signals or bugles, moved slowly downstream. They were now close to the métis country. The next day they reached Dumont's Crossing but made no effort to re-unite. Not far distant lay a small "nasty" ravine through which the road leading to Batoche descended. With a force of scouts and his two aides, Middleton rode ahead to reconnoitre. As he approached the ravine several shots rang out. "We saw a party of about fifty mounted men close to a bluff about 500 yards to our left, who fired a volley at us which, luckily, were aimed too high and rattled overhead among the trees," Middleton wrote.[42] Here, at Fish Creek, or Tourond's Crossing as the métis called it, where the French half-breeds had gathered to greet Riel on his return from Montana the year before, was the place where Dumont and his men had elected to stand and fight against Riel's enemies.

IV

When Riel returned to Batoche from Fort Carlton and Duck Lake, he felt his first task was to strengthen his own position among the métis. For the moment, at least, there appeared to be no danger of another attack from Crozier, and if the Canadian government was disposed to negotiate, it would be best to have a solid body of support behind him. The flight of Nolin had removed Riel's principal opponent among the métis. Riel was not sorry to see him go, particularly when he was able to point out to others Nolin's fate on his arrival in Prince Albert. But there were others besides Nolin who were opposed to him, or at best only lukewarm in their support. To obtain unity Riel had recourse to threats and arrests. But a unity whose foundation rested on intimidation was no unity at all. From time to time French-speaking half-breeds, including at least one member of the Exovedate, fled from Batoche. Fred Fidler, Louis Marion, Roger Goulet, Baptiste Boyer, Louis Riguidel, Gabriel Parenteau, Jean Baptiste Boucher, Jean Laplante, Octave Regnier and Joseph Bremner were among those who fell away from their allegiance to Riel or refused to fight for him.[43] Garnot, the young French-Canadian who sometimes acted as Riel's secretary after Jackson fell ill, declared that, within a fortnight of the formation of the Provisional Government, at least half of Riel's supporters were disposed to abandon his cause and remained loyal only because they feared for themselves or their families. Garnot himself was one of those who would not shoulder a rifle when the shooting started.[44] Riel was aware of the weakness of his position, and from time to time he lost his temper and berated his followers. One such instance was witnessed by Thomas Jackson, who heard Riel attack Albert Monkman with great bitterness, accusing him in strong words of "not doing his duty with the English half-breeds."[45] It was the act of a man who was nervous, excited and unsure of himself.

Far more effective than threats, arguments or scoldings were Riel's appeals to the religious mysticism of the métis. Even before the outbreak of fighting at Duck Lake, Riel had persuaded the Exovedate to recognize Bishop Bourget as the supreme pontiff. They even accepted Riel himself as a prophet of the Lord. On March 27, the Council deliberated upon the doctrine of everlasting punishment and resolved that "hell will not last forever" but "will come to an end one day by the

goodness and through the merits of Jesus Christ."[46]   On other occasions
the Exovedate spent its time discussing the doctrine of transubstantia-
tion, changing the names of the days of the week[47] and altering the signs
of the zodiac to remove their pagan background and give them some
religious meaning.[48]

During the weeks of April, 1885, Riel spent much of his time in
meditation. He confided many of this thoughts to paper, and in his
journal he described his visions and his communion with God. Each
morning he revealed them to the members of the Exovedate. "The
spirit of God has shown me that I could go on the battlefield alone," he
wrote at one time. At another he wrote, "I have seen a flock of dark
geese. They seemed hovering, but in reality they were stopped in the
sky. I have seen them divided as in two groups. Oh, warriors who are
fighting for bad principles, God will stop you in your soaring and in
spite of all you will go back with your defeats, your disasters and your
shames. Hear, listen, and obey." Later he wrote again, "My ideas
are just. They are upright on my gun, and my gun is exact. I have
been in a meeting with Maxime Lépine and another. I could see myself
in a glass of justice. Reason and intelligence illumined my countenance,
but Lépine seemed not to notice them. He was keeping away from me,
without leaving me altogether. Oh, Maxime, Maxime, it is your self
love that kills you." Again, "The Spirit of God told me, 'Your people
must be well placed and well guarded.' Oh, my God, please sustain me
in the Exovedate. Please sustain me in the army."[49]

There were those like Garnot who looked with a cold eye on these
prayers and spiritual visitations. A French-Canadian from Quebec,
educated at Bourget College at Rigaud, Garnot was more sophisticated
and more critical than were his métis colleagues at Batoche. He was
disposed to feel that Riel was deliberately playing on the ignorance and
superstititions of the French half-breeds to strengthen his own political
influence in the settlement. "The majority had such faith in these
prophecies," he said later, "that they would have hurled themselves in
the water if the Spirit of God had said so to Riel."[50] Louis Schmidt,
now very much opposed to his former schoolmate, wrote, "Riel wanted
to pass himself off in the eyes of the people as an inspired man and a
prophet. That is how he dragged so many innocent people to the
abyss."[51] Father Fourmond was particularly bitter against Riel,
probably because he himself had yielded earlier to Riel's personal charm
and to his political arguments. He wrote that Riel had deliberately
collected the métis at Batoche in order to "seduce them" and "to force
them to become apostates." Riel "was ever at my heels," declared

Fourmond, "to combat me and to fascinate my poor Christians who, almost all deceived by his airs of piety and continual prayers, looked upon him as a saint and an angel descended from heaven."[52]

It is easy enough for the sceptic to question Riel's sincerity. It is much harder to prove that he was sincere. And yet sincerity rather than insincerity fits the pattern of his life. Through all he did and uttered, there shone the light of inspiration. When the names of Emanuel Swedenborg or Joseph Smith are called to mind, who can seriously claim that Riel, the mystic, the man with the spiritual turn of mind, who had indulged in religious speculations from childhood, was not convinced of the reality of his spiritual visitations? It was this very conviction that made Riel so potent a force among the métis. He really believed his destiny was to lead his people to a new and better world, and to a Christian faith purged of the excrescences of "the old Roman." Deluded he may have been, but he was not a charlatan.[53] He carried a cross and not a sword. But in the vision of his own inner faith, he was as much a saviour sent to end the ills of his people as the youthful King David or Jeanne d'Arc.

"Priests are not religion," wrote Riel in his journal. "The Spirit of God has told me that this was, is, and always will be true."[54] This was his answer to the challenge that came to him from the priests who even yet constituted the greatest threat to his leadership of the métis. On April 5, Riel attended Mass at St. Anthony's. It was Easter. As Father Moulin spoke from the pulpit, Louis was tempted to rise and answer him; but he did not do so until the service was over. At the church door he tried to argue with Moulin; but the priest would have nothing to do with him and called him a heretic and an apostate.[55] Riel did not bother to reply. He did not have to worry about Moulin, whose influence had never been very great and whose activities were always under view. Much more dangerous were the priests at St. Laurent, some seven miles away. They were out of sight and could be carrying on the work of subverting the national movement without his knowing about it. Moreover, they might be in touch with men like Father André or even Charles Nolin in Prince Albert.[56] Father Vegreville in particular was the dangerous one, for he had made no secret about his hostility to Riel. Accordingly, when Vegreville visited Father Moulin on April 9, he was arrested by Riel's men and taken before the Exovedate and charged with activities inimical to the métis movement. Of Vegreville's unfriendliness there could be no doubt; but neither Riel nor his councillors were prepared to impose a penalty upon the priest, for such an act would arouse sympathy within the métis community. Vegreville was therefore merely ordered to remain at St. Anthony's. He was refused permission to return to St. Laurent, and to make sure that he would not escape, his horse and buggy were taken from him. He was then removed to Moulin's rectory and presented with a paper which he was asked to sign. Vegreville acquiesced. He felt he had no choice but to agree to the following undertaking, "I promise to keep perfectly neutral and I will not leave here without the consent of the Provisional Government."[57] Similar declarations were extracted later from Fathers Fourmond and Touze.

The arrest of Vegreville, and the news of the murders of Fathers Fafard and Marchand at Frog Lake, produced consternation at St. Laurent. The Grey Sisters in their convent felt their lives to be in danger, and with the assistance of Brother Piquet, they attempted to make their way to Prince Albert. But the journey was a nightmare of mishaps. They lost their way; they tipped over their wagon; they broke a wheel; they suffered from the cold; and then they made their way back to St. Laurent where they found that Riel had installed a guard in their quarters. It was no part of Riel's plans that the Sisters should go to Prince Albert, and he issued instructions to them that they should come, instead, to Batoche. When they arrived at the métis head-quarters, Riel treated them with every politeness and offered them every courtesy. He agreed that they might take up their residence in Moulin's rectory.[58]

By mid-April, Riel had under surveillance the greater part of the Catholic clergy who had served the métis community on the South Saskatchewan. The priests and nuns were free to carry out their religious duties; but they were, to all intents and purposes, prisoners. There would be no more tampering with the loyalty of the French half-breeds, either at St. Laurent or at Batoche. Only Father André remained free. But he was at Prince Albert, too far away to be within reach of Riel's soldiers.

Gabriel Dumont had no share in these activities. He was a man of action, not a man anxious to indulge in or understand abstract ideas, particularly those of a theological bent. He wanted to be about, moving. His scouts had told him that Canadian troops were gathering at Fort Qu'Appelle, that they were moving in force towards Humboldt and that they were close by Clarke's Crossing. He was anxious to take the field and carry on an active campaign of guerilla warfare. "I proposed to go ahead of the troops," he declared, "harass them by night, and above all prevent them from sleeping, believing this was a good way to demoralize them and make them lose heart."[59] Riel would not agree to this. His military ideas were summed up in a letter of instructions sent by Garnot to the various outposts:

The Exovedate are of the opinion that Middleton and his troops ought not to be treated as extraordinary. It would be better to watch well their moves, to let them come when they please—under the Almighty hand of Divine Providence—and when they are near enough to strike, and then to work until, with God's and Christ's help, we have conquered them. A complete success over Middleton, we have to ask from Our Lady, the Blessed Virgin Mary, and let us aim at such decisive success.[60]

Dumont grumbled, "I yielded to Riel's judgment, although I was convinced that, from a humane standpoint, mine was the better plan; but I had confidence in his faith and his prayers, and that God would listen to him."[61] Accordingly Dumont remained at Batoche, chafing under the restrictions imposed on him.

In spite of Riel's apparent self-confidence, and his obsessive concern with matters religious, there is no doubt that he shared the growing sense of tension within the environs of Batoche as Middleton's troops approached. He expressed it in his prayers. On April 21, he wrote:

I have seen the giant—he is coming. It is Goliath. I pray to intercept the communications of the enemies. Let them not be in accord. Let them move troops without discernment. Oh my God, grant us the favour of meeting so that we beat them one after another. Regulate our battles at such intervals as to give us time to take disposition and position, so that we open fire only at the moment and place chosen for us. . . . I pray you to keep away the sons of evil. Take away from them the resources of life. Strike them with stupefaction. Stagger them when the fight takes place so that when they hear the thunder they will know the Almighty is preparing to inflict retribution upon them.[62]

Finally Dumont reached the end of his patience. It was no longer practicable to follow Riel's "humanitarian counsels." Prayers were all right but they were not enough, and they could be the excuse for unnecessary delays. Dumont knew that his soldiers were uneasy and that an aggressive policy was necessary to maintain their morale. "I had it pointed out to Riel that he was giving the enemy too many advantages," Dumont said, "and I proposed to harry them during the night in order to hold up their progress and give our allies time to arrive."[63] He thereupon sent word to Big Bear and Poundmaker, and to the Sioux chief, White Cap, as well as to the Indians of the Eagle Hills. At the same time he set about preparing an ambush along the road from Clarke's Crossing to Batoche, at Tourond's Coulée at Fish Creek. He was going to deal with Middleton's soldiers as "we would buffalo." "All right!" said Riel, "do as you wish."[64]

V

It was at dusk, on the night of April 23, when Dumont set out to meet Middleton. "No one could believe the enthusiasm of the men," wrote Garnot.[65] But the actual number of armed métis was small, scarcely more than 200.[66] Forty others remained behind as a garrison for Batoche. The métis soldiers were not well armed. There were a few, like Dumont, who had modern rifles, but for the most part they were equipped with shot guns, some even with old muzzle-loaders. Riel rode at the head of the column with Dumont; but he was still unhappy about Dumont's plans. He had had a vision not long before, which told him to do battle with the Canadians "not far" from Batoche,[67] and at each halt he knelt to recite the rosary.[68] Dumont hoped to launch a night attack on Middleton's men, but the slowness of the march and the frequent halts imposed delays which he had not contemplated. Then, while the métis were having supper at Roger Goulet's farm—several of Goulet's cows were slaughtered for the purpose—two messengers dashed up on horseback. They had come from Batoche and carried word that Mounted Policemen were approaching the métis capital from the Qu'Appelle road and that reinforcements were urgently needed to withstand an attack. Dumont was inclined to discredit the rumour; but in the end he felt obliged to detach twenty-five horsemen and twenty-five foot soldiers and send them back under Riel's leadership.[69]

By this time it was too late to carry out a night attack. Nevertheless, Dumont went ahead with his proposal for an ambush in Tourond's Coulée. He placed his men—now reduced to about 130 since the withdrawal of men under Riel and by desertions from the ranks—on both sides of the road that wound through the ravine and on towards Batoche. With a small number of horsemen, he climbed the south side of the coulée in order to reconnoitre. The morning was dull and grey. There was a slight mist lying over the ground, and it was possible for Dumont to ride forward unobserved. Suddenly a group of Middleton's scouts appeared around the corner of a grove of trees, and Dumont, unable to restrain himself or his men, dashed forward firing his rifle. As the soldiers appeared in greater numbers, the métis turned and quickly made for cover, while the Canadians, led by Riel's one-time antagonist, the leader of the Portage party of 1870, Major Boulton, dismounted, threw themselves on the ground and returned Dumont's fire.[70] The engagement of Fish Creek was under way.

Dumont himself had muffed his chance of securing surprise, and the battle developed into a drawn-out and indecisive exchange of shots, the métis firing in the ravine from behind the cover of the trees and bush, while the Canadian troops took their positions near the crest. According to Middleton, "one Indian in full war paint, out of bravado, came dancing out and shouting his war cry and was immediately knocked over and fell in the open where the body remained. . . ." The Indian was a Teton Sioux, the first casualty of the day. As the battle continued, the troops could hear "the oaths and shouts of the excited métis and the war whoops of the Indians. . . ."[71] Dumont had considerable difficulty in maintaining the morale of his men. Outnumbered, in danger of being outflanked, outgunned and facing Canadian cannon, the métis felt isolated and helpless. To sustain their courage, one of the métis burst out singing the song of Pierre Falcon which his grandfathers had sung before him after Seven Oaks; others, like Maxime Lépine, interspersed their shots with prayers.[72] Dumont himself seemed to be everywhere, even setting fire to the prairie grass in an effort to cover his efforts to grab the rifles and cartridge cases of the fallen soldiers. The Canadian troops did succeed in penetrating the ravine and obtaining a foothold on the north bank, but the métis held on and succeeded, by their skilful use of cover, in holding up Middleton's advance. During the afternoon, help came for the beleaguered half-breeds, whose numbers had dwindled to no more than fifty-four men.[73] Edward Dumont heard the sound of the guns while at Batoche, and in spite of Riel's opposition, he declared "when my own flesh and blood are in danger I cannot stay here."[74] Gathering some eighty horsemen he hurried to Fish Creek and arrived in time to charge into the coulée and drive back the soldiers who had almost surrounded his brother's little force.

By this time the soldiers from the opposite bank of the Saskatchewan were making their way across the river, thus adding to Middleton's strength, and confirming the fact that the general had made a serious blunder when he had divided his force only a few days earlier. However, to the surprise of the métis huddled in the hollows among the bushes in the ravine, the Canadians did not press forward to the attack. Middleton was still uncertain of the strength of Dumont's force. He felt that his militiamen had suffered sufficient casualties already and that the elimination of the pockets of resistance in the ravine "will not affect the work of the day."[75] Dumont might talk of putting in a counter-attack, as the troops withdrew into their fortified camp; but his men, like the militiamen, were glad of a respite, for they were tired and chilled by the cold rain that had turned to sleet during the afternoon. Picking up their dead and wounded—their losses were four killed and two wounded, one of whom later died[76]—they withdrew to Batoche.

Both sides were satisfied with the outcome of the battle: Middleton, because his men had acquitted themselves well and because he had remained on the field; Dumont, because he had checked the Canadian advance and had gained time for the arrival of hoped-for reinforcements from other parts of the Territories.

Meanwhile, in Batoche, Louis Riel had sent his scouts to reconnoitre the Qu'Appelle road, only to find that the rumoured attack was baseless. Then, when the distant thunder of Middleton's guns reached the métis settlement, he gathered the people around him, women and children, and knelt in prayer. Raising his arms in the form of a cross, and turning his face upwards, he began to pray. When his arms became weary, two métis stepped forward and held them.[77] Then the miracle which he begged God to grant was conceded. Middleton was halted. Maxime Lépine did no more than express the general métis attitude when he said, "I think prayer did more than bullets."[78] With equal sincerity Dumont said simply, "I attribute our success to Riel's prayers; all during the engagement, he prayed with his arms crossed and he made the women and children pray, telling them that we could come to no great harm."[79]

During the next two weeks Riel turned his attention to his antagonists in the Roman Catholic Church. On April 26, at Riel's instigation, the Exovedate decided to substitute Saturday for Sunday as the day of religious observance. The motion was put by Parenteau and seconded by Carrière:

that the Lord's Day be replaced by the seventh day of the week as revealed by the Holy Ghost, through his servant Moses. That if any members of the Exovedate are not ready to vote for this resolution as yet, those of their brethren who today take the first step cordially invite them to join them as soon as they can conscientiously do so; and even if their adhesion takes some time to come, it will be received with the same fervour as if it was given today. May such adhesion soon render unanimous this act by which the Exovedate re-establishes in the name of God, the Lord's Holy day of rest.[80]

Three members of the Exovedate—Ouellette, Ross and Lépine—found it impossible to support the motion, but it was carried on a majority vote. This was followed by the decision to fix the day of Easter on May 1.

On April 30, the three priests who were held at Batoche denounced these innovations by the Exovedate and threatened with excommunication those who supported them. Riel replied on May 1. He subjected the priests to a tirade in which he denounced their actions, denied the infallibility of the Church and declared that he, Louis Riel, was the representative of the Holy Ghost come to reform Christ's church. Fourmond, Moulin and Vegreville attempted to defend their faith; but Louis spoke as a man inspired, and their arguments against him seemed flat and lifeless. "There remains only to strike us and have us put to death," wrote Vegreville gloomily.[81] Several days later, on May 4, Fourmond had another verbal encounter with the métis leader. But Fourmond was no match for Riel, even in a theological debate. "How can these poor people whom you try to deceive and mislead as to the truth of my divine mission," Louis cried, "for one moment believe you when they have the proof before them that you are a traitor to them and you are unworthy of their confidence? How dare you say that it is a crime to take up arms against the tyrant in defence of their rights?" When Fourmond talked of rendering unto Caesar the things that were Caesar's Riel replied, "Yes render to God, glory, honour and adoration, but to the tyrants of the world, render that which is due them. Sling back their authority, which they have usurped, in their teeth; tumble them from power; that is what God orders." Then, turning to those who were listening, he continued:

Listen to this priest who dares to tell you that it is a crime you are committing under my direction, in the fulfillment of my sacred mission; who dares to call rebellion your taking up arms in a sacred cause, a cause ordained and directed by God, the cause of your native land which lies bleeding, prostrate at the feet of tyrants, the sacred cause of the rights, the liberties, the lives of your wives and children for all time to come.

With Riel in the full tide of his inflammatory rhetoric, there was nothing that Fourmond could do but to appeal to those métis present to prove their loyalty to the faith of their fathers, by shouting in response, "Long live the old Roman."[82] But Fourmond shouted almost alone. Only Riguidel joined him; and Riguidel fled the next day to avoid arrest. This was the measure of Riel's success in his controversy with the clergy. He had challenged them and had emerged victorious. He had little to fear from them now.

But he had much to fear from other quarters. General Middleton was only a few miles away and he was making ready to resume his advance towards Batoche. As previously, Dumont wanted to attack the troops before they could get under way. "I knew well that if our men were to fight at Batoche, their resolution would be weakened by the cries and tears of the women and children," he later declared.[83] This time Riel would not yield. The battle must be fought at Batoche; his visions had told him this. Loyal to his chief, Dumont still believed in Riel's divine mission. Perhaps Riel might once more be able to produce the miracle of victory by prayer. But what the simple but indomitable Dumont did not know—at least there is no evidence to suggest it—was that Riel had his own doubts about his success. A sense of impending disaster seems to mark his writings at this time. He might appeal to

Poundmaker to hurry to Batoche with 300 men to help him "settle matters definitely" with Middleton,[84] but in his own journal he wrote, on May 6, three days before the fighting began at Batoche:

I wish to arouse those who slumber in the deep sleep of their sins. They do not understand. They do not hear. They do not obey me. The enemy comes up the river. He arrives. He proceeds to bombard the town. How is it going to resist? Nobody takes its interest to heart. It is going to fall into the hands of the conqueror for having first abandoned God. God also abandons it. It is all over with it.[85]

It was truer than most of his prophecies. On the same day he addressed an appeal for help to the people of the United States. But it did not reach its destination until the rebellion was at an end.[86]

Meanwhile Dumont and Michel Dumas were busy constructing rudimentary defence works in the shape of rifle pits and trenches. They were well-placed and sited to cover all the approaches by road and each trench could shelter several men. They were located on the reverse slope leading down to the South Saskatchewan River and were concealed among the trees and bushes that were so characteristic a feature of the river valleys in western Canada. The front line of defence works followed the wide curve made by the crest of the slope, extending from the cemetery, near St. Anthony's Church, to the east and north of the scattered group of houses called Batoche. But even with the best defences they could devise, the métis stood little chance of success against Middleton's soldiers. Without the support of Big Bear and Poundmaker, their numbers were far too few—probably not more than 250 or 300 men—and their armament was antiquated and their supplies of ammunition limited. It was a pitifully small force with which to attempt to achieve a revolution.

On May 7, General Middleton broke camp at Fish Creek. He moved towards his objective slowly. On his left the steamer *Northcote* had been fitted out with sacks and lumber stripped from Gabriel Dumont's nearby farm. The little stern wheeler was to co-operate in the attack on the métis capital. Dumont, however, had learned of the destruction of his farm buildings and the arrival of the *Northcote*, and he anticipated that the vessel was going to be used as a river gunboat. Accordingly, he placed a group of some thirty men opposite the Batoche church and warned others to lower the ferry cable when the boat appeared. The remainder of his force, about 175 men, he posted on the slopes of the hill in front of the town.[87] And then he waited.

As a result of a misunderstanding between Middleton and the captain of the *Northcote*, the battle for Batoche began on the river. It was planned that the boat and the troops should attack simultaneously; but the *Northcote* attacked first, fully an hour too early.[88]   As the boat approached the bend in the river, the defenders hurled their bullets into the protected side and the inadequately protected wheelhouse.   The helmsman immediately threw himself on the floor and the vessel drifted helplessly to a sandbank and back again into the main current of the river.   On his horse, Dumont rode hard along the bank shouting orders that the ferry cable should be lowered.   But his orders were carried out too slowly; and the cable only scraped the top of the wheelhouse and tore through the vessel's two smoke stacks.   A fire which was started on the deck was quickly doused, and the *Northcote* continued downstream. An effort was made to persuade the skipper to make another run, this time up the river.   He, however, had had enough.   In any event there was no chance that the vessel could ever pass the lowered ferry cable. Thus Western Canada's first and only prairie warship remained some miles below Batoche, well out of gunshot, until the battle was over.[89] It was not yet nine o'clock in the morning, when Middleton was due to make his first assault by land.

The troops approached Batoche cautiously.   From their trenches, the métis could see the infantry as they moved in skirmish order, and the gunners as they unlimbered their guns.   They could hear the blare of the bugles and the rattle of the Gatling gun.   Middleton was only about one-quarter of a mile away at Jean Caron's farm, about half a mile from Batoche.   Then the métis saw Father Moulin waving a white flag from the rectory door.[90]   The firing stopped, and Middleton approached the church.   His troops advanced at the same time and moved near the crest of the hill.   There was a furious exchange of shots as a few métis rushed forward in an effort to capture one of the Canadian cannon.   As the troops counter-attacked, the half-breeds slipped back through the bush, moving from rifle pit to rifle pit, leaving the impression of a strength far greater than they really possessed.   In the evening, when the troops withdrew, Dumont rushed to the rectory. He had seen wounded Canadians carried into the building and angrily demanded that they be surrendered.   But the wounded men had been carried away by their comrades, and Dumont found nothing.   He was convinced that the priests were hiding the Canadians, and that, in spite of their signed undertakings, they had violated their promises of neutrality by passing on information to the troops about the fundamental weakness of the métis position from the standpoint of numbers and ammunition.[91]

Such was the fighting on May 9.   On the 10th and 11th it was much the same.   The same skirmishing, the same bombardment, the same advance by the troops to the crest of the hill and the same withdrawal at night.   The casualties were few among the métis these three days; but the damage done by the cannon to various buildings was extensive. And yet, the fact that the guns had been unable to batter down the flag of the Holy Virgin, which flew over the Walters and Baker store, and the flag bearing the figure of Our Lord, which had been erected over the house in which the Exovedate held its sessions, seemed to suggest to the credulous métis that God might yet bring victory to the man who continued to walk about unarmed and unharmed, carrying his crucifix and encouraging those who fought on his behalf. [92]

The fourth day of the battle, May 12, began like all the others, with light skirmishing and sporadic shooting. But, by this time, the métis sharpshooters had to make every bullet count, for they had few cartridges left to them, and there was no hope of getting any more. Both Riel and Dumont knew that this was the day of decision. Riel was busy composing his prayers, while Dumont watched Middleton's men and wondered what the Canadian commander had in mind when he saw him making a wide sweep to the métis left with a force of infantry and mounted scouts. Did this suggest an attack from two widely separated points? If so, the battle would soon be over. By moving his men rapidly from one threatened spot to another, Dumont had held out for three days; he simply did not have the men to stretch his defences any thinner than they already were. Not only anticipating but fearing an all-out attack, Riel wrote a note to Middleton, "If you massacre our families, we are going to massacre the Indian agent and other prisoners." [93] He gave this note to John Astley, one of the prisoners whom Dumont had taken at Duck Lake. A similar message was given to Thomas Jackson, in case Astley should not get through the Canadian lines. [94] However Astley reached the general, who read the note and wrote in reply, "Mr. Riel, I am anxious to avoid killing women and children, and have done my best to avoid doing so. Put your women and children in one place, and let us know where it is, and no shot shall be fired on them. I trust to your honour not to put men with them." [95] After Astley returned, Riel sat scribbling notes to Middleton. One after another he tore them up. What he really wanted to do was bring about a cessation of the shooting before the attack began. But Dumont would have nothing to do with surrender, and when Riel conducted Astley back through the métis lines, he bore a note which contained nothing more than a promise to let Middleton know later where the women and children would be placed. [96] Then suddenly, just before Astley set out across the interval between the two contending forces, he scribbled on the envelope "I do not like war, and if you do not retreat and refuse an interview, the question remains the same as regards the prisoners." [97]

These preliminary attempts on Riel's part to bring the fighting to an end came too late.   The Canadian militiamen, restless and dissatisfied with Middleton's cautious leadership, took matters into their own hands. They started to run towards the cemetery near Moulin's rectory.   Then they poured over the crest of the hill.   The métis came out of their trenches to meet them—some of the defenders had no more cartridges to put in their guns—and here the bitterest fighting of the battle took place.   Here the defenders suffered their greatest number of casualties. It was in the final act of resistance that José Ouellette, 93 years of age, was killed by a bayonet, as well as Joseph Vandal, who was 75, Donald Ross, Isidore Boyer, Michel Trottier, André Batoche, Damase Carrière and others.[98]   It was only a matter of minutes before the troops reached the village and broke into Batoche's house to free the prisoners whom the métis, now on the run, were unable to take with them as they retreated.

In the church of St. Anthony, Father Fourmond was reciting his rosary. He had not completed his task when he heard the shouts of victory that marked the end of the fighting.   The battle of Batoche was over.   Two days later Father André wrote in his journal, "At last the dénouement so long awaited has arrived.   The rebellion has been crushed at Batoche on the spot where it was born on March 18th.   We are now free and the roads are open."[99]

VI

But the roads were not open for Riel and Dumont.   Like their companions, they had been caught up in a *sauve-qui-peut*.   From time to time little groups of métis gathered together and fired a few shots in the direction of Batoche; but the fight had gone out of them.   Not even Dumont's threats or Riel's arguments could rally them.   "What are we going to do," said Riel to his military commander.   "We are beaten." "We must die," replied Dumont.   "You must have known that in taking up arms, we should be defeated.   Very well, they must destroy us."[100] Taking charge, Dumont managed to find some blankets for Riel's wife— she was again with child—and for her two children.   Then he set out to find food and horses for the wanderers.   In the distance he could see many little white flags flying from the houses of the métis in Batoche. While Dumont was absent, Riel took his family to Moïse Ouellette's house on the west side of the river.   Then he returned to hide in the woods.   When Dumont came back he could not find his friend, and hearing that Riel had given himself up to the soldiers, he and Michel Dumas decided to make their way to the United States.   They crossed over the frontier into Montana.   They were taken into custody at Fort Assiniboine, were quickly released and made their way to Fort Benton.[101]

Louis Riel, May 1885, Under Guard after being Taken Prisoner

Louis Riel, July 1885, Standing in the Prisoner's Box, Court Room, Regina

Relatives of Louis Riel

Louis Riel, Sketch by Henri Julien

It was twelve months almost to the day since the same two men had passed through Benton on their way back to the Saskatchewan. At that time they had been accompanied by Louis Riel. Now they would never see Riel again.

It was not true that Riel had surrendered, at least it was not true when Dumont heard the report. On May 13, Middleton had written to Riel offering to receive him and his council and to give them protection until such time as the Canadian government might decide what was to be done with them. This letter was given to Moïse Ouellette who passed it first to Dumont and later to Riel. Dumont had, however, taken his resolve to try to escape, and he replied with characteristic defiance, "You tell Middleton that I am in the woods, and that I still have 90 cartridges to use on his men."[102] Riel did not reply until the 15th. He wrote, "I have received only today yours of the 13th instant. My council are dispersed. I wish you would let them go quiet and free. I hear that presently you are absent. Would I go to Batoche who is going to receive me? I will go to fulfil God's will."[103] There was no question in Riel's mind of reviving the métis resistance, as Dumont had talked wildly of doing. Nor was there any intention of trying to escape to Montana as Dumont actually did. He would not run away to die in exile. He would give himself up. He would plead his cause before the people of Canada. It was his destiny; he would not fight against it.

On the 15th, the day he wrote to Middleton, Riel gave himself up to three Mounted Police scouts. He was taken quietly to Middleton's headquarters and introduced laconically, "General, this is Mr. Riel." Middleton found him "a mild-spoken and mild-looking man, with a short brown beard and an uneasy frightened look about his eyes, which gradually disappeared as I talked to him. He had no coat on, and looked cold and forlorn, and as it was still chilly out of the sun, I commenced proceedings by giving him a military great coat of my own."[104] After this initial conversation, Riel was led to a tent erected next to that of the General. He was placed in the hands of Captain George Young, the son of the Methodist clergyman who, only fifteen years before, had pleaded in vain with Riel for the life of Thomas Scott. For two days Riel remained at Batoche speaking frequently with General Middleton and leaving the General with the impression of a man "imbued with a strong, morbid, religious feeling mingled with intense personal vanity."[105]

Finally, on May 17, Riel and Young embarked quietly on the *Northcote*. Their destination was the capital of the Territories, Regina. Six days later, Riel entered the North-West Mounted Police barracks in that town.[106] As the gates closed behind the métis leader, they closed, for the last time, on the hopes and aspirations of the New Nation.

CHAPTER 18

Trial

THE EVENTS in Saskatchewan were followed in other parts of Canada with an interest, friendly or hostile, according to the sympathies of those who read the newspaper despatches from the west. But in St. Vital, in Manitoba, where Riel's family lived, his mother, his brother Joseph, his sister Henriette and the others—his grandmother, Marie Anne Gaboury-Lagemodière, was now dead—the response was first one of apprehension and then of fear. What was going to happen to Louis? He had been spared death from a soldier's bullet; would he be spared by the government, which had pursued him so relentlessly in the 1870's, now that it had him in its power? Shortly after his arrival in Regina, Riel's mother wrote to him. It was a letter from her heart.

Dear child, my beloved Louis, for many years it has been God's will to fill the cup of his sorrows and bitterness for us. Today He offers it to us filled to overflowing . . . should it really be necessary for us to empty it in a single draught, Oh God, give me the strength and the will to do it. Ah Louis, to tell you what I am suffering, you will understand it as regards your own children, to paint for you a mother's grief is a thing impossible. I weep, yes, it is true, and yet I lift my head high; sadness does not cast me into the depths of despair . . . let us not lower our eyes to the ground, rather let us look towards heaven, there will we find our only refuge, our only consolation . . . again, once more, my dear son, courage, courage, in the great glory of God.[1]

Meanwhile Louis had written to his brother Joseph asking him not to be discouraged, telling him: "I was not taken prisoner. General Middleton wrote me and I gave myself up to him." Then he asked, "For the love of God try to come and help my family as soon as possible."[2] Joseph did not delay in fulfilling his brother's wishes. As soon as he was able, he set out for Batoche to find Marguerite and the two children, and take them back with him to St. Vital. While Joseph was en route to the Saskatchewan, Riel wrote to his mother. It was the first time in many months that he had taken the time to write to her. Now, in his hour of trouble, he turned to her again. He felt compelled by some filial urge to try to justify his conduct. So he laid the blame upon his enemies, the men who wanted to destroy the métis; upon the men who had even tried

340

to poison him on one occasion when he visited Prince Albert. He offered very few facts explaining the rebellion; he spoke only in generalities about "ill will" and "a faulty appreciation of events by certain public servants in the Saskatchewan." Then he asked his mother to send him a pair of shoes and a hat; he had only moccasins, and he had lost his hat at Batoche. Most of all, however, he wanted his brothers and his sisters to "redouble" their devotions: "please pray together, every morning and evening. . . ."³ None of the Riels needed such urging. They faithfully attended Mass, burned their candles and took the Holy Sacrament. "Our dear mother is resigned," wrote Henriette to her brother, "she excites the admiration of everybody; the Eucharistic bread is her greatest support. . . ."⁴

Finally Joseph returned to St. Vital with Louis's family, his wife Marguerite, his son Jean and his daughter Angélique. But none of them was in good health. They had undergone too many hardships in the cold and wet spring at Batoche; and Louis was informed that Marguerite was "thin, very much changed," and that she had been coughing blood.⁵ However she seemed to improve after her arrival at St. Vital, and Henriette was able, in July, to report that everybody seemed much better—"the children are very much alive. Jean plays from morning until night and really goes to sleep only because he is tired. He is big and fat." It was unfortunate that Angélique was not as healthy as her brother. It was true she had made considerable improvement, but she was still "very thin."⁶

Interestingly enough, Louis seems to have been less concerned about his future than was his family. He still believed in his star, and he showed no disposition towards melancholy in his conversations with Middleton, with Captain George Young or with the Reverend Charles Pitblado, all of whom saw and chatted with him until he was locked up in his cell in Regina. He told Young that "he was not so foolish as to imagine that he could wage war against Canada and Britain, but he hoped by the first success to compel the Canadian government to consider the situation or accede to his demands."⁷ He talked of matters theological, of Indian policy, of the events of 1869/70. Indeed, "he talked on almost every circumstance and subject . . ." said Young. "I found I had a mind against my own and fully equal to it; better educated and much more clever than I was myself."⁸ But when the door of his prison cell was locked behind him, Riel talked very little. His gaoler, Captain Burton Deane of the North West Mounted Police, was prepared neither to talk nor to listen to him; and he had no audience except himself and no means of communicating his thoughts except to scribble them on paper. The notes he made during his weeks in Regina were like those he had made at Batoche, a conglomeration of prayers, visions, confused past history and strange prophecies for the future.

While Riel was recording his visions or looking out of the little window of his cell at the blue prairie sky, his captors were preparing the indictment against him. Several of Canada's foremost lawyers were engaged to assist the Deputy Minister of Justice, W. G. Burbidge. The lawyers included Christopher Robinson, B. B. Osler, T. C. Casgrain and D. L. Scott. They were to handle the case against Riel. As far as the other métis prisoners were concerned, it was the government's strategy to induce them to plead guilty to minor charges and to concentrate all attention on the conviction of the man who had led them into rebellion, to place upon his shoulders the full responsibility for the North-West troubles and to make his associates appear in the role of dupes or victims.[9] Henry J. Clarke, who acted for the defence in the prosecution of several of Riel's associates, declared that such was the method of procedure. Writing to Macdonald in 1886, asking for an appointment to the bench, he made it clear that he had been the author of the depositions of Fathers André and Fourmond and Charles Nolin, "all of which have been or ought to have been of great use to the Government, placing as they do all the responsibility of the Rebellion on Riel and others, and all condemning him without stint."[10]

Meanwhile French-Canadians in Quebec were rallying to Riel's support. During the years 1870/74, Riel had been looked upon in Quebec as the leader of French survival in Western Canada. French-Canadians had identified him with themselves and the métis cause with their own. Since his stay in the mental hospital in Beauport, Riel had dropped out of Quebec politics and out of Quebec newspapers. His reappearance in Saskatchewan stimulated only a few memories and excited only limited comment; but with the outbreak of fighting, all the old sympathies revived. As he had been fifteen years before, Louis Riel once more became the symbol of the French-English quarrel in Canada. To those in Ontario, Riel again became a figure of criminality; to those in Quebec, a figure of innocence. And as before, the Riel question became the battle ground of Canadian party politics. Despite the fact that the Roman Catholic clergy, naturally inclined to uphold order and authority, were disposed to point the finger of guilt at Riel and blame him for the misfortunes suffered by the métis, including the murder of the two priests at Frog Lake,[11] the French-Canadian laity, generally, especially those of "nationalist" tendencies, openly expressed their regard for the métis leader. Even in April, while troops, including French-Canadian soldiers, were on their way to the battlefront, the Quebec legislature was debating a Liberal motion regretting the "sad events" in the North-West and attributing them to the vexatious and unjust policies of the Federal Conservatives.[12] It was more than a political manœuvre; but the introduction of party politics into the question of Louis Riel's fate was less calculated to serve Riel than it was the Liberal party.

Most active were Louis's old friends, the men who had been his school-mates and the men who had helped him in the 1870's. Some of the latter were gone. Mousseau's voice had been stilled by death and Masson's by his appointment as Lieutenant-Governor of Quebec. But there were other supporters, L. O. David, the president of the Riel Defence Committee; Charles Delorimier and R. Préfontaine, the vice-presidents; Charles Champagne, the secretary; and Jérémie Perrault, the treasurer. The members of the executive council of the new organization included Rodolphe LaFlamme, Pierre Rivard, Georges Duhamel, Adolphe Ouimet and others. In Ottawa there were Laurier, Beaubien, Trudel, Bellerose, Amyot, Bergeron and, of course, Fiset and Desjardins. It was the Riel Defence Committee that approached the lawyers François Lemieux, Charles Fitzpatrick and J. N. Greenshields and asked them to go to Saskatchewan to plead for Riel's life. When the lawyers agreed, it was Fiset, who had accompanied Riel into the House of Commons in March, 1874, when he signed the register as the member of parliament for Provencher, who wrote to tell Riel that all arrangements had been completed and that "it would be difficult" to find better counsel than Fitzpatrick and Lemieux.[13] Then the lawyers packed their bags and set out for the west. At St. Boniface they stopped long enough to visit the Riel family and receive a rosary from Henriette, as well as some water from the shrine at Lourdes to take to the prisoner in the police barracks at Regina.[14]

Louis was grateful to his friends for their help. After all, he had no money and no means of securing any. He had nothing for his counsel but advice. He therefore wrote a long rambling letter to Fiset and "the good lawyers of my defence," explaining that he had not been captured but had freely given himself up at Middleton's request and that he had been invited to go to the Saskatchewan and agitate on behalf of the people of the North-West. He blamed the heedless words of Lawrence Clarke for inciting the métis to take up arms and pointed out that at no time had he ever taken the offensive; he and the métis had merely waited and defended themselves when they had been attacked. "I desire that my trial should turn on the merit of my actions," he wrote, and that it should be held not at Regina but "before the Supreme Court."[15] In a letter to Lieutenant-Governor Dewdney, he made the same request. He asked that his trial should include specific charges, not only covering the events of 1885 but also those of 1869/70. Although he appreciated the distinction of the men who were to appear on his behalf before the court, he wondered whether the fact that they were all prominent Liberals was not a mistake.   He suggested to Dewdney that it would be better if he could have five counsel: one French-Canadian and one Irish-Canadian Liberal; one French-Canadian and one Irish-Canadian Conservative; and one English-Canadian Protestant "enjoying the confidence of the Conservative party and in particular of Sir John A. Macdonald."   "With God's help," he wrote, "my victory over the party of the Hon. Messrs. Blake and Mackenzie will be complete.   The triumph of the Conservative party over its antagonists will be great."[16] Several days later he explained to Sir John A. Macdonald his attitude towards the Roman Catholic Church, and argued that his "separation from Rome" did not imply any abandonment of the Christian faith. He had advocated such a course because he felt Pope Leo XIII was too much a politician to be a good bishop, and because a break with Rome "would lessen as much as was in my power the divisions, the disagreements between the religious denominations and the various nationalities."[17]   This was followed by another letter to the Prime Minister, laying the blame for the troubles in the North-West on Blake and Mackenzie.   The letter also expressed hope that he might be able to return to political life in Manitoba where "it would, perhaps, be of some use for me to become a minister" and where he could "continue with your government, the work begun here, fifteen years ago, by the Manitoba Act."[18]

By the time Fitzpatrick and Lemieux learned the nature of Riel's views and had talked seriously with their client, they knew what line their defence would have to take.   They could never deny that Riel had led an armed rising, although they could offer some arguments in extenuation of this fact: what they would do would be to prove that their client had been of unsound mind when he did so.   The kind of nonsense he was talking and writing in his notebooks in his cell left them no choice but to believe that he was very naive, very clever or—insane.[19]

II

Louis Riel spent eight weeks in prison waiting to be brought to trial. During this time the North-West Rebellion ground to a halt.   Poundmaker surrendered on May 14; and on May 28, General Strange's cannon drove Big Bear's Crees from their positions at Frenchman's Butte. Pursued into the north country, Big Bear's band disintegrated.   Finally the troops abandoned the chase and the old chief, having escaped all the soldiers sent to apprehend him, gave himself up to a Mounted Police sergeant at Fort Carlton on July 2. Four days later, on July 6, formal charges were laid against Louis Riel and the trial was fixed to take place on July 20 at Regina—at one time called Pile of Bones Creek before it had been elevated to the dignity of capital of the North-West Territories.

The trial opened at eleven o'clock on July 20. Hugh Richardson, the stipendiary magistrate, was to try the case. With him sat Henry LeJeune, Justice of the Peace. At the barristers' table, opposite the bench, sat the lawyers in their black gowns and white ties. To one side sat the sheriff, a brother of Adolphe Chapleau who had defended Lépine in 1873. The public seats were crowded. The trial had almost the appearance of a gala social occasion. The Lieutenant-Governor was in attendance and so, too, was the Commanding General of the Canadian Militia. And there were many ladies who came to see the famous "rebel," including Mrs. Middleton, Mrs. Richardson, Mrs. Forget, Miss Osler, Mrs. Watson and others. Here and there, amid the dark suits of the men and the light costumes of the ladies, were the brilliant scarlet tunics of the army officers, and assiduous law students and a dozen *blasé* reporters, all eager to take notes and discuss the case. Outside the court there was crowding and pushing, and the usual complaints of the ignorance, or insolence, or both, of the doorkeepers.[20]

When he took his seat, Judge Richardson called for Riel. Every possible precaution had been taken with the prisoner. There had been rumours current that the métis of Wood Mountain might attempt to free him, and all entries to the town of Regina were guarded by men of the Mounted Police, the Montreal Garrison Artillery and the 91st Battalion from Winnipeg. Riel himself was disguised as a Mounted Policeman and conducted in a carriage with a police escort across the Wascana, past Government House, and over the railway tracks to the court house. It was just a few minutes after the hour when he entered the courtroom. Dixie Watson, the clerk of the court, began the proceedings by intoning the charges in the solemn, imposing and traditional words. There was no specific mention of the fact that Riel was an American citizen, nor was it implied in the charge:

Louis Riel, then living within the Dominion of Canada and under the protection of our Sovereign Lady the Queen, not regarding the duty of his allegiance nor having the fear of God in his heart, but being moved and seduced by the instigation of the devil as a false traitor against our said Lady the Queen, and wholly withdrawing the allegiance, fidelity and obedience which he should and of right ought to bear towards our said Lady the Queen . . . together with divers other false traitors . . . most wickedly, maliciously and traitorously did levy and make war against our said Lady the Queen . . . and did then maliciously and traitorously attempt and endeavour by force and arms to subvert and destroy the constitution and government of this realm as by law established. . . .[21]

Before Riel was able to reply to the charge of high treason, Lemieux and Fitzpatrick challenged the jurisdiction of the court. Fitzpatrick argued that the North-West Territories Act of 1880, which provided for the trial of capital cases by a stipendiary magistrate and a jury of six men, was *ultra vires*. Judge Richardson would not, however, admit the validity of the argument. Only a short time previously, the very same argument had been raised in the case of one Connor, who had been convicted of murder in the North-West Territories, and the Appeal Court of Manitoba had confirmed the validity of the statute. Richardson therefore ordered the case to proceed. When the clerk repeated the question, "Louis Riel, are you guilty or not guilty?" Riel with dignity replied, "I have the honour to answer the court I am not guilty."[22]

The second day of the trial was taken up with arguments over a request for adjournment. Riel and Fitzpatrick and Lemieux all submitted affidavits complaining of the "utter impossibility" of conducting an adequate defence without the presence of the necessary witnesses. Riel asked for the appearance of Dumont, Dumas and Nault, who had fled to the United States, of Fathers André and Fourmond, and of Vankoughnet and Burgess, respectively the Deputy Ministers of Indian Affairs and of the Interior. But the court would not and could not guarantee the freedom of Dumont and the other métis, who themselves were under indictment, nor would it attempt to subpoena the two Deputy Ministers. The priests they would send for. Fitzpatrick was more successful when he asked for several alienists to bear witness to Riel's previous stay at Longue Pointe and Beauport. The Crown agreed to bear the costs of these witnesses, but it would not accept Fitzpatrick's request for an adjournment for one month. In the end, the defence was granted an adjournment of a week. The trial would be resumed on Tuesday, July 28. Some of the spectators were annoyed. "Just as it was becoming so interesting," remarked one young woman, "Oh, dear! that horrid man."[23]

While he was awaiting trial, Riel received a visit from his old friend and associate of 1869/70, the Abbé Georges Dugast, who had been sent by Archbishop Taché to see him. The two men talked together amicably in the presence of several policemen, and Dugast returned to St. Boniface convinced that the former métis leader was as "mad as a hatter."[24] The Archbishop was inclined to take the same view after he received a letter from his former protégé written on July 24.[25] It was a letter that revealed the intensity of Riel's religious mysticism and his continued belief in his divine mission. Riel argued, as he had argued many times before, that it was God's will that the papacy should remove from Rome, the capital of a "brigand king" and that the Pope should be freed from his captivity in the Vatican. He re-asserted his belief that the spirit of God had come to rest in the person of Ignace Bourget, and since Bourget's death, in the person of Archbishop Taché. "You are by divine election the successor of Archbishop Bourget," he wrote, "and while you are rendering the last honours to the mortal remains of the great servant of God, you are yourself becoming . . . the vicar of Jesus Christ on earth." St. Boniface was now the religious capital of Christendom, and the French-Canadian métis were Christ's chosen people. After Taché's death, the papacy would return to Montreal and remain there for "fifteen months and a week of years" after which it would return again to St. Boniface. This was the explanation, wrote Riel, "why I have separated from Rome and why I prayed that the métis would do as I do, if they wished." Then he went on. Taché should give over the North-West to the Catholic peoples of Europe, to the Bavarians, the Poles, the Italians, the Irish and others, and Colonel Irvine of the Mounted Police, should be appointed Lieutenant-Governor of this vast region. After sending this rather startling news to the Archbishop, Louis wrote to Henriette, his sister. It was a perfectly normal letter, the kind of letter any man might write. But this was always true of Riel; as long as he refrained from talking or writing about religion or politics, there was nothing to becloud his natural friendliness and normal conduct. All he did was thank Henriette for the rosary and the holy water she had sent him. "I am happy to learn that you are filled with courage," he said. "Your confidence is justified. And I do not think that it is misplaced."[26]

There was reason for the optimistic tone of Louis's letter to Henriette. The Ontarian, William Henry Jackson, his former secretary, had been tried on July 24 for complicity in the rebellion. Jackson had refused to plead. "I have always declared myself perfectly responsible, that is to say, as Riel's secretary," he said, "and I wish to share his fate whatever that may be."[27] The defence argued that Jackson was insane, a plea which the Crown did not seriously contest. Only three witnesses were called, Jackson's brother, Thomas Jackson, Dr. Jukes, the Mounted Police surgeon, and Dr. Cotton, a physician of Regina. In spite of William Jackson's protests that he was "perfectly sane," and his denials that he had ever been "a prisoner of Riel's," the jury returned a verdict of "not guilty on the ground of insanity."[28]

It was, therefore, with considerable confidence that Louis entered the dock to face his accusers on the morning of July 28. After several challenges, five on behalf of the accused and one—an Irish Catholic—on behalf of the Crown, a jury of six men was empanelled. There were no French-Canadians, no métis, among them.[29] B. B. Osler opened the case, making a great deal of Riel's note to Crozier demanding his surrender under threat of "a war of extermination," and attributing the whole rising to "the personal ambition and vanity of the man on trial." "The evidence will show," the Crown attorney declared, "that he desired blood, that his only object was to obtain money, or gratify his desire for power, and that he was altogether reckless of the means he employed to further his ends."[30]

Owing to the fact that Riel had not been himself a member of the Exovedate, it was incumbent upon the prosecution to prove that he was, nevertheless, both the inspiration and the director of the unhappy events of March and April. Accordingly, a number of witnesses were called to the stand to say, from their own observations, that it had been Riel who had given the orders to the métis, both before and after Duck Lake: Dr. Willoughby, the Saskatoon physician who had seen Riel and a number of armed men near Batoche on March 17, had heard Riel remark, "you see now I have my police; in one week that little Government police will be wiped out of existence";[31] Thomas McKay, to whom Riel declared that "it was blood; and the first blood they wanted was mine";[32] and John Astley, Harold Ross, Peter Tompkins, John Lash and George Ness, all of whom had been taken prisoners by Dumont and who were prepared to testify that at Duck Lake Riel had given the orders to the métis to fire. Astley's testimony was particularly damaging, as he had seen Riel beckoning the men to fall in line just before they set out for Duck Lake. And after Fish Creek, when Astley had offered to do what he could to arrange for an exchange of prisoners, Riel had answered, "If we gain another battle, the terms will be better. . . ."[33]

From the outset it was apparent what line Riel's lawyers intended to follow in defending their client. Dr. Willoughby was led by Fitzpatrick into telling the court about Riel's plan to subdivide the North-West Territory among the various peoples of Europe. It all sounded very odd. When Fitzpatrick asked, "It appeared to you a very rational proposition?" the witness replied, "No, it did not."[34] McKay then told about Riel's sudden and unreasonable bursts of temper and his equally sudden cooling off and invariable politeness afterwards. He also admitted that, as a half-breed, he felt that he was entitled to scrip and had never received it. Astley, however, was less inclined to follow Fitzpatrick's leads. He would not admit that Riel's actions were in any way unusual or eccentric. "He seemed intelligent and in many respects a clever man," said Astley.[35] Ness's evidence, too, was damaging to Riel, and Greenshields was moved to protest against the amount of hearsay that Judge Richardson seemed disposed to allow as evidence during the Crown examination.[36] Fitzpatrick, in cross-examination, tried to force Ness to say that Riel had endeavoured to keep the North-

West agitation within constitutional bounds. In this he failed, but he did draw from the witness an account of Riel's religious aberrations and the métis leader's declaration that "the Spirit of God was in him and that Rome had tumbled and he could tell future events."[37]

The first day ended with honours fairly even. The following day, the Crown produced George Kerr and Henry Walters to testify with regard to the seizure of their property; Hillyard Mitchell to show how he had tried to dissuade the métis from hostile action; and Thomas Jackson to prove that, during the engagement at Fish Creek, Riel had been in charge at Batoche and had urged his men "to fight" should they be attacked.[38] Then came Middleton, Crozier and Young. Once more the defence held to its course. Kerr told Fitzpatrick that he had attended a dinner at which Riel had "proposed the health of our Sovereign Queen Victoria"—he himself had contributed a dollar to the purse given Riel on that occasion.[39] Mitchell was a hostile witness, and he was not exposed to cross-examination. Jackson, however, seemed to offer a good opportunity to Fitzpatrick to discredit the testimony of the Crown witness. Why had Jackson destroyed the letter Riel had given him to circulate among the white settlers? Was it because it implicated Jackson himself? Was Jackson not one of Riel's white supporters? Jackson frankly admitted that "almost the whole of the people" in the District of Lorne had joined together for the purpose of agitating for "provincial rights principally, also for half-breed claims."[40] Then Fitzpatrick turned to discuss Riel's strange religious and political views. This was an error in tactics. To the lawyer's question of whether or not these revealed Riel as a peculiar individual, Jackson replied that Riel's religiosity was simply an "affectation of humility" and that he "spoke of religion but merely as ordinary men do."[41]

At this moment the Crown produced its star witness, Charles Nolin. Hitherto Riel had shown little interest in the proceedings. It is true that he had scribbled questions on pieces of paper and handed them to his legal advisers; but he had showed no annoyance when they were ignored. Now Riel was alert, interested. Nolin was his cousin. He had been his host in 1884 and his closest associate for many months. Nolin had, in fact, been called by the Mounted Police "the most dangerous" of the métis.[42] But Nolin had opposed him in 1870 and had deserted him in March of 1885. Now he was preparing to swear away Riel's life.

Nolin's hostility to his cousin was patent to all. He testified to Riel's demand for money, to Riel's refusal to allow him to tender for government contracts, to Riel's packing the meeting at which the métis leader had offered to return to Montana. Nolin could not be suppressed and in his answers went far beyond what was required by the questions put to him, sometimes to the embarrassment of the Crown attorneys. Since Nolin was speaking in French, Lemieux handled the cross-examination. He prodded Nolin into admitting his complicity in the agitation and his abandonment of Riel. The witness was also forced to admit that Riel was subject to visionary experiences and divine revelations and "inspirations that worked through every part of his body."[43] He told of Riel's proposals to divide Canada, giving "Quebec to the Prussians" and "Ontario to the Irish" and dividing the North-West between a variety of European nations.[44] He even conceded that when "the word police was pronounced" Riel "got very excited."[45] Then he related that when "Captain Gagnon passed in the country, and stopped at the prisoner's house to enquire what was the road to St. Laurent, and there was only the prisoner's wife and Mrs. Dumont in the house, and when the prisoner came back and was informed that Mr. Gagnon had been there, he got very much excited and the women could not explain what Gagnon had stopped for, and he got very excited, and the population generally got excited too."[46]

Riel jumped to his feet. "Your Honour," he asked, "would you permit me a little while." "In the proper time, I will tell you when you may speak to me, and give you every opportunity—not just now though," replied the judge. Riel persisted, "I wish you would allow me before this witness leaves the box."[47]

Fitzpatrick interrupted him, "I don't think this is the proper time, Your Honour, that the prisoner should be allowed to say anything in the matter."[48] Richardson agreed. Riel had the right to defend himself personally or by counsel, but once provided with a lawyer he could not interfere except to address the jury. But Riel did not want to wait. He did not like the way the cross-examination always seemed to lead towards one conclusion—that he was insane. He tried again to speak, "If you will allow me, Your Honour, this case comes to be extraordinary, and while the Crown, with the great talents they have at its service, are trying to show I am guilty . . . my good friends and lawyers, who have been sent here by friends whom I respect—are trying to show that I am insane—"[49] "Now you must stop," Richardson ordered.

But he would not stop. His counsel, he said, "come from Quebec, from a far province." They were obliged to put questions to men "with whom they are not acquainted, on circumstances which they don't know," and although he had offered them suggestions "they cannot follow the thread of all the questions that could be put to the witnesses. They lose more than three-quarters of the good opportunities."[50] When Richardson repeated that he could not put questions directly to the witness, that he would have to put them through his counsel, he replied, "I have too much to say.   There is too much to say . . . I have on cross-examination 200 questions."[51]

The Crown raised no objections to Riel's request—the prosecuting lawyers were prepared to allow Riel to put questions to the witnesses "if the prisoner's counsel are."[52]   But Fitzpatrick and Lemieux felt their professional dignity was involved, and they were convinced that Riel would do more harm than good to his own cause if given a free hand.   Accordingly, after a short adjournment, Lemieux informed the court that he and his colleagues would withdraw from the trial if their client was dissatisfied with their services; if they were to remain, then they must be permitted to conduct the case in the way they believed best without interruptions on Riel's part.   "I know from my good friends and my learned lawyers that it is a matter of dignity for their profession, and I consider if my intentions were not respectful for them and the friends who sent them, I would commit a great fault against my friends and against myself," replied Riel.   "The case concerns my good lawyers and my friends, but in the first place it concerns me. . . . I cannot abandon the wish that I expressed to the court, and I cannot abandon the wish that I expressed to retain my counsels. . . ."[53]   When Richardson urged him again to put his questions through his counsel, Riel felt the chains of formality were being drawn about him.   He did not want to be confronted with a choice of conducting his own case or surrendering it completely to Lemieux and Fitzpatrick.   But the regular courtroom procedure would allow no alternative.   He had to give in.   He had to leave the case to his lawyers.   But he did not give way willingly.   He would retain the services of his professional defenders; yet he could not suppress his protests.   "I cannot abandon my dignity," he cried.   "Here I have to defend myself against the accusation of high treason, or I have to consent to the animal life of an asylum.   I don't care much about animal life if I am not allowed to carry with it the moral existence of an intellectual being."[54]

The examination of Nolin continued.   Did Riel break with the Catholic clergy at Batoche?   Completely.   Were the métis a religious people?   They were.   Nolin sensed where he was being led.   Riel, he added, would "never have succeeded" in bringing the half-breeds with him had he "not made himself appear as a prophet."   Riel was not sincere, he had merely taken advantage of the "ignorance" and the "simplicity" of his people.[55]   The strength of Nolin's animosity was surprising even to those familiar with his attitude.   Richardson himself wondered if he was being completely fair to Riel when he stopped the prisoner once again from putting a question to Nolin.   This, at least, seems to be the meaning of the judge's remark, "If it were an ordinary criminal case, I should not hesitate, but this is beyond the ordinary run of cases that I have had to do with in my whole career."[56]

Two more witnesses were called, Thomas Sanderson and Robert Jefferson. This time Riel did not interrupt, not even when Jefferson identified him as the author of a letter to Poundmaker asking for help from the Indians. The two hundred questions he had formulated and would have liked to ask remained locked in his own mind.

After the court adjourned on the second day, a former magistrate, Matthew Ryan, wrote to Archbishop Taché telling him of the progress of the trial and of Riel's attempts to answer Nolin. "I for the first time felt deeply for him," Ryan wrote:

I had not been quite in sympathy with the style or mode of the defence, and when the prisoner urged with force and eloquence that these men "coming from afar" as he said, did not "understand the numerous circumstances of his case" with all my heart I could have helped him; and he seemed to understand it. Being near to him, he looked steadily, almost pitifully at me; but, alas! I was as powerless as himself.

Then he added "*Entre nous*—the lawyers are not to my taste, and they did not compare at all favourably with those of the Crown. Richardson (Judge) is, of course, cold and foxy."[57]

On Thursday, July 30, it was the defence's turn to summon witnesses. So far the emphasis had been laid upon Riel's irresponsibility. However, when André was called to the stand, he was questioned about the nature of the métis grievances and the failure of the government to redress them. Immediately Osler objected. After all, it was Riel, not the Government of Canada, who was on trial. Lemieux shifted his examination to the familiar line of Riel's attitude towards religion and politics. He was on safe ground here for, to André, Riel was quite insane: "It would seem as if there were two men in him, he lost all control of himself. . . . Many times, at least twenty times, I told him I would not speak on those subjects because he was a fool."[58] But when Casgrain asked, "Do you pretend that every man who has strange ideas on religious matters is a fool?" André answered, "No, I don't pretend that."[59] Casgrain pressed home the point he wished to make, "A man may be a great reformer of great religious questions without being a fool?" "I do not deny history," replied the priest.[60] Fourmond also testified to Riel's irrational statements and his excesses of temper when contradicted. Neither priest could be shaken in his conviction that Riel was not an accountable being. The trouble was that they were not experts—nor was Garnot who told the court, "I thought the man was crazy, because he acted very foolish."[61] Nevertheless their opinions carried weight, if only because they had lived with Riel and knew him.

However, the defence did have two expert witnesses to bolster its case, Dr. François Roy of Beauport and Daniel Clark of the Toronto Lunatic Asylum. Roy was, in fact, the key defence witness, and the Crown knew it. Osler's tactics were therefore to assume an attitude of bellicosity, to browbeat if not to confuse the witness. Hard pressed to answer Osler's questions in English, Roy fell back upon his own language, French, and in so doing lost much of his effectiveness as a witness, if only because of the difficulty of translating his evidence in a manner easily understood by the members of the jury. Yet no one could make him alter his opinion, "I do not believe that he [Riel] was in a condition to be the master of his acts. . . ."[62] Clark likewise expressed the view that Riel was insane; but he weakened the impact of his statement by adding, "I assume . . . that not only the evidence given is correct, but that he was not a deceiver."[63] Fitzpatrick cut the examination short. Osler, however, had not missed the significance of Clark's proviso. Were Riel's actions consistent with fraud? he asked. The doctor answered, "anything is consistent with fraud that is not discovered."[64]

Riel had listened to Roy's evidence with obvious irritation. He was pleased with the way Osler had handled the French-Canadian alienist. He had known Roy at Beauport in 1877. He knew, too, that his lawyers were depending greatly on Roy's evidence to prove their allegation of insanity. Speaking the next morning to Dr. Jukes, Riel remarked of Roy: "He put me into Beauport asylum under a false name, La Rochelle —he accused me of being insane. I told him then—that the present was not the only thing to be considered—and that the time would come when he would be ashamed—that time has come—that time came yesterday—and I was glad."[65]

The prosecution, too, attempted to produce its expert witnesses to rebut the evidence of Roy and Clark. They were Dr. James Wallace of Hamilton and Dr. Jukes of the Mounted Police. However, Wallace was easily disposed of when he was forced to admit that he had seen Riel only for half an hour and that "from what I have seen of him, I say that I have discovered no symptoms of insanity."[66] His evidence was too weak to be of any real value. Dr. Jukes, however, although no authority on mental illnesses, was a different proposition, and Fitzpatrick found that he had met his match. There was nothing belligerent about the witness; but he was able to turn the defence lawyer's questions back at him. "There are men who have held very remarkable views with respect to religion and who have been always declared to be insane until they gathered great numbers of followers and became leaders of a new sect, then they became great prophets and great men . . . take Mahomet for instance. . . ."[67]

III

The evidence was finished. Fitzpatrick stood to address the jury. His was a good speech, and it reflected the flamboyance of the man himself. He praised the citizen soldiers who had left their firesides to put down the rebellion; he spoke of the grievances of the North-West—of course such grievances did not justify rebellion, but "if there had been no rebellion, if there had been no resistance, is there any one of you that can say today, is there any one of you that can place his hand on his conscience and honestly say that the evils under which this country has complained would have been remedied?" He emphasized Riel's poverty, the constitutional character of his agitation and then the sudden change that indicated the onset of Riel's mental illness. He put forward the two alternatives, "Either this man is the lunatic that we his counsel have tried to make him, or he is an entirely sane man in the full possession of his mental faculties, and was responsible in the eyes of God and man for everything that he has done."[68] After Fitzpatrick had outlined all the evidence in favour of insanity, he concluded, "I know, gentlemen, that right will be done. I know you will do him justice, and that this man shall not be sent to the gallows by you, and that you shall not weave the cord that shall hang and hang him high in the face of all the world, a poor confirmed lunatic; a victim, gentlemen, of oppression or the victim of fanaticism."[69]

Fitzpatrick had made a strong appeal to the emotions of the six men who sat in the court to determine the facts and decide the guilt of the prisoner. Riel made an even stronger one. The tension had mounted as Fitzpatrick marshalled his arguments; but it was as nothing to the excitement which filled the courtroom as Riel rose to speak to the jury. Lemieux immediately disassociated himself and his colleagues from any statement that Louis might make. But he could not deny that the prisoner had the right to speak to the jury. Louis had been prevented from putting questions to the witnesses, but he was determined that he would speak when the proper time came. Now he had his opportunity to put his case, the métis case, not merely before the six men of the jury but before the whole of Canada. Human destiny might fail him; his divine mission never would.

After a moment of prayer, he began. At first he was nervous and hesitant in his speech. His sentences were short, jerky, incomplete. But none could question the sincerity of his words:

You have seen by the papers in the hands of the Crown, that I am naturally inclined to think of God at the beginning of my actions. I wish if you—If I do you won't take it as a mark of insanity, that you won't take it as part of a play of insanity. Oh my God, help me through Thy grace and the divine influence of Jesus Christ. Oh, my God, bless me, bless this honourable court, bless this honourable jury, bless my good lawyers who have come 700 leagues to try to save my life, bless also the lawyers for the Crown, because they have done, I am sure, what they thought their duty. They have shown me fairness which at first I did not expect from them. Oh my God, bless all those who are around me . . . change the curiosity of those who are paying attention to me, change that curiosity into sympathy with me.[70]

There was complete silence in the room. Riel continued, "The day of my birth I was helpless and my mother took care of me . . . the North-West is also my mother, it is my mother country. . . . I am sure that my mother country will not kill me more than my mother did forty years ago when I came into the world, because a mother is always a mother, and even if I have my faults, if she can see I am true she will be full of love for me."[71] Then Louis began a history of the North-West movement, the sufferings of his own people the half-breeds and the futile petitions to Ottawa. "It is true, gentlemen," he continued, "I believed for years I had a mission, and when I speak of a mission you will understand me not as trying to play the role of insane . . . so as to have a verdict of acquittal upon that ground. I believe that I have a mission, I believe I had a mission at this very time. What encourages me to speak to you with more confidence in all the imperfections of my English way of speaking, it is that I have yet and still have that mission."[72] He went back to his days in Manitoba, to his letters from Bishop Bourget and to the encouragement he had received from Father Eberschweiler of Fort Benton. He made no effort to hide the fact that he had been in a mental asylum but declared that, if it was to be his lot to die, it was his hope "I will not be reputed by all men as insane, as a lunatic." He defended his actions in the Saskatchewan and argued that there would have been no fighting, no bloodshed, had the métis not been attacked by the Mounted Police and by the militia. Riel's voice was strong now, and it was with pride that he cried, "I know that through the grace of God I am the founder of Manitoba."[73] Then he turned to his religious ideas. "What is my insanity about that?" he asked:

My insanity, your Honours, gentlemen of the jury, is that I wish to leave Rome aside, inasmuch as it is the cause of division between Catholics and Protestants. . . . If I have any influence in the new world it is to help in that way and even if it takes 200 years to become practical, then after my death that will bring out practical results, and then my children's children will shake hands with the Protestants of the new world in a friendly manner. I do not wish these evils which exist in Europe to be continued, as much as I can influence it, among the half-breeds.[74]

As to his claims to be a prophet—would the half-breeds have acknowledged him as a prophet "if they had not seen that I could see something into the future?" "We all see into the future more or less. . . . I say humbly, through the grace of God, I believe I am the prophet of the new world."[75]

Riel had been speaking for an hour, and although there were a few spectators who had been moved to sympathy, most of them grew bored. The day was warm, and the air was heavy in the crowded courtroom. He would have to bring his words to an end. And yet he had so much to say. There would have to be a few more words about the unrepresentative nature of the North-West Council.

If you take the plea of the defence that I am not responsible for my acts, acquit me completely, since I have been quarreling with an insane and irresponsible Government. If you pronounce in favour of the Crown which contends that I am responsible, acquit me all the same. You are perfectly justified in declaring that having my reason and sound mind, I have acted reasonably and in self-defence, while the Government, my accuser, being irresponsible, and consequently insane, cannot but have acted wrong. . . .[76]

He hesitated.

"Are you done?" asked Richardson wearily. Not yet. Just a few minutes more.

For fifteen years I have been neglecting myself. . . . The Reverend Father André has often had the kindness to feed my family with a sack of flour, and Father Fourmond. My wife and children are without means, while I am working more than any representative in the North-West. Although . . . I worked to better the condition of the people of the Saskatchewan at the risk of my life, to better the condition of the people of the North-West, I have never had any pay . . . If you say I was right, you can conscientiously acquit me, as I hope through the help of God you will. You will console those who have been fifteen years around me only partaking in my sufferings. What you will do in justice to me, in justice to my family, in justice to my friends, in justice to the North-West, will be rendered a hundred times to you in this world, and to use a sacred expression, life everlasting in the other.[77]

He had finished.

In complete silence Christopher Robinson stood up to present the argument for the Crown. He knew his case was won, that Riel had done more than any Crown witness to destroy the whole edifice of insanity Fitzpatrick had so carefully erected. But if the prisoner had not succeeded in saving his life, he had, at least, preserved his self-respect.

Robinson's speech was the antithesis of his opponent's. It was cold, clear and logical. There were no histrionics, none of the Irishman's passionate eloquence.   Perhaps it was all the more effective for that very reason, because the court had been drained of its emotions by Riel. Robinson challenged the argument of insanity, cited Nolin's evidence of Riel's demand for money and pictured the prisoner as "not merely a man of strong mind but unusually long-headed . . . a man who calculated his schemes and drew his plans with shrewdness, and was controlled by no insane impulse."[78]   He played down the evidence of Dr. Roy and set up against it that of Middleton, Young and others, who had daily observed Riel's demeanour since he had given himself up on March 15. Brick by brick, Robinson built up the structure of guilt skilfully using the evidence of Nolin, Willoughby, Lash, Astley, Crozier, McKay and the various documents that had been introduced to the court, such as Riel's note to Poundmaker, his ultimatum to Crozier, his appeals to the half-breeds of Battleford and Qu'Appelle.   "Those who are guilty of this rebellion and those who have not a proper excuse," he declared, "have taken the step upon their own heads, and they must suffer the punishment which the law from all time, and which the law for the last five centuries has declared to be the punishment of the crime of treason."

It was late in the afternoon of July 31 when Mr. Justice Richardson began his address to the jury.   So late that he had no opportunity to do more than define the nature of the charge and remind the jury of its duty to decide whether Riel was implicated in the acts charged against him and, if so, whether he was accountable for them.   The next morning the judge continued.   He dismissed the argument against the jurisdiction of the court and stressed the need for the defence to prove insanity beyond all question of doubt.

It was fifteen minutes past two o'clock when the jury retired.   Riel knelt in the dock and prayed fervently.   In the body of the courtroom the hum of conversation and the sound of Riel's voice, now faint, now loud, "sounded a contrast strange and even horrible," wrote Nicholas Flood Davin.[79]   Sometimes Riel would rise to speak to his counsel, and then sink back again upon his knees while newspaper reporters pushed and shoved and noisily prepared the messages to be sent to their papers. At three-fifteen in the afternoon the jury returned.   Riel jumped to his feet.   He gripped the railing of the dock and made a strenuous effort to appear cool and collected.   The clerk asked, "Gentlemen of the jury, is the prisoner guilty or not guilty?"   "Guilty," replied the foreman. He did not dare look at the prisoner, for there were tears in his own eyes, and he had argued in vain on Riel's behalf with the other jurymen.[80] Then he added, "Your Honour, I have been asked by my brother jurors to recommend the prisoner to the mercy of the Crown."   Without emotion Richardson replied, "I may say in answer to you that the recommendation which you have given will be forwarded in the proper manner to the proper authorities."[81]

Turning to Riel, Richardson put the routine question, "Louis Riel, have you anything to say why the sentence of the court should not be pronounced upon you, for the offence of which you have been found guilty?" There was a moment's pause. Then Riel answered, "Yes, your Honour."[82]

"Your Honours, gentlemen of the jury," Riel began. Richardson interjected abruptly, "There is no jury now, they are discharged." Riel hesitated only momentarily. "Well, they have passed away before me. . . . But at the same time I consider them yet still there, still in their seats." Now he began to speak with assurance.

The court has done the work for me, and although at first appearance it seems to be against me, I am so confident in the ideas which I have had the honour to express yesterday, that I think it is for good, and not for my loss. Up to this moment I have been considered by a certain party as insane, by another party as a criminal. . . . So there was hostility, and there was contempt, and there was avoidance. Today, by the verdict of the court, one of those situations has disappeared. I suppose that after having been condemned, I will cease to be called a fool. . . . I consider it is a great advantage. . . . I cannot fulfil my mission as long as I am looked upon as an insane being. . . . Should I be executed—at least if I were going to be executed—I would not be executed as an insane man. It would be a great consolation for my mother, for my wife, for my children . . . for my countrymen.

This desire to remove the stigma of insanity was almost an obsession with him, almost as much an obsession as his sense of divine mission. "And in some way, I think, that, to a certain number of people, the verdict against me today is proof that maybe I am a prophet. Maybe Riel is a prophet, he suffered enough for it. . . . I have been hunted as an elk for fifteen years."[83]

This, Riel's second speech in the courtroom in Regina, was more coherent, less emotional, than his earlier one. It would almost seem as if his first effort had been unprepared and delivered spontaneously in an effort to disprove the charge of insanity, while the second was more carefully prepared and thought out in advance. It may have been the speech he had intended to give in the first place. In any event, the second speech was an historical record of his actions in 1869/70, an effort to show that troubles in the Saskatchewan were not to be viewed "as an isolated fact" but were "the result of fifteen years' war" whose origin "lies in the difficulty of Red River." And so he talked about the Canadian commissioners sent to Red River in 1869/70, about Ritchot, Judge Black and the negotiations with Ottawa, and about the 1,400,000 acre land grant, one-seventh of the arable land of the Province of Manitoba, which had been given the half-breeds by the Manitoba Act. "God is the master of the universe," Riel declared, "and as a good father, he gives a portion of his lands to that nation, to that tribe, to everyone, that is his heritage, that is his share of the inheritance." Then turning to the half-breeds of the North-West, he argued that they, too, had a right to God's lands, their inheritance from their Indian forebears. "We are not birds," he said. "We have to walk on the ground."[84] As far as his own personal claims were concerned, "If Canada is just with me, if Canada respects my life, my liberty, my reputation, they will give me all they have taken from me"—for he had received nothing from the original half-breed grant in Manitoba. Nor had the Canadian Government ever accorded him the amnesty that had been promised, a real amnesty, not an amnesty that was no amnesty.

He stopped. Richardson looked up. "Is that all?" he asked. "No," replied Riel, "excuse me, I feel weak and if I stop at times, I wish you would be kind enough to—"[85]

Again he spoke about the people of the Saskatchewan. Surely they were entitled to one-seventh of the land of the Territories. If they should receive it, what objection could there be to settling it, as he had so often proposed, with the hard-pressed Catholic peoples of Europe? Then he talked about his own claims and traversed the familiar ground of his services during the Fenian Raids, his withdrawal as candidate in Provencher in favour of Sir George Cartier. But his own claims could never be isolated from those of his people. "I struggled not only for myself," he declared, "but I struggled for the rights, for the inauguration of the principles of responsible and constitutional government in Manitoba. That was conceded about the time I was banished."[86]

As he drew near the end of his speech, he demanded a special commission to try him on the charges of 1869/70 as well as on those of 1885. He could never quite rid himself of the haunting ghost of the Orangeman, Thomas Scott. "I wish," he asked, "to have a trial that will cover the space of fifteen years, on which public opinion is not satisfied. . . . I wish my career should be tried; not the last part of it." Then he asked that a commission of doctors might be appointed to examine him, not from the standpoint of sanity—the court had already decided that—but to determine whether or not he was an impostor. "I ask that a commission of doctors sit and if they examine me they can see if I was sincere or not." The notion that he might be looked upon as a deliberate impostor was as hateful to him as the suggestion that he was insane. He wanted to be cleared of the objectionable charge. "If I have been astray," said he, "I have been astray, not as an impostor, but according to my conscience."[87]

His effort exhausted him as it exhausted his audience. The speech made little impact on those who listened to it. The emotional excitement of the previous day evaporated once the jury's decision was made known, and everybody knew that nothing that Riel could say now would have any influence on his fate. Richardson's sentence was brief, cold, even brutal. "For what you did, the remarks you have made form no excuse whatever. For what you have done the law requires you to answer. . . . I cannot hold out any hope to you . . . that Her Majesty will, after what you have been the cause of doing, open her hand of clemency to you. . . ." Then came the awful and traditional words: "that you be taken now from here to the police guard-room at Regina . . . and that you be kept there till the 18th of September next, that on the 18th of September next you will be taken to the place appointed for your execution, and there be hanged by the neck till you are dead, and may God have mercy on your soul." [88]

The court rose.

CHAPTER 19

Execution

T HE WHOLE OF CANADA had watched the trial of Riel with a growing intensity of feeling. Broadly speaking, English-Canadians approved the verdict of guilty; some even wondered why the jury should have gone as far as to recommend the accused man to the mercy of the court. French-Canadians, however, taking their cue from Fitzpatrick, Lemieux and the writings of the clergy, were convinced that Riel was thoroughly insane, and they wondered why the jury should ever have convicted him. Since he had been convicted, and convicted by an English jury, the only explanation could be racial prejudice. As each day passed, public discussions grew more and more heated. To the English-Canadians, Riel was a double-dyed rebel—he had twice levied war on Canadians, and he was the murderer of the Orangeman, Thomas Scott. That there might be extenuating circumstances, some justification for Riel's agitation, few of them—there were a few, like Edward Farrer of the Toronto *Mail*—would concede. To the French-Canadians, Riel appeared more and more a patriot, a man who had stood up for the rights of the French métis both in Manitoba and in the Saskatchewan. It hardly helped to pacify them when they learned that not only Jackson but Riel's other English-speaking supporter who was brought to trial, the farmer from Red Deer Hill, Thomas Scott, who despite his name was in no way related to his Manitoba namesake, had been discharged. Riel, the French-Canadian, had been sentenced to hang; Scott, the English-Canadian, had been freed.

In Ottawa, the Prime Minister of Canada and his colleagues listened to the shouts for pardon and the shouts for death, and consulted their political futures. Macdonald was not alarmed. "The conviction of Riel is satisfactory," he telegraphed to Dewdney. "There is an attempt in Quebec to pump up a patriotic feeling about him—but I don't think it will amount to much."[1] For the moment, therefore, the government need take no stand, one way or the other; there was no need deliberately to provoke a political crisis over Riel, particularly while his case was still *sub judice*. Riel's appeal had gone to the Court of Queen's Bench in Manitoba. Macdonald did not think there would be any change in the verdict of the lower court, but there were those who did. Lemieux, Riel's chief counsel, was persuaded that Riel was insane, and he felt that the recommendation to mercy was obvious evidence of a real doubt in the minds of the men who had made up the jury, as to Riel's sanity.[2] But Lemieux's arguments and those of his colleagues, Charles Fitzpatrick and J. S. Ewart, proved no more convincing to the Court of Queen's Bench in Manitoba than they had to the Stipendiary Magistrate's Court in the Territories. The judges of the Manitoba Court looked on the Magistrate's Court as thoroughly competent to try a case of high treason, and they were not prepared to accept the argument that the weight of the evidence was in favour of Riel's insanity. Said Chief Justice Wallbridge, "The evidence upon the question of insanity shows that the prisoner did know that he was acting illegally and that he was responsible for his acts."[3] Joseph Dubuc, Riel's friend of earlier years, now a judge, did not attend the sittings of the court. He had obtained leave to attend an alumni reunion of his classmates at the College of Montreal.[4]

Owing to the time involved in carrying his case to appeal, Riel did not die on September 18. Nor did he die on October 16, the date to which his reprieve was extended. There was still another appeal, one to the Judicial Committee of the Privy Council. However, on October 22, the Judicial Committee ruled against the defence contention regarding the inadequacy of the court which tried Riel. With the question of Riel's sanity or insanity, the Judges of the Judicial Committee did not concern themselves. The editor of the *Times* in London declared:

It was certain before the Committee sat that their judgment would be in these terms. All that could be said on Riel's behalf was urged by his counsel on Wednesday, and when the arguments for the petitioner were concluded their Lordships announced that they were ready to pronounce judgment without calling on the Attorney-General to reply. This could mean only that the case for the petitioner had broken down and that nothing remained except to make a formal declaration of the opinion which the Committee had formed about it.

"That he has deserved death," continued the *Times* about Riel, "will be the universal opinion in this country and if the Canadian Executive see fit as a matter of policy to give effect to the capital sentence, there will be no question raised here as to the entire rectitude of their resolve."[5] There may have been such universal opinion in England, but there was no unanimity of view in Canada.

II

While the Canadian newspapers were fighting over his trial in Canada and his lawyers were arguing over his fate in Winnipeg and London, Riel remained quietly in his cell in the Mounted Police barracks in

Regina. He was always under guard, but he was permitted to attend
Mass on Sundays with the other métis prisoners and to exercise himself
in the small barrack square. The rest of his time he spent praying,
writing, noting his visions and recording his prophecies. On July 10,
Deane had written to Archbishop Taché asking for a chaplain, pointing
out that it was no part of the policy of the Mounted Police "to deprive
the prisoners of spiritual consolation."[6] In response to this appeal,
Taché first sent Father Dugast and, later, Father Cloutier to Regina,
and later still, Father Fourmond, Father Cochin and Father André.
Both Father Fourmond and Father Cochin talked frequently with Riel;
they argued with him about his religious deviations; they prayed with
him; they exhorted him. Finally they persuaded him to abjure what
they looked upon as his heresies. First verbally and then in writing,
Riel declared his willingness to return to the bosom of his mother
church, the church into which he had been born and in which he had
been raised. It was a great burden off his mind, for it meant that he
would once again be permitted to partake of the Blessed Sacrament,
which he loved and which meant so much to him.[7]

To Fourmond, Riel's recantation was a victory over the man who had
boasted that he had overthrown "the old Roman." Yet in some ways
it was a hollow victory. For Riel, if once more a practising Roman
Catholic, never abandoned his belief in his mission and his role as a
prophet. Fourmond and Cochin, and later André, recognized this fact,
but they did not try to press their victory too far. It was enough that
Riel was completely honest in his retraction, and that in those periods
of religious exaltation, when he once more saw visions and believed
himself to be in communication with the Holy Spirit, he was not himself.
It was a compromise, but it was not an unreasonable one. "Riel spends
all his time writing and praying," wrote Cochin. "When Mass is said
in prison, he assists with complete calmness and devotion. To see him
one would take him for a saint."[8] But André admitted, in another
letter, "as soon as one touches upon his weakness as far as religion and
prophecy are concerned, he is no longer the same, and his eyes and face
undergo a complete change." "He is a strange phenomenon," André
added, "I really don't know how to regard him."[9]

September 18, the day fixed for Riel's execution, approached with
frightening rapidity, although from time to time there were rumours of
a possible reprieve. Rumours or no rumours, Riel continued his
preparations to face death. His confessions and professions of faith
were always sincere, even though, as André remarked, "his mania for
prophesying . . . did not abandon him."[10] He was tense, worried and
restless, but he showed no fear of death. Rather, if we may believe a
notation in one of his notebooks, he looked forward to a "good death,"

for it would mean his union with Christ and the Blessed Virgin.[11]   Early in September various members of his family came from St. Vital to see him, his mother, his wife and his brother.[12]   Henriette could not leave St. Vital.[13]   These last farewells were trying, heart-rending experiences for all concerned; but Louis did not break down.   "Other men live unaware of the hour of their death," said he, "I know the hour of my death.   God has informed me of it."[14]

On September 17, Louis learned that the rumours of a reprieve were true.   His execution had been postponed for another month.   André brought him the news, and he broke down and sobbed hysterically. "All his moral strength abandoned him," said André.   "He had showed great strength of will, but he could no longer sustain the battle."[15] What was worse, he would once again, during the next four weeks, be forced to go through the purgatory of waiting.

As soon as he recovered himself, Louis wrote to St. Vital, to his mother and his wife, telling them the good news of the postponement.   It was a blessing he owed to their prayers, he believed, a blessing because it would give him "twenty-nine more days to prepare myself for death, and to enjoy life."[16]   It seemed more than a coincidence to Riel that the 17th was the birthday of his little daughter, Angélique.   "Blessed be this day when God deigns to look with charitable favour upon me; this day which was to have been the eve of my death has been changed to a beautiful day of thanksgiving," he wrote to Marguerite.[17]   Perhaps it was an omen for the future.   There was a new note of confidence in this letter, a confidence that was sufficiently contagious to affect André, who began to wonder if Riel would really be executed at all.[18]   "He has a particular talent for winning friends and gaining their sympathies," wrote André to Taché.   "People cannot help becoming interested in a man who is truly a phenomenon in himself."[19]

But if the load of concern for the immediate future had been lifted from his shoulders, there were other worries to tax his mind and dampen his joy.   Marguerite was not well.   The worry over her husband's fate, combined with the hardships she had experienced during the previous winter, had drained her strength and left her weak and listless.   And her cough never seemed to let up.   In his notebook, Louis bared his heart in a way he would not in conversation, even to his confessor.   "Oh my God!   If it be Thy will, please help to lengthen our days and help us to raise our dear little children in the holiness of Thy service.   If it please Thee, through Jesus, Mary, Joseph, grant us life.   Oh my God! save my dear wife."[20]

The strain of waiting was also telling on André.   Not only had he been obliged to give evidence in Riel's trial, and to serve as Riel's confessor, but he also had to attend the trials of the other métis prisoners, and he felt bitter that it should be a French-Canadian, Judge Charles Rouleau, who should prove so implacable an enemy of the poor, deluded métis brought before him.   In one of his letters André referred to Rouleau as "a vindictive man and a servile instrument in the hands of the government,"[21] and in another he wrote of his "malevolent" disposition.[22]   On October 12, André asked Archbishop Taché if a replacement could not be found, so that he might return to Prince Albert.[23] Moreover, he admitted that his sympathy for the man whom he had so strenuously opposed only a few months before, had grown to such an extent that it had led him to use language in some of his letters that had proved embarrassing both to the Archbishop and to himself.[24]   He wondered if his usefulness in Regina was not at an end.   Taché did not want to replace him; neither did Riel want to see him go.   Instead, Riel urged him to stay on at Regina as the prison chaplain.   In response to Riel's request, André resolved to play out his role until the fate of Riel should be decided.   "In spite of the terror," which the prospect of accompanying Riel to the scaffold inspired in him, he would continue to do his duty by the condemned man.[25]

Then came the second reprieve.   Surely Riel would not hang now.[26] Even Marguerite seems to have felt better, although her improvement was only temporary.[27]   More and more Louis devoted himself to his prayers and his prophecies, to the composition of an article on the nature of God and another on the interpretation of difficult portions of scripture.   He proposed to change the names of the planets and the stars to give them biblical rather than pagan names.   From time to time he recorded his revelations: Spain would come to the aid of the North-West; Manitoba would become entirely French-Canadian; in 500 years the métis population would number forty million; Bishop Bourget was "almost a thousand times" more saintly than Loyola; Louis XIV had attained heaven only after a long period in purgatory; Henry IV had been damned.[28]

As he wrote, there came a blow he had neither foreseen nor contemplated.   Marguerite, his wife, gave birth to her third child.   But the little boy lived only a few hours.   Marguerite herself survived, but the hand of death was upon her.   She would not live many months.[29]   It was the loss of the little child that hurt Louis most.   "The misery that I feel in seeing my little one taken from me without ever being able to embrace him, without ever being able to give him my love strikes to the innermost depths of my soul," he wrote to Henriette.   "I can only thank the good Lord in his charity, for having given the baby several hours of life, long enough for it to be baptized.   The pure water poured upon its infant forehead, the sacred words on its little spirit, have made it one of the children of God. My dear little one came into two worlds in a single day; this world and the next. He appeared on earth only long enough to receive the sign of our faith. . . ."[30] Riel never quite recovered from his sorrow. Perhaps that is why he prepared to go to the scaffold on November 10, resigned to the fate which was his.

Meanwhile the excitement in Canada continued. Macdonald could not have been more wrong when he said the agitation would not amount to much. Instead of declining, demands for Riel's pardon or for his death grew more and more raucous. It was no longer a question of whether Riel was innocent or guilty, it was whether he was sane or insane, whether he should live or die. Macdonald's friends—the Honourable John Norquay of Manitoba was one of them—wrote to remind him that any clemency shown Riel would lose the Conservative party the votes of English-speaking Canada.[31] But what of those hundreds of signatures on the petitions from Quebec?[32] As far as Macdonald himself concerned, he was prepared to stand firm; but would his French-Canadian colleagues in the cabinet do the same?[33] Finally, as a concession to Chapleau and Langevin, Macdonald agreed to grant Riel another reprieve until November 16 and to appoint a special commission to inquire into Riel's mental state.

On October 31, three medical men, Dr. Jukes of the Mounted Police, Dr. F. X. Valade of Ottawa, and Dr. M. Lavell, the Warden of the Kingston penitentiary, were appointed to examine Riel. It was patently impossible for the three physicians to determine whether or not Riel had been of unsound mind when he formed his Provisional Government in March and led his men to Duck Lake with his crucifix in his hands. All they could do would be to express their opinions as to whether or not Riel was normal when they examined him in November, six months later. It is difficult to look upon this medical commission as anything other than a meaningless political sop. The instructions given the physicians were too circumscribed, and they left too little room for any decision other than that Riel was an accountable, responsible being. In a private letter to Dr. Lavell, Macdonald reminded him:

Remember that the Jury have decided that he was sane when his treasons were committed and at the time of his trial. The Judge approved of the verdict and the Court of Queen's Bench at Manitoba on appeal confirmed it. You cannot therefore go beyond that verdict and your enquiry will be limited to the simple question whether he at the time of your report is sufficiently a reasonable and accountable being to know right from wrong.

Of course, added Macdonald, if Riel is possessed of a "raging dementia," the law humanely provided for a postponement of his execution "but if—

whatever illusions he may have—he still knows right from wrong the law should be allowed to take effect."[34]

Jukes had visited Riel often enough to have made up his mind about the métis leader. Valade and Lavell had never seen Riel before. Lavell was impressed by him. He found Riel with a "manly expression of countenance, sharp eyes, intelligent and pleasing address." "His conversational powers were remarkable," Lavell noted, "voice capable of any amount of modulation, with a rare charm about it. At times in conversation he manifested all the characteristics of his race, excitable and enthusiastic, while at other times, when speaking of circumstances having reference to his present condition and prospects, his voice was soft, mellow and sweet, interesting to a degree, drawing out the sympathies of the listener." Lavell did not reveal the nature of his mission to Riel. He merely posed as a newspaper man and questioned the condemned man on a variety of topics. Riel expounded all the familiar views; but what struck Lavell, throughout his conversation, was his real concern for his children, his fear of the disgrace that his execution as a criminal might have on them, his desire in some way to vindicate his actions so that his children "when they grew up should not feel ashamed of their father." Lavell, after several visits, parted from Riel "with depressed feelings." "The consciousness of the convictions I held as to his accountability gave me pain," wrote Lavell. "I became during my interviews with him very much interested. He impressed me as a notable character. With other characteristics I have mentioned he was enthusiastic and impulsive, and if those characteristics had been diverted into proper channels he would have made his mark for good in the great North-West."[35]

Dr. Jukes felt much the same as Lavell. He found Riel an interesting and attractive personality, a man suffering from illusions on matters of politics and religion, but otherwise a normal human being. Like Lavell, he felt drawn to the man. In a letter to Macdonald he wrote, "I confess I should be well pleased if justice and popular clamour could be satisfied without depriving this man of life."[36] Valade was more inclined to emphasize Riel's unsoundness of mind, as far as his hallucinations and illusions were concerned, than were his colleagues. But the burthen of the three reports was much the same: on matters other than religion and politics, Riel could distinguish right from wrong. Despite their variations, the doctors' reports were sufficiently alike to provide the government with good talking points on the hustings. So the cabinet, without any resignations on the part of its French-speaking ministers, decided that Riel should enjoy no clemency. "He shall hang," cried Macdonald, "though every dog in Quebec bark in his favour."[37]

III

Riel waited out his last hours with his confessor, with his rosary, his little bottle of water from Lourdes and a small statue of St. Joseph he had received from Father André. He had written to J. W. Taylor, and to President Cleveland of the United States, earlier during his imprisonment, and had received no reply.[38] There was no hope of help from the country of which he had become a citizen. On November 6, he wrote his will—not that he had anything to dispose of, but he could reiterate his submission to the Church and beg the forgiveness of his mother and his wife for all the distress he had caused them. And he could bestow his blessing upon his children. "I leave neither gold nor silver . . . but I pray God in his infinite mercy . . . to fill my mind and my heart with the truly paternal blessing that I wish to give them. Jean, my son, Angélique my daughter, I bless you in the name of the Father, Son and Holy Ghost, that you may devote yourselves to the knowledge of the will of God and faithfully carry it out in all piety and sincerity. . . ."[39] His body, he had told André some weeks before, was to be sent to Manitoba, to be buried beside that of his father in the church-yard of St. Boniface.[40] Then he turned to complete a "last mémoire" on the métis of the North-West, which he had started some weeks before.[41]

And before he realized it, the day was Sunday, November 15. The gallows had been erected in a fenced enclosure next to the guardroom. Tomorrow he would, in all probability, have to tread the scaffold, or so Father André told him. "*Laetatus sum in his quae dicta sunt mihi, in domum Domini ibimus*, I have rejoiced in the things that have been said to me, we will enter into the house of the Lord," he replied calmly.[42]

Only by a chance encounter with Irvine later in the day did André learn that the authority for the execution had come from Ottawa and that Riel's death would take place early the following morning. He rushed to Riel's cell to continue his ministrations. Later Dr. Jukes came to pay a last visit to the man whose fate he had himself helped to determine. As he had on previous occasions when Jukes had visited him, Riel began to talk about his visions. He had had a vision in Montana in which an angel had promised him that, like Christ, he would be raised on the third day after his death. Jukes did not argue with him. He could not agree with Riel; but he knew Riel well enough not to question the sincerity of the condemned man.

As they talked, Colonel Irvine entered with Sheriff Chapleau. Chapleau then told Riel that the sentence of execution would be carried out at eight o'clock the next morning. "I thought I had twenty-four hours," said Riel. But he displayed no emotion. "Riel's manner was dignified, calm and composed," wrote Jukes. "He spoke with his usual politeness and even laughed quietly at some remarks made by the Sheriff." To a query from Jukes, Riel replied that he had been sleeping well "but that tonight he would not sleep." When the doctor asked him if there was any delicacy he would like, Riel replied simply that three eggs would be acceptable; he had all the milk and other things he required. As Jukes turned to leave, Riel shook hands with him and thanked him for all the little kindnesses he had received. "I never saw him calmer, more resigned or more at ease," wrote Jukes.[43] With the assistance of André, and Father McWilliams, a priest he had known as a schoolboy, who was passing through Regina, Louis Riel spent the night in prayer and spiritual exercises. He prayed for his mother, for his wife, for his family, for his benefactors and even for his enemies, for Taché, for Grandin, for Pope Leo XIII and for Sir John A. Macdonald.[44]

Sometime after midnight he wrote a letter, his last letter, to his mother.[45] The old family loyalties, the close bond of blood relationship that had characterized his early life, and which, indeed, was the feature of all métis families, filled his heart to overflowing.

My dear Mother:

I received your letter with your holy blessing. Yesterday morning Father André put it on the altar, and said Mass for me in honour of Mary Immaculate, thus placing me, so to speak, in the shadow of her blessing. This morning the good father took your letter and placed it on my head at the moment in the Mass, when as celebrant, he gave the benediction and, uniting his blessing with yours, he thus transmitted to me the blessings of the Mass, with the many favours, spiritual and temporal, that you implored in my favour, in favour of my dear wife, my children, my beloved brothers and sisters, and my brothers- and sisters-in-law, my nephews and my nieces, all of whom are dear to me.

Dear mother, may the prayers of your eldest son, may my wishes and my prayers as a servant of God, mount to the throne of our Lord Jesus Christ, to the throne of Mary ever Virgin, and of St. Joseph, my dear and great protector; and may the mercy, the great consolation of God, of all that we know is dear in Paradise, be your lot forever.

May you be blessed from generation to generation for having been so good a mother to me.

May your faith, your firm hope, and your exemplary charity be like trees laden with good fruits in the future. And when your last day shall come, may God be so pleased with you that your pious spirit will leave the earth on the wings of the love of the angels.

It is two hours past midnight. Good Father André told me this morning to hold myself ready for tomorrow. I listen to him, I obey. I am prepared for everything according to his counsel and his recommendations.

But the Lord is helping me to maintain a peaceful and a calm spirit, like the oil in a vase which cannot become agitated.

I am doing everything I can think of to be ready for any eventuality, keeping myself in an even calm, according to the pious exhortations of the venerable Bishop Ignace Bourget.

Yesterday and today I have prayed God to strengthen you and grant you all his gentle comfort so that your heart may not be troubled by pain and anxiety.

I embrace you all with the greatest affection.

You, dear mother, I embrace you as a son whose soul is full of filial devotion.

You, my dear wife, I embrace you as a Christian husband in the Catholic spirit of conjugal union.

My dear little children, I embrace you as a Christian father, blessing you to the full extent of divine mercy both for the present and for the future.

You my dear brothers and sisters, brothers- and sisters-in-law, nephews, cousins and friends, I embrace you all with all the cordiality of which my heart is capable.

Please be joyful,

Dear Mother,

I am your affectionate, submissive and obedient son

Louis David Riel

Then it was back to his prayers and his rosary. He thought briefly of speaking from the scaffold, but he gave up the idea at André's request. In the early hours of the morning, he made his last confession. Mass was said, and Louis took Communion. At seven o'clock, André administered extreme unction, "I die Catholic and in the only true faith" were the last words Riel wrote.

Dawn broke slowly. Outside it was cold and clear. The hoar frost glittered in the morning sun. About eight o'clock, the Deputy Sheriff unlocked the door of the cell. It was the responsibility of Sheriff Chapleau, but the French-Canadian refused to play his role in the final tragedy. Riel looked up. "Mr. Gibson, you want me?" he asked. "I am ready." He was pale but calm. Father McWilliams, with his stole over his overcoat, went out first; Louis followed, carrying a small ivory crucifix which had been lent him by Mrs. Forget. Behind him came the Mounted Police escort in red tunics, and at the rear, Father André, a white surplice over his black soutane. Slowly they climbed the staircase towards the exit leading to the scaffold. The two priests recited the office of the dying. At the top, Riel knelt again with McWilliams, while André bestowed upon him a final absolution, "*Ego te absolvo peccatis tuis.*" He was nervous, and for a moment, but only for a moment. André wondered if Riel would succumb to the emotion he was trying hard not to show. The condemned man, however, made his responses in a firm voice. Asked if he willingly made the sacrifice of his life, he answered, "With all my heart, father."

"Do you quit this life with regret?"

"No. I thank God for having given me the strength to die well. I am on the threshold of eternity and I do not want to turn back."

"For the love of God do you forgive your enemies, all those who had desired and worked for your death?"

"I forgive them with all my heart as I would ask God to forgive me."

"Have you nothing in your heart against anybody, and is your conscience at peace?"

"I die at peace with God and with man, and I thank all those who had helped me in my misfortunes, and also the officers and the guards who have treated me with respect and compassion."[47]

Riel rose. The hangman approached and bound his hands behind his back. André kissed Riel, and together they walked towards the scaffold. Louis's face was set. He did not falter, showed no signs of weakness. "Courage, Father," he said to André, who could not keep back his tears. The mask and rope were placed over Louis's neck. "Say Our Father," said McWilliams. Riel bowed his head. André was weeping openly. Together Riel and McWilliams intoned the age-old prayer. Finally they reached the words "deliver us from evil. . . ."[48]

Outside the barracks a reporter from the Regina *Leader* watched the crowd. At the door of Colonel Irvine's house stood Lord Boyle and several uniformed officers, including Commissioner Irvine and Colonel McLeod. Near the enclosure behind which the métis tragedy was drawing to a close, there stood various groups of people, talking and grumbling because they could not see the hanging. As the moment of the execution approached, there was silence. Then a dull heavy sound as of a body falling. "The God damned son of a bitch is gone at last," said one voice. "Yes," said another, "the son of a bitch is gone for certain now."[49]

There followed some heartless laughter. But it was thin and brittle.

IV

After Riel's body had been viewed by the coroner's jury, it was placed in a rough, wooden coffin and locked in a small enclosure beneath the gallows.[50] Chapleau had told André that there would be no problem about sending the body to St. Boniface, but Colonel Irvine would not give his permission for its removal—not, at least, until he had received the necessary authority from the Lieutenant-Governor. Nor would Dewdney act until Ottawa had told him to do so.[51] "This poor unhappy

Riel," wrote André in bitterness to Archbishop Taché, "that the government seems to want to persecute and pursue in its hate, even in death."[52] Not until the 18th was the body released.

Meanwhile ugly rumours had started to circulate in Regina—rumours that some of Riel's enemies had mutilated the body of the dead man.[53] To put an end to these ghoulish stories, the coffin was opened late on the night of the 18th in the presence of Jukes, Irvine, McLeod and Pascal Bonneau,[54] a friend of Riel's who had come to take the body away. But it had not been touched or disturbed in any way.[55] The lid was then nailed on the coffin, and in the darkness the wooden box was borne by several Mounted Policemen to Bonneau's wagon which was standing by the barrack door. On the following morning, the 19th, a simple funeral was held in St. Mary's Church in Regina. The coffin was placed beneath the floor of the chapel.

On December 9th, Bonneau arranged for the transfer of the body to St. Boniface.[56] It was all done secretly and without arousing any attention. In a cold empty freight car, Riel returned to Red River, to the country of his birth, to the scene of his greatest political triumph. For two days he lay in state in his mother's house in St. Vital, while hundreds of métis filed past, paying their last respects to the man they have never ceased to honour as the greatest of their race. Several hundred miles away, Charles Nolin was wondering about running for parliament. But he would never do so. He had survived his cousin, but he was dead politically. His name would always stick in métis throats. Finally, on December 12, Riel's coffin was hoisted on strong loyal métis shoulders and carried six miles through the snow to St. Boniface. In the cathedral, a requiem Mass was sung by Father Dugast, assisted by Father Cloutier. On the Archbishop's throne sat Alexandre Taché, the prelate who had watched the young Louis at his studies and had chosen him to be a priest, who had sent him to be educated at Montreal, who had tried to obtain an amnesty for him in the troublous years of the 1870's. In the same chancel there could be seen the bearded face of Noel Ritchot, the Abbé who had encouraged and guided Riel during the days of the Provisional Government of Assiniboia, who had borne the burden of the negotiations that had led to the formation of the Province of Manitoba. Elsewhere sat hundreds of nameless métis who were Riel's friends.[57]

Louis Riel is buried in the grounds of the Basilica in St. Boniface. Two or three steps away are the graves of his father and those of the voyageur, Jean Baptiste Lagemodière, and his wife, Marie Anne Gaboury. Above the spot where Louis lies stands a brown granite tombstone. On it are inscribed the simple words, "RIEL, 16 NOVEMBRE 1885."

Bibliographical Note

This biography is based largely on contemporary materials rather than on secondary sources. The materials used are to be found in libraries and archives in Canada, the United States and Great Britain. In the Public Archives of Canada, the most obvious sources are the Department of Justice, Miscellaneous Riel Papers and the Macdonald Papers. In Manitoba, there are two important collections of documents. In Winnipeg, the Provincial Archives of Manitoba possess various Riel Papers, Dubuc Papers and Morris Papers: across the Red River, the Archiepiscopal Archives of St. Boniface contain the correspondence of Archbishop Taché and those who administered the archdiocese in his absence. The Historical Society of St. Boniface has in its possession the papers collected by the late Mgr. d'Eschambault. The library in La Maison des Oblats de Marie Immaculée in Edmonton contains a number of letters and other documents touching upon the events of 1884/85, including the personal accounts collected by the Abbé Cloutier at the request of Archbishop Taché. The Glenbow Foundation in Calgary has a small collection of Dr. Juke's Papers. There are also some Riel letters in the Bibliothèque Mallet, Union St. Jean-Baptiste, Woonsocket, Rhode Island. In Montreal, Major Masson kindly permitted me to examine a number of family records in his private collection of the Masson Papers. Other items relating to Louis Riel—such as his correspondence with Bishop Bourget—will be found in the Episcopal Archives of Montreal; still others will be found in the Archives of Laval University and in the Provincial Archives of Quebec. The papers of the Rev. J. B. Proulx are in the Library of the Seminary at Ste. Thérèse. In Kingston, the Library of Queen's University has a number of Charles Mair's Papers. The Library of the Royal Canadian Military Institute in Toronto contains various items of the Denison correspondence. The Library of the University of Saskatchewan has some of the papers of W. H. Jackson. In London, the Public Record Office, C.O. 42 series, contains correspondence between London and Ottawa relating to the Riel risings. The Archives of the Hudson's Bay Company should be consulted for material relating to the events in Red River. Consular despatches from Winnipeg are to be found in the Archives of the State Department, Washington, D.C.

Contemporary printed materials of the first importance include the *Debates* and *Journals* of the House of Commons and the *Sessional Papers*. Files of the *Nor'Wester*, *The New Nation*, *Le Métis*, *Le Manitoba* and the *Prince Albert Times* will be found in the Provincial Archives of Manitoba. The *Globe* and the *Mail* of Toronto are useful sources, as are *Le Nouveau Monde*, *La Minerve* and *L'Etendard* of Montreal. Files of the *Fort Benton Record* and the *Helena Herald* are located in the Library of the State Historical Society of Montana, Helena, Montana.

Of the secondary sources, little need be said. The most useful to the writer were the published memoirs and recollections of those who actually participated in the events described, such as the Rev. George Young,

BIBLIOGRAPHICAL NOTE

Major Boulton, Lord Wolseley, Alexander Begg, Gabriel Dumont and General Middleton. A vast quantity of pamphlet material is available in the Public Archives of Canada. This ranges from such useful and pertinent pamphlets as Taché's *L'Amnistie*, Riel's *Mémoire* and his *Poésies Religieuses et Politiques*, to the fugitive writings of the political polemicists of 1885 and 1886. Other secondary sources used by the author may be found in the references following this note.

Note on Plates

There are numerous photographs and sketches of Louis Riel in existence in various public archives, particularly those of Ottawa, Quebec, Winnipeg and Regina. In the selection used in this book, an effort has been made to show Riel at various periods of his life from his childhood to his death, and in so doing to avoid, as far as possible, reprinting the already familiar portraits that have appeared in volumes dealing with the history of western Canada.

The frontispiece is taken from a photograph of Riel published some time after 1876 as a special premium, by the cigar manufacturers, S. Davis and Sons of Montreal. The 1858 picture is taken from a photograph by Lapres and Lavergne of Montreal. (From the Public Archives of Canada, Ottawa.) The 1866 photograph was made by A. Bazinet of Montreal and was lent to me by M. Emile Falardeau of the same city. The 1875 portrait was taken by Glenton, of Nashua, New Hampshire. It is part of the Mallet collection, Union St. Jean-Baptiste, Woonsocket, Rhode Island.

The photograph of Riel and his associates was taken at Red River in the autumn of 1869. The photograph used here is a copy of one formerly belonging to W. H. Miller of Kingston and now in the library of Queen's University. The names were supplied to Mr. Miller by the Reverend George Young. It should be noted that some of the names differ from those used by the late Reverend A. G. Morice of St. Boniface in his history of the Red River insurrection: for Charles Larocque, Morice substitutes F. Guilmette; for Ambroise Lépine, Baptiste Beauchemin; and for H. F. O'Lone, Bob O'Lone. The Reverend George Young was a contemporary of the men portrayed: presumably he is the better authority.

There are several alleged photographs of Thomas Scott in the provincial archives of Manitoba. The one included here seems to portray the character of Scott better than the others. The word "alleged" is used only because of the reluctance of the provincial archivist to give positive identification. Although there seems to be little reason to question the identity of the alleged Scott photograph, there is room for argument about the photograph of the young woman. This photograph was found among the papers taken at Batoche and held for many years by the Department of Justice before being turned over to the Public Archives of Canada, Ottawa. It is not unreasonable to assume, in the absence of any other portrait of a young woman among Riel's papers, that the one in existence is that of his wife. All the more so as the photograph has been identified by Riel descendants as *not* being that of any of Louis Riel's sisters. Yet it must be admitted that the same descendants, as well as the son of Napoléon Nault, would not say positively that it *was* a photograph of Marguerite Riel, of whom no portrait has hitherto been known to exist.

The photograph of Julie Lagimodière-Riel is from the Union St. Jean-Baptiste, Woonsocket, Rhode Island; the photograph of Louis Riel, Sr., from the Manitoba Archives, Winnipeg. The photograph of Louis Riel, 1858, comes from the Quebec Archives. Louis Riel, about 1868, is from the Public Archives of Canada, Ottawa, as is Louis Riel, Member of Parliament, about 1873. Louis Riel, about 1884, is from the Saskatchewan Archives, Regina, and Charles Nolin's photograph is from the Manitoba Archives, Winnipeg. Louis Riel, May 1885, is from the Library, Royal Military College of Canada, Kingston. Louis Riel, July 1885, is from the Public Archives of Canada, Ottawa. The photograph of the relatives of Louis Riel belonged to the late Mgr. Antoine d'Eschambault, Genthon, Manitoba. The relatives are: Henriette Riel-Poitras (sister), Jean Marie Poitras (brother-in-law), Julie Lagimodière-Riel (mother), Angélique Riel (daughter) and Jean Riel (son).

The final illustration is from a sketch by the well-known Canadian artist and illustrator, Octave Henri Julien (1852-1908), who was employed for many years by the *Canadian Illustrated News* and the Montreal *Star*. This sketch was subsequently reprinted in post-card form. (From the St. Boniface Historical Society.)

Abbreviations

A.A.M.	*Archives de l'archevêché, Montréal*
A.A.Q.	*Archives de l'archevêché, Québec*
A.A.ST.B.	*Archives de l'archevêché, St. Boniface*
A.O.E.	*Archives des Oblats de Marie Immaculée, Edmonton*
A.S.D.	*Archives of the State Department, Washington*
A.U.ST.J.B.	*Archives de l'Union St. Jean-Baptiste, Woonsocket*
C.M.	*Collège de Montréal*
C.S.P.	*Canada Sessional Papers*
C.STE.T.	*Collège Ste. Thérèse*
H.B.C.	*Hudson's Bay Company Archives, London*
P.A.C.	*Public Archives of Canada*
P.A.M.	*Provincial Archives of Manitoba, Winnipeg*
P.A.Q.	*Provincial Archives of Quebec, Quebec*
P.A.S.	*Provincial Archives of Saskatchewan, Saskatoon*
P.A.ST.N.	*Parish Archives, St. Norbert, Manitoba*
P.J.M.	*Palais de Justice, Montréal*
P.P.	*Parliamentary Papers*
P.R.O.	*Public Record Office*
Q.U.L.	*Queen's University Library*
R.C.M.I.	*Royal Canadian Military Institute*
ST.B.H.S.	*St. Boniface Historical Society*
U.S.L.	*University of Saskatchewan Library*

Notes

CHAPTER ONE: Family

1. *St.B.H.S.*, Notes by Henriette Riel-Poitras, sister of Louis Riel.
2. The name also appears as Lagimonière. It was originally Lavimaudière. The Lagimodières were descended from Samuel Lecompte, Sieur de la Vimaudière, who married Marie-Jeanne Jérémie at St. Nicholas, July 28, 1705.
3. Rev. P. Dugast, "The First Canadian Woman in the North-West" (*Historical and Scientific Society of Manitoba*, No. 62, 1901).
4. In 1806 a white woman came to the west from the Orkneys disguised as a man. On December 29, 1806, she gave birth to a child at Pembina. Both the mother and the child were sent back to Scotland. (W. J. Healy, *Women of Red River* (Winnipeg. 1923),1.)
5. *St.B.H.S.*, Notes by Henriette Riel-Poitras.
6. Louis (1844-1885); Philomène and Elie (died in infancy); Sara (1848-1883); Marie (1850?-1873); Octavie (1852?-1890, married Louis Lavallée); Eulalie (1853-1931, married William Gladu); Charles (1854-1874); Joseph (1857-1892); Henriette (1860-1898, married Jean-Marie Poitras); Alexandre (1863-1903).
7. The oldest document relating to the Riels is the concession of a piece of land by Dame Louise Bissot, widow of Seraphin Marganne and seigneuresse of LaValtrie to Jean Riol dit l'Irelande, August 3, 1700, before the notary Antoine Adhémar. (See Rev. A. Champagne C.R.I.C., "Louis Riel avait-il sang irlandais" *L'Action Catholique*, November 25, 1951).
8. The marriage contract of Jean-Baptiste Riel *dit* l'Irelande and Louise Cottu was drawn up before the Rev. L. Chaigneau. Louise was the daughter of François Cottu. The contract is dated January 20, 1704. Their first child was Jean Baptiste, who was baptized at Ile Dupas, June 12, 1705. On October 6, 1710, the Sovereign Council registered the "lettres de naturalité accordeés par sa Majesté . . . au mois de mai" to some eighty persons, including "Jean-Baptiste Réel, irlandais, habitant de LaValtrie, marié à une française et ayant des enfants." (See letter, Rev. A. Champagne to G.F.G. Stanley, January 19, 1961). The Riel genealogy is as follows: J. B. Riel m. Louise Lafontaine (in Ireland); J. B. Riel m. Marie Sylvestre 1755, also m. Marie Amable Collin *dit* Laliberté 1767; J. B. Riel m. Marie Antoinette Eno 1783; J. B. Riel m. Marguerite Boucher 1815; L. Riel married Julie Lagimodière 1844; Louis Riel m. Marguerite Monet *dit* Bellehumeur 1882. This genealogical data was furnished the author by Rev. Pierre Picton of St. Boniface, and by M. Emile Falardeau of Montreal.
9. *St.B.H.S.*, Extract of Register of Baptisms, marriages and deaths, Parish of Ste. Geneviève de Berthier.
10. E. Coues, *New Light on the Early History of the Greater North-West: the manuscript journals of Alexander Henry and of David Thompson, 1799-1814*, (New York, 1897) I, 269.
11. R. G. MacBeth, *The Romance of Western Canada*, (Toronto, 1920), 35.
12. J. P. Pritchett, *The Red River Valley 1811-1849* (New Haven and Toronto, 1942), 104; Macdonell to Selkirk, July 17, 1813.
13. W. L. Morton, *Manitoba: A History* (Toronto, 1957), 50.
14. Oddly enough, none of the early explorers such as DuLhut, de Noyon or de la Vérendrye commented on the development of a métis population, although the records of the Hudson's Bay Company refer to it frequently. (See M. Giraud, *Le Métis Canadien* (Paris, 1945), 291, 429-430).

15. A. S. Morton, *A History of the Canadian West to 1870-71* (London and Toronto, 1939), 575; Alexander Macdonnell to Duncan Cameron, March 13, 1816.

16. Quoted in Chester Martin, *Lord Selkirk's Work in Canada* (Oxford, 1916), 109.

17. Falcon's song was first printed as an appendix in J. J. Hargrave, *Red River* (Montreal, 1871), 488-9. A slightly different version, with music and English translation, appears in E. Fowke, A. Mills and H. Blume, *Canada's Story in Song* (Toronto, n.d.), 122-3.

18. Alexander Ross says that the struggle with the North-West Company cost the Hudson's Bay Company £15,000 less than it cost the Canadian company. See Pritchett, *op. cit.*, 219.

19. Pritchett, 219.

20. Martin, *op. cit.*, Appendix B; Grant of Assiniboia to Lord Selkirk, June 12, 1811.

21. Giraud, *op. cit.*, 685.

22. "The Diary of Nicholas Garry," (*Transactions of the Royal Society of Canada*, 1900, Section II), 193.

23. E. H. Oliver, *The Canadian North-West, its Early Development and Legislative Records* (Canadian Archives, Ottawa, 1914), I, 267 note.

24. H. Y. Hind, *Narrative of the Canadian Red River Exploratory Expedition of 1857 and of the Assiniboine and Saskatchewan Exploring Expedition of 1858* (London, 1860), I, 177.

25. *C.S.P.*, 1871, V. No. 20; Census returns.

26. MacBeth, *op. cit.*, 76.

27. John McLean, *Notes of a Twenty-Five Years' Service in the Hudson's Bay Company Territories* (Champlain Society, Toronto, 1932), 378.

28. MacBeth, 91. Among the more substantial métis were men like Cuthbert Grant, Salomon Hamelin, François Bruneau, Pascal Breland, Urbain Delorme and Baptiste Larocque. These men not only had good farms but owned considerable numbers of horses and carts. (See Giraud, 881.)

29. A. Ross, *Red River Settlement: Its Rise, Progress and Present State* (London, 1856), 196.

30. In February, 1835, Bishop Provencher was appointed to the Council. The Rev. David Jones and the Rev. Wm. Cockran were already members. At a later date the Anglican bishop and the Rev. J. Smethurst were given Council appointments, along with the Rev. Louis LaFlèche. The first half-breed appointment was that of Cuthbert Grant.

31. Pritchett, 252.

32. *Ibid.*, 253.

33. E. E. Rich, *The History of the Hudson's Bay Company, 1670-1870* (London, 1959), II, 534.

34. *H.B.C.*, Public Correspondence, Simpson 1845-46; Simpson to the Governor and Committee, June 20, 1845. See also G.F.G. Stanley, *The Birth of Western Canada* (Toronto, 1960), 415.

35. Pritchett, 258.

36. Giraud, 918. Governor Simpson received a letter from Governor Christie dated April 21, 1846, stating that Belcourt had intervened "out of disappointment at not being licensed to take furs from the Indians" in payment of ecclesiastical dues. "This licence would have opened so wide a door for injurious intercourse with the Indians that I could not grant it," said Christie.

37. E. E. Rich, *London Correspondence Inward from Eden Colvile, 1849-1852* (London, 1956), lxxxiii-vi. The introduction to this collection of documents was written by W. L. Morton.

38. Belcourt was a restless man. Bishop Provencher wrote of him, "Il voit déjà fait en imagination ce qui ne se fera pas en dix ans, en sorte qu'il est toujours en avant en esprit, et en arrière en réalité": quoted in L. A. Prud'homme, "Georges Antoine Belcourt," (*Transactions of the Royal Society of Canada*, 1920, Section I), 25. See also J. M. Reardon, *George Anthony Belcourt, Pioneer Catholic Missionary of the North-West* (St. Paul, 1955).

39. Giraud, 930-31.

40. *H.B.C.*, Winnipeg Inward Correspondence, 1823-71; Belcourt to Riel, March 4, 1849, enclosed in Simpson to the Governor and Committee, June 30, 1849.

41. A. H. de Trémaudan, *Histoire de la Nation Métisse* (Montreal, 1935), 136.

42. *Colvile Correspondence, op. cit.*, lxxxiii. Bishop Provencher wrote, "Belcourt consulté repondit aux métis de soutenir leurs droits même par des armes si on prenait les armes contre eux." See Giraud, 921 note.

43. *H.B.C.*, Winnipeg Inward Correspondence, 1823-71; Sinclair to the court, May 17, 1848, enclosed in Simpson to the Governor and Committee, June 30, 1849. The "complaint" was signed by Sinclair, Peter Garrioch, Riel, Breland, Louis Batoche, Hamelin, Wm. McMillan, Wm. McGillis, Morin, Delorme and John Anderson.

44. Pritchett, 262.

45. *Colvile Correspondence*, lxxxix. The ten names included those of Wm. McMalen, Louis Rielle, Pascal Breland, Baptiste Fairjeu, Baptiste Larocque, Antoine Morin, Louis Letendre, Salomon Hamelin. Urbain Delorme and Wm. McMillan. The petition was dated June 2, 1849. It read in part, "We have used our utmost to restrain the people from resorting to any violence so as to induce him to leave, a point which they had determined upon, and we have only succeeded by urging them to await your decision."

46. *Ibid.*, cii. On November 27, 1850, Colvile wrote to Simpson: "Mr. Irelande alias Rielle, came to me about half an hour before the Court met—to say that the people were determined to keep Thom out. As we had no preparations made for a row, the Magistrates were all of opinion that it would be better for Thom to keep away. . . . (*Colvile Correspondence*, 199).

47. Provencher suggested the names of Narcisse Marion, Maximilien Dauphiné, François Bruneau, Salomon Hamelin and Pascal Breland. (*Colvile Correspondence*, lxxxix-xc).

48. Bruneau, Hamelin and Breland had been involved in the Sayer troubles as well as Riel. The most likely explanation would appear to be Colvile's dislike of Riel, whom he regarded as an agitator, and his sympathy for Thom, the man Riel was determined to drive out of the colony. The tone of Colvile's letter to Simpson, May 22, 1851, in which he mentions his intentions of recommending Bruneau as a councillor, reveals a strong bias against Riel. (*Colvile Correspondence*, 208).

49. Giraud, 953.

50. *P.A.M.*, Riel Papers, Riel to James Ross, September 10, 1861.

51. E. H. Oliver, *op. cit.*, I, 381.

52. *Ibid.*, I, 388.

53. *Ibid.*, I, 389.

54. Joseph Tassé *Les Canadiens de l'Ouest* (Montreal, 1878), II, 355. See also A. G. Morice, *Dictionnaire Historique des Canadiens et des Métis français de l'Ouest* (Quebec, 1913), 247.

55. *A.A.St.B.*, Riel to Fisher, Montreal, December, 1857; Riel to Fisher, Montreal, February 8, 1858.

56. *Ibid.*, Taché to the Grand Vicar, May 1, 1858. Taché wrote, "le bon Riel a mis à la base, il a accepté pour 200 louis une magnifique machine à fabriquer les étoffes qui vaut £1,000 et que Mme. Masson lui a, pour ainsi dire, donné. . . ."

CHAPTER TWO : Education

1. *P.A.M.*, G. B. Winship, Account of Events at Red River 1869-1870, Mss.

2. *St.B.H.S.*, Notes by Henriette Riel-Poitras.

3. *P.A.M.*, Riel Papers, Riel to Taché, July 24, 1885. In *P.A.C.*, Dewdney Papers, North-West Rebellion, M.G., 27, C.4, Vol. 1, is a note ln Riel's handwriting which says that he went to his first confession at seven years of age and made his first communion on March 25, 1856.

4. *St.B.H.S.*, Notes by Henriette Riel-Poitras.

5. *P.A.M.*, Riel Papers, Riel to Taché, July 24, 1885.

6. *St.B.H.S.*, Notes by Henriette Riel-Poitras.

7. *P.A.M.*, Riel Papers, Riel to Taché, July 24, 1885.

8. Dom Benoit, *Vie de Mgr. Taché, Archevêque de St. Boniface* (Montreal, 1904), I, 229: Taché to Bourget, May 22, 1851.

9. *Ibid.*, I, 280.

10. *P.A.M.*, Riel Papers, Riel to Taché, July 24, 1885.

11. Louis Schmidt, "Mémoires," (*Le Patriote de l'Ouest*, July 6, 1911).

12. Benoit, *op. cit.*, I, 300.

13. Schmidt, *Mémoires*, July 13, 1911.

14. *Ibid.*

15. *Ibid.*

16. For a history of the Collège de Montréal see Mgr. O. Maurault, *Le Petit Séminaire de Montréal* (Montreal, 1918).

17. Benoit, I, 376. On May 31, 1858, Taché wrote to his lawyer in Quebec, M. Cazeau, "Je viens d'écrire à M. LaFlèche et à M. Denis, directeur du Collège de Montréal de tirer sur vous, mais à mes depens, pour les frais de l'entretien de deux enfants que j'envoie l'un à Nicolet, l'autre à Montréal, ces maisons voulant bien leur donner l'éducation et la pension gratuitement. J'ai envoyé un troisième enfant à St. Hyacinthe; pour ce dernier vous n'aurez rien à payer."

18. *P.A.M.*, Joseph Dubuc, Autobiographie et Lettres, Mss.

19. The account of Riel's work at the Collège de Montréal is taken from the college records.

20. *C.M.*, students' records, April 10, 1863.

21. J. O. Mousseau, *Une Page d'Histoire* (Montreal, 1887) 7-8.

22. *P.A.M.*, Riel Papers, Riel to Taché, July 24, 1885.

23. *Ibid.*

24. Eustache Prudhomme in *L'Opinion Publique*, Montreal, February 19, 1870.

25. Mousseau, *op. cit.*, 5.

26. D. Frémont, *Les Secrétaires de Riel* (Montreal, 1953), 18.

27. *Ibid.*

28. Mousseau, 10.

29. *Ibid.*, 9.

30. Masson Papers, Riel to Mme. Masson, February 20, 1864.

31. *P.A.M.*, Riel Papers, Riel to his mother, February 23, 1864. A copy of this letter will be found in *P.A.C.*, Riel Papers, I.

32. *Ibid.*, Riel to his mother, March 21, 1864.

33. This poem was first published in *L'Opinion Publique*, February 19, 1870. See also P. de M., *L'Oeuvre Véridique de Louis Riel* (Montreal, 1934), 52-3.

34. Masson Papers, Atkinson to Mme. Masson, January 6, 1865.

35. Riel apparently went to live with his aunt, Mrs. John Lee (née Riel), if we may judge from a letter he wrote to George Cartier, February 24, 1865. This letter is in *P.A.Q.*, Chapais Collection.

36. *A.A.St.B.*, Lenoir to Taché, August 26, 1865.

37. R. Rumilly, *Histoire de la Province de Québec* (Montreal n.d.), I, 47-9.

38. *Ibid.*, 41.

39. Prudhomme, *op. cit.*

40. *A.A.St.B.*, Vanderburghe to Taché, July 16, 1865. Abbé Vanderburghe wrote, "Pauvre garçon! quand je l'ai vu avec sa chevelure herissé et avec un ton fort fashionable, je lui ai accordé peu de confiance."

41. *Ibid.*, Vanderburghe to Taché, August 18, 1865.

42. *P.A.Q.*, Chapais Collection, Riel to Cartier, February 24, 1865. In this collection there is also a letter in verse addressed to Cartier. Although the letter has the suggested date of 1868 written on it in pencil, Cartier is addressed as Procureur-Général du Bas-Canada, which would fix the date of writing prior to Confederation in 1867. Moreover the subject matter of the verses, namely the death of Riel's father, would suggest 1864 or 1865 as a more likely date.

43. A. N. Montpetit, *Louis Riel à la Rivière du Loup* (Lévis, 1885), 34. Montpetit wrote, "Je me rappelle avoir aperçue Riel à Montréal en 1866 ou 1867. On me dit alors qu'il étudiait le droit chez M. Laflamme."

44. Mousseau, 11-13. "Louis avocat aurait tenu son office dans son chapeau, et reçu sa clientèle sur le sommet de la montagne de Montréal."

45. *P.J.M.*, Contrat de Mariage entre M. Louis Riel et Mlle Marie Julie Guernon, June 12, 1866. The priest in charge was Isidore Tallet, pss.

46. This information was furnished G. F. G. Stanley by M. Emile Falardeau of Montreal, who learned of the circumstances from the nephew of Riel's fiancée, and who drew my attention to the existence of the marriage contract noted above. Mlle Guernon subsequently married Jean Malboeuf *dit* Beausoleil.

47. Schmidt, *Mémoires*, February 8, 1912.

48. Fréchette devoted one of the poems in his *La Légende d'un peuple* to Riel. It was entitled "Le Dernier Martyr."

49. W. L. Morton, *Alexander Begg's Red River Journal and other Papers Relative to the Red River Resistance of 1869-1870* (Champlain Society, Toronto, 1956), 35.

50. *St.B.H.S.*, Compte rendu de ses activités.

CHAPTER THREE: Red River

1. Benoit, *op. cit.*, I, 447.
2. Hargrave, *op. cit.*, 307.
3. Winship, *op. cit.*
4. *P.A.M.*, *Nor'Wester*, December 28, 1859.
5. A. C. Garrioch, *First Furrows, a History of the Early Settlement of the Red River Country* (Winnipeg, 1923), 225. R. G. MacBeth, *op. cit.*, 93, wrote, "I remember him when he was in the heyday of his physical strength, a tall giant, beside whose great stride I had to run. . . . Once when, in the tumultuous transition days, there was the usual riot, the crowd at a meeting made a rush for the platform where Schultz and others were sitting. The doctor rose, and, putting his foot on the bar of the big home-made oaken chair on which he had been sitting, wrenched it asunder as if it had been made of pipe stems; on seeing which the crowd concluded they would give up the rioting for that evening."
6. Hargrave, Chapter XXIX. See for instance, Schultz's dealings with McKenney and Ross. On January 10, 1865, Ross wrote to Schultz asking for the repayment of a loan, "I am sure you *must* feel the propriety of not making one wait for the repayment of a loan." This letter is quoted in J. B. Todd, "Sir John Schultz and the Canadian Expansionist Agitation in the Red River Colony, 1862-1871" (M.A. Thesis, University of Toronto, 1933), 32.
7. A Masonic lodge was organized in Red River of which Schultz became the "Worshipful Master" (Hargrave, 322).
8. W. L. Morton, *Manitoba*, 103.
9. A. S. Morton, *op. cit.*, 854.
10. Winship Mss.
11. Norbert Welsh, "The Waning Herds" (*Maclean's Magazine*, January 15, 1933).
12. This is her skipper's description. See Molly McFadden, "Steamboats on the Red" (*The Beaver*, June, 1950), 32.
13. For a discussion of railways and the Canadian and American Northwest development, see L. B. Irwin, *Pacific Railways and Nationalism in the Canadian American Northwest, 1845-1873* (Philadelphia, 1939).
14. *Nor'wester*, September 28, 1860.

15. *Ibid.*, October 1, 1860.
16. D. F. Warner, "Drang Nach Norden, the United States and the Riel Rebellion (*Mississippi Valley Historical Review*, March, 1953), 693.
17. St. Paul *Daily Times*, September 22, 1860.
18. R. W. Winks, *Canada and the United States, the Civil War Years* (Baltimore, 1960), 167.
19. For an account of Taylor, see T. C. Blegen, "James Wickes Taylor: a Biographical Sketch" (*Minnesota History Bulletin*, November, 1915), and H. C. Knox, "Consul Taylor of Winnipeg" (*The Beaver*, March, June, 1949).
20. Winks, *op. cit.*, 170.
21. Ruth E. Sandborn, "The United States and the British North-West, 1865-1870" (*North Dakota Historical Quarterly*, October, 1931), 13-14.
22. Blegen, *op. cit.*, 179-180. The Toronto *Globe* suggested prophetically that the Americans might try to annex the moon! In general the effect of the bill was to make Canadians more belligerently independent and to give an impetus to the movement towards Confederation.
23. Quoted in J. B. Brebner, *North Atlantic Triangle, the Interplay of Canada, the United States and Great Britain* (New Haven and Toronto, 1945), 165.
24. Irwin, *op. cit.*, 111.
25. *Ibid.*, 129.
26. Quoted in Sandborn, *op. cit.*, 14-15.
27. *Ibid.*, 15.
28. *Ibid.*, 16.
29. Sir R. H. Bonnycastle, *Canada and the Canadians in 1864* (London, 1846), 138.
30. Stanley, *op. cit.*, 21.
31. Rich, *The History of the Hudson's Bay Company*, II, 891.
32. *P.R.O.*, C.O. 42/677; Rose to Young, confidential, July 23, 1869.
33. MacBeth, 95.
34. A. S. Morton, 853.
35. *Nor'wester*, December 28, 1859.
36. *Ibid.*, February 28, 1860.
37. *Ibid.*, March 14, 1860.
38. *Ibid.*, October 1, 1860; February 5, 1862.
39. *Ibid.*, November 17, 1862. See also A. S. Morton, 858.
40. *A.A.St.B.*, Dallas to Taché, November 25, 1862.
41. Oliver, *op. cit.*, I, 514. See the Minutes of the meeting of the Governor and Council, November 25, 1862. The movers and seconders of the dismissal motions were William Mactavish and Bishop Taché, and Bishop Machray and John Inkster.
42. *Nor'wester*, November 29, 1862.
43. *A.A.St.B.*, Taché to Dallas, December 6, 1862.
44. For a detailed account, see Hargrave, Chapters XIX and XX.
45. *Nor'Wester*, March 21, 1864.
46. Hargrave, 285.
47. Oliver, I, 524, Minutes of a Meeting of the Governor and Council, April 28, 1863; McBeath, etc., to Dallas, April 28, 1863.
48. A. S. Morton, 853; and Rich, 813.
49. *H.B.C.*, London Inward Correspondence from Winnipeg, 1863; Bannatyne to Ellis, July 1, 1863.
50. *Nor'Wester*, April 17, 1865.
51. Hargrave, 405.
52. *Nor'Wester*, February 5, 1869.
53. Quoted in W. L. Morton, *Manitoba*, 114.

54. Toronto *Globe*, February 16, 1869, see letter by Charles Mair from Oak Point, dated January 20, 1869. The *Nor'Wester* did not mention the grasshoppers in its columns fearing, apparently, that confirmation of the news of the plague might discourage prospective settlers from Ontario.

55. *Ibid.*, September 4, 1868, see letter from Taché to the *Nor'Wester*, August 11, 1868.

56. *Ibid.*, December 19, 1868; Young to Sandford, November 27, 1868.

57. This report may be found in the *A.A. St. B.*

58. *C.S.P.*, 1869, II, No. 25; Lampson to Rogers, December 22, 1868.

59. See Justitia (Alexander Begg) to the *Globe*, November 10, 1869; H.S. Goldhawk to the *Owen Sound Times*, May 2, 1869 (reprinted in the *Globe*, June 28, 1869); also depositions by Bishop Taché and A. G. B. Bannatyne in the *Report of the Select Committee, Journals of the House of Commons, Canada*, VIII, Appx. 6, 1874.

60. Hargrave, 450.

61. *H.B.C.*, London Inward Correspondence from Winnipeg, 1870, Hargrave to Lampson, February 8, 1870. Hargrave wrote, "the Canadians belonging to the surveying and road-making parties lately arrived, lived among them [Schultz and his friends] and to the scandal of the well disposed, appeared to support them in their disorders. The result has been that the Canadians have made no progress in gaining the goodwill of the people."

62. *Perth Courier*, January 1, 1869; Mair to his brother, November 19, 1868. This letter subsequently appeared in *The Globe*, January 4, 1869.

63. G. Dugast, *Histoire Véridique des faits qui ont préparé le mouvement des métis à la Rivière Rouge en 1869* (Montreal, 1905), 28. See also *Begg's Red River Journal, 20.*

64. *Q.U.L.*, Mair Papers, Dawson to Taché, October 6, 1868.

65. Toronto *Globe*, February 16, 1869; letter from Charles Mair, January 20, 1869.

66. *Q.U.L.*, Mair Papers, Schultz to Mair, March 6, 1869. Again on March 19. Schultz wrote to Mair, "Canada *must* have the country—if not by peaceable adjustment with England, then in any way it can be got."

67. Schmidt, *Mémoires*, January 12, 1912.

68. *Ibid.*

69. *Begg's Red River Journal*, 399-402; L. R. to *Le Nouveau Monde*, February 25, 1869.

70. *A.A.St.B.*, Riel to Lachance, March 23, 1869, "Je vous écris afin de vous dire que si vous comptez toujours sur mon engagement, je serai prêt à partir."

CHAPTER FOUR: Provisional Government

1. Rich, *op. cit.*, II, 889.

2. Todd, *op. cit.*, 87, Schultz to J. McDougall, private, April 23, 1869.

3. *Nor'Wester*, September 7, 1869.

4. Alexander Begg, *The Creation of Manitoba, or a History of the Red River Troubles* (Toronto, 1871), 17, 25. In his deposition during the 1874 enquiry, Colonel J. S. Dennis swore on oath that Schultz told him that he and Snow had staked off and bought from the Indians lands near Oak Point to which the métis had laid claim, and that Schultz had asked him (Dennis) if the Canadian government would recognize their "rights" to these lands. (*Report of the Select Committee,* 1874)

5. *P.A.St.N.*, Notes de M. Ritchot, deuxième cahier.

6. *Ibid.* See also A. G. Morice, *A Critical History of the Red River Insurrection* (Winnipeg, 1935), 51.

7. *A.A.St.B.*, Dugast to Taché, July 29, 1869.

8. Ritchot, *op. cit.* Begg believed that the meeting had been prompted by Schultz, and he pointed out that Breland claimed he had never signed the original invitation. Begg says that the men who supported Dease were those who had staked out large tracts of land and hoped to establish their claims by paying nominal sums to the Indian or half-breed owners in order to secure title. (*Creation of Manitoba*, 89.)

9. *H.B.C.*, London Inward Correspondence from Winnipeg 1869, Mactavish to Smith, August 10, 1869.

10. *A.A.St.B.*, Dugast to Taché, August 24, 1869.

11. *Ibid.*

12. *Ibid.*, Dugast to Taché, August 14, 1869.

13. *Ibid.*, Dugast to Taché, August 24, 1869.

14. *Report of the Select Committee*, 1874, Dennis deposition. See also *Begg's Red River Journal*, 39.

15. *C.S.P.*, 1870, V, No. 12, Dennis to McDougall, August 21, 1869.

16. *Ibid.*, Braun to Dennis, October 4, 1869.

17. Ritchot, notes, 2 cahier.

18. *Begg's Red River Journal*, 411-13, Letter in *Le Courrier de St. Hyacinthe*, October 28, 1869.

19. *A.A.St.B.*, Dugast to Taché, September 4, 1869.

20. *Ibid.*, Lestanc to Taché, September 5, 1869.

21. *Ibid.*, Dugast to Taché, August 29, 1869.

22. Begg, *Creation*, 79-80.

23. *C.S.P.*, 1870, V, No. 12, Dennis, Memorandum of Facts and Circumstances connected with the active opposition by the French half-breeds in the Settlement to the prosecution of the Government surveys, October 11, 1869.

24. *Q.U.L.*, Mair Papers, Miscellaneous Notes by Charles Mair.

25. Howe wrote to McDougall from St. Paul on October 31, 1869, warning him against Schultz who, he said, had been passing "as a representative and confidential agent of the Canadian government," and telling McDougall that "it would be a great mistake to patronize the little clique of persons at war with the more influential elements of society." (This letter is quoted in full in Stanley, *The Birth of Western Canada*, 75.) Howe's letter did not reach McDougall until after he had been stopped by the métis. It is worth noting that Howe's appointment as Secretary of State for the Provinces had not met with the approval of Charles Mair's friend, G. T. Denison, who wrote to Mair on February 3, 1869, that Sir John Macdonald "has a great faculty for neglecting his friends and buying up his enemies, that is his strong suit, but it will be played out after a while." (*Q.U.L.*, Mair Papers.)

26. *P.A.M.*, Joseph Dubuc, Mémoires d'un Manitobain, Mss.

27. *C.S.P.*, 1870, V, No. 12. Dugast claimed that he drafted the order to McDougall (Morice, *op. cit.*, 162 note). There is, however, no mention of Dugast's name in Ritchot's notes. Dugast was a boastful man and was inclined to take much credit for the events of the métis rising.

28. Ritchot, *op. cit.*

29. *Ibid.*

30. Mactavish was suffering from tuberculosis. He died in Liverpool in 1870 while on his way to the south of France.

31. Oliver, *op. cit.*, I, 617: Minutes of a meeting of the Governor and Council of Assiniboia, October 25, 1869.

32. Ritchot, 2 cahier.

33. Oliver, I, 619, Minutes of a meeting of the Governor and Council of Assiniboia, October 30, 1869.

34. *Report of the Select Committee*, 1874, Lépine and Riel to Morris, January 3, 1873. This letter is also printed in the *Canadian Historical Review*, June ,1926, 137-160.

35. *A.A.St.B.*, Kavanaugh to Taché, November 1, 1869. Kavanaugh was an eyewitness of the Cameron episode. See also *C.S.P.*, 1870, V, No. 12, McDougall to Howe, November 4, 1869, and L. A. Prud'homme, *Monseigneur Noël-Joseph Ritchot* (Winnipeg, 1928), 69.

36. *C.S.P.*, 1870, V, No. 12, McDougall to Howe, November 5, 1869.

37. *Le Courrier de St. Hyacinthe*, October 28, 1869. (See note 18.)

38. Ritchot, 2 cahier.

39. *A.A.StB.*, Dugast to Taché, November 4, 1869; Dugast to Taché, August 31, 1869; Lestanc to Taché, October 23, 1869.

40. Masson Papers, Riel's notes of the Fort Garry Convention, enclosed in Riel to Masson, April 4, 1872.   Other copies may be found in the *P.A.M.*, and in *Begg's Red River Journal*, 420-30.

41. *P.P.* 1870, L(C 207).   Extract of Private Correspondence, November 2, 1869. According to George Young there were in the gun sheds at Fort Garry "four three-pdr. and four six-pdr. bronze field guns and fully a dozen iron guns in the bastions . . . there were also two small coehorn mortars to be used for curved fire." (See *University of Saskatchewan*, Historical Papers, 1869-70.)

42. There is evidence to show that this was at least contemplated.   James Mulligan, a pensioner, claimed he warned Dr. Cowan that the métis might try to seize the fort, and he offered to raise a force of men to protect it against such a contingency.   Had such a force been raised, there is no doubt that the Canadians would have been the first to offer their services.   (See Mulligan affidavit in *Debates of the House of Commons, Canada*, 1871, II, 1068-69.)

43. There seems to be some confusion about Mulligan's proposal noted above.   Begg says that Mulligan and another pensioner, Michael Powers, made their suggestion after and not before the fort was occupied by Riel (*Creation*, 74).   In a letter to the Secretary of State for War, Powers says that he made his offer after the fall of the fort (*P.R.O.*, C.O. 42/683, Power to the Secretary of State for War, November 8, 1869).   In the Canadian House of Commons, Donald A. Smith produced affidavits from Dr. Cowan and Judge Black that Mulligan's statements were untrue. (*Debates of the House of Commons, Canada*, 1875, I, 1061-71.)

44. Prud'homme, *Ritchot*, 71-2.

45. Begg, *Creation*, 48.   See also *Report of the Select Committee*, 1874, Dr. Cowan's deposition.

46. *Ibid.*, 49-50; also *C.S.P.*, 1870, V, No. 12.

47. Letter in Toronto *Globe*, December 1, 1869.

48. *Begg's Red River Journal*, 167-69.

49. Riel's notes of the Fort Garry Convention, *op. cit.*   (See note 40.)

50. *A.A.St.B.*, Lestanc to Taché, November 19, 1869.

51. Riel's notes of the Fort Garry Convention.

52. *Ibid.*

53. *Begg's Red River Journal*, November 26, 1869, 185.

54. *Ibid.*, November 27, 1869, 188.

55. Begg, *Creation*, 61.

56. *Begg's Red River Journal*, November 22, 1869, 177.

57. *C.S.P.*, 1870, V, No. 12, Schultz to McDougall, November 5, 1869; Snow to McDougall, November 9, 1869; Mair to McDougall, November 8, 1869.

58. *Ibid.*, McDougall to Mactavish, November 7, 1869; McDougall to Howe, November 14, 1869.

59. *Ibid.*, McDougall to Howe, December 2, 1869; McDougall to Howe, November 29, 1869.

60. Begg, *Creation*, 110.

61. Riel's notes of the Fort Garry Convention.

62. The list is printed in Begg, *Creation*, 110-111.

63. Riel's notes of the Fort Garry Convention.

64. *C.S.P.*, 1870, V, No. 12.   See also Begg, *Creation*, 131-33.

65. Henry Woodington, "Diary of a Prisoner in the Red River Rebellion" (*Niagara Historical Society*, No. 25, 1913), 43.

66. *C.S.P.*, 1870, V, No. 12, Dennis, Record of Proceedings under the commission from Lieutenant-Governor McDougall.   See also Dennis to Boulton, December 4, 1869, Dennis to Schultz, December 4, 1869, and Woodington, Diary, 39-40.

67. *Begg's Red River Journal*, December 7, 1869, 216; also Rev. George Young, *Manitoba Memories, Leaves from my Life in the Prairie Provinces* (Toronto, 1897), 110; and Schmidt, *Mémoires*, February 15, 1912.

68. *P.R.O.*, C.O. 42/677, Young to Granville, November 26, 1869.

69. *Ibid.*, C.O. 42/678, Macdonald to McDougall, November 27, 1869.

70. This is printed in Begg, *Creation*, 167-170.

71. This is based upon the recollections of Mrs. Bernard Ross, who was with Mactavish at the time (Healy, *Women of Red River*, 229).

CHAPTER FIVE : Donald A. Smith

1. This item was dated November 4 and was written from Pembina and signed "Spectator."

2. See, for instance, *Begg's Red River Journal*, November 22, 1869, 176; and November 30, 1869, 192; and December 27, 1869, 242; also Stutsman to Riel, December 25, 1869, 242. And in the *P.A.M.*, Stutsman to Riel, January 11, 1870.

3. These were the favourite hang-outs of the Americans. Emmerling was a German-American who came to the Red River in 1861. Hugh and Bob O'Lone were Americans who ran the Red Saloon.

4. Malmros, Robinson and Donaldson were Americans. According to *Begg's Red River Journal* "several applications for offices have been made to Riel by Americans—but have so far been put aside—one was to get H. S. Donaldson in as Postmaster" (January 6, 1870, 253). Later Malmros tried to persuade Riel to appoint Robinson as his secretary and Donaldson as his adjutant (*ibid.*, January 11, 1870, 258).

5. B. Willson, *The Life of Lord Strathcona and Mount Royal* (London, 1915), 291, Stutsman to President Grant, November 2, 1869. In a newspaper interview McDougall said, "In reply to our enquiry relative to the annexation feeling, the Governor said he did not think it existed to any extent. Stutsman was anxious to bring that about and he thought General Riel was similarly inclined, but the priests who really have more control than either were opposed to it." (St. Paul *Despatch* in the Ottawa *Citizen*, January 6, 1870.)

6. *A.A.St.B.*, Lestanc to Taché, October 23, 1869.

7. *The New Nation*, January 7, 1870. Begg wrote in his *Journal* on January 9, 1870: "Mr. Riel spoke to Major Robinson strongly against the tone of his newspaper in favour of Annexation to the States."

8. *Begg's Red River Journal*, 165 note. Lemay was believed to have been interested in *The New Nation*, but he and Stutsman had a falling out, and Lemay became a supporter of union with Canada.

9. *C.S.P.*, 1870, V, No. 12, W. E. Sanford to Howe, November 18, 1869.

10. *New York Times*, December 28, 1869.

11. Quoted in J. K. Howard, *Strange Empire, a Narrative of the Northwest* (New York, 1952), 137.

12. *Congressional Globe*, 41: 2, 3. The resolution was adopted December 8, 1869.

13. *A.S.D.*, Consular Despatches, Winnipeg, 1869-1871, Malmros to Davis, September 11, 1869.

14. *Ibid.*, Malmros to Davis, November 6, 1869.

15. *Ibid.*, Malmros to Davis, January 15, 1870.

16. Malmros to Ramsey, January 14, 1870, quoted in P. F. Sharp, *Whoop-Up Country, The Canadian West, 1865-1885* (Minneapolis, 1955), 307.

17. *A.S.D.*, Consular Despatches, Winnipeg, 1869-1871, Malmros to Davis, March 12, 1870.

18. Lampson to Northcote, January 31, 1870, quoted in D. G. Creighton, *John A. Macdonald, The Old Chieftain* (Toronto, 1955), 54.

19. R. Machray, *The Life of Robert Machray, Archbishop of Rupert's Land and Primate of All Canada* (London, 1909), 168.

20. McArthur, "Causes of the Rising," (*Manitoba Historical Society*, Winnipeg, 1882, No. 1), 1, 2.
21. *Report of the Select Committee, 1874*, Taché deposition.
22. Macdonald to Brown, October 14, 1869, quoted in Creighton, *op. cit.*, 43.
23. Macdonald to McDougall, December 8, 1869, quoted in Creighton, 44.
24. *C.S.P.*, 1870, V, No. 12, Smith to Howe, November 24, 1869.
25. *Ibid.*, Howe to Smith, December 10, 1869.
26. *P.A.C.*, Macdonald Papers, 516, Macdonald to Smith, December 12, 1869.
27. Charles Mair and Thomas Scott escaped January 9, 1870.   Dr. Schultz escaped January 23, 1870.
28. *Begg's Red River Journal*, December 23, 24, 1869, 238, 239.
29. *Ibid.*, December 22, 23, 1869, 236, 237.
30. *Ibid.*, December 22, 1869, 236; January 5, 251; January 6, 252; January 7, 254; and January 11, 1870, 258.
31. *Ibid.*, December 24, 25, 1869, 239, 240.
32. *Ibid.*, Stutsman to Riel, December 25, 1869, 242.
33. *A.S.D.*, Consular Despatches, Winnipeg, 1869-1871, Malmros to Davis, December 29, 1869.
34. *C.S.P.*, 1870, V, No. 12, Thibault to Howe, March 17, 1870.   This is Thibault's official report.
35. *P.R.O.*, C.O. 42/685, Smith to Howe, April 12, 1870.   This is a complete copy of Smith's report.   The version published in the *C.S.P.*, 1870, is an edited version with several omissions.
36. Smith's report.
37. *Begg's Red River Journal*, January 1, 1870, 250.
38. *Ibid.*, December 24, 1869, 239.
39. *A.A.St.B.*, Lestanc to Taché, February 3, 1870.
40. *Begg's Red River Journal*, January 1, 1870, 250.
41. A. H. de Trémaudan, *op. cit.*, 209.
42. Smith's report.   See also *Begg's Red River Journal*, January 17, 1870, 263.
43. *New Nation*, January 21, 1870.
44. Smith's report.   The references to Thibault and de Salaberry were deleted from the printed version of the report.
45. *A.A.St.B.*, Lestanc to Taché, February 3, 1870; Giroux to Taché, February 12, 1870.   Lestanc mentions his discussions with Angus McKay, one of Riel's opponents.   Fr. Giroux, who served as chaplain to Riel's soldiers, wrote that "sans le père Lestanc et le G. V. Thibault, le sang aurait coulé."
46. *Begg's Red River Journal*, January 20, 1870, 270.
47. *New Nation*, January 21, 1870.
48. *Ibid.*
49. *Ibid.*
50. *Ibid.*
51. *Begg's Red River Journal*, January 21, 22, 1870, 278, 279.
52. *Ibid.*, January 22, 1870, 279-80.
53. *A.A.St.B.*, Lestanc to Taché, February 3, 1870.
54. *Begg's Red River Journal*, January 26, 27, 1870, 287, 288.
55. *Ibid.*, January 27, 1870, 289.
56. A copy of the list will be found as an appendix to Smith's report.   See also Begg, *Creation*, 255-58.
57. *New Nation*, February 11, 1870.
58. *Ibid.*
59. *Begg's Red River Journal*, February 6, 1870, 297.

60. *A.A.St.B.*, Lestanc to Taché, February 3, 1870.
61. Smith's report. See also *Begg's Red River Journal*, February 6, 1870, 297-98.
62. *A.A.St.B.*, Giroux to Taché, February 12, 1870.
63. *Begg's Red River Journal*, February 7, 1870, 299.
64. *New Nation*, February 11, 1870.
65. *Ibid.*
66. *Ibid.*, February 18, 1870.
67. *Ibid.* See also *Begg's Red River Journal*, February 9, 1870, 301, and the evidence of Xavier Pagée at the trial of Ambroise Lépine (Elliot and Brokovski, *The Trial of Lépine* (Montreal, 1874), 74-5).
68. The committee included Louis Riel, W. B. O'Donoghue, Charles Nolin and James Ross, Thomas Bunn, Dr. Bird.
69. *New Nation*, February 18, 1870. See also Stanley, *op. cit.*, 420-1, note 37; and W. L. Morton's Introduction to *Begg's Red River Journal*, 99.
70. *New Nation*, February 18, 1870.
71. *Begg's Red River Journal*, February 10, 1870, 303.
72. *Ibid.*

CHAPTER SIX : Thomas Scott

1. For accounts of the imprisonment of the Canadians see Henry Woodington, *op. cit.*, 32-55, and A. W. Graham's manuscript diary in the *P.A.M.* The particular reference here is to Woodington, December 10, 1869.
2. Graham, *op. cit.*, December 11, 1869.
3. Woodington, December 13, 1869.
4. *Ibid.*, December 24, 1869.
5. *Ibid.*, January 4, 1870.
6. *C.S.P.*, 1870, V, No. 12, Dennis, "To all whom it may concern," December 9, 1869.
7. *Begg's Red River Journal*, January 10, 1870, 257.
8. Woodington, January 9, 1870.
9. MacBeth, *op. cit.*, 128-9.
10. Young, *op. cit.*, 119.
11. Major A. C. Boulton, *Reminiscences of the North West Rebellions* (Toronto, 1886), 101.
12. *Begg's Red River Journal*, February 12, 1870, 305.
13. Boulton, *op. cit.*, 104-5.
14. *Begg's Red River Journal*, February 11, 1870, 304.
15. *Ibid.*, February 12, 1870, 305.
16. *Ibid.*, February 15, 1870, 308.
17. *Ibid.*
18. *Ibid.*, February 16, 1870, 310.
19. Boulton, 105. See also *Begg's Red River Journal*, February 15, 1870, 307; and MacBeth, 150-51. According to MacBeth: "on the way down to the rendezvous, several houses of Riel's friends were searched for the rebel leader, and though some said they intended to secure him as a hostage, others openly declared that they would make short work of him."
20. Boulton, 106. See also George Young Mss. (Historical Papers, *University of Saskatchewan*).
21. One of the verses ran as follows:

> Hey, Riel are ye waking yet,
> Or are ye're drums a-beating yet,
> If ye're nae waking, we'll nae wait,
> For we'll take the fort this morning.

22. Boulton, 106.

23. *Begg's Red River Journal*, February 14, 1870, 306.

24. *P.A.M.*, Riel to Dease, February 15, 1870; Riel to Dease, February 16, 1870.

25. *P.A.C.*, Macdonald Papers, Vol. 102, 225-6, letter to Allan McDonald from his uncle, Red River, n.d.   The letter read in part: "We consider ourselves fully capable of making our own laws, and as we own the country and don't want to part with it, we came to the conclusion not to admit Gov. McDougall and suite."

26. *Ibid.*, 280-82, Jas. MacKay to Dr. Rowand, December 21, 1869.

27. MacBeth, 151-52.   MacBeth points out that while "the younger fry amongst us thought the whole thing a splendid idea," the older men of Kildonan felt that the project was "futile" and "likely to end in a useless shedding of blood," and that it "was also inopportune, inasmuch as the species of union effected between the opposing parties by the convention just held would be the most certain means of preserving peace. . . ."

28. The Toronto *Globe*, March 28, 1870, XYZ to the editor, February 22, 1870.

29. Hugh Sutherland was not a member of the Schultz-Boulton party, but merely happened to be passing by when Parisien, thinking him to be a pursuer, discharged his gun at him.   Parisien was simple-minded and was regarded by both sides as a spy.

30. Boulton, 108-9.   See also *New Nation*, February 18, 1870; and Healy, *Women of Red River*, 221-3.

31. *Q.U.L.*, Mair Papers, memoir by Charles Mair.

32. *P.A.M.*, Riel Papers, contains the original of this letter.   Printed versions are to be found in Boulton, 115-6; and in *Begg's Red River Journal*, 312.

33. Boulton, 112.

34. Mair memoir, *op. cit.*

35. *New Nation*, February 18, 1870.

36. *Ibid.*

37. *Ibid.*

38. Boulton, 114.

39. The names of the prisoners may be found in *New Nation*, February 18, 1870; and in *Begg's Red River Journal*, February 18, 1870, 316.

40. W. L. Morton, in his Introduction to *Begg's Red River Journal*, takes the view that it was an impulsive rather than a pre-meditated action.   On the other hand, Boulton, page 116, quotes O'Donoghue as saying that Riel ordered the attack. However, this may be answered by pointing out that by this time O'Donoghue was out of sympathy with Riel and was trying to discredit him.   It would seem reasonable, however, to believe that Riel's desire to seize Schultz would have been sufficient reason for him to have ordered the capture of the Portage party.

41. Boulton, 117, 119.

42. *Begg's Red River Journal*, February 19, 1870, 317.

43. *Ibid.*, February 20, 1870, 318.   "Everybody except the lady herself was disgusted," wrote Begg.

44. Boulton, 121; MacBeth, 155; Healy, 226-7; and *Begg's Red River Journal*, February 19, 1870, 316-17.

45. Smith's report.

46. Boulton, 123-4.

47. *Ibid.*, 124.

48. *Begg's Red River Journal*, February 24, 1870, 321.

49. There were frequent breaches of Riel's injunctions against the use of liquor by his men, and on March 2, two or three of them were imprisoned for drunkenness. According to Riel, "it was high time to make examples." (*Begg's Red River Journal*, March 2, 1870, 326.)

50. *Q.U.L.*, Mair Papers, excerpt of a letter of George Young, April, 1897, quoting a letter from Captain Rawe of Madoc, Ontario.

51. Mactavish to the Secretary, H.B.C., October 12, 1869, quoted in Begg, *Creation*, 79. Incidentally, Snow was rescued by two métis, Damase Harrison and Louis Blondeau.

52. *Trial of Lépine*, evidence of William Chambers, 54. Chambers said that Scott managed to get "half drunk" even when in prison.

53. *Begg's Red River Journal*, December 6, 1870, 212.

54. Dugast, *Histoire Véridique*, 114.

55. *P.A.C.*, Macdonald Papers, Vol. 517, Macdonald to Rose, March 11, 1870.

56. *P.A.Q.*, Chapais Collection, L. Riel, "Affaire Scott." This was a memorandum by Riel on the Scott affair which he sent to Masson. This document was published with an introduction by A. H. de Trémaudan in *The Canadian Historical Review*, VI, 1925, 222-234.

57. *Begg's Red River Journal*, March 1, 1870, 326.

58. See Paul Proulx to de Trémaudan in "Affaire Scott" (note 56) 231 footnote.

59. This account of Scott's trial is taken from Joseph Nolin's evidence at the trial of Lépine (*The Trial of Lépine*, 120-1).

60. Young, *Manitoba Memories*, 133.

61. *Ibid.*, 135.

62. Smith's report.

63. Young, 136.

64. *Ibid.*, 137.

65. *Begg's Red River Journal*, March 4, 1870, 328. Following Scott's execution, many stories circulated that he had not been killed but had died in his coffin , or even been buried alive. It is difficult to say how much truth, if any, there is in these stories. In all probability, they were "atrocity" stories, concocted by Riel's enemies in order to stir up feeling against him.

66. Riel, "Affaire Scott."

67. *Ibid.*

CHAPTER SEVEN : Bishop Taché

1. *Begg's Red River Journal*, March 9, 1870, 332.

2. *P.A.C.*, Macdonald Papers. Vol. 516, Macdonald to Rose, November 23, 1869. Macdonald wrote: "And to add to our troubles, Cartier rather snubbed Bishop Taché when he was here on his way to Rome."

3. *P.R.O.*, C.O. 42/694, Northcote to Granville, January 22, 1870.

4. *A.A.St.B.*, Macdonald to Taché, February 16, 1870. This letter is printed in *The Report of the Select Committee, 1874*.

5. Benoit, *op. cit.*, II, 59.

6. *A.S.D.*, Consular Despatches, Winnipeg, 1869-1871, Malmros to Davis, March 12, 1870. In this despatch, Malmros asked if he should give *de facto* recognition to the Provisional Government.

7. *Begg's Red River Journal*, March 8, 1870, 331; March 9, 1870, 332; March 10, 1870, 333.

8. *Ibid.*, March 10, 1870, 333.

9. *New Nation*, March 11, 1870.

10. *The Report of the Select Committee, 1874*, Taché deposition. Begg refers to Taché's visit to Riel in his *Red River Journal*, March 11, 1870, 334.

11. *Begg's Red River Journal*, March 11, 1870, 334; March 19, 1870, 339; March 28, 1870, 346.

12. *Ibid.*, March 13, 1870, 336.

13. *New Nation*, March 18, 1870.

14. *Begg's Red River Journal*, March 15, 1870, 337.

15. *New Nation*, March 18, 1870.

16. *Begg's Red River Journal*, February 11, 1870, 305.

17. Copies of these documents may be found in the *P.A.M.* There are printed copies in Begg's *Creation*, 323-29.

18. *Ibid.*, 325-29. See also Appendix XXIII in *Begg's Red River Journal*, 515-19.

19. *P.A.M.*, Ross Papers, Riel to Ross, February 21, 1870. Riel had borrowed a book on confederation from James Ross in February. See also *Begg's Red River Journal*, 516 note.

20. *A.A.St.B.*, Taché to Ritchot, March 21, 1870.

21. *Ibid.*, Taché to Riel, March 22, 1870.

22. *Ibid.*, Lemay to Taché, March 12, 1870.

23. The list published in the British Parliamentary paper, *P.P.* 1870 L(C 207) 130-1, was the list Judge Black took to Ottawa. This list was forwarded through diplomatic channels to London. Ritchot's list appears to have been for his own guidance in the negotiations with Ottawa. To have given it to the other delegates would have been to introduce a note of dissension, and there had been trouble enough in persuading Judge Black to act as a delegate.

24. The existence of this demand in the fourth list of rights was made public during the Manitoba School controversy. See Taché to the editor, December 22, 1889 (*Manitoba Free Press*, December 27, 1889).

25. *A.A.St.B.*, Taché to Ritchot, March 21, 1870.

26. *P.P.* 1870 L(C 207), Riel to Mactavish, March 28, 1870.

27. *Begg's Red River Journal*, April 5, 1870, 351. See also *New Nation*, April 15, 1870.

28. *Ibid.*, April 7, 1870, 352.

29. *New Nation*, April 8, 1870.

30. W.M. Davidson, *Louis Riel 1844-1885* (Calgary, 1955), 81.

31. *P.A.M.*, Proclamation aux peuples du Nord-Ouest, 9 avril, 1870. For the English translation, see *Begg's Red River Journal*, 354-5.

32. *New Nation*, March 11, 1870.

33. *Begg's Red River Journal*, May 7, 1870, 368; May 10, 1870, 369.

34. *Ibid.*, March 11, 1870, 334; March 12, 1870, 335.

35. *Ibid.*, April 20, 1870, 355. See also L. A. Prud'homme, "André Nault," (*Transactions of the Royal Society of Canada*, XX, 1928). O'Donoghue and several of his friends erected Schultz's pole in Fort Garry and hoisted the Provisional Government flag on it. *Begg's Red River Journal*, April 3, 1870, 362.

36. *New Nation*, April 8, 1870.

37. This and other oaths may be found in *New Nation*, April 8, 1870; and in Begg, *Creation*, 331-32.

38. *Begg's Red River Journal*, March 25, 1870, 343.

39. *Ibid.*, April 16, 1870, 358; April 18, 1870, 359.

40. J. N. O'Donnell, *Manitoba as I saw it* (Winnipeg, 1909), 104-5.

41. *Begg's Red River Journal*, Appendix XXIV, 520; N. P. Langford to J. W. Taylor, July 10, 1870.

42. *Ibid.*, March 27, 1870, 345.

43. *A.A.St.B.*, Riel to Ritchot, April 19, 1870.

44. *New Nation*, May 6, 1870.

45. *Ibid.*, May 27, 1870.

46. *Begg's Red River Journal*, April 18, 1870, 359. Begg wrote: "A number of the soldiers of the Provisional Government were paid off today and it is said that the most of them refused to re-enlist."

47. Captain Gay was a French adventurer who had served with Garibaldi or at least claimed that he had. With the outbreak of the Franco-Prussian War, he returned to France.

48. Riel's circular letter to the plainsmen and the mission of Patrice Breland illustrate Riel's anxiety to secure backing in case of necessity.   But when Patrice Breland reached Swan River, he found the métis indifferent to the Provisional Government. Breland's father, Pascal Breland, and Salomon Hamelin had urged peace and non-intervention at Red River (I. Cowie, *The Company of Adventurers, a Narrative of Seven Years in the Service of the Hudson's Bay Company, 1867-1874* (Toronto, 1913), 403-406, 412).   Colin Inkster stated that Riel returned to Fort Garry after a visit to the White Horse Plains much discouraged at his inability to counteract the moderating influence of Breland and Hamelin (G. T. Denison, *Reminiscences of the Red River Rebellion of 1869*, 27.)

49. *Begg's Red River Journal*, May 13, 1870, 370.

50. *A.A.St.B.*, Ritchot to Taché, May 12, 1870.

51. *Ibid.*, Riel to Ritchot, June 4, 1870.

52. News report from the correspondent of the New York *Herald*, who was on the boat, reprinted in the Toronto *Globe*, July 19, 1870.   See also *Begg's Red River Journal*, June 17, 1870, 382.

CHAPTER EIGHT : Manitoba

1. *P.A.C.*, Macdonald Papers, Vol. 102, D. R. Cameron to Macdonald, November 3, 1869; Cameron to Macdonald, December 6, 1869.

2. *Ibid.*, McDougall to Macdonald, November 8, 1869.

3. *Ibid.*, Vol. 516, Macdonald to Rose, January 3, 1870.

4. G. T. Denison, *The Struggle for Imperial Unity, Recollections and Experiences* (London, 1909), 11.

5. See Mair Papers in the Library of Queen's University.

6. Denison, *op. cit.*, 15.

7. Dr. Lynch had gone to Red River from Ontario in 1869.   He was with Schultz's party when they were made prisoners in December.

8. Denison, 22.

9. D. C. Thompson, *Alexander Mackenzie, Clear Grit* (Toronto, 1960), 114.

10. Denison, 24.

11. *Ibid.*, 25.

12. Toronto *Globe*, April 7, 1870.

13. *Ibid.*

14. Quoted in Denison, 26.

15. *Q.U.L.*, Mair Papers, Denison to Mair, February 3, 1869.

16. *A.A.St.B.*, Belcourt to Taché, April 4, 1870.   Senator Belcourt told Taché that the Cabinet had had a "très orageuse" session of seven hours in which Cartier "a menacé le Cabinet de donner sa résignation si ses collègues persistaient à vouloir envoyer des troupes à la Rivière Rouge."

17. *P.A.St.N.*, Ritchot journal, April 12, 1870.

18. *A.A.St.B.*, Ritchot to Taché, April 13, 1870.

19. Denison, 32.   See also *Q.U.L.* Mair Papers, Denison to Mair, April 20, 1870; and Ritchot journal, *op. cit.*, April 19, 1870.

20. *P.R.O.*, C.O. 42/685, Ritchot to Sir John Young, April 20, 1870.

21. *Ibid.*, Young to Granville, April 19, 1870.

22. Ritchot journal, April 23, 1870.

23. *A.A.St.B.*, Ritchot to Howe, April 21, 1870; Scott, Black and Ritchot to Howe, April 22, 1870.

24. Ritchot journal, April 25, 1870.

25. *P.A.C.*, Macdonald Papers, Vol. 517, Macdonald to Rose, February 23, 1870. On February 5, 1870, Macdonald wrote to Rose concerning Riel's delegation: "If we once get them here we will easily deal with them" (Macdonald Papers, Vol. 516).

26. This is just what Sir John hoped would happen. In his letter of February 23 to Sir John Rose, he wrote: "These impulsive half-breeds have got spoiled by this émeute and must be kept down by a strong hand until they are swamped by the influx of settlers."

27. *Report of the Select Committee, 1874,* Ritchot deposition. See also *A.A.St.B.,* Howe to Ritchot, Black and Scott, April 26, 1870.

28. Ritchot journal, April 27, April 29, 1870.

29. *Ibid.,* May 3, 1870. See also *A.A. St.B.,* Ritchot to Cartier, May 4, 1870. Re Macdonald, see Creighton, *Macdonald, The Old Chieftain,* 67-8.

30. *A.A.St.B.,* Ritchot to Bunn, May 14, 1870.

31. Ritchot journal, May 3, 1870.

32. *Ibid.* See also *Report of the Select Committee, 1874,* Ritchot deposition.

33. Quoted in Creighton, *op. cit.,* 68.

34. *R.C.M.I.,* Denison Papers, Schultz to Denison, May 30, 1870. Denison wrote, "Sir John is dying. Since yesterday fatal symptoms have come on, hectic fever and greater prostration, and Dr. Grant tells me that it is only a matter of a couple of days to the end."

35. *A.A.St.B.,* Ritchot to Taché, May 12, 1870.

36. *Ibid.,* Ritchot to Bunn, May 14, 1870.

37. *Report of the Select Committee, 1874,* Ritchot to Cartier, May 18, 1870.

38. *Ibid.* See also Ritchot journal, May 19, 1870.

39. *Ibid.,* Cartier to Ritchot and Scott, May 23, 1870.

40. *Ibid.,* Ritchot to Her Majesty the Queen, May 26, 1870.

41. *Ibid.,* Ritchot deposition. See also Ritchot journal, May 25, 26, 27, 28, 1870.

42. *Ibid.,* Ritchot deposition.

43. *Q.U.L.,* Mair Papers, Denison to Mair, August 11, 1869.

44. *P.A.C.,* Macdonald Papers, Vol. 102, McDougall to Macdonald, October 31, 1869; McDougall to Macdonald, November 8, 1869.

45. *P.R.O.,* C.O. 42/695, extract of a letter of Sir John Macdonald, January 26, 1870. See also *P.P.* 1870 L (C 207), Granville to Young, March 5, 1870.

46. *A.A.St.B.,* Taché to Howe, March 11, 1870.

47. *Begg's Red River Journal,* March 8, 1870, 331-32; March 23, 1870, 342. See also Morice, *Critical History,* 291-92.

48. *Ibid.,* April 30, 1870, 365.

49. *R.C.M.I.,* Denison Papers, Schultz to Denison, July 20, 1870.

50. Denison, 36-7.

51. *R.C.M.I.,* Denison Papers, Schultz to Denison, May 20, 1870.

52. *Debates of the House of Commons, Canada,* 1870, I, 1573.

53. *Report of the Select Committee, 1874,* Cartier memorandum, June 8, 1870.

54. *Ibid.,* Young to Granville, June 9, 1870.

55. *Ibid.,* Lynch to the Governor-General, July 1, 1870.

56. *Ibid.,* Young to Granville, July 6, 1870.

57. *Ibid.,* Ritchot deposition.

58. *Ibid.,* Ritchot to Cartier, June 18, 1870.

59. *Begg's Red River Journal,* June 18, 1870, 384.

60. *New Nation,* July 1, 1870.

61. *Ibid.*

62. *Ibid.*

63. *Begg's Red River Journal,* June 24, 1870, 384.

64. Quoted in F. W. Anderson, "Louis Riel, Patriot and Rebel" (*The Western Producer,* Saskatoon, August 4, 1955), 15.

65. *Report of the Select Committee 1874,* Taché deposition.

66. *Ibid.*
67. *R.C.M.I.*, Denison Papers, Schultz to Denison, July 20, 1870.
68. Denison, 37-8.
69. Report in the Toronto *Telegraph*, quoted in Denison, 43-4.
70. This motion was put by Hon. Wm. McDougall "in a vigorous and eloquent speech" (Denison, 42).
71. *Report of the Select Committee, 1874*, Taché deposition.
72. *Ibid.*, Taché to Young, July 25, 1870. Taché suggested that a garrison of "a couple of hundred men" should be stationed in the Red River Settlement "for a considerable period of time" as a means of calming the Indians and preventing any outbreak between the various sections of the population. The real objection that Taché had to sending the military expedition was that the force contained so large a proportion of Ontario volunteers.
73. *A.A.St.B.*, Taché to Riel, July 24, 1870. Denison printed an inaccurate version of this letter in his *Struggle for Imperial Unity*, 46.
74. *Report of the Select Committee, 1874*, Taché deposition.
75. *R.C.M.I.*, Denison Papers, Fred Denison to G. T. Denison, July 11, 1870.
76. *A.A.St.B.*, J. H. McTavish to Taché, July 31, 1870.
77. *Ibid.*, John Bruce to Taché, July 23, 1870.
78. *R.C.M.I.*, Denison Papers, Schultz to Denison, August 8, 1870.
79. *A.A. St.B.*, Lestanc to Taché, August 13, 1870.
80. *Report of the Select Committee, 1874*, Cartier to Taché, July 5, 1870.
81. *A.A.St.B.*, Bannatyne to Taché, August 6, 1870.
82. *Begg's Red River Journal*, July 22, 1870, 391-92; July 23, 1870, 392.
83. *Report of the Select Committee, 1874*, Riel to Taché, July 24, 1870.
84. *Q.U.L.*, Mair Papers, Eck to Stutsman, July 9, 1870.
85. *Report of the Select Committee, 1874*, Taché deposition.
86. A. H. de Trémaudan, "Louis Riel's Account of the Capture of Fort Garry" (*Canadian Historical Review*, June 1924), 157.
87. F. M. Viscount Wolseley, *The Story of a Soldier's Life* (Westminster, 1903), II, 217.
88. *Ibid.*, 220.
89. Dugast, *Histoire Véridique*, 192-93. See also Taché deposition and Schmidt, *Mémoires*, April 18, 1912. The man in question was James G. Stewart.
90. *Report of the Select Committee, 1874*, Taché deposition.
91. Col. G. J. Wolseley, "Narrative of the Capture of Fort Garry" (*Blackwood's Edinburgh Magazine*, CIX, January-June, 1871), 181. See also *Begg's Red River Journal*, Appendix XXI, 564.
92. Dugast, *op. cit.*, 193.

CHAPTER NINE: O'Donoghue

1. G. L. Huyshe, *The Red River Expedition* (London, 1870), 200. Huyshe says that the fugitives had only a few dried fish to eat, which they obtained from a métis farmhouse. It was this that prompted Riel to remark to a métis on the way to Red River, "Tell them that he who ruled in Fort Garry a few days ago, is now a homeless wanderer with nothing to eat but two dried suckers."
2. *P.A.M.*, Riel Papers, Sara Riel to her mother, August 31, 1870.
3. *Ibid.*
4. *Ibid.* Sara Riel to Louis Riel, September 9, 1870.
5. *Ibid.*, Taché to Riel, September 6, 1870.
6. *A.A. St.B.*, Riel to Taché, September 9, 1870.
7. *Ibid.*
8. *Ibid.*, LeFloch to Taché, September 7, 1870.

9. *Q.U.L.*, Mair Papers, Eck to Stutsman, July 9, 1870.

10. *A.A.St.B.*, LeFloch to Taché, September 7, 1870.

11. *Ibid.*, Smith to Taché, August 27, 1870.

12. Stanley, 142.

13. Young, *Manitoba Memories*, 190.   After making allowance for the puritanical strictures of a Methodist minister, there can be no doubt of the lawlessness and drunkenness of the soldiers and civilians. See also W. F. Butler, *The Great Lone Land* (London, 1873), 192-93; MacBeth, 163-64; A. Begg and W. R. Nursey, *Ten Years in Winnipeg 1870-1879* (Winnipeg, 1879), 33-4; Toronto *Globe*, September 9, 22, 27; October 3, 5, 11; November 18, 30, 1870.   The métis speak of disgusting orgies in addition to drunkenness and brawling (A. H. de Trémaudan, *Histoire de la Nation Métisse*), 258.

14. *Report of the Select Committee, 1874*, Archibald Memorandum on the Fenian Invasion of Manitoba in October, 1871.

15. *Ibid.*, Archibald to Macdonald, October 9, 1871.

16. Schultz blamed Goulet's death on the latter's inability to swim (see Schultz's *News Letter* as reported in the *Globe*, October 3, 1870).   The *Globe* took the view that he had been injured while swimming.   For additional material on Goulet, see *C.S.P.*, 1871, IV, No. 20, Archibald to Howe, September 17, 1871; and A. Begg, *History of the North West* (Toronto, 1894), II, 31.

17. *C.S.P.*, 1871, IV, No. 20, McConville to Archibald, September 27, 1871.   See also MacBeth, 164.

18. *A.A.St.B.*, Kavanaugh to Taché, March 13, 1870.   Kavanaugh wrote: "J'ai trop connu le pauvre Louis Riel pour approuver tout son passé."

19. Toronto *Globe*, September 14, 1870.

20. *A.A. St. B.*, Taché to Boucher de la Bruère, April, 21, 1871.

21. *Ibid.*, LeFloch to Taché, September 20, 1870.   Fr. Simonet at Pembina also wrote to Taché, on September 20, that Goulet's death "a couté cher au Canada."

22. J. P. Pritchett, "The so-called Fenian Raid on Manitoba" (*Canadian Historical Review*, March, 1929), 25.

23. *C.S.P.*, 1871, V, No. 20, Archibald to Howe, September 21, 1870.   See also *Debates of the House of Commons, Canada, 1876*, 797-98, for letter from O'Donoghue to the Speaker, February 26, 1875.

24. Pritchett points out the similarity of the wording of the "memorial and petition" and that of the letter of Riel and Lépine to Lieut. Gov. Morris, June 3, 1873. He concludes that this may be taken as evidence of the authorship of the "memorial."   Since Riel and O'Donoghue were the two best educated men at the meeting, it would be more reasonable to infer that they were the authors. Quite possibly Ritchot might have had a hand in it, if he were actually present.

25. G. F. G. Stanley, "Riel's Petition to the President of the United States, 1870," (*Canadian Historical Review*, December, 1939), 427.

26. Toronto *Globe*, October 18, 1870.

27. *A.A. St. B.*, LeFloch to Taché, September 29, 1870.

28. *Ibid.*, LeFloch to Taché, October 9, 1870.

29. Pritchett, 32.

30. Riel's petition, *op. cit.*, 428.

31. Pritchett, 35.

32. *A.A.St.B.*, O'Donoghue to Taché, October 25, 1870.

33. Pritchett, 33.   See also Toronto *Globe*, February 2, 1871 and *La Minerve*, February 6, 1871.   The explanation of Grant's unwillingness to take a more positive stand, with regard to O'Donoghue's petition, when it might be expected that the American president would have favoured annexation, may be found in J. W. Taylor's confidential letter of November 12, to Hamilton Fish.   Here Taylor gave the background story and stated that O'Donoghue had very little support in the Red River Settlement.   Taylor was at this time U.S. Consul in Winnipeg.

34. *Report of the Select Committee, 1874*, Girard deposition.
35. *A.A.St.B.*, Riel to Taché, September 30, 1870.
36. *Ibid.*, LeFloch to Taché, October 9, 1870.
37. *Report of the Select Committee, 1874*, Archibald to Cartier, September 3, September 10, October 14, 1870; Macdonald to Archibald, November 1, 1870; Cartier to Archibald, November 2, 1870.
38. *C.S.P.*, 1871, V, No. 20, Abstract of the census.
39. *R.C.M.I.*, Denison Papers, Schultz to Denison, December 20, 1870.
40. Riel sent a manifesto to Dubuc to be published in the *New Nation*, but the newspaper had been seized by the government and the manifesto to the métis never appeared.   (See *P.A.M.*, Dubuc to Riel, September 6, 1870.)
41. *P.A.M.*, Dubuc, Autobiographie et lettres Mss.
42. *Ibid.*, Dubuc Papers, Schmidt to Dubuc, April 27, 1870.
43. Dubuc, Autobiographie.
44. *P.A.M.*, Dubuc Papers, Riel to Dubuc, October 21, 1870; Dubuc to Riel, October 29, 1870.   See also *A.A. St. B.*, Taché to Kavanaugh, November 17, 1870.
45. *Ibid.*, Riel Papers, Proulx, Nault, etc., to Riel, November 7, 1870.
46. *A.A.St.B.*, Royal to Taché, November 6, 1870; also *P.A.M.*, Riel Papers, Royal to Riel, December 17, 1870.
47. *P.A.M.*, Riel Papers, Resolution of the métis adopted at St. Norbert, Pointe Coupée and St. Vital, November 27, 1870.
48. *Ibid.*, Dubuc Papers, Riel to the Electors of St. Vital, December 1, 1870.
49. *Ibid.*, Riel Papers, Giroux to Riel, December 15, 1870.
50. *Ibid.*, Royal to Riel, December 17, 1870.   See also *Report of the Select Committee, 1874*, Royal deposition.   According to Royal, Cartier suggested that Riel "go away from the country for five or six years so as to let the excitement pass away."
51. *Ibid.*, Lemay to Riel, January 2, 1871.
52. *A.A.St.B.*, Riel to Taché, January 18, 1871.
53. *Q.U.L.*, Mair Papers, Denison to Mair, January, 1871.
54. *R.C.M.I.*, Denison Papers, Fred Denison to G. T. Denison, March 15, 1871.   In a letter written January 1, Fred Denison said "the H.B. Co. would have moved heaven and earth rather than have been beaten by Dr. S."   He complained that the soldiers were allowed out of barracks only after the polls closed in Winnipeg.   Of Archibald, he wrote: "He does not appear popular with most of the loyal party as he has thrown himself into the arms of the other party."
55. *P.A.M.*, Riel Papers, Dubuc to Riel, January 12, 1871.   Dubuc reported a rumour that Dease had paid an Indian to poison Riel.   See also, *A.A.St.B.*, LeFloch to Taché, October 9, 1870.
56. *A.A.St.B.*, Allard to Forget, February 28, 1871.
57. *P.A.M.*, Riel Papers, Sara Riel to Louis Riel, February 20, 1871.
58. *Ibid.*, Sara Riel to Louis Riel, September 21, 1870.
59. *Ibid.*, Sara Riel to her mother, August 31, 1870; Sara Riel to Louis Riel, January 29, 1871.
60. *Ibid.*, Dubuc to Riel, April 12, 1871.
61. *Ibid.*, Riel to Dubuc, April 27, 1871.   See also *A.A.St.B.*, LeFloch to Taché, April 21, 1871; and *Report of the Select Committee, 1874*, Taché to Cartier, May 6, 1871.
62. *Report of the Select Committee, 1874*, Taché deposition.
63. *A.A.St.B.*, Girard to Taché, May 8, 1871.
64. *P.A.M.*, Riel Papers, Dubuc to Riel, March 20, April 12, 1871.
65. *Ibid.*, Dubuc Papers, Riel to Dubuc, June 5, 1871.
66. *P.A.Q.*, Chapais Collection, Clarke to Cartier, January 25, 1871.   Clarke wrote, "I can only congratulate Manitoba on having Sir George to fight her battles and lead her on again and again to victory.   Our triumph has been most complete. We will have a majority of at least six in the legislature."

67. F. H. Schofield, *The Story of Manitoba* (Winnipeg, 1913), I, 301-03.
68. *Report of the Select Committee, 1874*, Taché to Macdonald, January 25, 1873. For the opposite point of view, see *R.C.M.I.*, Denison Papers, F. C. Denison to G. T. Denison, March 15, 1871.
69. Toronto *Globe*, October 18, 1871. See also Pritchett, 38.
70. H. LeCaron, *Twenty Five Years in the Secret Service: The Recollections of a Spy* (London, 1892), 97-9. LeCaron was an associate of O'Neill during the Civil War and became a member of the Fenian Brotherhood. As a British agent, he kept both London and Ottawa informed of the activities of the Fenians.
71. Gilbert McMicken, "The Abortive Fenian Raid on Manitoba," (*Historical and Scientific Society of Manitoba*, Winnipeg, 1888), 7.
72. Schofield, *op. cit.*, 308.
73. *C.Ste.T.*, Rev. J. B. Proulx, "Invasion Fénienne," October 1, 1871.
74. *A.A.St.B.*, O'Donoghue to Taché, October 25, 1870; March 21, 1871; March 23, 1871. See also Taché to O'Donoghue, April 20, 1871.
75. *Ibid.*, Proulx to Taché, September 12, 1871.
76. The proclamation is printed in *C.S.P.*, 1872, VII, No. 26. A French version of the Proclamation was issued October 5.
77. Schofield, 310-11.
78. *Report of the Select Committee*, 1874, Taché deposition.
79. For various documents relating to the métis and the Fenian Raid, see A. H. de Trémaudan, "Louis Riel and the Fenian Raid of 1871," (*Canadian Historical Review*, June 1923), 132-144.
80. *Ibid.*, 134-35, meeting at St. Vital, September 28, 1871.
81. *Ibid.*, 137, meeting at Riel's, October 5, 1871.
82. *Ibid.*, 141, meeting at St. Vital, October 7, 1871.
83. *A.A.St.B.*, Dugast to Taché, October 9, 1871.
84. *Ibid.*, Ritchot to Archibald, October 4, 1871.
85. *Report of the Select Committee, 1874*, Archibald to Ritchot, October 5, 1871.
86. *P.A.M.*, Riel Papers, Riel, Lépine and Parenteau to Archibald, October 7, 1871. This letter is printed in the *Report of the Select Committee, 1874*.
87. *Report of the Select Committee, 1874*, Irvine to Archibald, October 8, 1871. Rev. J. B. Proulx, who was in St. Boniface at this time, wrote in his memorandum "Invasion Fénienne" (note 73) on October 9, 1871, that there were conflicting reports about the size of the Fenian force. Proulx regarded the whole episode as a bit of comic opera. He wrote: "Les Féniens sont formidables. Ils trainent avec eux quatre vingt canons, si gros qu'un homme peut se cacher dedans; ils ont des cartouches de trois pieds de long, hélas!"
88. *Ibid.*, Girard deposition. Proulx wrote in his "Invasion Fénienne" that Archibald "donna la main à tout le monde. Riel parla au nom de sa nation, le gouverneur se montra très satisfait et fit preuve dans ses paroles de beaucoup de prudence et de beaucoup de tact."
89. This was the general view of the "loyalists." One of Schultz's clerks, François Charette, in a affidavit, stated that Riel had urged the métis to support O'Donoghue. But affidavits from P. Parenteau, P. Vermette, A. Vermette and F. Roy, who were present, state that Riel urged them to support the government (*Le Métis*, November 2, 1871). Archibald, after "the most careful enquiry," concluded that Charette's statements "were untrue" (*Report of the Select Committee, 1874*, Archibald deposition).
90. *R.C.M.I.*, Denison Papers, Mair to Denison, October 9, 1871.
91. *Ibid.*, Harrison to Denison, January 23, 1872.
92. *Report of the Select Committee, 1874*, Address from the Legislative Council, January 17, 1872.
93. *Ibid.*, Archibald to Howe, January 20, 1872.
94. *Le Métis*, December 14, 1871.
95. Proulx, "Invasion Fénienne."

CHAPTER TEN : Member of Parliament

1. Toronto *Globe*, February 3, February 13, 1871.
2. *Ibid.*, January 20, 1871.
3. *Ibid.*, March, 1871.
4. Thompson, *op. cit.*, 131, 132.
5. *P.A.C.*, Macdonald Papers, Vol. 520, Macdonald to Rose, March 5, 1872.
6. *P.A.M.*, Riel Papers, Royal to Riel, December 17, 1870. See also *Report of the Select Committee, 1874*, Royal deposition.
7. *Report of the Select Committee, 1874*, Taché to Cartier, May 6, 1871.
8. *Ibid.*, Taché deposition.
9. *Ibid.*
10. *Ibid.*, Macdonald to Taché, December 27, 1871.
11. *Ibid.*, Taché deposition.
12. *Ibid.*, Archibald to Cartier, October 14, 1870.
13. *Ibid.*, Archibald to Cartier, February 24, 1872.
14. *A.A.St.B.*, Dubuc to Taché, December 11, 1871. See also *P.A.M.*, Pierre Parenteau and others to Archibald, December 9, 1871. A warrant for Riel's arrest had been sworn out by J. J. Setter in December, 1870, and A. M. Garrett tried to swear out a warrant for the arrest of Taché for having given hospitality to Riel. In November, 1871, Fr. Dugast reported that an effort was going to be made to serve the warrant against Riel. (Dugast to Taché, November 23, 1871.)
15. *Report of the Select Committee, 1874*, Taché deposition.
16. *Ibid.*, Taché to Riel and Lépine, February 16, 1872.
17. Stanley, *Birth of Western Canada*, 168. See also J. W. Bengough cartoon in *Grip*, October 25, 1873.
18. *P.A.M.*, Dubuc Papers, Riel to Dubuc, March 4, 1872; also Riel telegram to Dubuc, March 3, 1872.
19. *A.A.St.B.*, Riel to Taché, March 27, April 27, 1872.
20. *P.A.M.*, Riel Papers, affidavit of W. Devlin and J. Mager, St. Paul, March 20, 1872. See also *A.A. St. B.*, Riel to Taché, March 21, 1872.
21. *A.A.St.B.*, Riel to Taché, March 27, 1872.
22. Masson Papers, Riel to Masson, April 4, 1872.
23. *A.A.St.B.*, Royal to Taché, April 1, 1872.
24. *Ibid.*, Dugast to Riel, April 22, 1872. Dugast wrote, "Il faut taper sur Schultz." Taché wrote to Masson, on April 22, that Schultz had given $50.00 to prepare effigies. The other ringleader was Stewart Mulvey, a retired officer of the Ontario battalion and editor of Schultz's paper, the *Liberal*. See also *P.A.M.*, Riel Papers, Dubuc to Riel, April 27, 1872.
25. *Le Métis*, May 1, May 15, 1872.
26. *A.A.St.B.*, Riel to Taché, April 27, 1872.
27. A. H. de Trémaudan, "Riel and Lépine to Lieut. Gov. Morris, January 3, 1873," (*Canadian Historical Review*, June, 1926), 158.
28. *A.A.St.B.*, Riel to Taché, May 19, 1872.
29. *P.A.M.*, Riel Papers, Dubuc to Riel, January 31, 1872.
30. *Ibid.*, Dubuc to Riel, April 27, 1872.
31. *Ibid.*, Dubuc Papers, Riel to Dubuc, May 17, 1872.
32. *Report of the Select Committee, 1874*, Taché deposition.
33. *P.A.M.*, Dubuc Papers, Riel to Dubuc, June 18, 1872.
34. *A.A.St.B.*, Lacombe to Taché, July 5, 1872.
35. *P.A.M.*, Riel Papers, Dubuc to Riel, August 15, 1872.
36. *Le Métis*, August 21, 1872.

37. *Ibid.*, August 28, 1872.

38. *Ibid.*, September 4, 1872.

39. According to *Le Métis*, September 11, 1872, Cartier was defeated by "le programme rouge de l'hon. M. Dorion, communiste de Médéric Lanctot, et libératrice dr M. Doutre." See also R. Rumilly, *Histoire de la Province de Québec* (Montreal, n.d.), I, 210-223.

40. *Report of the Select Committee, 1874*, Macdonald to Archibald, September 4, 1872.

41. *Ibid.*, Archibald to Taché, September 5, 1872.

42. *Ibid.*, Taché deposition.

43. *Ibid.*, Archibald to Taché, September 12, 1872.

44. *Ibid.*, Macdonald to Archibald, September 12, 1872.

45. *Le Métis*, September 18, 1872.

46. *Report of the Select Committee, 1874*, Riel, Royal, Lépine and Dubuc to Cartier, September 14, 1872. See also Riel, Royal, Lépine, Dubuc, Beauchemin and Tourond to Cartier, September 14, 1872. (*A.A.St.B.*)

47. *Ibid.*, Macdonald to Archibald, September 13, 1872.

48. *P.A.M.*, Gunn Papers, Schultz to Gunn, September 23, 1872.

49. Cartier died in London, England, May 20, 1873. He was buried in Montreal.

50. *A.A.St.B.*, Macdonald to Taché, December 24, 1872.

51. Riel and Lépine to Lieut. Gov. Morris, January 3, 1873, *op. cit.*

52. *A.A.St.B.*, Langevin to Masson, January 15, 1873, enclosed in Masson to Taché, February 14, 1873.

53. *Report of the Select Committee, 1874*, Ritchot deposition; Ritchot to Macdonald, May 16, 1873.

54. *P.A.M.*, Morris Papers, Schmidt and Dubuc to Morris, November 6, 1872. The resignation was dated October 22, 1872. See also *Le Métis*, September 18, 1872.

55. *Ibid.*, Royal to Morris, March 1873; Morris to Macdonald, November 23, 1872.

56. *A.A.St.B.*, Cunningham to Taché, May 20, 1873.

57. *Ibid.*, Girard to Taché, May 26, 1873.

58. *Ibid.*, Royal to Taché, May 28, 1873.

59. *Ibid.*, Masson to Taché, July 25, 1873.

60. *Ibid.*, Forget-Despatis to Taché, August 3, 1873.

61. *Le Métis*, January 21, 1873.

62. *P.A.M.*, Morris Papers, Morris to Macdonald, June 1873.

63. *Ibid.*, Macdonald to Morris, June 4, 1873.

64. *Le Métis*, July 5, 1873.

65. *P.A.M.*, Dubuc Papers, Riel to the Electors of St. Vital, July 19, 1873.

66. *Ibid.*, Morris Papers, Morris to Campbell, August 19, 1873.

67. *Ibid.*, Campbell to Morris, August 21, 1873.

68. *Ibid.*, Dubuc papers, Riel to Dubuc, September 1873.

69. *A.A.St.B.*, Forget-Despatis to Taché, September 4, 1873.

70. *Ibid.*, Forget-Despatis to Taché, September 7, 1873.

71. *Ibid.*

72. *P.A.M.*, Morris Papers, Morris to Macdonald, September 17, 1873; Morris to Macdonald, September 20, 1873.

73. C. K. Sissons, *John Kerr* (Oxford, 1946), 187.

74. *Ibid.*, 182-7.

75. *A.A.St.B.*, Forget-Despatis to Taché, September 14-16, 1873.

76. M. McLeod, "Glimpses of Riel" (*Winnipeg Free Press*, Magazine Section, July 13, 1935).

77. *A.A.St.B.*, Dubuc to Kavanaugh, September 19, 1873. This letter was an invitation to attend the meeting.
78. *P.A.M.*, Morris Papers, Morris to Macdonald, September 22, 1873.
79. *Ibid.*, Morris to Macdonald, September 20, 1873.
80. *A.A.St.B.*, Langevin to Taché, September 19, 1873.
81. *Ibid.*, Langevin to Taché, September 20, 1873. See also *P.A.M.*, Morris Papers, Morris to Macdonald, September 20, 1873. Morris wrote, "Cornish's only motive can be the love of mischief, but he may have been prompted by the Ontario Opposition, with whom he is in close alliance in order to embarrass you."
82. *A.A.St.B.*, Forget-Despatis to Taché, September 18, 1873. When Dr. O'Donnell went to the Archbishop's house in St. Boniface, he was snubbed by Ritchot. (Forget-Despatis to Taché, September 21, 1873.)
83. *Ibid.*, Ritchot to Taché, September 24, 1873, "Nous avons été trahis par les lâches et infames qui se sont parjurés."
84. *Ibid.*, Proulx to Taché, n.d., 1873.
85. *Le Métis*, October 18, 1873.
86. *A.A.St.B.*, Taché to Forget-Despatis, October 11, 1873.
87. *Ibid.*, Forget-Despatis to Taché, October 17, 1873.
88. *P.A.M.*, Riel Papers, Dubuc to Riel, October 17, 1873.
89. *A.A.St.B.*, Forget-Despatis to Taché, October 14, 1873.
90. *Ibid.*, Forget-Despatis to Taché, October 17, 19-21, 1873.

CHAPTER ELEVEN : Outlaw

1. Morton, *Manitoba*, 170.
2. W. W. Folwell, *A History of Minnesota* (St. Paul, 1926), III, 60-1.
3. *Discours prononcé par l'hon. M. Mercier à l'assemblée législative de Québec sur la question Riel*, le 7 mars 1886 (Quebec, 1886), 56.
4. *Ibid.*
5. *A.A.St.B.*, Riel to Taché, January 1, 1874.
6. *Ibid.*
7. *P.A.M.*, Riel Papers, Riel to his mother, December 4, 1873.
8. *Ibid.*, Barnabé to Riel, January 19, 1874.
9. Riel, *Mémoire sur les causes des troubles du nord-ouest et sur les négociations qui ont amené leur reglement amiable* (Montreal, 1874). This was published early in 1874 by *Le Nouveau Monde* and was widely discussed in the Canadian press. The *Mémoire* was also printed in *Le Métis*, February 21, 28, 1874. *Begg's Red River Journal*, Appendix XXVII, contains an English translation.
10. *P.A.M.*, Riel Papers, Henriette Pierrette to Veuve Riel, January 25, 1874.
11. *A.A.St.B.*, Lucie Riel Lee to Taché, January 17, 1874.
12. *P.A.M.*, Riel Papers, Lachapelle to Riel, January 29, 1874.
13. *A.A.St.B.*, Lacombe to Taché, January 13, 1874.
14. *Ibid.*, Riel to Taché, January 18, 1874.
15. *Report of the Select Committee, 1874*, Dorion to Morris, January 2, 1874.
16. *Ibid.*, Taché to Dorion, January 3, 1874.
17. *Ibid.*, Taché deposition.
18. A. A. Taché, *L'Amnistie* (Montreal, 1874). This booklet appeared towards the end of March. A few days later an English translation was printed. In 1875, Taché published another pamphlet, *Encore l'Amnistie*.
19. *A.A.St.B.*, Lacombe to Taché, January 16, February 7, 1874.
20. *Ibid.*, Masson to Taché, February 5, 1874.
21. *Ibid.*, Lacombe to Taché, February 7, 1874.
22. *Ibid.*, Lacombe to Taché, February 18, 1874.

23. *Le Métis*, February 14, 1874.
24. The votes were cast as follows:

Parish	Riel	Hamelin
St. Vital	29	3
St. Norbert, nord	46	9
St. Norbert, sud	47	20
Ste. Agathe	20	25
Ste. Anne	53	11
	195	68

25. *P.A.M.*, Riel Papers, Dubuc to Riel, February 16, 1874.
26. *A.A.St.B.*, Lacombe to Taché, March 8, 1874.
27. *P.A.M.*, Lachapelle to Desjardins, March 26, 1874.
28. *Ibid.*, Dubuc, "Mémoires d'un Manitobain," Mss.
29. E. A. Collard, *Canadian Yesterdays* (Toronto, 1955), 43.   See also James Young, *Public Men and Public Life in Canada* (Toronto, 1912), II, 187-89.
30. *Ibid.*, 46.
31. Marchioness of Dufferin and Ava, *My Canadian Journal* (London, 1881), 137.
32. Thompson, 193-4.
33. The Committee included Smith (Selkirk), Cameron, Bowell, Abbott, Jones, Blake, Moss, Geoffrion and Masson.   It began its sittings on April 10 and concluded May 21.   The *Report* of the Committee was presented to the House of Commons by the chairman, F. Geoffrion, May 22.
34. *Journals of the House of Commons, Canada, viii,* 1874, 67-71.
35. *A.A.St.B.*, draft letter by Taché, May 2, 1874.
36. *Ibid.*, Lacombe to Taché, April 10, 1874.
37. *P.A.M.*, Morris Papers, Mackenzie to Morris, April 16, 1874.
38. *Ibid.*, Lachapelle to Desjardins, March 26, 1874.
39. Rumilly, *op. cit.*, I, 302.
40. *A. C. Ste. M.*, Riel to Desjardins, May 26, 1874.   See also *P.A.M.*, Lachapelle to Dubuc, June 9, 1874.   Lachapelle says Riel left Montreal on May 9.
41. *P.A.M.*, Dubuc Papers, Riel to Dubuc, May 27, 1874.
42. *Ibid.*, Lachapelle to Dubuc, May 7, 1874.
43. See *Report of the Select Committee, 1874.*
44. Rumilly, I, 301, "Les Trés Honorable John A. Macdonald a menti (excusez le mot) comme ferait un voyou."
45. *P.A.M.*, Dubuc Papers, Lachapelle to Dubuc, September 1, 1874.
46. *Ibid.*, Riel Papers, L. Bourget to Riel. May 30, 1874.
47. *Ibid.*, Desjardins to Riel, June 13, 1874.
48. *Ibid.*
49. *Ibid.*, Dubuc Papers, Riel to Dubuc, July 13, 1874.   See also Schofield, I, 327.
50. *Ibid.*, Lachapelle to Dubuc, August 14, 1874.
51. *Ibid.*   See also *A.A. St.B.*, Deschamps to Forget-Despatis, August 18, 1874.
52. *Ibid.*, Riel to Dubuc, September 10, 1874; Lachapelle to Dubuc, June 9, 1874.
53. *Ibid.*, Lachapelle to Dubuc, September 1, 5, 1874.   See also *P.A.M.*, Riel Papers, Riel to Dugast, August 13, 1874.
54. *Ibid.*, Riel to Dubuc, September 7, 1874.
55. *A.A.St.B.*, Lachapelle to Ritchot, August 17, 1874.
56. *P.A.M.*, Riel Papers, Dubuc to Riel, September 7, 1874.
57. *Le Métis*, September 5, 1874.
58. *A.A.St.B.*, Riel to Ritchot, October 5, 1874.
59. *P.A.M.*, Riel Papers, Desilets to Riel, September 24, 1874.   See also *A.A.Q.*, Riel to Taschereau, January 20, 1875.

60. *A.A.St.B.*, Riel to Taché, November 23, 1874. This letter was written from St. Paul. Another letter, written by Riel to Bishop Bourget on November 25, was given the dateline of Chicago. (*A.A.M.*, Bourget Gen. Corresp., Riel to Bourget, November 25, 1874.)

61. Masson Papers, Royal to Masson, July 9, 1874.

62. Rumilly, I, 323.

63. See Elliot and Brokovski, *Preliminary Investigation and Trial of Ambroise D. Lépine for the murder of Thomas Scott, op. cit.*

64. *Ibid.*, John Bruce evidence, 59.

65. *Ibid.*, Joseph Nolin evidence, 58-9.

66. *Ibid.*, François Charette evidence, 64.

67. Masson Papers, Royal to Masson, November 9, 1874.

68. *Trial of Lépine*, 126-27.

69. *C.S.P.*, 1875, VII, No. 11, Dufferin to Carnarvon, December 10, 1874.

70. C. W. de Kiewiet and F. H. Underhill, *Dufferin-Carnarvon Correspondence, 1874-1878* (Toronto, 1955), 113, Dufferin to Carnarvon, December 4, 1874.

71. *C.S.P.*, 1875, VII, No. 11, Dufferin to Carnarvon, December 10, 1874.

72. On leaving prison, Ambroise Lépine moved first to Saskatchewan and then later returned to his home in Manitoba, where he died in 1922.

73. *Debates of the House of Commons, Canada, 1875*, February 11, 1875, 50.

74. *Ibid.*, February 12, 1875, 136. The Liberals claimed that this solution was satisfactory to Archbishop Taché. It was not. Taché telegraphed Masson on February 15, 1875, "Am not satisfied. Amnesty promised. Not banishment. Thanks for claiming justice. Sorry you failed." On the same day Taché wrote a long letter expanding his telegram. (Masson Papers.)

CHAPTER TWELVE: Fugitive

1. Mason Wade, *The French Canadians 1760-1945* (Toronto, 1955), 341.

2. *Ibid.*, 340.

3. *A.A.St.B.*, Lacombe to Taché, January 11, 1874, January 13, 1874. It was on January 8 that Riel met Bourget. See L. Pouliot, S.J., "Correspondence Louis Riel–Mgr. Bourget," (*Revue d'Histoire de L'Amérique Française*, December 1961), 430.

4. *P.A.M.*, Riel Papers, Bourget to Riel, July 14, 1875. See also Pouliot, *op. cit.*, 437.

5. *A.U.St.J-B.*, Bibliothèque Mallet, Barnabé to Mallet, November 29, 1874.

6. *P.A.M.*, Riel Papers, Barnabé to Riel, December 9, 1874.

7. Gabriel Nadeau, *L'Oeuvre Historique d'Edmond Mallet*, n.d., 3.

8. C. K. Clarke, "A Critical Study of the Case of Louis Riel," (*Queen's Quarterly*, April, 1905), 384. See also H. Gilson, "Etude sur l'Etat Mentale de Louis Riel," (*L'Encéphale, Journal des Maladies Mentales et Nerveuses*, Paris, 1886, 54).

9. *Le Travailleur* (Worcester, Mass.), December 24, 1874.

10. *Ibid.*, June 10, 17, 24, 1875. Lalime was appointed Canadian immigration agent on the instigation of Mgr. Taché (Benoit, II, 295).

11. *A.A.M.*, Bourget Gen. Corresp., Riel to Bourget, January 18, 1875.

12. Taschereau had disapproved of A. B. Routhier's *Catholic Programme* as contrary to the declared policy of the Canadian Church of avoiding active participation in politics. Bourget, on the other hand, had written to F. X. Trudel on June 6, 1871: "La présente est pour certifier à qui voudra l'entendre, que j'approuve en tout point le Programme Catholique et qu'il n'y a rien dans ce programme qui soit dans mon opinion digne de blâme . . . j'ajoute que je considère ce programme comme la plus forte protection du vrai parti conservateur et le plus ferme appui des bons principes qui doivent gouverner une société chrétienne." (R. P. Papin Archambault, *Le Sénateur Alphonse Desjardins, journaliste et homme public, 1841-1912* (Montreal, 1941), 25-6.)

13. *A.A.Q.*, Riel to Taschereau, January 20, 1875.
14. *P.A.M.*, Riel Papers, Barnabé to Riel, January 18, 1875.
15. *P.A.St.N.*, Riel to Ritchot, February 11, 1875.
16. *Debates of the House of Commons*, Canada, 1875, February 24, 322.
17. *P.A.M.*, Lachapelle to Riel, January 22, 1875.
18. *Ibid.*, Lachapelle to Riel, February 25, March 25, 1875.
19. *A.A.M.*, Bourget. Gen. Corresp., Riel to Bourget, January 18, 1875. Riel also wrote to Bourget on March 23, 1875. See also Pouliot, 434-35.
20. *P.A.M.*, Desjardins to Riel, April 9, 1875.
21. *A.U.St.J-B.*, Bibliothèque Mallet, Riel to Mallet, May 10, 1875.
22. *Ibid.*
23. The manifesto is dated April 20, 1875. A copy may be found in the Riel Papers in the *P.A.M.*
24. *A.A.St.B.*, Thibault to Taché, April 28, 1875.
25. Riel's letter to Mallet dated May 10, 1875, was written from Keeseville, N.Y.
26. *P.A.M.*, Riel Papers, Barnabé to Riel, June 16, 1875. Barnabé addressed this letter to Suncook.
27. *A.U.St.J-B.*, Bibliothèque Mallet, Riel to Mallet, July 2, 1875. This letter was written from Keeseville.
28. *P.A.M.*, Lachapelle to Riel, June 29, 1875. See also Barnabé to Riel, June 29, 1875. Barnabé wrote: "Je pense que vous serez assez sage pour vous manger un peu—laissez les affaires pour quelques jours. Il vous faut de repos."
29. *Ibid.*, Riel Papers, Riel to his mother, July 12, 1875. Riel wrote this letter from Worcester.
30. *A.A.St.B.*, Riel to Ritchot, July 15, 1875.
31. *P.A.M.*, Lachapelle to Riel, October 23, 1875.
32. *A.A.M.*, Riel Dossier, Riel to Bourget, September, 1875. Riel wrote "Je laisse votre ville épiscopale si généreuse et si bienfaisante."
33. *P.A.M.*, Riel Papers, Mallet to Riel, October 22, 1875.
34. *Ibid.*, Riel to his Mother, July 12, 1875.
35. *P.A.C.*, Riel Papers, II, Bourget to Riel, July 14, 1875. See also *A.A.M.*, Riel to Bourget, December 6-7, 1875. Riel wrote: "Une chose ne me sort pas de l'esprit; c'est votre lettre du 14 juillet . . . j'accepte avec le plus grand bonheur la mission que vous m'annoncez."
36. *A.A.M.*, Riel Dossier, Riel to Bourget, April 20, 1876. Riel wrote: "De toutes vos lettres je n'en fais qu'une, et c'est là le livre de ma guidance. Je la porte sur mon cœur durant le jour et la place au chevet de mon lit durant la nuit. Je médite continuellement les paroles de mon directeur. Je me dites continuellement vos paroles. . . ."
37. *Ibid.*, Riel to Bourget, December 6-7, 1875.
38. *P.A.M.*, Riel Papers, Riel to Hon. O. P. Morton, October 31, 1875.
39. *A.U.St.J-B.*, Bibliothèque Mallet, Mallet's notes on Riel.
40. *Ibid.*
41. Olive Knox, "The Question of Louis Riel's Insanity," (*Papers read before the Historical and Scientific Society of Manitoba*, 1951), 24.
42. In an undated letter to Mallet, Riel wrote: "A virgin has helped me during the greatest part of the time which I have spent writing this earnest appeal to your charity . . . the Virgin, so candid and fair, has sometimes knelt down near me, sometimes stood over my desk. She has watched my words closely. . . ." (*A.U. St.J-B.*, Bibliothèque Mallet.) It is said that Riel came to Washington with $1000 given him by Bishop Bourget, and that he gave it to a blind Italian beggar who sat daily in front of the Presbyterian church. Because of this excess of generosity, Mallet had to borrow money from Fr. Keane, later Bishop of Richmond, to send Riel north. This story is told by W. F. Bryant in *The Blood of Abel* (Hastings, Nebraska, 1885). Despite its gory title, this small book contains useful information about Riel, which the author obtained after Riel's death

from Joseph Riel, Edmond Mallet and others.   In his letter of July 14, Bourget had written: "vous ne vous réserverez rien de ce qui vous appartient, de ce qui vous touche."   Riel referred to this injunction in his letter to Bourget of May 9, 1876 (*A.A.M.*, Riel Dossier).   Possibly Bourget's remark may explain Riel's action with regard to his money, if the Bryant story is true.

43.   *A.U.St.J-B.*, Bibliothèque Mallet, Primeau to Mallet, December 31, 1875.

44.   *A.A.M.*, Lettres de Mgr. Bourget, tome 24, Bourget to Riel, January 2, 1876. See also Pouliot, 442.

45.   *A.A.St.B.*, Riel to Taché, January 8, 1876; *P.A.St.N.*, Riel to Ritchot, January 14, 1876.

46.   *A.U.St.J-B.*, Bibliothèque Mallet, Barnabé to Mallet, December 29, 1875.

47.   *L'Etendard* (Montreal), April 26, 1886, Affidavit by John Lee April 22, 1886. John Lee married Lucie Riel, sister of Louis Riel (father), October 23, 1849, in Montreal.   During 1863-4, the Lees lived at Côte St. Louis near Mile-End and later in St. Jean Baptiste village.   They were neighbours of Joseph Guernon who lived at Côte St. Louis until 1865, when he moved to St. Jean Baptiste village. Lee was a carpenter and undertaker and was, for a time, an alderman.   He died February 25, 1915.

48.   *Ibid.*

49.   *Ibid.*

50.   *Ibid.*, July 13, 1886, "Histoire médicale de Louis David Riel," by Dr. H. Howard.

51.   *A.A.M.*, Riel Dossier, Riel to Bourget, May 15, 1876.

52.   *Ibid.*, Riel to Bourget, May 1, 1876.

53.   *Ibid.*, enclosed in Riel to Bourget, May 15, 1876.

54.   Howard, "Histoire Médicale de Louis David Riel," *op. cit.*

55.   *P.A.C.*, Department of Justice Miscellaneous Riel Papers, R. G. 13, B 2 II, contains a certificate signed by Dr. Lachapelle, May 15, 1876.   See G. F. G. Stanley, "A Footnote to History: Was Louis Riel an American Citizen?" (*Canadian Historical Review*, March, 1948), 40, note 2.

56.   Lee affidavit, *op. cit.*

57.   Of the contemporary alienists, Dr. François Roy regarded Riel as insane.   Dr. F. X. Perrault took the view that he was simulating madness.   Dr. Howard felt that Riel could distinguish between right and wrong but that, as he was criminally inclined, he was insane "par suite d'un défaut tératologique dans son organization psychologique."   Others, who wrote on Riel's insanity included Dr. Daniel Clark (*American Journal of Insanity*, July, 1887-88), Dr. H. Gilson (*Encéphale*, Paris, 1886), and Dr. W. W. Ireland (*Through the Ivory Gates*, Edinburgh, 1889).

58.   D. Clark, "A Psycho-Medical History of Louis Riel," (*American Journal of Insanity*, Utica N.Y., 1887-88), 38.   See also, A. A. Chiel "Louis Riel, Prophet of the New World" (*The Jewish Post*, September 15, 1955).   Riel claimed that his name was David Mordecai.   Riel refers to this in his letter to Taché, January 8, 1876.   (*A.A.St.B.*)

59.   Howard.   See also *A.A.M.*, Riel Dossier, Riel to Bourget, May 15, 1876.   Riel wrote that God had told him "tu beugleras de ma fureur . . . tu briseras les lustres du lampion brisé; tu dépouilleras les autels souillés de ma demeure. . . ."   After he broke the altar ornaments, Riel was forbidden to attend Mass.   In consequence, he went on a three day hunger-strike.

60.   Howard.   Howard found Riel standing naked with his arms outstretched like a crucifix.   See also *A.A.M.*, Riel Dossier, Riel to Bourget, May 11, 1876.   In his letter, Riel said he had been told by the Holy Spirit "tous immoler, mes plaisirs, mes gouts, ma volonté je me mets tout à vos pieds.   Même je suis tout nu, car je me tout dépouillé de mes habits."

61.   *A.A.St.B.*, Bolduc to Taché, December 4, 1876.

62.   Copies of Riel's scribblings during his period of alienation will be found in the Dubuc Papers in the Manitoba Archives; in the archives of Laval University; and in the Riel Dossier in the archiepiscopal archives of Montreal.   Riel told Dr. Samson at a later date; "J'en étais à me croire prophète ou quelque chose

d'analogue. Il me semblait que la papauté devait laisser le sol vermoulu de l'Europe pour un monde plus jeune. . . . Il me semblait que le tour de l'Amérique était venu, et je me croyais un role important dans ce nouvel ordre de choses." ("Le peuple contre sir John," *Polémiques et documents touchant le Nord-Ouest et l'exécution de Louis Riel*, published by *L'Etendard*, Montreal, 1886, 6.)

63. This will be found in the archives of Laval University.

64. Masson Papers, Lacombe to Masson, May 1, 1876.

65. Lee Affidavit.

66. *A.A.St.B.*, Riel to Bolduc, July 30, 1876.

67. *Ibid.*, Bolduc to Taché, December 4, 1876.

68. *P.A.Q.*, Riel to C. Vincelette, February 1, 1877. Riel asked particularly for Bouillet's *Dictionnaire Historique.*

69. O. D. Skelton, *Life and Letters of Sir Wilfrid Laurier* (Toronto, 1921), I, 294.

70. On his discharge from Beauport, Riel freely discussed his illness with his physicians. When he asked if his mental trouble would recur, Dr. Dansereau told him that he would have nothing to fear if he kept away from anything that might excite him, in particular, politics. (*C.S.P.*, 1886, XII, No. 43F, Dansereau and Milette to the Governor-General, March 8, 1886.)

71. *The Queen vs. Louis Riel* (Ottawa, 1886), Roy 154.

72. *A.A.M.*, Riel Dossier, Riel to Bourget, May 15, 1876.

73. *L'Etendard*, March 1, 1886; Riel to Lachapelle, February 9, 1878.

74. *A.A.St.B.*, Bolduc to Taché, February 4, 1878.

75. *P.A.M.*, Riel Papers, Lachapelle to Riel, February 17, 1878.

76. *A.A.St.B.*, Riel to Taché, February 4, 1878.

77. *P.A.St.N.*, Riel to Ritchot, March 1, 1878.

78. This was one of Riel's purposes in writing to Taché on February 4, note 74.

79. *P.A.M.*, Riel Papers, Barnabé to Riel, April 8, 1878.

80. *Ibid.*, A. V. (Vincelette[?]) to Riel, March 17, 1878; Marian (St. Onge) Vincelette to Riel, June 20, 1878.

81. *Ibid.*, Barnabé to Riel, October 11, 1878.

82. *Ibid.*

83. *Ibid.*, Barnabé to Riel, November 11, 1878.

84. *A.U.St.J-B.*, Bibliothèque Mallet, Barnabé to Mallet, October 12, 1878.

85. *P.A.M.*, Riel Papers, Barnabé to Riel, January 7, 1879. Barnabé enclosed a copy of his letter to Bishop Ireland in this letter.

86. *Ibid.*, Barnabé to Riel, February 1, 1879. Barnabé wrote that he had received no reply from Ireland. On March 16, Barnabé wrote again to Riel, attributing Ireland's lack of interest to a fear that Barnabé and Riel would become too much involved in Riel's half-breed problems to do very much about Ireland's colonization scheme.

87. *Ibid.*, Payette to Barnabé, February 1, 1879. This letter was forwarded by Barnabé to Riel.

88. In his letters to Riel of February 1, and February 19, 1879, Fr. Barnabé speaks of his sister's illness (*P.A.M.*, Riel papers).

89. Healy, *Women of Red River*, 226-27.

90. *P.A.C.*, Department of Justice Miscellaneous Riel Papers, II, Evelina Barnabé to Riel, April 13, 1879. In this letter Evelina asked Riel not to mention the engagement in letters to her as she always read his letters to her mother and brother.

91. *Ibid.*, Evelina Barnabé to Riel, October 4, 1878.

92. *P.A.M.*, Riel Papers, Evelina Barnabé to Riel, October 21, 1878.

93. *P.A.C.*, Department of Justice Miscellaneous Riel Papers, II, Evelina Barnabé to Riel, January 9, 1879.

94. *P.A.M.*, Riel Papers, Evelina Barnabé to Riel, May 13, 1879.

95. *Ibid.*

CHAPTER THIRTEEN : American Citizen

1. F. G. Roe, *The North American Buffalo, A Critical Study of the Species in its Wild State* (Toronto, 1951), 442.

2. W. T. Hornaday, "The Extinction of the American Bison" (*Smithsonian Report*, 1887, Washington, 1891), 512.

3. *A.A.St.B.*, Lacombe to Taché, June 18, 1878.

4. See, for instance, *ibid.*, Kavanaugh to Taché, May, 1870.

5. *Ibid.*, LeFloch to Taché, August 13, 1872.

6. *Ibid.*, LeFloch to Taché, September 28, 1873.

7. *Ibid.*, LeFloch to Taché, June 2, 1873.

8. Giraud, *op. cit.*, 1116-24.

9. E. Lecompte, *Sir Joseph Dubuc 1840-1914* (Montreal, 1923), 166-7.

10. Dubuc, Mémoires d'un Manitobain, Mss.

11. *Ibid.*

12. *Ibid.*

13. *A.A.St.B.*, Dubuc to Taché, January 21, 1879.

14. *Ibid.*, Dubuc to Taché, February 20, 1879.

15. *P.A.M.*, Riel Papers, Dubuc to Riel, March 5, 1879.

16. *A.A.St.B.*, Dubuc to Taché, February 20, 1879.

17. *P.A.M.*, Riel Papers, Riel to Dubuc, April, 1879.

18. L. D. Riel, *Poésies Religieuses et Politiques* (Montreal, 1886).   The poem about Macdonald is dated: St. Joseph, August, 1879.   It reads in parts a follows:

> Le candidat battu de Kingston s'est permis
> Plus d'une ruse en sa carrière.
> C'est ainsi qu'il ternit sa réputation;
> Un renard hors de sa tannière
> Fait aussi bien des tours digne de mention.

19. Fort Benton *Record*, December 19, 1879.

20. *A.A.St.B.*, Lépine to Taché, January 2, 1880.   See also Hugonard to Taché, January 13, 1880.

21. Fort Benton *Record*, September 17, 1880; *Yellowstone Journal*, August 21, 1880; Fort Benton *Record*, August 24, 1882.

22. *P.A.M.*, Riel Papers, Riel to the editor, Helena *Independent*, May 29, 1882.

23. *Ibid.*, Riel Papers, O'Hanlon to Riel, March 4, 1880.

24. Turner, *The North West Mounted Police*, I, 409-11, 501-2.

25. *Le Droit*, February 10, 1943, contains a letter from Riel to his mother, probably written about 1882, in which Louis said: "Je dois vous apprendre, bien chère Maman, que je suis marié depuis plus d'un an.   J'ai pris une fille de la prairie . . . une métisse Canadienne française.   Elle s'appelle Marguerite.   Elle est la fille aînée d'un monsieur que vous n'avez jamais, je pense bien, ni vu ni connu.   Jean Monet dit Bellehumeur est son nom. . . ."   In one of his random verses, Louis wrote:

> Je vous ai marié, Oh ma fille,
> En dix huit cent quatre vingt un
> Au désert, près de la coquille,
> Devant Dieu, par le droit commun.
> Aussitôt que viendra le Prêtre,
> Nous nous rendons ensemble à lui,
> Nous irons rencontrer, peut-être,
> Jusqu'à Benton, saint appui.

The reference to "la coquille" seems to suggest that the marriage took place near the Musselshell, south-east of Fort Benton.

26. *P.A.M.*, Riel Papers, contain a copy of Riel's wedding certificate dated March 6, 1882.

27. *St.B.H.S.*, Riel to his mother, August 9, 1882.   In this letter Riel wrote: "ma femme m'a donné un petit garçon bien portant, Dieu merci."   The boy was born May 4, 1882.   He was named Jean.   After Riel's death, Jean Riel was brought up as Jean Monet by Riel's mother.   He received an education in Montreal. Honoré Mercier, Honoré Beaugrand and Alf. Pelland were interested in him. He married Laure Cazeau and worked with the Grand Trunk Railway.   He died July 30, 1908, without issue.

28. *Ibid.*, Evelina Barnabé to Henriette Riel, May 14, 1882.

29. *P.A.C.*, Department of Justice, Miscellaneous Riel Papers, II, Evelina Barnabé to Riel, October 15, 1882.

30. *Ibid.*, see various drafts of Riel's letter to Evelina.

31. *P.A.M.*, Riel Papers, Sr. Marguerite Marie (Sara Riel) to Mme. Riel, January 4, 1883.

32. Riel's naturalization certificate is in the *P.A.M.*   See also G. F. G. Stanley, "Was Riel an American citizen," *op. cit.*

33. Winnipeg *Free Press*, June 28, 1883.

34. Winnipeg *Daily Sun*, June 29, 1883.

35. *Ibid.*

36. *P.A.C.*, Department of Justice, Miscellaneous Riel Papers, II, Riel to his wife, July 14, 1883.   Ritchot gave Riel a gift of $50 to assist him, "un don de quelques amis," (Ritchot to Riel, July 29, 1883.)

37. A. G. Morice, *Dictionnaire Historique, op. cit.*, 207.   See also Davidson, *op. cit.*, 132-6; and *C.S.P.*, 1886, XIII, No. 52, Queen vs Parenteau and 25 others.

38. Turner, I, 410.

39. Great Falls *Tribune*, July 16, 1885.

40. Fort Benton *Record*, October 17, 1879.

41. Helena *Weekly Herald*, April 12, 1883, Riel to the editor.

42. *P.A.M.*, Riel Papers, draft petition to General Miles, August 6, 1880.   This petition was referred to in the Montana press.

43. *P.A.C.*, Department of Justice, Miscellaneous Riel Papers, II, Riel to U.S. Marshal Alexander Botkin, June 20, 1882.

44. Broadwater wrote to Martin Maginnis, the Democratic member of Congress for Montana, demanding a redrawing of the boundaries of the Indian reserves to assist Broadwater's interests in "choice spots."   He coupled his demands with the threats "both I must have, or damned if I don't go back on you next election." (P. F. Sharp, *Whoop-Up Country, op. cit.*, 154.)

45. *P.A.C.*, Department of Justice, Miscellaneous Riel Papers, II, Riel to Botkin, June 20, 1882.

46. Alexander Botkin, "The John Brown of the Half-Breeds (*Rocky Mountain Magazine*, September 1900, Helena Montana), 18.   See also the *Boulder Monitor*, July 24, 1920.

47. *P.A.C.*, Department of Justice, Miscellaneous Riel Papers, II.   In a scribbled memo, Riel wrote "the Republicans have accepted us as voters, as witnesses, thereby acknowledging our political and civil rights.   They have even done me the honour of appointing me special deputy marshal.   They are themselves opening the way to the half-breed element in defending them practically at the polls, in listening to them practically in the courts, and appointing some of them to offices. . . ."

48. *P.A.M.*, Riel Papers, Louis Riel to Joseph Riel, January 4, 1884.

49. *Ibid.*, Riel to the editor of the Helena *Independent*, May 29, 1882.

50. Helena *Weekly Herald*, October 26, 1882, Riel to Maginnis open letter.

51. *Ibid.*, November 9, 1882.

52. *Ibid.*, November 23, 30; December 7, 1882. In an undated memorandum (probably 1883), Riel wrote: "that power of wrong is principally represented by the Democratic party. I respectfully except from such a peremptory charge all that class of good citizens who follow the Democratic party in a fortuitous way and who get along with them more as companions than as supporters. My intention is to be equally deferential towards those who may side with the Democratic party for personal considerations, in good faith, under the influence of unstudied motives uncalculatingly, without knowing the dangerous drifts of Democracy. It is probable that there are even amongst the Democratic political leaders some honest men who happen to be there more by circumstance than by choice. I acknowledge them and I honor their character. My wish and my hope is that before long all those good elements will unite with the Republicans where they belong and where they ought to be. . . . When the electoral campaign opened last fall in Montana, the bulk of the Democratic party left aside the legitimate means of canvassing. Their wealthy leaders spent amongst the railroad men in Custer and Dawson counties the colossal bribe of thousands of dollars and fixed up matters in such a shape as to open the ballot box to any kind of illegal votes that might be thrown on the market. . . ."

53. Helena *Weekly Herald*, December 21, 1883, Riel to the editor.

54. *Ibid.*, November 23, 1882.

55. Fort Benton *Record*, November 30, 1882.

56. *Ibid.*, March 27, 1883.

57. See Sharp, *op. cit.*, 114-15. Healy had presided "like a feudal baron" at Whoop-Up but had left on the appearance of the N.W.M.P. By 1876, Healy was desperate and wrote to Maginnis, "I am a total wreck financially." With Maginnis's help, he became Democratic party chairman in Choteau county in 1877 and Sheriff in the same year.

58. Fort Benton *Record*, May 19, 1883.

59. *Ibid.* It was after his arrest that Riel went to St. Vital to try to sell some land.

60. Helena *Weekly Herald*, August 23, 1883.

61. Fort Benton *Record*, September 1, 1883.

62. Helena *Weekly Herald*, June 11, 1885, H. P. Rolfe to the editor.

63. Fort Benton Record, April 19, 1884.

64. L. B. Palladino, *Indians and Whites in the North West* (Baltimore, 1894), 191. See also W. N. Bischoff, *The Jesuits in Old Oregon* (Caldwell, 1945), 91-2.

65. Fr. Damiani, S.J., had persuaded a group of métis to settle at St. Peter's and there was already a small settlement at the mission in 1883. (See *Jesuit Archives, Mount St. Michael's, Spokane,* "Historia St. Petri ap ad Pedes Negros.")

66. *P.A.C.*, Department of Justice, Miscellaneous Riel Papers, II, Lavallée to Riel, February 3, 1884; Joseph Riel to Louis Riel, May, 1884; and Riel's mother to Louis Riel, December 31, 1883.

67. Botkin, *op. cit.*, 19.

68. *P.A.C.*, Department of Justice, Miscellaneous Riel Papers, II, Mrs. M. C. Murphy (Mitchell Ranch) to Riel, March 3, 1884.

69. *Ibid.*, Riel to R. P. Penoda, June 3, (1884).

70. *Ibid.*, Riel to Bourget, February 26, 1884.

71. *Ibid.*, Macdonald Papers, Vol. 105, Riel to the delegates, June 5, 1884. There is another copy of this letter in the *P.A.M.*

72. *P.A.M.*, "Dumont's mémoire dictated to A. H. de Trémaudan."

73. *Sun River Sun*, June 12, 1884.

74. David McAstocker, S.J. "Introduction" to Bischoff, *op. cit.*, xvi, xvii. McAstocker personally knew Fr. Eberschweiler. After the rebellion, Gabriel Dumont returned to Fort Benton where he met Eberschweiler and told him that he had escaped death during the fighting "as a favor from the good God" because he had gone to confession to Fr. Eberschweiler just before setting out for the Saskatchewan with Riel (Fr. David McAstocker, S.J., to G. F. G. Stanley, August 15, 1954).

CHAPTER FOURTEEN : North Saskatchewan

1. W. S. Gladestone, a former H.B.C. employee, stated: "We all traded whisky. Well, the Hudson Bay Company traded rum up to the year 1860. I have seen as many Indians drunk at Edmonton and Rocky Mountain House as ever I seen anywhere else . . ." (Sharp, 35).

2. Sharp, 40-1.

3. Stanley, *The Birth of Western Canada*, 199-200.

4. Alexander Morris, *The Treaties of Canada with the Indians of Manitoba and the North West Territories* (Toronto, 1880), 272.

5. Stanley, 214.

6. *A.S.D.*, Consular Despatches, Winnipeg, V, Taylor to Seward, March 25, 1878.

7. Norman to Dewdney, December 27, 1882, quoted in Stanley, 234-5.

8. Fort Benton *Record*, May 7, 1880.

9. Dewdney to the Supt.-General, October 24, 1883, quoted in Stanley, 235-36.

10. Turner, I, 381, 408-11. See also Fort Benton *Record*, January 31, 1879; March 5, 1880; October 1, 1880; and Fort Benton *River Press*, January 15, 1881.

11. Stanley, 282.

12. Fort Benton *Record*, April 11, 1879; May 7, June 25; October 8, 1880. On May 7, the paper reported: "The Blackfeet to the number of 200 lodges, under the leadership of Big Crowfoot are camped at a point south-east of the Little Rockies near the Punchette. The Bad Boy with 30 lodges of North Peigans have gone towards the Blackfoot camp. All these camps and bands are suffering fearfully from hunger and they feel their poverty more, perhaps, than any other tribe."

13. Reed to Dewdney, December 28, 1883, quoted in Stanley, 285.

14. *P.A.C.*, Department of Justice, Miscellaneous Riel Papers, II, N.C.W. to Riel, May 18, 1884.

15. G. F. G. Stanley, "The Half-Breed Rising of 1875," (*Canadian Historical Review*, December, 1936), 399-412.

16. For an account of the métis migration westward, see Giraud, 1134ff.

17. *C.S.P.*, 1885, XIII, No. 116, petition of John Fisher and others May 5, 1873. See also *Le Métis*, October 10, 1874.

18. *Ibid.*, George McKay and others to the Gov.-General, 1878.

19. *Ibid.*, J. S. Dennis, Confidential paper to the Minister of the Interior, December 20, 1878. A copy of this was sent to Taché.

20. *Ibid.*

21. *A.A.St.B.*, Dennis to Taché, December 23, 1878.

22. *Ibid.*, McKay to Taché, January 20, 1879.

23. *Ibid.*, Taché to Dennis, February 3, 1870.

24. See Stanley, *Western Canada*, Chapter XII.

25. Not really as bad! C. B. Rouleau had been appointed magistrate in 1883 to succeed Matthew Ryan, a former magistrate who had been appointed by the Liberal administration of Alexander Mackenzie and had been dismissed in 1881.

26. Morris to Mackenzie, August 20, 1877; quoted in L. H. Thomas, *The Struggle for Responsible Government in the North West Territories, 1870-1897* (Toronto, 1956), 81.

27. Laird to Mackenzie, July 10, 1877; quoted in *ibid.*, 82.

28. *A.A.St.B.*, Lestanc to Taché, August 2, 1879.

29. *P.A.S.*, Morris-Macdonald Correspondence, Morris to Macdonald, November 16, 1872: "there is a split among the French half-breeds, and . . . a section have elected Pascal Breland as their chief . . . Breland is an anti-Rielite."

30. Morris to Langevin, June 8, 1878; quoted in Thomas, *op. cit.*, 83.

31. Grandin to Langevin, June 13, 1884; quoted in Giraud, *op. cit.*, 1191.

32. *Report of the Department of Agriculture*, 1881, 41; quoted in A. S. Morton, *History of Prairie Land Settlement* (Toronto, 1938), 78.

33. *Report of the Department of Agriculture, 1883*, 107; quoted in *ibid.*, 68-9.

34. *Le Manitoba*, June 19, 1884, letter from Joseph Royal.

35. Smith to White, October 31, 1885; quoted in Stanley, *op. cit.*, 262.

36. The Winnipeg *Daily Sun*, December 6, 1883.

37. *Ibid.*, December 19, 20, 1883. See also Morton, *Manitoba*, 211-3.

38. For various complaints, see the issues of the *Vidette* for 1884.

39. See The Edmonton *Bulletin* for 1883 and 1884.

40. *C.S.P.*, 1885, XIII, No. 116, Extract from MacDowall letter, in Dewdney to Macdonald, March 27, 1882.

41. *The Prince Albert Times*, February 28, 1883.

42. *Ibid.*, June 3, 1883.

43. *Ibid.*, March 21, 28, 1883.

44. L. B. Duff, "The Amazing Story of the Winghamite Secretary of Louis Riel" (*Western Ontario History Nugget*, No. 22, University of Western Ontario, 1955), 4.

45. A report from the Registrar's office of the University of Toronto, June 13, 1879, shows that W. H. Jackson stood sixth in a class of eleven in the second year of the University, with first class standings in mathematics and chemistry. He had more scientific skill than judgment—his standing in logic was third class. This document is to be found among the Jackson papers in the Library of the University of Saskatchewan.

46. Duff, *op. cit.*, 5.

47. Donatien Frémont, *Les Secrétaires de Riel*, 77.

48. *U.S.L.*, Jackson Papers, Jackson letter, n.d.

49. *Ibid.*

50. *The Prince Albert Times*, June 13, 1883.

51. *Ibid.*, October 17, 1883.

52. *Debates of the House of Commons, Canada, 1885*, IV, 3083, speech by Hon. Edward Blake, July 6, 1885. See also Stanley, *op. cit.*, 265.

53. *Prince Albert Times*, March 14, 1883. MacDowall had done so by endorsing demands put forward by Charles Nolin at a meeting of the métis at Moise Ouellette's place early in March.

54. *A.O.E.*, Témoinage de Charles Nolin et de Maxime Lépine. The statements of various participants in the rebellion were collected by the Abbé Cloutier, who was sent to investigate the unhappy events in the Saskatchewan valley by Archbishop Taché. A copy of Cloutier's report is in *A.A.St.B.*

55. *Prince Albert Times*, May 10, 1884. See also editorials for March 2, and May 23, 1884.

56. *A.O.E.*, Mémoire de Philippe Garnot. Garnot wrote of Nolin: "un homme plein d'intrigues qui n'est capable ni de parler ni agir ouvertement."

57. Edmonton *Bulletin*, February 22, 1884.

58. *Prince Albert Times*, May 30, 1884. See also Nolin and Lépine, Témoinage, *op. cit.*

59. *C.S.P.*, 1886, XII, No. 43 H, Resolutions in re sending a delegation to Louis Riel.

60. *P.A.C.*, Macdonald Papers, Vol. 106, T.Z. to Riel, May 20, 1884. For the original of this letter, see Department of Justice, Miscellaneous Riel Papers, RG 13, B 2, Vol. II, 425-431. The initials would appear to be T. L. rather than T. Z., as given in the translation in the Macdonald Papers: the writer was Régnier, the schoolmaster who wrote the letter for Maxime Lépine.

61. *Prince Albert Times*, May 30, 1884.

62. *A.O.E.*, Grandin circular letter, June 10, 1884.

CHAPTER FIFTEEN: Agitator

1. *A.O.E.*, Nolin and Lépine, Témoinage.
2. *P.A.M.*, Riel Papers, L. Riel to J. Riel and L. Lavallée, n.d., 1884. See also *P.A.C.*, Department of Justice, Miscellaneous Riel Papers, II.
3. *Missions des Oblats de Marie Immaculée*, XXIII, 1885, Fourmond to the Superior General, December 27, 1884.
4. *Le Manitoba*, July 24, 1884.
5. Schmidt, Mémoires, May 23, 1912.
6. *P.A.C.*, Dewdney Papers, Riel letters, J. A. Macrae to Dewdney, July 2, 1884.
7. Schmidt, Mémoires, May 23, 1912.
8. *U.S.L.*, Jackson Papers, Riel to Jackson, September 29, 1884.
9. Nolin and Lépine, Témoinage.
10. *Prince Albert Times*, July 18, 1884. See also *Le Manitoba*, July 24, 1884.
11. Nolin and Lépine, Témoinage. See also Jackson Papers in the *U.S.L.*
12. At Jackson's trial in July of 1885 at Regina, T. E. Jackson denied that his brother had been Riel's secretary (*C.S.P.*, 1886, XIII, No. 52, *The Queen vs Jackson*, 341). But this was probably said in order to exculpate W. H. Jackson from complicity in Riel's movement. In the same trial W. H. Jackson (page 340) definitely called himself Riel's secretary. For a short, although inaccurate, biography of Jackson, see the Toronto *World*, May 22, 1885.
13. Nolin and Lépine, Témoinage.
14. *A.A.St.B.*, André to Lacombe, January 9, 1886.
15. *P.A.C.*, Department of Justice, Miscellaneous Riel Papers, Riel to the Gentlemen who kindly invite me to hold a public meeting in Prince Albert, July 18, 1884.
16. Toronto *Globe*, September 4, 1884, T. E. Jackson to the *Globe*, August 19, 1884.
17. Nolin and Lépine, Témoinage. See also Rev. J. Le Chevallier, *Batoche* (Montreal, 1941), 48.
18. *P.A.C.*, Dewdney Papers, Vol. 6, André to Riel, n.d. See also *A.A. St.B.*, André to Lacombe, January 9, 1886; also Stanley, *op. cit.*, footnote 13, 440-1.
19. *Prince Albert Times*, July 18, 1884, see letter signed "Gyges."
20. *Ibid.*, July 25, 1884.
21. *Ibid.*
22. *P.A.C.*, Macdonald Papers, Vol. 105, André to Dewdney, July 21, 1884.
23. *P.A.M.*, Riel Papers, L. Riel to J. Riel and Louis Lavallée, n.d., 1884.
24. Winnipeg *Daily Sun*, July 22, 1884.
25. *P.A.C.*, Macdonald Papers, Vol. 105, Jackson to Riel, July 23, 1884. See original in *P.A.C.*, Department of Justice, Miscellaneous Riel papers, II.
26. *Ibid.*
27. *P.A.C.*, Department of Justice, Miscellaneous Riel Papers, W. H. Jackson to the Citizens of Prince Albert, July 28, 1884.
28. *Ibid.*
29. Stanley, 286-88.
30. *Ibid.*, 288-89.
31. *P.A.C.*, Macdonald Papers, Vol. 107, Rae to Dewdney, July 29, 1884; Macrae to Dewdney, August 5, 1884. See also Louis Schmidt, "Notes sur le mouvement des métis à St. Laurent, Sask., T.N.O., en 1884," enclosed in Schmidt to Taché, March 7, 1885 (*A.A.St.B.*).
32. *P.A.C.*, Macdonald Papers, Vol. 105, Brooks to Crozier, August 14, August 21, 1884. Re Jackson's statement see Stanley, 303.
33. *Ibid.*, Macdonald Papers, Vol. 107, Dewdney to Macdonald, August 8, 1884.
34. Stanley, 291.

35. Reed to the Superintendent-General, January 23, 1885; quoted in Stanley, 293-94.

36. *Prince Albert Times*, September 26, 1884. Regarding the press Jackson wrote in his manifesto (note 27), "Our local press is not to be relied on. It is in the hands of a few governmental favorites who inspire its editorials. . . ."

37. Schmidt, Notes, *op. cit.*

38. *Ibid.*

39. *Ibid.*

40. *P.A.C.*, Macdonald Papers, Vol. 107, Rouleau to Dewdney, September 5, 1884.

41. *U.S.L.*, Jackson Papers.

42. Schmidt, Notes.

43. *Ibid.*

44. *U.S.L.*, Jackson Papers, Riel to T. E. Jackson, August 25, 1884.

45. *P.A.C.*, Macdonald Papers, Langevin to Macdonald, 1884-1891, Langevin to Macdonald, November 6, 1884.

46. *P.A.M.*, Riel Papers, Isbister to Riel, September 4, 1884.

47. Nolin and Lépine, Témoinage. See also Le Chevallier, *op. cit.*, 51.

48. *Ibid.*

49. Turner, *The Royal North West Mounted Police*, II, 77. See *P.A.C.*, Macdonald Papers, Vol. 105, for reports of Keenan and Brooks.

50. Schmidt, Notes. See also Fourmond to Fabre, December 27, 1884; quoted in Le Chevallier, 52, and Forget to Dewdney, September 18, 1884, in *P.A.C.*, Macdonald Papers, Vol. 107.

51. *Ibid.* See also *P.A.C.*, Macdonald Papers, 105, Keenan to Crozier, September 7, 1884.

52. *La Petite Chronique de St. Laurent*, cited in Le Chevallier, 52. Schmidt in his "Notes" says that Riel managed this business very cleverly, dramatically taking one Ludger Gariault, a French-Canadian and Paul Schley, a Frenchman from Belfort, by the hand and leading them forward, as symbolic of the unity of the three groups, métis, French and French-Canadian. For another account of this meeting, see E. Jonquet, *Mgr. Grandin, premier évèque de Saint Albert* (Montreal, 1903), 375-6; also P. E. Breton, *Vital Grandin* (Montreal, 1960), 296-7.

53. *P.A.C.*, Macdonald Papers, Vol. 107, Forget to Dewdney, September 18, 1884.

54. *Ibid.*

55. *Ibid.*

56. *Ibid.*, Dewdney to Macdonald, September 19, 1884.

57. *Missions des Oblats de Marie Immaculée*, XXIII, Fourmond to the Superior-General, December 27, 1884.

58. Schmidt, Notes. Schmidt wrote: "De son coté, le bon P. Fourmond, qui est assez poète et musician en ses heures, voulut rehausser la solemnité par un chant de sa composition. Mais son enthousiasme est si grand qu'il entonne son cantique qui lui seul connaît du reste, sur un ton d'un octave trop haut, et il étouffe à chaque verset."

59. Le Chevallier, 53.

60. *A.A.St.B.*, Grandin to Taché, September 8, 1884.

61. *P.A.M.*, Riel Papers, Taché to Riel, October 4, 1884.

62. Schmidt, Notes.

63. *U.S.L.*, Jackson Papers, Affidavit by J. Slater, July 28, 1885.

64. *P.A.M.*, Riel Papers, W. H. Jackson to Riel, December 18, 1884.

65. *Colonial Office, North America, 113, Correspondence respecting the Rising in the North West Territory, confidential*, Jackson and Spence to Chapleau, December 16, 1884. The original letter and petition will be found in *P.A.C.*, Department of Interior, Dominion Lands Branch, Correspondence, file 83808.

66. Jackson to Riel, January 27, 1885; quoted in Stanley, 307.

CHAPTER SIXTEEN : Exovedate

1. *A.O.E.*, Nolin and Lépine, Témoinage.
2. *C.S.P.*, 1886, XII, No. 43 c, *The Queen vs Riel*, 199.
3. Schmidt, Notes.
4. *Prince Albert Times*, November 28, 1884.
5. *Ibid.*, December 5, 1884.
6. *A.A.St.B.*, Végreville to Taché, December 16, 1884.
7. Schmidt, Notes.
8. Fr. Morice in *Histoire de l'Eglise Catholique dans l'Ouest Canadien du Lac Supérieur au Pacifique* (St. Boniface, 1921) II, 73, says that Riel was excluded from the sacraments. This is not the version given in *La Petite Chronique de St. Laurent*. Fr. Le Chevallier in his *Batoche*, page 56 follows *La Petite Chronique*.
9. Nolin and Lépine, Témoinage.
10. *P.A.C.*, Macdonald Papers, Vol. 107, MacDowall to Dewdney, December 24, 1884.
11. *Ibid.*, André to Dewdney, January 7, 1885; enclosed in Dewdney to Macdonald, January 11, 1885.
12. *Ibid.*, Macdonald Papers, Vol. 105, Howe to Crozier, December 24, 1884; enclosed in Crozier to Dewdney, January 7, 1885.
13. *Queen vs Riel*, Nolin, 125.
14. Garnot, Mémoire, *op. cit.*
15. *P.A.C.*, Macdonald Papers, Vol. 107, André to Dewdney, January 21, 1885.
16. *Ibid.*, Macdonald Papers, Vol. 250, MacDowall to Dewdney, January 28, 1885.
17. *Ibid.*, Macdonald Papers, Vol. 107, MacDowall to Dewdney, February 2, 1885. Riel spoke of an indemnity of $35,000 (*The Queen vs. Riel*, 220).
18. *Ibid.*, André to Dewdney, February 6, 1885.
19. *Le Manitoba*, February 26, 1885. The correspondent in question was Louis Schmidt.
20. *Debates of the House of Commons, Canada, 1885*, IV, 3118. For an account of Macdonald's reaction to Riel's claims, see D. G. Creighton, *John A. Macdonald, The Old Chieftain* (Toronto, 1955), 412-17.
21. *P.A.C.*, Macdonald Papers, Vol. 105, MacPherson to Dewdney, February 4, 1885.
22. *La Petite Chronique de St. Laurent*, quoted in Le Chevallier, 59.
23. *A.A.St.B.*, Végreville to Taché, February 26, 1885.
24. Garnot, Mémoire.
25. Schmidt, Notes.
26. *Queen vs Riel*, Nolin, 126.
27. Schmidt, Notes.
28. *A.A.St.B.*, Végreville to Taché, February 19, 1885.
29. Schmidt, Notes.
30. *A.A.St.B.*, Grandin to Taché, September 8, 1884.
31. *Ibid.* This idea is also expressed in Giraud, *Le Métis Canadien*, 1202.
32. Schmidt, Notes.
33. Nolin and Lépine, Témoinage.
34. *Ibid.*
35. Garnot, Mémoire.
36. *P.A.C.*, Macdonald Papers, Vol. 105, Crozier to Dewdney, January 7, 1885.
37. *A.A.St.B.*, T. A. Bernier to P. B. de la Bruère, May 27, 1885.
38. Garnot, Mémoire.
39. *A.A.St.B.*, Grandin to Taché, September 8, 1884.
40. *Queen vs Riel*, 197, 224. Riel called himself a prophet during his trial.

41. In September, 1884, Nolin had demanded the despatch of an ultimatum to Ottawa under the threat of taking up arms (*P.A.C.*, Macdonald Papers, Vol. 105, Keenan to Crozier, September 25, 1884). According to Sgt. Keenan, N.W.M.P., "This man Nolin is the most dangerous of the half-breeds for the reason that he is strongly in favour of tampering with the Indians." See also E. J. Chambers, *The Royal North West Mounted Police* (Montreal-Ottawa, 1906), 83.

42. Schmidt, Notes.

43. *Queen vs Riel*, Nolin, 126.

44. Nolin made this promise following his wife's recovery from a serious illness (*Le Manitoba*, March 5, 1885). On February 8, Nolin and his wife, Rosalie Lépine, swore to the miraculous cure, which they attributed to the intercession of Notre Dame de Lourdes. The certificate attesting to the cure was signed by Charles Nolin, Rosalie Lépine, Maxime Lépine and Andrew Spence, the last-named a Protestant. See *La Petite Chronique de St. Laurent*, 1885.

45. During this period, Superintendent Gagnon, N.W.M.P., while riding to St. Laurent, stopped at the Riel house to inquire directions. Riel was not at home. This harmless episode was twisted into a scandal, since there were only two women in the house, and Riel became greatly excited. (*Queen vs Riel*, Nolin, 130; see also Davidson, Louis Riel, *op. cit.*, 153.)

46. Stanley, 442, footnote 67.

47. *Queen vs Riel*, Nolin, 127. See also *La Petite Chronique de St. Laurent*, 1885.

48. *A.O.E.*, Végreville to Grandin, March 12, 1885.

49. *La Petite Chronique de St. Laurent*, 1885.

50. Garnot, Mémoire.

51. Gagnon to Irvine, March 10, 1885; cited in Chambers, 85 and Stanley, 321.

52. Crozier to Irvine, March 11, 1885, *ibid.*

53. *P.A.C.*, Macdonald Papers, Vol. 107, Dewdney to Macdonald, March 11, 1885.

54. Crozier to Dewdney, March 14, 1885; quoted in Chambers, 85.

55. White to Irvine, March 15, 1885; *ibid.*

56. Garnot, Mémoire.

57. *Ibid.*

58. *Queen vs Riel*, Willoughby, 54-5.

59. *Ibid.*, 56, 58.

60. For a discussion of Lawrence Clarke's statement, see Stanley, 443, footnote 69.

61. *Queen vs Riel*, Tompkins, 86, Lash, 91.

62. *Ibid.*, Ness, 96.

63. In his *Histoire de la Nation Métisse*, 411, de Trémaudan wrote that Riel took possession of the church with Fr. Moulin's permission. However, on July 7 of 1885, Moulin wrote to Fr. Soullier giving the account used above. Moreover, Garnot wrote in his "Mémoire": "prise de l'église malgré les protestations du P. Moulin." See also Le Chevallier, 69.

64. *A.O.E.*, André to Grandin, March 22, 1885.

65. *Queen vs Riel*, Walters, 104-5.

66. *U.S.L.*, Jackson Papers. In this letter Jackson urged his mother "to recollect the necessity of an authorized interpretation of Scripture and consider the suitability of giving that power to Peter, who, having been taught humility was specially fitted to command and whose epistles are in marked accordance with the Sermon on the Mount." Jackson also wrote: "I am confident that God has at last led me to the place where he wishes me to work." It should be added that after his baptism Jackson adopted the French form of Henri Jaxon for his name. To this form he adhered, although in later years he called himself Honoré Joseph Jaxon. He worked as a labour organizer in the U.S. and died in poverty in New York, January 21, 1952. See Duff, "The Amazing Story of the Winghamite Secretary of Louis Riel," *op. cit.*

67. *La Petite Chronique de St. Laurent*, 1885. See also Chevallier, 70.

68. *Ibid.*

69. During his trial, Riel said: "The 19th century is to be treated in certain ways, and it is probably for that reason I have found the word '*exovede*,' I prefer to be called one of the flock; I am no more than you are, I am simply one of the flock, equal to the rest." (*Queen vs Riel*, 197.)   See also *ibid.*, Young, 172.

70. *Ibid.*, Nolin, 127.   The men who arrested Nolin on Riel's orders were Philippe Gariépy, David Tourond, François Vermette and Joseph Flemoine.

71. Garnot, Mémoire.

72. *Queen vs Riel*, Nolin, 127-8.   See also Schmidt, Notes and *La Petite Chronique de St. Laurent*, 1885.

73. Giraud, 1209.

74. *P.A.C.*, Macdonald Papers, Vol. 110, deposition of Azarie Gariault, Angélique Dumont, J-B Boucher, G. Parenteau, Norbert Turcotte.

75. *Ibid.*, Department of Justice, Miscellaneous Riel Papers, III, Lépine affidavit, May 14, 1885.

76. Minutes of the Exovedate, see Davidson, 157.

77. Le Chevallier, 72.

78. They included a mounted squadron with "A" Troop officered by Capt. C. F. Young and Lieuts. T. N. Campbell and J. D. Wilson; and "B" Troop under Capt. H. S. Moore and Lieuts. Edward Stanley and John Gordon.   The infantry company was under Capt. Thos. McKay and Lieut. J. J. Campbell.

79. This Company was designated No. 1, Coy. Prince Albert Volunteers.   It had as its officers, Capt. H. S. Moore, formerly of the Irish Militia, 1st Lieut. C. F. Young, formerly of the 5th Regiment of Foot and 2nd Lieut. John Morton, formerly of the 32nd Bruce Rifles.   The sergeants were T. N. Campbell and J. D. Wilson, formerly with the Perth Regiment and Alex McNab, retired Adjutant of the 32nd Bruce Rifles.

80. *Queen vs Riel*, Mitchell, 107.

81. *Ibid.*, McKay, 61.

82. *Ibid.*, 61, 62.

83. *Ibid.*, Exhibit 5, Riel to Crozier, March 21, 1885.

84. *Queen vs Scott*, McNiven, 88; Ross, 137.

85. *Ibid.*, McNiven, 90.

86. *Ibid.*, Ross, 139.

87. *Ibid.*, Ross, 140; Paquin, 145.

88. This letter is quoted in full in Stanley, *Birth of Western Canada*, 318.

89. *Queen vs Scott*, Matheson, 125.

90. *Ibid.*, Craig, 93.

91. Quoted in Stanley, 318-9; see also 443 footnote 77.

92. This letter was addressed to the English half-breeds at St. Andrews and St. Catherine's on March 23, 1885.   It is quoted in full in Stanley, 319-20.

93. *Queen vs Scott*, exhibit, Scott to the French Council, March 23, 1885.

94. *Ibid.*, Nolin, 149.

95. *Ibid.*, Nolin, 151; Miller, 155-6.

96. *Ibid.*, Miller, 155. In the P.A.C., Department of Justice Miscellaneous Riel Papers, is a document entitled "Credentials of delegates to Louis Riel, March 26, 1885" appointing Isbister and Sanderson to see Riel.

CHAPTER SEVENTEEN: North-West Rebellion

1. *Queen vs Riel*, McKay, 64-6.

2. *C.S.P.*, 1886, VI, No. 8, Irvine to Macdonald, December 31, 1885.   A letter to the Winnipeg *Sun* (June 2, 1885) stated that Lawrence Clarke had accused Crozier of cowardice.   This is the view expressed by N. F. Black in his *History of Saskatchewan and the Old North West* (Regina, 1913), 1, 281-2.

3. The prisoners included J. W. Astley, a surveyor and Harold Ross, deputy sheriff

of Prince Albert. See *Queen vs Riel*, Astley, 69; also G. F. G. Stanley, "Gabriel Dumont's Account of the North West Rebellion, 1885," in the *Canadian Historical Review* September, 1949, 251.

4. *Queen vs Riel*, Astley, 69; Ross, 76.

5. *Ibid.*, Astley gave the number at 400.

6. Dumont's Account, *op. cit.*, 253.

7. This is based upon an interview with Joseph "Gentleman Joe" McKay, published in the Prince Albert *Daily Herald*, March 26, 1935: "Duck Lake Battle fought 50 years ago today." Black's *History of Saskatchewan, op. cit.*, 277, gives a similar version. Riel claimed that the N.W.M.P. fired first (*Queen vs Riel*, Astley, 69). Crozier claimed that the métis fired the first shots (*C.S.P.*, 1886, VI, No. 8, Irvine to Macdonald, April 1, 1885).

8. *Queen vs Riel*, Astley, 69; Ross, 77; Sanderson, 139.

9. *P.A.C.*, Department of Justice, Miscellaneous Riel Papers, III; John Kummerfield to Sally, March 30, 1885.

10. Dumont's Account, 255.

11. The names of the N.W.M.P. and the P. A. Volunteers casualties may be found in Turner, II, 115. The métis casualties included J-B Montour, Joseph Montour, Auguste Laframboise, Isidore Dumont and the Indian Assiyiwin. The métis and Indian are buried in the cemetery at St. Anthony's church, Batoche. For an account of the engagement at Duck Lake, see *Prince Albert Times*, July 10, 1885.

12. Dumont's Account, 255.

13. *Queen vs Riel*, Astley, 73-4.

14. Dumont's Account, 255.

15. Stanley, *Birth of Western Canada*, 329-330; Turner, *North West Mounted Police*, II, 114.

16. Dumont's Account, 256.

17. *P.A.C.*, Department of Justice, Miscellaneous Riel Papers, V, C. Nolin to Marguerite Nolin, June 26, 1885. Nolin wrote: "J'ai la triste nouvelle vous apprendre que je suis prisonnier depuis 40 jours. Ce n'est pas un cas pour déshonour mes parents, c'est la faute de ce maudit Riel." See also Schmidt, Notes.

18. *Ibid.*, Dewdney Papers, Vol. 6, Minutes of the Exovedate, March 31, 1885. The métis did not apparently disturb Fr. Moulin at his church on their return (see Moulin to Soullier, July 7, 1885, cited in Le Chevallier, 177). The métis soldiers were required to take the following oath: "Faites-nous serment devant Dieu que vous serez fidèle au mouvement des métis canadien-français et à leur Gouvernement Provisoire, et faites-nous serment de garder la route que vous avez à surveiller, et à être fidèle aux devoirs que l'Exovidat vous impose aux nom de Dieu." (*P.A.C.*, Riel Papers, II.)

19. *Ibid.*

20. The original Riel journal was handed to Deputy Sheriff Hanafin, who had it translated into English by Alex Stewart who made two copies. One of these copies is in the possession of the Prince Albert Historical Society.

21. *Queen vs Riel*, Sanderson, 140.

22. *P.A.C.*, Department of Justice, Miscellaneous Riel Papers, III, Minutes of the Exovedate, March 27, 1885.

23. *Queen vs Riel*, Sanderson, 140.

24. *Ibid.*, Exhibit 20, 232. The original is in P.A.C. Department of Justice, Miscellaneous Riel Papers, III.

25. *P.A.C.*, Department of Justice, Miscellaneous Riel Papers, Evidence Books, Ross statement. Incidentally, no physician responded to Riel's request.

26. *Queen vs Riel*, Jackson, 110.

27. *U.S.L.*, Jackson papers, Riel to the English who have come to look for their dead, March 29, 1885. A draft in Riel's handwriting will be found in *P.A.C.*, Department of Justice, Miscellaneous Riel Papers.

28. *Queen vs Riel*, Jackson, 111.

29. *Ibid.* See also Jackson's statement in *P.A.C.* Department of Justice, Miscellaneous Riel Papers, Evidence Books.

30. Turner, 1, 408-413, 443, 501-2.

31. *P.A.C.*, Department of Justice, Miscellaneous Riel Papers, Evidence Books, Jackson statement. According to Jackson, Big Bear and Boss Bull had an interview with Riel at Jackson's house in Prince Albert in July of 1884.

32. *P.A.C.*, Macdonald Papers, Vol. 105, Crozier to Dewdney, January 7, 1885.

33. For an account of the Indian rising, see Stanley, *Birth of Western Canada*, Chapter XV.

34. *Queen vs Riel*, Exhibit 7, 227.

35. *Ibid.*, Exhibit 9, 228.

36. *Ibid.*, Exhibit 8, 228.

37. Sir Joseph Pope, *Correspondence of Sir John Macdonald* (Toronto, 1921), 354-6; Macdonald to Lansdowne, August 28, 1884; Lansdowne to Macdonald, August 31, 1884.

38. The military force used in the North-West Rebellion was made up of Canadian Militia and not of British regulars. Enlistment was voluntary. The official report of the campaign will be found in *The Report on the Suppression of the Rebellion in the North West Territories and matters in connection therewith*, presented to the Canadian Parliament in May, 1886. General Middleton wrote his own account, which was published in the *United Services Magazine*, November–December 1893. This latter account was edited by G. H. Needler and republished in 1948 by the University of Toronto Press.

39. The public reaction to the North-West Rebellion on the part of the people of Kingston, Ontario, will be found in G. F. G. Stanley, "Kingston and the North West Rebellion" (*Historic Kingston*, IX, 1960).

40. Major-General Sir Fred Middleton, *Suppression of the Rebellion in the North West Territories of Canada 1885* (G. H. Needler editor, Toronto, 1948), 19.

41. *Ibid.*, 20.

42. *Ibid.*, 32.

43. *P.A.C.*, Macdonald Papers, Vol. 110, depositions by various métis taken by the Royal Commission on Rebellion Losses. See in particular the deposition of Patrice Tourond.

44. Garnot, Mémoire. According to Garnot, Riel said to him: "vous me contrariez beaucoup, et j'ai même des suspicions contre vous. Vous savez sans doute que si vous n'aviez pas consenti à agir comme sécrétaire, au commencement de cette affaire, on était pour prendre les moyens de vous punir. Vous savez aussi que chaque parole que vous dites contre moi et contre la religion que j'essaie à réformer me fait beaucoup de tort et que vous ne faites ou ne dites rien sans que l'Esprit de Dieu m'avertisse de vos intentions."

45. *Queen vs Riel*, Jackson, 112.

46. *P.A.C.*, Department of Justice, Miscellaneous Riel Papers, III, Minutes of the Exovedate.

47. *Ibid.*, Dewdney Papers, Vol. 6. The new names were Christ Aurore, Vierge Aurore, Joseph Aube, Divine Aurore, Deuil Aurore, Calme Aurore, Vive Aurore. See also Department of Justice, Miscellaneous Riel Papers, I.

48. The signs of the zodiac were to be called "les diamants de son Diadème."

49. Riel, journal.

50. Garnot, Mémoire.

51. Schmidt, Notes.

52. *La Minerve*, March 10, 1886; Fourmond to the Directors of the Congregation for the Propagation of the Faith.

53. De Trémaudan, *Histoire de la Nation métisse*, 421. Riel's efforts during his trial to convince people that he was not an imposter seem sincere (*Queen vs Riel*, 224-5).

54. Riel, journal.

55. Moulin to Soullier, July 7, 1885; quoted in Le Chevallier, 177.
56. De Trémaudan, 412-3.
57. *P.A.C.*, Dewdney Papers, Vol. 6. See also *A.O.E.*, Végreville's journal.
58. *A.O.E.*, Journal des Sœurs Fidèles Compagnons de Jesus de St. Laurent, April–May, 1885.
59. Dumont's Account, 256.
60. Davidson, *op. cit.*, 167.
61. Dumont's Account, 257.
62. Riel, Journal.
63. Dumont's Account, 258.
64. *Ibid.*, 259.
65. Garnot, Mémoire.
66. Garnot stated that there were 105 horsemen and 100 men on foot. Dumont gave the number at 200 (Dumont's Account, 259).
67. Garnot, Mémoire.
68. Dumont's Account, 259.
69. *Ibid.*
70. Boulton, *Reminiscences of the North West Rebellions*, 225-26.
71. Middleton, *op. cit.*, 32.
72. *P.A.C.*, Dewdney Papers, Vol. 6, Report of Maxime Lépine on the engagement at Fish Creek. Lépine wrote: "Suddenly I heard a young man singing in French the Song of the Bois Brulé, Falcon's song. That gave me courage. . . ."
73. Dumont's Account, 262. See also Lépine Report. The numbers dropped as a result of desertions rather than casualties.
74. *Ibid.*
75. Boulton, 236.
76. Dumont's Account, 262. Dumont wrote: "We lost only 4 men; that is to say: 2 Sioux, my nephew St. Pierre and José Vermette. Two others were wounded; François Boyer, my nephew and Michel Desjarlais, who died three days later."
77. Garnot, Mémoire.
78. Lépine, Report.
79. Dumont's Account, 262.
80. *P.A.C.*, Department of Justice, Miscellaneous Riel Papers, IV, Minutes of the Exovedate.
81. *A.O.E.*, Végreville Journal.
82. *C.S.P.*, 1886, XIII, No. 52, *The Queen vs Joseph Arcand et al*, Fourmond, 396.
83. Dumont's Account, 264.
84. *P.A.C.*, Department of Justice, Miscellaneous Riel Papers, Riel to Poundmaker, May 1, 1885.
85. Riel Journal.
86. *The Irish World*, November 21, 1885. Riel's letter to *The Irish World* is dated May 18, 1885. This is taken from newspaper clippings in the Bibliothèque Mallet (*A.U.*, *St. J-B.*).
87. Dumont's Account, 265.
88. Stanley, *Birth of Western Canada*, 448, footnote 49.
89. Was this the beginning of the naval tradition of the prairies, which led so many prairie boys to enlist in the R.C.N. during the War 1939-45? *The New York Herald*, May 10, 1885, had as one of its headlines "Loyal Navy Disabled."
90. Middleton, 46. See also Le Journal des Sœurs Fidèles Compagnons de Jesus de St. Laurent.
91. The "traitors" to whom Dumont referred in his Account (265-66) were the clergy.
92. Dumont's Account, 265.
93. *Queen vs Riel*, Exhibit 1, 225.

94. *Ibid.*, Exhibit 2, 226.
95. *Ibid.*, endorsement on Exhibit 1, 226.   See also Astley evidence, 70.
96. *Ibid.*, Exhibit 3, 226.
97. *Ibid.*, Exhibit 4, 226.
98. Dumont's Account, 266.
99. *A.O.E.*, André Journal.   See also Le Chevallier, 207.
100. Dumont's Account, 267.   Dumont blamed the métis defeat on the shortage of ammunition and the work of the priests in persuading men to lay down their arms in return for safe conduct.   Dumas likewise blamed defeat on the lack of ammunition.   See Dumont and Dumas interview in *The River Press*, Fort Benton, June 10, 1885.
101. *The River Press*, June 10, 1885.
102. Dumont's Account, 268.
103. *Queen vs Riel*, Exhibit 19, 232.
104. Middleton, 56.
105. *Ibid.*, 57.
106. Riel and Young travelled by boat to Saskatoon and then overland by wagon to Moose Jaw.   From Moose Jaw to Regina they journeyed by train.   On Sunday, May 17, Robert Hazelton, Staff Sergeant to Surgeon Lt.-Col. Ryerson, was called to see Riel at Young's request.   Hazelton later wrote, "At a small bell-shaped tent there were two sentries walking.   Each had a loaded gun with fixed bayonet on his shoulder . . . the prisoner was lying down as I entered.   He scrambled to his feet as I came in.   His small piercing eyes were so bright and so searching that I almost forgot to survey the powerful physique that confronted me.   He greeted me in a low musical voice and placed rather a delicate soft hand in mine.   His hat was off showing a great mass of brown hair, all well kept . . . he wore a gray Northwest Mounted Police shirt . . . a pair of bull-hide moccasins, gray tweed pants and vest completed his apparel." (*Brantford Courier*, January 28, 1904.)

CHAPTER EIGHTEEN : Trial

1. *St.B.H.S.*, Julie Riel to Louis Riel, May 27, 1885.
2. *P.A.C.*, Department of Justice, Miscellaneous Riel Papers, IV, Louis Riel to Joseph Riel, May 25, 1885.
3. *Ibid.*, Riel to his mother, June 9, 1885.
4. *St.B.H.S.*, Henriette Riel-Poitras to Louis Riel, June 12, 1885.
5. *Ibid.*, Henriette Riel-Poitras to Louis Riel, June 30, 1885.
6. *Ibid.*, Henriette Riel-Poitras to Louis Riel, July 7, 1885.
7. *Queen vs Riel*, Young, 171.
8. *Ibid.*, 172.
9. According to Garnot, the Crown approached the métis suggesting that they plead guilty to the lesser charge of treason-felony rather than not guilty to treason. Garnot and several others refused, and then yielded.   Garnot wrote: "Un jour ils vinrent et nous demandèrent tous ensemble et nous expliquèrent la différence entre l'accusation de haute trahison, pour laquelle nous devions infailliblement subir sentence de mort, et celle de trahison félonie, pour laquelle on pouvait subir emprisonnement à partir d'une journée à la vie. . . . Ils nous dirent ensuite, 'On est décidé à vous condamner et nous ne voyons aucun moyen de vous sauver, car vous n'aurez certainement pas justice. La couronne nous offre que si vous plaidez coupables, on vous accusera de trahison-félonie, mais si vous refusez, vous serez accusés de haute trahison et plusieurs d'entre vous seront exécutés." (Frémont, 151.)   Carey to Taché, August 3, 1885, reported that all the half-breeds would plead guilty to charges of treason-felony, which was a good thing "Regina juries being very hostile" (*A.A.St.B.*).
10. *P.A.C.*, Macdonald Papers, Vol. 110.   Clarke to Macdonald, August 30, 1886. Clarke had offered his services to the Government as early as March (Macdonald Papers, Vol. 106, Clarke to Macdonald: March 24, 1885).

11. *Le Véritable Riel* (Montreal, 1887). This pamphlet presents the case of the Hierarchy against Riel. See André's letter to *La Minerve* under the pseudonym "Testes Fideles." See also Fourmond's letter to *La Semaine Religieuse*. See also *P.A.C.*, Caron Papers, Grandin to Caron, July 12, 1885. Grandin wrote: "J'ai souffert de voir nos bons métis trompés et terrorisé par un misérable maniaque." In *Le Manitoba*, July 9, 1885, Fr. Piquet wrote: "Riel ne mérite pas la sympathie des Canadiens français, c'est un apostat."

12. *Journals of the Legislative Assembly, Quebec, 1885*, XIX, 162-63. See also Rumilly, *Histoire de la Province de Québec*, V, 26-8.

13. *St.B.H.S.*, Fiset to Riel, May 22, 1885.

14. *Ibid.*, Henriette Riel-Poitras to Louis Riel, July 12, 1885.

15. *P.A.C.*, Department of Justice, Miscellaneous Riel Papers, IV, Riel to Fiset, Fitzpatrick and Lemieux, June 16, 1885. Riel made the same request in a telegram dated June 18, 1885, adding that the trial should be in Lower Canada.

16. *Ibid.*, Riel to Dewdney and Deane, June 24, 1885; Riel to same June 27, 1885. See also Macdonald Papers, Vol. 107.

17. *Ibid.*, Macdonald Papers, Vol. 107, Riel to Dewdney and Macdonald, July 6, 1885.

18. *Ibid.*, Riel to Macdonald, July 16, 1885. Riel, incidentally, spoke highly of Captain Deane in this letter.

19. *A.A.St.B.*, Lemieux, Fitzpatrick and Greenshields to Taché, July 15, 1885. Riel's lawyer expressed the view that Riel was "un maniaque religieux, et aussi désireux de commander et d'exercer le pouvoir . . . la cause de Riel est une de vie ou de mort." Fitzpatrick told Dugast that Riel was "un fou ou un sacré hypocrite—peut-être les deux." (Dugast to Taché, July 17, 1885.)

20. Regina *Leader*, July 21, 1885.

21. *Queen vs Riel*, 14-16.

22. *Ibid.*, 37.

23. Regina *Leader*, July 21, 1885.

24. *A.A.St.B.*, Dugast to Taché, July 17, 1885. Dugast said that Riel was "un fou à double platine." Riel wrote a song to celebrate Dugast's visit, part of which went as follows:

> Prêtre, George Dugast, nous sommes
>   Et nous serons en bon rapports,
> Tant que l'homme entendra les hommes
>   Applaudir aux nobles efforts:
> Mes vues, mes idées, vos lumières
>   Se repoussent en s'alliant,
> Comme les eaux de deux rivières
>   Arrivées à leur confluent.

This poem was sent to Dugast in a letter dated July 19, 1885.

25. *P.A.M.*, Riel Papers, Riel to Taché, July 24, 1885.

26. *St.B.H.S.*, Riel to Henriette Riel-Poitras, July 27, 1885.

27. *C.S.P.*, 1886, XIII, No. 52, *Queen vs Jackson*, 340.

28. *Ibid.*, 344. Jackson was taken to the asylum in Selkirk, Manitoba, from which he escaped November 6, 1885. He fled to the U.S. On November 16, he wrote to his sister asking her to send a telegram to Sir John A. Macdonald offering himself for execution in place of Louis Riel. Later he sent a letter to his lawyer expressing his firm belief in Riel's divine mission.

29. Michael Sullivan was challenged by the Crown. (See *A.A.St.B.*, Lemieux to Taché, August 5, 1885.) There was one French name among those summoned for jury service in the case of Riel, that of Benjamin Limoges; but Limoges was not selected. Since French names appear in the juries which tried Scott and Jackson, it is clear that a jury equally divided between French and English could have been found. Such a course would have gone far towards lessening the racial bitterness and political recriminations which followed Riel's conviction by a purely English-speaking jury.

30. *Queen vs Riel*, 54.

31. *Ibid.*, Willoughby, 55.
32. *Ibid.*, MacKay, 61.
33. *Ibid.*, Astley, 70.
34. *Ibid.*, Willoughby, 59.
35. *Ibid.*, Astley, 74.
36. *Ibid.*, 98.
37. *Ibid.*, Ness, 100.
38. *Ibid.*, Jackson, 112.
39. *Ibid.*, Kerr, 103.
40. *Ibid.*, Jackson, 115.
41. *Ibid.*, Jackson, 117.
42. *P.A.C.*, Macdonald Papers, Vol. 105, Keenan to Crozier, September 15, 1885.
43. *Queen vs Riel*, Nolin, 129.
44. *Ibid.*, 130.
45. *Ibid.*
46. *Ibid.*
47. *Ibid.*, Riel, 130.
48. *Ibid.*, Fitzpatrick, 131.
49. *Ibid.*, Riel, 131.
50. *Ibid.*, 132.
51. *Ibid.*
52. *Ibid.*, 131.
53. *Ibid.*, Riel, 133-134.
54. *Ibid.*, 134.
55. *Ibid.*, Nolin, 135.
56. *Ibid.*, Richardson, 136.
57. *A.A.St.B.*, Ryan to Taché, July 29, 1885.
58. *Queen vs Riel*, André, 146.
59. *Ibid.*, 147.
60. *Ibid.*, 148.
61. *Ibid.*, Garnot, 150.
62. *Ibid.*, Roy, 155.
63. *Ibid.*, Clark, 162.
64. *Ibid.*
65. *Glenbow Foundation*, Riel Papers, Jukes Memorandum.
66. *Queen vs Riel*, Wallace, 164.
67. *Ibid.*, Jukes, 169, 170.
68. *Ibid.*, Fitzpatrick, 182.
69. *Ibid.*, 191.
70. *Ibid.*, Riel, 192.
71. *Ibid.*
72. *Ibid.*, 193.
73. *Ibid.*, 195.
74. *Ibid.*, 196.
75. *Ibid.*, 196, 197.
76. *Ibid.*, 198.
77. *Ibid.*, 199.
78. *Ibid.*, Robinson, 203.
79. Regina *Leader*, August 31, 1885.
80. The foreman was Francis Cosgrave.   His daughter is the authority for the statement that he argued on behalf of Riel, and that he felt that "Riel should have been set free and allowed to go somewhere in the North West Territories and have a place of his own with other métis."   (*The Globe and Mail*, July 22, 1955.)

81. *Queen vs Riel,* Richardson, 213.
82. *Ibid.,* Riel, 213.
83. *Ibid.,* 214.
84. *Ibid.,* 217, 218.
85. *Ibid.,* 218.
86. *Ibid.,* 221.
87. *Ibid.,* 225.
88. *Ibid.,* Richardson, 225.

CHAPTER NINETEEN : Execution

1. *P.A.C.,* Macdonald Letter Book 23, Macdonald to Dewdney, private, August 17, 1885.
2. *A.A.St.B.,* Lemieux to Taché, August 5, 1885.   The correspondent of the Toronto *Mail* wrote: "Three of the jurors in Riel's case tell me that the meaning of the recommendation to mercy is that in their opinion Riel should not be hanged, as they think that, while he is not absolutely insane in the ordinary accepted meaning of the word, he is a very decided crank." (The Toronto *Mail,* August 3, 1885.)   Edward Blake received a letter written by one of the jurymen who stated: "In recommending him to the mercy of the court, we did so because we considered that while the prisoner was guilty and we could not by any means justify him in his acts of rebellion, at the same time we felt that had the Government done their duty and redressed the grievances of the half-breeds of the Saskatchewan . . . there never would have been a second Riel Rebellion, and consequently no prisoner to try and condemn." (*House of Commons Debates, Canada,* March 19, 1886, 255.)
3. Wallbridge, C. J., in the *Queen vs Riel* in the Appeal Court of the Queen's Bench, Manitoba, September 2, 1885.
4. Rumilly, 80.   "Mon père me disait qu'un grand-oncle par mariage, le juge Joseph Dubuc, par répugnance de toute l'affaire, avait refusé de présider le procès car le sujet l'avait grandement chagriné" (Dolorès Normandin to G. F. G. Stanley, January 27, 1960).
5. The *Times* (London, England), October 23, 1885.
6. *A.A.St.B.,* Deane to Taché, July 10, 1885.
7. *Ibid.,* Riel to Fourmond, August 5, 1885.   See also Cochin to Taché, August 7, 1885.   This letter contains sixteen questions asked Riel, and Riel's replies to them.
8. *Ibid.,* Cochin to Taché, August 11, 1885.
9. *Ibid.,* André to Taché, August 12, 1885.   On August 14, Cochin wrote to Taché that Riel looked upon himself as another Moses come to lead his people to the promised land, another St. Peter come to raise the church from its depths.
10. *Ibid.,* André to Taché, September 16, 1885.
11. *P.A.M.,* Riel's notebooks.
12. *A.A.St.B.,* Cloutier to Taché, September 10, 1885.   Riel's mother and wife stayed in Regina with Pascal Bonneau.   Bonneau's daughter later said: "When they were in our house they were both silent and sorrowful . . . Riel's mother was dressed in the black stuff dress and head shawl of the native people, and although she was a white woman, looked more like a métis than Riel's wife, who of course had Indian blood in her veins." (Z. M. Hamilton to G. F. G. Stanley, October 4, 1947; Z. M. Hamilton was the husband of Bonneau's daughter.)   Re Pascal Bonneau, see note 54 below.
13. *St.B.H.S.,* Henriette Riel-Poitras to Louis Riel, September 14, 1885.   Believing that Riel was about to be executed, she referred to her letter as "the last evidence of our love that you will receive."
14. *A.A.St.B.,* Cloutier to Taché, September 10, 1885.

15. *Ibid.*, André to Taché, September 21, 1885.
16. *P.A.M.*, Riel Papers, Riel to his mother, September 17, 1885.
17. *Ibid.*, Riel to Marguerite Riel, September 17, 1885. A copy of this letter is to be found in *P.A.C.*, Dewdney Papers, II.
18. *Ibid.*, André to Taché, September 21, 1885.
19. *Ibid.*, André to Taché, October 6-7, 1885.
20. *Ibid.*, Riel's notebooks.
21. *A.A.St.B.*, André to Taché, August 20, 1885. Of Richardson, André wrote, he was "un homme juste et impartiale et je lui donne le témoinage que j'y aimerais bien que nos gens soient jugé par lui que par le juge Rouleau."
22. *Ibid.*, André to Taché, October 6-7, 1885.
23. *Ibid.*, André to Taché, October 12, 1885.
24. *Ibid.*, Taché to Désiré Giroux, August 21, 1885. Taché explained that André had written a letter to Lemieux that had been published in the press. Taché favoured strict neutrality in matters of politics, but he was disposed to agree with André that affairs in the North-West had not been conducted with the knowledge and impartiality necessary for good administration. He wrote: "Moi, j'ai parlé tout bas! Je regrette de le dire; mes paroles n'ont pas été entendus, tandis que la pensée du Père André se repercute avec un bruit et un effet tout particulier." Giroux was a supporter of Macdonald who had expressed surprise to Taché at André's remarks. See also André to Taché, September 7, October 12, 1885.
25. *Ibid.*, André to Taché, October 12, 1885. See also *A.O.E.*, André to Lacombe, October 15, 1885.
26. *Ibid.*, André to Taché, October 19, 1885. Even as late as October 11, former magistrate Matthew Ryan wrote to Taché, "There is a general feeling in town that Riel is not to die."
27. *St.B.H.S.*, Henriette Riel-Poitras to Louis Riel, October 15, October 17, October 21, 1885.
28. *P.A.M.*, Riel's notebooks.
29. Riel's wife died in 1886, within six months of the execution of her husband. The cause of death was what was called "consumption" (i.e., tuberculosis). His daughter, Angélique, died in 1894 while still a child. Re his son Jean, see note 27, Chapter XIII.
30. *St.B.H.S.*, L. Riel to Henriette Riel-Poitras, October 26, 1885.
31. *P.A.C.*, Macdonald Papers, Vol. 108. See letters and telegrams from J. White, August 28; G. A. Kirkpatrick, September; N. F. Davin, September 1; John Norquay to Fred White, September 14; John Boyd, September 17; J. C. Gilroy, October 29, and others. Gilroy wrote, to tell Macdonald that if Riel were not hanged "in a few months there will be the greatest rebellion, one of the mightiest struggles for freedom and liberty from French domination by the loyal, intelligent, Protestant people of Ontario that our beloved Dominion has ever witnessed." These were words as strong as Riel had used!
32. For a list of petitions, see *C.S.P.*, 1886, XII, No. 43f. In *ibid.*, No. 43 e, there is a list of petitions asking that Riel's sentence not be disturbed. These latter were far fewer in number than the former. It is hard to believe today that a commutation of Riel's sentence by Macdonald would have had the serious consequences Macdonald apparently apprehended.
33. For the reaction of the French-Canadian ministers and the electors of Quebec to the Riel crisis, see Stanley, *The Birth of Western Canada*, Chapter XVII, and Rumilly, *Histoire de la Province de Quebec*, V, Chapters II and III.
34. *Q.U.L.*, Lavell correspondence, Macdonald to Lavell, October 31, 1885. Correspondence regarding the insanity commission will also be found in *P.A.C.*, Macdonald Papers, Vol. 106.
35. *Ibid.*, private memorandum by Dr. Lavell on Louis Riel. See also *A.A.St.B.*, André to Taché, November 9, 1885. André wrote: "Le Dr. Valade, après deux entrevues avec Riel s'est carrément prononcé pour sa folie, mais Riel avec sa folie est une intelligence supérieur au Dr. Lavell, qui est un méthodiste enragé, à l'esprit étroit et borné. . . . Il reconnait que Riel est fou en religion et en politique, mais tout en le reconnaissant fou il le reconnait responsable. Trouvez la solution à une pareille enigme."

36. *Glenbow Foundation,* Riel Papers, Jukes to Macdonald, November 9, 1885.
37. G. R. Parkin, *Sir John A. Macdonald* (London and Toronto, 1908), 244.
38. *A.S.D.,* Consular despatches from Winnipeg, VI, Riel to Taylor, July 21, 1885; Riel to President Cleveland, enclosed in Riel to Taylor, September 12, 1885. See also *L'Indépendent,* Fall River, Mass., August 31, 1885. In 1888, Henriette Riel-Poitras wrote to W. F. Bryant, comparing her brother's trial with that of Jeanne d'Arc, and complaining of President Cleveland's indifference (Bryant, *The Blood of Abel,* 114). Ex-editor of *Le Travailleur* (Worcester, Mass.), Ambroise Coquet sent a copy of Riel's naturalization certificate to Washington, and Edmond Mallet wrote to Cleveland assuring him that Riel was an American citizen (*L'Independent,* November 2, 1885). See also G. F. G. Stanley, "Was Louis Riel an American Citizen?" *op. cit.*
39. *St.B.H.S.,* Riel's testament, November 6, 1885. This is printed in de Trémaudan, *Histoire de la Nation Métisse,* 431-34.
40. *Ibid.,* Riel to André, September 14, 1885. See also *A.A.St.B.,* André to Dewdney, November 18, 1885.
41. De Trémaudan, 434-48.
42. *A.A.St.B.,* André to Taché, November 16, 1885.
43. *Glenbow Foundation,* Riel Papers, Jukes Memorandum, November 15, 1885.
44. *A.A.St.B.,* André to Taché, November 16, 1885.
45. *P.A.M.,* Riel Papers, Riel to his mother, November 15, 1885.
46. The *New York Herald,* November 17, 1885, contains a letter by Riel to McWilliams, November 16, 1885. Fr. C. A. McWilliams was a priest in the Kingston diocese at this time.
47. *A.A.St.B.,* André to Taché, November 16, 1885.
48. The Regina *Leader,* November 17, 1885; The Toronto *Mail,* November 17, 1885.
49. *Ibid.,* November 19, 1885. John Henderson, a former prisoner of Riel's in the first uprising, did duty as hangman, for which the sheriff paid him fifty dollars. (Robert Sinton, "Looking Backward from the Eightieth Milestone, 1935-1854" Mss. 27.)
50. *Glenbow Foundation,* Riel Papers, Jukes memorandum, November 18, 1885.
51. André applied for Riel's body on November 16 (Dewdney to Macdonald, telegram, November 16, 1885). Hon. J. A. Chapleau wanted the body buried in Regina (Chapleau to Macdonald, November 16, 1885). Dewdney believed that it should be buried in the guard room square and later sent to St. Boniface, after the agitation in Quebec and Ontario had calmed down (Dewdney to Macdonald, private, November 18, 1885). These letters will be found in *P.A.C.,* Macdonald Papers, Vol. 106. The rope used to hang Riel was destroyed. The pieces of rope allegedly used in the hanging to be found in various museums can hardly be authentic!
52. *A.A.St.B.,* André to Taché, November 18, 1885.
53. *P.A.C.,* Macdonald Papers, André to Dewdney, November 18, 1885.
54. Pascal Bonneau was a French-Canadian contractor who worked on the construction of the main line of the Canadian Pacific into Regina. He was a strong Conservative and a friend of Riel, even though he had had no sympathy whatsoever with the proceedings at Batoche.
55. *Glenbow Foundation,* Riel Papers, Jukes Memorandum, November 18, 1885. The body was also viewed at a different hour by Père André, N. F. Davin and Sheriff Chapleau (*Supplement to the Leader,* Regina, November 19, 1885; see also *P.A.C.,* Macdonald Papers, Vol. 106, André to Macdonald, telegram, November 19, 1885).
56. "Pascal Bonneau, whom I knew very well, interviewed me in regard to assisting him in loading a heavy box into a car then standing near the Albert Street crossing, the box to arrive about 11 p.m. the same evening. At the hour named, Mr. Bonneau arrived driving a pony and jumper, with the box. After placing the box in the car and fastening the door, we asked Mr. Bonneau what the box contained. He replied that it contained the body of Riel, and that he was himself accompanying the body which was to be buried in Riel's former home town. He also asked me to treat the matter as strictly confidential." (Robert Sinton, "Looking Backward," 28.)
57. *Le Manitoba,* December 17, 1885.

Index